FOUNDATION PRESS

HUMAN RIGHTS ADVOCACY STORIES

Edited By

DEENA R. HURWITZ
Associate Professor of Law, General Faculty
University of Virginia School of Law

MARGARET L. SATTERTHWAITE
Associate Professor of Clinical Law
New York University School of Law

With

DOUG FORD
Lecturer, General Faculty
University of Virginia School of Law

FOUNDATION PRESS

THOMSON
WEST

2009

Cover: New Delhi, INDIA: Narmada Bachao Andolan (NBA) leader, Medha Patkar (center), along with members and activists of the NBA, blocks the entrance of the Indian Social Justice and Empowerment Ministry office in New Delhi, 02 January 2007. Hundreds of activists demanded that the height of the Sardar Sarovar Dam in the central state of Madya Pradesh should not be raised and that more than 24,000 families in 177 villages displayed by the construction of the dam should be rehabilitated immediately. (*See* Chapter 10: *The Story of Narmada Bachao Andolan: Human Rights in the Global Economy and the Struggle Against the World Bank*, by Smita Narula.) RAVEENDRAN/AFP/Getty Images

This publication was created to provide you with accurate and authoritative information concerning the subject matter covered; however, this publication was not necessarily prepared by persons licensed to practice law in a particular jurisdiction. The publisher is not engaged in rendering legal or other professional advice and this publication is not a substitute for the advice of an attorney. If you require legal or other expert advice, you should seek the services of a competent attorney or other professional.

Nothing contained herein is intended or written to be used for the purposes of 1) avoiding penalties imposed under the federal Internal Revenue Code, or 2) promoting, marketing or recommending to another party any transaction or matter addressed herein.

© 2009 By THOMSON REUTERS/FOUNDATION PRESS
    195 Broadway, 9th Floor
    New York, NY 10007
    Phone Toll Free 1–877–888–1330
    Fax (212) 367–6799
    foundation–press.com
Printed in the United States of America

ISBN 978–1–59941–199–6

TEXT IS PRINTED ON 10% POST CONSUMER RECYCLED PAPER

HUMAN RIGHTS ADVOCACY STORIES

Introduction 1

    Margaret L. Satterthwaite & Deena R. Hurwitz

Part One: NGO Advocacy and the Development of Human Rights Norms 13

Chapter 1:

    Outlawing Torture: The Story of Amnesty International's Efforts to Shape the U.N. Convention against Torture 15

    Jayne Huckerby & Sir Nigel Rodley

Chapter 2:

    The Story of the *TAC* Case: The Potential and Limits of Socio–Economic Rights Litigation in South Africa 43

    Amy Kapczynski & Jonathan M. Berger

Part Two: Culture and Identity: Individual and Collective Rights 81

Chapter 3:

    The Stories of *Dudgeon* and *Toonen*: Personal Struggles to Legalize Sexual Identities 83

    Mark Bromley & Kristen Walker

Chapter 4:

    Gaining Legal Recognition of Indigenous Land Rights: The Story of the *Awas Tingni* Case in Nicaragua 117

    S. James Anaya & Maia S. Campbell

Chapter 5:

    The Law of the Republic Versus the "Law of the Brothers": A Story of France's Law Banning Religious Symbols in Public Schools 155

    Karima Bennoune

Part Three: International Standards and the Role of Criminal Law in Protecting Human Rights 191

Chapter 6:

    Engendering Genocide: The *Akayesu* Case Before the International Criminal Tribunal for Rwanda 193

    Beth Van Schaack

Chapter 7:

    The Story of *Samuel Hinga Norman* in Sierra Leone: Can Truth Commissions and Criminal Prosecutions Coexist After Conflict? 229

    Ari S. Bassin & Paul Van Zyl

Chapter 8:

    Universal Jurisdiction and the Dilemmas of International Criminal Justice: The Sabra and Shatila Case in Belgium 267

    Deena R. Hurwitz

Chapter 9:

    Arresting Juxtapositions: The *Story of Roper v. Simmons*   315

    Alison J. Nathan

Part Four: Globalization, Foreign Policy and the Economy   349

Chapter 10:

    The Story of Narmada Bachao Andolan: Human Rights in the Global Economy and the Struggle Against the World Bank 351

    Smita Narula

Chapter 11:

    The Story of *Sale v. Haitian Centers Council*: Guantánamo and *Refoulement* 385

    Harold Hongju Koh & Michael J. Wishnie

Chapter 12:

    The Story of *Doe v. Unocal*: Justice Delayed But Not Denied 433

    Katie Redford & Beth Stephens

Part Five: Human Rights in a World at War 463

Chapter 13:

    Inspiring and Inadequate: the *Krstić* Genocide Conviction through the Eyes of a Srebrenica Survivor 465

    Doug Ford

Chapter 14:

    The Story of Hamid Karzai: The Paradoxes of State-building and Human Rights 505

    Aziz Z. Huq

Chapter 15:

    The Story of *El–Masri v. Tenet*: Human Rights and Humanitarian Law in the "War on Terror" 535

    Margaret L. Satterthwaite

Contributors to *Human Rights Advocacy Stories* 579

*

FOUNDATION PRESS

HUMAN RIGHTS ADVOCACY STORIES

*

Introduction

Margaret L. Satterthwaite & Deena R. Hurwitz

As much as any area of the law, human rights involves narratives—the stories of individuals, groups, and movements of people—who engage in different ways with the strategies, institutions, and legal frameworks that we refer to as international human rights. But perhaps more than many other fields of law, human rights norms and standards develop as much through individual and collective vision and action in the world as through cases before courts and tribunals. By making real the stories of collective action behind human rights advocacy, developing norms, and enforcement mechanisms, *Human Rights Advocacy Stories* illustrates the dynamic interactions between advocacy and legal doctrine.

The chapters in this volume tell the stories of individuals and groups whose bodies, minds, lives, identities, communities, and cultures are threatened at the hands of governments, corporations, armed groups, or communities. They are the stories of people who are brave, desperate, determined, or just angry enough to stand up against those abuses. What unites these stories is not only the abuse and resistance, but also the forms that the resistance takes.

International human rights law encompasses wide-ranging venues, subjects, and strategies. The law is interpreted and applied not only in courts and tribunals, but also in villages, boardrooms, and international institutions. This is a field of law shaped by legislatures and judges, as well as by grassroots movements, pioneering "norm entrepreneurs,"[1] and scholars. As a result, we have chosen to interpret human rights "cases" broadly enough to include cases that have been adjudicated by a court or commission, as well as specific controversies that were decided outside the confines of a courthouse. We believe this broader approach is necessary in a field that is defined, in part, by the dearth of institutions entrusted with binding decision-making power.

---

1. *See* Harold Hongju Koh, *The 1998 Frankel Lecture: Bringing International Law Home*, 35 Hous. L. Rev. 623 (1998).

Rather than attempting to present a chronological or doctrinal history of human rights, we approached this *Stories* volume with key themes, controversies, and developments that are frequently used as organizing concepts in international human rights classes and textbooks. These include the development of human rights norms and the work of human rights organizations; the function of individual and collective identities in human rights struggles; the role of international criminal norms in protecting human rights; globalization, foreign policy, and the economy; and human rights in a world at war. Within these themes, we chose cases and case studies that illustrate some cross-cutting issues, including:

- The role of the lawyer and the law in human rights struggles;
- The dynamic interplay of formal and informal modes of protest;
- The relationship between domestic and international law;
- The role of the law and legal institutions in crafting solutions to mass atrocities that provide both truth and justice.

We also intentionally selected cases that illustrate the full range of human rights—from civil and political to economic, social, and cultural. Finally, we approached these themes through issues that have contemporary resonance. Consistent with the rest of the *Stories* series, we intend to give the reader a sense of the dynamism behind the legal controversies that shape the discipline.

Perhaps more than some other volumes in this series, we focused carefully on the role of advocacy of all types—formal and informal, legal and extralegal—in defining, advancing, and protecting international human rights. In this vein, we intentionally sought out authors who were actively engaged in the cases and issues about which we invited them to write. Rather than seeking formal objectivity, we asked our authors to honestly assess and analyze the successes and failures of advocacy efforts in which they had some stake. In cases where an author was a protagonist—as lawyer or central advocate—we asked a second author to join in the writing effort. We felt this would ensure that there was enough distance between the main character and the story to encourage clear analysis.

Human Rights Advocacy Stories includes fifteen chapters, organized in five sections. This Introduction presents a brief overview of these sections and chapters. We conclude with a note to professors and students.

INTRODUCTION

Part One: NGO Advocacy and the Development of Human Rights Norms

Part One, *NGO Advocacy and the Development of Human Rights Norms*, presents human rights through some of its most enduring and successful strategies and players: non-governmental organizations ("NGOs") and their efforts to create new norms and mechanisms of accountability. These chapters present the stories of two very different human rights organizations: Amnesty International ("AI"), one of the oldest and largest international organizations in the modern age of human rights, and the Treatment Action Campaign, a community-based AIDS advocacy organization formed in 1998 in South Africa. In the stories presented here, each organization uses different strategies to advance separate causes. Amnesty International engages with the United Nations to push for the creation of a binding treaty outlawing torture, and the Treatment Action Campaign combines civil disobedience and community education with constitutional litigation to advance the right to health.

Chapter One, "Outlawing Torture: The Story of Amnesty International's Efforts to Shape the U.N. Convention against Torture," chronicles AI's fight in the 1970s and 1980s to strengthen and codify the prohibition of torture and other forms of cruel, inhuman or degrading treatment or punishment. Examining the crucial steps along the way, the Chapter explores AI's strategies for influencing the treaty-drafting process, suggesting that a combination of public pressure, adept lobbying, and impeccable preparation for substantive debate were the secrets of AI's success. This Chapter was written by two individuals who are leaders in their respective generations in the fight against torture: Sir Nigel Rodley, Professor of Law and Chair of the Human Rights Centre, University of Essex and the former U.N. Special Rapporteur on Torture; and Jayne Huckerby, Research Director of NYU's Center for Human Rights and Global Justice, whose work has focused on ending the use of torture in the "War on Terror." Sir Nigel Rodley was the Legal Director of Amnesty International during the drafting of the Torture Convention, and the story reveals fascinating details about the treaty's negotiation, including the internal policies and positions taken by Amnesty International, its relationship with other key organizations, and its determination to ensure the Convention included a strong universal jurisdiction clause.

Chapter Two takes on similar themes, examining the efforts of HIV/AIDS activists in South Africa to ensure that poor HIV-positive mothers have access to the drug Nevirapine to prevent transmission of the virus to their newborn children. "The Story of the TAC Case: The Potential and Limits of Socio–Economic Rights Litigation in South Africa" focuses on an HIV-positive mother, Busisiwe Maqungo, whose child died after her HIV status was concealed and she was discharged from a government-run clinic without having been given Nevirapine. Joining forces with the Treatment Action Campaign ("TAC"), a community-based AIDS activist organization, Maqungo and others like her sued the South African government, arguing that the Constitutional right to health care required the government to make Nevirapine available to poor women. The authors of this Chapter explore the efforts of the TAC—both inside and outside the courtroom—to ensure that the socio-economic rights promised in the South African Constitution are made a reality through government programs and services. Through their historical win, TAC and its members symbolize the power of advocacy backed by legally-enforceable human rights norms. The story is told by Amy Kapczynski, Assistant Professor of Law at the University of California Berkeley School of Law and an expert on the intersections between international law, intellectual property, and global health; and Jonathan M. Berger, Senior Researcher and Head of Policy and Research at the AIDS Law Project in Johannesburg, South Africa.

Part Two: Culture and Identity: Individual and Collective Rights

Part Two, *Culture and Identity: Individual and Collective Rights*, includes three contemporary stories concerning individual and collective rights that raise critical questions of identity, gender, culture and agency. Together, these chapters demonstrate that advocates continue to challenge international human rights law and institutions to respond fully to the variety of identities, practices, and choices that individuals and communities make. Two of the chapters tell the stories of community members who seek the support of human rights advocates, courts, and commissions in their quest to live their lives fully—and sometimes differently than other members of their various communities. The third chapter examines the quest of a community to gain international legal support for its collective claims.

Chapter Three, "The Stories of *Dudgeon* and *Toonen*: Personal Struggles to Legalize Sexual Identities," narrates the tales of Jeffrey Dudgeon and Nick Toonen, two gay men—one from Northern Ireland and the other from Australia—whose commitment to living open lives as equal citizens led them to challenge their respective countries' anti-sodomy laws before international human rights bodies. Each man was part of a larger struggle defined by community-based organizing for the equality of lesbian, gay, bisexual, and transgender ("LGBT") people. These movements, which vary across time, geography, and culture, have grown enormously in recent years in visibility and strength, drawing on the language and norms of international human rights. This Chapter tells the story of the *Dudgeon* case before the European Court of Human Rights, decided in 1981, and its impact on the later *Toonen* case, decided

INTRODUCTION

by the U.N. Human Rights Committee in 1994. It was written by two experts on LGBT rights: Mark Bromley, founder of the Council for Global Equality, an NGO dedicated to advancing LGBT rights, and Kristen Walker, Associate Professor of Law at the University of Melbourne and a barrister with a wide-ranging human rights practice.

Chapter Four, "Gaining Legal Recognition of Indigenous Land Rights: The Story of the *Awas Tingni* Case in Nicaragua," explores the efforts of an indigenous community in Nicaragua to gain legal title to the land it has used for generations. Along the way, the community—with the help of legal allies including co-author S. James Anaya, who was counsel to the community during the legal battle examined in this Chapter and now serves as the U.N. Special Rapporteur on the Human Rights of Indigenous Peoples[2]—sets a groundbreaking legal precedent before the Inter–American Court of Human Rights. This story examines the contours of the right to property as a human right, the status of indigenous claims under international human rights law, and the role of transnational legal coalitions in vindicating the rights of small communities. This Chapter was co-written by Professor S. James Anaya and Maia S. Campbell, project attorney for the University of Arizona Indigenous Peoples Law and Policy Program, which advocates before international bodies for the Awas Tingni Mayangna community in Nicaragua and the Maya communities of Toledo District, Belize.

Chapter Five, "The Law of the Republic Versus the 'Law of the Brothers': A Story of France's Law Banning Religious Symbols in Public Schools," presents the voices of "women's rights activists, journalists, religious figures, and scholars of Muslim, Arab or North African heritage living in France who support the Law on Religious Symbols," enacted in 2004. The author of the Chapter, Karima Bennoune, Professor of Law and the Arthur L. Dickson Scholar at the Rutgers School of Law–Newark, is a noted human rights scholar who has many years of experience in hands-on human rights work. Through interviews and in-depth examination of the context for the debate over the 2004 Law, Professor Bennoune tells a story that has not been heard in the Anglophone literature examining the so-called "headscarves controversy." The story that unfolds here is complex and richly layered, weaving together interviews conducted in France and an analysis of the relevant human rights norms to reflect a contextual approach to religious expression and questions of religious fundamentalism.

---

2. Professor Anaya's full title is United Nations Special Rapporteur on the Situation of Human Rights and Fundamental Freedoms of Indigenous People.

Part Three: International Standards and the Role of Criminal Law in Protecting Human Rights

Part Three, *International Standards and the Role of Criminal Law in Protecting Human Rights*, highlights the role of emerging norms of international criminal law on efforts to protect human rights. In the past two decades, enormous progress has been made by the international community to advance international criminal law as a method to check grave abuses and to bring those responsible for such abuses to justice. At the same time, those efforts have been questioned by critics who are concerned that criminal justice is sometimes pursued at the expense of transitional justice. These debates are being played out both before international criminal tribunals such as the International Criminal Tribunal for Rwanda and before mixed—or "hybrid"—criminal tribunals set up by the international community in countries that have experienced upheaval such as Sierra Leone. Another set of debates surrounds the enforcement of international criminal norms by domestic courts. Under the principle of universal jurisdiction, national courts are empowered to investigate, try, and punish perpetrators of crimes that occurred far from their territory. The exercise of such powers has been celebrated by the human rights community but assailed by others, who charge that the exercise of universal jurisdiction too easily becomes politicized. Finally, international norms concerning how criminal law issues such as the death penalty should be handled are increasingly influencing domestic courts, even when those courts do not rely directly on such rules. The chapters in this section explore these issues, as well as cross-cutting themes including gender and conflict, litigation strategy, and the role of international lawyers in advancing international criminal law and transitional justice.

Chapter Six, "Engendering Genocide: The *Akayesu* Case Before the International Criminal Tribunal for Rwanda," presents the story of the first conviction following trial for genocide under international law since the crime was defined more than five decades ago. Along the way, the case is also credited with landmark decisions on core issues in international criminal law, including incitement and the constitutive elements of the crime of genocide. This Chapter discusses these issues, but focuses on another groundbreaking element of the case: its recognition—a first in international criminal law—of the concept of genocidal rape. The importance of this decision is explored alongside a discussion of the efforts of feminist legal activists to achieve and expand this victory. The Chapter was written by a leading expert in international criminal law: Beth Van Schaack, Associate Professor of Law at Santa Clara University School of Law. Professor Van Schaack teaches and writes in the areas of human rights, transitional justice, and international criminal law, and is co-author (with Ronald C. Slye) of *International Criminal Law and Its Enforcement* (published by Foundation Press).

INTRODUCTION

Chapter Seven is entitled "The Story of *Samuel Hinga Norman* in Sierra Leone: Can Truth Commissions and Criminal Prosecutions Coexist After Conflict?" This Chapter examines the tension that erupted between the two central post-war transitional justice institutions created in Sierra Leone with the assistance of the international community: the Special Court for Sierra Leone and the Sierra Leone Truth and Reconciliation Commission ("TRC"). These two bodies, set up to address the mass human rights abuses that took place during Sierra Leone's ten-year-long civil war, were themselves confronted with a conflict when Samuel Hinga Norman, a high-profile defendant before the Court, asked to testify publicly before the Truth Commission. As this Chapter shows, "what ensued illustrated the potential for tension between TRCs and court prosecutions. It was also entirely avoidable." The authors are especially well-positioned to narrate the events that led to the tension and to suggest ways around similar problems in the future: Paul Van Zyl, co-founder and Executive Vice–President of the International Center for Transitional Justice (ICTJ), also directs the Transitional Justice Program at NYU School of Law, and Ari S. Bassin is a Project Officer with the International Organization for Migration's Police Reform Project in Aceh, Indonesia, working on post-conflict security sector reform.

Chapter Eight, "Universal Jurisdiction and the Dilemmas of International Criminal Justice: The Story of the Sabra and Shatila Case in Belgium" opens by describing a massacre that left more than 2000 people dead, hundreds—or more—disappeared, and thousands of survivors traumatized. The story picks up twenty years later, when stateless victims with no recourse to justice sought redress through a model criminal statute providing extraterritorial jurisdiction for war crimes, crimes against humanity and genocide. This Belgian law, which had no statute of limitations and allowed for no possibility of immunity for heads of state or "official acts," seemed to provide the opening the survivors sought. Armed with well-documented and incontrovertible evidence pointing to responsible individuals, the case seemed unassailable. By the time the Sabra and Shatila case was filed in 2001, the law had been used to prosecute individuals responsible for abuses in Rwanda and the Democratic Republic of the Congo. Unlike those cases, this complaint concerned a politically controversial incident: Israel's role in the 1982 massacres in the Beirut refugee camps of Sabra and Shatila. Moreover, the complaint alleged war crimes, crimes against humanity, and command responsibility by then-Israeli Prime Minister Ariel Sharon, among others. Two years of intense legal and political maneuvers ensued, including a series of Belgian legal and legislative "clarifications" concerning the scope of the law. The case was impacted by political assassination, by a decision by the International Court of Justice, and by intense pressure on Belgium from Israel and the United States. Professor Deena R. Hurwitz, co-editor of this volume, worked on the case with her students at the Yale Law School human rights clinic.

Chapter Nine, "Arresting Juxtapositions: The Story of *Roper v. Simmons* and the Advocacy of International Human Rights Before the United States Supreme Court," examines a different aspect of the relationship between criminal law and human rights. In *Roper v. Simmons*, the U.S. Supreme Court held that the imposition of the death penalty on offenders who were younger than eighteen years of age at the time of their crime was prohibited by the Eighth Amendment. Presenting the story behind this decision, this Chapter considers the impact of human rights advocacy and arguments in a case that was ultimately decided on the basis of a U.S. constitutional standard. As the Chapter explains, the Court's "articulation of the Eighth Amendment protection sounds in the discourse of human rights not only because it invoked human dignity as the core, unassailable value, but also because it casts the state's obligation not as a negative restriction, but as an affirmative obligation on the part of the state to protect the human dignity of all, even those judged guilty and sentenced to death." This Chapter was written by Alison J. Nathan, an Alexander Fellow at NYU School of Law, whose scholarship focuses on the death penalty, habeas corpus, and civil procedure.

Part Four: Globalization, Foreign Policy and the Economy

Part Four collects stories about attempts to influence the human rights impacts of globalization, including the negative influence on refugees of foreign policy decisions about migration, the displacement of populations as a result of large internationally-financed infrastructure projects, and corporate complicity in grave human rights violations. These advocacy efforts have produced new forms of transnational litigation—explored here through the stories of two cases brought in U.S. federal court by U.S. litigators working closely with partners from other countries—one under the Alien Tort Statute and the other using U.S. constitutional and statutory norms in combination with treaty law. Efforts to redress the harms of globalization have focused on distilling new norms to hold non-state actors—including corporations and multilateral development banks—to account for the human rights impact of their endeavors. Finally, advocacy has also centered on the need for new institutions, such as the World Bank Inspection Panel.

Chapter Ten, "The Story of Narmada Bachao Andolan: Human Rights in the Global Economy and the Struggle Against the World Bank," explores the organizing efforts of a coalition of community-based organizations in India that gathered under the banner "Narmada Bachao Andolan" (Save Narmada Movement). These organizations, and the

INTRODUCTION 9

charismatic leaders who delivered their message, employed direct nonviolent action to oppose a series of enormous dams on the Narmada River that threatened to submerge their villages. Their tactics included sit-ins, hunger strikes, and—rarely and most controversially—sacrifice by drowning. The group also sought redress through litigation before the Indian Supreme Court. Because the project was backed by the World Bank, protests called on the Bank to review the project and address the concerns of the Narmada Bachao Andolan. In 1991, the Bank created a commission to review the project; the review ultimately led to the Bank's withdrawal. Further, the pressure brought by the movement, combined with the calls of advocates from around the world for World Bank accountability, led to the creation in 1993 of the World Bank Inspection Panel, empowered to review complaints by communities affected by Bank projects. This Chapter was written by Smita Narula, Associate Professor of Clinical Law at NYU School of Law, a Faculty Director of the Center for Human Rights and Global Justice at NYU, and a recognized expert on human rights in India.

Chapter Eleven is entitled "The Story of *Sale v. Haitian Centers Council*: Guantánamo and *Refoulement*." This Chapter tells the David and Goliath story of a Yale Law School clinic that sued the United States to halt its policy of housing HIV-positive refugees at Guantánamo and returning them to Haiti—almost twenty years before Guantánamo became famous as a prison camp in the "War on Terror." These refugees, who had fled a violent military government in Haiti, faced almost certain persecution because of their political opinion were they returned. While partnering with their clients at Guantánamo, the Yale clinic invented a new model of human rights litigation. This Chapter was written by Dean Harold Hongju Koh and Professor Michael J. Wishnie of Yale Law School. Each is in an incomparable position to tell the tale: Dean Koh, as Co–Director of the Allard K. Lowenstein International Human Rights Clinic at Yale, was Professor Wishnie's teacher at the time of the *Sale* case. As a law student, Wishnie was a member of the team that litigated the case. Further, Dean Koh later served as U.S. Assistant Secretary of State for Democracy, Human Rights and Labor, giving him a unique vantage point from which to reflect on this case, which was laden with foreign policy concerns. Professor Wishnie now supervises clinic students at Yale in litigation concerning immigration, labor and employment, and habeas corpus.

Chapter Twelve, "The Story of *Doe v. Unocal*: Justice Delayed But Not Denied," presents the compelling story of three law students who joined together with Burmese human rights activists and villagers to take on the powerful U.S. oil company, Unocal. Unocal had entered into a lucrative contract with the Burmese government and another company to build a natural gas pipeline. Despite the international opprobrium of the government of Burma, the contract specified that the government would provide security for the pipeline project. But, the government began to force villagers to provide manual labor on the pipeline, relocated villagers under duress, and severely restricted freedom of movement in the pipeline region. After painstaking and risky fact-finding work was completed by the U.S. law students (by then licensed lawyers) and Burmese activists, they filed a lawsuit in federal court, alleging under the Alien Tort Statute (ATS) that Unocal had aided and abetted the government of Burma in human rights violations including forced relocation, forced labor, rape, torture and murder. This Chapter is narrated by Katie Redford, one of the three law students in the story who became a co-founder of EarthRights International and now serves as the director of the organization's U.S. office, and Beth Stephens, Professor of Law at the Rutgers–Camden School of Law, a recognized expert on the ATS and a former staff attorney at the Center for Constitutional Rights, where she litigated ATS cases for many years.

Part Five: Human Rights in a World at War

Part Five presents several issues of contemporary interest and enduring import: the intersection of human rights, humanitarian law, and national security policy in key war and post-conflict policies such as humanitarian intervention, state-building, and treatment of transnational terrorism suspects. Through stories about the international community's failure to prevent or respond adequately to the genocide in Bosnia, U.S.-led state-building efforts in Afghanistan, and the wrongful extraordinary rendition of a German national, the chapters in this section examine the inter-relationships between the legal frameworks operable in war and peace and the political considerations of major world powers.

Chapter Thirteen, "Inspiring and Inadequate: The Story of the Krstić Conviction in the Eyes of a Srebrenica Survivor," tells the harrowing tale of the massacre at Srebrenica from the perspective of a survivor, and her reaction to the conviction of General Radislav Krstić by the International Criminal Tribunal for the Former Yugoslavia on charges of genocide. The story of Mirsada Malagić is—tragically—like many others. Although she and her two youngest children made it out of Srebrenica alive, her husband, teenage sons, and other male relatives were all slaughtered by Serb forces in July 1995. Her reaction to the conviction of Krstić was also emblematic of the feelings of many survivors of the genocide: while Malagić welcomed the conviction, she felt strongly that justice was not served when Krstić was given a sentence of fewer than forty years in prison. This Chapter, written by Doug Ford, Lecturer at the University of Virginia School of Law and collaborator on this volume, who worked in Bosnia–Herzegovina identifying bodies through ante-mortem data, presents Malagić's story as the outcome not only of the genocide, but also of failed policies by the international community, including the U.N., NATO, and the world's leading states. The Chapter also examines the development of the doctrine of humanitarian intervention, and its recent incarnation in the responsibility to protect.

Chapter Fourteen is entitled "The Story of Hamid Karzai: The Paradoxes of State-building and Human Rights." This Chapter dramatizes another side of the debate over humanitarian intervention, asking whether military action that is aimed at both halting terrorism and building a new rights-respecting state is so inherently contradictory as to be untenable. Narrating the choices facing Hamid Karzai as he took up the reins of the state of Afghanistan after the U.S.-led ouster of the Taliban, the Chapter also examines the role of the many multinational actors, NGOs, and consultants who swoop into post-conflict situations with high ideals and large grants. The Chapter's author, Aziz Z. Huq, who will join the faculty of the University of Chicago as an Associate Professor of Law in September 2009, directs the Liberty and National Security project at the Brennan Center for Justice at NYU School of Law, and worked as a senior consulting analyst for the International Crisis Group in Afghanistan in 2002–03.

Chapter Fifteen, entitled "The Story of *El–Masri v. Tenet*: Human Rights and Humanitarian Law in the 'War on Terror'," tells the story of a German man who was mistakenly abducted while on vacation in Macedonia and then secretly detained by the CIA for several months before being released without apology or acknowledgment in the hills of Albania. Despite being told not to reveal what had befallen him, Khaled El–Masri was determined to fight for his rights and the rights of others caught up by the U.S. extraordinary rendition and secret detention program. With the help of a German lawyer and the ACLU, El–Masri made his story known and became the human face of this controversial program. This Chapter places El–Masri's story in context, explaining the relationship between human rights law and international humanitarian law in counter-terrorism operations, and explores the legal strategies adopted by the ACLU and its allies in their transnational efforts to combat extraordinary rendition. This Chapter was written by Margaret L. Satterthwaite, co-editor of this volume and Associate Professor of Clinical Law at NYU School of Law and a Faculty Director of the NYU Center for Human Rights and Global Justice, who represents several individuals who have experienced extraordinary rendition and has written extensively on the practice.

Note to Professors and Students

Professors and the students they teach face special dilemmas concerning international human rights, because—though the modern field is barely three-quarters of a century old—it comprises a vast and evolving array of topics and issues. Despite the expansive nature of international human rights, professors teaching an introductory course are expected to cover the basics of black letter international human rights law as well as the history, politics, and institutional debates surrounding that law. At the same time, students are expected to grasp this wide array of issues and controversies while simultaneously absorbing the doctrinal contours of international human rights.

This volume is designed to respond to these dilemmas. It can be used as a complement to any of the leading international human rights textbooks, or it may be used as a stand-alone text or supplement to a course pack. In selecting our chapters, we analyzed the leading textbooks, alongside syllabi from more than a dozen professors teaching international human rights law at leading universities—in law schools and graduate programs in foreign affairs and political science. While the texts and courses follow diverse organizational schemes, they contain themes that we drew on in crafting those that organize the stories in this volume.

Our objective is to expose readers to key topics, actors, and critical issues in international human rights law; provide knowledge of basic human rights mechanisms, institutions, and methodologies; and above all, give the reader a sense of the dynamism and constant development in the field of international human rights. We hope this book will bring some of the key issues, stories, and characters to life for the reader.

We would like to thank all of the authors for their hard work in narrating these important stories. Our appreciation to John Bloomquist, Ryan Pfeiffer, Robb Westawker and Jim Coates at Foundation Press, for their stewardship of the book. We owe a debt of gratitude to the students who assisted with citations and proof-reading: Adam Abelson and Mitra Ebadolahi at NYU School of Law, and Suzanne Sam Libby, Nilakshi Parndigamage, Alyssa Petroff, Shaunik Panse, and Meredith Van Tine at the University of Virginia School of Law.

Part One

NGO Advocacy and the Development of Human Rights Norms

*

1

Outlawing Torture: The Story of Amnesty International's Efforts to Shape the U.N. Convention against Torture

Jayne Huckerby & Sir Nigel Rodley*

Introduction

Several years after its formation in 1961,[1] Amnesty International ("Amnesty") began its official push to transform torture into an act as legally and morally unacceptable and "as unthinkable as slavery."[2] Central to achieving this goal was the creation of an international human rights instrument that would unequivocally and plainly codify the prohibition on torture. After devoting the best part of a decade of work to this groundbreaking treaty, the instrument—the United Nations

---

* The authors would like to thank the staff in Records Management at Amnesty International, International Secretariat for their support for this project.

1. Amnesty International was founded by British lawyer Peter Benenson after he learned that two Portuguese students had been imprisoned for toasting a drink to freedom. In May 1961, the *Observer* provided a platform for the "Appeal for Amnesty 1961" campaign when it published Benenson's article, "The Forgotten Prisoners." In 1962, Amnesty was established as a permanent organization and its headquarters, the International Secretariat, was set up in London in 1963. Amnesty is based on worldwide voluntary membership and consists of "... sections, structures, international networks, affiliated groups and international members," with an International Executive Committee (IEC) responsible for its "leadership and stewardship" (*see* Articles 5 and 7 of Amnesty's Statute). *See generally* Amnesty International, *The History of Amnesty International*, *available at* http://www.amnesty.org/en/who-we-are/history; Statute of Amnesty International, as amended by the 28th International Council, meeting in Morelos, Mexico, Aug. 11–17, 2007; Peter Benenson, *The Forgotten Prisoners*, Observer, May 28, 1961; Stephen Hopgood, Keepers of the Flame: Understanding Amnesty International 55 (2006).

2. Amnesty Int'l, *Conference for the Abolition of Torture, Paris, Dec. 10–11, 1973, Final Report*, 10 (1974) [hereinafter *Paris Conference Final Report*] (citing Seán MacBride, Chairman of Amnesty's IEC). *See also* Ann Marie Clark, Diplomacy of Conscience, Amnesty International and Changing Human Rights Norms 39 (2001).

("U.N.") Convention against Torture and Other Cruel, Inhuman or Degrading Treatment or Punishment ("Convention" or "Torture Convention")—opened for signature in December 1984.

The story of Amnesty's work on the Torture Convention demonstrates the power of moral vision when backed by thousands of individuals around the world who organize themselves as members of a single movement. The story also provides key insights into the organization itself and the role of human rights non-governmental organizations ("NGOs") more generally in developing international norms at the U.N. At the time of the drafting of the Torture Convention, Amnesty had been at the forefront of revealing torture as a worldwide practice—from the increased use of torture in Latin America to the torture following the military coup in Greece in 1967, to the torture and death of South African black consciousness leader Steve Biko.[3] With the drafting of the Convention, Amnesty could extend its traditional work on behalf of individual prisoners to a push for international norms through a U.N. convention that would address the very violations that such prisoners suffered.

Recently, some States have sought to undermine the full protections of the torture prohibition in the context of the "War on Terror." In many ways, these attempts have been nuanced. They have not challenged the fact that international law prohibits torture and cruel, inhuman or degrading ("CID") treatment or punishment. Instead, they have sought to narrowly construe what the prohibition encompasses, relying on restrictive interpretation tools to read the Torture Convention as prohibiting less than what it intends.[4] The story of Amnesty's work on the Torture Convention provides important substantive and tactical insights to combat such efforts and to ensure that the full scope of the torture prohibition is observed.

---

3. *See, e.g.*, AMNESTY INT'L, ANNUAL REPORT 1975–76 49 (1976); J. HERMAN BURGERS & HANS DANELIUS, THE UNITED NATIONS CONVENTION AGAINST TORTURE: A HANDBOOK ON THE CONVENTION AGAINST TORTURE AND OTHER CRUEL, INHUMAN OR DEGRADING TREATMENT OR PUNISHMENT 13 (1988); CLARK, *supra* note 2, at 39–43; IAIN GUEST, BEHIND THE DISAPPEARANCES: ARGENTINA'S DIRTY WAR AGAINST HUMAN RIGHTS AND THE UNITED NATIONS 76–86 (1990); MARGARET E. KECK & KATHRYN SIKKINK, ACTIVISTS BEYOND BORDERS: ADVOCACY NETWORKS IN INTERNATIONAL POLITICS 104 (1998); WILLIAM KOREY, NGOS AND THE UNIVERSAL DECLARATION OF HUMAN RIGHTS, "A Curious Grapevine" 172 (1998); NIGEL RODLEY, TREATMENT OF PRISONERS UNDER INTERNATIONAL LAW 21, 24–26, 41 (2d ed. 1999).

4. *See, e.g.*, U.S., *List of issues to be considered during the examination of the second periodic report of the United States of America: Response of the United States of America* 1–7 (2006) [hereinafter *Response to Comm. Against Torture List of Issues*]; Scott Shane, David Johnston & James Risen, *Secret U.S. Endorsement of Severe Interrogations*, N.Y. TIMES, Oct. 4, 2007, at A1. *See further* Karen J. Greenberg, THE TORTURE PAPERS: THE ROAD TO ABU GHRAIB (2005); Manfred Nowak, *What Practices Constitute Torture? U.S. and U.N. Standards*, 28 HUM. RTS. Q. 809 (2006); Nigel Rodley, *The Prohibition of Torture; Absolute Means Absolute*, 34 DENV. J. INT'L L. & POL'Y 145 (2006).

Amnesty's Early Involvement on the Torture Issue

Amnesty's push against torture officially started several years after its formation when it determined that it would address all uses of torture and not just torture in situations of political imprisonment. The organization recognized the need for an international instrument that would reflect this conviction as a matter of treaty law. At Amnesty's request, in August 1971, a U.K. barrister prepared a Draft Convention on Torture and the Treatment of Prisoners for Amnesty's International Executive Committee.[5] When Amnesty launched its renowned Campaign for the Abolition of Torture on December 10, 1972, its dual aims were to increase public awareness of torture and to promote international machinery to proscribe the practice.[6] Indeed, this Campaign "stimulated" some governments to bring the question of torture before the U.N. General Assembly.[7] On November 2, 1973 the General Assembly adopted Resolution 3059 (XXVIII), which "[r]ejects any form of torture and other cruel, inhuman or degrading treatment."

A little over one month later, Amnesty published its first comprehensive *Report on Torture*.[8] The report surveys practices in more than sixty-five countries and assesses the arguments being advanced both for and against the use of torture. These arguments have not changed much over time. For example, the *Report on Torture* identifies the ticking time bomb scenario as "the most effective presentation of the argument justifying torture today"[9] and describes it in terms very similar to those used recently in connection with the "War on Terror:"[10]

> The classic case is the French general in Algiers who greeted visiting dignitaries from the metropolis with: 'Gentlemen, we have in our hands a man who has planted a bomb somewhere out in that city. It

---

5. *See* Amnesty Int'l, *Draft Convention on Torture and the Treatment of Prisoners* (Aug. 1971) (on file with Amnesty International). This draft contained provisions that, *inter alia*, outlined the status of torture as a crime under international law and envisaged enforcement mechanisms consisting of an International Commission on Torture and the Treatment of Prisoners, as well as an International Court to try crimes under international law in breach of the Convention.

6. *See* CLARK, *supra* note 2, at 18, 43–55; HOPGOOD, *supra* note 1, at 81–82; KOREY, *supra* note 3, at 171.

7. *See* BURGERS & DANELIUS, *supra* note 3, at 13.

8. AMNESTY INT'L, REPORT ON TORTURE (Am. ed. 1975).

9. *Id.* at 23.

10. As demonstrated more than thirty years ago by Amnesty, it has again been incumbent on NGOs to resist this line of argument. *See, e.g.,* The Assoc'n for the Prevention of Torture, *Defusing the Ticking Bomb Scenario: Why we must say No to torture, always* (2007), *available at* http://www.apt.ch/content/view/109/lang,en/.

will go off within four hours. Would you not use every means to save the lives of innocent people?"[11]

The report had a dramatic impact. It was covered by the press even before its release when *Time* magazine published an article in July 1973 that announced Amnesty's upcoming "worldwide survey" of torture practices.[12] Amnesty also had plans to follow-up the report's release with a large Conference for the Abolition of Torture to be held one week later in Paris. Amnesty's Secretary General Martin Ennals gave the job of running the conference to Eric Abraham, a nineteen-year-old refugee from South Africa, who had been active in the National Union of South African Students ("NUSAS").

This was a huge task, made more difficult when one week before the Conference, the U.N. Educational, Scientific and Cultural Organization ("UNESCO") withdrew its promise to host. UNESCO argued that Amnesty's *Report on Torture* was part of the conference and thus "breached the UNESCO contract rule that its member states may not be criticized."[13] As soon as Amnesty heard of the decision, Ennals, Amnesty's Legal Officer, Nigel Rodley (one of the co-authors of this Chapter) and the Chair of Amnesty's French section, Marie–José Protais, met with UNESCO's top leadership—on a Saturday—to discuss how the issue could be resolved. UNESCO's Director–General was in Morocco on mission, so the Amnesty delegation promised UNESCO's Deputy Director–General that it would keep the *Report on Torture* out of the conference. However, despite a sympathetic hearing, UNESCO rejected Amnesty's offer by the end of the same weekend, confirming Amnesty's suspicion that its decision was due to pressure from governments and not actually because of a problem with the contract. In the end a balance was struck, with Amnesty holding the conference at the new Tour Olivier de Serres Center and UNESCO providing translation services and equipment. A few months later Amnesty's request to be granted formal "consultative relations" with UNESCO was agreed.

With this crisis averted, on December 10, 1973, one week after the *Report on Torture*'s release, 300 delegates and participants attended the conference in Paris. The Conference coincided with the twenty-fifth anniversary of the Universal Declaration of Human Rights and was convened to shape the second phase of Amnesty's Campaign.[14] In particular, Amnesty had to make a decision about whether and how to continue leading the campaign to end torture. The organization was

---

11. AMNESTY INT'L, *supra* note 8, at 23–24.

12. *Amnesty for the Defense*, TIME, July 9, 1973, *available at* http://www.time.com/time/magazine/article/0,9171,907502,00.html.

13. Amnesty Int'l, *Paris Conference Final Report, supra* note 2, at 10.

14. *See* Amnesty Int'l, *Campaign for the Abolition of Torture, Strategy for 1973*, Act. 42/IEC 73, Agenda Item 9(c) (1973) (on file with Amnesty International).

divided. On the one hand, the *Report on Torture* and the Campaign's first phase had had an enormous impact. However, by late 1973, the International Secretariat was urging Amnesty's International Executive Committee to shift responsibility for the torture issue to another NGO or NGOs. It argued that the torture work was not restricted to political imprisonment, which was the main focus of Amnesty's mandate, and that torture had become such a big issue that it might dominate Amnesty's work. International Executive Committee member Eric Baker, one of Amnesty's founders, strongly resisted the International Secretariat's attempts to hand off the torture issue. His efforts were successful. From both the Paris conference and the International Executive Committee meeting held in Paris at around the same time, there was a "predominant feeling" that Amnesty should continue to lead the Campaign.[15] With this new mandate, Amnesty established its Campaign Department "[w]ithin 24 hours of the end of the Conference...."[16]

Amnesty in Transition

Amnesty's evolving approach to the torture issue exemplified its transition during the 1970s. Established in response to a single instance of human rights violation, the organization had developed a case-based methodology by which it would "adopt" cases of prisoners of conscience (those imprisoned for expressing their beliefs without advocating violence) on whose behalf the organization and its national sections would work. It now faced a transition from being a case-driven lobbying group to becoming a norm-oriented *human rights* organization that looked beyond situations of political imprisonment. This transformation necessarily meant increased attention to international law and universal human rights *principles*.

The genius of Amnesty's approach lay in how it would integrate this newer focus on international institutions and principles with the work of its national sections on behalf of prisoners of conscience worldwide. The possibilities were endless and exciting. Amnesty's increased attention to universal human rights principles assisted national sections' case-based activism because it showed that Amnesty was independent and above national politics.[17] At the same time, Amnesty could use its campaign work to authoritatively contrast its worldwide factual findings on torture and disappearances with the international human rights principles that existed in documents such as the Universal Declaration of Human Rights.[18] This campaigning built consensus in the minds of the "public

---

15. *See* Amnesty Int'l, *Post Paris CAT*, Act. 04/IEC 73, Agenda Item 12 (1973) (on file with Amnesty International).

16. *See* Amnesty Int'l, *Paris Conference Final Report*, *supra* note 2, at 17.

17. *See* GUEST, *supra* note 3, at 78; KECK & SIKKINK, *supra* note 3, at 88.

18. *See* CLARK, *supra* note 2, at 37.

and [among] elites" that new norms were necessary.[19] Later, as these new norms took shape, Amnesty would utilize its national sections to mobilize their governments on contentious drafting issues, such as whether there should be universal jurisdiction for torture offenses.[20]

Amnesty knew that to maximize its work at the international level, it would need additional expertise and a more planned and professionalized approach toward the U.N.[21] Amnesty had gained U.N. Economic and Social Council ("ECOSOC") consultative status—the official means by which the NGOs can provide input to U.N. bodies—quite quickly (about three years after Amnesty's formation).[22] However, Amnesty had no permanent staff representation in either Geneva or New York and relied primarily on its volunteers for its U.N. work.[23] This situation changed when in early 1973, before adding the Campaign Department, Amnesty added a Legal Officer, Nigel Rodley.[24] Within Amnesty this appointment was perceived as recognition of its increased attention to international law to safeguard the human rights of prisoners of conscience. Accordingly, direct responsibility for work with the U.N. shifted from the organization's Secretary General to Rodley.[25] As an experienced international lawyer, Rodley was well placed to lead Amnesty's new focus to develop international norms at the U.N.[26]

The Lead–Up to the Drafting of the Torture Convention

This new focus yielded a number of results over the next few years. For example, during 1974 and 1975, Amnesty played a critical role in the formulation of professional codes of conduct for police, military, prison and medical personnel prohibiting torture.[27] Amnesty also demonstrated its ability to make both substantive and strategic contributions on the

---

19. Id.

20. See, e.g., Virginia Leary, *A New Role for Non–Governmental Organizations in Human Rights: A Case Study of Non–Governmental Participation in the Development of International Norms on Torture*, in U.N. LAW/FUNDAMENTAL RIGHTS: TWO TOPICS IN INTERNATIONAL LAW 197, 206 (Antonio Cassese ed. 1979).

21. See, e.g., Amnesty Int'l, *Minutes of the International Organizations Sub–Committee* (May 31, 1978) (on file with Amnesty International).

22. See U.N. Econ. & Soc. Council [ECOSOC], *List of non-governmental organizations in consultative status with the Economic and Social Council as at 31 August 2006*, 10, U.N. Doc. E/2006/INF/4 (Oct. 26, 2006).

23. See CLARK, supra note 2, at 7.

24. The title switched from Legal Officer to Legal Adviser around 1975.

25. See Amnesty Int'l, Int'l Executive Comm. Int'l Orgs. SubComm., *Strategy, Planning and Structure of AI work at the UN*, Agenda Item 11(a) (June 1978) (on file with Amnesty International).

26. See Leary, supra note 20, at 206.

27. See Amnesty Int'l, *Paris Conference Final Report*, supra note 2, at 14, 17.

question of torture in its work on the Declaration on the Protection of All Persons from Being Subjected to Torture and Other Cruel, Inhuman or Degrading Treatment or Punishment ("Declaration"). The Declaration was adopted at the Fifth U.N. Congress on the Prevention of Crime and the Treatment of Offenders in the first half of September 1975. Amnesty's role included submitting a sixteen-page document containing recommendations; circulating that document, accompanied by a personal message, to fifty governments in advance of the Congress; mobilizing national sections to press their governments to support the recommendations; and sponsoring two events at the Congress on the torture issue.[28]

While Amnesty "had a virtual monopoly, as a non-governmental organization authority speaking the language of universal human rights,"[29] other organizations were also working toward an international instrument prohibiting torture. Amnesty's approach to these other groups was to work very closely with the Geneva-headquartered International Commission of Jurists ("ICJ") and participate in larger informal multilateral NGO collaborations as necessary.

ICJ and Amnesty had a close institutional relationship because Seán MacBride, one of Amnesty's founders, was both Chairman of Amnesty's International Executive Committee (from 1961 to 1974) and ICJ Secretary–General (from 1963 to 1970). MacBride had also acted as a "liaison and an inside 'ear' for Amnesty International in the early days of its U.N. consultative status," i.e., from 1964 onward.[30] By the time the draft torture convention was on the table, Rodley's main counterpart at the ICJ was MacBride's successor, Niall MacDermot. MacDermot was occasionally impulsive and a very forceful character, and "[n]o one talked down to MacDermot, and no one ignored him. Diplomats deferred to him and dreaded his rebukes."[31] However, these personality traits did not interfere with a relationship between MacDermot and Rodley that was for the most part extremely collaborative and productive.

In addition to this close relationship with the ICJ, Rodley and Amnesty were also active in informal NGO collaborations that were working toward entrenching the legal prohibition of torture. The question of how best to coordinate such action was comprehensively discussed at an International Symposium on Torture held at the Institut

---

28. *See generally* AMNESTY INT'L, ANNUAL REPORT 1975–76, *supra* note 3, at 40; Amnesty Int'l, *Report on Geneva Congress* (Oct. 14, 1975) (on file with Amnesty International); Helena Cook, *Amnesty International at the United Nations*, *in* "THE CONSCIENCE OF THE WORLD": THE INFLUENCE OF NON-GOVERNMENTAL ORGANISATIONS IN THE U.N. SYSTEM 181, 190 (Peter Willetts ed., 1996); Leary, *supra* note 20, at 202–204.

29. *See* HOPGOOD, *supra* note 1, at 54.
30. *See* CLARK, *supra* note 2, at 7.
31. *See* GUEST, *supra* note 3, at 112.

Henry–Dunant in Geneva on May 5 and 6, 1977. Among the twenty persons who participated was Amnesty's Dick Oosting, who presented the possibilities for increased coordination and cooperation among NGOs opposing torture.[32]

His presentation inspired an informal luncheon meeting approximately two weeks later between representatives of Amnesty, the ICJ, the International Committee of the Red Cross ("ICRC"), the World Council of Churches' Commission of the Churches on International Affairs ("WCC"), and Michael A.S. Landale of the Australian Mission to the U.N.[33] It was agreed at this meeting that the four NGOs would meet regularly (every four to six weeks), that representation at these meetings would be high level, and that the collaboration would be kept informal (e.g. there would no permanent secretariat).[34] The ICRC in particular insisted on the latter requirement, as they would have been unable to participate in a formal collaboration.[35] This arrangement also suited Amnesty. Driven by concerns about independence and impartiality, Amnesty also had a general policy of only occasional formal cooperation with other NGOs on substantive issues, especially on country-specific matters.

The group called itself the Informal Liaison Group on Torture and held its first meeting on July 8, 1977 at the Institut Henry Dunant in Geneva.[36] From the outset, the meetings focused on the substantive and strategic issues surrounding the three draft proposals for a torture convention[37]—the Swiss Committee Against Torture's ("Swiss Committee") draft Convention concerning the Treatment of Persons Deprived of their Liberty (May 1977), the International Association of Penal Law's ("IAPL") Draft Convention for the Prevention and Suppression of Torture,[38] and the text being prepared by the Swedish government.

---

32. *See Symposium on Torture*, 195 INT'L REV. RED CROSS 330, 330–331 (1977).

33. *See, e.g.,* Nigel Rodley, Amnesty Int'l, *Report on Visit to Geneva–19–22 May, 1977* (May 23, 1977) (on file with Amnesty International).

34. *Id. See also* Letter from A–Dominique Micheli, Delegate to Int'l Orgs., Int'l Comm. of the Red Cross, to Martin Ennals, Sec'y Gen., Amnesty Int'l (June 20, 1977) (on file with Amnesty International).

35. *See* Rodley, *supra* note 33.

36. *See* Letter from Micheli to Ennals, *supra* note 34; Minutes, Meeting of Informal Liaison Group on July 8, 1977 in Geneva, Switzerland (undated) (on file with Amnesty International).

37. The Group also addressed other relevant standard-setting activities being conducted at the time, such as the draft Code of Conduct for Law Enforcement Officials and the Principles of Medical Ethics relevant to the Role of Health Personnel, particularly Physicians, in the Protection of Prisoners and Detainees against Torture and Other Cruel, Inhuman or Degrading Treatment or Punishment.

38. *See* U.N. ESCOR, Comm'n on H.R., submitted by Int'l Ass'n of Penal Law, *Draft Convention for the Prevention and Suppression of Torture*, E/CN.4/NGO/213 (1978).

Amnesty provided input on all three texts. However, in August 1977, the organization withdrew its "openly active support" for the draft prepared by the Swiss Committee.[39] It made this decision primarily because it "long regarded an international convention through the highest inter-governmental body, the United Nations, allowing the widest participation without compromising on effectiveness, as a necessary and urgent target."[40] Jean–Jacques Gautier, the founder of the Swiss Committee, was not well pleased. He had proposed the core idea embodied in the draft—that empowering a commission to conduct regular inspections of States would prevent ill-treatment—and was devoted to the proposal. It fell to MacDermot of the ICJ to manage the situation. He proposed to Gautier that the draft first be promoted outside of the U.N. process. Gautier agreed and he and the ICJ championed his proposal at the European level.

These efforts resulted in the European Convention for the Prevention of Torture and Inhuman or Degrading Treatment or Punishment, which opened for signature on November 26, 1987, over a decade after Gautier put forward his original plan. That Convention provides for a preventative system to protect detainees from ill-treatment by establishing a European Committee for the Prevention of Torture and Inhuman or Degrading Treatment or Punishment that undertakes visits to places of detention. The Swiss Committee's draft was also turned into a proposed optional protocol to the draft torture convention. Costa Rica formally submitted this draft to the U.N. Commission on Human Rights on March 6, 1980 with the request that it be considered after the Convention's adoption. In 1991, Costa Rica re-submitted the draft, and it eventually formed the basis for the Optional Protocol to the Torture Convention adopted by the U.N. General Assembly in December 2002. Given that the Swiss Committee's proposal was taken forward in these different ways, Gautier did not try to change Amnesty's position on the Swiss Committee's draft. It was also relevant that by June 1978 Amnesty had officially decided not to support any of the specific drafts produced for the Convention.

With Amnesty's eye firmly on the U.N., one of its and the Informal Liaison Group's first goals was to try to influence which U.N. body would produce the Torture Convention. The challenge was to dissuade the Swedes, and in particular, then Under–Secretary for Legal and Consular Affairs of the Swedish Ministry of Foreign Affairs, Hans

---

39. *See* Letter from Martin Ennals, Sec'y Gen., Amnesty Int'l, to Jean–Jacques Gautier, Founder, Swiss Comm. Against Torture (Aug. 1, 1977) (on file with Amnesty International).

40. *See* Amnesty Int'l, *AI Position on the Jean–Jacques Gautier Proposal for Use by Swiss Section* (Aug. 24, 1977) (on file with Amnesty International).

Danelius,[41] from asking the General Assembly to task the U.N. Commission on Human Rights with this role.[42] It was Amnesty's aim to convince Sweden and other governments that the drafting of the Convention should instead be dealt with at the 1980 U.N. Congress on the Prevention of Crime and the Treatment of Offenders. The Commission was a politicized body, composed of diplomats who would more readily see the significance of the draft convention and potentially block its progress. In contrast, the Congress was composed of technocrats acting primarily in their capacity as officials involved in the administration of justice and law enforcement. They were not as affected by the political divides of the Commission and could not easily oppose the subject matter of the proposed convention as torture was a crime in most, if not all, of their jurisdictions.

Promoting Principles for Inclusion in the Draft Convention

Despite these efforts, on December 8, 1977, the General Assembly requested the U.N. Commission on Human Rights to draw up a draft convention against torture and other CID treatment or punishment. On January 15, 1978, the IAPL submitted its Draft Convention for the Prevention and Suppression of Torture and three days later the Swedish government submitted its draft.[43] A little less than two weeks later, on January 30, 1978, Amnesty's International Executive Committee Sub-Committee on International Organizations ("Sub-Committee") met in London to formulate its recommendations to the International Executive Committee on how Amnesty should approach the drafting of the Torture Convention.

Amnesty's International Executive Committee adopted the Sub-Committee's recommendations in early June 1978, agreeing that Amnesty's position on the draft convention would follow five key elements:

I. AI welcomes the decision of the General Assembly to develop a convention against torture and hopes this will be produced without undue delay.

II. AI has taken no stand, and will take no stand, on the various drafts or texts produced for this convention.

---

41. *See* BURGERS & DANELIUS, *supra* note 3, at vi.

42. *See, e.g.*, Draft Minutes, Meeting of Informal Liaison Group on Torture on Oct. 5 1977 in Strasbourg, France (undated) (on file with Amnesty International); Draft Minutes, Meeting of Informal Liaison Group on Torture on Aug. 26 1977 in Geneva, Switzerland (undated) (on file with Amnesty International).

43. U.N. ESCOR, Comm'n on H.R., submitted by Sweden, *Draft International Convention against Torture and Other Cruel, Inhuman or Degrading Treatment or Punishment,* U.N. Doc. E/CN.4/1285 (1978).

III. AI hopes, however, that when the convention is adopted it will include the following principles:

a. Every state should be obliged to either extradite, or itself to try, alleged torturers within its jurisdiction.

b. There should be universality of jurisdiction in respect of alleged torturers.

c. There should be an effective implementation mechanism to deal with allegations of torture.

d. The question of cruel, inhuman or degrading treatment or punishment should be addressed.

IV. When and where appropriate, AI should voice this position (I, II and III) above. Expert AI members or staff can in their individual private capacities enter into textual details of this convention, so long as they make clear this is done in their personal capacity.

V. AI should devote more of its resources to exposing the continuing practice of torture and the non-adherence of governments to the UN declaration against torture than to the formulation or adoption of the convention.[44]

Amnesty's participation in the drafting process was particularly guided by elements II, III and IV. In November 1981, the International Executive Committee confirmed that Amnesty would continue to focus on the four principles in element III—extradition or trial of alleged torturers, universal jurisdiction over torture, implementation of the torture prohibition, and inclusion of the prohibition of CID treatment or punishment—as well as the issue of how "lawful sanctions" should be dealt with in the Torture Convention's definition of torture.[45]

"II. AI has taken no stand, and will take no stand, on the various drafts or texts produced for this convention."

At its meeting on January 30, 1978, the Sub–Committee had before it the IAPL and Swedish drafts. Following a lengthy discussion on the IAPL draft, the Sub–Committee decided to recommend that Amnesty adopt the principle that it would avoid associating with a particular text.[46] This recommendation was taken up by the International Execu-

---

44. *See* Amnesty Int'l, *Report of IEC,* June 2–4, 1978 (on file with Amnesty International).

45. *See, e.g.,* Letter from Stephanie Grant, IEC Member, Amnesty Int'l, to Walter Kälin, Swiss Section, Amnesty Int'l (Feb. 2, 1982) (on file with Amnesty International).

46. *See* Amnesty Int'l, *Report from the Sub–Committee on International Organisations held in London on Jan. 30 1978*, AI Index IOR 41/03/79 [hereinafter *Report from the Sub–Comm. on Int'l Orgs*] (on file with Amnesty International).

tive Committee and from this point onward Amnesty officially saw it as its "role to support principles which should be incorporated in such drafts."[47]

Amnesty continued to adhere to this position even when the Swedish draft was the only text being considered at the U.N. It was a deliberate policy choice in favor of impartiality. In November 1981, at the request of the organization's Swiss and German sections,[48] the International Executive Committee revisited its June 1978 decision and determined that, despite developments (i.e., the fact that only the Swedish draft was being considered), the organization's position should not change. This was because of Amnesty's belief that public association with government texts could damage its reputation for impartiality.[49]

This commitment to independence, balance and political neutrality was the cornerstone of Amnesty's identity.[50] Indeed, in the lead up to the thirty-ninth session of the General Assembly in 1984, Margo Picken, Amnesty's representative in New York, had expressed concern that Amnesty should not be perceived as the "non-governmental wing of the Dutch,"[51] the government that was responsible for shepherding the Torture Convention through its final drafting and adoption phases. Fortunately, some enlightened governments were less worried about the risk of appearing to be the governmental wing of Amnesty or the ICJ and closely collaborated with both organizations at all stages.

Despite the obvious benefits of this collaboration, Amnesty and others (including the Dutch) were nevertheless concerned that Amnesty should not appear to be too closely associated with the draft. This concern pointed in two different directions: either that Amnesty would insist too much on improved language (such as in the area of "lawful sanctions"), encouraging some governments sensitive to Amnesty's per-

---

47. *See* Letter from Thomas Hammarberg, Sec'y Gen., Amnesty Int'l, to Niall MacDermot, Sec'y–Gen., Int'l Comm'n of Jurists (June 1, 1984) (on file with Amnesty International).

48. *See* Letter from Walter Kälin, Swiss Section, Amnesty Int'l, to IEC, Amnesty Int'l (Oct. 1981) (on file with Amnesty International); Letter from Luise Scherf, Board Member, German Section, Amnesty Int'l, to IEC, Amnesty Int'l (Nov. 11, 1981) (on file with Amnesty International).

49. *See* Letter from Grant to Kälin, *supra* note 45; Letter from Stephanie Grant, IEC Member, Amnesty Int'l, to Luise Scherf, Board Member, German Section, Amnesty Int'l (Feb. 2, 1982) (on file with Amnesty International). The fact that the letter was signed by Grant may reflect Rodley's disaffection with an application of the principle he found bureaucratic and difficult to reconcile with the aim of effective reconciliation with other NGOs.

50. *See* GUEST, *supra* note 3, at 78; HOPGOOD, *supra* note 1, at 61–62; KECK & SIKKINK, *supra* note 3, at 88.

51. *See* Margo Picken, Amnesty Int'l, *Note on lunch meeting with Alphons Hamer (Netherlands), 4 April 1984* (Apr. 6, 1984) (on file with Amnesty International).

spective to re-open already satisfactorily decided issues and potentially expose the entire draft to re-negotiation; or that the interests of Amnesty as a human rights organization would be so closely identified with the text that non-cooperative governments would become intractable in their opposition to the draft. Amnesty had to balance these concerns against its interest in working closely with the drafters to ensure that the principles in the International Executive Committee's June 1978 decision were included in the final text. Amnesty's compromise in the lead up to the Convention's adoption in 1984 was to draw attention to any remaining concerns it had regarding the text, while simultaneously making it very clear that the organization did not want to jeopardize the Convention's adoption.[52]

"IV. Expert AI members or staff can in their individual private capacities enter into textual details of this convention, so long as they make clear this is done in their personal capacity."

Amnesty's decision not to submit draft text stemmed from similar concerns that motivated its position on not supporting specific drafts, such as the importance of impartiality, as well as apprehension about the capacity of the national sections to negotiate complicated textual details.[53] This position also was aimed at preventing Amnesty from being too closely associated with the weak and compromised text that is often the product of government negotiations.[54]

This caution meant two things in practice. First, that Amnesty provided observations but would not promote these observations in the form of textual amendments and second, that Rodley primarily provided textual input in his personal capacity. Indeed, when recollecting the contribution of NGOs like Amnesty to the drafting process, Amnesty receives credit as an organization but contributions are also remembered in terms of what individual representatives like Rodley and Niall MacDermot of the ICJ did and said.[55]

However, neither of these approaches was static in practice. For example, Amnesty's policy of providing observations could not prevent situations when an Amnesty comment inadvertently became a textual

---

52. *See, e.g.,* Amnesty Int'l, *AI's concerns at the 39th Regular Session of the UN General Assembly New York, September–December 1984*, AI Index IOR 41/06/84 (July 9, 1984) (on file with Amnesty International).

53. *See* Letter from Grant to Kälin, *supra* note 45; Letter from Grant to Scherf, *supra* note 49.

54. *See* Cook, *supra* note 28, at 191.

55. Telephonic Interview with Erika Feller, Assistant High Commissioner–Protection, United Nations High Commissioner for Refugees (July 2, 2007). Ms. Feller had arrived in Geneva in 1980 as First Secretary in the Australian Mission to the U.N.

amendment. For example, Article 12 of the original Swedish draft addressed the right to compensation, but had not specified that compensation would include "rehabilitation." A meeting of medical groups at Amnesty's International Secretariat in London inspired Rodley to make an oral statement on rehabilitation at the 1980 session of the Commission's Working Group on the draft convention. The Greek Chair of the session, Anestis Papastefanou, said that he would put in the Amnesty "amendment" and the Working Group ultimately adopted the article with the term "rehabilitation" in square brackets (signaling non-agreement within the Working Group).[56]

Additionally, the policy that expert Amnesty members or staff should only submit text in a personal capacity was not so rigid as to prevent Amnesty as an organization from proposing text on the Torture Convention's fundamental provisions. As demonstrated below, Amnesty departed from its policy twice during drafting, proposing textual modifications in Amnesty's name on the issues of "lawful sanctions" and CID treatment or punishment.

Amnesty's Position on the Content of the Treaty

Trial or Extradition and Universal Jurisdiction

It was Amnesty's hope that the Torture Convention would include two principles on jurisdiction over the offense of torture: first, that "Every state should be obliged to either extradite, or itself to try, alleged torturers within its jurisdiction" and second, that "There should be universality of jurisdiction in respect of alleged torturers." The aim of both principles was to fight impunity for torturers, a cornerstone of any Convention that would truly seek to outlaw torture. Indeed, when the Convention was considered by the U.N. Commission on Human Rights in 1984, Amnesty's Secretary General Thomas Hammarberg gave a statement that heralded the Convention's "crucial principle" of universal jurisdiction and emphasized that there should be "no safe haven for torturers."[57]

This "crucial principle" was understood by all of those involved in drafting the Torture Convention to be contained in its Article 5. Article 5 provides a number of bases for establishing jurisdiction, including where the State does not extradite an offender present in its territory. While strictly speaking Article 5 does not provide for "pure" universal jurisdiction (in which no nexus to the State would be required), "universal

---

56. *See* BURGERS & DANELIUS, *supra* note 3, at 68–69.

57. *See* Thomas Hammarberg, Sec'y Gen., Amnesty Int'l, *An International Convention Against Torture* (1984) (on file with Amnesty International).

jurisdiction" became the simplified way to refer to the "wide domestic jurisdiction" set out in Article 5 of the Torture Convention and in Article 8 of the original Swedish draft.[58]

It was somewhat remarkable that the original Swedish draft included such wide-ranging bases for establishing jurisdiction over torture. When Sweden submitted its original draft there was virtually no precedent for universal jurisdiction to be included in an international human rights instrument intended to be binding on States. There were similar provisions in other instruments, such as the Geneva Conventions in the international humanitarian realm and in conventions dealing with international terrorism. While there was also a universal jurisdiction provision in the International Convention on the Suppression and Punishment of the Crime of Apartheid, which had opened for signature on November 30, 1973; this instrument was largely discredited at the time of drafting the Torture Convention. Nor did universal jurisdiction appear in the Declaration on which much of the initial Swedish draft was based.[59] Instead, in large part, it was NGOs that were pushing for the linking of universal jurisdiction and torture—for example, the IAPL's draft that preceded the original Swedish text by three days included a wide basis for the exercise of jurisdiction in its Article IX.

According to Hans Danelius, the Swedes' decision to include the principle of universal jurisdiction in their original draft was based primarily on similar provisions in other conventions at the time, e.g., conventions dealing with terrorism.[60] While these provisions evidently provided some guidance, it was still a significant step to include a provision originally designed to eliminate loopholes for those suspected of (mainly transnational) crimes of terrorism in a treaty designed to eliminate impunity for those suspected of crimes of torture—often crimes carried out by State officials within their own countries. Indeed, apart from the International Convention on the Suppression and Punishment of the Crime of Apartheid, the Torture Convention would be the first international human rights convention to include such wide criterion for establishing jurisdiction over human rights violations.

This achievement was all the more marked given that the Swedes, particularly the Ministry of Justice, did not want the Torture Convention to explicitly mention that torture was a crime under international law, in addition to being an act that the Convention required States to criminalize under domestic law. There was a moment of hope that the Swedes would change their position on this point. At around the time the original Swedish draft was being prepared in December 1977, the

---

58. *See* BURGERS & DANELIUS, *supra* note 3, at 58.

59. *Id.* at 35.

60. Telephonic Interview with Hans Danelius, former Justice of the Supreme Court of Sweden (July 6, 2007); *see also* BURGERS & DANELIUS, *supra* note 3, at 35–36.

Swedish Attorney–General, Helga Romander, was participating in the IAPL drafting committee in Siracusa. At that meeting he told Rodley that he strongly supported the IAPL draft's principle of universality of jurisdiction, giving Amnesty hope that Sweden might also agree to explicitly categorize torture as a crime under international law in the draft text.[61]

However, Sweden continued to oppose this approach. A number of other governments were in a similar position—positive about the idea of a Torture Convention, but either uncomfortable or unfamiliar with the concept of a "crime under international law."[62] There was a general lack of clarity concerning both what constituted a crime under international law and the legal implications that flowed from so classifying an act.[63]

Amnesty representatives believed that torture already had acquired the status of a crime under customary international law, but that a treaty was needed to make this "absolutely clear" and to identify the consequent legal obligations.[64] At the same time, they were well aware that efforts to draft treaties explicitly recognizing particular violations as international crimes had seen limited success thus far. In particular, there was some embarrassment around the existence of the International Convention on the Suppression and Punishment of the Crime of Apartheid, which had defined apartheid and related acts as "violating the principles of international law." Having been pushed through by the African States (with the support of the Soviet Union and others) over Western objections, it did not have wide support and its legal drafting was considered deficient. Countries did not want to be put in the inconsistent position of promoting one convention that referred to the enumerated violations as an international crime, but not another.[65]

In light of all of these factors, Amnesty decided to uphold its policy that torture should be classified as a crime under international law but to stop actively lobbying for this to be explicitly recognized in the Convention.[66] It was ultimately more important to ensure that the text

---

61. *See* Nigel Rodley, Amnesty Int'l, *Report on a visit to Geneva, Siracusa and Paris, 15–19, December 1977* (internal) (undated) (on file with Amnesty International).

62. *See* Nigel Rodley, Amnesty Int'l, *Proposed Convention on Torture: Crime under International Law*, Int'l Org. Sub–Comm., Agenda Item 11e (1978) (on file with Amnesty International); Letter from Nigel Rodley, Legal Adviser, Amnesty Int'l, to Karl–Walter Bluhm (Oct. 6, 1980) (on file with Amnesty International).

63. *See* Rodley, *Proposed Convention on Torture: Crime under International Law*, *supra* note 62.

64. *Id.*

65. *Id.*

66. *See* Amnesty Int'l, *Report from the Sub–Comm. on Int'l Orgs*, *supra* note 46; Rodley, *Proposed Convention on Torture: Crime under International Law*, *supra* note 62; Letter from Rodley to Bluhm, *supra* note 62.

stipulate core obligations rather than explicitly recognize the concept of an international crime itself. This position was also taken by other groups, notably the ICJ.

By deciding to focus on core obligations, Amnesty could direct its lobbying efforts toward those key governments that were particularly resisting the Convention's inclusion of universal jurisdiction. This included, for example, Australia and the Netherlands. In relation to the latter, Amnesty faced a big challenge because J. Herman Burgers, a member of the Netherlands delegation to the Commission, and chairperson-rapporteur of the Commission's Working Group between 1982 and 1984,[67] particularly had reservations about the concept of universal jurisdiction as applied to the crime of torture.

This was reflected in the Netherlands's position in the early stages of the drafting process. For example, in 1980 the Netherlands supported making universal jurisdiction contingent on the rejection of an extradition request, a move which would have limited the extent to which the Convention would prevent safe havens for torturers. By 1981, the Netherlands was no longer advocating this position, but still sought to make the exercise of universal jurisdiction contingent "upon complaint by any interested party."[68] In 1982 this proposal was withdrawn and J. Herman Burgers as chairperson-rapporteur worked diligently to find a compromise on universal jurisdiction that would bring all parties together. During this process, Amnesty's efforts at the international level were supplemented by its Dutch national section, which partnered with the Dutch section of the ICJ to get a motion favoring universal jurisdiction through the Dutch parliament.

The import of the Torture Convention's jurisdiction provisions cannot be overstated. The Torture Convention's principle of *aut dedere aut punire* (extradite or punish on the basis of simple presence in the forum country), along with its application to acts of public officials, were key factors in the 1999 landmark decision of the U.K. House of Lords that Senator Augusto Pinochet did not have immunity for certain crimes committed during his previous tenure as Chile's head of state. This result was possible because the original Swedish draft convention provided for universal jurisdiction. The explicit inclusion of the concept was so contested throughout the Commission's Working Group's sessions that, had it not been in the original text, it surely would not have been added at a later stage. From Amnesty's perspective—and indeed that of any NGO—it was much easier to defend existing text rather than having to advocate for the introduction of such a far-reaching principle. This was

---

67. *See* BURGERS & DANELIUS, *supra* note 3, at vi.

68. *Id.* at 72.

also the lesson of the long battle about how the Convention would apply to CID treatment or punishment, explored later in this Chapter.

Implementation

Along with universal jurisdiction, implementation provisions were a major sticking point during drafting, and a major priority for Amnesty. In his speech before the plenary Commission in 1984, Hammarberg emphasized the importance of the implementation provisions of the Torture Convention in the following terms: "The purpose of a convention against torture should ... be to ensure the *enforcement* of the international prohibition on torture."[69]

The draft convention that was sent to the General Assembly for adoption in 1984 contained four implementation procedures. Two of these procedures were optional, meaning that they required states to declare that they recognized the competence of the Committee against Torture to receive complaints against it from other states (Article 21) and from individuals (Article 22). The other two implementation procedures were more integral to the Convention, and also more controversial. Article 19 provided for periodic reporting to the Committee and the Committee's consideration of these reports. While this was in essence a standard treaty body function, there was disagreement over the sub-paragraphs which set out what the Committee could do in respect of the state reports received.[70] These sub-paragraphs, along with the fourth implementation procedure in Article 20, were the *only* provisions of the draft convention that were unresolved when sent to the General Assembly.[71]

The fact that Article 20 caused so much disagreement was unsurprising. Article 20 established a procedure by which the Committee was empowered to initiate a confidential inquiry into allegations of systematic torture in a state. This was an innovation for a U.N. human rights treaty and a radical one at that. Delegations differed significantly on whether the procedure should be mandatory or optional.

Amnesty took the former position and focused its lobbying efforts to emphasize the importance of the inquiry system being mandatory. These efforts continued right up until the eleventh hour at the U.N. General Assembly, when the Swedes told Hammarberg that to overcome the Soviet Union's objection to the mandatory nature of the Article 20 inquiry procedure they were going to accept a provision (now Article 28) by which states could "opt out" of Article 20. Hammarberg telephoned

---

69. *See* Hammarberg, *An International Convention Against Torture, supra* note 57.
70. *See* Burgers & Danelius, *supra* note 3, at 97.
71. *Id.* at 96–107.

Rodley to consult on this proposal, who thought it a very good solution to what was otherwise proving to be an intractable problem. Rodley guessed that many states that would not have supported the Article 20 procedure would be loath to make the requisite declaration in order to opt out of it. Amnesty therefore agreed with the Swedish proposal and the text moved forward to adoption.

Cruel, Inhuman or Degrading Treatment or Punishment

Amnesty's commitment to including CID treatment or punishment in the draft convention was heavily influenced by the fact that the 1975 Declaration on the Protection of All Persons from Being Subjected to Torture and Other Cruel, Inhuman or Degrading Treatment or Punishment deals with both torture and CID treatment or punishment. The Declaration's approach itself reflected the unfortunate but all too real distinction that the European Commission of Human Rights had made in the *Greek Case* (1969), defining torture to be an aggravated form of CID treatment or punishment.[72] Making this distinction was unfortunate because it ran contrary to the intention of the framers of the Universal Declaration of Human Rights who used the holistic phrase of "torture or cruel, inhuman or degrading treatment or punishment" (in Article 5) to have a flexible formula that could encompass practices such as medical experiments of the Holocaust.[73] Three months after the adoption of the U.N. Declaration, the European Court of Human Rights confirmed this distinction by holding that five specific interrogation techniques the Commission had found to be torture in *Ireland v. United Kingdom* (1976)[74] were not sufficiently aggravated to be so categorized. Rather, the Court found them to be "inhuman and degrading treatment."[75] Amnesty's position was also consistent with the U.N. General Assembly Resolution that had requested the Commission to draft a convention against torture and other CID treatment or punishment.

In accordance with the language in the Declaration and the Resolution, the original Swedish draft had contained a number of references to CID treatment or punishment. Article 1(2) of the original Swedish draft defined torture as an "aggravated and deliberate form of cruel, inhuman or degrading treatment or punishment" and virtually all of its substantive articles applied to both torture and CID treatment or punishment. However, the revised Swedish draft of February 19, 1979[76] addressed

---

72. Greek Case, 1969 Y.B. Eur. Conv. on H.R. 1, 186 (Eur. Comm'n H.R.).

73. *See* RODLEY, *supra* note 3, at 75.

74. Ireland v. United Kingdom, 1976 Y.B. Eur. Conv. on H.R. 512 (Eur. Comm'n H.R.).

75. Ireland v. United Kingdom, 2 Eur. H.R. Rep. 25, 165–168 (1978).

76. U.N. ESCOR, Comm'n on H.R., submitted by Sweden, *Revised text of the substantive parts of the Draft Convention Against Torture and Other Cruel, Inhuman or Degrading Treatment or Punishment*, U.N. Doc. E/CN.4/WG.1/WP.1 (1979).

CID treatment in a more limited way. The draft bracketed the reference to CID treatment or punishment in Article 1(2), reflecting that it was disputed. It also removed other references to CID treatment or punishment in the substantive guarantees, e.g., *non-refoulement* and criminalization provisions. Instead, there was a new Article 16 that stated that the "Convention shall be without prejudice to any provisions in other international instruments or in national law which prohibit cruel, inhuman and degrading treatment or punishment."

Before the end of the 1979 session of the Commission's Working Group, MacDermot suggested to Danelius that the revised Swedish draft should also stipulate a general duty to prevent CID treatment or punishment not amounting to torture.[77] In the lead up to the January 1980 session of the Working Group, MacDermot and Rodley corresponded on this new draft language. At Rodley's suggestion, they agreed that MacDermot's proposed general duty statement should be followed by text specifying which articles in the Convention applied to CID treatment or punishment. After some back and forth, they agreed that the draft provision should specify seven such articles: Articles 3 (*non-refoulement*), 10 (education), 11 (review of practices with a view to prevention), 12 (right of complaint), 13 (prompt and impartial investigation), 14 (compensation) and 15 (non-use of evidence obtained under torture) of the Swedish revised draft of February 19, 1979. Given the importance of ensuring that the Torture Convention would not only stipulate a general duty to prevent CID treatment or punishment not amounting to torture, and the need to cooperate effectively with the ICJ, Amnesty departed from its policy of not submitting draft text. Accordingly, at the 1980 session of the Commission's Working Group, Amnesty and the ICJ jointly[78] submitted the following proposal for a second paragraph in Article 16:

> 2. Each State Party shall take effective measures to prevent in any territory under its jurisdiction other acts of cruel, inhuman or degrading treatment or punishment which do not amount to torture as defined in Article 1. In particular, the obligations contained in articles 3, 10, 11, 12, 13, 14, and 15 shall apply with the substitution for references to torture of references to other forms of cruel, inhuman or degrading treatment or punishment.[79]

---

77. *See* Letter from Niall MacDermot, Sec'y–Gen., Int'l Comm'n of Jurists, to Hans Danelius, Under–Sec'y for Legal and Consular Affairs, Swedish Ministry of Foreign Affairs (Oct. 29, 1979) (on file with Amnesty International).

78. This submission has previously been incorrectly referred to as the sole initiative of the ICJ: *see* Burgers & Danelius, *supra* note 3, at 70–71.

79. Amnesty Int'l & the Int'l Comm'n of Jurists, *Suggestion for an additional paragraph to Article 16*, H.R. (XXXVI)/W.G.10/W.P.5 (1980), *in* Burgers & Danelius, *supra* note 3, at 70.

Based on developments at the Working Group's session, Amnesty and the ICJ then submitted a revised draft of this paragraph for insertion as the first paragraph in Article 16:

1. Each State Party shall undertake to prevent in any territory under its jurisdiction other acts of cruel, inhuman or degrading treatment or punishment which do not constitute torture as defined in Article 1, when such acts are committed by or at the instigation of or with the consent or acquiescence of a public official or other person acting in an official capacity. In particular, the obligations contained in Articles [3], 10, 11, 12, 13, [14] and [15] shall apply with the substitution for reference to torture of references to other forms of cruel, inhuman or degrading treatment or punishment.[80]

The square brackets denoted disagreement among the delegations about whether the obligations of *non-refoulement* (Article 3), compensation (Article 14) and non-use of evidence obtained under torture (Article 15) should apply to CID treatment or punishment. While Rodley wanted all of these articles to be included, he was particularly concerned about the potential omission of Article 14, which he regarded as essential to ensuring enforcement of the prohibition on CID treatment or punishment. The United Kingdom was the main opponent to Article 14's inclusion, so both before and after the 1980 Working Group, Amnesty and Paul Sieghart of Justice (an ICJ affiliate in the U.K.) lobbied the U.K. government in London and Geneva. This was to no avail. In addition to Article 14, none of the other articles that were put in square brackets in 1980 made it into the final version of Article 16 of the Torture Convention.

The failure of Amnesty and ICJ's proposal that Article 16 include reference to Article 3 has adversely impacted the consistency of state practice on inter-state transfer of individuals. In particular, the United States has argued that the only treaty obligation it has with respect to *non-refoulement* is contained in Article 3 of the Convention and has stressed that the obligation only applies to torture and not to CID treatment or punishment.[81] The United States has also sought to undermine the prohibition on *refoulement* to torture, not by disputing that there is such a prohibition, but through the asserted use of "diplomatic assurances" to effect transfer,[82] and restrictive standards to assess the

---

80. *See* Amnesty Int'l & the Int'l Comm'n of Jurists, H.R. (XXXVI)/W.G.10/W.P.5/Rev. 1 (1980), *in* BURGERS & DANELIUS, *supra* note 3, at 71.

81. U.S., *Written Response to List of Issues to Be Taken Up in Connection with the Consideration of the Second and Third Periodic Reports of the United States of America* [hereinafter *Written Response to Human Rights Comm.*] 16–18 (2006); U.S., *Response to Comm. Against Torture List of Issues*, *supra* note 4, at 49–50.

82. *See, e.g.*, Condoleezza Rice, U.S. Sec'y of State, Remarks Upon Her Departure for Europe (Dec. 5, 2005) (transcript available at http://www.state.gov/secretary/rm/2005/57602.htm).

likelihood of torture upon transfer.[83] These challenges to the scope of the prohibition on transfer both to torture and to CID treatment or punishment are believed to have been made with a view to enabling the "rendition" or "extraordinary rendition" of terrorism suspects to countries for coercive interrogation.[84] More generally, the Convention's separate treatment of torture and CID treatment or punishment has given States an incentive to argue that certain acts do not meet the definition of torture contained in Article 1, but rather should be treated as CID treatment or punishment.

Amnesty and other groups working on the Convention could not have fully contemplated or guarded against the unscrupulous ways in which states would seek to exploit the text's distinction between torture and CID treatment or punishment. Indeed, Amnesty argued strongly at the time that because this distinction had been made by an influential international human rights body (the European Court of Human Rights), the Torture Convention needed to address both forms of ill-treatment. It is impossible to guess in hindsight what would have happened if the Convention had either not addressed CID treatment at all or had dealt with it in the same way as the prohibition on torture. Nor is it necessarily realistic given that the General Assembly Resolution had requested the Commission to draft a convention against torture and other CID treatment or punishment and the trend by the time of drafting was to distinguish between the two components in some way.

However, it is possible that, in pursuing its position, Amnesty was unduly influenced by the approach taken in the Declaration and the European Court of Human Rights, as well as the fact that the original Swedish draft included CID treatment or punishment in its very definition of torture. In retrospect, it may have been better to work for CID treatment or punishment to be left out of the Torture Convention altogether, as was the case nearly a decade later with the Inter-American Convention to Prevent and Punish Torture. The Article 1 definition of torture in the Convention would have been sufficient to catch the behavior that the Torture Convention was aiming to stop.

Lawful Sanctions

Another contentious issue in the drafting of the Convention was how "lawful sanctions" would be excluded from the definition of torture. Article 1 of the Declaration states that torture "... does not include

---

83. For example, the United States utilizes a "more likely than not" standard to assess the likelihood that an individual will be subject to torture.

84. *See, e.g.,* U.N. Human Rights Committee [hereinafter Hum. Rts. Committee], *Concluding Observations: United States of America,* ¶ 16, U.N. Doc. CCPR/C/USA/CO/3/Rev.1 (Dec. 18, 2006).

pain or suffering arising only from, inherent in or incidental to, lawful sanctions to the extent consistent with the Standard Minimum Rules for the Treatment of Prisoners." Article 1 of the original Swedish draft followed the Declaration and similarly excluded lawful sanctions from the definition of torture "to the extent consistent with the Standard Minimum Rules for the Treatment of Prisoners."

The language in both the Declaration and the original Swedish draft strikes a careful balance between two competing concerns. On the one hand, the exclusion of "lawful sanctions" reflects the fact that neither the Declaration nor the draft convention sought to unduly interfere with a country's penal sanctions.[85] Indeed, the exclusion of "lawful sanctions" from the Declaration's definition of torture was apparently a response to states that sought to maintain such practices as corporal punishment.[86] On the other hand, the requirement that "lawful sanctions" be consistent with the Standard Minimum Rules for the Treatment of Prisoners seeks to avoid a potential loophole by which states could try to allow acts effectively amounting to torture by legalizing them as penal sanctions under its domestic law.

Amnesty's focus on the issue of "lawful sanctions" was prompted by events at the Commission's Working Group in 1979. This Working Group had before it the original Swedish draft and in the opening days of the Working Group, several participants objected to its reference to the Standard Minimum Rules for the Treatment of Prisoners. MacDermot in particular strongly supported removing the reference, arguing that a non-legal document should not be mentioned in a legal definition and that the reference was vague. It was one of the few occasions on which Amnesty and the ICJ departed significantly on the substance of the text. At this time, Amnesty's Secretary General, Martin Ennals, was attending the Working Group session on Amnesty's behalf. Although Ennals knew that the removal of the reference would be detrimental, he was not equipped to resist the forceful approach of MacDermot. By the time Rodley joined the session on February 8, 1979, much of the damage on "lawful sanctions" had been done and Amnesty would spend the next five years trying to mitigate its impact.

Amnesty efforts on this front commenced during that Working Group's session. On February 23, 1979, Rodley delivered a statement proposing several solutions to this problem, including "to delete the exemption altogether and make no reference to lawful punishment."[87]

---

85. *See* BURGERS & DANELIUS, *supra* note 3, at 121.

86. *See* RODLEY, *supra* note 3, at 31.

87. *See* Amnesty Int'l, Transcript of a Statement of Nigel Rodley in respect of Article 1 of the Revised Swedish Draft Convention Against Torture Before the Working Group on

MacDermot robustly resisted this position again, with the result that the Article 1 definition of torture was amended to provide that torture "does not include pain or suffering arising only from, inherent in or incidental to lawful sanctions" without referencing the Standard Minimum Rules for the Treatment of Prisoners or any other international standards.

For the next few years, Amnesty continued to denounce the Article 1 amendment as an "invitation to legislate the rack"[88] and to promote the suggestions set out in its February 23, 1979 statement. Ultimately, in June 1984, Amnesty decided to seek deletion of the lawful sanctions exclusion, and failing that, to seek an amendment of the text to specify that only sanctions lawful under international law would be excluded from the torture definition.[89] The latter approach was deemed more realistic than seeking reinstatement of the reference to the Standard Minimum Rules for the Treatment of Prisoners, and would have substantially the same effect. In articulating this position, the International Executive Committee Sub–Committee on International Organizations noted that:

> To this end, although AI does not usually make a practice of drafting texts, in this case certain specific textual proposals might give governments an idea as to how to proceed with suggested modifications of the text. But this should not be done in such a way as to cause AI to appear to be approving or disapproving of particular texts as such.[90]

Despite the efforts of Amnesty and others on this front, the text remained as it was adopted in 1979. In lieu of modifying the text, Amnesty had also advocated that other measures should be taken to clarify that the definition of torture would only exclude sanctions lawful under both domestic and international law. One such measure was for governments to indicate to the U.N. General Assembly the view that "lawful" had to be read to mean "lawful under international law." At least four countries (Italy, Netherlands, the United Kingdom and the

---

Drafting the Convention of the UNHCR (Feb. 23, 1979) (on file with Amnesty International).

88. *See, e.g.,* Letter from Nigel Rodley, Legal Adviser, Amnesty Int'l, to Mr. M.K.O. Simpson–Orlebar, Esq., U.K. Foreign and Commonwealth Office (Dec. 5, 1979) (on file with Amnesty International).

89. *See, e.g.,* Letter from Wolfgang Heinz, IEC Member, Amnesty Int'l, to Reinhard Marx, Chairperson, German Section, Amnesty Int'l (June 19, 1984) (on file with Amnesty International); Letter from Nigel Rodley, Legal Adviser, Amnesty Int'l, to Michael Landale, Counsellor, Australian High Comm'n. (July 23, 1984) (on file with Amnesty International).

90. *See* Amnesty Int'l, IEC Int'l Orgs. Sub–Comm., *AI and the UN* (June 1984) (on file with Amnesty International).

United States) did, in fact, affirm this position in their comments on the draft to the 1984 General Assembly.[91]

Disappearances?

The question of disappearances was not on Amnesty's list of principles for inclusion in the Torture Convention. This was not because Amnesty felt the Convention should not properly encompass disappearances. Rather, it was in part because Amnesty's U.N. work on disappearances was being directed through other processes that were happening at the same time as the drafting of the Convention, such as the establishment of the U.N. Working Group on Enforced or Involuntary Disappearances in 1980. It also owed to the fact that these U.N. efforts on disappearances were not then focused on standard-setting.[92] Defining disappearances was a normative challenge that had not yet been resolved and which may have unduly complicated the Convention drafting process.

In retrospect, there may also have been a strategic concern that raising the issue of disappearances in the drafting of the Torture Convention might open the text up to the type of sabotage being experienced on the disappearance question elsewhere in the U.N.[93] Again, it would have been difficult for the NGOs and delegations involved to predict the consequences of failing to push for the explicit inclusion of the prohibition on enforced disappearances in the Convention. Currently the United States disputes the relationship between enforced disappearances and torture, queries the extent to which the Convention prohibits *incommunicado* detention, and argues that Article 3's *non-refoulement* protection does not explicitly prevent return of individuals to countries where they might be disappeared.[94] This is

---

91. See RODLEY, *supra* note 3, at 322.

92. For example, the issue of disappearances was very nearly left out of the Body of Principles for the Protection of All Persons under Any Form of Detention or Imprisonment during its drafting in the U.N. Sub–Commission on Prevention of Discrimination and Protection of Minorities of the Commission on Human Rights. It was only included when quite late in the drafting process, Rodley drew attention to its omission over lunch with MacDermot and the Sri Lankan member of the Sub–Commission, the latter of whom subsequently raised the issue when the Sub–Commission resumed after the lunch-break and thereby secured its inclusion.

93. See generally GUEST, *supra* note 3, for an excellent account of efforts, particularly by Argentina's military government from 1976 to thwart the ability of the U.N. machinery to address disappearances.

94. *See, e.g.*, U.S., REPLY OF THE GOVERNMENT OF THE UNITED STATES OF AMERICA TO THE REPORT OF THE FIVE UNHCR SPECIAL RAPPORTEURS ON DETAINEES IN GUANTANAMO BAY, CUBA, 34 (Mar. 10, 2006) *available at* http://www.asil.org/pdfs/ilib0603212.pdf; U.S., *Response to Comm. Against Torture List of Issues*, *supra* note 4, at 44–5.

despite the fact that the international law prohibiting torture clearly prohibits enforced disappearance and the human rights violations it entails.[95] It is a perverse outcome that some of the very practices which helped inspire the drafting of the Convention (e.g., disappearances and other violations in Chile and Argentina)[96] have resurfaced in relation to the U.S. secret detention program for terrorism suspects that it not only admits running, but claims to be lawful.[97]

Looking Back to Look Forward

In many ways, the challenges faced by Amnesty and other NGOs to outlaw torture are the same as those faced by NGOs currently grappling with how to challenge governments' increased resort to illegal coercive interrogations, renditions and disappearances in connection with the "War on Terror." As with the period covered by this Chapter, no government today would seriously dispute that torture is illegal. Instead the more nuanced strategy of governments like the United States has been to simultaneously stress that torture is abhorrent,[98] while narrowing the very notion of what torture is understood to encompass.[99] This narrowing has occurred through manipulation of (national) law; but it has also been achieved through attempts to persuade the public by means of legal argument, however specious, that certain measures are exceptional and justified against certain persons in order to protect security and to save lives.

In resisting these attempts, some human rights organizations have not been as vigilant in how they argue against torture as Amnesty was more than thirty years ago. In the post-September 11, 2001 environment, some organizations seek to make the case against torture by arguing both that it is illegal and that it is ineffective. Use of the latter argument is often justified on the basis that it is not enough in the current environment to show that torture is illegal, and that to truly make gains in the eyes of the public and governments, NGOs need to

---

95. *See, e.g.,* U.N. Committee Against Torture, *Conclusions and Recommendations of the Committee Against Torture: United States of America,* ¶ 17, U.N. Doc. CAT/C/USA/CO/2 (July 25, 2006); Hum. Rts. Committee, *Concluding Observations, supra* note 84, at ¶ 12.

96. *See supra* note 3.

97. At least under U.S. law: *see, e.g.,* News Release, White House Office of the Press Sec'y, President Discusses Creation of Military Commissions to Try Suspected Terrorists (Sept. 6, 2006), *available at* http://www.whitehouse.gov/news/releases/2006/09/20060906-3.html.

98. *See, e.g.,* Condoleezza Rice, U.S. Sec'y of State, Remarks Upon Her Departure for Europe, *supra* note 82; White House Office of the Press Sec'y, President Discusses Creation of Military Commissions to Try Suspected Terrorists, *supra* note 97.

99. *See supra* note 4.

also show that torture does not work. However, by the very act of engaging in this argument, NGOs lose significant ground and also embark on a slippery slope toward the notion that there are some forms of torture that are justified and legal. This much was clearly stated by Amnesty in 1973:

> One argument that has been presented in the past and is often heard today is that torture is inefficient ... This line of argumentation based on inefficiency is totally inadmissible. To place the debate on such grounds is to give the argument away; in effect it means that if it can be shown to be efficient it is permissible.[100]

Such public information elements of Amnesty's Campaign still have clear relevance, as does the second phase of Amnesty's Campaign, the focus on international norms. Indeed, the strategy of nailing down the illegality of torture was, and should continue to be, seen as a way of sidelining the inevitably inconclusive moral-philosophical discussion. Current efforts to entrench the illegality of torture and CID treatment or punishment can also usefully consider Amnesty's practice of advocating principles rather than drafts and text. This approach can help avoid complicity in the drafting of laws, such as those on preventive detention, that purport to resolve "War on Terror" and human rights challenges, but actually do so in ways that violate fundamental human rights guarantees.

However, the overall lesson from the drafting of the Convention and the events that inspired it is that as much as there is history of governments violating rights, there is also one about resistance to such abuses. The story of Amnesty International's influence on the Torture Convention is one piece of that history that advocates can draw upon to help defend the human rights guarantees that are inviolable but often under threat.

---

100. *See* AMNESTY INT'L, REPORT ON TORTURE, *supra* note 8, at 24.

*

2

The Story of the *TAC* Case: The Potential and Limits of Socio–Economic Rights Litigation in South Africa

Amy Kapczynski & Jonathan M. Berger

Introduction

I gave birth to an HIV positive baby who should have been saved. That was my experience, the sad one, and I will live with it until my last day.[1]
Busisiwe Maqungo
Mfuleni, Cape Town, South Africa

When Busisiwe Maqungo walked into an antenatal clinic in Cape Town in 1999, she knew that there were medicines that could be used to reduce the risk of transmitting the human immunodeficiency virus ("HIV")—the virus that causes Acquired Immune Deficiency Syndrome ("AIDS")—from mothers to their children. She had learned this, in fact, from television. But she did not think she might be at risk of HIV infection. Not a single health care provider at the clinic said anything about an HIV test during her visit, even though at the time, more than one in five pregnant women attending public antenatal clinics in South Africa was HIV-positive.[2] Busisiwe worried when she saw the word "positive" on her antenatal chart, but a nurse explained it away: "Something to do with iron," she was told.[3]

At the age of one month, Busisiwe's daughter Nomazizi fell gravely ill with pneumonia and diarrhea. When doctors diagnosed Nomazizi with

---

1. Affidavit of Busisiwe Maqungo, Submitted in Support of the Applicants in *Minister of Health & Others v. Treatment Action Campaign & Others (No. 2)* 2002 (5) SA 721 (CC) (S. Afr.) at para. 7 (Aug. 2001) [hereinafter Maqungo Aff.]. This affidavit, as well as most of the record of the *TAC* case, is available at http://www.tac.org.za/Documents/MTCTCourtCase/MTCTCourtCase.htm.

2. *See* REPUBLIC OF S. AFR. DEP'T. OF HEALTH, NATIONAL HIV AND SYPHILIS SERO-PREVALENCE SURVEY OF WOMEN ATTENDING PUBLIC ANTENATAL CLINICS IN SOUTH AFRICA (2000), *available at* http://www.doh.gov.za/docs/reports/2000/hivreport.html (reporting that in 1999, 22.4% of all women attending public antenatal clinics in South Africa were HIV-positive).

3. Maqungo Aff., *supra* note 1, at para. 5.

HIV, they told Busisiwe that her daughter would die, and that nothing could be done.[4] After that, her baby was always sick. Busisiwe explained: "I had to borrow money from her father's parents, to take her to hospital.... Sometimes my baby would be out of hospital for a week and then she would be sick again. I never had enough time with her."[5]

In time, Busisiwe would learn that she had been tested for HIV without her consent, and that no one had informed her of the results or even what the test was for. And no one, of course, had offered her a medicine called Nevirapine—which had been offered to the state at no cost. Nor had she been told that just two doses might well have prevented the transmission of HIV to her little girl.[6]

The clinic that Busisiwe attended was not unusual in this regard. At the time, the South African government had refused to commit to a public sector program to prevent mother-to-child-transmission of HIV (a "PMTCT" program). As a result, an estimated 89,000 children were born with HIV in South Africa in 1999.[7] Without access to medicines for treating HIV infection, all of these children would die. In 1999, at the age of just nine months, Nomazizi became one of them.

This would not, however, be the end of Nomazizi's story. Busisiwe became a member of a South African AIDS activist organization known as the Treatment Action Campaign ("TAC"). TAC is a community-based organization that campaigns for the health and rights of people living with HIV/AIDS in South Africa.[8] Founded in 1998, it now has approximately 12,000 members in more than 200 branches around the country.[9] The organization is perhaps best known for its high-profile campaigns

---

4. Children with HIV can live long and healthy lives if they have access to antiretroviral ("ARV") treatment. In South Africa in 1999, however, children and mothers like Nomazizi and Busisiwe did not have access to the necessary treatment. *See, e.g.,* Mark Heywood, *Shaping, Making and Breaking the Law in the Campaign for a National HIV/AIDS Treatment Plan, in* DEMOCRATIZING DEVELOPMENT: THE POLITICS OF SOCIO-ECONOMIC RIGHTS IN SOUTH AFRICA 181, 212 (Peris Jones & Kristian Stokke eds., 2005) [hereinafter Heywood, *Shaping, Making and Breaking*].

5. Maqungo Aff., *supra* note 1, at para. 9.

6. *See* Laura A. Guay et al., *Intrapartum and Neonatal Single–Dose Nevirapine Compared with Zidovudine for Prevention of Mother-to-Child Transmission of HIV–1 in Kampala, Uganda: HIVNET 012 Randomized Controlled Trial,* 354 LANCET 795, 799 (1999) (detailing study which found that Nevirapine lowered risk of HIV–1 transmission during first fourteen to sixteen weeks of infants' lives by nearly fifty percent in breastfeeding population) [hereinafter Guay].

7. Affidavit of Quarraisha Abdool Karim, Submitted in Support of the Applicants in *Minister of Health & Others v. Treatment Action Campaign & Others (No. 2)* 2002 (5) SA 721 (CC) (S. Afr.), at paras. 37–39 (Aug. 13, 2001) [hereinafter Karim Aff.], *available at* http://www.tac.org.za/Documents/MTCTCourtCase/MTCTCourtCase.htm.

8. For further information, *see* the Treatment Action Campaign website at http://www.tac.org.za/.

9. The TAC national office is located in Cape Town. In addition to its provincial offices, located in the Western Cape, Gauteng, Eastern Cape, KwaZulu–Natal, Limpopo and

seeking access to treatment for people with HIV/AIDS. Equally important, though, is TAC's lesser known work, which strives to improve HIV prevention efforts, combat discrimination, cultivate leadership of people living with HIV/AIDS, and build national and global networks of like-minded activist groups.[10] The organization's tactics range from legal filings, to civil disobedience, to community-based treatment literacy work that has educated tens of thousands of people around the country about the science of HIV prevention and treatment.[11]

In 2001, after repeated attempts over a number of years to convince the government to provide comprehensive PMTCT services had failed, TAC filed a lawsuit contending that the government was violating the South African Constitution. In an affidavit filed by TAC as an integral part of its court papers, Busisiwe—and a number of other women like her—told their stories. With the help of these women, TAC won what has become one of the most celebrated human rights cases in the world: *Minister of Health & Others v. Treatment Action Campaign & Others (No. 2)* ("*TAC* case").[12] In its judgment, the Constitutional Court of

---

Mpumalanga provinces, TAC has district offices in Lusikisiki and Queenstown (Eastern Cape), Pietermaritzburg (KwaZulu–Natal), Khayelitsha (Western Cape) and Ekhurhuleni (Gauteng). Comprised of more than 200 branches across the country, the TAC offices encompass a wide range of locales, from the poorest Eastern Cape communities (such as Lusikisiki), to wealthy institutions such as the University of Cape Town. Most TAC volunteers and staff members reside in the communities in which they work. The internal dynamics, leadership, and decision-making within the TAC organization fall outside the scope of this Chapter. For more information on these matters, *see generally* Steven Friedman & Shauna Mottiar, *Rewarding Engagement?: The Treatment Action Campaign and the Politics of HIV/AIDS: A Case Study for the UKZN Project Titled Globalisation, Marginalisation, and New Social Movements in South Africa* (Ctr. for Civ. Soc. and Sch. of Dev. Stud., Univ. of Kwazulu–Natal, 2004), *available at* http://www.ukzn.ac.za/ccs/files/FRIEDMAN%20MOTTIER%20A%20MORAL%20TO%20THE%20TALE%20LONG%20VERSION.PDF. *See also* Steven Friedman & Shauna Mottiar, *A Rewarding Engagement? The Treatment Action Campaign and the Politics of HIV/AIDS*, 33 POL. & SOC. 511, 513 (2005).

10. TREATMENT ACTION CAMPAIGN, CONSTITUTION art. IV (1998), *available at* http://www.tac.org.za/Documents/Constitution/Constitution13Dec04.PDF.

11. The "Treatment Literacy Program" is TAC's largest operation; as of this writing, the organization has trained over 300 of its members to become experts on the science of HIV prevention and treatment. Currently, about 250 of these experts provide treatment literacy services on almost a daily basis to health facilities and other institutions around the country. Consistent with the TAC's mission, the Treatment Literacy Program emphasizes the view that the provision of HIV prevention and treatment education increases the number of people with HIV who seek timely assistance from the public health system, and improves adherence to ARV and other HIV-related treatment. This information was provided by Nathan Geffen, the former head of TAC's policy, research and communications work and its recently elected Treasurer. Email from Nathan Geffen to Jonathan Berger (Sept. 1, 2008) (on file with authors).

12. 2002 (5) SA 721 (CC) (S. Afr.) [hereinafter *TAC (No. 2)*]. This and other South African Constitutional Court cases are available online at the Court's official website, http://www.constitutionalcourt.org.za.

South Africa held that the government's failure to develop and implement a comprehensive PMTCT program breached the express constitutional guarantee of access to health care services, in particular the state's positive obligations in respect of that right. The Court ordered the government to take a series of steps aimed at ensuring access to comprehensive PMTCT services in the public health sector, "without delay."[13]

For most commentators, the story of the *TAC* case has been a story about courts, and the role that they can or should play in socio-economic rights litigation. Scholars in South Africa, for example, have said "[t]he Court's order . . . demonstrates that socio-economic rights can offer important protections to the vulnerable against unreasonable government policies," but they have at the same time criticized the decision for not going far enough in its remedial aspect.[14] Scholars in the United States, in contrast, have marveled at the strength of the ruling and remedy in the *TAC* case, and have suggested that the result can be explained by the fact that this was an exceptionally simple and compelling case.[15]

Little has been written about how the case came into being or the impact it has had on the life options and experiences of people living with and affected by HIV in South Africa.[16] Consider here three facts: the *TAC* case was brought only after four years of sustained lobbying and organizing efforts demanding PMTCT programs in South Africa. The suit itself was framed by carefully orchestrated advocacy work and mass demonstrations that caused dramatic change in the government's policy even during the litigation. Years after the stunning victory in the *TAC* case, and despite claims by some that the government "quickly implemented the orders of the Constitutional Court,"[17] reliable estimates

---

13. *Id.* at para. 135.

14. David Bilchitz, *Towards a Reasonable Approach to the Minimum Core: Laying the Foundations for Future Socio–Economic Rights Jurisprudence*, 19 S. AFR. J. HUM. RTS. 1, 2 (2003).

15. Mark V. Tushnet, *New Forms of Judicial Review and the Persistence of Rights- and Democracy-Based Worries*, 38 WAKE FOREST L. REV. 813, 826 (2003) (arguing that the "case was a perfect one for exercising judicial review. The government's position was discredited and had been abandoned. The Constitutional Court could pretty much do whatever it wanted in the case.").

16. This article draws heavily upon one of the best articles on the prelude to the case: Mark Heywood, *Preventing Mother-to-Child HIV Transmission in South Africa: Background, Strategies and Outcomes of the Treatment Action Campaign's Case Against the Minister of Health*, 19 S. AFR. J. HUM. RTS. 278, 282 (2003) [hereinafter Heywood, *Preventing Mother-to-Child HIV Transmission*].

17. Richard J. Goldstone, *A South African Perspective on Social and Economic Rights*, 13 HUM. RTS. BRIEF 4, 5 (2006) (referring to *TAC (No. 2)* and "other cases where the court has ruled against [the government].").

indicate that only about thirty percent of women in South Africa who need medicine to prevent the transmission of HIV to their children are receiving it.[18]

These facts alone demonstrate that to describe the *TAC* case in terms that focus on courts or legal texts alone is to miss the true story of the case. That story is less about a judgment or a doctrine than it is about a movement. More specifically, it is about the power that an organized movement can have if it makes strategic use of constitutionally entrenched and justiciable human rights, lays the groundwork necessary to give those abstract guarantees meaning, and energetically builds broad public support for its cause. TAC did the political and technical work to make the Constitutional Court's judgment seem both legally obvious and morally necessary, and thereby created a precedent that helped bring real improvements in access to PMTCT services in South Africa, and that was also likely central to the establishment of a public sector HIV treatment program for the country. But the ultimate promise of the case—that all women in South Africa have access to quality medicines and services to prevent the transmission of HIV to their children—still awaits fulfillment. The judgment alone could not guarantee the result that it declared constitutionally required. For that, it needed a movement. And unfortunately, the Court very likely overestimated the work that the movement in question could do to implement the Court's judgment. That, too, is part of the legacy of the *TAC* case. In the end, then, the story of the *TAC* case is less a story about the power and limits of courts than it is a story about the power and limits of the Treatment Action Campaign.

Social and Medical Background

HIV is a retrovirus that attacks the human immune system. It can be transmitted through blood, semen, or other bodily fluids, for example through unsafe sex or injecting drug use with shared needles. Children can contract HIV from their mothers before they are born, during delivery, or while breastfeeding. Collectively, these forms of transmission are known in the field as "mother-to-child-transmission of HIV" ("MTCT"). Studies in South Africa show that, absent any medical intervention, one-fifth to one-third of children will contract HIV from a mother infected with HIV.[19]

---

18. *See, e.g.*, World Health Organization Progress Report, Towards Universal Access: Scaling Up Priority HIV/AIDS Interventions in the Health Sector (2007), *available at* http://www.who.int/hiv/mediacentre/universal_access_progress_report_en.pdf; *see also infra* note 135.

19. *See* Anna Coutsoudis et al., *Method of Feeding and Transmission of HIV–1 from Mothers to Children by 15 Months of Age: Prospective Cohort Study from Durban, South Africa*, 15 AIDS 379, 383 fig.1 (2001) (showing infection rates at fifteen months of about

Adults infected with HIV can live for many years without any symptoms of the disease, as the immune system and the virus battle one another. The same cannot be said for children—and particularly infants—with HIV infection, who may decline much more quickly.[20] Eventually, if a person is not treated with the antiretroviral ("ARV") medicines that prevent the replication of the virus, his or her immune system will be weakened, and he or she will begin to develop illnesses characteristic of AIDS, such as tuberculosis and cryptococcal meningitis.[21] Absent treatment, AIDS is fatal.

First identified in 1981, AIDS is now the leading cause of death in many countries around the world. Approximately 33 million people around the world are living with HIV, two-thirds of them in sub-Saharan Africa.[22] Two million people died of AIDS-related illnesses in 2007, including an estimated 270,000 children under the age of fifteen.[23] During the same period, there were an estimated 2.7 million new

---

19% for children who were never breastfed, 24% for children who had been exclusively breastfed, and 36% for children who were fed a mix of breast milk and other food); *see also id.* at 386 (hypothesizing reasons for higher rate of transmission for children who were fed a mix rather than exclusively breastfed, e.g. that mixed feeding compromises the child's digestive system).

20. For example, a relatively old study showed that nearly half of all children who contracted HIV from their mothers and went untreated would die by the age of two. *See* Rosemary Spira et al., *Natural History of Human Immunodeficiency Virus Type 1 Infection in Children: A Five-Year Prospective Study in Rwanda*, 104 PEDIATRICS e56, *3 (1999). With early access to ARV treatment, however, survival rates increase significantly. Interim data from a recent Children with HIV Early Antiretroviral Therapy ("CHER") study "found a significant increase in survival among infants who received immediate ARV therapy (96%) compared to infants who received therapy later (84%) based on declining immune function linked to a defined CD4+ T-cell count and/or clinical progression." NATIONAL INSTITUTES OF HEALTH, NATIONAL INSTITUTE OF ALLERGY AND INFECTIOUS DISEASES, QUESTIONS AND ANSWERS, CHILDREN WITH HIV EARLY ANTIRETROVIRAL THERAPY (CHER) STUDY: TREATING HIV–INFECTED INFANTS EARLY HELPS THEM LIVE LONGER, para. 8 (2007), *at* http://www3.niaid.nih.gov/news/QA/CHER_QA.htm (describing the results of the 2007 DSMB review of the CHER interim data regarding infant survival rates).

21. For access to basic information on HIV/AIDS that is focused on the U.S., *see* http://www.thebody.com/; *see also* http://www.cdc.gov/hiv/topics/basic/index.htm. For access to information on HIV/AIDS with a focus on South Africa, see TREATMENT ACTION CAMPAIGN, HIV IN OUR LIVES: A BOOK OF INFORMATION SHEETS FOR PEOPLE LIVING WITH HIV, SUPPORT GROUPS AND CLINICS (2007), *available at* http://www.tac.org.za/community/files/file/InOurLives/HIV InOurLivesEnglish.pdf (providing a guide to living with HIV in the form of a series of worksheets); TREATMENT ACTION CAMPAIGN, ARVS IN OUR LIVES: A HANDBOOK FOR PEOPLE LIVING WITH HIV AND TREATMENT ADVOCATES IN SUPPORT GROUPS, CLINICS AND COMMUNITIES (2006), *available at* http://www.tac.org.za/documents/arvsinourlives.pdf (providing a detailed guide to antiretroviral treatment, aimed at people with advanced treatment literacy skills).

22. *See* JOINT UNITED NATIONS PROGRAM ON HIV/AIDS ("UNAIDS"), AIDS EPIDEMIC UPDATE 32 (2008), *available at* http://www.unaids.org/en/KnowledgeCentre/HIVData/Global Report/2008/2008_Global_report.asp.

23. *Id.* at 32, 37.

infections, with approximately 370,000 of these in children under the age of fifteen.[24]

In South Africa alone, an estimated 11.2% of the population, approximately 5.4 million people, were living with HIV/AIDS in 2006.[25] Approximately 346,000 deaths in South Africa—out of an estimated total of 737,000 deaths from all causes, both natural and unnatural—were attributed to the epidemic in 2005.[26] Importantly, these deaths were not evenly distributed across the population as a whole. As noted by a discussion document published by the South African Presidency, "[t]he most affected in this regard are able-bodied citizens in the prime of their lives. These would most likely be parents of young children and possibly breadwinners of extended families who are also among the most skilled within the population."[27]

As far back as the mid-to-late-1990s, scientists began to make enormous progress in learning how to treat and prevent HIV with the use of ARV medicines. In 1994, for example, it was discovered that ARV medicines such as zidovudine ("AZT") could dramatically reduce the risk of MTCT.[28] ARV combination therapy emerged in 1996, and it quickly became clear that it could keep people with HIV/AIDS alive and healthy, perhaps indefinitely.[29] The subsequent development of simplified

---

24. *Id.* 31–31.

25. R.E. Dorrington et al., The Demographic Impact of HIV/AIDS in South Africa—National and Provincial Indicators for 2006 8 (Cape Town Ctr. for Actuarial Research, S. Afr. Med. Research Council and Actuarial Soc'y of S. Afr. eds., 2006) (estimating a total of 5,372,000 HIV infected persons, rounded to the nearest thousand, in a chart entitled "HIV and AIDS Indicators at mid–2006") [hereinafter Dorrington].

26. *Id.* at 11 (estimating, in a chart entitled "Mortality Indicators, 2006," that out of a total 737,000 deaths in South Africa in 2005, 391,000 were non-AIDS related, and 346,000 were AIDS deaths).

27. POLICY COORDINATION AND ADVISORY SERVICES ("PCAS") & THE PRESIDENCY, A NATION IN THE MAKING: A DISCUSSION DOCUMENT ON MACRO-SOCIAL TRENDS IN SOUTH AFRICA 65 (2006), *available at* http://www.thepresidency.gov.za/main.asp?include=docs/reports/microsocial/index.html.

28. *See* Edward M. O'Connor et al., *Reduction of Maternal–Infant Transmission of Human Immunodeficiency Virus Type 1 with Zidovudine Treatment*, 331 NEW ENG. J. MED. 1173, 1173 (1994). At the time of this study, AZT as well as a small number of other ARV medicines had already received FDA marketing approval for the treatment of HIV infections.

29. *See e.g.*, Frank J. Palella et al., *Declining Morbidity and Mortality Among Patients with Advanced Human Immunodeficiency Virus Infection*, 338 NEW ENG. J. MED. 853, 853 (1998) (showing that AIDS-related mortality dropped by about 70% in the two years after combination therapies were adopted in the United States). ARV medicines work by interfering with the replication of the virus. If they are not taken in the proper combinations and at the prescribed times, however, the virus can evolve to become resistant to the medicines.

PMTCT regimens in 1998 and 1999 meant that such programs could be implemented in even the most resource-poor settings.[30]

The most important such regimen for the purpose of the *TAC* case was confirmed by a Ugandan study in 1999, in which scientists showed that just one dose of Nevirapine given to the mother during labor, and one dose given to the child directly after birth, could reduce the risk of MTCT by up to fifty percent.[31]

In 1998, at least 70,000 infants in South Africa were infected with HIV as a result of MTCT.[32] A universal PMTCT program using Nevirapine thus had the potential to prevent up to 35,000 pediatric HIV infections each year, if not more. Yet the government refused to implement such a program. This refusal was not based on cost—the government's internal documents showed that the intervention was cost-effective, because the cost of the double dose of the medicine was low and the lives and medical costs saved so substantial.[33] Rather, as Mark Heywood of the TAC has written, the primary motivation behind the government refusal appears to have been the "sometimes hidden, sometimes open, relationship . . . between the President and AIDS denialists."[34]

AIDS denialists—not to be confused with those who are simply in denial about their own risk (or the implications) of HIV infection—believe that AIDS is caused not by HIV, but rather by a hodge-podge of circumstances that weaken the immune system, such as recreational drug use, malnutrition, and ARV medicines themselves. No credible

---

30. *See, e.g.,* Nancy A. Wade et al., *Abbreviated Regimens of Zidovudine Prophylaxis and Perinatal Transmission of the Human Immunodeficiency Virus,* 339 NEW ENG. J. MED. 1409, 1412 (1998) (showing that even abbreviated AZT regimens reduced the risk of MTCT).

31. Guay, *supra* note 6, at 795. More sophisticated regimens have significantly higher success rates. *See, e.g.,* Scott Nightingale, *Evidence behind the WHO Guidelines: Hospital Care for Children: What Antiretroviral Agents and Regimens are Effective in the Prevention of Mother-to-child Transmission of HIV?,* 52 J. TROPICAL PEDIATRICS 235 (2006) (reviewing the success of more complex regimes in developing country settings).

32. Founding Affidavit Submitted in Support of the Applicants in *Minister of Health & Others v. Treatment Action Campaign & Others (No. 2)* 2002 (5) SA 721 (CC) (S. Afr.), at para. 22 (Aug. 21, 2001) [hereinafter Founding Aff.] *available at* http://www.tac.org.za/Documents/MTCTCourtCase/ccmfound.rtf. Estimates such as these inevitably vary somewhat, according to the presumptions and data-gathering methods used. TAC's expert estimated the number of child infections in 1999 to be 87,000. *See* Karim Aff., *supra* note 7, and accompanying text.

33. M. Henscher, *Confidential Briefing: The Costs and Effectiveness of Using NVP or AZT for the Prevention of Mother to Child Transmission—Current Best Estimates for SA,* TAC Founding Affidavit, Annexure T at 381.

34. Heywood, *Preventing Mother-to-Child HIV Transmission, supra* note 16, at 282. Heywood is also Executive Director of the AIDS Law Project, which is a sister organization to the TAC, and which serves as its legal representative in many key public interest cases. For further information, *see* the AIDS Law Project website at http://www.alp.org.za/.

medical evidence supports this position.[35] But for reasons that are still unclear, in 1999 denialism gained a powerful foothold in the ruling party in South Africa, apparently stemming from the views of President Mbeki himself.[36] As the use of ARVs caused AIDS deaths to plummet in wealthy countries and AIDS activists began to organize globally to demand the extension of HIV treatment to developing countries, the South African government seized upon denialist arguments about the toxicity of such medicines to justify delay.[37] This set the stage for a profound conflict between the TAC and the government that would eventually make its way to the South African Constitutional Court.

Legal Background

The South African Constitution is widely hailed as one of the most progressive constitutions in the world. It was adopted in 1996,[38] after a long debate over the proper scope of constitutional rights in a new democracy and the feasibility of judicial enforcement of socio-economic rights.[39] The debates were resolved in favor of the view that political and civil rights and social and economic rights go hand in hand. The

---

35. For documents reviewing the scientific evidence that the HIV virus causes AIDS, *see* NATIONAL INSTITUTES OF HEALTH, THE EVIDENCE THAT HIV CAUSES AIDS, *at* http://www.niaid.nih.gov/factsheets/evidhiv.htm. *See also* http://www.aidstruth.org (website developed by HIV/AIDS research scientists and community advocates to counter AIDS denialists and promote use of ARVs). Also notable is the decision of the Supreme Court of South Australia in *R v. Parenzee* (2007) SASC 143 (S. Austl.) where, in dismissing the "evidence" of prominent AIDS denialists, Justice Sulan holds as follows: "I am satisfied that no jury would conclude that there is any doubt that the virus HIV exists. I consider no jury would be left in any doubt that HIV is the cause of AIDS...." *Id.* at 372.

36. Mbeki, for example, invited prominent denialists to join a Presidential AIDS Advisory Panel to "debate" the causes of AIDS. *See* Heywood, *Preventing Mother-to-Child HIV Transmission, supra* note 16, at 281. For further discussion of AIDS denialism in South Africa, *see* EDWIN CAMERON, WITNESS TO AIDS 97–100 (2005); Edwin Cameron & Jonathan Berger, *Patents and Public Health: Principle, Politics and Paradox*, 131 PROC. BRIT. ACAD. 331, 361 (2005).

37. Heywood, *Preventing Mother-to-Child HIV Transmission, supra* note 16, at 282–83, n. 26.

38. S. AFR. CONST. 1996, *available at* http://www.info.gov.za/documents/constitution/index.htm. South Africa's transitional constitution, which governed the region's first democratic elections on April 27, 1994, included a provision for a post-apartheid Parliament to draft a "final" Constitution. Interestingly, the Interim Constitution, which was negotiated prior to the 1994 elections and later adopted by the apartheid Parliament, largely did not recognize socio-economic rights. *See* S. AFR. (Interim) CONST. 1993 ch. 3 s. 7–35 ("Fundamental Rights") *available at* http://www.constitutionalcourt.org.za/site/constitution/english-web/interim/ch3.html.

39. *See, e.g.*, Dennis M. Davis, *The Case Against the Inclusion of Socio–Economic Demands in a Bill of Rights Except as Directive Principles*, 8 S. AFR. J. HUM. RTS. 475 (1992); Nicholas Haysom, *Constitutionalism, Majoritarianism, and Socio–Economic Rights*, 8 S. AFR. J. HUM. RTS. 451 (1992); Etienne Mureinik, *Beyond a Charter of Luxuries: Economic Rights in the Constitution*, 8 S. AFR. J. HUM. RTS. 464 (1992).

Constitution thus includes some of the strongest socio-economic rights protections in the world. For example, section 27—which draws much inspiration from Article 12 of the International Covenant on Economic, Social and Cultural Rights ("ICESCR")[40]—provides as follows:

(1) Everyone has the right to have access to—

(a) health care services, including reproductive health care;

(b) sufficient food and water; and

(c) social security, including, if they are unable to support themselves and their dependents, appropriate social assistance.

(2) The state must take reasonable legislative and other measures, within its available resources, to achieve the progressive realization of each of these rights.

(3) No one may be refused emergency medical treatment.[41]

In many constitutional systems, rights to health care services, food, or social security are non-existent, non-justiciable, or subject to only very minimal judicial review. One prominent school of jurisprudential thought contends that courts simply do not have the resources, expertise, and wherewithal to interpret and enforce such rights. Typically, the argument goes, such matters involve technical expertise that courts simply do not have, and require decisions about resource allocation that are better suited to the legislative branch.[42] This issue marks a critical fault line in the theory and law of human rights. If socio-economic rights cannot be litigated, one important tool for their realization is eliminated. The argument against the justiciability of such rights also often implicitly works to reinforce the notion that civil and political rights are more fundamental than socio-economic rights.

---

40. International Covenant on Economic, Social and Cultural Rights, G.A. Res. 2200A (XXI), art. 2(1), U.N. Doc. A/6316 (Dec. 16, 1966), *available at* http://www.unesco.org/education/pdf/SOCIAL_E.PDF [hereinafter ICESCR]. One important distinction should be noted between the two documents. Whereas Section 27 of the South African Constitution of 1996 guarantees a right to have access to health care services, Article 12 of the ICESCR entrenches a right "to the enjoyment of the highest attainable standard of physical and mental health." (ICESCR art. 12(1)). This distinction is evident in the manner in which the Constitutional Court understands minimum core obligations—an integral part of the ICESCR—as "possibly being relevant to reasonableness under Section 26(2) [of the South African Constitution], and not as a self-standing right conferred on everyone under Section 26(1)." *TAC (No. 2)* 2002 (5) SA 721 (CC) at para. 34 (S. Afr.) (citing Justice Yacoob in *Government of the Republic of South Africa & Others v. Grootboom & Others* 2001 (1) SA 46 (CC) (S. Afr.)). Further, the ICESCR has yet to be ratified by South Africa's Parliament.

41. S. AFR. CONST., *supra* note 39, ch. 2, s. 27.

42. *See, e.g.*, Davis, *supra* note 39.

The South African Constitutional Court (along with the U.N. Committee on Economic, Social and Cultural Rights as well as supreme courts in countries such as India) has firmly rejected the argument that socio-economic rights are categorically non-justiciable, and insisted on the interdependence between social, economic, political, and civil rights. In a series of cases that have become milestones in the global debate over socio-economic rights, the Constitutional Court has declared that such rights, as they are enshrined in the South African Constitution, are fully justiciable, and in fact that South African courts are *obliged* to test the constitutional adequacy of the government's programs against these guarantees and to provide adequate remedies for all constitutional violations. Few courts have done as much to interpret and enforce socio-economic rights, and as a result, "South Africa's role in the social rights adjudication debate is seen as revolutionary and heroic by proponents of justiciability and as irresponsible and doomed by its detractors."[43]

Two foundational cases structure the basic framework of socio-economic rights litigation in South Africa, forming the backdrop to the decision in the *TAC* case. *Soobramoney v. Minister of Health, KwaZulu-Natal* was the first socio-economic rights case to come before the Constitutional Court.[44] It was brought by a man with late-stage kidney failure who was in urgent need of dialysis, but who had been rejected from his local hospital because he did not satisfy the strict medical criteria being used to ration scarce time available on the hospital's limited number of dialysis machines.

The Court in *Soobramoney* ruled that the hospital's guidelines limiting access were reasonable and non-discriminatory,[45] and that it would "be slow to interfere with rational decisions taken in good faith by the political organs and medical authorities."[46] Further, the Court held that the reality of limited resources will at times require the state to "adopt a holistic approach to the larger needs of society rather than to focus on the specific needs of particular individuals within society."[47]

In the second foundational case, *Government of the Republic of South Africa and Others v. Grootboom and Others*,[48] members of an informal ("squatter") settlement who were facing eviction sued the government under, *inter alia*, Section 26 of the Constitution, which

---

43. Eric C. Christiansen, *Adjudicating Non-Justiciable Rights: Socio-Economic Rights and the South African Constitutional Court*, 38 COLUM. HUM. RTS. L. REV. 321, 321 (2007).
44. 1998 (1) SA 765 (CC) (S. Afr.).
45. *Id.* at para. 25.
46. *Id.* at para. 29.
47. *Id.* at para. 31.
48. 2001 (1) SA 46 (CC) (S. Afr.).

provides that "everyone has the right to have access to adequate housing," and that the state must "take reasonable legislative and other measures, within its available resources, to achieve the progressive realization of this right." The Court unanimously ruled against the government, established that the socio-economic rights in the South African Constitution are clearly judicially enforceable,[49] and set forth the basic inquiry in socio-economic rights cases, instructing courts to determine simply "whether the measures taken by the state to realize the right ... are reasonable" in the circumstances.[50]

"Reasonableness" is obviously a malleable concept, and *Grootboom* established the case-by-case approach that has come to characterize the Constitutional Court's review of socio-economic rights issues generally. But it also established several principles that courts must use when assessing the reasonableness of a government plan, including the notion that the needs of the poor "require special attention,"[51] and the requirement that such plans must be "capable of facilitating the realization of the right," must allocate appropriate financial resources for the program, and must seek to achieve their goal "expeditiously."[52]

Applying those standards to the facts in the case, *Grootboom* held that the government's housing program was not reasonable because it failed "to recognize that the state must provide for relief for those in desperate need."[53] The Court then ordered the government to "devise and implement within its available resources a comprehensive and coordinated program progressively to realize the right of access to adequate housing."[54]

Because the court ordered the government to produce a plan, but specified very little about the precise parameters of that plan and did not make it automatically subject to further judicial oversight, scholars from traditions characterized by a presumption against the justiciability of socio-economic rights have hailed the decision as invoking a new form of judicial review that is democratically experimental,[55] or that adopts a

---

49. *Id.* at para. 20 ("The question is ... not whether socio-economic rights are justiciable under our Constitution, but how to enforce them in a given case. This is a very difficult issue which must be carefully explored on a case-by-case basis.").

50. *Id.* at para. 33.

51. *Id.* at para. 36.

52. *Id.* at paras. 39, 41, 46.

53. *Id.* at para. 66.

54. *Id.* at para. 99.

55. *See, e.g.*, Tushnet, *supra* note 15, at 822 (suggesting that *Grootboom* "can be seen as a version of a broader type of weak-form judicial review that Michael Dorf and Charles Sabel identify with what they call democratic experimentalism").

flexible "administrative law model of socioeconomic rights."[56] Within South Africa, however, the decision has been routinely criticized for the weakness of its remedy. Ultimately, while *Grootboom* did lead to some limited relief for the individual plaintiffs, it has resulted in few meaningful improvements in housing for the poor.[57] As a result, the years leading up to the decision in the *TAC* case were characterized by significant academic debate within South Africa over the role of the Constitutional Court and in particular the remedial adequacy of the order in *Grootboom*.[58]

The Story of the Case

The current situation, in which women with HIV are unable to take appropriate measures to protect their health and that of their infants, has a devastating impact on their lives. That situation is avoidable.[59]
Siphokazi Mthathi
Mowbray, Cape Town, South Africa

Prelude

The efforts that led to the *TAC* case began in 1997, four years before the litigation papers were drawn up. A coalition including the AIDS Law Project, the AIDS Consortium and the Perinatal HIV Research Unit at the University of Witwatersrand, Johannesburg, began lobbying the government to urge the creation of a national policy and program for PMTCT.[60] In 1998, results of the trials that demonstrated the viability of short-course AZT therapy for PMTCT were released, making a comprehensive national program seem significantly more feasible. Around the same time, TAC itself was created, and "one of its primary objectives [was] a demand that government implement a programme to prevent MTCT."[61]

---

56. *See* Cass R. Sunstein, Designing Democracy: What Constitutions Do 234 (2001) (italics omitted).

57. *See, e.g.*, Kameshni Pillay, *Implementing Grootboom: Supervision Needed*, 3 ESR Rev. 16, 17 (2002) *available at* http://www.escr-net.org/caselaw_more/caselaw_more_show.htm?parent_id=401409 (noting that after a year of inaction, the government's response was "limited to putting together a plan to deal with the permanent resettlement of the Wallacedene Community. There is a clear lack of understanding that the judgment requires systemic changes to national, provincial and local housing programmes to cater for people in desperate and crisis situations.").

58. *See, e.g.*, David Bilchitz, *Giving Socio–Economic Rights Teeth: The Minimum Core and its Importance*, 119 S. Afr. L. J. 484 (2002); Pillay, *supra* note 56.

59. Founding Aff., *supra* note 32 at para. 238.

60. Heywood, *Preventing Mother-to-Child HIV Transmission*, *supra* note 16, at 280.

61. *Id.* at 281.

In its initial response to the TAC demands regarding PMTCT, the government seemed cooperative, with the high price of AZT appearing to be the main obstacle. The medicine was under patent in South Africa, meaning that the company Glaxo Wellcome possessed the exclusive right to make, sell, or import it into the country. As a result, the company could effectively charge whatever price it liked, and the medicine was priced exorbitantly. In an April 1999 meeting, TAC and the government agreed that the "government would name an affordable price for the implementation of AZT to pregnant mothers and report within six weeks on the price and other issues pertaining to the prevention of mother-to-child transmission," and that TAC and other civil society organizations would call on Glaxo Wellcome to "unconditionally lower the price of all HIV/AIDS medications to an affordable price for poor people and countries."[62]

Over the next year, TAC focused significant energy on securing affordable prices for AZT and other HIV-related medicines. Its members marched, protested, met with drug companies, and intervened on the side of the government in a lawsuit brought by patent-based drug companies that challenged a law designed to reduce the prices of medicines in South Africa. These efforts met with significant success. Facing an avalanche of pressure, patent-holding companies began reluctantly to reduce their prices. They also withdrew their lawsuit against the South African government, in significant part due to a worldwide campaign urging them to do so and to TAC's intervention in the case.[63]

But at the same time that this advocacy was creating the conditions for comprehensive PMTCT and ARV treatment programs in South Africa, AIDS denialism was taking hold at the highest levels of government. The first signs came shortly after the April 1999 meeting, which just preceded national and provincial elections and the inauguration of a new president. In September, the new Health Minister, Dr. Mantombazana ("Manto") Tshabalala–Msimang, told TAC that the government was committed to a PMTCT program, but that there were concerns about the safety and efficacy of Nevirapine.[64] Despite mounting evidence to the contrary, Tshabalala–Msimang told Parliament in November of

---

    62. Founding Aff., *supra* note 32, at para. 233.

    63. Mark Heywood, *Drug Access, Patents and Global Health: "Chaffed and Waxed Sufficient,"* 23 THIRD WORLD Q. 217 (2002).

    64. Nevirapine was known to cause, in a very small number of cases, serious and life-threatening side effects when used in continuous, long-term ARV treatment. These side-effects were considered rare enough, and the benefits significant enough, that the drug had been registered for treatment in South Africa in 1996. Furthermore, a Ugandan PMTCT trial found only two adverse events that were "possibly, but unlikely to be" attributable to the drug, out of 310 women studied. Guay, *supra* note 6. Nevertheless, TAC was aware at the time that there were some uncertainties about the possible long-term effects of single-dose Nevirapine on women who later wished to begin ARV treatment, as well as about the

that year: "we simply do not have enough information, either on the affordability or on the appropriateness of [using] the [ARV] drugs [for PMTCT] to make any decisions that might have long term health effects on the lives of children born to HIV positive mothers."[65]

In November 1999, President Mbeki publicly questioned whether AZT was too toxic to be of medical benefit, and announced that he had ordered an inquiry into the matter.[66] When the South African Medicines Control Council ("MCC") completed its review and concluded that AZT's health benefits outweighed the risks, the report was first rejected and then ignored.[67] When the results of the South African Intra-partum Nevirapine Trial ("SAINT") began to emerge in early 2000, and showed Nevirapine to be as safe and efficacious as indicated in an earlier Ugandan PMTCT study, the South African government continued to stall.[68] Around the same time, the government also declined to take up an offer from the drug company Boehringer Ingelheim for a five-year free supply of Nevirapine for PMTCT.[69]

In July 2000, the Thirteenth International AIDS Conference was held in Durban, South Africa, creating a platform for TAC and other AIDS activist groups to stage the first global march for treatment access. Thousands strong, the marchers demanded, among other things, that the South African government "immediately implement a country-wide program to reduce the risk of mother-to-child transmission of HIV using AZT or Nevirapine."[70] But President Mbeki's opening speech for the

---

efficacy of Nevirapine in cases where it is not feasible to use baby formula ("formula feed"). A careful review of the medical evidence demonstrated that Nevirapine's benefits outweighed its risks in settings where more efficacious medical regimens for PMTCT were not available. Founding Aff., *supra* note 32, at paras. 83–91, 92–107 and 117–119 respectively.

65. Dr. M.E. Tshabalala–Msimang, MP, Minister of Health, *Statement to the National Assembly on HIV/AIDS and Related Issues* (Nov. 16, 1999), *at* http://www.info.gov.za/speeches/1999/0001131124a1002.htm.

66. Heywood, *Preventing Mother-to-Child HIV Transmission*, *supra* note 16, at 282.

67. *Id.* at 283.

68. *See id.* at 285; Founding Aff., *supra* note 32 at para. 233; *see also* D. Moodley et al., *A Multicenter Randomized Controlled Trial of Nevirapine Versus a Combination of Zidovudine and Lamivudine to Reduce Intrapartum and Early Postpartum Mother-to-Child Transmission of Human Immunodeficiency Virus Type 1*, 187 J. INFECTIOUS DISEASES 725 (2003).

69. *See* Press Release, Boehringer Ingelheim, Boehringer Ingelheim Offers VIRAMUNE® (nevirapine) Free of Charge to Developing Economies for the Prevention of HIV-1 Mother-to-child Transmission (July 7, 2000), *available at* http://www.boehringer-ingelheim.com/hiv/news/ndetail.asp?ID=101; *see also* Pat Sidley, *Drug Firm is to Supply AIDS Drug Free in South Africa*, 323 BRIT. MED. J. 7311, 7311 (2001) (noting the government's initial failure to take up the offer).

70. TAC and HealthGAP Coalition, *Global Manifesto* (July 9, 2000), *available at* http://www.actupny.org/reports/durban-access.html. The manifesto included numerous ad-

conference did not highlight AIDS as a specific problem for Africa, and offered no indication that the government would move forward with PMTCT programs.[71]

In August 2000, the health minister and her nine provincial counterparts announced that the government would continue to avoid the use of AZT for PMTCT, and that Nevirapine-based PMTCT programs would not be considered until the drug was registered for the purpose in South Africa, and then used for two years at a limited number of "pilot sites" around the country.[72]

This was a clear signal that the government had no intention of moving forward with a comprehensive PMTCT program with any speed. But it would still be more than a year before TAC filed its suit. As Mark Heywood of the TAC describes:

> At the International AIDS Conference, TAC seriously considered bringing an urgent High Court application for access to Nevirapine on behalf of several women in the late stages of pregnancy. However, despite scientific consensus on its safety and efficacy, the medicine was not yet registered in South Africa for the prevention of MTCT. AZT was registered, but it was felt that with the greater cost of the medicine, together with the more complicated drug regimen (AZT must be taken daily from 36 weeks of pregnancy) made successful litigation more difficult. TAC's legal counsel cautioned against commencing litigation before Nevirapine was registered.[73]

TAC could have relied upon the fact that Nevirapine was registered for other uses in the country, and that "off label" prescribing (where a doctor prescribes a medicine for uses other than those for which the drug is registered) is widely accepted, but the organization believed that this was asking the court to "invit[e] compromise in the system of medicine registration." Heywood continues: "There was no option for TAC but to continue the campaign, but delay the litigation. Pressure was now

---

ditional demands, for instance, that drug companies reduce their prices, that wealthy countries support HIV treatment and prevention programs in the South, that all trade pressures being exerted on developing countries seeking to override patents and use generic AIDS medicines be halted, and that international agencies such as UNAIDS and WHO "proceed rapidly with viable programs to increase medication access." *Id.*

71. Heywood, *Preventing Mother-to-Child HIV Transmission, supra* note 16, at 285–86.

72. *Id.* at 286. TAC later learned, through leaked minutes, that the health Member of the Executive Council came to this conclusion despite the fact that the country's Chief Director for HIV/AIDS had recommended the immediate implementation of a country-wide PMTCT program, and pointed out the ethical importance of providing Nevirapine to women immediately. *Id.* at 288.

73. *Id.* at 286.

turned to the MCC to speed up registration of the drug and on government to clarify its programme."[74]

Neither task proved simple. There were numerous delays in establishing the pilot sites, and continued acrimony between the Health Minister and advocacy groups.[75] After inexplicable delays, Nevirapine was expressly approved for PMTCT use in April 2001.[76] With thousands of preventable infant HIV-infections taking place each month and the necessary registration for Nevirapine in place, TAC recruited some of the country's leading constitutional lawyers, and prepared a comprehensive letter of demand to the Minister of Health and the political heads of the nine provincial health departments. It requested that the government immediately permit doctors—where capacity existed—to prescribe Nevirapine in the public sector and expand beyond the pilot sites to create a national PMTCT program.[77] The Health Minister refused both requests, citing resource constraints, anticipated problems with Nevirapine-induced viral resistance to HIV medicines, concerns about the lack of safe alternatives to breastfeeding, and questions about sustainability.[78] The Campaign had finally exhausted all options, and so commenced a constitutional suit.

Litigation and Rulings

On August 21, 2001, TAC filed suit in the Pretoria High Court, along with two other plaintiffs: the Children's Rights Centre in Durban and a coalition of concerned pediatricians known as "Save Our Babies." Some external groups and allies, such as the Congress of South African Trade Unions, were quietly supportive, but "reluctant publicly to endorse taking 'our' government to court."[79] TAC members were not so reticent. Here it is worth reflecting on another precondition of a successful lawsuit. Before a court can enforce a right, it needs a willing plaintiff. In post-apartheid South Africa, many organizations have been reluctant to challenge directly the overwhelmingly popular African National Congress government, and unwilling to use the courts and the Constitution in their struggle for social change.

In their pleadings, TAC and its co-applicants contended that the government's refusal to extend PMTCT programs beyond the pilot sites

---
74. *Id.*

75. *Id.* at 290.

76. TAC learned through documents obtained in litigation that the internal MCC decision that the drug was safe and effective had occurred in November 2000. *Id.* at 289.

77. *Id.* at 289–91.

78. *Id.* at 291.

79. *Id.* at 300.

and its refusal to permit doctors—where capacity existed—to prescribe Nevirapine for PMTCT in the public health sector violated sections 27(1) and (2) of the Constitution, as well as other constitutional provisions dealing with rights to life, equality, dignity, bodily and psychological integrity, and children's rights.[80] The application also argued that the government's policy violated the Universal Declaration on Human Rights (which South Africa recognized as forming part of customary international law), as well as several human rights treaties that had been signed and ratified by South Africa: the International Covenant on Civil and Political Rights, the African Charter on Human and People's Rights, the Convention on the Elimination of All Forms of Discrimination Against Women, the Convention on the Rights of the Child and the International Convention on the Elimination of All Forms of Racial Discrimination.[81]

In the months before the case was filed, TAC had paved the road by recruiting various experts who could show that PMTCT programs were effective and affordable. For example, a professor of economics presented data that she had prepared demonstrating the cost-effectiveness of a Nevirapine-based regime compared with the costs of treating the children who would otherwise contract HIV.[82] A professor of medicine and Principal Medical Specialist for the Provincial Administration of the Western Cape reviewed the existing evidence to demonstrate that Nevirapine was a cheap, effective, safe, and internationally recommended intervention for PMTCT.[83] A former National Director of the HIV/AIDS and Sexually Transmitted Diseases program in South Africa submitted an affidavit providing evidence about rates of HIV infection in the country.[84]

TAC also ensured that the case addressed the human consequences of the government's failure to act by including affidavits from women such as Busisiwe Maqungo, nurses who worked in antenatal clinics and

---

80. Founding Aff., *supra* note 32, at paras. 268–75.

81. *Id.* at paras. 284–91. The founding affidavit also referred to the ICESCR, which South Africa has signed but not yet ratified. Interestingly, the only reference to international human rights law in the Constitutional Court's decision is its refusal to adopt the concept of minimum core obligations arising out of various interpretations of the ICESCR.

82. Affidavit of Professor Nicoli Jean Nattrass, Submitted in Support of the Applicants in *Minister of Health & Others v. Treatment Action Campaign & Others (No. 2)* 2002 (5) SA 721 (CC) (S. Afr.), at paras. 7–23 (Aug. 15, 2001), *available at* http://www.tac.org.za/Documents/MTCTCourtCase/MTCTCourtCase.htm.

83. Affidavit of Professor Robin Wood, Submitted in Support of the Applicants in *Minister of Health & Others v. Treatment Action Campaign & Others (No. 2)* 2002 (5) SA 721 (CC) (S. Afr.), at paras. 17–50 (Aug. 16, 2001), *available at* http://www.tac.org.za/Documents/MTCTCourtCase/MTCTCourtCase.htm.

84. Karim Aff., *supra* note 7.

cared for children with HIV, and doctors who were unable to prescribe Nevirapine to their patients and who spoke of the untenable ethical position which they consequently faced.

The government offered a response of more than a thousand pages justifying its policy. First, it argued that a comprehensive PMTCT program was unaffordable, in part because of the cost of Nevirapine, but also because of the costs of counseling, testing, and training healthcare providers.[85] While it admitted that Nevirapine had been registered for PMTCT, the government also suggested that its use could nonetheless be "catastrophic for public health" because it could lead to widespread resistance to ARV medicines.[86] Further, the government stressed that even if Nevirapine were used, some of the drug's effect would be undone through breastfeeding, for example, where women were not able to use baby formula ("formula feed") because of lack of access to clean water.[87]

TAC enlisted support from a variety of experts to counter each of these points in its replying papers. For example, it relied upon the Director of the Centre for Health Policy at the University of the Witwatersrand to identify the capacity that did exist within the healthcare system to provide PMTCT services.[88] The claim was substantially helped by the fact that one "rogue" province, the Western Cape, had already submitted an affidavit detailing its plans to create a comprehensive PMTCT program that would reach 90% of the population in need in 2002, and 100% of that population by 2003.[89]

TAC did not limit its enlisted support to South African experts. As Heywood also recounts,

> [C]ontact was made with Dr. Mark Wainberg, one of the world's leading virologists, based in the United States, who agreed to depose to an affidavit countering the selective quotation of one of his own

---

85. *TAC v. Minister of Health* 2002 (4) BCLR 356 (T) (High Court judgment describing submission of Dr. Ntsaluba). *See also* Heywood, *Preventing Mother-to-Child HIV Transmission, supra* note 16, at 297.

86. Answering Affidavit Submitted in Support of the Respondents in *Minister of Health & Others v. Treatment Action Campaign & Others (No. 2)* 2002 (5) SA 721 (CC) (S. Afr.), at para. 816 (Oct. 20, 2001), *available at* http://www.tac.org.za/Documents/MTCT CourtCase/MTCTCourtCase.htm.

87. Heywood, *Preventing Mother-to-Child HIV Transmission, supra* note 16, at 296.

88. Affidavit of Helen Schneider, Submitted in Support of the Applicants in *Minister of Health & Others v. Treatment Action Campaign & Others (No. 2)* 2002 (5) SA 721 (CC) (S. Afr.), at paras. 6–23 (Nov. 4, 2001), *available at* http://www.tac.org.za/Documents/MTCT CourtCase/MTCTCourtCase.htm.; *see also* Heywood, *Preventing Mother-to-Child HIV Transmission, supra* note 16, at 299.

89. Heywood, *Preventing Mother-to-Child HIV Transmission, supra* note 16, at 295. In response to this affidavit, the plaintiffs no longer sought any order against that province.

articles by [Director–General of the Department of Health] Ntsaluba around the issue of Nevirapine resistance. Similarly, Dr. Laura Guay, the principle investigator on the [Ugandan Nevirapine] trial, was contacted and supplied an affidavit countering a number of distortions made with regard to this clinical trial.[90]

It was these efforts, along with the affidavits accompanying the initial filing, that made a complicated set of disputes about medical evidence, programmatic structure, and cost-benefit calculation seem simple. Importantly, the successful mobilization by TAC of political sentiment against the government's policy also framed the case in profound ways. Throughout the period that the suit was pending, TAC continued to advocate for a national PMTCT program as well as a comprehensive national ARV treatment program. It held workshops with its volunteers to explain the case, and organized a national treatment summit that took place several days before the High Court hearing, bringing together more than 600 people from civil society, government, and the health care sector.[91] Rallies and marches were held throughout the country. The night before the hearing, 600 TAC supporters stood vigil outside the courthouse.[92]

The ruling issued by High Court Judge Chris Botha on December 14, 2001 did not disappoint. It rejected the government's suggestion that Nevirapine was too toxic or would cause long-term resistance for women, concluded that breastfeeding would not fully negate the benefits of Nevirapine, found that there was "incontrovertible evidence that there is a residual or latent capacity in the public sector outside the eighteen pilot sites to prescribe Nevirapine," and asserted that the cost of the drug was not a concern because it was "minimal."[93] Justice Botha concluded that the government's policy in "prohibiting the use of Nevirapine outside the pilot sites in the public health sector [was] not reasonable and that it [was] an unjustifiable barrier to the progressive realization of the right to health care."[94]

Justice Botha ordered the government to make Nevirapine available in the public health system, and to "plan an effective comprehensive national programme to prevent or reduce mother-to-child transmission for HIV" that included voluntary testing and counseling services, access to Nevirapine and formula feed.[95] In addition, he instructed the respondents to lodge plans detailing the steps that they had taken—and

---

90. *Id.* at 298–99.
91. Heywood, *Shaping, Making and Breaking*, *supra* note 4, at 188–89.
92. *Id.*
93. *TAC v. Minister of Health* 2002 (4) BCLR 356, 384 (T).
94. *Id.*
95. *Id.* at 387.

planned to take—to implement his order. Such plans were to be lodged with the court by the end of the first quarter of 2002, with the TAC and its allies being given an opportunity thereafter to comment on them and the state a further opportunity to reply.[96]

The government quickly indicated its intent to appeal, effectively putting the order on ice. For most of the next four months, a fierce battle over whether the government had to provide Nevirapine—but not implement a comprehensive PMTCT program—pending that appeal ensued. In response to an application to compel interim implementation notwithstanding the government's application for leave to appeal, the High Court ordered the government to permit state doctors to provide the medicine where it was medically indicated. In so doing, Judge Botha noted that the plaintiffs had shown the "irreparable harm" required for interim implementation because ten children a day would needlessly contract HIV in the absence of the intervention, with the "harm" to the state of implementing pending an appeal being essentially an inconvenience if anything at all.[97] The government sought to appeal this interim order too, but was several times denied leave—including by the Constitutional Court itself a little less than a month before the merits of the appeal were argued.[98]

Yet at the same time, the government seemed publicly to signal a change in its approach to PMTCT. Gauteng province started to expand its PMTCT program beyond the two pilot sites, and despite criticism from the Health Minister, quietly continued.[99] And just over two weeks before the main appeal was argued before the Constitutional Court, Mbeki's Cabinet officially shifted gear, stating, in an official Cabinet press statement:

> Where there is capacity to provide the package of care that is needed, and where the demands of research dictate, sites are being extended. Towards the end of the year, tests will be done on the babies and mothers being monitored, for us to then consider moving to universal access of Nevirapine. A Universal Roll-out Plan in this regard is being worked on and will be released in due course.[100]

But the appeal in the *TAC* case continued, as did TAC mobilization. The group organized protests in several South African cities in the days before the hearing in Constitutional Court, including a march in Johan-

---

96. *Id.*

97. *TAC v. Minister of Health*, TPD Case No. 21182/2001 (Mar. 8, 2002) 12–13 (on file with authors).

98. Heywood, *Preventing Mother-to-Child HIV Transmission, supra* note 16, at 304.

99. *Id.*

100. *Summary of Government's Position on HIV/AIDS* (Apr. 17, 2002), *available at* http://www.info.gov.za/issues/hiv/govposition02.htm.

nesburg on the first day of the hearing that drew 5000 people.[101] On that day, activists waited on long lines and filled the courtroom, many wearing the "HIV-positive" t-shirts that had come to be the hallmark of TAC.

On July 5, 2002, the Constitutional Court unanimously found in favor of TAC, squarely rejecting each of the government's arguments about efficacy, safety, resistance, and capacity. The Court's findings and arguments merit close consideration because they point to TAC's success in defining the contours of reasonable debate about PMTCT, and the government's approach to the issue. Importantly, the judgment relied on the factual evidence provided by TAC, and, wherever it could, on the government's own admissions and actions—many of which had been prompted by pressure from TAC and its co-plaintiffs. The Court noted, for example, that the "decision of the government to provide Nevirapine to mothers and infants at the research and training sites is consistent only with government itself being satisfied as to the efficacy and safety of the drug."[102]

The Court carefully skirted the resource-allocation issue in similar fashion, pointing out that the government admitted that the cost of Nevirapine was "within the resources of the state,"[103] and that it had admitted "at the hearing of the appeal that the government has made substantial additional funds available for the treatment of HIV, including the reduction of mother-to-child transmission.... This means that the budgetary constraints referred to in the affidavits are no longer an impediment."[104] Thus, despite a well-documented history of state inaction, the Court portrayed the limited PMTCT program as one that had been freely chosen by the state. This made the court's jurisprudential job considerably easier, and was made possible by the comprehensive campaigning of TAC.

In its legal analysis, the Court forcefully rejected the government's argument that the right to have access to health services is not justiciable.[105] But, it also declined expressly to adopt the jurisprudential approach taken by the U.N. Committee on Social, Economic and Cultural Rights in interpreting the ICESCR. This so-called "minimum core" approach—designed to make socio-economic rights easier to apply— posits that states must respect an essential "core" of social and economic rights, despite the broad caveat in the ICESCR (Article 2) that obliges a state party to respect such rights to "the maximum of its available

---

101. Heywood, *Preventing Mother-to-Child HIV Transmission*, supra note 16, at 310.
102. *TAC (No. 2)* 2002 (5) SA 721 (CC) at para. 62 (S. Afr.).
103. *Id.* at para. 71.
104. *Id.* at para. 120.
105. *Id.* at para. 106.

resources, with a view to achieving progressively the full realization of the rights recognized." As described by the Committee:

> The concept of progressive realization constitutes a recognition of the fact that full realization of all economic, social and cultural rights will generally not be able to be achieved in a short period of time. In this sense the obligation differs significantly from that contained in article 2 of the International Covenant on Civil and Political Rights which embodies an immediate obligation to respect and ensure all of the relevant rights. Nevertheless, the fact that realization over time, or in other words progressively, is foreseen under the Covenant should not be misinterpreted as depriving the obligation of all meaningful content.[106]

To ensure this, the Committee went on to conclude that the treaty imposes a "minimum core obligation" on all states to ensure "minimum essential levels of each of the rights."[107] As a result, "a State party in which any significant number of individuals is deprived of essential foodstuffs, of essential primary health care, of basic shelter and housing, or of the most basic forms of education is, prima facie, failing to discharge its obligations under the Covenant," even if the state argues that it lacks resources or is working towards this goal in progressive fashion.[108]

An *amicus curiae* in the *TAC* appeal urged the Constitutional Court to read section 27(1) of the South African Constitution to create its own "minimum core" to which individuals are entitled without regard to the "progressive realization" and "available resources" qualifications of section 27(2).[109] In declining to do so, the Court relied on the text of section 27 and its worry that "courts are not institutionally equipped to make the wide-ranging factual and political enquiries necessary for determining what the minimum core standards ... should be."[110] Importantly, the Court did not abandon the concept of minimum core entitlements completely. Instead, it reaffirmed the position stated in *Grootboom* that the idea of minimum core is potentially relevant "in determining whether measures adopted by the State are reasonable."[111]

---

106. U.N. Committee on Economic, Social and Cultural Rights [hereinafter CESCR], *General Comment 3: The Nature of States Parties Obligations (Article 2(1))*, para. 9, U.N. Doc. E/1991/23 (Dec. 14, 1990).

107. *Id.* at para. 10.

108. *Id.*

109. *TAC (No. 2)* (5) SA at para. 26. *See also Government of the Republic of South Africa & Others v. Grootboom & Others* 2001 (1) SA 46 (CC) at paras. 27–33 (S. Afr.) [hereinafter *Grootboom*].

110. *TAC (No. 2)* (5) SA at para. 37.

111. *Grootboom* (1) SA at para. 33; *see also TAC (No. 2)* (5) SA at para. 34 (suggesting that the minimum core is "relevant to reasonableness under section 26(2)").

In other words, the failure to provide a minimum set of benefits in a particular context may indeed constitute unreasonable—and thus unconstitutional—conduct.[112]

Relief Granted

With these preliminary interpretive issues decided, the Constitutional Court was now in a position to answer the two key legal questions of the case. First, was the state entitled to limit the provision of Nevirapine for PMTCT to eighteen identified sites, "even where it was medically indicated and adequate facilities existed for the testing and counseling of the pregnant women concerned"? Second, had the state "devise[d] and implement[ed] within its available resources a comprehensive and coordinated programme to realise progressively the rights of pregnant women and their newborn children to have access to health services to combat . . . [MTCT]?"[113] Applying the reasonableness test set forth in *Grootboom*, the Court held in favor of the TAC on both issues.[114] Its analysis was highly case-specific, eschewing any broad statements about the nature of the constitutional right to health services and simply concluding that—absent any real resource constraints or safety issues, and given the existing capacity in the health sector—the government's position was unreasonable.[115]

What remedy should follow? The Court stated the general principle that "[w]here a breach of any right has taken place, including a socio-economic right, a court is under a duty to ensure that effective relief is granted,"[116] and noted the courts' obligations to be flexible and creative in crafting effective remedies, because " '[p]articularly in a country where so few have the means to enforce their rights through the courts, it is essential that on those occasions when the legal process does establish that an infringement of an entrenched right has occurred, it be effectively vindicated.' "[117]

---

112. In this regard, *see N v. Government of Republic of South Africa (No. 1)* 2006 (6) SA 543 (D), in which the failure to provide prisoners at a particular facility with access to ARV treatment was held to be unreasonable, and therefore unconstitutional.

113. *TAC (No. 2)* (5) SA at para. 135.

114. For further discussion of the *TAC* case, *see* Heywood, *Preventing Mother-to-Child HIV Transmission, supra* note 16. *See also* Mark Heywood, *Contempt or Compliance? The* TAC *case after the Constitutional Court Judgment*, 4 ESR Rev. 7 (2003) [hereinafter Heywood, *Contempt*].

115. *TAC (No. 2)* (5) SA at para. 80.

116. *Id.* at para. 106.

117. *Id.* at para. 102 (citing *Fose v. Minister of Safety and Security* 1997 (3) SA 786 (CC) at para. 69 (S. Afr.)).

The Court then ordered the government "without delay" to permit doctors to prescribe Nevirapine in state clinics and hospitals; to "facilitate" the use of Nevirapine for PMTCT; and to take "reasonable measures" to expand testing and counseling programs in the state sector to facilitate the use of Nevirapine.[118] But it also vacated the lower court's order that the government return to court to submit its new plan. Part of the Court's reluctance to grant the supervisory order plaintiffs had sought appears rooted in the fact that by the time the case was argued, the state's official position had changed. As we have already mentioned, the government had already—albeit reluctantly—expressly committed itself to the universal rollout of PMTCT services, and certain provinces had started to implement such programs.[119] The Court wrote:

> Government policy is now evolving. Additional sites where Nevirapine is provided with a full package to combat mother-to-child transmission of HIV are being added. In the Western Cape, Gauteng and KwaZulu–Natal, programmes have been adopted to extend the supply of Nevirapine for such purpose throughout the province. What now remains is for the other provinces to follow suit. The order that we make will facilitate this.[120]

Formally, the Court justified its decision by holding that supervisory orders should issue only when "necessary," and by noting that "the government has always respected and executed orders of this Court. There is no reason to believe that it will not do so in the present case."[121]

This statement is notably incongruous with the history of denialism and obstructionism within the South African government that initially led to the *TAC* case. The Court's expressed confidence was clearly in part intended as a performative statement, to produce the compliance that the Court desired. But it also hints at an implicit delegation of the enforcement of the decision—to civil society, and specifically to the TAC itself. If the government did not comply with the decision, or stalled in its implementation, the Court may have presumed that TAC would simply return to court, judgment in hand, and demand its enforcement. If so, the presumption overstated the capacity of the TAC, as we will see.

---

118. *Id.* at para. 135.

119. *See* Jonathan Michael Berger, *Litigation Strategies to Gain Access to Treatment for HIV/AIDS: The Case of South Africa's Treatment Action Campaign*, 20 WIS. INT'L. L. J. 595, 601–03 (2002).

120. *TAC (No. 2)* (5) SA at para. 132.

121. *Id.* at para. 129 (footnote omitted). Interestingly, the Court relied in part on the decision of the Nova Scotia Court of Appeals in *Doucet–Boudreau v. Nova Scotia (Dep't of Educ.)* (2001) NSCA 104, 128, stating: "Canadian courts have also tended to be wary of using the structural injunction," *TAC (No. 2)* (5) SA at para. 110. The *Doucet-Boudreau* decision has since been overruled by the Supreme Court of Canada ("SCC"). *See Doucet-Boudreau v. Nova Scotia (Minister of Educ.)*, (2003) 3 S.C.R. 3.

Outcome and Impact

Since the Constitutional Court judgment, tens of thousands of mothers and children have received the single-dose Nevirapine regimen in South Africa. It is beyond rational question that thousands of young lives and immeasurable suffering have been spared.[122]

Justice Edwin Cameron
Bloemfontein, South Africa

Analysis and Response

Activists responded to the ruling with immediate elation, singing and dancing outside of the Court and the TAC's Johannesburg offices.[123] The Health Minister's response was more equivocal. In an interview she gave at the Fourteenth International AIDS Conference in Barcelona, Tshabalala–Msimang was reported to have "described drugs used to prevent transmission of HIV from mother to child as poison."[124] But in another interview, the Minister declared that the government would accept the ruling of the Court, and even insisted that its ruling in fact "confirmed the approach of her department in planning to extend the availability of Nevirapine."[125] The reality seems to be that the ruling was, as the *Financial Times* noted, "a crushing defeat for the government."[126]

Since it was handed down, the decision in the *TAC* case has been widely hailed as a deeply significant judgment and as a symbol of the power that courts can have on the terrain of socio-economic rights. One TAC lawyer, for example, declared that the case "shows that the Constitution creates a powerful tool in the hands of civil society, to ensure that the government gives proper attention to the fundamental needs of the poor, the vulnerable and the marginalised."[127] Other legal

---

122. CAMERON, *supra* note 36, at 117.

123. *See, e.g., Court Ruling on Supply of Aids Drugs Welcomed*, BBC NEWS, July 5, 2002. *See also* Nicol Degli Innocenti & Geoff Dyer, *Court Victory for Aids Campaigners*, FIN. TIMES (LONDON), July 6, 2002, at 8 (citing TAC leader Zackie Achmat's statement: "We are elated by the ruling ... [b]ut there is an element of sadness too, because we had to fight government for five years and it was a totally unneccessary battle.") [hereinafter Innocenti & Dyer].

124. *See, e.g.,* Laurie Garrett, *Anti-HIV Drug Poison, Summit Told*, THE AGE, July 9, 2002, *available at* http://www.theage.com.au/articles/2002/07/08/1025667115671.html. Unsurprisingly, this comment was later denied.

125. Carmel Rickard, *Human Rights Triumph As State Loses AIDS Battle*, SUNDAY TIMES (JOHANNESBURG), July 7, 2002, *available at* http://www.aegis.com/news/suntimes/2002/ST020701.html.

126. Innocenti & Dyer, *supra* note 123, at 8.

127. Geoff Budlender, *A Paper Dog with Real Teeth*, MAIL & GUARDIAN (S. AFR.), July 12, 2002, *available at* http://www.tac.org.za/Documents/Other/geoff_budlender.txt.

commentators agreed that the ruling demonstrated conclusively the importance of socio-economic rights, but criticized the Court for failing to retain supervisory jurisdiction, effectively leaving it up to TAC to ensure government compliance. In addition, they criticized the decision's failure to adopt the minimum core approach, as described above.[128]

Another group instead found remarkable how strong the court's order and judgment in fact were, especially when compared to the order in *Grootboom*.[129] *Grootboom*, after all, ordered the government only to develop a *plan* to address the housing needs of the poorest and most vulnerable people; the decision in the *TAC* case instead ordered the government to provide Nevirapine "without delay" in the public health sector, and to build the counseling and testing services needed to make the PMTCT program effective.[130] Several commentators have offered the same explanation of the difference between the two results: The *TAC* case, they state, was much easier. As one wrote:

> The crucial factor that separates *TAC* from *Grootboom* is not greater assertiveness on the part of the Court, but the fact that extending an entitlement to Nevirapine—where the drug is medically indicated and where, if necessary, testing and counseling are available—had only limited cost-implications and did not involve issues involving great expertise.[131]

---

128. *See, e.g.*, Sandra Liebenberg, *Enforcing Basic Rights*, FINANCIAL MAIL (S. AFR.), July 12, 2002, *available at* http://www.queensu.ca/msp/pages/In_The_News/2002/July/basic.htm; Bilchitz, *supra* note 14; Marius Pieterse, *Resuscitating Socio–Economic Rights: Constitutional Entitlements to Health Care Services*, 22 S. AFR. J. HUM. RTS. 473, 474 (2006).

129. *See* Jonathan Klaaren, *A Remedial Interpretation of TAC*, 20 S. AFR. J. HUM. RTS. 455, 460–61 (2004) (stating "[T]he judges took their role of evaluation very seriously. Governmental objections were assessed against evidence and found wanting.... The case was an example of a willingness to closely scrutinize the government's decisions with respect to access to socio-economic rights. In administrative law terms, TAC was a hard-look case."); Mark Tushnet, *Social Welfare Rights and the Forms of Judicial Review*, 82 TEX. L. REV. 1895, 1906 (2004) (calling *TAC* an example of enforcement of a "strong social welfare right," i.e., one that "courts will enforce ... fully, without giving substantial deference to legislative judgments, whenever they conclude that the legislature has failed to provide what the constitution requires").

130. *TAC (No. 2)* 2002 (5) SA 721 (CC) at para. 135 (S. Afr.).

131. Murray Wesson, Grootboom *and Beyond: Reassessing the Socio–Economic Jurisprudence of the South African Constitutional Court*, 20 S. AFR. J. HUM. RTS. 284, 296 (2004). *See also* Tushnet, *supra* note 15, at 826 (crediting the decision to the fact that "South African legal elites knew that the government's policy was motivated in large measure by President Thabo Mbeki's expressed view that AIDS was not caused by HIV," as well as to the fact that Nevirapine had been approved "through the ordinary processes for the approval of drugs," the government's concession that Nevirapine was affordable, and the government's decision to "make Nevirapine generally available by the time the Constitutional Court decided the case").

But, it seems just as odd to present the *TAC* case as an inherently "easy case" as it is to present the judgment as the result of a sudden assertiveness on the part of the Constitutional Court. The issue of PMTCT services in South Africa did not start out as a simple one. The pre-history of the *TAC* case demonstrates that the result relied crucially on concerted and savvy advocacy that made an initially difficult issue appear simple, and morally imperative. And the Court must have been attuned to the very real possibility that such a decision would have significant financial implications beyond PMTCT, in particular regarding government policy on ARV treatment and access to other HIV-related services.

As the narrative above demonstrates, the case for these programs was built by a large coalition over many years. It involved not only legal expertise, but also scientific, medical, and economic expertise, and a broad public consensus in favor of PMTCT. It also required recognition of the AIDS denialism that had taken hold in the government. Had TAC brought its case several years earlier, before it had, for example, worked to ensure the timely registration of Nevirapine for PMTCT, and to mobilize healthcare providers and women to demand PMTCT services, the case would not have been an easy one at all.

Immediate and Practical Impact on PMTCT

The importance of reading *TAC*—the case—through the lens of TAC—the movement—becomes even more evident when we look to the aftermath of the decision. The political and symbolic significance of the decision in the *TAC* case cannot be overemphasized. It dealt a decisive blow to denialism within the government, and ensured that the Ministry of Health could no longer simply refuse to provide comprehensive PMTCT services in the public sector.[132] But, in terms of its immediate and practical impact on the provision of PMTCT services, the record is significantly less spectacular.

Since the Court's decision in July 2002, implementation of the PMTCT program has been patchy at best. Although the government

---

132. As late as October 24, 2000, the Minister of Health stated: "There is a narrow view again that continues to associate prevention of mother to child transmission of HIV with the use of antiretrovirals only.... We know there are other medical interventions.... We know ... [ARV medicines] are toxic." *See* Steven Swindells, *South Africa Limits Role of Key Drugs in AIDS Fight*, REUTERS NEWS MEDIA, Oct. 24, 2000, *available at* http://www.aegis.com/news/re/2000/RE001017.html. A day later, UNAIDS recommended that PMTCT programs constitute a base level of care for pregnant women with HIV and their children. *See* Press Release, UNAIDS, Preventing Mother-to-Child HIV Transmission: Technical Experts Recommend Use of Antiretroviral Regimens Beyond Pilot Projects (Oct. 25, 2000), *available at* http://www.thebody.com/content/treat/art651.html.

insisted that it was complying with the ruling, it also refused to give TAC information about its plans and progress. Only after TAC threatened further legal action did the government provide it with information about what had been done to comply.[133] In general, "TAC found that . . . in provinces where there was already a commitment to establishing a comprehensive PMTCT program . . . the judgment unshackled health departments and politicians and opened the door to implementation."[134] In other provinces, the result was decidedly otherwise. In Mpumalanga province, for example, implementation only began after the TAC held a public demonstration and filed contempt of court proceedings.[135]

Most disturbing is that six years later, the PMTCT program in South Africa still has a long way to go to reach universal coverage. While the state claims relatively high levels of coverage,[136] a sizeable disconnect between the estimated numbers of pregnant women in South Africa with HIV and those actually accessing the full PMTCT package of services appears to remain.[137] As the South African Health Review 2006 explains:

> PMTCT data from the 53 health districts in [South Africa] for 2004 indicated that a relatively low proportion of mothers actually got tested for HIV, resulting in many deliveries of women of unknown HIV serostatus and missed opportunities to prevent MTCT.[138]

In other words, the programs that do exist are not reaching many of the women who need them, apparently in significant part because women either are not being offered HIV tests or because they are not agreeing to be tested. This need not be the case, however. For instance, 95% of women who attend the Cape Town Médecins Sans Frontières

---

133. Heywood, *Contempt, supra* note 112, at 9.

134. *Id.*

135. *Id.* at 10.

136. *See* REPUBLIC OF S. AFR., PROGRESS REPORT ON DECLARATION OF COMMITMENT ON HIV/AIDS (Reporting Period Jan. 2006 to Dec. 2007) (Prepared for the U.N. Special Session on HIV and AIDS) 24–25 (Mar. 4, 2008) [hereinafter S. AFR. PROGRESS REPORT 2006-07], *available at* http://data.unaids.org/pub/Report/2008/south_africa_2008_country_progress_report_en.pdf.

137. The South African Country Progress Report for the U.N. Special Session on HIV and AIDS appears to misrepresent the data. For example, the report claims that "[t]he total number of HIV-positive pregnant women identified and enrolled into the PMTCT programme in 2006 was 186,646 (72.7%)"—out of an estimated 256,700 HIV-positive pregnant women who attended antenatal services in the public health sector that year. However, an earlier draft of the country report (on file with the authors) indicated that only 69,952 HIV-positive women accessed ARV medicines for PMTCT in 2006. Using that number, coverage of comprehensive PMTCT services in 2006 was below 30%. It appears as if the state is using the wrong numerator in its calculations. S. AFR. PROGRESS REPORT 2006-07, *supra* note 134, at 24.

138. Arthi Ramkissoon et al., *Options for HIV Positive Women*, in SOUTH AFRICAN HEALTH REVIEW 2006, 315, 323 (P. Ijumba & A. Padarath eds., 2006).

PMTCT program in Khayelitsha agree to be tested, in part because of the quality of the counseling offered.[139] The result of a substandard regimen,[140] the lack of testing uptake, the low rates of ARV access, and the persistence of breastfeeding as a mode of transmission, is that an estimated 64,000 children contracted HIV from their mothers in 2006.[141]

It has also long been clear that PMTCT interventions are far more successful if they use several ARVs than if they use only one. More drugs means more expensive—and potentially more complicated—programs, but a consensus has emerged since the *TAC* case that simple multi-drug regimens are sufficiently cost effective and should now be the standard in developing countries, many of which are already implementing significantly more complex ARV treatment programs. World Health Organization ("WHO") guidelines now officially recommend such regimens.[142] But until relatively recently, all but one province in South Africa—the Western Cape—still relied upon a single-dose Nevirapine regimen.

The new national *HIV & AIDS and STI Strategic Plan for South Africa, 2007–2011* ("National Strategic Plan") recognizes the centrality of improving the PMTCT program, and the importance of moving to more efficacious drug regimens.[143] Once again, however, the presence and

---

139. Médicins Sans Frontièrs, Activity Report, *Providing HIV Services Including Antiretroviral Therapy at Primary Health Care Clinics in Resource–Poor Settings: The Experience from Khayelitsha* 14 (2003) (showing an over 95% acceptance rate for 2002 and 2003), *available at* www.msf.org/source/countries/africa/southafrica/2004/1000/khayelitsha 1000.pdf.

140. The new PMTCT protocol, adopted on February 11, 2008, is much improved. While it still falls short of international good practice, early indications suggest that it will result in a significant reduction in HIV incidence amongst infants. In this regard, *see* Louise Flanagan, *Gauteng sees progress in mom-and-baby programme*, INDEPENDENT ONLINE (JOHANNESBURG), Sept. 2, 2008, *available at* http://www.iolhivaids.co.za/index.php?fSection Id=1591&fArticleId=4589806. To view the 2008 protocol, *see* The National Department of Health, *Policy and Guidelines for the Implementation of the PMTCT Programme* (Feb. 11, 2008) *available at* http://www.doh.gov.za/docs/policy/pmtct.pdf.

141. *See* Dorrington, *supra* note 25, at ii.

142. WORLD HEALTH ORGANIZATION, ANTIRETROVIRAL DRUGS FOR TREATING PREGNANT WOMEN AND PREVENTING HIV–INFECTIONS IN INFANTS: TOWARDS UNIVERSAL ACCESS, RECOMMENDATIONS FOR A PUBLIC HEALTH APPROACH, 27 (2006), *available at* http://www.who.int/hiv/pub/guidelines/pmt ctguidelines3.pdf.

143. SOUTH AFRICAN NATIONAL AIDS COUNCIL, HIV & AIDS AND STI STRATEGIC PLAN FOR SOUTH AFRICA, 2007–2011 (2007) [hereinafter NATIONAL STRATEGIC PLAN 2007], *available at* http://www.info.gov.za/otherdocs/2007/aidsplan2007/khomanani_HIV_plan.pdf. The National Strategic Plan was adopted by the newly constituted South African National AIDS Council ("SANAC") on April 30, 2007, and by Mbeki's Cabinet two days later, was developed under the leadership of Deputy President Phumzile Mlambo–Ngcuka, former Deputy Minister of Health Nozizwe Madlala–Routledge, and Dr Nomonde Xundu, chief director of HIV and AIDS, TB and STIs in the national Department of Health. The plan states: "[e]xtending prevention programmes and getting them to work ... is critical [to] reducing long-term morbidity and costs. A simple example is PMTCT. If this programme

activity of a movement to hold the government accountable has been critical. In August 2007, the AIDS Law Project wrote to the health minister on behalf of a group of concerned health care workers, the Southern African HIV/AIDS Clinicians' Society and TAC, demanding that the PMTCT regimen be updated. The minister did not respond. Instead, her department informed the South African National AIDS Council ("SANAC") some three months later that "dual therapy"[144] would become the minimum PMTCT regimen in the country.[145] Despite promising to finalize the amended protocol within two weeks, the process took a further three months.[146]

Despite the Constitutional Court's somewhat misplaced trust in government's willingness to comply with its judgment, as well as its apparent faith in the TAC's tenacity and ability to hold the state to account, the state's failure properly to implement a comprehensive PMTCT program has shown how important it is for courts to be mindful of the fact that even the strongest of civil society organizations do not have unlimited resources and capacity. In retrospect, the Court's order in the *TAC* case did not "ensure that the rights enshrined in the Constitution are protected and enforced,"[147] and was thus not an "appropriate" remedy for the constitutional harm.[148]

---

was functioning properly, it would radically reduce paediatric AIDS cases...." NATIONAL STRATEGIC PLAN 2007 at 122. Goals 3.1 and 3.2 include the following: "Broaden existing mother to child transmission services to include other related services and target groups" and "Scale up coverage and improve quality of PMTCT to reduce MTCT to less than 5%." *Id.* at 73–74.

144. Although technically incorrect, the term "dual therapy" is widely used in South Africa to refer to a two-drug regimen—ordinarily AZT and Nevirapine—for PMTCT. Such a regimen is not therapy, but rather prophylaxis.

145. Telephonic communication from Mark Heywood, Deputy Chairperson, SANAC, to Jonathan Berger (Nov. 28, 2007).

146. Media communiqué issued by the Government Communications and Information Service (GCIS) on behalf of SANAC (Nov. 29, 2007) (on file with authors). At the same time, the KwaZulu–Natal Department of Health started to take disciplinary action against Colin Pfaff—a public sector doctor—for providing better PMTCT services at Manguzi Hospital in the rural north of the province. Manguzi Hospital was able to do so because it had received donor funds from a U.K.-based organization. The charges against Pfaff were later dropped. *See* Kerry Cullinan, *Doctor in Trouble for His Attempt to Reverse "Miserable Lives" of HIV Babies*, HEALTH-E NEWS SERVICE, Feb. 16, 2008, *available at* http://www.health-e.org.za/news/article.php?uid=20031882; Kerry Cullinan, *KZN Drops Misconduct Charges Against Doctor*, HEALTH-E NEWS SERVICE, Feb. 21, 2008, *available at* http://www.health-e.org.za/news/article.php?uid=20031889.

147. *Fose v. Minister of Safety and Security*, 1997 (3) SA 786 (CC) at para. 19 (S. Afr.).

148. For more on what constitutes appropriate relief, *see* Kent Roach & Geoff Budlender, *Mandatory Relief and Supervisory Jurisdiction: When is it Appropriate, Just and Equitable?*, 122 S. AFR. L. J. 325 (2005).

As an organization that has used the law, advocacy campaigns and public mobilization effectively to compel the state to invest billions of rands into the provision of health care services, even the TAC was not able to ensure proper implementation of the Court's judgment. In part, its "failure" to hold the state to account lies in its focus on the broader campaign for comprehensive HIV treatment services. Had the organization not been fighting the government on a range of other fronts, it would have been able to work with the Court's decision to ensure proper implementation—just as it has been able to use the national treatment plan to ensure that ARV treatment is provided to greater numbers of people in the public sector.

The *TAC* case shows why socio-economic rights claimants have to ensure that sufficient evidence is placed before courts regarding the broader social and political context within which their decisions are made. Had the Constitutional Court been more attuned to the broader campaign for access to ARV treatment, or more responsive to the clear history of obstruction within the government, it may well have realized that TAC was not in a position to do what was expected of it. Even if it was wary of granting supervisory jurisdiction in circumstances which had witnessed a significant government retreat in relation to PMTCT policy, the Court should—at a bare minimum—have required the state to report publicly on its progress in implementing the order. In the absence of such information, the TAC was unable to expend the necessary resources to ensure compliance.

Impact on Broader HIV/AIDS Policy

It is no accident that the decisive legal victory in the *TAC* case was used to support the organization's campaign to compel a reluctant state to develop and implement a comprehensive public sector ARV treatment program. Simply put, the case was conceptualized—from the very beginning—as an integral part of the broader treatment access campaign. While the issue of PMTCT was—and remains—of paramount importance, the TAC always conceived of the case as a stepping stone towards the provision—at state expense—of comprehensive HIV treatment services.[149]

Subsequent developments have vindicated the TAC approach, with the case arguably providing the kick-start that was needed to shift the state into action. The first breakthrough came in the Cabinet statement of April 17, 2002 where, in addition to a commitment to implement a comprehensive PMTCT program, the government pledged to ensure the availability of post-exposure prophylaxis services in the public health

---

149. *See* Heywood, *Shaping, Making and Breaking, supra* note 4.

sector.[150] For the first time, government publicly recognized the utility of ARV medicines in treating HIV infection, acknowledging that they "can improve the quality of life of People Living with AIDS, if administered at certain stages in the progression of the condition and in accordance with international guidelines and protocols."[151]

The skeptic may argue that this action, coming just short of two weeks before the hearing of the appeal in the *TAC* case, was a transparent—and apparently successful—attempt to influence the Constitutional Court. But regardless of intention, the commitment was indeed followed by further action. Shortly after the Court handed down its decision, the government established a Joint Health and Treasury Task Team charged with "examining treatment options to supplement comprehensive care for HIV and AIDS in the public health sector."[152] In an apparent reference to the work of the Task Team, another Cabinet statement issued some three months later on October 9, 2002 claimed that the government was working "to create the conditions that would make it feasible and effective to use antiretrovirals in the public health sector."[153]

But, as has unfortunately been the hallmark of the South African government's response to HIV/AIDS for some time, progress from this point to the adoption of the national treatment plan some thirteen months later was hardly smooth—or inevitable. Among other events that formed part of the TAC intensified program of action, two stand out: a powerful march of 20,000 people on the opening of Parliament in February 2003, and a nationwide campaign of civil disobedience that began little more than a month later on the eve of Human Rights Day. Drawing on a repertoire of protest that evoked the struggle against apartheid, protesters marched on government buildings, staged sit-ins, peacefully provoked arrest, and laid charges of culpable homicide against two government ministers—one for failing to take lawful action to override patents and bring the prices of HIV medicines down, and the other for failing to prevent loss of life through the development and implementation of a treatment program.[154]

---

150. Post-exposure prophylaxis uses ARV medicines to reduce the risk of HIV transmission following rape and other forms of sexual assault.

151. Government Communications and Information Service, *Statement of Cabinet on HIV/AIDS*, Apr. 17, 2002, *available at* http://www.tac.org.za/newsletter/2002/ns18_04_2002.txt

152. OPERATIONAL PLAN FOR COMPREHENSIVE HIV AND AIDS CARE, MANAGEMENT AND TREATMENT FOR SOUTH AFRICA at 13 [hereinafter OPERATIONAL PLAN 2003], *available at* http://www.info.gov.za/issues/hiv/careplan.htm.

153. Government Communications, *Update on Cabinet's Statement of 17 April 2002 on Fighting HIV/AIDS* (Oct. 9, 2002) *available at* http://www.info.gov.za/issues/hiv/updateoct02.htm.

154. The decision to make March 21 Human Rights Day was a deliberate one. Formerly known as Sharpeville Day, the date marks the anniversary of a particularly

The campaign produced results. The Cabinet called a special meeting in which it was decided that "the Department of Health should, as a matter of urgency, develop a detailed operational plan" that would provide ARV treatment in the public sector.[155] On November 19, 2003, Cabinet adopted such a plan, officially committing the government to provide ARV treatment in the public healthcare system.[156] This too was part of the legacy of the *TAC* case. As government experts themselves recognized, the *TAC* case and its predecessors, such as *Grootboom*, helped to inform the government's sense that it was obliged to provide such treatment.[157]

Broader Impact

While it is difficult to measure with precision the extent to which the decision in the *TAC* case was responsible for the development, adoption and subsequent implementation of South Africa's national treatment plan, the evidence points in the direction of significant influence. In addition to strengthening the public campaign of TAC, and assisting the state to think through its constitutional obligations in respect of the treatment of HIV infection, the case was instrumental in solidifying the foundation for further litigation, advocacy, mobilization and campaign work that were necessary for the country to reach the point where the new National Strategic Plan could be developed in a truly consultative manner.

The emerging health rights jurisprudence—to which the *TAC* case makes a significant contribution—has been used successfully by the TAC in at least three further matters relating to access to treatment for HIV infection: *Hazel Tau v. GlaxoSmithKline South Africa (Pty) Ltd. and*

---

bloody attack in 1960 by police officers on peaceful protesters of the apartheid regime. In Gauteng province, the TAC civil disobedience campaign involved a march to the local Sharpeville police station to lodge the culpable homicide charges.

155. Government Communications, *Statement on Special Cabinet Meeting: Enhanced Programme Against HIV and AIDS* (Aug. 8, 2003), *available at* http://www.info.gov.za/speeches/2003/03081109461001.htm.

156. OPERATIONAL PLAN, *supra* note 152, at 246.

157. GOVERNMENT OF THE REPUBLIC OF SOUTH AFRICA, REP. OF THE JOINT HEALTH AND TREASURY TASK TEAM CHARGED WITH EXAMINING TREATMENT OPTIONS TO SUPPLEMENT COMPREHENSIVE CARE FOR HIV/AIDS IN THE PUBLIC HEALTH SECTOR (Aug. 1, 2003) [hereinafter TASK TEAM REP.], *available at* http://www.info.gov.za/otherdocs/2003/treatment.pdf. Other noteworthy cases in this regard are *Soobramoney v. Minister of Health (KwaZulu–Natal)* 1998 (1) SA 765 (CC) (S. Afr.), and *Government of the Republic of South Africa & Others v. Grootboom & Others* 2001 (1) SA 46 (CC) (S. Afr.). An Appendix of the TASK TEAM REPORT indicated that these cases "outlined some principles which are relevant to the question of whether and in what manner antiretroviral drugs should be supplied in the public health sector." *See* TASK TEAM REP. App. at 2 (internal citation omitted)

Boehringer Ingelheim (Pty) Ltd.;[158] litigation threatened in March 2004 to compel the state to procure an interim supply of ARV medicines pending the finalization of a formal state tender for the national treatment program; and *N v. Government of Republic of South Africa (No. 1)*, *N v. Government of Republic of South Africa (No. 2)*, and *N v. Government of Republic of South Africa (No 3)*.[159]

The first case, brought by the TAC and others, sought to use competition law to challenge the pricing practices of two multinational pharmaceutical companies, and directly resulted in increasing access to a sustainable supply of affordable ARV medicines. In the second matter, the TAC succeeded in compelling the Minister of Health to procure an interim supply of ARV medicines, and this gave provinces with existing capacity the space to implement the national treatment plan with urgency, saving many lives that would have been lost in the year that it took the government to procure ARV medicines through a formal state tender.[160] The last cases were brought by TAC lawyers on behalf of prisoners living with HIV who needed access to ARVs. As a result of these cases, there has been a significant—although still insufficient—increase in the number of prisoners accessing ARV treatment.[161]

Thus, much of the broader impact of the *TAC* case was not determined until well after the ink was dry on the opinion. Once again, that impact has been significantly shaped by the existence of a strong social movement that has been able to weave the judgment—and the South African Constitution—into a series of ongoing advocacy efforts to improve the lives of people living with, or at risk of being infected by, HIV. Indeed, because AIDS is still an everyday catastrophe in South Africa, and because that movement is stronger than ever, much of the history of the *TAC* case undoubtedly remains to be written.

---

158. Complaint before the Competition Commission of South Africa, case no. 2002Sep226.

159. 2006 (6) SA 543 (D) (S. Afr.); 2006 (6) SA 568 (D) (S. Afr.); 2006 (6) SA 575 (D) (S. Afr.).

160. For example, Gauteng province began to provide ARV treatment only days after the Minister's capitulation on the issue. Other provinces followed shortly thereafter.

161. For further detail on *N*'s case, *see* Lukas Muntingh & Christopher Mbazira, *Prisoners' Right of Access to Anti-Retroviral Treatment*, 7(2) ESR Rev. 14, 16 (2006); *see also* Adila Hassim & Jonathan Berger, *Case Review: Prisoners' Right of Access to Anti-Retroviral Treatment*, 7(4) ESR Rev. 18, 21 (2006); Adila Hassim, *The '5 Star' Prison Hotel? The Right of Access to ARV Treatment for HIV Positive Prisoners in South Africa*, 2 Int'l J. Prisoner Health 157 (2006).

Conclusion

One of the greatest health and social challenges our country faces is the HIV/AIDS epidemic. Former President Nelson Mandela said, "AIDS is no longer (just) a health issue, it is a human rights issue".... It is a human rights issue that babies continue to be infected by their HIV positive mothers because the clinic sister has neglected to tell the pregnant mother about how she could reduce the risk of her baby being infected.[162]
Former Deputy Minister of Health Nozizwe Madlala–Routledge
Cape Town, South Africa

Much of what the *TAC* case has to offer, both in terms of lessons learned and a possible way forward, lies beyond the academic debates that ordinarily focus narrowly on legal doctrine and ideology. Considering it in its totality—from the initial advocacy before the TAC was even established, through the recent adoption of South Africa's National Strategic Plan (which includes a renewed focus on PMTCT)—shows the *TAC* case as a tool in a broader campaign, rather than simply a case.

For lawyers working in the field of human rights and social justice litigation, the *TAC* case merely reinforces what many have long realized—that, while law and legal institutions have the potential to be used as tools of social change, their impact in large part depends on how and by whom they are used. As much work as is needed to prepare for litigation, much more is needed to ensure that a successful court decision translates into successful societal outcomes. And regardless of how far courts are prepared to go in fashioning their orders, those fighting to create change can rely only on themselves to ensure that jurisprudential victories put bread on the table, or pills in mouths, or roofs over people's heads. While courts may make the job of civil society much easier through the use of creative remedies, ultimately enforcement requires active participation from an organized and mobilized populace.

For economists, scientists, researchers and academics, to name but a few relevant professions, the *TAC* case shows how knowledge needn't—and shouldn't—be produced in a vacuum. Instead, valuable research can and must be used to benefit society more broadly, and to ensure that public policy is well-informed, evidence-based and responsive to real needs. But perhaps more important, the *TAC* case shows that we cannot take science and scientific thought for granted and that, on their own, they are highly vulnerable to the raw muscle of politics.

For poor people, the *TAC* case shows the power of organization, mobilization and voice. In the context of South Africa in particular, it

---

162. Nozizwe Madlala–Routledge, foreword, HEALTH & DEMOCRACY: A GUIDE TO HUMAN RIGHTS, HEALTH LAW AND POLICY IN POST-APARTHEID SOUTH AFRICA (Adila Hassim et al. eds., 2007). A transcript of the former Deputy Minister's speech at the formal launch of the book can be found at http://www.doh.gov.za/docs/sp/2006/sp1027.html.

demonstrates the crucial link between civil and political rights on the one hand, and socio-economic ones on the other. Without the political space to assemble, express views contrary to unreasonable state policy, and popularize and clarify demands through a free press, the socio-economic demands of TAC regarding access to state resources for addressing people's health needs would most likely not have been realized. And without giving expression to the voices of people like Busisiwe Maqungo, the real impact of the impugned policy may not have been clearly understood.

For all of us, the *TAC* case shows that successful struggles for social justice are interrelated. While Irene Grootboom—the first applicant in the landmark housing rights case discussed above who passed away in August 2008—may not have seen any significant improvement in her living conditions, her case has proved an indispensable part of ensuring that the South African state begins taking its responsibilities in respect of health care services seriously. In just six years, the *TAC* case has played an instrumental role in helping to catalyze fundamental shifts in state policy, resource allocation and the balance of power between the state and those in whose name and on whose behalf it exists.

Yet the story of the *TAC* case is far from complete. It will remain so for as long as hundreds of thousands of people each year in South Africa are infected with HIV and die from AIDS-related illnesses, and access to comprehensive health care services remains a luxury enjoyed primarily by the rich. The *TAC* case is thus at once a victory, a tool for future activism to protect basic human rights, and a promise waiting to be redeemed.

Part Two
Culture and Identity: Individual and Collective Rights

3

The Stories of *Dudgeon* and *Toonen*: Personal Struggles to Legalize Sexual Identities

Mark Bromley* & Kristen Walker**

Introduction

The initial legal battles in the effort to vindicate the human rights of lesbian, gay, bisexual and transgender ("LGBT")[1] communities have focused on challenging laws—many of them archaic and rarely enforced—that criminalize consensual, same-sex sexual activity. Even if these colonial-era laws are no longer enforced in many parts of the world, their mere existence creates a dangerously hostile legal and social environment.[2] They make it more difficult for LGBT communities to

---

* With this contribution, I would like to recognize Jeffrey Dudgeon for standing up for the rights I now take for granted, my husband for giving me the courage to stand up for myself, and the many women and men who are still fighting to legalize their own existence in countries around the world.

** I would like to thank Nick Toonen, Rodney Croome, Wayne Morgan and, as always, Miranda Stewart.

1. "LGBT" is an acronym that is commonly used by those who self-identify as lesbian, gay, bisexual or transgender. The terms "lesbian," "gay" and "bisexual" refer to a person's sexual orientation, including those whose sexual attraction is to individuals of the same-sex (homosexual) or to both sexes (bisexual). As an identity-based term, "LGBT" focuses on those who self-identify with these categories and does not include all men who have sex with men ("MSM") or all women who have sex with women ("WSW"). While also an identity-based term, "transgender" is not specifically about sexual orientation. It is a generic term used by those whose deeply felt gender identity or whose gender expression differs from their biological sex at birth. Transgender people may or may not elect surgery or hormonal treatments to help align their biological sexual organs and physical appearance with their own personal sense of their gender identity. Transgender people may be heterosexual, lesbian, gay or bisexual in their sexual orientation. At the international level, some experts avoid using "LGBT" because these identity-based references do not translate well across the world's regions, cultures and languages. International human rights activists increasingly speak of human rights violations committed on the basis of "sexual orientation or gender identity." *See* discussion of the *Yogyakarta Principles*, *infra* note 137.

2. Depending on the exact interpretation of some outdated laws, approximately eighty-five countries still criminalize consensual, same-sex sexual activity, and at least seven countries still apply the death penalty. *See* statistics of the International Lesbian and

claim a public identity or seek protection from human rights abuses, many of which involve physical violence and are perpetrated by non-state actors, with the complicity or indifference of the police, the courts or other government officials. This Chapter describes the stories behind the *Dudgeon* and *Toonen* decisions, the two cases that led the international decriminalization movement and ultimately influenced the U.S. Supreme Court.

At the beginning of his legal story, Jeffrey Dudgeon was a thirty-year-old civil servant and gay-rights activist living in Belfast. He was also a liberal-leaning unionist in the harshly divided politics of the day. But his true activism was in support of gay rights in Northern Ireland. At the time, he was serving as the treasurer of the Northern Ireland Gay Rights Association ("NIGRA"), and he was later a founding member of the International Lesbian and Gay Association ("ILGA").[3] The case opens in January 1976 when the Royal Ulster Constabulary raided a number of homes of gay men, using warrants for drug-related investigations, to question more than twenty adult men, all members of three gay organizations in Northern Ireland.[4] The raids clearly targeted those who were active in the movement to decriminalize homosexuality.[5] Dudgeon's home was one of those that was raided.

Half-way around the world, starting in mid-August 1988, the Tasmanian Gay Law Reform Group ("TGLRG"—later re-named the Tasmanian Gay and Lesbian Rights Group) set up a stall in the Salamanca Market, a popular weekly market held in Hobart, Australia. The stall was intended to help publicize the ongoing campaign to decriminalize homosexual activity in Tasmania and to collect signatures on a petition to the Tasmanian Parliament seeking law reform. The market already hosted other political stalls, such as the Tasmanian Wilderness Society, Greenpeace and Amnesty International. But a month after the stall opened, the Hobart City Council banned TGLRG from the market,

---

Gay Association, *available at* www.ILGA.org. In many countries, the laws are not actively enforced but may still be used by law enforcement to intimidate, coerce or extort bribes. Even where the laws have not been enforced in recent times, repeal efforts are often met with significant public hostility. *See* AMNESTY INTERNATIONAL, LOVE, HATE AND THE LAW: DECRIMINALIZING HOMOSEXUALITY (2008), exploring the different legal approaches to criminalizing homosexuality and the wide range of abuses that such laws engender.

3. The International Lesbian and Gay Association ("ILGA") is a worldwide network of LGBT groups that has been working for nearly thirty years to promote LGBT equality.

4. Brief submitted by applicant to the European Court of Human Rights in Dudgeon v. The United Kingdom, 45 Eur. Ct. H.R. (ser. A) (1981) (on file with authors) [hereinafter Dudgeon's Legal Brief].

5. Conversation with Jeffrey Dudgeon, Belfast, Ireland (Aug. 8, 2007); *see* Michael T. McLoughlin, *Crystal or Glass?: A Review of Dudgeon v. United Kingdom on the Fifteenth Anniversary of the Decision*, 3 MURDOCH UNIVERSITY ELECTRONIC JOURNAL OF LAW 4, para. 15 (1996).

deciding that TGLRG's campaign was offensive and political, and that it promoted an illegal activity.[6] When members of the TGLRG and their supporters defied the ban, many of them were arrested for trespass, though charges were never brought.[7] In late 1988, over a period of several months, there were more than 120 arrests in the Salamanca Market of activists—some gay, some lesbian, some straight—seeking the repeal of Sections 122 and 123 of the Tasmanian Criminal Code, which criminalized homosexual activity. Nick Toonen's then long-term partner, Rodney Croome, was one of the men arrested. Although he was one of the organizers of the protests, Nick Toonen was never himself arrested. He was concerned about the impact an arrest might have on his employment, and as a known member of the TGLRG, he knew that he faced almost certain arrest if he simply entered the market.

The stories of these two men—Jeffrey Dudgeon and Nick Toonen—ultimately led to legal victories that are still impacting the fight for LGBT rights around the world. *Dudgeon* was the first international case to apply the European Convention for the Protection of Human Rights and Fundamental Freedoms ("European Convention")[8] to find a violation of the right to privacy in a case challenging the "buggery" and "gross indecency" laws in Northern Ireland. That decision was reinforced by the U.N. Human Rights Committee in 1994, when it decided, in *Toonen v. Australia*,[9] that such laws violated rights to privacy and equality in the International Covenant on Civil and Political Rights ("the ICCPR").[10]

As detailed in poignant terms in the stories behind these two leading international cases, criminalization of sex between men (and often also of sex between women) has placed a great burden on many people's lives; and in many cases it has led to imprisonment, illness, depression and death. Many brave men and women (straight and gay) have campaigned against such laws, and this Chapter tells the story behind two of the most important international legal campaigns. The stories in turn me-

---

6. Communication to the Human Rights Committee by Nicholas Toonen, Dec. 25, 1991 (copy on file with the authors) [hereinafter Toonen Communication].

7. It was later discovered that the Council had no jurisdiction to ban the stall from the market, the place where the market was held never having been gazetted as part of Council land. Interview with Rodney Croome, Hobart, Australia (Mar. 8, 2007).

8. European Convention for the Protection of Human Rights and Fundamental Freedoms, *concluded* Nov. 4, 1950, 213 U.N.T.S. 221 [hereinafter European Convention].

9. Toonen v. Australia, U.N. Hum. Rts. Comm., No. 488/1992, U.N. Doc. CCPR/c/50/D/488/1992 (1994).

10. The ICCPR has general international application and 192 state parties, including the United States. International Covenant on Civil and Political Rights, *opened for signature* Dec. 16, 1966, 999 U.N.T.S. 171 (ratified by the United States June 8, 1992).

morialize their namesakes, both gay rights activists who fought calculated battles to legalize their own existence.

As demonstrated by the stories behind these cases, legalizing homosexual activity is a crucial step in protecting LGBT communities. Otherwise, the act that significantly defines a whole class of persons is criminal, making it awkward if not legally impossible to extend broader non-discrimination protections to LGBT individuals and families. The legal challenges described in this Chapter lent crucial momentum to the ongoing movement toward full recognition of the basic human rights of LGBT communities worldwide.

Today, many international human rights organizations are actively promoting LGBT human rights protections, just as the United Nations and other human rights institutions are simultaneously struggling to extend longstanding principles of privacy, non-discrimination, personal and bodily integrity, health and social development to the complexities of gender and human sexuality. It is an effort that many consider to be one of the most important new challenges in the modern human rights movement.

Criminalizing Identity through Sodomy Laws

Sex between men has been the subject of criminal sanction for hundreds of years. These laws are often vague and may prohibit acts described as "sodomy," "buggery," "gross indecency" or "crimes against nature." In many countries, the laws were first introduced by colonial authorities—a point noted with irony in a 2004 petition to the United Nations by African LGBT activists representing sixteen African countries. The petition emphasized that "[p]olitical leaders say these laws defend 'African cultural traditions'—even though, without a single exception, these laws are foreign imports, brought by the injustice of colonialism."[11]

Many of the more antiquated laws are curiously silent when it comes to criminalizing sex between women. But even when a law is silent on sex between women, it almost always exposes lesbians to similar, sometimes even greater, levels of public homophobia, violence and social exclusion. All too often these laws provide legal cover for a wide range of human rights abuses targeting LGBT communities, including physical violence, committed by both state and non-state actors; discrimination, whether officially sanctioned or socially enforced; and sexual violence, an all-too-common weapon used by families, neighbors and police to "punish" those who challenge gender stereotypes.

---

11. The Johannesburg Statement on Sexual Orientation, Gender Identity, and Human Rights, *adopted* Feb. 13, 2004, *available at* http://www.hrw.org/lgbt/pdf/joburg_statement021304.htm.

Fortunately, the enforcement of sodomy laws is indeed lapsing in many countries, a trend that may often reflect a political preference for allowing the laws to fade into history without ever affirmatively repealing them. But as long as they technically remain in force, they can always be invigorated at a later moment, or used to intimidate, extort, harass or otherwise to justify a broad range of human rights abuses. In Uganda, for example, after Sexual Minorities Uganda ("SMUG") introduced an LGBT tolerance campaign called "Let Us Live in Peace," Ugandan government officials began calling for the full enforcement of the country's sodomy law, a provision that criminalizes consensual same-sex sexual activity with up to life in prison.[12] Some Ugandan officials have called for even harsher laws.[13]

Since the 1960s, however, LGBT activists worldwide, together with their straight allies in the human rights movement, have pushed for decriminalization. Most Western countries decriminalized during this period—some through legislative changes and some through litigation. In the United States, the trend over the past few decades was one of state-by-state legislative decriminalization, culminating with the 2003 decision of the U.S. Supreme Court in *Lawrence v. Texas*, which is explored at the end of this Chapter.[14]

Dudgeon v. United Kingdom

At the time of Jeffrey Dudgeon's interrogation in 1976, the harassment of gay activists in Northern Ireland was increasing, although the law reform movement was also gaining strength. Activists were encouraged by the earlier decriminalization victory in England and Wales, where the Sexual Offences Act of 1967 stripped the "buggery" and "gross indecency" articles of their general application for consenting adults over the age of twenty-one.[15] In Scotland, the law had not yet been reformed, but successive Lord Advocates had stated in Parliament that they would not prosecute cases that would not be criminal if the 1967 Act of England and Wales applied also in Scotland.[16] And before the *Dudgeon* case was even decided, a 1980 amendment finally brought Scottish law into conformity with England and Wales.[17] Gay rights activists in Belfast were eagerly anticipating similar progress.

---

12. *See* Human Rights Watch, *Letter to Congressional Caucus About U.S. Support for Ugandan Homophobia,* Oct. 11, 2007, *available at* http://hrw.org/english/docs/2007/10/11/uganda17079.htm.

13. *See id.*

14. Lawrence v. Texas, 539 U.S. 558 (2003).

15. Dudgeon v. United Kingdom, 45 Eur. Ct. H.R. (ser. A) at para. 16 (1981).

16. *Id.* at para. 18.

17. *Id.*

On January 21, 1976, the police searched Dudgeon's home with a warrant issued under the Misuse of Drugs Act.[18] The police found some marijuana, but a roommate in the house, not Dudgeon, was ultimately charged with drug possession.[19] At the same time, the police also seized all of Dudgeon's diaries and his personal papers.[20] With information from those diaries, he was questioned at the police interrogation center for four and a half hours about his homosexuality. As later noted in the case, he was never questioned about the use of drugs.

During those hours of police interrogation, he was repeatedly insulted by the police. In a first effort to protect his rights, he immediately filed a complaint protesting his mistreatment.[21] No criminal or disciplinary action was ever taken against the police.[22] But with names obtained from the diaries, the police later brought in even more LGBT activists for questioning.[23]

During the interrogation, Dudgeon signed a statement admitting to being a homosexual, even after he was warned that the statement could be used against him.[24] This act of publicly asserting his identity when he could have remained silent—and likely avoided some legal complications—was only one of many times during the more than five years of the case when Dudgeon would stand up and proclaim his homosexual identity. In the legal proceedings before the European Commission and European Court of Human Rights, Dudgeon would have many more opportunities to assert his identity as a proud gay man. And in many respects, that was the entire point of the case.

With the diaries and the information Dudgeon freely admitted during his interrogation, the police sent a request to the Director of Prosecutions recommending that charges be brought against him based on his sexual activity.[25] The Prosecutor and the Attorney General in London deliberated on the issue for more than a year, waiting until February 1977 to inform Dudgeon that they would not press charges.[26] His personal papers—marked up and annotated by the police—were also

---

18. *Id.* at para. 33.

19. Dudgeon's roommate received a suspended sentence. Conversation with Jeffrey Dudgeon, *supra* note 5. *See* Report of the Commission of Mar. 13, 1980, *Dudgeon*, Series B, No. 40, at para. 43 [hereinafter European Commission].

20. *Dudgeon*, 45 Eur. Ct. H.R. (ser. A) at para. 33.

21. European Commission, *supra* note 19, at para. 44.

22. *Id.*

23. Conversation with Jeffrey Dudgeon, *supra* note 5.

24. European Commission, *supra* note 19, at para. 43.

25. *Dudgeon*, 45 Eur. Ct. H.R. (ser. A) at para. 33.

26. *Id.*

finally returned to him after a year.[27] During that entire time, Dudgeon lived with the very real fear that he could be prosecuted for his sexual identity, which he had already freely admitted, while the police eagerly marked up his personal diaries for use as evidence against him.

With the assistance of NIGRA, Dudgeon formally lodged his case with the European Commission of Human Rights in May 1976, arguing that the existence of laws criminalizing homosexual conduct, together with the police investigation and interrogation he endured in January of that year, constituted an unjustified interference with his right to respect for his private life under Article 8 of the European Convention. He also argued that he suffered discrimination on the basis of his sex, sexuality and residence in violation of the non-discrimination provision of Article 14 of the European Convention.

In July 1976, six months after Jeffrey Dudgeon's home was raided by the police, and two months after he filed his case with the European Commission of Human Rights, the government of the United Kingdom announced in Parliament that Westminster would consider a law reform package for Northern Ireland. (Northern Ireland was then under direct rule from London.) The reforms would address a range of social issues, including divorce and homosexuality, which the United Kingdom had originally intended to leave to the decision of a devolved government in Northern Ireland.[28] But the political stalemate in Northern Ireland made that devolution process increasingly unlikely.

After nearly two years of consultations, in July 1978, the United Kingdom published a draft law that was intended to bring the Northern Ireland law into conformity with England and Wales.[29] The forward to the proposed decriminalization package recognized that homosexuality was an issue "about which some people in Northern Ireland hold strong conscientious or religious opinions," but that the "present law is difficult to enforce, that fear of exposure can make a homosexual particularly vulnerable to blackmail and that this fear of exposure can cause unhappiness not only for the homosexual himself but also for his family and friends."[30]

Local opposition to this London-driven reform package quickly grew. The opposition was led by Reverend Ian Paisley, a leading political figure in Northern Ireland who was head of the growing Democratic Unionist Party, a rival to the then-dominant Ulster Unionist Party. Paisley was also the founder of his own conservative Presbyterian church, and his

---

27. Id.
28. *Dudgeon*, Eur. Ct. H.R. (ser. A) at para. 22.
29. *Dudgeon*, Eur. Ct. H.R. (ser. A) at para. 24.
30. Id.

forces collected 70,000 signatures to "Save Ulster from Sodomy."[31] While never publicly appearing together, many of Paisley's bitter political enemies joined him in his high dudgeon, including Roman Catholic leaders and bishops, some of whom were encouraged by officials in London to submit a similar statement opposing the law reform package. A Catholic statement eventually warned that the reformers were actually seeking larger social acceptance of an "alternative sexual life-style,"[32] which was certainly true, although the European Court later tried to deflect that point by cautioning that its decision in favor of decriminalization "does not imply approval."[33]

It is indeed ironic that one of the very few points around which political rivals in the midst of the violence of Northern Ireland could all agree was their common fear of "sodomites." The Northern Ireland Office in Belfast soon began promoting this unusual point of sectarian cooperation on the anti-sodomy campaign.[34] And when the Labor Government was forced into an election in April 1979, Margaret Thatcher became Prime Minister, and her new Secretary of State for Northern Ireland—obviously influenced by the conservative backlash—dropped the legalization proposal altogether.[35] But by closing the door to legislative reform, the Thatcher Government gave a boost to Dudgeon's pending legal case and to the worldwide decriminalization movement.

Dudgeon's case was considered first by the European Commission of Human Rights, which then forwarded the case to the European Court of Human Rights for a binding decision.[36] The Commission declared Dudgeon's complaints admissible in March 1978,[37] and by a unanimous decision found a violation of Dudgeon's right to respect for his private life in March 1980.[38] After referring the matter from a regular panel to a

---

31. *Dudgeon*, Eur. Ct. H.R. (ser. A) at para. 25.

32. European Commission, *supra* note 19, at para. 35; McLoughlin, *supra* note 5, at para. 37.

33. *Dudgeon*, Eur. Ct. H.R. (ser. A) at para. 61.

34. Conversation with Jeffrey Dudgeon, *supra* note 5.

35. *See Dudgeon*, Eur. Ct. H.R. (ser. A) at para. 26.

36. Until 1998, individuals could not apply directly to the European Court of Human Rights. Applications were filed first with the European Commission of Human Rights, which was empowered to consider the admissibility of the case and make a non-binding decision on the merits. The Commission then had the authority to refer cases to the European Court of Human Rights for a binding decision on the merits. Protocol 11 to the European Convention for the Protection of Human Rights and Fundamental Freedoms abolished the Commission, expanded the Court and provided a system of direct application. Protocol No. 11 to the Convention for the Protection of Human Rights and Fundamental Freedoms, E.T.S. 155, *entered into force* Nov. 1, 1998.

37. European Commission, *supra* note 19.

38. *Dudgeon*, Eur. Ct. H.R. (ser. A) at para. 96.

plenary panel for such a clearly contentious case,[39] the European Court in 1981 agreed, finding a human rights violation by a wide margin of fifteen votes to four.[40] Despite that strong margin of support for the decision, the actual court proceedings were far more contentious. At the very beginning of the case, when Dudgeon tried to walk into the courtroom with his legal team, he was sternly sent out to the public gallery.[41] And at the last moment, the Court decided not to allow Dudgeon's lawyers to provide expert testimony to discredit the Nazi-era social science studies that the Commission had cited in rejecting earlier gay rights cases.[42] The courtroom tensions were clear.

The first decision from the European Commission was probably the most remarkable, because as gatekeeper to the Court, the Commission had for thirty years rejected numerous gay-rights cases, finding them to be "manifestly ill-founded."[43] As recently as 1975, in an admittedly less sympathetic sodomy challenge that included allegations of sexual conduct with persons under twenty-one years of age, the Commission rejected a complaint from Germany, noting "the existence of a special social danger in the case of masculine homosexuality."[44] The Commission's unanimous decision just two and a half years later, finding such a clear violation of the right to privacy in the *Dudgeon* case, was nearly astounding. What caused that reversal?

As with many groundbreaking litigation efforts, the *Dudgeon* case had four crucial factors going for it: good facts, good timing, an indifferent adversary, and a court that was gradually becoming more confident and more assertive in responding to the rights in issue (here privacy rights). The facts in the case helped the members of the Commission understand that Dudgeon was indeed the victim of a human rights violation, even though no charges were ever filed against him.[45] Timing was also crucial. The case came at a unique historical moment in the larger decriminalization movement in the United Kingdom and at a politically awkward period in Westminster's direct rule over Northern

---

39. *Dudgeon*, Eur. Ct. H.R. (ser. A) at para. 5; Dudgeon's Legal Brief, *supra* note 4.

40. *Dudgeon*, Eur. Ct. H.R. (ser. A) (1981).

41. Conversation with Jeffrey Dudgeon, *supra* note 5.

42. *Dudgeon*, Eur. Ct. H.R. (ser. A) at para. 10; Dudgeon's Legal Brief, *supra* note 4.

43. Donna Gomien, David Harris & Leo Zwaak, Law and Practice of the European Convention on Human Rights and the European Social Charter 232–33 (1996).

44. X. v. Federal Republic of Germany, Application No. 5935/72, 3 D.R. 51, at 56 (1975); *see also* Peter Van Dijk, *The Treatment of Homosexuals under the European Convention on Human Rights*, in Homosexuality: A European Community Issue, 194 (Kees Waaldijk & Andrew Clapham eds., 1993).

45. The facts in this case certainly stand in stark contrast to the molestation charges that the Commission considered in its review of German sodomy laws in the case of X. v. Federal Republic of Germany, *supra* note 44.

Ireland. And the government of the United Kingdom was itself indifferent to the outcome in the case, since at least some within the government were happy to let others take the political fallout for what by then had become a political and legal headache. This indifference must have helped in convincing the Commission and then the Court that the social and political backlash to the case would not be as extreme as might otherwise be expected. Finally, the Court itself was by then taking a more aggressive approach in building its own case law. So the facts were good, the timing was right, the government of the United Kingdom was indifferent and the Commission and Court were assuming a more assertive posture. Dudgeon could not have seen it when he filed his case, but he had everything going for him.

Framing the Legal Arguments in Dudgeon

There were two significant legal questions in the *Dudgeon* case. The first threshold question was essentially one of standing: whether Dudgeon could be considered a victim of a human rights abuse. The second was whether the government could permissibly intrude on Dudgeon's private life for the "protection of health or morals," or "the protection of the rights and freedoms of others," two of the express limitations on the right to privacy that are specifically listed in the European Convention.[46]

The United Kingdom decided to fight aggressively on the second question, claiming the right to intrude on Dudgeon's privacy because decriminalization would be "damaging to the moral fabric of Northern Irish society."[47] Since the laws had already been reformed in much of the rest of the country, the government was forced to emphasize the "profound differences of attitude and public opinion between Northern Ireland and Great Britain in relations [sic] to questions of morality."[48] The government also claimed that the prohibition protected "the rights and freedoms of others" by safeguarding young persons and vulnerable members of society, a claim the Court merged with the general "protection of morals" defense.[49]

Surprisingly, the United Kingdom decided not to fight as aggressively on the first—and probably more convincing—legal question of standing. In the proceedings before the European Commission and the European Court, the United Kingdom did not significantly challenge Dudgeon's claim of victim status under Article 25 of the European Convention. Without fully conceding the point, the United Kingdom accept-

---

46. European Convention, *supra* note 8, at art. 8, para. 2.
47. *Dudgeon*, Eur. Ct. H.R. (ser. A) at para. 46.
48. *Dudgeon*, Eur. Ct. H.R. (ser. A) at para. 56.
49. *Dudgeon*, Eur. Ct. H.R. (ser. A) at paras. 45, 47.

ed that Dudgeon was directly affected by the laws and "entitled to claim to be a 'victim' thereof."[50] Instead, the United Kingdom tried to argue that the cumulative effect of the laws was not significant enough to interfere in a meaningful way with Dudgeon's private life.[51] Most of the dissenting opinions in the European Court took issue with that legal concession on victim status; and even the majority opinions for both the Commission and the Court struggled with the question. The judges had to reconcile the fact that before *Dudgeon* and its progeny of decriminalization cases, the case law of the European system had been fairly strict in defining victimhood. An applicant could not claim that the mere existence of a law violated the applicant's rights. The law must have been applied "to his detriment."[52]

The United Kingdom based its surprisingly timid arguments around admissibility on the fact that the laws criminalizing homosexuality had not been applied "in recent years" to prosecute private consensual acts involving persons over the age of twenty-one, concluding rather astoundingly that the laws did not therefore prohibit Dudgeon from engaging in such acts.[53] Given that contorted logic, it remains difficult to find any other than narrow political calculations to explain why the United Kingdom attempted to defend the Northern Irish laws. But, fortunately, the unique facts of the case made even that admittedly half-hearted defense look rather ridiculous. Dudgeon had been subjected to hours of humiliation and police questioning; the authorities spent a year deciding whether to prosecute him; and his personal papers and diaries were seized and marked up by the police. Clearly the laws were applied to his great detriment.

To supplement the facts in the case, Dudgeon submitted two powerful affidavits describing the challenges and distress he endured as a direct result of the laws criminalizing his existence. He noted that he had known he was homosexual since he was fourteen years old; that he had experienced fear, suffering and distress as a direct result of the law; and that he also suffered psychological trauma and fear of legal action, harassment, blackmail, and prejudice.[54] In addition, he candidly noted that the laws, and the resulting social stigma, affected his relationship with his family and limited his social and career advancement, resulting in direct economic loss.[55]

---

50. European Commission, *supra* note 19, at para. 84; *Dudgeon*, Eur. Ct. H.R. (ser. A) at para. 40.

51. European Commission, *supra* note 19, at para. 84.

52. *Id.* at para. 85.

53. *Id.* at para. 89.

54. *Id.* at para. 42.

55. *Id.* at para. 42.

Based on a lifetime of both psychological and economic harm, Dudgeon sought £10,000 in damages and additional legal fees to compensate for this personal suffering and career loss.[56] The Court, in a subsequent decision on the question of damages, rejected his compensation claim, along with a parallel £5,000 claim for the distress, suffering and anxiety caused by Dudgeon's police interrogation, finding that the Court's decision in itself provided just satisfaction for Dudgeon's claims.[57] It did, however, award limited legal fees.[58]

Even in this highly sensitive case, the facts demonstrating harm were hard to ignore, and both the Commission and the Court concluded that the law had been applied to Dudgeon's detriment. In the Commission's view, the harm was evident when the police took the first steps toward prosecuting Dudgeon.[59] The Court, noting the law was not "dead" and that private individuals could initiate criminal prosecutions under Northern Irish procedure, was even blunter and, ultimately, less attached to the Commission's first-step-toward-prosecution justification for intervening.

Private Life Includes Sexual Life

In remarkable terms considering the novelty of the case and the rigid definition of victim in the case law, the European Court of Human Rights found that "the maintenance in force of the impugned legislation constitutes a continuing interference with the applicant's right to respect for his private life (which includes his sexual life)."[60] While seemingly obvious to many courts and jurists today, that simple parenthetical insertion was crucial, and it has transformed the way much of the world looks at privacy rights. One's sexual life, at least across much of Europe, was now firmly protected within the sphere of privacy, including for homosexuals over twenty-one years of age.[61] That recognition would lead to many more legal advances in Europe and beyond.

The European Court continued by setting out Dudgeon's paradox for all to see: "the very existence of this legislation continuously and directly

---

56. *Dudgeon*, Eur. Ct. H.R. (ser. A) at para. 71.

57. Dudgeon v. United Kingdom (Article 50), 59 Eur. Ct. H.R. (ser. A) (1983).

58. *Id.*

59. European Commission, *supra* note 19, at para. 96.

60. *Dudgeon*, Eur. Ct. H.R. (ser. A) at para. 41.

61. The legal age of consent was lower than twenty-one years for heterosexuals in many European countries at the time, but the European Court would not rule until much later—in January 2003—that unequal age of consent laws for heterosexual and homosexual persons constitute a separate violation of non-discrimination protections under Article 14 of the European Convention. L. and V. v. Austria, App. Nos. 39392/98 and 39829/98 (2003), and S.L. v. Austria, App. No. 45330/99 (2003).

affects his private life ... either he respects the law and refrains from engaging—even in private with consenting male partners—in prohibited sexual acts to which he is disposed by reason of his homosexual tendencies, or he commits such acts and thereby become[s] liable to criminal prosecution."[62] The legal response to that paradox—that the law did in fact have a detrimental effect on him—was a groundbreaking legal conclusion that paved the way for the subsequent decisions in *Toonen* and *Lawrence*.

The next European Court case to test the reach of *Dudgeon* was *Norris v. Ireland*, involving a similar challenge to criminal laws by the founder and chairman of the Irish Gay Rights Movement in the Republic of Ireland.[63] In that case, the applicant had never been prosecuted or subjected to any criminal investigation, but he still claimed to be a victim of a human rights violation because of the mere existence of laws criminalizing homosexual acts.[64] The European Court agreed, firmly embracing the precedent of *Dudgeon* and finding that "[a] law which remains on the statute book, even though it is not enforced in a particular class of cases for a considerable time, may be applied again in such cases at any time."[65] In *Lawrence*, the U.S. Supreme Court would go on to say that the mere existence of these laws "demeans the lives of homosexual persons."[66]

Setting the Historical Context and the Legacy of Dudgeon

It is impossible to consider the story behind *Dudgeon* without also considering the unique history of the period. During the five years of litigation, the laws and social attitudes toward homosexuality were changing quickly. The government initially stalled the case by engaging in protracted negotiations over a friendly settlement, hoping the issue might be resolved by other means.[67] During this period, the government even sought to amend the law, until national politics and the standoff in the devolution debate led London to back away from legal reform. But the government in London was clearly indifferent toward the outcome of the case, and from Dudgeon's perspective, London was only arguing the point to advance its own domestic political agenda and build support among political adversaries in Belfast. Indeed, Dudgeon would later write that "the British government spent an estimated half million

---

62. *Dudgeon*, Eur. Ct. H.R. (ser. A) at para. 41.
63. Norris v. Ireland, 13 Eur. Ct. H.R. (ser. A) at para. 9 (1988).
64. *Id.* at para. 29.
65. *Id.* at para. 34.
66. *Lawrence*, 539 U.S. at 575.
67. Jeff Dudgeon, *The U.K. Supreme Court*, THE SOCIALIST, Mar. 5, 1984.

pounds on their own defense in the full knowledge they were going to, and ought to lose."[68]

The case also came at a unique moment for the European Commission and the Court. When drafting Article 8 of the European Convention, the original word that was debated was the "inviolability" of the right to private and family life, a term that was later changed to "the right to respect" for one's private and family life, in an apparent attempt to weaken the scope of the protection.[69] But the European Convention case law was gradually building up this weakened term, and the *Dudgeon* decision represented an important step in that direction. The case came at an important moment in the expansion of privacy doctrine in Europe, and at a time when the European Commission and the Court seemed determined to build their own case law by accepting more controversial cases.[70] The European human rights experiment was gaining ground quickly and Dudgeon's case was carried along by some of that momentum.

While the *Dudgeon* case was remarkable for the time, the reluctance of both the European Commission and the Court to find a violation of the non-discrimination provision in Article 14 of the European Convention also demonstrates how legally narrow the decision is from today's perspective.[71] The omission was significant, because Dudgeon actually changed his legal team after the Commission's decision in an effort to emphasize the non-discrimination aspects of the case in his argument before the Court.[72] The administrative bureaucrats at the European Court were apparently unhappy with this emphasis and continued for months to deal with his former legal team, forcing Dudgeon to launch a parallel battle for recognition of his new lawyers.[73] Dudgeon is still convinced that his determination to emphasize the non-discrimination argument in the case resulted in the Court's refusal to hear his witness on the non-discrimination point, and in the Court's broader hostility

---

68. *Id.* at para. 8.

69. Gomien, *supra* note 43, at 228.

70. In the 1975 case of X. v. Federal Republic of Germany, in which the Commission had just two and a half years earlier rejected an application challenging Germany's sodomy laws, the Commission already signaled that it was paying attention to the decriminalization movement in Europe, pointedly noting that a committee of experts of the Council of Europe was studying the decriminalization of homosexuality. X. v. Federal Republic of Germany, *supra* note 44, at 54.

71. *Dudgeon*, 45 Eur. Ct. H.R. (ser. A) at para. 69 (finding that "there is no useful legal purpose to be served in determining whether he has in addition suffered discrimination as compared with other persons who are subject to lesser limitations on the same right.").

72. Conversation with Jeffrey Dudgeon, *supra* note 5; Jeff Dudgeon, *supra*, note 67.

73. Jeff Dudgeon, *supra*, note 67.

toward his claims for damages and legal fees.[74] Indeed, the final decision specifically—almost shockingly—says that decriminalization is not the same as acceptance, and that it should not be taken as precedent in demanding full legal or social equality for LGBT persons.[75] It also shut down any notion of a gay "family life," despite the broad definition of family life in the European case law.[76] Those broader concepts of lesbian, gay and transgender equality and family life are still being debated in Europe and beyond.

The European decriminalization cases, led first by *Dudgeon* and then including *Norris* in 1987, helped build the LGBT legal movement in Europe. The cases also lent support to subsequent legal battles in Australia, the United States, and today in countries like India, where colonial sodomy laws remain in place.[77] Several human rights experts—gay and straight alike—also built their human rights credentials on the early decriminalization cases. Mary Robinson, who went on to become President of Ireland and then a widely respected United Nations High Commissioner for Human Rights, was lead counsel in the *Norris* case,[78] and she later filed an influential *amicus* brief that the U.S. Supreme Court cited in the *Lawrence* case.[79]

After *Dudgeon* and *Norris*, the doors were open to more robust European cases built on notions of equality. And in 1992, Australian Nick Toonen took those arguments to the global level through the United Nations. By the time of *Lawrence*, the legal landscape had changed so dramatically that even a conservative U.S. Supreme Court issued a 6-3 decision that was more sweeping in scope, and more similar to *Dudgeon* in staking out a clear privacy argument, than either side had anticipated.[80] When Justice Kennedy read the *Lawrence* decision from the bench of the U.S. Supreme Court in June 2003, many of the gay

---

74. *Id.*

75. *Dudgeon*, 45 Eur. Ct. H.R. (ser. A) at para. 61.

76. One of the dissenting opinions emphatically states that "[t]here is no suggestion that any point relating to family life arises in this case." *Dudgeon*, 45 Eur. Ct. H.R. (ser. A) at para. 7 (Walsh, J., partially dissenting); Peter Van Dijk, *supra* note 44, at 190 (noting that family life is not restricted to married relationships, but also includes unmarried couples with a common household and other family relationships).

77. *See* Alok Gupta, *Section 377 and the Dignity of Indian Homosexuals*, ECONOMIC AND POLITICAL WEEKLY, Nov. 18, 2006, *available at* http://www.iglhrc.org/files/iglhrc/program_docs/Section%20377,%20 gupta.pdf.

78. Norris v. Ireland, 13 Eur. Ct. H.R. (ser. A) (1988).

79. *Lawrence*, 539 U.S. at 576-77.

80. Linda Greenhouse, *The Supreme Court: Homosexual Rights; Justices, 6-3, Legalize Gay Sexual Conduct in Sweeping Reversal of Court's '86 Ruling*, N.Y. TIMES, Jun. 27, 2003, at A1 (noting that "few people on either side of the case expected a decision of such scope.").

rights supporters who packed the courtroom were moved to tears by the breadth of the opinion.[81]

Toonen v. Australia

Decriminalization of sex between men started somewhat later in Australia than in Britain, Europe and the United States. It was not until 1972 that an Australian state (South Australia) first decriminalized private sexual conduct between adult men. Other states followed suit in the 1980s, and by 1990, Tasmania was the only state in Australia still to criminalize private consensual sex between adult men.[82]

The *Toonen case* was brought by Nicholas Toonen against Australia before the United Nations Human Rights Committee.[83] It was an important step in a long battle to achieve decriminalization in Australia as a nation;[84] a battle that led to the transformation of Tasmania from the state with the most homophobic laws to one of the few states to provide almost full equality to its gay and lesbian citizens in all areas of life, including relationship recognition and parenting. Nick Toonen and other members of the Tasmanian Gay Law Reform Group ("TGLRG"—later re-named the Tasmanian Gay and Lesbian Rights Group) played an essential role in that battle.

The *Toonen case* concerned two sections of the Tasmanian Criminal Code, Sections 122 and 123. Those sections outlawed all sexual relations between men.

Section 122 provided:

> Any person who—
>
> (a) has sexual intercourse with any person against the order of nature;
>
> (b) has sexual intercourse with an animal;

---

81. JEFFREY TOBIN, THE NINE: INSIDE THE SECRET WORLD OF THE SUPREME COURT 190 (2007).

82. Although various states retained unequal age of consent laws through the 1990s.

83. The U.N. Human Rights Committee reviews general treaty compliance by countries that have ratified the International Covenant on Civil and Political Rights ("ICCPR"). The Human Rights Committee may also receive and consider individual petitions alleging specific violations of the ICCPR that are submitted against countries that have also ratified the First Optional Protocol to the ICCPR. The United States has ratified the ICCPR but not the First Optional Protocol. Optional Protocol to the International Covenant on Civil and Political Rights, *opened for signature* Dec. 16, 1966, 999 U.N.T.S. 302 (entered into force on Mar. 23, 1976) [hereinafter Optional Protocol].

84. For a more academic and theoretical analysis of the Communication to the Human Rights Committee and the Committee's decision, *see* Wayne Morgan, *Identifying Evil for What it Is: Tasmania, Sexual Perversity and the United Nations*, 19 MELB. U. L. REV. 740 (1994).

(c) consents to a male person having sexual intercourse with him or her against the order of nature, is guilty of a crime.

Section 123 provided:

Any male person who, whether in public or in private, commits any indecent assault upon, or any other act of gross indecency with, another male person, or procures another male person to commit an act of gross indecency with himself or any other male person, is guilty of a crime.

Each offense was punishable by up to twenty-one years in prison, although at the time that Toonen's communication ("Communication") was filed, there had been no prosecutions for consensual sexual activity between men for some ten years. Section 122(a) also potentially criminalized lesbian sexual activity, although the law's application to lesbians had never been decided under Tasmanian law and there appear to be no instances of lesbians being prosecuted for violation of Section 122(a). But lesbians still experienced discrimination, and popular sentiment considered their conduct equally illegal. Lesbians were involved in the TGLRG and its campaigns.[85]

Calls to repeal Sections 122(a) and (c) and 123 began in the late 1970s, but the orchestrated campaign by the Tasmanian gay and lesbian community started in the late 1980s, driven by the TGLRG. The Tasmanian Gay Law Reform Group actually started life as the Law Reform Committee of the Gay University Students of Tasmania Organization ("GUSTO"). Early in 1988, a group of about ten gay men, fed up with the discrimination and secrecy surrounding their lives, decided to act. They formed the GUSTO Law Reform Committee and started lobbying and speaking out, though at the time many were reluctant to use their own names publicly.[86] That Committee soon separated from the university group and renamed itself the TGLRG. It then quickly achieved visibility at the Third National AIDS Conference held in Hobart (the capital of Tasmania) in August 1988, at which several participants, including Justice Michael Kirby (then President of the New South Wales Court of Appeal, now a Justice of the High Court of Australia), called for repeal of laws criminalizing sex between men.[87] This was the true start of the campaign for law reform. The group also began to communicate

---

85. As Wayne Morgan observes, there is little attention to lesbians in the initial Communication made by Toonen, but this is to some extent addressed in the Final Submission made by Toonen to the Human Rights Committee, where stories of lesbian experiences of discrimination are included. The ultimate decision of the Committee mentions "homosexual men and women" twice. *See Id.* at 750.

86. MIRANDA MORRIS, PINK TRIANGLE: THE GAY LAW REFORM DEBATE IN TASMANIA 7 (1995).

87. *Id.* at 8.

with politicians, churches, the gay community and the broader public about the importance of decriminalization.

Taking the Law Reform Struggle to the Marketplace

In August 1988, the TGLRG took the decriminalization campaign to the Salamanca Market in Hobart, setting up a stall alongside other politically-oriented groups including the Tasmanian Wilderness Society, Greenpeace, and Amnesty International. Less than a month later, the Hobart City Council banned the group from the market on the basis that the TGLRG was offensive, political, and promoted a banned activity. Though some members defied the ban and were arrested, Nick Toonen faced a precarious situation that he later explained in his appeal to the Human Rights Committee:

> [W]hen I, as an identifiable gay activist, entered Salamanca Place during the period October 22nd 1988 to December 10th 1988, I was asked to leave that market; and had I refused to leave, I would have been arrested for trespass on a public street. I believe that by compelling me to leave Salamanca market, by applying the sanction of arrest if I refused, the Hobart City Council and the Tasmania Police were violating my right to freedom of association, my right to freedom of assembly and my right to freedom of speech—all rights which are guaranteed by the [ICCPR]. The fact that this repression occurred in the name of section 122(a) and (c) and 123 of the Tasmanian Criminal Code is an indictment of those criminal laws.[88]

In hindsight, it seems extraordinary that peacefully advocating law reform could lead to a person's arrest in a recognized democracy; but in Australia there is no Bill of Rights, and at that time there was no constitutional protection for freedom of political speech.[89] The very idea of decriminalizing gay male sex was so controversial that discussion of it was considered unsuitable for a public marketplace. It was clear that the Hobart City Council had no intention that Salamanca also become a Socratic marketplace of ideas.

The decision to ban the TGLRG stall from the market was fortunate in many respects, as it attracted considerably more attention than the mere presence of the stall might otherwise have done. As word spread of the prohibition, more advocates joined the stall and subjected themselves to arrest. Given the legal consequences, however, many other gay men felt they could not risk arrest, and this realization caused even more

---

88. Toonen Communication, *supra* note 6.

89. An implied constitutional protection for political speech was first located in the Australian Constitution in 1992, in Australian Capital Television v. Commonwealth 177 C.L.R. 106 (1992).

intense personal conflict for some.[90] Nonetheless, hundreds protested from outside the market precinct, until they, too, were threatened with arrest.[91] At the height of the protests, police were arresting people who merely wore badges in support of the TGLRG or gay and lesbian rights, and those who simply approached the stall.[92] On some occasions even bystanders who had come to the market to shop and inadvertently strayed too close to the TGLRG stall found themselves under arrest.[93] The City Council continued to insist that any person refusing to leave the market when required to do so by police would never be permitted to enter the market again. The penalty for flouting the expulsion was immediate arrest.

Eventually, on December 10, 1988, the Council relented and permitted the TGLRG to claim its stall, an important victory in the organization's larger campaign to claim a legal identity for gays and lesbians. The Salamanca protests were successful in drawing broad public attention to the plight of gay men in Tasmania. While not all of that attention was sympathetic, much of it was. The *Hobart Mercury* ran an editorial comparing the political censorship of TRLG to that experienced under apartheid South Africa and the German Third Reich.[94]

Extending the Struggle to the Legislature

Although the TGLRG found some political support for its reform proposals,[95] when the members first launched their campaign, a conservative Tasmanian government was in power that was vehemently opposed to any change in the law. But the Labour Party opposition was supportive, and in 1989, with the help of the Greens, the Labour Party took control of the government. Both parties had a more liberal attitude to issues of sexuality and were, broadly speaking, sympathetic to the push for law reform. After extensive lobbying by the TGLRG, the new government was persuaded that reform should proceed.

---

90. Bob Brown, for example, now the only out gay member of the federal Parliament in Australia, decided he could not risk arrest, although he visited the stall. *See* Morris, *supra* note 86, at 20.

91. Toonen Communication, *supra* note 6.

92. *Id.*

93. *Id.*

94. Morris, *supra* note 86, at 16 (*quoting Editorial*, Hobart Mercury, Sept. 29, 1988).

95. Judy Jackson, a Labour member of the lower house, presented the first TGLRG petition for law reform to parliament on Aug. 23, 1988. *See* Morris, *supra* note 86, at 27. She also, as Attorney General for Tasmania, introduced a raft of law reform in the early 2000s that achieved almost complete equality for lesbian and gay relationships and families.

During the years 1989–1991, there was much debate about gay law reform in Tasmania. The health sector supported decriminalization, particularly AIDS organizations and those working with HIV-positive individuals. Some churches also supported law reform, although often out of pity rather than support for gay rights.[96] There was vehement opposition to law reform from other churches and from conservative politicians. Several anti-law reform groups were established, including FACT ("For A Caring Tasmania"), TasAlert, CRAMP ("Concerned Residents Against Moral Pollution") and HALO ("Homophobic Activist Liberation Organization"—a satirical but nonetheless anti-reform group).[97] These organizations not only favored retaining Sections 122 and 123, they were also preoccupied with the larger legal consequences of the debate. In a letter to a Tasmanian newspaper, TasAlert stated its views:

> Decriminalization is saying that the State accepts homosexuality as an alternative lifestyle. Next they'll be demanding equal rights to legally marry and adopt children. They'll see decriminalization as an opportunity to introduce their practices into the school curriculum. If this move is successful it will rock the moral foundations of society and hasten the fall of Australia.[98]

Once again, the opposition's fears were justified. Once decriminalization was achieved, lesbians and gay men did start calling for legal recognition of their relationships, the right to have children (whether by adoption or through assisted conception), and the introduction of appropriate educational material in schools. These battles are still ongoing in Australia, where Tasmania is now leading the way in extending legal equality for lesbians and gay men.

In December 1990, the Labour Party introduced legislation in Parliament to repeal Sections 122 and 123. The proposal was contained within a package of HIV/AIDS law reform,[99] which the TGLRG described as "closet homosexual law reform,"[100] because it tucked decriminalization of sexual relations into a bill dealing principally with HIV/AIDS testing and prevention. As expected, the debate over the decriminalization aspect of the bill was heated and at times vitriolic. But many members of Parliament spoke in favor of the legislation. Don Wing, an independent M.P., gave voice to the reform effort by noting:

---

96. See MORRIS, *supra* note 86, at 45.

97. Morgan, *supra* note 84, at 751–52.

98. See MORRIS, *supra* note 86, at 35 (*citing* Hobart, SUNDAY EXAMINER, June 11, 1989).

99. The HIV/AIDS Preventative Measures Bill 1990, which dealt with issues such as HIV testing, confidentiality and preventive programs.

100. MORRIS, *supra* note 86, at 76.

> There are good and bad people in all walks of life with all sorts of sexual orientations, and homosexual people are no different except for their sexual orientation. They play important roles in the life of the community and, as with heterosexual people, are in the main ordinary, decent citizens.[101]

But there were also contributions like these:

> If we had a bull like that, I know where he would end up if he would not serve the females—he would be in the mall tomorrow among the sausages.[102]

And:

> [W]e ought to be looking in the other direction: not decriminalizing—we ought to be tightening up the laws, making them a bit more drastic than they are now—a little more draconian, and maybe we will influence a few of them to take the plane north to those places where they can do what they like ... Do not let them sully our state with their evil activities.[103]
>
> . . .
>
> The truly compassionate course is to use every means possible to deflect people from a lifestyle that causes spiritual, emotional and medical misery.[104]
>
> . . .
>
> While we cannot legislate for morality we can legislate against immorality. While the law cannot enforce good it can restrain evil.... [T]he law cannot make people sexually pure but it can restrain sexual perversity.... Further, even if the law can do nothing else, the law ought to identify evil for what it is.[105]

Others used the AIDS crisis to argue against law reform. One contributor relied on the work of Paul Cameron, the American anti-gay activist:

> This well-researched and candid exposé dares to present the real facts: placing the blame of this disease precisely where it falls, on the shoulders of willfully promiscuous homosexuals and our timid government. [Cameron] exposes the homosexual sinister success in

---

101. Australia, Tasmania, Legislative Council, Hansard, at 1224 (July 2, 1991).

102. *Id.* at 1225 (July 3, 1991); *see also* Second Submission supplied to the Committee Concerning the Impact of SS 122 and 123 on the Author, July 14, 1991 (copy on file with the authors) [hereinafter Second Submission].

103. Legislative Council, Hansard, at 1246 (July 3, 1991); *see also* Second Submission, *Id.*

104. Legislative Assembly, Hansard, at 6122–23 (Dec. 19, 1990).

105. *Id.* at 6121; *see also* Morgan, *supra* note 84, at 740.

controlling government health officials and how the 'gay community' is succeeding in its evil agenda in legitimizing perversion in the eyes of youngsters.[106]

Members of the TGLRG watched the parliamentary debates. Rodney Croome said he was "physically sickened by the debate, and other observers could do nothing but weep as the Legislative Council tore our lives to shreds."[107] He and others left the chamber noisily in protest. On July 11, 1991, a more organized protest occurred.

> Eleven lesbians, gay men and their supporters who were sitting in the Legislative Council's visitors' gallery stood up, removed their jumpers and revealed T-shirts, each with a letter that collectively read "Hypocrites!" After tossing white feathers—symbolizing cowardice—into the chamber, they joined the 50 or so people who were laying flowers and wreaths on the steps of the Legislative Council to commemorate all those who had committed suicide as a result of homophobia in Tasmania or died from AIDS-related illness—both in Tasmania and in exile.[108]

Ultimately, in July 1991, the law reform package was passed in the lower house with seventeen for, seventeen against, and the casting vote of the chair in favor.[109] But the clauses repealing Sections 122 and 123 did not pass the upper house, where only four out of nineteen members voted for repeal of Section 122 and six for repeal of Section 123.[110] The reform had stalled, with no prospect of passage in the near future.

Appealing to the International Community

A breakthrough for the TGLRG came toward the end of 1991, when the Australian federal government announced that it would ratify the First Optional Protocol to the International Covenant on Civil and Political Rights, which allows individuals to appeal directly to the UN Human Rights Committee for violations of human rights standards protected under the terms of the ICCPR.[111] The TGLRG immediately saw an opportunity for further action in relation to their law reform activities. If the Tasmanian Parliament would not act, they would seek action

---

106. Legislative Assembly, Hansard, at 6092 (Dec. 19, 1990).
107. Interview with Rodney Croome, Hobart, Australia (Mar. 8, 2007).
108. MORRIS, *supra* note 86, at 100.
109. *Id.* at 77.
110. Toonen Communication, *supra* note 6. The upper house—the Legislative Council—was highly malapportioned and undemocratic, with some electorates containing over 20,000 electors and others containing fewer than 5000 electors. *See* Second Submission, *supra* note 102.
111. Optional Protocol, *supra* note 83.

from the international community, through the United Nations Human Rights Committee ("the Committee"). A communication to the Committee needed to be brought by an individual, so Nick Toonen was chosen as the person to make the Communication; but it was, in truth, a claim on behalf of all gay men in Tasmania, as Nick Toonen later explained:

> The idea all along was that it should be a group effort and seen as a gay community and Gay and Lesbian Rights Group complaint; but it had to be from an individual. And choosing that individual was quite a difficult thing.... Rodney [Croome] shouldn't do it because he was (and still is, to a large extent) the primary spokesperson for the Gay and Lesbian Rights Group, and he would be presenting the community's point of view on the complaint. So we wanted someone else, whose name was actually deemed to be a victim, as the UN deemed me. Well, there were a number of criteria, one of which was we wanted someone who had been born and lived in Tasmania all their life, so there was no question about it being a 'ring-in' sort of thing. Secondly, we wanted someone who was committed to staying as long as the process took, which is, for young gay men, not an easy commitment necessarily to make in Tasmania.... And thirdly, they had to be publicly and openly and positively gay in the media and so forth. Which really brought it down [to me].[112]

The TGLRG prepared the Communication with assistance from legal academic Wayne Morgan, then at the University of Melbourne. They had it ready and waiting well before ratification of the First Optional Protocol occurred; and they sent it to the Committee in Geneva on the day Australia's ratification took effect (December 25, 1991). Toonen had not been prosecuted under the law, so one issue was whether the case was admissible. Was Toonen really a "victim" of a human rights violation? Following the arguments in the *Dudgeon* case, the submissions filed by Toonen emphasized the various ways in which the criminal law contributed to discrimination against gay men. One important aspect was the criminal law's impact on the mental health of young gay men and lesbians:

> Because of the criminalization of all male homosexual acts between consenting adults in private, it was impossible for me, while in late secondary school, to access the information and support I needed to allow me to develop a positive self image and to counter the negative ideas about my sexuality which I had internalised.[113]

> [A]lthough I knew from a very early age that I was gay, I had no way of forming a positive self-identity around my sexuality and I internalised much of the fear, hatred and contempt of homosexuality

---

112. Morris, *supra* note 86, at 101.
113. Toonen Communication, *supra* note 6.

that pervaded my childhood and adolescent world. The isolation that I felt because of the silence and ignorance that surrounded my sexuality compounded the sense of loathing I internalised. Having experienced what it is like to grow up in a world completely antagonistic to something which I knew to be an intrinsic and inalienable part of my identity, it is not hard for me to understand why at least one in three people under the age of twenty-one attempt[s] suicide because of hostility to their homosexuality from peers and family members.[114]

Toonen also referred to the general atmosphere of discrimination, harassment and violence experienced by lesbians and gay men in societies in which homosexual activity is criminalized:

[A]long with other homosexual people in Tasmania, I have faced condemnation, denunciation and vilification from public figures because of my sexual orientation and because my sexual activity is against the law. I have also experienced verbal and physical harassment and abuse because of my sexual orientation—motivated, I believe, at least in part, by the stigma which the criminal law attaches to my sexual orientation.[115]

Toonen explained in his Communication that he had been threatened and abused by a group of youths with cricket bats after a rally in support of decriminalization, and how he was only saved from serious physical harm by the arrival of a television crew. He attributed this incident to the youths' knowledge that he was a gay man and, thus, a criminal. He observed that he also lived with the fear of police action:

[W]hile these laws exist, it is possible for the police to enter my house and arrest me—and for me to be tried and imprisoned—all for sexual activity which I believe is not only victimless but which for me is natural and good. By posing a constant threat to my liberty and freedom, these laws place an unnecessary burden and stigma upon me from which it is impossible to escape while I live in Tasmania.[116]

Toonen also stated that after lodging his initial Communication, he lost his employment as a manager with the Tasmanian AIDS Council, a development he attributed to pressure from the Tasmanian government as a result of his high profile role in the complaint.[117] The Committee concluded that Toonen was sufficiently affected by the law to bring the

---

114. Second Submission, *supra* note 102.

115. Toonen Communication, *supra* note 6.

116. *Id.*

117. Final submissions made to the Committee, Jan. 26, 1993 (copy on file with the authors) [hereinafter, Final Submission].

case, consistent with the approach of the European Court of Human Rights in *Dudgeon*.

At the merits phase, Toonen and the TGLRG took the opportunity to present numerous stories of discrimination, harassment and violence to the Committee, while also carefully addressing the legal arguments in the case. Indeed, for those involved, one of the important features of the Communication was the opportunity it provided to tell their personal stories and emphasize the common indignities suffered by so many real people. Interestingly, Australia (as the respondent to the Communication) conceded that the Tasmanian laws violated the right to privacy. But Tasmania itself, though not a party to the Communication, was permitted to submit its own material to the Committee to try to justify its state-level laws.[118]

It was a long wait for a result, but in March 1994, the Committee concluded that Australia was in breach of its human rights obligations under the ICCPR, principally on the basis of the right to privacy under Article 17. The Committee also took the view that discrimination on the basis of sexual orientation was a form of sex discrimination prohibited by the ICCPR.[119] The Committee stated:

> 8.4 [...] the Tasmanian authorities submit that the challenged laws are justified on public health and moral grounds, as they are intended in part to prevent the spread of HIV/AIDS in Tasmania, and because, in the absence of specific limitation clauses in article 17, moral issues must be deemed a matter for domestic decision.
>
> 8.5 As far as the public health argument of the Tasmanian authorities is concerned, the Committee notes that the criminalization of homosexual practices cannot be considered a reasonable means or proportionate measure to achieve the aim of preventing the spread of AIDS/HIV. The Australian Government observes that statutes criminalizing homosexual activity tend to impede public health programmes "by driving underground many of the people at the risk of infection". Criminalization of homosexual activity thus would appear to run counter to the implementation of effective education programmes in respect of the HIV/AIDS prevention. Secondly, the

---

118. Like the United States, Australia is a federal nation. This means that Australia, the nation, is a party to treaties, rather than the individual states. Thus the proper respondent to a communication under the ICCPR is Australia, rather than the State of Tasmania, and only the parties to a communication are usually entitled to make submissions to the Human Rights Committee in relation to the communication. The decision by the Australian government to forward Tasmania's views on the case was unusual, and it was triggered more by domestic political concerns rather than any legal right of Tasmania to put submissions forward for consideration.

119. *See* Toonen v. Australia, U.N. Hum. Rts. Comm., No. 488/1992, U.N. Doc. CCPR/c/50/D/488/1992 at para. 8.7 (1994) [hereinafter Toonen v. Australia].

Committee notes that no link has been shown between the continued criminalization of homosexual activity and the effective control of the spread of the HIV/AIDS virus.

8.6 The Committee cannot accept either that for the purposes of article 17 of the Covenant, moral issues are exclusively a matter of domestic concern, as this would open the door to withdrawing from the Committee's scrutiny a potentially large number of statutes interfering with privacy. It further notes that with the exception of Tasmania, all laws criminalizing homosexuality have been repealed throughout Australia and that, even in Tasmania, it is apparent that there is no consensus as to whether Sections 122 and 123 should not also be repealed. Considering further that these provisions are not currently enforced, which implies that they are not deemed essential to the protection of morals in Tasmania, the Committee concludes that the provisions do not meet the "reasonableness" test in the circumstances of the case, and that they arbitrarily interfere with Mr. Toonen's right under article 17, paragraph 1.

Even though the Committee had reached its decision, the battle was not over. The Tasmanian government (by then, once again, a conservative government) refused to accept the decision, and it took considerable effort and lobbying to convince the federal government to intervene by passing legislation to override the Tasmanian Criminal Code. Even then, the Tasmanian government maintained that its legislation was valid. Litigation was then commenced in the High Court of Australia, this time with Rodney Croome and Nick Toonen both as plaintiffs.

In September 1994, Croome and others presented themselves to the police to confess their breaches of the criminal law. Croome named Toonen as his sexual partner, and Toonen was brought into the criminal investigation when the police asked him to come in for an interview. However, the Director of Public Prosecutions declined to press charges.[120] In the case that followed, the Tasmanian government tried, unsuccessfully, to assert that Croome and Toonin were not sufficiently affected by sections 122 and 123 to bring the case, since they had not been prosecuted.[121] In their 1997 judgment, three members of the Australian High Court rejected this argument and observed that "[t]he conduct by the plaintiffs of their personal lives in significant respects is overshadowed by the presence of ss 122 and 123 of the [Criminal] Code."[122] After

---

120. *See* Croome v. Tasmania (1997) 191 C.L.R. 119 at 131.

121. *See id.* For an analysis of the litigation *see* Kristen Walker, *International Human Rights Law and Sexuality: Strategies for Domestic Litigation*, 3 N.Y. City L. Rev. 115 (1998).

122. *Croome*, 191 C.L.R. at 138.

the government's defeat in the High Court, the Tasmanian Parliament finally repealed Sections 122 and 123 in May 1997.[123]

Toonen's Communication to the Human Rights Committee had always acknowledged that repeal of Sections 122 and 123 would not be a panacea:

> I know that the repeal of sections 122(a) and (c) and 123 will not make all this hatred, and personal pain go away. The belief that heterosexuality is inherently superior to homosexuality is deeply ingrained in our society and section 122(a) and (c) and 123 ... are only one manifestation of this kind of chauvinism in amongst the fears, lies, distortions, discrimination, harassment and violence which upholds heterosexual supremacy.
>
> However, the law is the most fundamental expression of the nature of social interaction in any community, so while anti-gay prejudice may take on any number of more immediately and obviously self-destructive manifestations than the criminal laws in question, these laws are still this society's most fundamental expression of its belief in the privilege and well-being of one sexual group at the expense of the basic rights and survival of another.[124]

Yet, the Committee's decision was a major breakthrough for lesbian and gay rights in Tasmania, Australia, and the world. In Tasmania, it paved the way for future non-discrimination laws, formal recognition of gay and lesbian relationships, and legal recognition of gay and lesbian co-parents. Other states in Australia have begun similar law reform processes, and Australia's national Human Rights and Equal Opportunity Commission recently recommended a raft of legislative changes to ensure greater equality for lesbians and gay men.[125] The U.N. Committee's view that the ICCPR's guarantee of equality before the law extends to sexual orientation has been an important tool in these law reform debates.

The Impact of Dudgeon *and* Toonen *in the United States:* Lawrence v. Texas

The successful decriminalization efforts in Europe and Australia had lasting impacts around the world. In the United States, the U.S. Su-

---

123. This occurred before the High Court had an opportunity to rule on the substance of the Tasmanian government's case. But it was widely believed in the Australian legal community that the Tasmanian government had no prospects of succeeding in defending the validity of its laws in the face of conflicting federal law.

124. Second Submission, *supra* note 102.

125. *See* Human Rights and Equal Opportunity Commission, *Same–Sex: Same Entitlements: National Inquiry Into Discrimination Against People in Same–Sex Relationships: Financial and Work–Related Entitlements and Benefits*, at 41 (May 2007), *available at* www.humanrights.gov.au/human_rights/samesex/report/pdf/SSSE_Report.pdf.

preme Court found the international trend toward decriminalization—as well as some of the reasoning behind the *Dudgeon* and *Toonen* cases—relevant to its decision in the 2003 case of *Lawrence v. Texas*. In *Lawrence v. Texas*, the U.S. Supreme Court overturned its own 1986 decision in *Bowers v. Hardwick*[126] by striking down a homosexual sodomy statute in the state of Texas. Indeed, it was almost inevitable that the Supreme Court should refer to the *Dudgeon* case—decided more than 20 years earlier—to overturn *Bowers v. Hardwick*.[127] The U.S. Supreme Court found an "emerging awareness that liberty gives substantial protection to adult persons in deciding how to conduct their private lives in matters pertaining to sex."[128] Citing international practice and the decision of the European Court of Human Rights in *Dudgeon v. United Kingdom*,[129] and recognizing that sometimes "laws once thought necessary and proper in fact serve only to oppress," the Court found that its earlier decision "demeans the lives of homosexual persons," and that the Texas statute violated the right to liberty under the Due Process Clause of the U.S. Constitution.[130]

Following the reasoning of *Toonen v. Australia*,[131] the U.S. Supreme Court also went beyond a pure privacy argument and found a link between privacy rights and equality. The Supreme Court noted that "[e]quality of treatment and . . . respect for conduct protected by the substantive guarantee of liberty are linked in important respects, and a decision on the latter point advances both interests."[132]

In his now famous dissent in the *Lawrence* case, Justice Scalia railed against the Court's role in supporting a "homosexual agenda," arguing that the "Court has taken sides in the culture war, departing from its role of assuring, as neutral observer, that the democratic rules of engagement are observed."[133] His point was simple. Gradual social acceptance should come through democratic elections and legislative reform, not court-ordered protection. And in his view, such acceptance was still far off. "Many Americans," he wrote, "do not want persons who openly engage in homosexual conduct as partners in their business, as scout-

---

126. 478 U.S. 186 (1986).

127. *Lawrence*, 539 U.S. at 578.

128. *Id.*, at 572.

129. *Dudgeon*, 45 Eur. Ct. H.R. (ser. A).

130. *Lawrence*, 539 U.S. at 575, 578–79 (2003).

131. Toonen v. Australia, U.N. Hum. Rts. Comm., No. 488/1992, U.N. Doc. CCPR/c/50/D/488/1992 (1994).

132. *Lawrence*, 539 U.S. at 575 (2003).

133. *Id.*, at 602.

masters for their children, as teachers in their children's schools, or as boarders in their home."[134]

But for those whose very existence is criminalized, it remains exceedingly difficult to meet the majority population openly and honestly to convince them, through the democratic rules of engagement, that sexual orientation and gender identity have very little bearing on one's capacity to become a business partner, educator or gracious lodger. And it is even more difficult, if not altogether impossible, to build electoral momentum for law reform when one faces criminal sanction for simply standing up and asserting one's right to exist. The experiences of Nick Toonen and those arrested in the Salamanca Market for promoting legal reform in Australia underscore that very point.

Jeff Dudgeon and his lawyers responded to the majoritarian argument many years before Justice Scalia ever posed it. In philosophical terms befitting the novelty of their case, they concluded their response brief by noting that the application was designed "to help bring about equality under the law for gay people of all ages.... To view public morality as if gays are not part of the public ... is to fail to see that such standards must either be a compromise between minorities and majorities, or they must emerge from an acceptance of different and perhaps occasionally antagonistic moral outlooks."[135]

Conclusion

Dudgeon and *Toonen* made tremendously important contributions to international human rights law concerning sexuality. They paved the way for general decriminalization of same-sex sexual activity in Europe and Australia, protections that now apply to the half-billion people living in all twenty-seven countries of the European Union and to the more than twenty million people living across Australia. The decisions have also influenced the jurisprudence of other countries around the world, including the United States. China decriminalized in 1997. Ecuador, Fiji, Portugal, South Africa, Sweden and Switzerland have all taken these protections a step further by embedding even broader non-discrimination protections in their national constitutions. And the U.N. Human Rights Committee now regularly raises the issue with countries that maintain laws criminalizing private consensual same-sex expression, even when they are not enforced.[136]

---

134. *Id.*

135. Dudgeon's Legal Brief, *supra* note 4.

136. Indeed, several years before the *Lawrence* decision, the U.N. Human Rights Committee in its 1995 examination of U.S. compliance with the ICCPR noted the "serious infringement of private life in some states which classify as a criminal offence sexual relations between adult consenting partners of the same sex carried out in private, and the

In addition, twenty-nine leading human rights experts from twenty-five countries around the world gathered in 2006 to proclaim the "Yogyakarta Principles," which were named after the conference location in Yogyakarta, Indonesia. The Principles apply binding human rights standards to issues of sexual orientation and gender identity. The principles recognize the fundamental importance of the decriminalization effort, while simultaneously calling on governments to ensure that other more general laws are not used as substitutes for sodomy laws in an attempt to *de facto* criminalize consensual sexual activity among persons of the same sex who are over the age of consent.[137] The Yogyakarta Principles are now being discussed more broadly at the United Nations and have been endorsed by activists worldwide.

The reforms that have followed decriminalization, including the implementation of non-discrimination laws, the registration of same-sex relationships, and the recognition of lesbian, gay and transgender parented families, could not have occurred without the initial step of decriminalization. Indeed, the authors wish to acknowledge the impact of these cases on our own lives, as we have had the advantage of living most of our adult lives in a milieu in which criminalization of same-sex sexual activity is considered a human rights violation, not a legitimate moral stance.

But international human rights law has not yet fully honored the initial spirit of *Dudgeon* and *Toonen*. While international law now generally recognizes that discrimination against lesbians and gay men is contrary to norms of non-discrimination in the ICCPR and in regional human rights treaties, there have been set-backs. In 1999, for example, the U.N. Human Rights Committee held, in a disturbingly brusque decision, that the right to marry and found a family contained in the ICCPR does not require states parties to provide same-sex marriage rights.[138] A year later, however, in *Young v. Australia*, the Human Rights Committee did find a violation of the non-discrimination provision of the ICCPR where state benefits were denied to same-sex couples that were otherwise granted to unmarried heterosexual couples.[139]

---

consequences thereof for their enjoyment of other human rights without discrimination." CONSIDERATION OF REPORTS SUBMITTED BY STATES PARTIES UNDER ARTICLE 40 OF THE COVENANT, U.N. Doc. CCPR/C/79/Add.50 at para. 287 (1995). More recently, the Human Rights Committee welcomed the U.S. Supreme Court's decision in *Lawrence*. CONSIDERATION OF REPORTS SUBMITTED BY STATES PARTIES UNDER ARTICLE 40 OF THE COVENANT, U.N. Doc. CCPR/C/USA/Q/3/CRP.4 at para. 9 (2006).

137. The *Yogyakarta Principles*, Principle 6, *available at* www.yogyakartaprinciples.org.

138. Joslin v. New Zealand, Human Rights Comm., No. 902/1999, para. 8.3, U.N. Doc. CCPR/C/75/D/902/1999 (2002).

139. Young v. Australia, Human Rights Comm., No. 941/2000, U.N. Doc. CCPR/C/78/D/941/2000 (2003).

The progression of cases from *Dudgeon*, where the European Court refused to consider an equality argument, to *Toonen*, where the U.N. Human Rights Committee entertained a limited equality argument, to *Lawrence*, where the U.S. Supreme Court found the two arguments to be fundamentally linked, is significant. This expansion from privacy to equality seems logical, but, ironically enough, all three decisions sought also to limit their own impact, cautioning that they should not be read too broadly or otherwise interpreted as requiring anything close to full equality. The *Dudgeon* Court warned that decriminalization was not the same as approval,[140] while the Human Rights Committee declined to consider a broader free-standing non-discrimination argument.[141] And the *Lawrence* Court warned that the case "does not involve whether the government must give formal recognition to any relationship that homosexual persons seek to enter."[142] In all three cases, even the judges in the majority seemed to recognize that the most logical outcome of their argument extended beyond the more limited legal points they were conceding, and all of them emphasized the still evolving social and political attitudes toward homosexuality. Many of those larger battles for equality have yet to be fought—and won.

Jeff Dudgeon and Nick Toonen could have walked away from their fights, but they chose not to. Their defiance made them heroes in the gay rights movement; and today their names are nearly synonymous with the ongoing legal battle for LGBT equality. But there are untold stories of other less prominent campaigners. In 2008, approximately eighty-five countries still criminalized same-sex sexual activity, in some cases with a penalty of death.[143] In many countries, the fight for decriminalization continues.[144] Dudgeon and Toonen's legal challenges allow today's equal-

---

140. *Dudgeon*, 45 Eur. Ct. H.R. (ser. A) at para. 61.

141. The Committee declined to consider whether there was a violation of the Covenant's free-standing non-discrimination provision under Article 26. Toonen v. Australia, *supra* note 119, at para. 11.

142. *Lawrence*, 539 U.S. at 578.

143. *See* DANIEL OTTOSSON, INTERNATIONAL LESBIAN AND GAY ASSOCIATION, STATE-SPONSORED HOMOPHOBIA: A WORLD SURVEY OF LAWS PROHIBITING SAME SEX ACTIVITY BETWEEN CONSENTING ADULTS (2007).

144. For example, even as this Chapter is being written, human rights advocates in India are fighting to extend the same protections to another billion or more people by using arguments from *Dudgeon* and *Toonen* to challenge Section 377 of the Indian Penal Code, a colonial-era provision that prohibits "carnal intercourse against the order of nature." Section 377 of the Indian Penal Code reads as follows: "Unnatural sexual offences:— Whoever voluntarily has carnal intercourse against the order of nature with any man, woman or animal, shall be punished with imprisonment for life or with imprisonment of either description for a term which may extend to ten years, and shall also be liable to fine. Explanation—Penetration is sufficient to constitute the carnal intercourse necessary to the offence described in this section." For details of the legacy of this law, *see* ARVIND NARRAIN &

ly heroic campaigners to argue, just as the U.S. Supreme Court finally recognized in the *Lawrence* case, that "[t]he State cannot demean their existence or control their destiny by making their private sexual conduct a crime."[145]

Yet, there is still a long way to go before international law fully recognizes and respects LGBT lives as truly equal to heterosexual lives. Nick Toonen summed it up poignantly when he stated that:

> [W]ith the lifting of the unnecessary burden I and other gay Tasmanians constantly carry, I will be able to live with dignity, without the threat of the invasion of my privacy by the police, with less fear of stigmatization, vilification, physical violence and the violation of my basic democratic rights, and with greater institutional support and personal fulfillment. But above all, I know I will be in a better position to endure, and eventually free myself, my gay brothers and lesbian sisters, and my whole community, from the pain of ignorance and bigotry that cripples us.[146]

Commenting on a 2006 poll showing that fully 88% of the population in Northern Ireland now believes that there should be no discrimination against gay men or lesbians, Jeff Dudgeon noted that the dramatic increase in tolerance can be explained by an increase in visibility.[147] Such visibility would not have been possible if homosexual identities were still criminalized. Dudgeon recognized that attitudes had become far more tolerant because "[s]traight people meet more gay people these days."[148] Jeff Dudgeon and Nick Toonen helped make those acquaintances possible.

The global struggle for a fully legal existence is hardly over. And for many transgender or gender-nonconforming individuals, similar demands to define and legalize their bodies, as well as their existence, are even more complicated. Nonetheless, the common refusal of LGBT communities worldwide to allow anyone else, especially the government

---

BROTOTI DUTTA, NAZ FOUND. INT'L, MALE-TO-MALE SEX AND SEXUALITY MINORITIES IN SOUTH ASIA: AN ANALYSIS OF THE POLITICO-LEGAL FRAMEWORK (2006).

The law is rarely used to prosecute consensual sex but casts a very broad net of illegality and generalized persecution in the country. *See* Gupta, *supra* note 77. In September 2006, more than 100 leading film stars, writers, and academics joined that fight by signing a petition arguing that India's colonial-era law should finally be abandoned. Randeep Ramesh, *India's Literary Elite Call for Anti-gay Law to Be Scraped*, THE GUARDIAN (U.K.), Sept. 18, 2006.

145. *Lawrence*, 539 U.S. at 578.

146. Second Submission, *supra* note 102.

147. Henry McDonald, *Hain Moves to Outlaw Prejudice Against Gays*, THE OBSERVER (U.K.), Jul. 30, 2006, at 1.

148. *Id.*

or the legal system, to demean their bodies, their families or their identities has spawned an unmistakable new global movement in support of full LGBT equality.

*

4

Gaining Legal Recognition of Indigenous Land Rights: The Story of the *Awas Tingni* Case in Nicaragua

S. James Anaya* & Maia S. Campbell

In their simple quest to keep the lands they consider their own, the people of the remote Nicaraguan community of Awas Tingni did not set about to forge an international legal precedent with implications for indigenous peoples throughout the world. Yet, that is what they did. Awas Tingni is one of numerous Mayangna, or Sumo,[1] indigenous communities in the isolated Atlantic Coast region of Nicaragua.[2] Most of its 1,100 or so members live in a village of dispersed wood-plank, stilted houses close to the Wawa River, at the edge of a dense tropical forest. Few of the community's adults have formal education past elementary school, but they are rich in the knowledge of the slash and burn farming techniques and the skills of hunting and freshwater fishing that have sustained them. Once little known, the community's identity is now merged with that of a landmark case, *The Case of the Maya[n]gna (Sumo) Awas Tingni Community v. Nicaragua*, decided by the Inter–American Court of Human Rights on August 31, 2001.[3]

The demands of indigenous peoples worldwide are now prominent within the international human rights agenda; the assertion of commu-

---

* The authors would like to thank the Awas Tingni community for its continued perseverance in the face of adversity, without which this story would not exist. Parts of this chapter are adapted from Jame Anaya's contribution to an earlier piece he co-authored: S. James Anaya & Claudio Grossman, *The Case of Awas Tingni v. Nicaragua: A New Step in the International Law of Indigenous Peoples*, 119 Ariz J. Int'l & Comp. L. 1 (2002).

1. The people of Awas Tingni prefer to call themselves Mayangna, as opposed to Sumo, a commonly used designation. They regard the latter term as one imposed by outsiders.

2. The Atlantic Coast region of Nicaragua is generally understood to include roughly the eastern third of the country. The geographically isolated region has a unique history and cultural milieu. The region is home to the Miskito, Mayangna (Sumo), Rama Indians and to a substantial Black Creole population. For a demography and history of the Atlantic Coast region, *see* CARLOS M. VILAS, DEL COLONIALIMSO A LA AUTONOMIA: MODERNIZACION CAPITALISTA Y REVOLUCION SOCIAL EN LA COSTA ATLANTICA 19–127 (1990).

3. The Case of the Mayagna (Sumo) Awas Tingni community v. Nicaragua, Inter–Am. Ct. H.R. (ser. C) No. 79 (Judgment on the Merits and Reparations of Aug. 31, 2001) [hereinafter Judgment].

nal or collective rights over lands and natural resources has been a common feature of these demands. Indigenous peoples around the world, practically as a matter of definition, have been dispossessed of the lands that have historically sustained them as a result of colonizing forces and the modern legacies of those forces.[4] The multiple human rights dimensions of these past and, all too often, ongoing patterns of dispossession are well-known and have been the subject of numerous accounts given by indigenous peoples to international and regional institutions concerned with human rights. Basic rights to life, health, culture, and self-determination are all implicated in the struggle of indigenous peoples to maintain their connections with their traditional lands. It is these lands from which they have derived sustenance, within which their patterns of social interaction have been organized and developed, and upon which their ability to pursue their own destinies has depended. The demand of indigenous peoples to secure their rights in traditional lands, moreover, can be seen as grounded in the human right to property.

In the *Awas Tingni* case, the Inter–American Court held that the international human right to enjoy the benefits of property, particularly as affirmed in the American Convention on Human Rights (Article 21), includes the right of indigenous peoples to the protection of their traditional land and resource tenure. The Court held that the State of Nicaragua violated the property rights of the Awas Tingni community by granting to a foreign company a concession to log within the community's traditional lands and by failing to otherwise provide adequate recognition and protection of the community's customary tenure. This was the first legally binding decision by an international tribunal to uphold the collective land and resource rights of indigenous peoples in the face of a state's failure to do so. It effectively applied the standard of indigenous land rights to be adopted years later, on September 13, 2007,

---

4. Hence the rubric of "indigenous peoples" has developed internationally to address the concerns of groups that have experienced such historical forces and their ongoing legacy. The issues and groups that fall within this rubric are indicated by the following widely cited passage of a major United Nations study:

> Indigenous communities, peoples and nations are those which, having a historical continuity with pre-invasion and pre-colonial societies that developed on their territories, consider themselves distinct from other sectors of the societies now prevailing in those territories, or parts of them. They form at present non-dominant sectors of society and are determined to preserve, develop and transmit to future generations their ancestral territories, and their ethnic identity, as the basis of their continued existence as peoples, in accordance with their own cultural patterns, social institutions and legal systems.

Study of the Problem of Discrimination Against Indigenous Populations, U.N. Doc. E/CN.4/Sub.2/1986/7/Add. 4, ¶ 379 (1986) (*prepared by* José Martínez Cobo, Special Rapporteur).

by the U.N. General Assembly as a key part of its Declaration on the Rights of Indigenous Peoples.[5]

As of July 2008, the judgment in *Awas Tingni* was still not yet fully implemented—a manifestation of the difficulties in implementing the far-reaching reforms called for in the judgment. Still, the case laid the groundwork for an expanding jurisprudence on indigenous rights within the Inter–American human rights system. It also strengthened a contemporary trend in the broader processes of international law and policy that led to adoption of the Declaration and that helps to empower indigenous peoples as they press their demands for self-determination as distinct groups with secure territorial rights.

The Path to the Inter–American Court of Human Rights

The MADENSA Logging Initiative, the World Wildlife Fund, and Awas Tingni's Demand for Land Tenure Security

It was May 1993 when Jamie Castillo, Charlie Mclean, and other Awas Tingni leaders met at the village with representatives of the Nicaraguan government. They were joined at the meeting by Dr. Guillermo Castilleja, a program officer of the World Wildlife Fund ("WWF"), and James Anaya, co-author of this Chapter. To escape the drizzling rain typical of that time of year, they all gathered under the awning of the Moravian church building. These distinctive red and white churches are a feature common to all indigenous communities of the Atlantic Coast, which for decades have been the object of Christian missionary activity. They discussed logging plans being promoted by Maderas y Derivados, S.A. ("MADENSA"), a Dominican-owned company. Representatives of the company were also present.

Dr. Castilleja had contacted Anaya, who was then on the faculty of the University of Iowa College of Law and had previous experience working with the indigenous peoples of Nicaragua, and asked him to make the trip to Awas Tingni to help evaluate the implications of the MADENSA logging initiative for the community. The WWF had for some time been working with the government forestry agency to develop an effective regulatory regime conducive to sustainable forestry. When Dr. Castilleja, himself a forester, first learned of the MADENSA initiative for large-scale logging of valuable tropical hardwoods in an area of approximately 43,000 hectares, he had also learned that most of this area was territory claimed by the Awas Tingni community on the basis of traditional use and occupancy.

---

5. United Nations Declaration on the Rights of Indigenous Peoples, G.A. Res. 61/295, U.N. Doc. A/RES/61/295 (Sept. 13, 2007).

At the meeting in May 1993, Awas Tingni leaders made clear their view that the land belonged to the community. They told those present that the community, while not opposing the logging if it proceeded on that understanding, had as its foremost concern gaining official government recognition and documentation of the community's rights to its traditional lands. Jamie Castillo spoke in his native Mayangna language in his capacity as the community's *síndico*, its principal leader within the traditional governing structure that is common, with some variation, to all Atlantic Coast indigenous communities. His words were interpreted into Spanish by Charlie Mclean, one of the few adult villagers whose formal education extends beyond elementary school. Mr. Mclean's own leadership post in the community was that of Forest Manager. They both stressed the linkage between the need for official recognition of Awas Tingni rights in traditional lands and the demand of the community to benefit fairly under any logging initiative.

In the absence of a paper title or other official recognition of Awas Tingni land rights, government land and natural resource management authorities had continued to designate Awas Tingni traditional land as state-owned. Such was the precarious land tenure situation shared by most of the Atlantic Coast indigenous communities, despite provisions in the constitution adopted by Nicaragua in 1987, which explicitly recognized the distinctive character of the Atlantic Coast communities and their rights to maintain their distinctive cultural attributes and forms of organization, communal forms of property, and the enjoyment of the natural resources on their communal lands.[6] These rights were further affirmed and elaborated upon within a regime of decentralized governance provided for in the Statute of Autonomy for the Atlantic Coast Regions of Nicaragua,[7] enacted the same year. With these reforms, adopted in the face of an indigenous insurgency that had arisen alongside a broader civil war in the 1980s, Nicaragua came to be regarded by many as being at the forefront of countries turning toward progressive indigenous policies. However, legal affirmation of indigenous land rights had not translated into practical application or effective protection for those rights, as the Awas Tingni situation illustrated.

In the months following the May 1993 meeting at the village, government officials from the Ministry of Environment and Natural Resources ("MARENA") decided to bypass the concerns expressed by Awas Tingni leaders. They proceeded unilaterally to grant MADENSA a thirty-year concession for logging within the 43,000 hectare area on the assumption that the land targeted for logging was entirely state-owned.

---

6. Constitución Política de la República de Nicaragua [Cn.] [Constitution] tit. IV, ch. VI, arts. 89, 90, 180, La Gaceta [L.G.] 9 January 1987 (Nicar.).

7. Estatuto de Autonomía las Regiones Autónomas de la Costa Atlántica de Nicaragua, Ley No. 28, La Gaceta [L.G.], Diario Oficial No. 238, 30 October 1987.

This outraged the community leaders, who protested both to the government and to the WWF. Under pressure from the WWF, the government accepted the suspension of the concession until an agreement could be negotiated with the Awas Tingni community and adequate environmental controls could be established.

The Iowa Project

Responding to the community's concerns, and at the urging of its leaders, the WWF helped develop and fund a project of the University of Iowa College of Law (the "Iowa project"), directed by James Anaya, to assist the community in negotiations with the government and MADENSA. Anaya secured the help of three key individuals: Maria Luisa Acosta, a Nicaraguan lawyer who had recently completed a law degree at the University of Iowa, where she had conducted research on the Atlantic Coast under Anaya's supervision; Hans Åkesson, a forester with extensive experience in his native Sweden and various other countries, and who had previously worked for the Nicaraguan government forestry agency; and, on a pro bono basis, Todd Crider, a New York attorney and long-time friend of Anaya who specializes in complex business transactions. Together they embarked on an adventure with many unexpected turns.

A few weeks after he had first travelled to Awas Tingni, Anaya once more made the journey to the village, this time with Acosta and Åkesson. It was a trek they would each make many more times. From the regional capital of Bilwi (Puerto Cabezas), a town with a frontier feel, it was a three to five hour truck ride, depending on the weather and number of pot-holes in the badly maintained dirt road, followed by a forty-five minute walk. Sheltered in the community school house from intermittent heavy rain, Anaya, Acosta and Åkesson met for several hours with community leaders and members, gathered in their traditional assembly through which all major decisions are made, to explain the MADENSA initiative and the various actors involved. The offer of assistance by the Iowa project team was then discussed at length by the traditional assembly well into the night, while the three outsiders sat sipping coffee on the porch of a nearby thatched-roof house. When the three were prompted to return to the school house, the community, through its traditional assembly, enthusiastically and ceremoniously accepted the offer of assistance. The community thus moved into the highly unusual position—unusual for Atlantic Coast indigenous communities as well as for the government and industry in their dealings with communities—of having the backing of its own legal and technical team.

With the counsel of the Iowa Project experts, the community proceeded through several rounds of often contentious discussions to negotiate a trilateral agreement with MARENA and MADENSA for sustainable timber harvesting within the 43,000–hectare area. In May 1994, an agreement was finally signed. It provided for economic benefits for the community and committed the government to a process by which it would definitively identify and title the community's traditional lands.[8] Additionally, under the agreement, the government undertook to refrain from any action that would prejudice or undermine the community's land claim.[9] The WWF and other environmentalists hailed that agreement as a model of sustainable forestry respectful of indigenous rights.

The SOLCARSA Concession

The government's commitment to a process of land titling in favor of Awas Tingni, however, proved illusory. Even as the government was formalizing this commitment in a written agreement, it was engaged in discussions with a second logging company, Sol del Caribe, S.A. ("SOL-CARSA"), a Korean-owned firm, which was soliciting the government for a concession to log an area of 63,000 hectares of land adjacent to the MADENSA management area. While in the forest hunting, Awas Tingni community members spotted strangers counting trees and soon learned of the SOLCARSA initiative. By the time the Awas Tingni community leaders became aware of these plans in July 1995, the government had already granted SOLCARSA an exploration license and preliminary approval of the concession. Through a letter signed and submitted by Maria Luisa Acosta, Awas Tingni protested the SOLCARSA initiative, arguing that most of area sought by SOLCARSA was within the community's traditional territory.

Weeks passed with no response by the government to the community's written protest as all pretense of cooperation between the community and the Iowa project, on the one hand, and the government, on the other, dissipated. The government's unresponsiveness—and worse—continued for months while Awas Tingni leaders, usually accompanied by Acosta or Anaya, met with government officials at all levels, even on one occasion with the Nicaraguan President, Arnoldo Alemán. Beyond grant-

---

8. Convenio de Aprovechamiento Forestal entre la Comunidad de Awas Tingni; Maderas y Derivados de Nicaragua, S.A.; y el Ministerio del Ambiente y los Recursos Naturales, 15 de mayo de 1994 (on file with the authors). The process leading to this agreement and its content are summarized in S. James Anaya & S. Todd Crider, *Indigenous Peoples, The Environment, and Commercial Forestry in Developing Countries: The Case of Awas Tingni, Nicaragua,* 18 HUM. RTS. Q. 345 (1996).

9. Article 3.2 of the agreement provides: "MARENA promises to facilitate the definition of the communal lands and not to undermine the territorial aspirations of the community ... Such definition of lands should be carried out according to the historical rights of the community and within the relevant legal framework." (Translation from Spanish).

ing audiences and occasionally promising to address the community's concerns, the officials did nothing to respond to concerns. Rather, they allowed the status quo to coalesce into a firm government posture behind the SOLCARSA concession and against the community.

Awas Tingni leaders and community members became increasingly alarmed by the presence of SOLCARSA agents, who were conducting an inventory of the timber resources within lands that were used by the community for agriculture and for subsistence hunting and gathering. When it became apparent that the government was determined to go ahead and grant SOLCARSA the concession under the assumption that the lands in question were entirely state-owned, the community decided to stand its ground. Community leaders convened an assembly to explore options and called on Anaya and Acosta to participate. After extensive debate, the community decided to take unprecedented legal action as an alternative to physically confronting the SOLCARSA agents.

Jim Anaya had significant experience litigating in the United States, but none in Nicaragua. He and Maria Luisa Acosta studied the Nicaraguan *amparo* procedure, which provides for judicial relief from constitutional infractions. They discussed with community leaders how an *amparo* petition might be framed to allege violations of constitutional provisions that generally affirm indigenous communal land rights, something that had never before been done. One night in September 1995, Anaya worked through the night at the modest guesthouse where he stayed in the regional capital of Bilwi to complete a draft of the *amparo* petition. The following morning, Acosta helped to finalize it and then proceeded to file it in the Court of Appeals in Matagalpa, a city outside the Atlantic Coast region and, for all practical purposes, worlds away from Awas Tingni.

The Court took just a few days to reject the *amparo* action, not allowing it to proceed to the Nicaraguan Supreme Court for a determination on the merits. With an irony that befits this story, the Court of Appeals ruled that the *amparo* action was procedurally barred because of what it found to be constructive acquiescence by Awas Tingni in the granting of the SOLCARSA concession. The Court relied on a procedural rule that allows an inference of acquiescence when a petition is not presented within thirty days of when the claimant becomes aware of the matter. Further, in accordance with the rule, the community's knowledge of the SOLCARSA concession was deemed to be acquiescence. On this point, the Court referred to Awas Tingni's letter of protest to the government, which had been appended to the *amparo* petition to demonstrate the required exhaustion of administrative remedies. An appeal to the Nicaraguan Supreme Court was summarily rejected. Yet, even before the appeal, the Awas Tingni community had taken its complaint to the

Inter–American Commission on Human Rights ("Inter–American Commission").

Filing the Petition in the Inter–American Human Rights System

The decision to petition the Inter–American Commission on Human Rights was born more out of a sense of limited options than from faith in the possibility of a successful and effective outcome. Complaints to the Commission must be grounded in the American Convention on Human Rights, the American Declaration of the Rights and Duties of Man, or select provisions of other inter-American human rights instruments.[10] None of these instruments explicitly provided for a collective right to land on the basis of traditional land tenure, or any other collective right of indigenous peoples. Neither the Inter–American Commission nor the Inter–American Court of Human Rights had clearly or explicitly found such a right to stand alone on the basis of these instruments. The Commission previously had addressed indigenous land issues, but only in the context of physical violence and involving violations of individual rights readily found in the inter-American instruments.[11]

Proceedings before the Commission can move at a notoriously slow pace and, what is more, a final decision on the merits of a petition is in formal terms only a recommendation. Further still, it is up to the

---

10. Rules of Procedure of the Inter–American Commission on Human Rights, art. 23, Oct. 16–27, 2006, *reprinted in* Basic Documents Pertaining to Human Rights in the Inter-American System, OAS/Ser.L/V/I.4, rev. 9 (2003), *available at* http://www.cidh.oas.org/Basicos/basic16.htm; *see also* American Convention on Human Rights, arts. 41–55, Nov. 22, 1969, O.A.S.T.S. No. 36, 1144 U.N.T.S. 123 (entered into force July 18, 1978); *see generally* Statute of the Inter–American Commission on Human Rights, arts. 19–20, O.A.S. Res. 447 (IX–0/79), O.A.S. Off. Rec. OEA/Ser.P/IX.0.2/80, vol. 1, at 88.

11. One such case, in fact, concerned the Miskito Indians, the largest of the indigenous groups of the Atlantic Coast region. Inter–Am. C.H.R., *Report on the Situation of Human Rights of a Segment of the Nicaraguan Population of Miskito Origin and Resolution on the Friendly Settlement Procedure Regarding the Human Rights Situation of a Segment of the Nicaraguan Population of the Miskito Origin*, O.A.S. Doc. OEA/Ser.L/V/II.62, doc. 10, rev. 3 (1983), OEA/Ser.L/V/II.62, doc. 26 (1984), in which the Commission addressed alleged human rights violations arising from the violence in the Atlantic Coast region during that country's civil war during the early 1980s. In doing so, it pointed to the need for Nicaragua to address the land claims of the Miskito and other indigenous peoples of the region as part of a comprehensive solution to the conflicts. The Commission, however, stated that it was "not in a position to decide on the strict legal validity of the claim of the Indian communities to their ancestral lands." *Id.* at Sec. F, ¶ 6. *See also* Yanomami v. Brazil, Case 7615, Inter–Am. C.H.R., Report No. 12/85 (1984–85) (discussing the rights of the Yanomami to permanent possession of the lands they inhabit under the Constitution and laws of Brazil, but limiting its findings to violations of the rights to life, health, and residence, due to construction of a highway; authorization to exploit subsurface resources; abrupt and uncontrolled entrance of outsiders, and proceedings to displace the Yanomami from their lands, among other government actions).

Commission or the state concerned, not the petitioner, to take the case to the Inter–American Court of Human Rights for a legally binding ruling, but only after the Commission procedures are completed. At the time (1995), just a handful of the literally hundreds of cases submitted to the Commission every year made their way to the Inter–American Court.[12]

Having been advised of these limitations, the Awas Tingni community nonetheless resolved to take their case to the Commission and authorized their attorneys accordingly. Jim Anaya worked with Todd Crider and his associate Jeffrey Bullwinkel, of the law firm Simpson Thacher and Bartlett in New York, to draft the petition. They advanced a theory of Awas Tingni land rights centering on Article 21 of the American Convention on Human Rights, which provides that "[e]veryone has the right to the use and enjoyment of his property."[13] In an effort to see Awas Tingni's traditional land tenure system validated on its own terms, the petition argued that this general human right to property be interpreted in light of relevant international developments, including the Commission's own recent draft American Declaration of the Rights of Indigenous Peoples, which recognized that "[i]ndigenous peoples have the right to the recognition of their property and ownership rights with respect to lands and territories they have historically occupied."[14]

Filed on October 2, 1995, the petition alleged violations of Awas Tingni's right to property by virtue of the SOLCARSA concession and the state's more general failure to recognize and respect the community's traditional land tenure. It also averred violations of the rights to equality (Article 24) and to participate in government (Article 23). To bolster the claim, the petition referred as well to Nicaragua's obligations under the International Covenant on Civil and Political Rights ("ICCPR"), alleging violation of the right to cultural integrity (Article 27). The petition requested that the Commission assist the community in its effort to stop the concession to SOLCARSA and to achieve secure land tenure.[15]

---

12. Since then, the Commission amended its Rules of Procedure to establish a presumption in favor of submitting to the Court cases in which the Commission's recommendations have not been followed, and the petitioner desires the case be heard by the Court. See Rules of Procedure of the Inter–Am. C.H.R., *supra* note 10, art. 44(1), (2)(a).

13. American Convention on Human Rights, *supra* note 10, art. 21.

14. Draft of the Inter–American Declaration of the Rights of Indigenous Peoples, art. XVIII(2), approved by the IACHR at the 1278th session held on Sept. 18, 1995, OEA/Ser./L/V/II.90, Doc. 9 rev. 1 (1995). The Inter–American Commission subsequently amended the draft declaration. See American Declaration on the Rights of Indigenous Peoples, Inter–Am. C.H.R., art. VI(1), O.A.S. Doc. OEA/Ser.L/V/II.95, doc. 7 rev., (Mar. 14, 1997).

15. See S. James Anaya, *The Awas Tingni Petition to the Inter–American Commission on Human Rights: Indigenous Lands, Loggers, and Government Neglect in Nicaragua*, 9 St. Thomas L. Rev. 157 (1996) (including full text of petition).

As the case proceeded through the Inter–American human rights system, adding to the pro bono assistance of attorneys from Simpson Thacher and Bartlett was the backing of the Indian Law Resource Center ("ILRC") and, later, the Indigenous Peoples Law & Policy Program of the University of Arizona James E. Rogers College of Law, whose faculty Anaya joined in 1999.[16] The ILRC, a U.S.-based non-governmental organization, had long been involved in aggressively advocating indigenous rights in Nicaragua, principally through its Latin American Projects director, Armstrong Wiggins, himself a Miskito Indian from Nicaragua's Atlantic Coast. Anaya, who continued as the lead attorney for Awas Tingni, worked as special counsel to the ILRC.

It was several months before the Inter–American Commission initiated proceedings on the case and forwarded the petition to the government of Nicaragua, asking for a response. Soon thereafter, the Commission convened a meeting with the parties at its offices in Washington D.C. Awas Tingni leaders made the first of several trips to Washington and, with their lawyers, sat face to face with the Nicaraguan Ambassador to the Organization of American States ("OAS") in the presence of Commission delegates. The Commission offered its good offices to mediate a solution to the dispute, pursuant to the "friendly settlement" procedure provided in the American Convention on Human Rights and the Commission's Rules of Procedure.[17] Both sides accepted. However, the process never amounted to much more than each side arguing its position in the presence of a member of the Commission or its staff. As a mediated solution remained elusive, the Awas Tingni lawyers continued to advocate the case before the Commission and provide it with new information as events unfolded.

Documenting Awas Tingni Land Tenure

An important component of the legal actions taken by Awas Tingni at the national and international levels was the detailed mapping and a related ethnographic study. The initial terms of reference for the WWF-funded Iowa Project included assisting Awas Tingni to compile the data to support its claim to traditional lands. This data would be the basis of discussions with the government that in turn was expected to lead to

---

16. The Indian Law Resource Center is a U.S.-based organization that provides legal assistance to indigenous peoples in several countries throughout the Hemisphere. *See* http://www.indianlaw.org for further information. Information on the University of Arizona's Indigenous Peoples Law & Policy Program is *available at* http://www.law.arizona.edu.

17. American Convention on Human Rights, *supra* note 10, arts. 48(f), 49; *see generally* Statute of the Inter–Am. C.H.R., *supra* note 10, arts. 19–20; Rules of Procedure of the Inter–Am. C.H.R., *supra* note 10, arts. 38(4), 41.

titling or other official recognition of Awas Tingni lands. The data instead became the basis of contentious legal proceedings that reached the highest level of adjudication within the inter-American human rights system.

In its early phases, the Iowa Project established a cooperative relationship with Harvard's Weatherhead Center for International Affairs in order to assist Awas Tingni to document the historical, ethnographic, and geographic data relevant to its land claim. Theodore Macdonald, an anthropologist from the Weatherhead Center, had previously worked with Jim Anaya in Nicaragua when they were both involved in peace negotiations between the government and warring Miskito Indian groups in the 1980s. He spent several weeks in 1995 and 1996 in Awas Tingni conducting research in collaboration with a team of community members that included Jamie Castillo and Charlie Mclean.

Even before all of this, community leaders had sketched a map of the Awas Tingni traditional lands without any outside assistance. With this sketch map as an initial point of reference, Dr. Macdonald worked with the community researchers to document Awas Tingni's historical and continuing land tenure patterns. Using a simple hand-held electronic device, a Magellan Geographical Positioning System ("GPS"), the community researchers—who, for reasons that remain vague to the authors, called themselves *Los Elefantes*—located relevant geographic coordinates, which became the basis for the map illustrating Awas Tingni's historical land tenure.

At the time the Awas Tingni community discovered the plans for the SOLCARSA concession, in mid–1995, this research was ongoing. After Awas Tingni filed its complaint with the Inter–American Commission in October 1995, a preliminary ethnographic report and accompanying map in support of the community's land claim was completed. As revealed by Dr. Macdonald's report, the boundaries of the community's historical land use area had fluctuated over time and were, to an extent, porous in relation to the land uses of neighboring communities. Drawing a line around the land now claimed by the community represented its understanding, rightly or wrongly, that a finite boundary was needed to assert the claim and to achieve land tenure security. Therefore, in addition to designating Awas Tingni's historical use area, the map contained a line demarcating the land now claimed.

The preliminary report and map were submitted to the Inter–American Commission and to relevant Nicaraguan government institutions, including MARENA and the regional governing body of the North Atlantic Autonomous Region. At the same time it submitted the preliminary report and map, in a written communication to the government in early 1996, Awas Tingni again raised its concern over the SOLCARSA concession, and proposed that consideration of the concession be suspended pending resolution of the community's land claim or an agreement with the community.

Ignoring the community's submissions and proposal, the government proceeded—through MARENA—with its plans and formally granted the concession to SOLCARSA on March 13, 1996. In response to the mounting threat of logging under the SOLCARSA concession, the community leaders developed yet another map. This map, which was sketched by hand, detailed the land and resource tenure patterns of the community within the concession area, and it also was submitted to the Inter–American Commission and relevant government authorities.

The Nicaraguan government maintained the position that the land claimed by Awas Tingni was excessive, although the government never contested the data and maps presented by the community. Faced with this evidence at a hearing before the Inter–American Commission in October 1997, government representatives conceded that at least part of the land within the SOLCARSA concession area was Awas Tingni communal land.

Simultaneous Nicaraguan Domestic Proceedings

While the case was proceeding at the international level before the Inter–American Commission on Human Rights, the SOLCARSA concession became the subject of an additional legal proceeding within the Nicaraguan judicial system. In 1996, at the request of the Awas Tingni community, two members of the Regional Council of the North Atlantic Autonomous Region filed another *amparo* action with the Nicaraguan Supreme Court. Jim Anaya and Maria Luisa Acosta, the community's attorneys, assisted them in again demanding that SOLCARSA's concession be revoked, though on different grounds. Remarkably, this *amparo* action—brought by regional authorities and based on an alleged procedural infraction rather than a violation of communal land—was successful. The Nicaraguan Supreme Court declared the SOLCARSA concession unconstitutional in February 1997 on the ground that the Regional Council had not approved the concession as required by Article 181 of the Constitution. By then the controversy concerning the concession was brewing among other indigenous communities and concerned local non-governmental organizations, with significant media coverage. Article 181 of the Constitution gave the Supreme Court a way of nullifying the concession without addressing the thorny issue of land ownership.

But instead of cancelling the SOLCARSA concession, MARENA officials sought to "cure" the constitutional defect by securing a post hoc ratification of the concession by the Regional Council. In a divided vote, the Regional Council approved the concession in October 1997. Around this time, MARENA and Foreign Ministry officials appeared before the Inter–American Commission in Washington asserting that the government intended to follow the Nicaraguan Supreme Court's decision, implying that they intended to cancel the concession. Faced with this development, Awas Tingni initiated a third action in the Nicaraguan courts, this one against the Regional Council members who voted to ratify the concession and the central government officials who promoted that ratification. Although this suit was filed just days after the Regional Council vote, the Nicaraguan Supreme Court delayed twelve months before dismissing the case on October 14, 1998 on the ground that it was untimely, as the concession had been granted more than a year earlier.

However, yet another domestic legal action *did* result in the SOLCARSA concession being cancelled. The Awas Tingni lawyers assisted dissenting members of the Council in filing for execution of the Supreme Court's earlier decision declaring the concession unconstitutional because it was not preceded by Regional Council approval. The Supreme Court acceded and, on February 3, 1998, issued an order that the Nicaraguan president himself direct the nullification of the concession. According to the Court, the concession was in the first instance invalid because of a defect in the process by which it was granted that could not be cured by a subsequent Regional Council vote. Shortly after the execution order, but almost a year after the initial determination of unconstitutionality, on February 13, 1998 the MARENA officials notified SOLCARSA that its concession had been made null.

The eventual nullification of the SOLCARSA concession was a notable success for the Awas Tingni community and for other sectors of Nicaraguan civil society that opposed the concession. Still, the underlying land tenure issue remained unresolved, and the government's disposition toward justly resolving it remained questionable at best. Awas Tingni, like the majority of other indigenous communities of the Atlantic Coast, still lacked official demarcation of its traditional territory or other official, specific recognition of traditional land and resource tenure. And it did not look like they could count on the government to take remedial action without additional pressure of some kind.

The Commission's Findings in the Absence of a Mediated Settlement

Meanwhile, the friendly settlement process before the Inter–American Commission was going nowhere. Between early 1996 and late 1997, the Commission convened a number of friendly settlement meetings between representatives of Awas Tingni and the Nicaraguan government, followed by two formal adversarial hearings before panels of

Commissioners. It was apparent throughout that the government was not prepared to concede the validity of Awas Tingni's claim in anything but the vaguest of terms, and that it was not willing to commit to specific action to recognize and secure the community's property rights. When it appeared that the government was bent on allowing the logging by SOLCARSA to go forward, the Commission issued Precautionary Measures, calling on Nicaragua to suspend the concession given by the government to SOLCARSA to carry out forestry work within Awas Tingni lands because of the threat of immediate and irreparable harm that the logging presented.[18] This was an extraordinary step, as it was the first time that the Commission issued Precautionary Measures in an incident not involving a threat to physical life or safety.

At a final, informal meeting between the government and the community at OAS headquarters in Washington the day after the October 1997 Commission hearing, Nicaragua's Ambassador to the OAS openly disparaged the Awas Tingni leaders who were present with their attorneys for having denounced Nicaragua internationally. He criticized the lawyers for meddling and for instigating the dispute. No Commission delegates were present.

The government's attitude did not change after MARENA's grudging nullification of the SOLCARSA concession. With efforts at a meditated solution having failed, the Inter–American Commission completed its investigation of the case and in March 1998 delivered to the Nicaraguan government a confidential report finding it responsible for violating the human rights of the members of the Awas Tingni community, including the right to property as the community's attorneys had argued. Although the SOLCARSA concession had been cancelled, Awas Tingni remained without secure rights in its traditional lands, and that in itself was a violation of the Convention, according to the Commission. The government's response to the Commission failed again to provide guarantees of prompt and definitive steps toward changing that situation, but rather stated a general intention to address land issues concerning all the indigenous communities of the Atlantic Coast.[19] Dissatisfied with this response, and at the urging of the Awas Tingni lawyers in consultation with community leaders, the Commission decided to submit the case to

---

18. *See* Annual Report of the Inter–American Commission on Human Rights 1997, OEA/Ser.L/V/II.98 doc. 6 rev., Ch. III (2)(A) (Apr. 13, 1998).

19. The Commission's recommendations to the government from its confidential report and the government's response are extracted in the *Complaint by the Inter–American Commission on Human Rights, Submitted to the Inter–American Court of Human Rights in the Case of the Awas Tingni Mayagna (Sumo) Indigenous Community Against the Republic of Nicaragua*, ¶¶ 67–68, June 4, 1998, *available in English and original Spanish at* www.law.arizona.edu/depts/iplp/advocacy_clinical/awas_tingni/inter_american.htm [hereinafter Complaint].

the Inter–American Court of Human Rights. This was a significant move, given the relatively few cases that the Commission submitted to the Court at the time. The Commission considered it a case with both immediate and potentially far-reaching implications for the rights of indigenous peoples in relation to lands and resources.

The Proceedings Before the Court

In June 1998, the Inter–American Commission named as its assistants the Awas Tingni lawyers[20] and filed a complaint against Nicaragua before the Inter–American Court of Human Rights. The Commission designated its member, Claudio Grossman, as its delegate to the Court for the case. Bertha Santoscoy, the Commission's staff attorney who had overseen the processing of the case by that body, now worked closely with Jim Anaya to draft the complaint and subsequent submissions to the Court, as well as to prepare for and represent the Commission at the Court hearings, along with commissioners Grossman and Helio Bicudo.

In its complaint, the Inter–American Commission charged Nicaragua with essentially the same violations of international human rights that were articulated by Awas Tingni in its earlier petition to the Commission, including violations of the right to property (considered in relation to other human rights), plus a violation of the right to judicial protection.[21] The Commission adopted as its own the positions and legal theory that had been advanced by the community's attorneys, and for the most part, these were the positions and legal theory ultimately adopted by the Court. Relying on the ethnographic research and mapping described above, as well as a host of other documentation, the Inter–American Commission requested that the Inter–American Court order Nicaragua to establish and implement a procedure that would result in the prompt demarcation and specific recognition of Awas Tingni

---

20. Under the Rules of Procedure of the Inter–American Court of Human Rights then in effect, neither the victims of alleged human rights abuses nor their lawyers were permitted direct participation in the proceedings in cases before the Court, other than in the proceedings on reparations subsequent to a finding of state responsibility. However, the Rules of Procedure permitted the Inter–American Commission to appoint as its assistants the legal representatives of the victims and thereby allow their participation in the proceedings under the authority of the Commission. *See* Rules of Procedure of the Inter–American Court of Human Rights, art. 23, Basic Documents Pertaining to Human Rights in the Inter–American System (1997), OEA/Ser.L/V1.4 Rev.7 (adopted in 1996, repealed 2001) [hereinafter 1996 Rules of Procedure]. The revised Rules of Procedure of the Court, effective as of June 1, 2001, allow the victims and their legal representatives to participate directly and autonomously in all phases of the proceedings. Rules of Procedure of the Inter–American Court of Human Rights, art. 23, Basic Documents Pertaining to Human Rights in the Inter–American System (2001), in OEA/Ser.L/V/1.4 Rev.8, *available at* www.oas.org.

21. *Complaint*, *supra* note 19.

communal lands, in accordance with the community's traditional land tenure patterns, and to provide monetary compensation to Awas Tingni for the infringement of its territorial rights.[22]

Nicaragua argued for dismissal on the grounds that Awas Tingni had failed to exhaust all available domestic remedies. On February 1, 2000, the Inter–American Court unanimously ruled against Nicaragua's preliminary objections and held the case admissible.[23] As the case proceeded before the Court on the merits, the government of Nicaragua settled on a defense that rested, essentially, on the following assertions: Awas Tingni could not claim an ancestral entitlement to land because the existence of the community's village at its present location dates back only to the 1940s; the area claimed by the community is too large in proportion to the community's membership; and neighboring indigenous communities have rights to at least parts of the same area.[24]

It was never in dispute that the people of Awas Tingni moved their principal village to its present location in the 1940s. However, as the evidence presented by the Commission demonstrated, the community moved from a location a relatively short distance away within a contiguous territory that includes both the older and newer settlements and that corresponds with a pattern of land use and occupancy that dates back generations. The government never provided any documentation or testimony to disprove the evidence of Awas Tingni's historical and

---

22. The Commission's position was further elaborated, in light of the oral testimony at the hearing on the merits, in its Post–Hearing Brief. *See Final Written Arguments of the Inter–American Commission on Human Rights Before the Inter–American Court of Human Rights in the Case of the Mayagna (Sumo) Indigenous Community of Awas Tingni Against the Republic of Nicaragua*, Aug. 10, 2001, *available in English and original Spanish at* www.law.arizona.edu/depts/iplp/advocacy_clinical/awas_tingni/inter_american.htm [hereinafter Final Written Arguments of the Inter–American Commission].

23. Caso de la Comunidad Mayagna (Sumo) Awas Tingni, Excepciones Preliminares, sentencia de 1 de febrero de 2000, Corte IDH (Ser. C.) No. 67, ¶¶ 40, 51, 56, 60 (admissibility). The Nicaraguan government argued that the Awas Tingni community had not exhausted all available domestic legal remedies, and had failed to properly bring a timely legal action to assert its rights. Further, the government declared that the community did not address its request for titling to the competent central government authority, but rather to a third party without competence to adjudicate the matter. The Commission argued that the state had waived its right to assert the community's failure to exhaust domestic legal remedies by not raising the objection with sufficient specificity early in the proceedings. Alternatively, the Commission argued, even if the state had not waived its right to raise the objection, the community had, in fact, exhausted all available domestic remedies.

24. *See Reply of the Republic of Nicaragua to the Complaint Presented Before the Inter–American Court of Human Rights in the Case of the Mayagna Community of Awas Tingni*; *Final Written Arguments of the Republic of Nicaragua on the Merits of the Issue* (Case No. 11.577—Mayagna Community of Awas Tingni), *both available in English and original Spanish at* www.law.arizona.edu/depts/iplp/advocacy_clinical/awas_tingni/inter_american.htm).

continuing land tenure within the territory claimed, although it challenged the completeness of the evidence of the community's land tenure. Nor did it present any specific proof of any land entitlement on the part of neighboring communities that would trump Awas Tingni's claim, although it was undisputed that those communities asserted claims on the basis of traditional use patterns to *parts* of the same land claimed by Awas Tingni.

From the time Awas Tingni first began legal action to confront the government over the SOLCARSA concession and to assert communal land rights, officials within MARENA had sought vigorously to turn neighboring indigenous communities against Awas Tingni by emphasizing to them the dimensions of Awas Tingni's claim in relation to the surrounding geography. This tactic did give rise to tensions with and even some opposition from these neighboring communities, which are all ethnic Miskito communities, while Awas Tingni is ethnic Mayangna. But thanks especially to assistance from Maria Luisa Acosta and Armstrong Wiggins of the Indian Law Resource Center, himself a Miskito, Awas Tingni managed to build understanding with the neighboring communities and avoid confrontation over conflicting land claims, although the seeds of that confrontation would later sprout after the Inter–American Court's judgment in favor of Awas Tingni. Significantly, in the proceeding leading up to the judgment, most of these same neighboring communities joined in an *amicus curiae* submission to the Court supporting Awas Tingni and urging a comprehensive settlement of the land claims of all the indigenous communities in the region.[25]

Notwithstanding its references to the land interests of the neighboring communities, throughout the Inter–American Court's proceedings the government asserted broad authority over and discretion in the management of lands that are not yet officially titled to any individual or group. This position was based on a presumption against the existence of indigenous land and resource rights absent definitive proof within a set of narrow state-defined criteria that do not necessarily correspond with the concept of traditional tenure. Such an approach, with its underlying presumption against the existence of indigenous land or resource rights, has been shared by governments throughout the world with the result that, over time, indigenous peoples have lost effective use and enjoyment of ever greater parts of their traditional lands. In the Awas Tingni case, the government of Nicaragua was confronted with an effort to hold it to

---

25. *See* Organization of Indigenous *Síndicos* of the Nicaraguan Caribbean (OSICAN), *amicus curiae* brief, submitted to the Inter–Am. Ct. H.R. (Jan. 27, 1999). Other *amicus curiae* briefs were submitted by the Assembly of First Nations (Canada); International Human Rights Law Group (USA); Mohawk Indigenous Community of Akwesasne (USA); and National Congress of American Indians (NCAI) (USA) *all available in English and original Spanish at* http://www.law.arizona.edu/Journals/AJICL/AJICL2002/vol191.htm.

a different presumption—one in which indigenous peoples are presumed entitled to the lands they in fact have used and occupied in accordance with longstanding cultural patterns.

The clash of understandings about indigenous-state relations concerning lands and resources was nowhere more evident than in the public hearing on the merits of the case, a remarkable event that took place over two and a half days at the Court's seat in San José, Costa Rica.[26] Some thirty members of the Awas Tingni community, who had traveled to San José by bus from their remote village in Nicaragua, crammed the small courtroom along with at least an equal number of other observers. An additional thirty or so onlookers watched the event from another room through a video link set up especially for the overflow audience. The Commission presented twelve witnesses, including Awas Tingni and other indigenous leaders from the Atlantic Coast; the anthropologist Theodore Macdonald, who had assisted the community with its ethnographic study and mapping; and several others—some qualified by the Court as expert witnesses—with relevant knowledge on conditions among indigenous peoples in the Atlantic Coast and more generally on indigenous-state relations in the hemisphere.

From the testimony of the indigenous leaders unfolded a story of people and land, and of a struggle to maintain the connection between the two. The following exchange between Antonio Cançado Trindade, the President of the Court, and Awas Tingni leader Charlie Mclean illustrates the poignant nature of this testimony.

> **PRESIDENT CANÇADO TRINIDADE:** I do have just one question, I would like to ask the Secretary to project the map again. You mentioned, Mr. Mclean, that Urus Asang Hill and Kiamak Hill are sacred places, isn't that right?
>
> **WITNESS CHARLIE MCLEAN:** Yes.
>
> **PRESIDENT CANÇADO TRINIDADE:** ... I would like to know a little more about the sacred nature of those hills.
>
> **WITNESS CHARLIE MCLEAN:** Okay, this Urus Asang Hill [pointing to the map on the screen]. Do you know Mono?
>
> **PRESIDENT CANÇADO TRINIDADE:** No.
>
> **WITNESS CHARLIE MCLEAN:** Well, that is Mono [Monkey], Mono Hill. Why did they name it that way? Our grandfathers lived in that hill, so they had as their animals those that are the monkeys. Yes, so, then that grandfather died there and there they buried him. The other, Kiamak, is a sacred hill. This one also sacred. This other

---

26. *See* Transcript of the Public Hearing on the Merits (Nov. 16–18, 2000) *available in unofficial English translation and original Spanish at* http://www.law.arizona.edu/Journals/AJICL/AJICL2002/vol191.htm [hereinafter Transcript of Hearing].

is sacred. The utensils of war of our ancestors, our grandfathers, were the arrows....

PRESIDENT CANÇADO TRINIDADE: Thank you. And when you refer to our grandfathers, that is to say, "our dead," to how many generations do you refer?

WITNESS CHARLIE MCLEAN: My grandfather told me it can be some three hundred cycles, centuries, pardon, because there they have lived all the time in their life. Yes; in addition if we base it on the history, it extends over many places too, yes.

. . .

PRESIDENT CANÇADO TRINIDADE: Yes, do you have any type of homage or any symbolic homage to past generations, to your ancestors?

WITNESS CHARLIE MCLEAN: Yes.

PRESIDENT CANÇADO TRINIDADE: What do these commemorations or symbolisms to past generations consist of?

WITNESS CHARLIE MCLEAN: Yes, ... there is a part, it doesn't appear here, because it is a rustic map [he points to a sketch map projected on the screen].... So here it exists—inside of that area there is a place, it is called Quitiris—there exists a symbol that our grandfathers had a place to meet, a special place. It currently exists; the chairs there are made of stone and such.

PRESIDENT CANÇADO TRINIDADE: So you show your respect to your dead, in the Community?

WITNESS CHARLIE MCLEAN: Yes, we have respect. When we go there, we pass by greeting silently with respect. Also, our grandfathers had this ... relationship with Asangpas Muigeni. Do you know Asangpas.... [sic] ?

PRESIDENT CANÇADO TRINIDADE: No. Can you explain? I am very interested in knowing.

WITNESS CHARLIE MCLEAN: Asangpas Muigeni is the spirit of the mountain; it is the same form as a human, but it is a spirit always lives [sic] under the hills. And it has a relationship, if we base it on history, we have to speak about many things there, yes.[27]

Jaime Castillo, Awas Tingni's *síndico*, and Wilfredo Mclean, the mild-mannered director of the school and by virtue of that position a community leader and spokesman, added to the description of the community's relationship to the lands it claimed with accounts of the importance of the territory for the community's subsistence. They pro-

---

27. *Id.* at 155–156 (Nov. 16).

vided details about the community's protests of the SOLCARSA concession and the multiple fruitless efforts to have the government recognize and respect the community's rights in its traditional lands. The Awas Tingni leaders' testimony was reinforced by several persuasive indigenous advocates, including Brooklyn Rivera, the charismatic Miskito Indian coordinator of the umbrella indigenous organization, Yatama, and an official in the former central government administration. Rivera told of the feeble and ultimately ineffective government responses to indigenous land claims generally. Humberto Thompson, another Miskito leader and then a member of the Northern Atlantic Regional Council, also testified about the efforts of the central government to influence the Council to favor the logging interests, including with bribes. Guillermo Castilleja, the World Wildlife Fund officer who was present from the beginning, gave an account of the failed commitment the government made to secure Awas Tingni's land rights when it promoted and validated the MADENSA deal.

The social science and legal experts gave context for this story. Their testimony provided insights into its broader implications and validated the perspective of territorial tenure advanced by the indigenous leaders. Among the expert witnesses were the renowned anthropologist and sociologist Rodolfo Stavenhagen who, in 2001, became the first United Nations Special Rapporteur on the Human Rights and Fundamental Freedoms of Indigenous People; Roque Roldán, a Colombian lawyer with expertise and practical experience on legal developments concerning indigenous land tenure throughout Latin America; and Lottie Cunningham, a Miskito lawyer and director of the Center for Justice and Human Rights of the Atlantic Coast of Nicaragua, a non-governmental legal services organization that addresses land and other issues facing indigenous communities throughout the Atlantic Coast region.

Other expert witnesses included anthropologists Charles Hale and Galio Gurdian, whose expertise on the indigenous peoples of Nicaragua was well-known. They led a study in 1998 on indigenous land claims in the Atlantic Coast region and on the government responses to those claims. The study was commissioned by the government itself, under pressure from the World Bank and with Bank funding. In its written submissions to the Court, the government selectively cited this study in an effort to show that it had acted reasonably to address indigenous land tenure. Although the study had not been made public, once the government referred to it, the entire study became open to discussion in the Court proceedings. As Hale and Gurdian testified, the study as a whole demonstrated quite the opposite of what the government was attempting to show. In a significant blow to the government's defense, it detailed the various state policies, actions, domestic laws, and regulations that suppressed or neglected traditional indigenous land tenure.[28]

The government defaulted in its timely presentation of a witness list to the Court and hence was not permitted to present witnesses of its own. However, the Court itself called one of the government officials that Nicaragua had proposed as a witness: the General Director from the government office of Rural Titling of Nicaragua. The General Director in effect served as a government witness, and the government lawyers who cross-examined the Commission's witnesses persisted in advancing the perspective of state dominance over territory, fully ignoring the dimensions and significance of the indigenous presence. The following exchange between a government lawyer and Jaime Castillo, who signed the initial petition to the Inter–American Commission, is particularly telling.

[Government of Nicaragua] (GON): Mr. Castillo, could you tell us what distance you normally cover to hunt and fish?

WITNESS JAIME CASTILLO FELIPE (through [Mayagna] interpreter): In all the area over which we have the run of the land, we make use of different activities, without other options to work them there.

GON: Excuse me, what distance do you cover to hunt, to fish?

WITNESS JAIME CASTILLO FELIPE: He does not specify the distances, but rather he takes all the area which belongs to him, so he is not interested right now in saying from here to there.

GON: Really, the State of Nicaragua is interested in knowing that distance.

WITNESS JAIME CASTILLO FELIPE: In this case it is the government's obligation to go and recognize or know the terrain and not be asking the length without seeing things.

GON: Let's make it, eh ... we would like to emphasize that the witness refuses to answer.

PRESIDENT CANÇADO TRINIDADE: Maybe the question could be restated in relation to the extension of the area in which he moves around....

GON: It is very difficult ... he refuses....

PRESIDENT CANÇADO TRINIDADE: In a last attempt at an effort to obtain a response to that question, in hours it takes to

---

28. General diagnostic study on land tenure in the indigenous communities of the Atlantic Coast (March 1998) (*prepared by* the Central American and Caribbean Research Council) (on file with the authors).

walk, how much time does it take to move to engage in the work or the activities or the type of fishing to which the state referred?

. . .

WITNESS JAIME CASTILLO FELIPE: His normal hunting distance is a trip of fifteen days; they go to work or go to hunt and, after, they return knowing where their surrounding territories are.

PRESIDENT CANÇADO TRINIDADE: The question is answered.

GON: The question is answered, Your Honor, and let's pass to the next one within the time allotted. In order to fish or hunt in a zone with abundant fauna, in a zone with many rivers and fish, the very tributary in which Mr. Castillo lives, Mr. Castillo, is it necessary for you to walk so much to get a fish to feed your children?

WITNESS JAIME CASTILLO FELIPE: In order to maintain the territory, even if there is an abundance of animals, types of animals, the Community does not expend its resources, but rather selects what it is going to consume and, in that way, it uses a broad expanse of territory but it does not destroy and only recognizes the existence of its surrounding riches.[29]

Despite such episodes, the government remained undaunted. In his closing argument, the government's chief lawyer, Edmundo Castillo, a private sector attorney who the Foreign Ministry had contracted specifically for this case, summarized the state's assessment. He declared emphatically that Awas Tingni does not possess ancestral lands.[30] As those words were uttered, gasps could be heard from the rows in which Awas Tingni people sat, tears of pain and perhaps of rage visible in the eyes of many.

The Court's Judgment

In the end, the Inter–American Court accepted Awas Tingni's account of its relationship to the territory and ruled that the community does possess legal entitlement to the lands. After soliciting and receiving post-hearing final written arguments from the Commission and the government, the Court rendered its decision on August 31, 2001, finding Nicaragua violated relevant provisions of the American Convention on Human Rights and ordering reparations.

The Court first found that Nicaragua had violated the Convention by failing to make effective the rights of indigenous peoples to lands and

---

29. Transcript of Hearing, *supra* note 26, at 139–140 (Nov. 16).
30. *Id.* at 296–299 (Nov. 18).

resources that are recognized in general terms by the Nicaraguan Constitution and legislation. The Court pointed to the absence of an adequate state mechanism to respond to the Awas Tingni community's requests for the titling of its lands and the failure of the Nicaraguan courts to proceed on the community's legal actions in a timely manner. In this regard, the Court found violations of Article 25 of the Convention, which affirms the right to judicial protection, in connection with Articles 1 and 2, which obligate state parties to adopt the measures necessary to secure the enjoyment of fundamental rights. The Court thus established that the faithful implementation of domestic legal protections for the rights of indigenous peoples is an obligation under the American Convention on Human Rights and that states may incur international responsibility if they fail to make those rights effective.

Going beyond that part of its decision predicated on a prior existing domestic legal norm, the Court additionally found a violation of Article 21 of the Convention: the right to property. In what is the most significant and far-reaching part of its decision, the Court held that the concept of "property" as articulated in the American Convention on Human Rights includes the communal property of indigenous peoples as defined by their customary land tenure. Thus, the Court suggested that such property may exist apart from what domestic law has to say. Although it stressed that, in the case of Nicaragua, domestic law does recognize indigenous communal property, the Court affirmed that the rights articulated in international human rights instruments have "autonomous meaning that cannot be limited by the meaning attributed to them by domestic law."[31]

The Court accepted the Commission's view of the international human right of property, determining that in its meaning autonomous from domestic law, this right embraces the communal property regimes of indigenous peoples as defined by their own customs and traditions. The Court thus held that "possession of the land should suffice for indigenous communities lacking real title to property of the land to obtain official recognition of that property."[32] In arriving at this conclusion the Court employed what it termed an "evolutionary" method of interpretation, taking into account normative international develop-

---

31. Judgment, Inter–Am. Ct. H.R. (Ser. C), No. 79 at ¶ 146 (2003). The Inter–American Commission had pressed this point in its written submissions, invoking the jurisprudence of the European Court of Human Rights regarding the analogous property rights provision of the European Convention on Human Rights, and referencing developments elsewhere in international law, and institutions specifically concerning indigenous peoples' rights over land resources. *See Final Written Arguments of the Inter–American Commission, supra* note 22, at ¶ 62.

32. Judgment, *supra* note 3, at ¶ 151.

ments both within and outside of the Inter–American system.[33] In his concurring opinion,[34] Judge García Ramírez expounded upon this interpretive methodology, making reference to several key texts, including: the Commission's draft American Declaration on the Rights of Indigenous Peoples;[35] the first complete draft of the United Nations Declaration on the Rights of Indigenous Peoples, which had yet to be adopted;[36] and the International Labour Organization Convention (No. 169) on Indigenous and Tribal Peoples.[37] Judge García Ramírez further admonished due regard for indigenous peoples' own values in relation to lands and resources.

With this case, the Inter–American Court upheld an international standard of protection of indigenous land rights, affirmed that the faithful implementation of both this international standard and any domestic legal protections for the rights of indigenous peoples is a positive obligation under the American Convention on Human Rights, and established that states may incur international responsibility if they fail to make those rights effective. Exercising its authority under Article 63(1) of the American Convention on Human Rights to order reparations, the Court instructed Nicaragua to develop an adequate procedure for the demarcation and titling of the traditional lands of indigenous communities "in accordance with their customary laws, values, customs, and mores"; to proceed to demarcate and title Awas Tingni's traditional lands in particular within fifteen months; and, until the titling was complete, to refrain from allowing or tolerating any act that would affect the community's use and enjoyment of its rights over those lands.[38]

While marking a bold path in the doctrine of international law to embrace indigenous peoples' rights over land and natural resources, the Court was notably timid and less careful in its assessments of monetary reparations and the recoverable costs incurred by Awas Tingni in the

---

33. *Id.* at ¶ 146.

34. Judgment, Inter–Am. Ct. H.R. (Ser. C), No. 79 at ¶¶ 6–9 (2003) (Sergio García Ramirez, concurring).

35. *See* American Declaration on the Rights of Indigenous Peoples, *supra* note 14, and text.

36. Judge Garcia Ramirez cited the draft of the Declaration developed by the U.N. Working Group on Indigenous Peoples Peoples (erroneously calling it, however, the Proposed Declaration on Discrimination Against Indigenous Populations), then still under consideration within the UN. *See* Draft United Nations Declaration on the Rights of Indigenous Peoples, *adopted by* the U.N. Sub–Commission on the Prevention of Discrimination and Protection of Minorities, 26 August 1994, U.N. Doc. E/CN.4/Sub.2/1994/2/Add.1.

37. Convention (No. 169) Concerning Indigenous and Tribal Peoples in Independent Countries, June 27, 1989, art. 13, International Labour Conference (entered into force Sept. 5, 1990) [hereinafter ILO Convention No. 169].

38. Judgment, *supra* note 3, at ¶¶ 138, 153, 164, 173.

domestic and international proceedings. With broad reparations authority, the Court has frequently ordered non-monetary remedial measures, as it did in this case by ordering Nicaragua to demarcate and title indigenous lands. The Court also has ordered monetary relief to compensate for material and moral harm to victims and monetary compensation for legal and other costs incurred by victims in seeking vindication of their rights.[39] In prior cases, the Court had conducted extensive proceedings, sometimes over a period of months, subsequent to finding a violation of the Convention in order to determine reparations. The Rules of Procedure in effect when the Awas Tingni case was initiated before the Court reflected this practice of having a separate phase of proceeding on reparations subsequent to the merits phase.[40] Relying on this practice and the Court's Rules of Procedure then in effect, the Commission had foregone presenting specific evidence and arguments on compensable damages and costs and instead in its complaint to the Court had explicitly reserved the right to present such evidence and arguments at a subsequent reparations phase.

In the Awas Tingni case, however, the Court skipped a reparations phase, following its now preferred practice of merging consideration of the merits and reparations. Prior to issuing its decision on the merits of the case, the Court requested the Inter-American Commission and Nicaragua to provide written arguments and documentary evidence on damages and costs, and it set a deadline allowing them a mere ten days to do so. Because of an internal administrative error, the Commission did not notify the community's legal representatives of the Court's request or otherwise act on it until after the deadline had passed. Even though the community, acting autonomously through its own legal counsel, did submit a brief on damages and costs a few days after being notified by the Commission of the Court's request,[41] the Court ignored that brief in its decision. The Court referred only to the Commission's own submission on reparations, which incorporated by reference the community's arguments, and ruled it inadmissible for being untimely.[42]

Without confronting the community's or the Commission's arguments for much larger sums, and without otherwise allowing the submission of specific evidence on damages and costs, the Court ordered that, "in accordance with equity," Nicaragua invest the total sum of U.S. $50,000 "in works or services of collective interest for the benefit of the

---

39. *See generally* Dinah Shelton, *Reparations in the Inter-American System*, *in* THE INTER-AMERICAN SYSTEM OF HUMAN RIGHTS (David Harris & Stephen Livingston, eds., 1998).

40. *See* 1996 Rules of Procedure, *supra* note 20, art. 23 (stating that "[At] the reparations stage, the representatives of the victims or of their next of kin may independently submit their own arguments and evidence.").

41. *See* S. James Anaya, *supra* note 15.

42. Judgment, *supra* note 3, at ¶ 159.

Awas Tingni community" and that it pay the community U.S. $30,000 for its expenses and costs.[43] The community's post-judgment request to the Court that it reconsider its reparations decision and provide for a full reparations proceeding was summarily rejected in a terse note written by the Court's Secretary. The note admonished that neither the community nor its attorneys had standing before the Court because, under the Court's Rules of Procedure in effect at the time the case began, the victims were permitted to participate autonomously only in a reparations phase. Of course, in this case there was no reparations phase.[44]

Despite this outcome in regard to monetary reparations, the Court's decision stands on balance as a victory for Awas Tingni and other indigenous communities of Nicaragua. Furthermore, it is as an important development for all indigenous peoples in their efforts to secure rights over land and natural resources.

Implementation of the Awas Tingni Judgment

What perhaps most attests to the far-reaching nature of the Inter-American Court's judgment are the difficulties that have persisted in its implementation. Implementation has required the adoption of new administration procedures, the creation of new institutions, and the deployment of substantial financial resources to shift the matrix of entrenched policies and practices on land tenure that gave rise to the problems manifested by the *Awas Tingni* case.

Typical of countries throughout the world, Nicaragua's law and policies affecting indigenous peoples were built upon colonial-era assumptions that exclude consideration of indigenous peoples as entitled to continue as distinct, culturally differentiated communities with secure entitlements to traditional lands. Even the introduction of a new constitutional order in 1987, which recognized the indigenous communities of the Atlantic Coast and affirmed their traditional property regimes, did not accomplish an adequate departure from the legacies of the past, as the *Awas Tingni* case illustrates. Nicaragua's continuing neglect of indigenous peoples and the demands of respect for traditional land

---

43. *Id.* at 440–442, ¶ 173(6–7).

44. Note from Manuel E. Ventura Robles, Secretary, Inter–American Court of Human Rights, to Professor S. James Anaya, Legal Representative of the Awas Tingni community (December 4, 2001) (stating that the Court's decision was rendered under Regulations adopted on September 16, 1996 and that "despite the fact that Article 23 of the applicable Regulations confers *locus standi* to the representatives of the victims in the reparations phase, in the *Awas Tingni* case there was no separate reparations phase, and thus, the Court had no obligation to invoke one, neither did it have the power to receive from the community a separate brief regarding its claims in that regard.") (original Spanish note on file with the authors).

tenure came up against a newly emerging international norm that the Inter–American institutions were prepared to embrace and promote. But, as the *Awas Tingni* case further illustrates, it is one thing for norms upholding the rights of indigenous peoples to be affirmed by the international legal system; it is quite another thing for those norms, even when backed by a legally binding judgment, to take hold in people's lives.

The Court gave Nicaragua fifteen months to demarcate and title the area traditionally used and occupied by Awas Tingni; and that time came and went without the state providing the community with legal security over its lands. In fact, it was five months after the judgment that the government formally announced its adherence to the Court's orders and agreed to meet with the Inter–American Commission and the community's representatives to initiate steps toward implementation.

On February 22, 2002, government and Awas Tingni representatives met at the Washington D.C. offices of the Inter–American Commission, where the Nicaraguan Ambassador to the OAS handed the Commission a check for $30,000 to comply with the Court's order to pay the community's litigation costs. At a day-long meeting on April 16, 2002, held in a highly formal setting at the Nicaraguan Foreign Ministry in Managua, delegates of various government agencies, representatives of the Awas Tingni community, and the Inter–American Commission met to discuss implementation of the remaining aspects of the Court's judgment.

A new leader joined the community's delegation to the April 2002 meeting. Melba Mclean, sister of Charlie Mclean, was then the only university educated member of Awas Tingni. Her presence at the meeting that day was soft-spoken but powerful, and she emerged from the meeting a key figure in the subsequent efforts to secure the land title mandate by the Inter–American Court's judgment. Another new face at the meeting was Luis Rodriguez–Piñero, whom Jim Anaya had recruited to join the legal team to assist with the judgment's implementation. He would become a trusted advisor to Mclean and other community leaders and come to spearhead much of the legal work in the implementation process. Also joining Awas Tingni's legal team during the later implementation phase would be Lottie Cunningham, the Miskito lawyer who had testified at the Court hearing in the case.

The meeting started with a tense debate about basic concepts of international state responsibility and the meaning of the judgment. Thanks in no small measure to Ms. Mclean, the atmosphere eventually softened and a cooperative spirit emerged, ultimately leading to the formation of two joint government-community commissions to negotiate the terms of implementation. The first joint commission dealt with the Court's order to invest $50,000 in social services for the community, which was invested in a boarding house for Awas Tingni children who must travel to Puerto Cabezas to attend school.[45] The other commission, which handles the most essential aspect of the judgment—the mandate to secure Awas Tingni in the possession of its land through a deed of title and other measures—is a longer story.

The Sluggish Progress Toward Domestic Compliance

Undoubtedly, the case has resulted in an important step toward ensuring land tenure security more generally for the indigenous communities of Nicaragua. In January 2003, the Nicaraguan General Assembly adopted the much-awaited *Law 445, Communal Property Regime Law of the Indigenous and Ethnic Communities of the Atlantic Coast Region of Nicaragua and the Rivers Bocay, Coco, Indio and Maiz*[46] ("Law 445"). With this law, Nicaragua affirms indigenous land occupation, usufruct and natural resource use rights, and traditional tenure. It also establishes the administrative bodies responsible for titling communal lands: the National Commission for Demarcation and Titling (*Comisión Nacional de Demarcación y Titulación*, "CONADETI"), which was created in June 2003; and three "intersectoral" commissions of demarcation and titling (each referred to as a "CIDT"), which were created in August 2003. Upon the enactment of the new law, the Nicaraguan government declared that it complied with that part of the Inter–American Court's decision in the *Awas Tingni* case requiring the adoption of an "effective mechanism" for demarcating and titling indigenous lands in Nicaragua. However, thus far, Law 445 has not proven to be such an effective mechanism. Establishing a new legal framework to process indigenous land claims based on customary tenure is a complex process, often at odds with the domestic regime, that is unaccustomed and, in fact, formerly hostile to recognizing and protecting these kinds of claims.

According to Law 445, a community must submit a "diagnostic study" of its land tenure and socio-economic characteristics along with its titling application.[47] The government insisted on a new study of Awas

---

45. *See* Ministerio de Relaciones Exteriores, Informe a la Corte Interamericana de Derechos Humanos en el caso de la Comunidad Mayagna Awas Tingni 2–4 (Feb. 21, 2005).

46. Ley del Régimen de Propiedad Comunal de los Pueblos Indígenas y Comunidades Étnicas de las Regiones Autónomas de la Costa Atlántica de Nicaragua y de los Ríos Bocay, Coco, Indio y Maíz, Ley N° 445, La Gaceta Diario Oficial No. 16 del 23 de enero de 2003.

47. *Id.* at art. 46 (requiring that the study is to consist of: a) The historical background of the petitioning community; b) The demographic social, economic and cultural characteristics of the petitioning community; c) The traditional forms of management, use and tenancy for the requested area; d) The names of the indigenous or ethnic communities and other entities or persons occupying the land adjacent to the requested areas; e) Any possible conflicts that may arise between the petitioning community or communities and the neighboring communities or with third parties).

Tingni, rejecting as incomplete and biased the mapping and ethnographic work done by the community prior to the Court's judgment. With the community's agreement, the government commissioned the Awas Tingni diagnostic study to private consultants financed by Proyecto de Ordenamiento de la Propiedad (PRODEP), the World Bank's Land Administration Project in Nicaragua. The study was undertaken in June and July of 2003 by a consultant group composed of Alistar–Nicaragua, the Centro de Investigación y Documentación de la Costa Atlántica ("CIDCA") of the Universidad Centroamericana ("UCA"), and Idaho State University, with community participation under the supervision of government technicians. It confirmed that the lands claimed by Awas Tingni were part of a territory in which the Mayangna people have lived for some 6,000 to 8,000 years. Its final assessment of Awas Tingni's present use of its ancestral territory indicated that the community occupies, and in some manner uses or projects influence over, a territory of 125,000 hectares, which includes areas of economic and productive use as well as areas of historic and cultural value. Further, the study showed that 41,000 hectares of this same area were also claimed by neighboring Miskito communities.

Awas Tingni maintained the position that the government was obligated to demarcate and title their lands by virtue of the judgment of the Inter–American Court, without the community itself having to take any further initiative to that effect. Nonetheless, in the face of continuing government inertia, on November 11, 2003 Awas Tingni submitted an application for titling under the newly-enacted Law 445, along with the government-sanctioned diagnostic study. It was the first application to be submitted under the law. The five-stage demarcation process established by Law 445 consists of application, conflict resolution, demarcation, titling, and title clearance.[48] Despite the fact that Law 445 requires applications to be initially reviewed and acted upon within thirty days, the community's request was before the initial processing agency, the local CIDT, for more than a year with no action. At that time the CIDT still had no internal procedures by which to process applications. Once these measures were established and the application was processed, CIDT mistakenly transferred it to CONADETI, the final titling agency, rather than to the Regional Council, which under Law 445 must first resolve any existing overlapping land claims before the application is considered for demarcation and titling. In December 2004, CONADETI in turn referred the community's application to the Demarcation Commission of the Regional Council. Although Law 445 states that the Regional Council must resolve the dispute in three months, it did not initiate the conflict resolution stage until March 2005 and did not finalize the process until February 2007, almost two years later.

---

48. *Id.* at arts. 39–51.

Certainly, the institutions in charge of processing indigenous land claims under Law 445 have been hamstrung by technical and financial limitations and influenced by political pressures, which are all largely beyond their immediate control. Among the more measurable factors contributing to the inefficiency of Law 445 are the lack of adequate training for the members of institutions responsible for land demarcation; the lack of sufficient financial support for the demarcation and titling processes; and a central government that for years appeared at best ambivalent to any commitment to title indigenous lands according to the criteria of traditional land tenure mandated both by the Inter-American Court and Law 445. The representatives of the institutions created by Law 445 have had little or no prior technical experience, support, or training in the areas of land demarcation. CIDT and CONADETI had no operational budget, paid staff, or permanent facilities in 2003 and 2004, since the central government did not create the fund authorized to finance these institutions at the time Law 445 was enacted. Similarly, the Demarcation Commission of the Regional Council did not receive funds for its conflict resolution activities until 2005.

The implementation process has also been influenced by the shifting of political forces in power since the Inter-American Court's decision. CONADETI and CIDT are composed of elected representatives of the various indigenous and ethnic groups in the Atlantic Coast, as well as representatives from all levels of government, which makes maintaining political neutrality throughout their largely technical mandate a difficult proposition.

The Problem of Overlapping Land Claims

Exacerbating the delays in processing the Awas Tingni land titling application were the overlapping land claims of three neighboring Miskito communities, Francia Sirpi, Santa Clara, and la Esperanza (known collectively as Tasba Raya), which had surfaced during the litigation leading to the judgment. These communities first arrived in the area close to Awas Tingni when the Nicaraguan Agrarian Institute ("INRA") resettled them from the Rio Coco area to the north in the 1970s. INRA issued them titles to relatively small portions of land adjacent to areas that Awas Tingni has continued to use and occupy. On the basis of their projected needs, coupled with expanding land use patterns, these Miskito communities eventually claimed areas extending well beyond their titled lands and into Awas Tingni ancestral territory. The claims of the Tasba Raya communities were documented and mapped in the 1998 *General Diagnostic of Land Tenure of the Indigenous Communities of the Atlantic Coast*, produced by the Central American and Caribbean Research Council ("CACRC") under the coordination of anthropologists Charles Hale and Galio Gurdian. This is the study the government selectively cited during the Inter–American Court proceedings.

The problems arising out of the overlapping land claims originate in part from the demarcation process itself, which tends to impose fixed boundaries between indigenous communal lands when those boundaries traditionally have been fluid and have even recognized shared use areas and joint access to natural resources. Correspondingly, the two-dimensional process of mapping is inherently limited in its ability to represent the complexity of indigenous customary land tenure patterns. The CACRC maps depicting the Tasba Raya and other communities' claims represented the overlapping claims with intersecting lines and boxes and, in doing so, perhaps over-simplified and obscured the multi-faceted nature of customary indigenous land tenure. Thus, the very process of demarcating and titling Awas Tingni lands ignited tensions between it and the neighboring communities and aggravated fears on the part of the Tasba Raya communities that official recognition of Awas Tingni lands would negate their rights within the overlap area. This was despite the spirit of cooperation and coexistence that had prevailed between the indigenous communities for years. If anything, the actions of Nicaraguan officials fomented the conflict, as government lawyers attempted to do during the Inter–American Court proceedings. Government officials have repeatedly cited the conflict between Awas Tingni and its neighbors as the reason Awas Tingni lands still are not titled, diverting attention from the lack of institutional capacity and political will necessary to advance the demarcation and titling process.

Beginning in 2005, well after Awas Tingni submitted its land titling application under Law 445 and the overlapping claims became apparent, the Demarcation Commission of the Northern Atlantic Regional Council held a series of sessions with representatives of the Tasba Raya and Awas Tingni communities to attempt to mediate a solution to the overlapping land claims. Until then, both the Demarcation Commission and the Regional Council had remained mostly idle with respect to their duties under Law 445 to resolve overlapping claims. When the efforts at a mediated solution finally failed in late 2006, the Regional Council moved to dictate its own resolution to the conflict in accordance with Law 445. On February 15, 2007, the Regional Council divided the 41,000 hectares of the overlap area between the communities, assigning 20,000 hectares for the exclusive use of Awas Tingni.[49] The remaining 21,000 hectares, excluding the Awas Tingni sacred sites and places still inhabited by Awas Tingni families (such as its historical settlement of Tuburus), were divided equally among the three Tasba Raya communities.[50]

---

49. Consejo Regional de la Región Autónoma del Atlántico Norte, Resolución No. 0—14–02–2007 (Feb. 14, 2006).

50. *Id.* at art. 2.

Finally, the resolution called upon CONADETI to proceed to demarcate and title all of Awas Tingni lands in accordance with the official diagnostic study and the settlement of the overlapping claims.[51]

In determining the rights of the Awas Tingni and the Tasba Raya communities in the overlap area, the Regional Council did not distinguish between the Mayangna indigenous groups, which have maintained a long-standing use of the overlap area, and the Miskito communities, which were relocated to the area by the Nicaraguan government in the 1970s. Rather, the Regional Council concluded that both the Mayangna and Miskito are indigenous groups that "have maintained a historical continuity of the now-called Autonomous Region of Nicaragua."[52] By treating the Awas Tingni community and the Tasba Raya communities as equal rights-holders within the overlap area, the Regional Council implicitly concluded that their divergent customary land tenure claims warrant equivalent protections under Law 445.

The Council resolution provided an overly simplistic solution to a complex problem. Still, this process makes clear that the government institutions charged with the far-reaching mandate of demarcating and titling indigenous lands according to customary land tenure are grappling with their own limitations and still evolving to fulfill their mandate. In the meantime, the Awas Tingni community has been forced to adapt its claim to fit the limited and not fully developed legal and administrative regimes in order to proceed with the demarcation and titling of its ancestral territory.

The next stages of the process will consist of demarcation, titling, and title clearance of Awas Tingni traditional lands. The title clearance stage refers to the duty of the state to recognize the Awas Tingni territory free and clear of any prior questionable or illegal titles, registrations or recognitions that were provided to non-community members either implicitly or expressly. This stage can be expected to create further difficulties, since it will deal with the rights and presence of third parties on Awas Tingni lands, including non-indigenous peasant farmers who have recently moved there from other parts of the country with government encouragement. For some time, the Nicaraguan government failed to deal with this problem and in fact contributed to its exacerbation, even in the aftermath of the Inter–American Court's judgment. In several cases, government authorities issued permits to outsiders to log or even settle on Awas Tingni lands, despite the Court's order to the contrary.

In response to the encroachment of its lands by third parties, the community requested a new intervention by the Court less than a year

---

51. *Id.* at art. 3.
52. *Id.*

after the 2001 decision. In September 2002, the Inter-American Court issued a Provisional Measures Resolution—a type of resolution issued by the Court only in cases of "extreme gravity and urgency."[53] The Court ordered the Nicaraguan government to adopt affirmative measures to protect the lands and natural resources of the Awas Tingni community.[54] Despite this, the destructive actions of third party loggers and settlers, in fact, intensified for a period. The community has considered arrangements with some loggers and settlers, such as leasing agreements, though problems can be expected to continue with groups who claim the government awarded them land titles within Awas Tingni territory.

The situation became even more complex in the aftermath of Hurricane Felix, which passed like a bullet over the Awas Tingni community in September 2007 and reduced almost all of their ancestral rainforest to an impenetrable mass of tree trunks and sticks. In this sad twist in the Awas Tingni story, the community lost within a matter of hours the forest and resources that it had fought for years to protect. Community members fear that others will take advantage of the chaos to further exploit resources within Awas Tingni lands; in fact, various logging companies have approached individuals with proposals to extract the valuable fallen hardwood. Nevertheless, the community remains focused on moving forward the physical demarcation and titling of their lands—though now this process is combined with efforts to rebuild their thatch-roof houses and livelihoods and to begin the slow process of rehabilitating their forest ecosystem.

Importance of the Case in Shaping Human Rights Law

The delays associated with the implementation process have raised significant questions about the administrative measures necessary to transform legal recognition of indigenous property rights into a practical protection of those rights. Even though the 2001 decision of the Inter-American Court did not by itself immediately and conclusively resolve the land claims of Awas Tingni and other indigenous communities in Nicaragua's Atlantic Coast, the decision has been a significant catalyst towards that end. The Court's intervention prompted Nicaragua to accept that specific measures are needed to secure indigenous peoples' land rights in accordance with contemporary norms. What is more, it fostered greater awareness and the deployment of greater government

---

53. Statute of the Inter-American Court of Human Rights, art. 25, O.A.S. Res. 448 (IX–0/79), O.A.S. Off. Rec. OEA/Ser.P/IX.0.2/80, Vol. 1 at 98.

54. Provisional Measures Solicited from the Government of Nicaragua by the Representatives of the Victims, Resolution of the Inter-American Court of Human Rights, Sept. 6, 2002, *available at* http://www.law.arizona.edu/depts/iplp/advocacy/awastingni/documents.cfm?page=advoc.

energies toward meeting that need, however inadequate they still may be.

The Inter–American Court's judgment in *Awas Tingni*, moreover, represents a significant step in the development of international human rights law, especially as it concerns indigenous peoples regionally and globally. In the years since this landmark decision, the Court has reaffirmed and built upon its holding that indigenous peoples' have property rights based on their traditional land tenure and that these rights are protected as a matter of law under the American Convention on Human Rights, in particular in a series of cases against Suriname and Paraguay.[55] In *Sawjoyamaxa Indigenous Community v. Paraguay*, the Inter–American Court reviewed and synthesized its jurisprudence on the land rights of indigenous peoples, affirming that within the Inter–American human rights system:

(1) [t]raditional possession by indigenous peoples of their lands has the equivalent effect of full title granted by the state;

(2) traditional possession gives the indigenous the right to demand the official recognition of their land and its registration;

(3) the members of indigenous peoples that for reasons outside their will have left or lost possession of their traditional lands maintain their right to the property, even when they do not have legal title, except when the lands have been legitimately transferred in good faith to third persons; and

(4) members of indigenous peoples that involuntarily lost possession of their lands which have been legitimately transferred to innocent third parties, have the right to recover them or to obtain other lands of equal size and quality.[56]

In its own adjudication of cases since *Awas Tingni*, the Inter–American Commission has contributed a jurisprudence that builds upon that judgment, including through the case of the *Maya Indigenous Communities v. Belize*. Unlike in Nicaragua, the legal system in Belize provided no recognition of indigenous land rights on the basis of traditional tenure. Rather, Belize's legal system supported the active neglect of the Maya communities' traditional land tenure and the granting of concessions to log and explore for oil on their lands. Yet, in a 2004 decision, the Inter–American Commission reaffirmed the existence of an "autonomous" property right irrespective of state recognition. In this

---

55. *See, e.g.* Moiwana Cmty. v. Suriname, Inter–Am. Ct.H.R (Ser. C) No. 124 (2005); Yakye Axa Indigenous Cmty. v. Paraguay, Inter–Am. Ct.H.R. (Ser. C) No. 125 (2005); Sawhoyamaxa Indigenous Cmty. v. Paraguay, Inter–Am. Ct.H.R. (Ser. C) No. 146 (2006); Saramaka People v. Suriname, Inter–Am. Ct.H.R. (Ser. C) No. 172 (2007).

56. *Sawhoyamaxa*, Inter–Am. Ct.H.R. (Ser. C) No. 146 (2006), at ¶ 128.

case, the Commission construed the right to property of Article XXIII of the American Declaration of the Rights and Duties of Man. It made clear that "the property rights of indigenous peoples are not defined exclusively by entitlements within a state's formal legal regime, but also include that indigenous communal property that arises from and is grounded in indigenous custom and tradition."[57] On October 18, 2007, the Supreme Court of Belize handed down a landmark decision affirming the rights of the indigenous Maya communities of Belize to the land and resources that they have traditionally used and occupied and declared that these rights are protected under the Belize Constitution in light of relevant international law.[58] The judgment in favor of the Maya communities was significantly informed throughout by the 2004 final report of the Commission in the case of the Maya of Belize, and the Supreme Court stated that, although the recommendations were not in themselves binding, it could "hardly be oblivious to them: and may even find these, where appropriate and cogent, to be persuasive."[59]

Likewise, in its final report in the case of *Mary and Carrie Dann v. the United States*, the Inter–American Commission built upon the *Awas Tingni* decision and explicitly linked the interpretation of the property rights provisions of the American instruments with the broader universe of developments and trends in the international legal system regarding the rights of indigenous peoples.[60] On the basis of these developments, the Commission identified "general international legal principles developing out of and applicable inside and outside of the inter-American system."[61] These principles of general international law include essentially the same principles summarized by the Inter–American Court in the *Sawjoyamaxa* case referred to above.

---

[57]. Maya Indigenous Cmty. of the Toledo District, Belize, Case No. 12.053 (Belize), Inter–Am. C.H.R. Report No. 40/04 (merits decision of Oct. 12, 2004), at ¶ 117.

[58]. Claims No. 171, 172 (2007), Aurelio Cal and Manuel Coy et al. v. The Attorney General of Belize and the Minister of Natural Resources and Environment (Oct. 18, 2007).

[59]. *Id.* at ¶ 22.

[60]. Mary and Carrie Dann, Case 11.140 (United States), Inter–Am. C.H.R. Report No. 75/02 (merits decision of Dec. 27, 2002).

[61]. *Id.* at ¶ 131. The Commission cited the following general principles: the right of indigenous peoples to legal recognition of their varied and specific forms and modalities of their control, ownership, use and enjoyment of territories and property; the recognition of their property and ownership rights with respect to lands, territories and resources that they have historically occupied; and where property and user rights of indigenous peoples arise from rights existing prior to the creation of a state, recognition by that state of the permanent and inalienable title of indigenous peoples relative thereto and recognition that such title may only be changed by mutual consent between the state and respective indigenous peoples when they have full knowledge and appreciation of the nature or attributes of such property. This also implies the right to fair compensation in the event that such property and user rights are irrevocably lost. *Id.*

As suggested by the Commission, the *Awas Tingni* case and the jurisprudence it has spawned simultaneously draws from an array of international developments and helps to consolidate them into a norm that is part of both conventional and general, or customary, international law. Prominent among these developments is the adoption in 1989 by the International Labour Organization of its Convention (No. 169) Concerning Indigenous and Tribal Peoples in Independent Countries; the adoption by the U.N. General Assembly on September 13, 2007 of the United Nations Declaration on the Rights of Indigenous Peoples;[62] and the discussions of the Organization of American States toward the adoption of a declaration on indigenous rights.[63] ILO Convention No. 169 affirms the "rights of ownership and possession of the [indigenous] peoples concerned over the lands which they traditionally occupy and use," and it provides related guarantees.[64] The text of the U.N. Declaration on the Rights of Indigenous Peoples and the draft American Declaration on the Rights of Indigenous Peoples, which is still under discussion, affirm indigenous land rights in even stronger terms. The *Awas Tingni* decision effectively extended the reach of the land rights norm articulated in ILO Convention 169 beyond the eighteen states that thus far have ratified it. The case also helped to transform discussions on the U.N. Declaration, which led to its eventual adoption, and helped to shift the ongoing discussions on the proposed American Declaration toward a focus on what the international norm of indigenous land rights already is and not just what it should be.

So, the remote hamlet of Awas Tingni has catalyzed a process for the defense of lands and access to life-sustaining resources. That process has yielded a now often-cited decision by the Inter–American Court of Human Rights, a decision affirming that states are obligated to recognize and adopt specific measures to protect indigenous peoples' rights to land and natural resources in accordance with their own traditional use and occupancy patterns. That the Court grounded this obligation in the right to property of the American Convention on Human Rights has implications for states beyond those that are parties to that treaty. The right to property is affirmed in numerous other international human rights

---

62. United Nations Declaration on the Rights of Indigenous Peoples, *supra* note 5. For a description and analysis of other norm-building developments concerning the rights of indigenous peoples, including land rights, *see* S. JAMES ANAYA, INDIGENOUS PEOPLES IN INTERNATIONAL LAW 156 (2d ed. 2004).

63. Proposed American Declaration on the Rights of Indigenous Peoples (Approved by the Inter–Am. C.H.R. on February 26, 1997, at its 1333rd session, 95th Regular Session), OEA/Ser./L/V/.II.95 Doc.6 (1997). Later draft provisions for American Declaration on the Rights of Indigenous Peoples are in *New Compendium of Proposals for the Phase of Review of the Draft American Declaration on the Rights of Indigenous Peoples*, OEA/Ser.K/XVI, GT DADIN/doc.276/06 rev. 4 (Dec. 8, 2006).

64. ILO Convention (No. 169), *supra* note 37.

instruments—including the American Declaration of the Rights and the Duties of Man, which is considered as expressive of the human rights obligations of all members of the OAS; and the Universal Declaration of Human Rights, which is regarded as customary international law.

Furthermore, the *Awas Tingni* case reinforces broader developments and helps to crystallize a specific norm of general or customary international law upholding indigenous land rights. The case signals that indigenous peoples' rights to ancestral lands and resources are a matter of already existing international law derived from the domain of universally applicable human rights. The community of Awas Tingni's successful invocation of the universal human right to property calls on states and the international community to avoid the discrimination of the past and embrace indigenous modalities of property, rather than exclude them. In doing so, it marks a new path for understanding the rights and status of the world's indigenous peoples.

*

5

The Law of the Republic Versus the "Law of the Brothers:" A Story of France's Law Banning Religious Symbols in Public Schools

Karima Bennoune*

"Simplicity is killing us."
Malika Zouba, Algerian journalist living in France

Religious fundamentalisms represent one of the greatest contemporary threats to human rights, including the human rights of women.[1] Yet, this topic remains largely obscured in much of the human rights literature outside of the specialized field of women's human rights. International human rights scholarship and critique has often instead fetishized issues of identity and portrayed a range of complex socio-

---

* The author would like to thank James McGhee and Emily Anderson for excellent research assistance. Moreover, she is deeply grateful for the help of Marieme Hélie–Lucas and Jeanne Favret–Saada, and for the time of all those who spoke with her in France. This Chapter was supported by funding from the Dean's Research Fund at the Rutgers School of Law, Newark.

1. *See, i.e.*, HILARY CHARLESWORTH & CHRISTINE CHINKIN, THE BOUNDARIES OF INTERNATIONAL LAW: A FEMINIST ANALYSIS 249 (2000). "Fundamentalism" is a term used by parts of the international women's human rights movement. Here it refers to "political movements of the extreme right, which, in a context of globalization ... manipulate religion ... in order to achieve their political aims." Marieme Hélie–Lucas, *Dossier 23/24: What is Your Tribe? Women's Struggles and the Construction of Muslimness*, WOMEN LIVING UNDER MUSLIM LAWS, 2001, *available at* http://www.wluml.org/english/pubsfulltxt.shtml?cmd$87)=i–87–2789. One advantage of the language of fundamentalisms is that it speaks across religious boundaries about movements within many traditions, including Christianity, Hinduism, Islam and Judaism. Note that those interviewed here often used the French terms *"Islamistes"* and *"intégristes"* to refer to the movements they described. The author alone is responsible for the specific language used in the English translation as most interviews were conducted originally in French, and translated by her into English.

political questions as simple matters of difference and individual rights to freedom of religion. No topic has more thoroughly manifested these shortcomings than the regulation of headscarves in French public schools.

In the polarizing post-September 11 environment, many international human rights advocates and other critical voices have understandably been concerned with not appearing to be "Islamophobic"[2] or to buy into the Bush Administration's failed terrorism narrative. To avoid these pitfalls, such voices have often responded with a thin anti-racist account of the headscarf controversy in France, an account simply pitting a racist French state against headscarved Muslim girls who are being hampered from expressing their individual religious beliefs.[3] In this narrative, the mass of white French citizens support the law, while the undifferentiated "Muslims" oppose it. All of the internal politics and debate among Muslims, and those of Muslim, North African, and Arab heritage, on this topic are thereby "disappeared." The aim of this Chapter is to complicate the simplified human rights story of the 2004 French Law on Religious Symbols ("the 2004 Law" or "the Law"),[4] and to place the issue firmly within the context of contemporary struggles over and with religious fundamentalisms.

---

2. The term "Islamophobia" denotes hostility toward Islam and Muslims generally, and has been argued to be a part of European society since the Eighth Century. *See* COMMISSION ON BRITISH MUSLIMS AND ISLAMOPHOBIA, ISLAMOPHOBIA: ISSUES, CHALLENGES AND ACTION 7–8 (2004), *available at* http://www.insted.co.uk/islambook.pdf. Undoubtedly, discrimination against people of Muslim origin has been a grave challenge to human rights in the era of the "War on Terror." *See* Combating Defamation of Religions, Comm'n on Human Rights Res. 2004/6, ¶¶ 6, 16, U.N. Doc. E/CN.4/RES/2004/6 (Apr. 13, 2004). However, some prominent dissidents of Muslim heritage have staunchly criticized the concept of Islamophobia as "confus[ing] criticism of Islam as a religion and stigmatization of those who believe in it." See, *e.g.*, *Writers Issue Cartoon Row Warning*, BBC NEWS, Mar. 1, 2006, *available at* http://news.bbc.co.uk/1/hi/world/europe/4763520.stm. These criticisms of the term "Islamophobia" are shared by some interviewed here. *See* discussion at note 63.

3. For example, *see* Peter Danchin, *Suspect Symbols: Value Pluralism as a Theory of Religious Freedom in International Law*, 33 YALE J. INT'L L. 1, 21–25 (2008); Jane Freedman, *Women, Islam and Rights in Europe: Beyond a Universalist/Culturalist Dichotomy*, 33 REV. INT'L STUDIES 29–44 (2007); JOAN SCOTT, THE POLITICS OF THE VEIL (2007); Johnathan Sugden, *A Certain Lack of Empathy*, HUMAN RIGHTS WATCH (July 1, 2004), *available at* http://www.hrw.org/english/docs/2004/07/01/turkey8985.htm; *Memorandum to the Turkish Government on Human Rights Watch's Concerns with Regard to Academic Freedom in Higher Education, and Access to Higher Education for Women who Wear the Headscarf*, Human Rights Watch Briefing Paper, 26–29, 37–38 (June 29, 2004), *available at* http://hrw.org/backgrounder/eca/turkey/2004/headscarf_memo.pdf [hereinafter *Memorandum to the Turkish Government*].

4. Law No. 2004–228 of March 15, 2004, Journal Officiel de la République Française [J.O.] [Official Gazette of France], Mar. 17, 2004, p. 5190, *available at* http://www.legifrance.gouv.fr/WAspad/UnTexteDeJorf?numjo=MENX0400001L.

This human rights law story is told primarily through conversations conducted in 2007 with women's rights activists, journalists, religious figures, and scholars of Muslim, Arab or North African heritage living in France who support the Law on Religious Symbols. Their voices have mostly been left out of the Anglophone version of this debate, and they provide particular insights into the difficult questions raised.[5] This Chapter does not purport to represent the full spectrum of opinions in the Muslim population or in France generally concerning the 2004 Law.[6] The opposition of some Muslims to the French ban on religious symbols in public schools has already been highly publicized. Telling the often overlooked "other" side of the story demonstrates that the policy debate about headscarves in school is not just a question of identity, but of political choices with political consequences. The voices of those interviewed here should also serve as a reminder that, in the field of human rights, we need to be wary of making easy assumptions about the correlation between identity and opinion and that we cannot proceed blind to context.

This story also underlines the need to complexify the concept of identity whenever we address it. Identity is multi-faceted, shifts over time and place, and may be affected by politics and context in a range of ways. It is not necessarily immutable. This is made clear by the words of a North African woman activist recounted to the author during this research. She reportedly said, "When I arrived in France I was told I was an immigrant. Then I became Moroccan. And now we are all called Muslims, whether we are practicing or not."[7]

---

5. Opinions critical of the Law have already received a great deal of airtime and can be found elsewhere in the literature. *See, for example,* the interviews of veiled girls and women conducted in Adrien Katherine Wing & Monica Nigh Smith, *Critical Race Feminism Lifts the Veil? Muslim Women, France and the Headscarf Ban*, 39 U.C. DAVIS L. REV. 743 (2006) and FRANÇOISE GASPARD & FARHAD KHOSROKHAVAR, LE FOULARD ET LA RÉPUBLIQUE (1995).

6. Most of those interviewed here are of North African or Arab origin and from regions that have historically produced the largest Muslim and Arab immigration to France. Some seventy percent of France's Muslim population of 5–6 million are from Algeria, Morocco and Tunisia. *See Muslims in Europe: Country Guide*, BBC NEWS ONLINE, Dec. 23, 2005, *available at* http://news.bbc.co.uk/2/hi/europe/4385768.stm. This significant North African presence in part explains the interrelationship between developments in the Maghreb and France that many of those interviewed here describe. Note, however, that the French Muslim population is becoming increasingly diverse as Turkish and South Asian immigration increases. The use of the term Muslim "population," rather than Muslim "community" in this Chapter is a deliberate choice intended to reflect this frequently overlooked diversity. *See* Saleh Bachir and Hazem Saghieh, *The "Muslim community": A European invention*, openDemocracy, Oct. 16, 2003, *available at* http://www.open democracy.net/conflict-terrorism/community_2928.jsp.

7. One estimate suggests that of the approximately five million members of what is called France's Muslim community, only 700,000 are actually practicing Muslims. *See* John

The French Law on Religious Symbols in Public Schools: A Brief History and Overview

Many of those interviewed stressed the importance of precision in describing the 2004 Law. They felt that the Law's scope had been overblown by its opponents. Concerned with setting the record straight, they wanted to make clear that under the 2004 Law, the headscarf, and any other "ostentatious" religious symbols of any denomination, are banned only in public schools.[8] The Algerian journalist and activist Malika Zouba—who lives in France—stressed, "[pro-veil] activists make people believe that the veil has been banned everywhere."[9] It is not prohibited in any other public space or even in public universities.

The 2004 Law may be translated as follows: "In [primary] schools, junior high schools and high schools, signs and dress that conspicuously show the religious affiliation of students are forbidden."[10] It was adopted on March 15, 2004, and entered into force in September 2004, just in time for the start of the school year. The broader effect of the Law, including on Sikhs in France, merits consideration but lies beyond the scope of this Chapter, which focuses solely on the relationship between the 2004 Law and the headscarf. Given the approach taken by the European Court of Human Rights in Şahin v. Turkey,[11] it is most likely that the Court would find the French law to be in accordance with the European Convention on Human Rights. In Şahin, the Court found Turkey's ban on Islamic headscarves and beards in public universities

---

Lichfield, *So were the French right all along?*, THE INDEPENDENT (London), Oct. 19, 2006 at 36.

8. Note that even prior to the adoption of the 2004 Law, civil servants were prohibited from displaying religious symbols, including the veil, while carrying out their official duties.

9. Interview with Malika Zouba, in Paris, France (June 8, 2007) (notes on file with the author). Only the first quote from an interview will be footnoted. Each subsequent quote from the same individual is drawn from the same cited interview, unless otherwise noted.

10. This translation is from *French Lawmakers Overwhelmingly Back Veil Ban*, MSNBC, Feb. 10, 2004, http://www.msnbc.msn.com/id/4231153/print/1/displaymode/1098/. The relevant portion of the original French law reads: "Dans les écoles, les collèges et les lycées publics, le port de signes ou tenues par lesquels les élèves manifestent ostensiblement une appartenance religieuse est interdit." Law No. 2004–228 of March 15, 2004, *supra* note 4.

11. Leyla Şahin v. Turkey, App. No. 44774/98, Eur. Ct. H.R., Fourth Section (June 29, 2004). The judgment was affirmed by the Grand Chamber in Leyla Şahin v. Turkey, App. No. 44774/98, Eur. Ct. H.R. (Nov. 10, 2005), *available at* http://www.echr.coe.int/echr. The Court's approach here has been criticized by some in the human rights world. *See, e.g.*, Sugden, *supra* note 3 and *Şahin*, App. No. 44774/98, at ¶ 11 (dissenting opinion of Judge Tulkens). For a defense of the reasoning in *Şahin*, see Karima Bennoune, *Secularism and Human Rights: A Contextual Analysis of Headscarves, Religious Expression, and Women's Equality Under International Law*, 45 COLUM. J. TRANSNAT'L. L. 367–426 (2007).

not to be a violation of human rights. The Court emphasized the particular importance of secularism to the protection of human rights in the Turkish context and the margin of appreciation to be afforded governments in matters concerning the relationship of religion and state.

In French schools, the controversy that led to the adoption of the 2004 French Law erupted in September 1989 when three girls were expelled from a high school in Creil for refusing to remove the *foulard islamique*,[12] which their principal found to contravene the principle of *laïcité*.[13] *Laïcité*, a particularly French notion of secularism, is a basic principle governing the French state about which there appears to be a high degree of public consensus.[14] It was forged in the historic battle over the role of the Catholic Church in France that culminated in the 1905 Law separating church and state.[15] Following the Creil controversy, in November 1989, the Conseil d'État[16] ruled that the wearing of religious symbols in schools did not per se contradict the principle of *laïcité*. According to that ruling, displaying such symbols in school contravened *laïcité* only when the symbol as worn constituted an act of pressure, provocation, or proselytizing, or threatened the rights of another student, or otherwise disturbed public order. Between 1989 and 1994, three ministerial circulars attempted to clarify the matter further. The first held that teachers should determine the acceptability of symbols like the headscarf on a case-by-case basis; the second reaffirmed secularism in public schools; and the third suggested the permissibility of banning "ostentatious" religious symbols, including the headscarf.

---

12. The *foulard islamique*, known in Arabic as the *hijab*, covers the hair, neck and shoulders, and often the outer rim of the face. It is sometimes accompanied by a long dark cloak, or *djilbab*, which conceals the shape of the body, and it is sometimes worn with gloves. The even more restrictive *niqab* covers everything but the eyes. Famously, the *burka* hides even those. Joan Scott has argued that the headscarf and the veil are not the same thing and that the difference between these terms is elided in discussions of the 2004 Law. Joan Scott, *Symptomatic Politics: The Banning of Islamic Headscarves in French Public Schools*, 23 FRENCH POLITICS, CULTURE & SOC'Y 106, 108 (2005). Nevertheless, these two terms appear interchangeably for stylistic reasons in this Chapter. Though the author recognizes that each of the named garments is distinct, this range of clothes—chosen for their "modesty"—raises many similar issues.

13. On the history of the Law, see the detailed exposition in Hanifa Chérifi, *Rapport à monsieur le ministre de l'éducation nationale de l'enseignement supérieur de la recherche, Applications de La Loi du 15 Mars 2004 Sur le Port des Signes Religieux Ostensibles dans les Établissements d'Enseignement Publics*, 30–33 (July 2005) [hereinafter Chérifi Report].

14. For further information, *see* HENRI PENA-RUIZ, SECULARITY AND THE REPUBLIC (2007).

15. Law of Dec. 9, 1905 Journal Officiel de la République Francaise [J.O.] [Official Gazette of France], Dec. 11, 1905 (concerning the separation of church and state), *available at* http://www.assemblee-nationale.fr/histoire/eglise-etat/sommaire.asp#loi.

16. The Conseil d'État is the highest administrative court in France, with final jurisdiction over cases involving executive actions. It also serves a range of legislative, administrative and judicial functions.

However, far from resolving the matter, the controversy only grew, particularly subsequent to the media coverage of the first episode. By 1994, some 3000 girls were seeking to wear the headscarf in French schools. During that period, the issue was dealt with largely on a case-by-case basis, usually involving negotiation. For some, this represented the ideal way to resolve such disputes. For others, this produced a piecemeal approach that, they argue, resulted in more girls being excluded from school for wearing headscarves before the adoption of the 2004 Law than were excluded after it came into effect. Many teachers and principals were unsure how to proceed. Numerous disputes arose, complete with strikes both by those supporting the veil and by teachers opposing it, and protracted administrative proceedings. When girls faced problems in schools for wearing headscarves, they were vigorously supported by Muslim fundamentalist organizations which campaigned for the "right to veil."[17]

These Muslim fundamentalist organizations enthusiastically promoted their agenda among high school students in particular. Girls facing discipline for seeking to veil in school were often given great media attention and regarded as heroes by their supporters. Some girls veiled because they wanted to or believed it to be an expression of their religious beliefs. Others wore the headscarf because they were coerced by family members, neighbors or others in the community. Some veiled out of teenage rebellion against teachers or more liberal parents, some to express protest against the French state or international events like the Iraq war. Others donned the veil to express pride in their heritage, or because they had internalized misogynist views about modesty, or to gain respect, or because they clearly supported a theocratic agenda, and many for a combination of some or all of these reasons.[18] Regardless of the individual motivations, for many teachers, the resulting disputes were terribly difficult to resolve. One such fracas in 2000 concerned an eight-year-old girl whose Iranian father and French mother wanted her to go to school veiled. When this possibility was rejected by her teachers, she was moved to a different school.

In July 2003, in light of what some interpreted as mounting attacks on the principle of *laïcité*, French president Jacques Chirac created the Stasi Commission. This body included some prominent individuals of Muslim heritage, and its mandate was to investigate the application of *laïcité* in France and make recommendations to the President. In its December 2003 report, the Commission recommended, *inter alia*, the

---

17. Chérifi Report, *supra* note 13, at 32.

18. For discussion of the range of motives claimed by school girls seeking to wear the *foulard islamique, see* Wing, *supra* note 5, and GASPARD & KHOSROKHAVAR, *supra* note 5.

adoption of a law banning religious symbols in schools—a law similar to the one subsequently adopted in 2004.[19]

When the Law was promulgated, some of its opponents predicted that near civil war would result in France. International reaction was highly charged. Some human rights groups criticized the Law using rights-based arguments.[20] Meanwhile, a group calling itself "The Islamic Army in Iraq" abducted two French journalists on August 20, 2004, and these hostages were shown on Al Jazeera pleading for President Chirac to lift the headscarf ban and save their lives. The abduction produced a backlash among Muslim opponents of the ban in France, many of whom felt it was a matter for the population of France to decide without outside interference—especially of such a coercive and violent nature.

On the first day of the academic year in fall 2004, a total of 240 religious symbols appeared in schools. All were Muslim headscarves except for two Christian crosses and one Sikh turban.[21] Of these, only seventy students refused to remove the symbol in question. Subsequently, during the first weeks of the school year, the number of religious symbols in schools slowly rose. However, the Law's supporters largely viewed the process of implementing the ban as a success. For example, Hanifa Chérifi, an education expert of Algerian origin who authored the official report on the implementation of the Law for the French Minister of Education in July 2005, stressed the importance of the preparation of the teacher corps and the seriousness of the dialogue that was carried out with students.[22] According to the Minister of Education's 2004 implementation circular for the Law, dialogue was always to precede discipline.

Ultimately, during the 2004–2005 academic year, forty-four students were suspended for wearing the headscarf and three for wearing the Sikh turban, usually after long processes of dialogue and negotiation with students and families were exhausted (according to Chérifi, that is nearly 100 fewer than the number of students who were expelled in 1994–95 under the previous educational policy.) Another ninety-six students are reported to have either transferred to private schools, enrolled in correspondence courses or left school (only those over sixteen). The analogous numbers for the subsequent school years are difficult to

---

19. COMMISSION DE RÉFLEXION SUR L'APPLICATION DU PRINCIPE DE LAÏCITÉ DANS LA RÉPUBLIQUE, RAPPORT AU PRÉSIDENT DE LA RÉPUBLIQUE (Dec. 11, 2003) *available at* http://lesrapports.ladocumentationfrancaise.fr/BRP/034000725/0000.pdf.

20. *See, e.g., France, in* AMNESTY INTERNATIONAL, ANNUAL REPORT 2005, *available at* http://web.amnesty.org/report2005/fra-summary-eng; Press Release, Human Rights Watch, *France: Headscarf Ban Violates Religious Freedom* (Feb. 27, 2004), *available at* http://hrw.org/english/docs/2004/02/26/france7666.htm.

21. Chérifi Report, *supra* note 13, at 11.

22. *Id.* at 7–10.

obtain as there has been no official follow-up to the Chérifi report.[23] While the expulsions and departures are a most unfortunate result, the numbers were much lower than predicted. Furthermore, these statistics do not quantify the number of girls who, thanks to the Law, felt less coercion in school because the ban reinforced their personal choice not to wear the headscarf, despite familial or community pressure to do so. Concern in human rights circles has been almost exclusively for the welfare of those girls seeking to veil, with little thought to the human rights of those who did not wish to be coerced into doing so.

The story of the politics surrounding the 2004 Law requires careful decoding. Supporters of the Law come from across the political spectrum, including both the truly Islamophobic and members of the far-right with an anti-immigrant agenda, and principled champions of secularism, leftwing anti-fundamentalists and progressive women's rights campaigners including many of Muslim and North African heritage. Some *beur*,[24] immigrant and Muslim organizations—such as the Council of Democratic Muslims, and the Federation of Amazighe (Berber) Associations of France, as well as some women's rights groups with significant North African membership like *Ni Putes, Ni Soumises* (Neither Whores, Nor Submissives), and anti-racist groups like *S.O.S. Racisme* and Africa 93— came out in support of the Law in the name of women's rights, integration and secularism. The Law's opponents are also diverse, including Muslim fundamentalists, some practicing and secular Muslims, some on the left and the far left, and some human rights activists and feminists. Most often, these opponents characterize the Law as a violation of religious or academic freedom, an expression of racism, or simply a bad idea. Much like the nasty debates about legal regulation of pornography and prostitution among feminists, the debate about the 2004 Law has been highly polarized and divisive. However, it has not followed the simple lines of white French (pro) versus Muslim (con), as has been painted in much of the English-language literature. Like many human rights stories, this is a debate that goes beyond identity and one that is heavily grounded in the Law's context.

Understanding the French Law on Religious Symbols in Context: Feminist and Anti–Fundamentalist Stories about the 2004 Law

The Core Question of Fundamentalism

In most of the stories told about the 2004 Law by those interviewed for this Chapter, the single most important factor was the emergence of

---

23. A British news report in October 2006 claimed that by then only forty-five Muslim girls in France had "been forcibly excluded from school for refusing to bare their heads." Lichfield, *supra* note 7.

24. This term, adopted from Parisian slang for "Arabs," refers to persons of North African/*maghrebi* descent who have grown up in France.

Islamic fundamentalism both internationally and in France. In the era of globalization, these stories conceptualize the debate as one that is inherently transnational. What happens in Algeria,[25] Iran, Lebanon, or other countries on these issues has tremendous significance in France. Hence, for many of the experts interviewed here, the growth and power of religious extremist movements, both internationally and in France, and their stance vis-à-vis women's rights imbue the struggle over headscarves in schools with particular political meaning. This should complicate the human rights response. In France, the ideology of the Muslim Brotherhood[26] has permeated numerous civil society associations and federations, becoming a powerful force. Hanifa Chérifi has argued that these groups have chosen to focus on questions of identity that have a powerful resonance with a young generation suffering from the failures of integration.[27] The fundamentalists seek the implementation of their own repressive version of Islamic law over Muslim populations and countries, advocate the separation of the sexes, oppose women's human rights and equality, and have sometimes used or advocated violence to achieve these ends or to punish those who oppose their agenda.

For Algerian journalist Mohamed Sifaoui, famous for having infiltrated Al Qaeda in France,[28] the contemporary issue of the veil in French schools can only be understood in the context of the rise of fundamentalist Islam.[29] Though certain forms of veiling such as the old-school *haik* (a

---

25. Throughout most of the 1990s, a violent struggle raged between the Algerian government, backed by the military, and armed fundamentalist groups seeking to create a theocratic state. The fundamentalist project of creating a theocratic state in Algeria represented a particular assault on basic human rights, including the rights of women. In practice, both sides committed atrocities, but the fundamentalists particularly targeted secularists, intellectuals, journalists, artists, women activists and unveiled women for assassination and carried out large scale massacres of villagers. As many as 200,000 people may have lost their lives during the conflict. *See, i.e.*, Hugh Roberts, *Under Western Eyes: violence and the struggle for political accountability in Algeria*, MIDDLE EAST REPORT, 39–42 (Spring 1998); MAHFOUD BENNOUNE, ESQUISSE D'UNE ANTHROPOLOGIE DE L'ALGÉRIE POLITIQUE (1998); Louisa Ait–Hamou, *Women's Struggle Against Muslim Fundamentalism in Algeria: Strategies or a Lesson For Survival?*, in WARNING SIGNS OF FUNDAMENTALISMS 117–124 (Ayesha Imam et al. eds., 2004); and, *Compilation of Information on the Situation in Algeria*, WOMEN LIVING UNDER MUSLIM LAWS, No. 1 March 1995 (on file with author).

26. Founded in Egypt in 1928 by Hasan al-Banna, the Brotherhood views its own radical interpretation of Islam as a comprehensive way of life and political system.

27. *ISLAM Rencontre* (Interview with Hanifa Cherifi), SOCIÉTÉ, Nov. 20, 2001, available at http://www.humanite.fr/popup_imprimer.html?id_article=253771.

28. *See* MOHAMED SIFAOUI, MES "FRÈRES" ASSASSINS: COMMENT J'AI INFILTRÉ UNE CELLULE D'AL-QAÏDA (2003).

29. Interview with Mohamed Sifaoui, in Paris, France (June 8, 2007) (notes on file with the author).

loose white silk cloak worn with a lace kerchief over the lower face) were advocated by some North African traditionalists, the wearing of the *foulard islamique* was taken up by fundamentalist groups as part of their broader agenda.[30] Sifaoui traces this back to the late 1980s, a time which also corresponds to the rise of fundamentalist groups in Algeria. The liberal former Mufti of Marseille, Soheib Bencheikh, who is now director of that city's *Institut Supérieur des Sciences Islamiques*, agrees with Sifaoui. Bencheikh underscores that, "[w]e are not talking about any veil. We are talking about an Iranian-style or Saudi-style garment; sometimes even worn with gloves. This is the avant-garde of a creeping ideology."[31] Dress became symbolically important and powerful in the political struggle within the Muslim population. Some of the young, male fundamentalists began to wear long robes and skull caps, and to grow prominent beards. As *beur* anti-racist activist Mimouna Hadjam joked, "they looked like the representatives of God on earth. You with your Western outfit, how can you compete?"[32]

Making a clear distinction between traditional or practicing Muslims and those for whom Islam is part of a political project aimed at theocracy, Sifaoui carefully delineates that, "this is not a question of Islam, but of Islamism." Chérifi has also warned of the danger of confusing someone who is merely a believer with a fundamentalist.[33] This mistake is to be avoided, but not by pretending fundamentalism does not exist. Sifaoui criticizes not only those who fail to recognize fundamentalism, but also those "on the other side in the extreme right who say that the Qu'ran is all about violence. We must find a balance." For him the Qu'ran is an important and valuable source of spirituality, but not of law or politics. Lalia Ducos, a retired Algerian beautician and feminist who has lived in France for many years, points to the tremendous confusion in public discourse in the post September 11 era between Arabs, Muslims, fundamentalists and even terrorists. In her view, this has had a very negative impact on young people of Muslim or Arab heritage in France.[34]

---

30. Note that the *foulard islamique* is not a traditional garment for North Africans or for many of Muslim heritage from other parts of the Muslim world. *See* Marieme Hélie-Lucas, *International Veils*, WOMEN LIVING UNDER MUSLIM LAWS, Oct. 23, 2006, *available at* http://www.wluml.org/english/newsfulltxt.shtml?cmd[157]=x-157-539225.

31. Interview with Soheib Bencheikh, in Marseille, France (June 11, 2007) (notes on file with the author).

32. Interview with Mimouna Hadjam, in Paris, France (June 12, 2007) (notes on file with the author).

33. *ISLAM Rencontre, supra* note 27.

34. Interview with Lalia Ducos, in Paris, France (June 8, 2007) (notes on file with the author).

Zazi Sadou, a well-known women's rights advocate and founder of the *Rassemblement Algérien des Femmes Démocrates*, also sees the problem of headscarves as grounded in the emergence of fundamentalism. "The first generation [of North African women immigrants to France] came in traditional clothes with perhaps a small scarf over part of their hair. But the first Islamic veil appeared in France at exactly the same time as the rise of the Islamic Salvation Front (FIS) in Algeria."[35] Making a literal connection in this regard, Mimouna Hadjam, who works with the anti-racist NGO Africa 93 in the northern Paris *banlieues*, [36] said that in those neighborhoods, fundamentalist activists became particularly visible in 1991 and 1992.[37] This occurred as the Algerian government cracked down on such groups and individuals at home and many fled to France, where they gained asylum more easily than did their secular opponents.[38] Hadjam exclaimed, "I am all for the right to asylum, but why did these guys get visas when women in danger [from the fundamentalist groups] could not get them?"

For Sifaoui, the Islamic veil is a symbol of militancy, regardless of the individual motivations of the women wearing such garb. The underlying fundamentalist political agenda is linked to the effect of the veil on personhood. In his estimation, "A woman under a burka or veil whose face or head we cannot see ... has been reduced to a thing." He asks, "Is uniforming Muslim women a good idea?" According to Sifaoui, this is the ultimate form of depersonalization.

The choice in France is stark, as Sifaoui sees it. "Either we leave our Muslim fellow citizens at the mercy of the fundamentalists and suffer the consequences. Or we help our Muslim fellow citizens to join the train of modernity, even while staying attached to their traditions." Meanwhile, as he describes it, on the other side, groups like the *Union des Organisations Islamiques de France* (UOIF) and the *Conseil Européen des Fatwas et de la Recherche*—which issues *fatwas*, or Islamic law rulings, concerning Muslims throughout Europe—have been pushing ceaselessly for Muslim women in Europe to wear the veil in all contexts.

---

35. Interview with Zazi Sadou, in Marseille, France (June 11, 2007) (notes on file with the author).

36. This term, which roughly translates as "suburbs," now refers specifically to the "depressing, outer-city high-rise housing estates which have become identified with France's working-class and multiethnic postcolonial populations." Carrie Tarr, *Maghrebi–French (Beur) Filmmaking in Context*, in BEUR IS BEAUTIFUL: A RETROSPECTIVE OF MAGHREBI-FRENCH FILMMAKING 2 (Cineaste 2007).

37. For a more detailed account of Hadjam's views on the headscarf controversy in the context of fundamentalism, *see* Mimouna Hadjam, *L'Islamisme contre les femmes partout dans le monde*, PENSAMIENTO CRÍTICO, Oct. 6, 2004, *available at* www.pensamientocritico.org/mimhad0405.htm.

38. *See* LEILA HESSINI, FROM UNCIVIL WAR TO CIVIL PEACE: ALGERIAN WOMEN'S VOICES 19 (1998).

For an example of the strident advocacy of veiling to which Sifaoui refers, consider the *fatwa* issued by the *Conseil Européen des Fatwas et de la Recherche* regarding the duty of Muslim women and girls in Europe to cover their heads. It proclaims:

> We are determined to convince the Muslim woman that covering her head is a religious obligation. God has prescribed this modest dress and the scarf for the Muslim woman so that she can be distinguished from the non-Muslim woman and the non-practicing woman. Thus, by her dress, she presents herself as a serious and honest woman who is neither a seductress nor a temptress, who does no wrong either by her words or by any movement of her body, so that he whose heart is perverse cannot be tempted by her....[39]

The *Cercle d'Étude de Réformes Féministes*, a French women's group that studies and promotes women's rights, commented on this *fatwa*.

> The first of the reasons cited [for women to cover] is the visibility of the Muslim woman, and making an obvious distinction between her and other women. The marking of distinction which constitutes discrimination or makes discrimination possible ... is understood here as a positive objective. Moreover, it is about marking the difference from, or even the superiority over, other women who are neither "serious nor honest" or who "do wrong"....[40]

Lalia Ducos, who is currently an activist with the group *20 Ans Barakat*,[41] also traces the evolution of the hijab question in France to the rise of Algerian fundamentalist groups, drawing a long historical arc. For her, this history is crucial to understanding the situation today. She stresses the grim reality that many Algerian women and others have paid with their lives for not wearing the veil. To illustrate, she tells the story of Warda Bentifour, an Algerian teacher who was killed in front of her students by an armed fundamentalist group during the 1990s conflict in Algeria for refusing to veil. Many Algerians in France support the Law, she argues, because they "have fled fundamentalism and atrocities [in Algeria] and don't want to see the same problems reproduced in their country of asylum...." Soheib Bencheikh, who is also of Algerian origin, echoes the sentiment that, especially those who come from countries that have seen the rise of fundamentalism (Algeria, Iran,

---

39. *Conseil Européen des Fatwas et de la Recherche*, fatwa No. 6, in *Recueil de Fatwas*, Série No. 1, Avis Juridiques Concernant les Musulmans d'Europe 7 (2002) *available at* www.c-e-r-f.org/fao–180bis.htm, along with commentary on the *fatwas* by the *Cercle d'Étude de Réformes Féministes* [translated by the author].

40. *Id.*

41. This organization focuses on the reform of discriminatory family law in North Africa, and in Algeria in particular. For more information, *see* http://20ansbarakat.free.fr/.

etc.), recognize the danger.[42] Such immigrants and refugees warn that, based on their experiences in their home countries, if the fundamentalists are victorious in schools, this problem will only spread.

Education is a deliberate target of fundamentalist struggle within many religious traditions around the world.[43] For example, American science teachers now reportedly shy away from teaching evolution to avoid disputes with Christian fundamentalists.[44] Given this centrality of education in fundamentalist strategy, Marieme Hélie–Lucas, an Algerian sociologist who now lives in France, agrees with Bencheikh and others that the danger is not only the Muslim fundamentalist demand to allow the headscarf in schools, but that this is only the first of escalating demands. As she says, the fundamentalists "always start with women. That is a weak point because everyone is prepared to trade women's rights."[45] As she and others view it, the demand for "the right to veil" is part of a broader fundamentalist agenda to force Muslim children to eat *halal* meat in school, to keep Muslim schoolchildren out of physical education, co-educational swimming and situations involving *mixité* (mixing of the sexes), and even to restrict or change curricular content, especially in the sciences, a demand familiar to Americans. Furthermore, for Hélie–Lucas, if one gives in on the question of the headscarf in school, this will strengthen the hand of the fundamentalists in achieving these other goals, and demanding even more.[46] As she notes ironically, the fundamentalists claim "the right to be different, and then the right to persecute those who want to be different [from them]." Indeed, for Asma Guénifi, a psychologist who volunteers with the women's group *Ni Putes, Ni Soumises* (Neither Whores Nor Submissives), the insertion of the veil in schools is part of an Islamist project that has as its goal a society based on separation between the sexes.[47] Sadou also adjures that

---

42. *See*, for example, CHAHDORTT DJAVANN, BAS LES VOILES! (2003).

43. *See, e.g.*, KEVIN PHILLIPS, AMERICAN THEOCRACY: THE PERIL AND POLITICS OF RADICAL RELIGION, OIL, AND BORROWED MONEY IN THE 21ST CENTURY (2006), CHETAN BHATT, LIBERATION AND PURITY: RACE, NEW RELIGIOUS MOVEMENTS AND THE ETHICS OF POSTMODERNITY 242–244 (1997) and Karima Bennoune, *"A Disease Masquerading as a Cure": Women and Fundamentalism in Algeria, An Interview with Mahfoud Bennoune, in* NOTHING SACRED: WOMEN RESPOND TO RELIGIOUS FUNDAMENTALISM AND TERROR 75, 80, 88 (Betsy Reed ed., 2002).

44. Cornelia Dean, *Evolution Takes a Back Seat in U.S. Classes*, N.Y. TIMES, Feb. 1, 2005, at F1.

45. Interview with Marieme Hélie–Lucas, in Marseille, France (June 11, 2007) (notes on file with the author).

46. On a related note, for a view of the adoption of the Law as a blow to the Muslim fundamentalist movements in France, see the comments of Nadia Chaabane from the Assocation of Tunisians of France in ASFAD, FACE AUX INTÉGRISTES, FACE AU SEXISME, DIX ANS DE LUTTE POUR LES DROITS DES FEMMES DU MAGHREB, ICI ET LÀ-BAS 65 (2005).

47. Interview with Asma Guénifi, in Paris, France (June 12, 2007) (notes on file with the author).

if the veil is normalized in school, the fundamentalists will then move on to their next demand—perhaps the banning of sex education. It is the failure of critics of the Law to see this context that is most disconcerting to those interviewed here.

Ducos expressed her great frustration with those such as the anti-racist organization *Les Indigènes de la République*, who justly criticize racism in France but fail to equally critique Muslim fundamentalism. She also articulated her dismay that anti-fundamentalist voices do not get a hearing in the media. Malika Zouba, a journalist who was forced to flee Algeria during the 1990s and now has asylum in France, notes that "if you demonstrate against the cartoons of the Prophet Mohamed[48] you'll get shown on TV, but if I demonstrate against the Family Code,[49] I won't get any attention." Hélie–Lucas, who founded the network of Women Living Under Muslim Laws, notes that there had been very few demonstrations of veiled women against the Law inside France, and many demonstrations in support of the Law, including by people of Muslim heritage. However, precisely the opposite has been portrayed by the media outside of France. Furthermore, both Sifaoui and the Tunisian-born anthropologist Jeanne Favret–Saada maintain that what Muslim fundamentalists say, including about the question of women and the veil, needs to be studied carefully and made widely known.[50] They argue that these groups have played on the lack of knowledge of their ideology and strategy, especially in liberal and human rights circles.

Indeed, a common theme for progressive anti-fundamentalist *beurs*, Muslims, and North African immigrants who support the Law is their frustration with some Western leftists, liberals and human rights advocates who they feel do not support them—their logical counterparts—in the struggle against fundamentalism. These particular left, liberal and human rights voices are seen not to recognize both that the fundamentalists' project for Europe is antithetical to their own professed values

---

48. This refers to the cartoons of the Prophet Mohamed published in Denmark in 2005 that sparked worldwide protest and controversy. *See* JEANNE FAVRET-SAADA, COMMENT PRODUIRE UNE CRISE MONDIALE AVEC DOUZE PETITS DESSINS (2007).

49. Here she refers to Algeria's gender discriminatory family law which has been the subject of a protracted struggle by the women's movement. For more information *see* Karima Bennoune, *Between Betrayal and Betrayal: Fundamentalism, Family Law and Feminist Struggle in Algeria*, 17 ARAB STUDIES QUARTERLY 51 (1995) and Karima Bennoune, *The International Covenant on Economic, Social and Cultural Rights as a Tool for Combating Discrimination Against Women: General Observations and a Case Study on Algeria*, 184 INT'L. SOC. SCI. J. 351, 360–363 (2005).

50. Interview with Jeanne Favret–Saada, in Marseille, France (June 11, 2007) (notes on file with the author). For these two authors' most recent written contributions to that end, *see* FAVRET-SAADA, *supra* note 48, and MOHAMED SIFAOUI, COMBATTRE LE TERRORISME ISLAMISTE (2007).

and is central to the headscarf debate.[51] Developing this critique, Favret–Saada identifies some Muslim fundamentalist groups as important allies of the Catholic Church in its opposition to women's rights and homosexuality.[52] This Catholic Church social project is often clearly opposed by those same Western leftwing, liberal and human rights figures. However, Mohamed Sifaoui argues that such linkages are overlooked. He explains to French leftists and *"droits de l'hommistes"* that "the Muslim fundamentalists are *our* extreme right." As Favret–Saada acerbically notes, "the Islamists are happy to meet Europeans who are so naïve ... and talk only about [religious] discrimination." Zazi Sadou opines that "those who see [the Law] only as racism do not understand fundamentalism and the pro-veil campaign of the fundamentalists. Hence, they understand the veil only as a cultural sign, but not as an ideological uniform." It is perhaps logical that this political matrix is more visible to critics of Muslim heritage than to Western liberals and human rights advocates. As Mimouna Hadjam explains, "We did not discover Islamic fundamentalism on September 11, 2001. We have been living with it for 20 years."

Interestingly, though sharing much of the analysis of the other commentators, Zouba specifically views the headscarf as not only a question of fundamentalism but also a trope for the desperate situation of many immigrants and their children in the French *banlieues* (slums where many Muslim populations live). She sees it as "a way to have an identity in a country where you are blocked, where you do not exist." Though she is a vigorous opponent of the veil, as well as a supporter of the Law, she also understands headscarving in France as a way for the dispossessed to widen the gap between themselves and the rest of society in protest, "to frighten them with our veils." Ultimately, paradoxically, it is a way for them to render discrimination against themselves more visible.[53] At the same time, she also underscores the influence of fathers, brothers, and of mosques on girls who veil. And she too points a finger at the Iranian revolution and Algerian fundamentalist groups in explaining how the demand to veil in schools became such a big issue when it was

---

51. For further elaboration of this key point, *see also Statement to the World Social Forum*, WOMEN LIVING UNDER MUSLIM LAWS, Jan. 20, 2005, *available at* http://www.wluml.org/english/newsfulltxt.shtml?cmd[157]=x-157-103376 and Marieme Hélie–Lucas, *The Enemy of My Enemy is Not My Friend: Fundamentalist Non State Actors, Democracy and Human Rights*, WOMEN LIVING UNDER MUSLIM LAWS, Sept. 3, 2006, *available at* http://www.wluml.org/english/newsfulltxt.shtml?cmd[157]=x-157-544539.

52. *See* Carla Power, *The New Crusade: Fighting for God in a secular Europe, conservative Christians, the Vatican and Islamic militants find a common cause*, NEWSWEEK, Nov. 8, 2004, *available at* http://www.newsweek.com/id/55637/page/2.

53. For a more detailed exposition of Zouba's thoughtful views on the subject, *see* Malika Zouba, *Un débat difficile et miné*: *Voile et dépendance*, 59 CONFLUENCES MÉDITERANÉE 33 (Fall 2006).

not so for earlier generations of Muslim immigrants. Similarly, Bencheikh, who does indeed identify the headscarf as "a subject of ideology," also recognizes that it may be the "clothing of the poor," as it "hides whether you have had your hair done or have fashionable clothes."

As these analyses might suggest, Hélie–Lucas and others blame the failures of the French state for the success of fundamentalist movements in France. "Like in Algeria, when the French state refuses to provide services, the fundamentalists rush in, and they also provide their ideology. When the state is not doing its job, it leaves space to these fascist organizations." She and others particularly highlight the terribly high, disproportionate rate of unemployment in the *banlieues*, which creates a fertile ground for fundamentalist recruitment and conditions ripe for the manipulation of legitimate grievances. While the general rate of unemployment in France is at about ten percent, it is reported to be at least fifty percent among youth in the *banlieues*.[54] Sifaoui points out that all of this has allowed the fundamentalists to say to Muslims in France, "Look, we told you the French would not consider you citizens. Come back to us and we will defend you." Favret–Saada comments that if the Socialists in power in the 1980s had responded effectively to the demands of the anti-racist and immigrant rights movements at the time of the *Marche des Beurs*,[55] the Muslim fundamentalists could never have been so successful in Diaspora populations in France. Ducos warns ominously that it is very dangerous not to resolve these pressing social problems. Her point has been hammered home dramatically by the renewal of urban violence in the *banlieues* in November 2007.[56]

The Difficult Question of Racism

This brings us to the question of the role of racism in the dynamics surrounding the Law. Many in the international human rights community, as well as other commentators, have dismissed the ban on religious symbols in public schools (usually referred to simply and mistakenly as the ban on headscarves) as a manifestation of French racism, xenophobia, or exclusionary conceptions of citizenship, particularly in the post-

---

54. *See Crisis in France*, BUSINESS WEEK, Nov. 21, 2005, *available at* http://www.businessweek.com/magazine/content/05_47/b3960013.htm.

55. On Dec. 3, 1983, 100,000 people marched in Paris for equality and against racism and police violence. This movement was notable for its progressive coalition of blacks, *beurs* and whites. *See* Boris Thiolay, *Vingt ans après la Marche des beurs*, L'EXPRESS.FR, Dec. 3, 2007, *available at* http://www.lexpress.fr/info/societe/dossier/integration/dossier.asp?ida=412853.

56. *See* Hugh Schofield, *The hyper-president's biggest problem*, BBC NEWS, Nov. 28, 2007, *available at* http://news.bbc.co.uk/2/hi/europe/7116978.stm.

September 11 world.[57] Even a well-known supporter of the Law like Fadela Amara, a founder of *Ni Putes, Ni Soumises* who became France's Urban Affairs Minister in 2007, has warned that "the issue of the veil has become for some a new political argument for stigmatizing Muslims and the *banlieues*."[58] France has a terrible history of colonialism and colonial manipulation of the concept of women's rights in many of the countries like Algeria, from which its Muslim immigrants came. In today's France, racism against those who originate from such countries and their descendents persists and constitutes a systemic obstacle to their enjoyment of human rights. How should this affect the thinking and advocacy strategies of the human rights community concerning the 2004 Law? While some restrictions on religious expression are consonant with human rights law, according to the UN Human Rights Committee, permissible restrictions cannot be "imposed for discriminatory purposes or applied in a discriminatory manner."[59]

On the other hand, Chérifi claims that, despite the stereotypical portrayals of the views of Muslims in France in the international media, a majority support the Law. For others, like Mimouna Hadjam, whose human rights career began in the French anti-racist movement working against discriminatory police violence in the 1980s,[60] racism against Muslims, Arabs or immigrants is too simple an explanation for the adoption of the Law. Certainly, in her opinion, racism endures in France, especially in the field of employment, though she feels that discrimination is a problem shared by the working class of any background. Despite her view that racism is not the motivation for the Law, she recognizes that veiled women and girls are indeed sometimes the target of discrimination. For example, she stressed that if she found out that a veiled girl had been attacked by racists on a train, she would be the first one to defend her.

Echoing a common refrain among many of those interviewed for this Chapter, Malika Zouba argues that rather than the 2004 Law being racist, it is racist to assume that the veil is "naturally" to be found on Muslim and North African women's heads. "Yes, racism here is a real problem," she concedes, "and you have to be careful not to be used by the Islamophobes. But, allowing another discrimination [veiling] is not

---

57. *See, e.g.*, Leti Volpp, *The Culture of Citizenship*, 8 THEORETICAL INQUIRIES IN LAW 571 (2007) and JOAN SCOTT, *supra* note 3.

58. FADELA AMARA & SYLVIA ZAPPI, NI PUTES, NI SOUMISES 107 (2003) (author's translation).

59. U.N. Human Rights Committee, *General Comment No. 22: The Right to Freedom of Thought, Conscience and Religion (Art. 18)*, ¶ 8, U.N. Doc. CCPR/C/21/Rev.1/Add.4 (July 30, 1993).

60. This violence proved deadly and sparked widespread unrest. *See* FAUSTO GIUDICE, ARABICIDES: UNE CHRONIQUE FRANÇAISE 1970–1991 (1992).

fighting discrimination. Banning the veil is not against Islam. It is against discrimination against girls [and women]." Jeanne Favret–Saada cautions that the actual racism against immigrants in France "does not mean that a victim of racism is incapable of being himself an oppressor." Furthermore, Zouba argues that the real struggle against all forms of discrimination begins with the Law, but must not stop there. Otherwise, "the Islamophobes will have won." As she explains:

> My struggle goes beyond the veil. It starts with the struggle against the veil, but does not stop there. Otherwise, I am looking at my community as a racist, if I am blind to other suffering and discrimination besides the veil. Any youth with an Arab name applying for a job will have a 15–20% chance of actually getting it. (I am being optimistic here.)

This recalls Leti Volpp's important point that the Stasi Commission made many other recommendations for improving the situation of Muslims in France beyond the adoption of the Law, including the creation of an anti-discrimination authority and the adoption of official school policies against racism. So far, the Law on Religious Symbols is the only recommendation to be adopted by the legislature.[61] Zouba also points out that, while opposing the scarf and the coercion sometimes used to purvey it, one has to be very careful not to perpetuate the stereotype of all immigrant Muslim men in the *banlieues* as "thieves, rapists and veilers" [*voleurs, violeurs, voileurs*].[62] She is clear that she wants nothing to do with those "who are on my side [of the headscarf issue] because it gives support to their prejudices against Muslims."

Those interviewed expressed diverse opinions about the very concept of what is called "Islamophobia."[63] Zouba uses the term "Islamophobia" freely, and Ducos has used it in her writing. In contrast, Hadjam is uncomfortable with the word, as she considers the concept an artificial construct. Hélie–Lucas rejects it altogether, preferring instead to speak of racism. She absolutely agreed that racism in France needs to be fought, but as a form of discrimination, not as Islamophobia. She sees the use of the notion of "Islamophobia" as a hallmark of the fundamentalist strategy. "When one confronts the fundamentalist agenda, they [fundamentalists and their supporters] say that what you are doing is

---

61. Volpp, *supra* note 57, at 593. President Sarkozy and Minister Fadela Amara have recently promised a controversial new "Marshall Plan for the *banlieues*" that is supposed to improve life in the suburbs by promising more law enforcement, employment, transportation and better schools. *See* Tracy McNicoll, *Fadela Amara: Madame Marshall Plan*, NEWSWEEK, Mar. 1, 2008, *available at* http://www.newsweek.com/id/117816.

62. She borrowed this framework from Thierry Leclère, *En stigmatisant les garçons des cités, le mouvement Ni putes ni soumises a-t-il faussé le débat?*, TÉLÉRAMA, Numéro 2865 2004-12-11.

63. *See* discussion above, *supra* note 2.

against Islam." The concern with the concept of Islamophobia largely emanates from the fear that it may confuse legitimate criticism of a religion or religious practices with discrimination against adherents of the religion. Bencheikh, a former Mufti with a religious education from Al Azhar University in Cairo,[64] describes the problem as follows: "We must preserve the debate on religion itself, but protect Muslims from attacks." While religious discrimination is a real problem, spurious allegations of such prejudice must not be allowed to disable human rights-based critique of what is claimed to be religious practice when it violates the rights of women or others.

The Meanings of the Veil

At the heart of this debate is the meaning of the headscarf itself. Some, like U.S. academic Joan Scott, have imputed positive significance to the veil, perhaps in an attempt to counter prejudice against Muslims in the West.[65] However, for those interviewed here, the meaning of the veil was almost unfailingly negative. Hanifa Chérifi comprehends the headscarf as the visible sign of inferior status for women which affects the dignity of the person. For Sifaoui, "the Islamist veil clings to the body and becomes a part of the personality." According to him, in the *banlieues*, some adolescent boys and their fathers, having listened to radical Imams telling them that their women must veil, pushed their sisters and daughters to do so. Some other girls then decided to veil of their own volition, so as to not be treated as prostitutes or "loose" in their neighborhoods. For many, the veil, often accompanied by baggy clothing, became a kind of *laissez-passer*, allowing a girl to go out or to move around safely (Zouba calls it a kind of "visa"). This underscores the point that the *banlieues* had become a zone governed not by the law of the republic, but rather where individual men in the community enforced the "law of the brothers." The headscarf was one way women and girls could negotiate and avoid punishment under this informal "law." Often girls are said to change clothes at the borders of their neighborhoods. In fact, Zouba says that "ironically, the veil is a means to do what is prohibited. It makes it possible to go out with boys, for example, because you are anonymous."

In recent years, in the *banlieues*, Zouba argues that "the law of the brothers has prevailed." Lalia Ducos explains that, even before the 2004 Law, "in the *cités*,[66] there was a law imposed by men on women. Girls

---

64. Founded in 988 A.D., Al Azhar is one of the most prestigious centers of Islamic learning in the world.

65. *See* Scott, *Symptomatic Politics*, *supra* note 12, at 106, 116, and Scott, The Politics of the Veil, *supra* note 3.

66. This term refers to the large apartment complexes found in the *banlieues*.

did not dare to dress freely. [Under this 'law,' girls] had to veil and wear big baggy clothes to hide their shape. This was the only way to be left alone in the daily life of a woman." Such unofficial "laws" raise basic questions about democracy for Hélie–Lucas. She asks, "are we having laws that are not voted on by the people?" The strength of the informal "law" constraining women's choice about dress suggests that a lack of government restrictions on headscarves may not actually produce the result seemingly desired by many of the 2004 Law's opponents: for women to be able to wear what they choose. In this context, the formal 2004 Law may be understood as a way to counter this parallel "law" of brothers, fathers or neighbors. Hence, for some women of Muslim or North African heritage who support the 2004 Law, its adoption represents the government fulfilling a basic democratic obligation that it had neglected previously. This flags a larger concern about the government's abdication of responsibility for human rights in the *banlieues*. Hadjam says, we "need the state to be engaged [in the *banlieues*]." Ducos actually is concerned that the government is not fully implementing the 2004 Law now, leaving some girls without protection from coercion. Such a perspective is almost never heard in English language accounts of the headscarf issue.

While the Islamic veil is particularly associated with and promoted by fundamentalist movements, veiling in general is also the product of traditional ideas about female virtue and male lust and sexual agency—ideas that are all too familiar to women in many societies. For Zazi Sadou, the veil is most often the product of pressure from fathers and older brothers. Girls are told that wearing the veil is the only way to be respected. "It reassures men that their daughters are proper, even in a liberal Western society. Thus, a woman's body is used as a symbol of morals. Some men then think, 'I am a good Muslim because my daughter wears the veil.'" As Asma Guénifi says, "I am Algerian and I am proud of it. But the veil is the submission of women." This view was repeated by Hadjam.

For Anglophone and academic opponents of the 2004 Law like Joan Scott, the veil may simply be a cloth, and other understandings of it are somewhat hysterical.[67] However, for Asma Guénifi and others, "the scarf is not just a cloth. It is an ideology." Malika Zouba also explains the issue in terms of the trajectory of women's rights. She asks:

> Why should we accept this going backward? . . . My father veiled my two [older] sisters and my mother. This was a way of telling the French, 'we are different.' I was ten at the independence [of Algeria,

---

67. *See generally* SCOTT, THE POLITICS OF THE VEIL, *supra* note 3, and Joan Scott, Presentation at panel on Veiling and the Law, Yale Law School (Oct. 31, 2007) (notes on file with the author).

in 1962] and never wore the veil. I should have been veiled at the age of 13 or 14, but I was not. Why? My country made a step forward. I went to school and university [in Algeria]. This is quite different from my two older sisters. My two younger sisters also went to school.... However, in the 1980s [after the Iranian revolution] we began to go backwards.

The "duty" to veil is drawn from interpretation of religious texts by Islamists, according to Lalia Ducos, and as Malika Zouba emphasizes, these are mostly interpretations by men.[68] Some girls may become convinced that such "modesty" is the only way to save their souls. From a religious point of view, Bencheikh asserts that veiling is not one of the five pillars of Islam; therefore it can be limited. Interpretation and re-interpretation of religious doctrine over time and subject to context are key themes for him. A Muslim fundamentalist once told the author of this Chapter that there is no such thing as interpretation, an idea common to many fundamentalisms. On the contrary, for Sifaoui and Bencheikh, the meaning of the veil must be carefully rethought in the contemporary French context. Sifaoui suggests that wearing it in France has paradoxical results. Whereas the veil was originally intended to "protect" women from the gaze of men and strangers, in the West it draws the gaze and garners attention. In a radical rethink, Bencheikh suggests that it is school itself that serves today as the functional equivalent of the veil historically. Education is now the best way to protect one's daughter and ensure her safe future.[69]

One of the concerns of those who oppose the 2004 Law is that by banning the headscarf in schools the Law stigmatizes veiled girls and women in French society. However, supporters of the Law turn this argument on its head, postulating that the wearing of the veil in school by some stigmatizes other unveiled girls as bad Muslims, a view confirmed by the fatwa from the *Conseil Européen des Fatwas et de la Recherche* quoted above.[70] While certainly not the fault of individual veiled women, in the broader social context, "not-being-veiled is a condition that can only exist in the presence of veiling."[71] Not-being-veiled has led to a range of terrible consequences for women and girls, including social stigma, family pressure and violence, attacks in the community, and even death. Young *beur* women in the *banlieues* have been attacked and gang raped, in the ritual known as the *tournante*, and

---

68. On the myriad of interpretations of women's rights under Islamic law, *see Knowing Our Rights: Women, family, laws and customs in the Muslim world, available at* http://www.wluml.org/english/pubsfulltxt.shtml?cmd$87)=i–87–16766.

69. *See* Soheib Bencheikh, Marianne et le Prophète: L'Islam dans la France Laïque 144–145 (1998).

70. *Conseil Européen des Fatwas et de la Recherche, supra* note 39.

71. Bennoune, *Secularism and Human Rights, supra* note 11, at 426.

even murdered for wearing miniskirts, appearing "loose," or being disobedient.[72] Algerian school-girls were gunned down by the Armed Islamic Group in the 1990s for refusing to cover their heads—something that is well known among Algerians living in France.[73]

Scholars like Scott or Volpp who oppose the 2004 Law often argue that for some girls, the veil is simply a personal choice and should be respected as such. Some of those interviewed here are willing to recognize the possibility that veiling is a choice in a limited number of cases, but emphasize that the Law preserved a wide field for the expression of that choice. As Guénifi says, "We respect the choice. You can wear the veil anywhere, except in public school." Hadjam, too, stresses that the Law "does not keep a girl from veiling in the street." Furthermore, given that headscarves are not banned in universities, for her, "the reasoning of the French Law is that at 18, a girl can choose." Sadou evinces the view that "when you are 20 or 30 you can say it is a choice, but these are not adults. These are minors, children in school."

Others problematize the notion of free choice in this context. "Don't tell me the veil is a choice," says Lalia Ducos. "There are a million ways to manipulate the spirit to wear the veil." "I question the word 'choice,'" agrees Malika Zouba. "It seems a girl has the choice. But she did not decide. Men decided she should wear the veil and she is following their views. Maybe not her father or brother, but at the mosque, on Arab TV where they have sermons all day long."

Others have argued that, paradoxically, the headscarf may be a way for girls to rebel against more liberal or assimilated parents. For Favret–Saada, those who see the headscarf in school as merely a harmless sign of such adolescent revolt "do not see that in rebelling against their parents [this way], they end up with something worse than their parents." Similarly, Sifaoui posits that it is wrong to think that the veil is a way of opposing rules; he says, "the veil is a way of following rules, submitting to rules." For others, it may be both at the same time, a phenomenon perhaps magnified by the 2004 Law.

The Contextual Approach to Restrictions on Headscarves in Public Education

To ground the interviews on the 2004 Law conducted in France in the framework of human rights law, this section summarizes the rele-

---

72. *See* French Muslims Fail to Enter Mainstream and Suffer from Poverty, Discrimination and Sexism, National Public Radio broadcast (Feb. 26, 2003); SAMIRA BELLIL, DANS L'ENFER DES TOURNANTES (2002); AMARA & ZAPPI, *supra* note 58, at 5–7.

73. *See* KARIMA BENNOUNE, S.O.S. ALGERIA: WOMEN'S HUMAN RIGHTS UNDER SIEGE, IN FAITH AND FREEDOM: WOMEN'S HUMAN RIGHTS IN THE MUSLIM WORLD 184, 187 (Mahnaz Afkhami ed., 1995).

vant human rights norms and the contextual approach to evaluating headscarf regulation in light of these norms. Tackling this issue as a matter of human rights requires the rationalization of conflicting rights claims, those based on freedom of religion and those based on sex equality.

Freedom of religion is a fundamental human right. Article 9(1) of the European Convention on Human Rights, to which France has adhered, sets out that:

> Everyone has the right to freedom of thought, conscience and religion; this right includes freedom to change his religion or belief and freedom, either alone or in community with others and in public or private, to manifest his religion or belief, in worship, teaching, practice and observance.[74]

As Bencheikh, former Mufti of Marseille, began his interview, "Muslims, like all others, have the right to exercise their religion in beauty and dignity." However, this right to religious freedom also includes the right to be free of religion if one chooses. Moreover, expression of religious belief can be subjected to some limitations under human rights law itself, as the *Şahin* case reminds us. According to Article 9(2) of the European Convention,

> Freedom to manifest one's religion or beliefs shall be subject only to such limitations as are prescribed by law and are necessary in a democratic society in the interests of public safety, for the protection of public order, health or morals, or for the protection of the rights and freedoms of others.[75]

At the same time, sex equality is also a fundamental human right, and one from which no derogation is permissible.[76] The Convention on the Elimination of All Forms of Discrimination against Women, to which France is also a state party, requires that states "take all appropriate measures to eliminate discrimination against women by any person, organization or enterprise."[77] On an even more ambitious note, the Convention mandates states to "modify the social and cultural patterns of conduct of men and women, with a view to achieving the elimination

---

74. Eur. Convention on Human Rights, Nov. 4, 1950, 213 U.N.T.S. 221, art. 9(1). This right is also protected by the Int'l Covenant on Civil and Political Rights (ICCPR) art. 18; Int'l Covenant on Civil and Political Rights, Dec. 16, 1966; S. Treaty Doc. No. 95–20, 999 U.N.T.S. 171.

75. Eur. Convention on Human Rights, *supra*, note 74, at art. 9(2).

76. The ICCPR requires states to respect and ensure the rights set out in the convention on the basis of equality between women and men and prohibits derogations that involve discrimination on the basis of sex. *See* ICCPR, *supra* note 74, at arts. 2–4.

77. Convention on the Elimination of All Forms of Discrimination against Women, art. 2(e), Dec. 18, 1979, 1249 U.N.T.S. 13.

of prejudices and customary and all other practices which are based on . . . the inferiority or the superiority of either of the sexes or on stereotyped roles for men and women."[78]

Human rights law offers insufficient guidance on resolving conflicts between the right to religious freedom and the right to gender equality. In practice, as Marieme Hélie–Lucas comments, all too often women's rights give way in the face of religious justifications for sex discrimination. There has been some—mostly vague—mention of the intersection of women's equality and religion in recent standards. For example, the U.N. Commission on Human Rights in 1998 urged states to "take all necessary action to combat hatred, intolerance and acts of violence, intimidation, and *coercion* motivated by intolerance based on religion or belief, including practices which violate the human rights of women and discriminate against women."[79] The Vienna Declaration and Programme of Action, adopted at the World Conference on Human Rights in 1993, "stresse[d] the importance of . . . the eradication of any conflicts which may arise between the rights of women and the harmful effects of certain traditional or customary practices, cultural prejudices and religious extremism."[80] In its 2000 General Comment on gender equality, the U.N. Human Rights Committee extolled the idea that freedom of religion "may not be relied upon to justify discrimination against women. . . ."[81]

Furthermore, as many of those interviewed here contend, the mainstream human rights movement has failed to come to terms with the meaning of the human right to freedom of religion in the face of political movements that deploy religious arguments—and do so to support political projects that aim to curtail the rights of others. Both universal and regional human rights instruments prohibit the misuse of human rights to destroy the rights of others.[82] Analyzing these complex norms is further complicated by what are indeed racist and xenophobic discourses on headscarves, fundamentalism, terrorism and women's rights in the Muslim world, discourses which have proliferated since 9/11. Yet, often human rights narratives only recognize the religious freedom issue and

---

78. *Id.* at art. 5(a).

79. Comm'n on Human Rights, *Implementation of the Declaration on the Elimination of All Forms of Intolerance and of Discrimination or Belief*, Res. 1998/18, ¶ 4(c), U.N. Doc. E/CN.4/1998/18 (Apr. 9, 1998) (emphasis added).

80. World Conference on Human Rights, June 14–25, 1993, *Vienna Declaration and Programme of Action*, ¶ 22, U.N. Doc. A/CONF.157/23 (July 12, 1993).

81. U.N. Human Rights Committee, *General Comment No. 28: Equality of Rights Between Men and Women (Art. 3)*, ¶ 21, U.N. Doc. CCPR/C/21/Rev.1/Add.10 (Mar. 29, 2000).

82. *See, e.g.*, Eur. Convention on Human Rights, *supra* note 74, at art. 17, and ICCPR, *supra* note 74, at art. 5.

in its most simple iteration, reducing the very real complexities of headscarf regulation in schools to a more comfortable—and false— simplicity.

Given these tensions and conflicts, the subject of government restrictions on the wearing of veils and other "modest" garments in public education is too complex to give rise to an easy bright line rule for compatibility with human rights norms.[83] While a bright line rule seems more objective and easier to apply, it produces a formalistic approach blind to the complex reality on the ground. Instead, a contextual approach enables a thick analysis and maximizes the ability to effectively address particular challenges to human rights in a specific context.

Using the contextual approach, human rights advocates weighing restrictions on "modest" garments for Muslim women and girls in public schools under international law should look carefully at the meanings and impact of the symbols in context. In doing so, they should consider a range of factors, including the impact of the garments on other women (or girls) in the same environment; coercion of women in the given context, including activities of religious extremist organizations; gender discrimination; related violence against women in the location; the motivation of those imposing the restriction; religious discrimination in the given context; the alternatives to restrictions; the possible consequences for human rights both of restrictions and a lack thereof; and whether or not there has been consultation with impacted constituencies (both those impacted by restrictions and by a lack of restrictions on such garments). Though this formula forces consideration of a multiplicity of issues, this matrix also enables a truly intersectional approach more likely to produce substantively rights-friendly results for the greatest number of women and girls in the long run.

The first question to ask is whether the wearing of the religious symbol causes, magnifies, or otherwise constitutes discrimination against women in that particular locale. If it does not, obviously restrictions on the symbol are not justifiable on these grounds. If it does, the second

---

83. For further discussion, including of the relevant international human rights law, see Bennoune, *Secularism and Human Rights*, *supra* note 11. The difficulty in establishing a bright line rule on the regulation of religious symbols has been recognized by the U.N. Special Rapporteur on freedom of religion. She has suggested a sophisticated approach to the regulation of religious symbols involving the consideration of a range of general criteria to balance the competing rights at stake. The first category of "aggravating indicators," such as discriminatory intent, suggest incompatibility of particular attempts to regulate religious symbols with human rights law. An alternate list of "neutral indicators" indicate that the restrictions in question may not violate human rights standards, including when "the language of the restriction . . . is worded in a neutral and all-embracing way," or when "the interference is crucial to protect the rights of women. . . ." *Report of the Special Rapporteur on freedom of religion or belief*, U.N. Doc. E/CN.4/2006/5 (Jan. 9, 2005) at 11–19, 17–18 (*prepared by* Asma Jahangir).

question to ask is whether the specific restrictions are likely to violate freedom of religion, especially on discriminatory grounds. If the answer is no, and the restrictions are otherwise in accordance with human rights law (including the requirements that they are necessary to protect the rights of others, proportionate and prescribed by law), they should be deemed acceptable under the European Convention on Human Rights, the International Covenant on Civil and Political Rights, and other relevant standards.[84]

If the answer to both questions is yes, i.e., where both discrimination against women and against Muslims is at play, the situation becomes more difficult to resolve. There, the deciding factor ought to be coercion. The state should not interfere with the right of adults to dress as they please in public schools, unless coercive social forces (in the family or the community) that mandate the use of the veil or other forms of "modest" dress are active to that end in the location. In such a situation, the state can interfere to protect women from coercion, and is actually mandated by human rights law to do so. This principle is important for human rights advocates to remember, given that all too often what are deemed religious or cultural rights take precedence over women's rights when the two are seen to conflict. For girls, a lower standard for what constitutes coercion can apply, given their greater sensitivity to peer pressure and less-developed agency.

Mainstream human rights advocates who focus traditionally on state conduct more than on the impact of non-state actors on human rights may have a tendency to overlook the human rights imperative to check coercion by non-state groups in the community, such as fundamentalist organizations. Given this emphasis, the mainstream human rights movement is prone to respond only to one dress code (the state's restrictions on the headscarf) but not the other (pressure to cover from family, community and social movements).

In any case, gender-sensitive and anti-racist education and community dialogue must accompany any restrictions. Furthermore, any constraints on dress must be imposed with religious and, where relevant, racial and ethnic sensitivity. However, this issue cannot be seen as involving religious freedom alone. Gender equality remains at the heart of the matter. Human rights law requires states to act affirmatively to end discrimination against women. This prescription must be remembered, along with what human rights law says about religious freedom.

---

84. France is a state party to a number of related international human rights treaties, including the ICCPR (acceded to in 1980), the Convention on the Elimination of All Forms of Discrimination against Women (ratified in 1983), the Int'l Convention on the Elimination of All Forms of Racial Discrimination (acceded to in 1971), the Convention on the Rights of the Child (ratified in 1990) and the Eur. Convention on Human Rights (ratified in 1974).

Critique of the Human Rights Response to the 2004 Law

Both Amnesty International and Human Rights Watch, along with a number of other international human rights groups, like the International Federation of Human Rights (FIDH), have been outspokenly critical of the French Law.[85] Moreover, some prominent international human rights lawyers[86] have been involved in recent cases defending the "right to veil" at school. One example is the recent case in nearby England in which the father of a twelve-year-old-girl unsuccessfully sought for her to be able to wear the *niqab*, which covers the full face, to school.[87] These positions taken by some international human rights advocates were strongly criticized by many of those interviewed for this law story.

For example, Chérifi retorts that the problem of the veil in school should not be understood simply as a question of women dressing the way they want to, but rather as a symbol of a status that subordinates women. She asks, "Do we defend this lower status for women in the name of human rights? Liberty does not mean you have to allow everything. Some human rights NGOs do not have a historical perspective on this question." Lalia Ducos feels that some human rights advocates have forgotten how this issue came to be a controversy, focusing on it, mistakenly, as a question of respect for culture and diversity. Even a religious leader like Bencheikh warned that human rights advocates should not "use liberty against liberty, as a sort of Trojan Horse."

Sifaoui is even more critical of the positions of human rights detractors of the 2004 Law and avers that some positions seem to reflect the attitude that "human rights are good for me, but for Muslims to oppress their women is fine because it is written in a holy book." In his view, those human rights groups that are critical of the Law do not seem to realize the consequences of their positions on these issues. He agrees that "we must be very attached to individual liberty." However, for Sifaoui, "the choice also involves taking into consideration the freedom

---

85. *See, e.g.*, AMNESTY INTERNATIONAL, *supra* note 20, and HUMAN RIGHTS WATCH, *supra* note 20.

86. For example, lawyers associated with London's prestigious Matrix Chambers, a group known for its human rights expertise, have been involved in several such cases.

87. *British girl, 12, loses fight to wear full-face veil at school*, AGENCE FRANCE PRESSE, Feb. 21, 2007. The garment implicated in this case is distinct from the headscarf, which does not cover the entire face. However, as noted above, this range of "modest" clothes raises some similar issues. Moreover, some women's rights advocates fear escalating claims for "modest" clothing in schools. Today this is a live issue. Several other European countries now struggle with whether to allow the burka, which covers even the eyes, in school. *See, e.g., Germany Mulls School Uniforms, Burka Ban*, UNITED PRESS INT'L, May 8, 2006.

of others." This view was echoed by an unveiled Turkish woman engineer who stressed that, "when I see women all covered up like that, I feel pressure."[88]

The rights of non-veiled Muslim girls are just as implicated in this controversy as the rights of girls who wish to veil. As Hélie–Lucas submits, the claims move rapidly from "the right to veil" to the right to beat up those who do not.[89] This reality is often overlooked by human rights critiques, which focus only on the individual wishing to veil and not on those around her. In fact, according to many of those interviewed for this Chapter, one of the most important constituencies supporting the Law consists of unveiled Muslim girls who wish to be free from pressure to veil in school. During the collection of input for the preparation of the Stasi Commission Report, Zazi Sadou spoke to many unveiled school girls who argued that public school was their best chance to emancipate themselves. Sadou says many appealed to the Stasi Commission to recommend a law against the headscarf in school, saying: "We are the silent majority. Our brothers will force us to wear the veil if you leave us alone in the face of pressure from family and community." Soheib Bencheikh further emphasized the constraints placed on many unveiled Muslim girls to induce them to veil. "They are menaced, threatened." This coercion, in his view, leads many unveiled Muslim girls to support the Law. "It is possible that non-Muslim women tolerate [the presence of the veil in school], but not that [unveiled Muslim women] do."

For some secular North African supporters of the 2004 Law, the human rights arguments for the veil in school are a kind of cultural relativism, ironically emanating from a human rights movement putatively committed to universality. Some interviewed here see it as a failure of the human rights movement to appreciate the importance of secularism for human rights. Hadjam and others perceive some of the mainstream human rights stances on the headscarf as a manifestation of post-colonial guilt. Zouba, an ardent defender of universality, says,

> Of course I understand that human rights activists are torn. The problem is that those women and girls who are forced to wear the veil are not appearing in the same human rights reports.[90] All

---

88. Comments of Turkish woman engineer, in Istanbul, Turkey (June 15, 2007) (notes on file with the author).

89. According to Hélie–Lucas, just this sort of violence has been visited upon children for not following religious dietary restrictions at school. *See, e.g.,* Union des Familles Laïque, *Un enfant de huit ans tabassé pour avoir mangé du porc à la cantine de l'École,* Mar. 14, 2007, *available at,* http://www.ufal29.infini.fr/spip.php?article739.

90. For example, in Amnesty International's 2005 Annual Report, the only criticism of dress codes for women is in the entry on France which notes the restrictions on religious symbols in schools. Neither Saudi Arabian nor Iranian provisions that penalize women for

attacks on human rights should be denounced, provided that you are not denouncing an attack on human rights by allowing another attack on human rights.

Conclusions About the 2004 Law

As noted, most of those interviewed for this Chapter supported the 2004 Law, though their explanations for their support varied. Chérifi supported the Law without reservation and, while recognizing that the French government had much more to do to make amends for its historic failures toward immigrants, she believed that the 2004 Law's implementation has been a success. For her, this success is based on the spirit of the Law, the universality of its approach which does not target any one religion, and the extensive preparations carried out before the Law entered into force.

Sifaoui raises a question of proportion. Of the five million Muslims in France, only 3000 or so had sought to wear the veil in school, and of these only a small number left school rather than give it up.[91] He asks if the secularism of the entire society should be called into question for such a small minority of girls. Ultimately, for him, the concept of *laïcité* and the 2004 Law that defends it are about *vivre-ensemble*, an idea designed to enable France's diverse population to live together.[92] Sifaoui's conclusion about the Law seems to be based both on his views about the discriminatory nature of the veil itself, as well as on his committed secular republicanism (the latter views coexist with his being a practicing Muslim). For him, personal choices are inherently limited in a public space like the public school, which "belongs to everyone." Here the young person is not a Muslim or a Christian, but simply a student among students, and among whom one does not distinguish on the basis of religion. Zazi Sadou strongly supports the Law as a way to protect girls who do not wish to veil and as a means to fight against fundamentalism. She also approves of the 2004 legislation because, "the intrusion of all religious symbols, especially the headscarf, represents the invasion of public space by religious practice."

"Among feminists, we were split over the Law," says Lalia Ducos. "Some thought it would be discriminatory. At first I was shocked. Then I realized that it was an epic struggle between republican laws and those who oppose them." Ducos stressed that most veiled girls did not leave school after the Law went into effect, but rather removed their scarves

---

failing to cover, including through internationally unlawful corporal punishments, are enumerated as specific concerns. *See* AMNESTY INTERNATIONAL, *supra* note 20.

91. For a discussion of available statistics, *see supra* text at notes 21–23.

92. This can be translated as "living together in a spirit of cooperation or coexistence," a concept often emphasized in French public discourse.

at school. When asked if she believes the 2004 Law takes the right approach, Malika Zouba said, "I guess so. At least you can prevent some of the girls from being veiled, which is a major victory. If 10% of the would-be-veiled girls could escape, then I agree with the Law. Even veiled, I am glad to see a woman in the street; but I ask, is there anything I can do before she wears the veil?"

Jeanne Favret Saada was against the Law initially and, like Françoise Gaspard whose views are summarized below, preferred negotiated solutions to such problems. However, when the issue became a major political contest, and when pro-veil groups like the *Union des Organisations Islamiques de France* and others organized a huge campaign for veiling in school and against the proposed law, "you had to stop the epidemic of veils in schools." If the government had yielded, it would have represented a major victory for those [pro-veil, fundamentalist] forces, in her view. She hopes that the Law can afford some protection to girls who are coerced into wearing the veil. As she said, "If it concerns a girl who gives in to the neighborhood, at least they [fundamentalist activists, members of community and family] cannot bother her in class."

Marieme Hélie–Lucas initially wondered if a new law was needed and if instead the 1905 Law on the separation of church and state would suffice. The old Law, which was in no way targeted at Muslims, but rather concerned the Catholic Church, could simply have been applied to the current problem in schools. As she says, "You do not have a particular religious identity when you are training to be a citizen of the Republic." Ultimately, she has become a supporter of the 2004 Law. Her support comes in part from concern about decreasing secularism in France and about more young people trying to wear not only the headscarf, but also other religious symbols like the *kippah* (Jewish skullcap) and the cross in school.

In the words of Soheib Bencheikh, a codified law is useful because, "once the Law was adopted, there was no more controversy." He stresses that "the choice to be French means to respect the law." Turning to French history, he argues that many young Muslims "do not know how much the Third Republic did to liberate science and knowledge from the domination of the Jesuits" and how much of a struggle had occurred to secularize education in the Christian context. For him, this is an important part of the backdrop to the 2004 Law. He, too, was particularly struck by how few girls have continued to insist on wearing the veil in school since the adoption of the Law.

Marc Saghie, a Lebanese journalist living in Paris, proposes that the French government should not have dealt with the veil in school generically as a religious symbol, but rather directly as a question of discrimination against women.[93] Indeed, there has been some slippage between the arguments that has perhaps contributed to criticism of the Law. One position in the debate is to defend *laïcité* in principle from the interjection of all religious symbols in schools (the veil being, of course, the most prominent and widespread). The alternate view expressed is that the Law is justified because the veil is discriminatory, girls need to be protected from it in school, and the only acceptable way of doing so is by banning all religious symbols equally. Sometimes, as noted above, these arguments are interwoven. For Ducos and Sifaoui, the 2004 Law is clearly about the veil, though Ducos particularly recognized that it was helpful to put the proscription in the context of regulations on the symbols of other religions as well. By contrast, Chérifi posits the Law as a universal construct to defend *laïcité*, which is about all religions equally. However, Sadou submits that "even here [in France] it is presented as a law against the veil." Asma Guénifi laughed at her own gaffe in referring to it as "the Law against the scarf," saying, "Even I make the mistake. It is the Law against religious symbols."

In any case, there have been difficult consequences for some of Muslim and North African heritage who have come out in support of the Law and against fundamentalism, like those interviewed here. Mohamed Sifaoui was reportedly attacked by fundamentalists linked to Algerian armed groups in Paris on June 13, 2008, and a civil society campaign currently seeks to convince the French state to renew his police protection.[94] According to Guénifi, "We have been called racists, unbelievers and against our own culture. We received death threats and phone threats." For a woman who had lost her brother to the fundamentalist armed groups in Algeria during the 1990s, these threats carried a particular resonance. The organization with which she works, *Ni Putes, Ni Soumises*, was initially divided over the ban. However, its members realized that the consequences for their own struggles for women's rights would be very negative if the Law was not adopted. "We are fighting for *mixité* (the mixing of the sexes); we are fighting for girls to have the same opportunities, the same rights." For her, the advocates of veiling in France were the same kind of fundamentalists as in Algeria, such as her fundamentalist neighbor who had pressured her to wear the *djilbab* during the 90s. "We refuse this male chauvinist project. We refuse the separation of men and women and the crushing of a woman so she does not exist anymore."

---

93. Interview with Marc Saghie, in Paris, France (June 12, 2007) (notes on file with the author).

94. *See* SIAWI (Secularism is a Women's Rights Issue), *France must ensure police protection for Mohamed Sifaoui*, August 19, 2008, *available at* http://www.siawi.org/article 507.html and Mohamed Sifaoui, *Mon agresseur formellement identifié*, June 15, 2008, *available at* http://www.mohamed-sifaoui.com/article-20459573.html.

However, for *Ni Putes, Ni Soumises*, the veil itself is not the sole priority. Similar to the view expressed by Zouba, the 2004 Law is important to the organization, but only one issue among many to be addressed. The activists of *Ni Putes, Ni Soumises* are organizing in the *cités* and *banlieues*, working on human rights education for girls, providing legal information, opposing forced marriages and FGM, working to support women survivors of domestic violence and also supporting the rights of women back home in their countries of origin.[95] In regard to the latter task, Ducos argues that the struggles of Diaspora women in France can indeed have an important impact on women's struggles in their countries of origin. The same was true of the Algerian independence movement historically—support for independence flourished among Algerian migrant workers in France. Many of those interviewed here emphasized that the debate about the headscarf should be understood in its regional and transnational contexts.

Mimouna Hadjam explains that her organization, Africa 93, did not initially take a position calling for a law on religious symbols in schools. This was due to skepticism about the social efficacy of legislation, because in the group's experience "laws against racism have not ended racism." However, the group came out in favor of the Law in December 2003 when they saw the Islamist demonstrations against it. "It scared me. If these people saw that the Law did not pass, they would have thought they had won." She expressed that many progressive women like her in her working class neighborhood were very afraid that the Law would not pass. Still she stresses that, "For us the Law is not a panacea. It is a minimum. We want anti-sexist education in school, from the very beginning." Moreover, Hadjam cautioned that she was indeed concerned about what would happen to the veiled girls themselves in the wake of the Law's adoption. "The expulsion of a girl [from school] is a failure." Still, she concludes that, overall, the Law has been a success. Finally, she also recognizes that the Law may mean very different things to different people. "I have a feminist vision of the Law. Chirac had a republican vision." When asked if she thought the ban had increased fundamentalist pressure on women, as some have suggested, she said, "It clarified things, which always heightens tensions. Women's struggle always increases social tension, as de Beauvoir wrote."

A Brief Rejoinder from Françoise Gaspard

Just as many Muslims and North Africans support the ban on religious symbols in schools, complicating the simplistic narrative critiqued above, some non-Muslim French oppose it. Françoise Gaspard is a prominent French sociologist who carried out groundbreaking research

---

95. For more information on these projects, *see* http://www.niputesnisoumises.com.

on the views of veiled girls in French schools. She is also the current member of French nationality on the U.N. Committee on the Elimination of All Forms of Discrimination against Women. Though a staunch critic of veiling itself, she opposed the 2004 Law, thinking that "it was counter-productive" and could result in the "double stigmatization of girls and Islam."[96] Gaspard preferred that the matter of headscarves be dealt with through negotiation with individual girls in school, for example, asking them in class to lower their scarves to their shoulders as a matter of politeness. For her, this should be "a social debate, not a legal question." However, even she feels that it should be forbidden to cover the face, for "it is useful in a society to see the face." Moreover, she completely accepts that teachers should not be able to wear headscarves to school out of respect for neutrality as this could seem like a kind of pressure.

As to the escalating demands of the fundamentalists on other issues in school, Gaspard was adamant that children should not be able to refuse to take certain classes or to be exempt from sports on religious grounds. Her primary concern was the exclusion and self-exclusion of veiled girls from school. She also questioned what progress could have been made by the Law when, in her view, there might not be any veils in school, but many veils remain visible outside school in the same neighborhoods. Furthermore, she believes that fundamentalist pressure on women has gotten worse because of the debate; though overall she speculates that a progressive Islam is gaining on fundamentalist movements.

Interestingly, even an opponent of the Law like Gaspard believes that the question is settled for now in France. "The answer is not abrogation of the Law. It is dangerous to re-open the question now. We must live with it." The best way of doing this, for her, is to directly support girls themselves. For her, the question of fundamentalist pressure on unveiled girls is a complicated one. She too feels that, in France, "We have left power to the bearded ones [the fundamentalists] and they made the law [in the neighborhoods]." During the 2007 presidential elections, several veiled girls told her they would vote for Nicolas Sarkozy because he would bring order and, in their words, they were "tired of our brothers bringing order."[97]

Still, like many of the Law's opponents, Gaspard views the debate over the headscarf that led to the Law as a reflection of the "xenophobia

---

96. Interview with Françoise Gaspard, in Paris, France (June 10, 2007) (notes on file with the author).

97. President Sarkozy has been criticized, however, for a past pattern of tolerating and cooperating with fundamentalist organizations like the *Union des Organisations Islamiques de France*. Claude Askolovitch, *Les Illusions perdues de Sarkozy*, NOUVEL OBSERVATEUR, Feb. 14–20, 2008, at 24.

of the general French population," and in particular, its fear of immigration by previously colonized peoples. To thoroughly examine the 2004 Law, one must give serious consideration to the arguments made by its supporters, such as those discussed here, as well as those made by thoughtful opponents like Gaspard.

Some Final Thoughts on the Contexts of the Headscarf Debate

The presentation of the female body remains a contentious issue across many cultures. Like all societies, France is complex and these issues are contested. In keeping with her universalist leaning, Malika Zouba frames the headscarf debate in both the specific and global contexts. "The veil is linked to the supremacy of Muslim men. All over the world, men attempt to dominate women. And all throughout the world, women struggle against this. Male domination is not specific to Muslims. It is universal, as is the struggle of women for greater freedom." It is helpful to understand the headscarf debate in this broader context too. Indeed, it is to this global reality Zouba describes that the Beijing Declaration responds when it proclaims that "Women's rights are human rights."[98]

One can continue to imagine a world in which women can wear what they choose and can do so in substantive equality.[99] This seems to be the concern of some who oppose the Law. Yet, the question is how to apply international human rights standards so as to ensure that women can wear what they choose in the actual contexts in which women live, like in France. In the context of fundamentalist, community or familial pressure on women to cover, pressures that some women may indeed internalize, the removal of government restrictions on headscarves in school may not necessarily lead to the freedom or enjoyment of human rights that one imagines.

As the interviews in this Chapter indicate, some feminists of Muslim and North African origin argue that the wearing of headscarves by some girls in schools, especially schools with a high percentage of Muslim students, can indeed have a negative impact on the human rights of other Muslim girls. Moreover, allowing such "modest" garments to be

---

98. Beijing Declaration, adopted by the Fourth World Conference on Women, ¶ 14 (September 15, 1995). This declaration was adopted in 1995 by governments around the world at the U.N. Fourth World Conference on Women in Beijing.

99. Substantive equality "addresse[s] the realities of context and determine[s] equality and discrimination against women in terms of eliminating disadvantage in result." SAVITRI GOONESEKERE, THE CONCEPT OF SUBSTANTIVE EQUALITY AND GENDER JUSTICE IN SOUTH ASIA 13, *available at* http://www.unifem.org.in/PDF/The%20Concept%20of%20Substantive%20 Equality%20–final%20–%2031–12–07.pdf. This concept is embodied in the Convention on the Elimination of All Forms of Discrimination against Women, *supra* note 77, arts. 1 and 3. Substantive equality is often defined in opposition to formal equality, which stresses identical treatment instead of equality in result.

worn in schools risks leaving girls vulnerable to coercion aimed at pressuring them to do so—coercion that has been documented in many instances in France. Thus, some limits on the wearing of headscarves in school in this particular context may indeed be required by human rights norms guaranteeing substantive gender equality. Such restrictions also come within the exceptions to the right to express religious belief as found, *inter alia*, in Article 18(3) of the International Covenant on Civil and Political Rights. Therefore, they are consonant with human rights law. Human rights critics of the French law usually reject this possibility out of hand, but such a legal approach may produce more substantive enjoyment of human rights by women in France's Muslim population in the long run.

There is no question that finding the right balance for addressing the issue of headscarves in school in the contemporary moment is incredibly difficult and requires one to tightrope walk over perilous waters, making use of a vocabulary heavily laden with political meaning. One must somehow find a space for opposition to fundamentalism and racism, to sex discrimination and religious or ethnic discrimination, to the Muslim far right and the French far right. This requires an anti-racism which is unabashedly feminist, a feminism which is unequivocally anti-racist and a thick analysis of human rights. In today's world, it is perhaps convenient to take a narrow anti-racist or religious freedom position on the Law, looking at it through only one human rights lens. Zouba characterizes this attitude on the part of some human rights advocates as follows: "They want to fight origin discrimination, so let [the girls] wear the veil as a kind of [anti-racist] corrective, because they don't want to deal with this other problem [of discrimination against women]. This is the only discrimination they want to tackle." The stories told here about the 2004 Law make clear that such limited approaches are mistaken. The struggles for women's equality and against religious extremism must also be factored into any useful human rights analysis of these headscarf regulations.

Moreover, the failure of human rights forces to comprehend and respond forcefully to the menace of religious fundamentalisms—in this particular manifestation, to Muslim fundamentalist pressure on women and girls to cover—needs to be addressed. This deficiency makes one particularly sympathetic to the Law's supporters quoted here. Clearly, we need a human rights account of religious extremism, and that account needs to be brought to the center of our analysis of the 2004 Law.

As this law story comes to an end, it is worth pondering Hadjam's admonishment of the French progressives in her local government who funded Muslim fundamentalist associations, but not her anti-racist and anti-fundamentalist group, Africa 93. She said: "I am a counter-weight to [fundamentalism]. I represent feminism and secularism, yet you do not support me." This is a pattern that is all too often replicated elsewhere. It is imperative for human rights advocates to find thoughtful ways to support those who are working democratically for human rights and against fundamentalism within Muslim countries and Diaspora populations, like those interviewed here.[100] Collectively, their endeavors represent one of the most important human rights struggles of our time.

---

100. A similar engagement is needed with their counterparts who organize against fundamentalisms in other religious traditions. *See, e.g.*, RIGHTS & DEMOCRACY (INTERNATIONAL CENTRE FOR HUMAN RIGHTS AND DEMOCRATIC DEVELOPMENT), FUNDAMENTALISMS AND HUMAN RIGHTS, REPORT OF THE MEETING, Montréal, 12–14 May 2005, *available at* http://www.dd-rd.ca/site/_PDF/publications/fundamentalism_hr.pdf.

Part Three

International Standards and the Role of Criminal Law in Protecting Human Rights

*

6

Engendering Genocide: The *Akayesu* Case Before the International Criminal Tribunal for Rwanda

Beth Van Schaack*

Introduction

Gender crimes and crimes of sexual violence are no longer as invisible as they once were thanks largely to the work of feminist scholars, practitioners, and activists, and to the landmark case against Jean Paul Akayesu before the International Criminal Tribunal for Rwanda ("ICTR" or Tribunal). The case against Akayesu is credited with establishing many "firsts" in international criminal law. For one, it resulted in the first adversarial conviction for genocide under international law since that crime's inception fifty years prior. It also established a number of important jurisprudential precedents concerning the law of incitement, complicity, cumulative charging, individual criminal responsibility in non-international armed conflicts, and the constitutive elements of the crime of genocide. Most importantly for the purposes of this volume, the case was the first to recognize the concept of genocidal rape—the subject of vigorous discussion and advocacy among the feminist legal and activist community at the time.

Akayesu was *bourgmestre* (mayor) of Taba Commune and one of its most powerful people in April 1994 when genocide engulfed the small mountainous country of Rwanda. The primary allegations against Akayesu were not that he personally engaged in acts of violence. Rather, he was charged with ordering, inciting, or instigating international crimes.

---

* The author is indebted to Timothy Kennedy, Jessica Tillson, and Pami Vyas for their expert research assistance. In addition, the author would like to thank Susan Lamb and Aritha Wickramasinghe of the ICTR for their assistance in gathering original materials and transcripts; Rhonda Copelon and Isabelle Solon Helal for sharing their thoughts, files and memories; and Michelle Oberman, Susana SáCouto, and Patricia Viseur–Sellers for their generous and helpful comments.

As one witness described it, "Akayesu did not kill with his own hands, but with his orders."[1]

During the course of the proceedings against Akayesu, advocates for gender justice in Rwanda and elsewhere intervened to urge that Akayesu be held responsible for the rapes perpetrated in Taba Commune and that these acts be recognized as predicate acts for the genocide charge. This outcome would not have been possible had the original indictment against Akayesu not been amended in crucial ways, enabling the Tribunal to rule on the genocidal rape allegations. This story will highlight the role that advocates played in encouraging the Tribunal to consider genocidal rape in Rwanda and the limitations such advocates have faced in piercing the prosecutorial and adjudicative process.

For its rulings on rape and genocide, *Akayesu* has been heralded as "the most important decision rendered thus far in the history of women's jurisprudence."[2] Given subsequent developments before the Rwanda tribunal, however, *Akayesu*'s gender justice legacy—at least vis-à-vis victims in Rwanda—is more modest. The full story of the impact of the case must await the work of the International Criminal Court. At this point, however, there is no doubt that the case ratcheted up the expectations and aspirations of advocates for international gender justice.

History of the Rwandan Conflict

A brief history of Rwanda is necessary to understand the 1994 genocide.[3] Anthropologists and historians have shown that the people of Rwanda (and Burundi) descended from three distinct populations: one known as the Hutu, who resembled the Bantu people of the region; a second, the Tutsi, who resembled the Cushitic or Nilotic people of the Horn of Africa; and a third, the Twa, related to local pigmy populations. Over time, these groups intermixed and developed a common language and culture. The groups were differentiated by occupation, economic means, and political status and were more fluid than fixed.

---

1. Press Release, Fondation Hirondelle, Akayesu Found Guilty of Genocide (Sept. 2, 1998), *available at* http://www.hirondelle.org/hirondelle.nsf/caefd9edd48f5826c12564cf004f793d/f12757ecc6d866d1c12566730041e5ae?OpenDocument.

2. Kelly Askin, *Women's Issues in International Criminal Law: Recent Developments and the Potential Contribution of the ICC*, *in* INTERNATIONAL CRIMES, PEACE, AND HUMAN RIGHTS: THE ROLE OF THE INTERNATIONAL CRIMINAL COURT 47, 52 (Dinah Shelton ed., 2000).

3. This historical account is drawn from the factual findings in Prosecutor v. Akayesu, Case No. ICTR–96–4–T, Judgment, at paras. 54, 78–129 (Sept. 2, 1998) [hereinafter *Akayesu*]. *See generally* ELIZABETH NEUFFER, THE KEY TO MY NEIGHBOR'S HOUSE: SEEKING JUSTICE IN BOSNIA AND RWANDA (2001); PHILIP GOUREVITCH, WE WISH TO INFORM YOU THAT TOMORROW WE WILL BE KILLED WITH OUR FAMILIES: STORIES FROM RWANDA (1998).

During the colonial era, from approximately 1890 to 1962, Belgian colonial administrators solidified these distinctions by "assigning" individuals an "ethnicity" on a state-issued identity card. The Hutu represented about eighty-four percent of the population, the Tutsi constituted about fifteen percent, and the Twa about one percent. At first, the colonizers favored individuals identified as Tutsi—for reasons grounded in racism, some have argued, as such individuals had more Caucasian features. As a nascent independence ethos began to develop among the Tutsi elite in the 1940s, the Belgian colonizers shifted their allegiance to the Hutus in an effort to prolong their rule over the region. This coincided with the Catholic Church's promotion of a political awareness among the Hutu populace. Hutu intellectuals soon published revolutionary manifestos outlining the political, social, and economic oppression suffered by the Hutu populace at the hands of the minority Tutsi group. In 1956, the U.N. Trusteeship Council pressured Belgium to organize elections on the basis of universal suffrage. These elections elevated Hutu individuals for the first time into local and national positions of political power. Rwanda achieved its independence in 1962 under the leadership of the Belgium-installed Grégoire Kayibanda, a Hutu leader who imposed ethnically-based quotas for access to schools, some industries, and the civil service that significantly limited Tutsi participation in these sectors.

More systematic violence began to break out between the two groups in the wake of these policies and the inequities they generated.[4] Many Tutsi individuals fled to neighboring countries, especially Uganda, Burundi, and Congo. Some of these exiles organized themselves into militia to carry out cross-border raids at night, embracing what later became the epithet *Inyenzi*, meaning "cockroach." These raids provoked violent reprisals against Tutsis within Rwanda. Tutsi exiles in Uganda further organized themselves into the Rwandese Patriotic Front ("RPF"), with the Rwandan Patriotic Army ("RPA") as its military wing. Their goals were the return of exiles to Rwanda and eventually the overthrow of the Hutu-dominated regime, later led by President Kayibanda's successor, General Juvénal Habyarimana, who took power in a coup on July 5, 1973. Habyarimana at first installed a one-party state with automatic national membership in his *Mouvement Républicain National Pour La Démocratie et le Développement* (the National Revolutionary Movement for Democracy and Development, or MRND). Habyarimana eventually capitulated to internal and external pressure to allow multipartyism. This opened the way for the rise of Hutu-power political groups, such as the *Coalition pour la Défense de la République* ("CDR").

---

4. This account belies the tendency of some to describe the killing in Rwanda as an expression of so-called "age-old tribal animosities." This facile explanation masks the role that political elites played in manipulating differences to consolidate political power.

The RPF launched a devastating attack in October 1990, further destabilizing Habyarimana's regime. Hutu-power political parties began to form and train paramilitary units, such as the MRND's *Interahamwe* ("those who stand together") and the CDR's *Impuzamugambi* ("those who share a single goal"). Together, the groups stepped up anti-Tutsi violence and propaganda, particularly through the Hutu-dominated *Radio Télévision Libre des Milles Collines* ("RTLM") and a pictorial magazine, *Kangura* ("Wake Up"). After several failed ceasefires, the RPF and the Government of Rwanda agreed to the Arusha Peace Accords on August 4, 1993, providing for the establishment of a transitional government to include the RPF, the partial demobilization and integration of the two opposing armies, the creation of a demilitarized zone, and the deployment of a two-year U.N. peace-keeping force composed of 2,500 soldiers (the United Nations Assistance Mission for Rwanda ("UNAMIR")) to help implement the Accords.

As President Habyarimana and Burundian President Cyprien Ntaryamira were returning on April 6, 1994 from a meeting in Tanzania on the implementation of the Arusha Peace Accords, their plane was shot down over Kigali Airport. The identity and the precise motive of the assassins remain unknown. Many speculate that Hutu nationalists, angered that President Habyarimana had capitulated during the peace process, were responsible.

Radios immediately proclaimed the end of the last ceasefire and government agents set up roadblocks around the country. Massacres of Tutsi and moderate Hutu individuals began in Kigali and soon spread to other parts of the country. Fueled by genocidal propaganda broadcast over the radio and facilitated by the ubiquitous identity cards, many Hutu citizens turned against their Tutsi friends, neighbors, and compatriots. Even children were not spared. By the end of April, corpses clogged rivers and streams and lay in heaps around the country. Because ammunition was eventually in short supply, many deaths were accomplished with machetes and other rudimentary farm implements. Eventually, 500,000–800,000 individuals were left dead, almost seventy-five percent of the Tutsi population.[5]

In the face of this bloodshed, the international community remained largely silent. In January 1994—several months before the genocide began—Major–General Roméo Dallaire, the Canadian force commander of UNAMIR, had learned from a high-level informant that the extermination of the Tutsi populace was being planned. Dallaire made several requests to expand his mandate, but in fact, the opposite ensued. On

---

5. HUMAN RIGHTS WATCH, LEAVE NONE TO TELL THE TALE: GENOCIDE IN RWANDA, *available at* http://www.hrw.org/reports/1999/rwanda/Geno1-3-04.htm (citing various estimates of the number of deaths).

April 7, 1994, the Rwandan Army executed ten Belgian peacekeepers (so called "blue helmets"), apparently in order to provoke Belgium's withdrawal. Belgium complied and recalled the rest of its troops on April 19. On April 21, the U.N. Security Council reduced UNAMIR's force size to a few hundred individuals. The international community employed a series of semantic contortions to avoid using the term "genocide," afraid that the Genocide Convention would require state parties to intervene. Six weeks after the genocide began, the U.S. State Department finally permitted the use of the term.

In 1993, the Security Council had established an ad hoc international tribunal to prosecute individuals accused of committing international crimes in the ongoing war in the former Yugoslavia—the International Criminal Tribunal for the Former Yugoslavia ("ICTY"). Responding to calls that Africans deserved international justice, too, especially in the face of atrocities committed on an exponential scale, the Security Council established the International Criminal Tribunal for Rwanda ("ICTR")[6] with jurisdiction over genocide, crimes against humanity, and certain war crimes. Before the Tribunal, rape—like crimes such as murder, torture, or arbitrary detention—was not prosecutable as a freestanding crime; rather, it could only be charged as a crime against humanity or a war crime. Nor was rape an enumerated predicate of genocide, although the actus reus of the latter crime was broadly defined.

As originally designed, the two ad hoc tribunals shared a Chief Prosecutor and an Appeals Chamber. The first Chief Prosecutor was Justice Richard Goldstone, a jurist with a long history fighting human rights abuses in Africa. Below the Chief Prosecutor, separate prosecutorial offices and deputy prosecutors staffed the two institutions. At the moment, the two tribunals are subject to Security Council-ratified Completion Strategies that originally envisioned all trial proceedings completed by the end of 2008 and all appellate proceedings completed in 2010. In the context of establishing these Completion Strategies, the Security Council appointed a Chief Prosecutor dedicated to the ICTR.

Jean Paul Akayesu

In April 1993, Akayesu had been appointed *bourgmestre* of Taba Commune, located a mere 11 miles from the capital of Kigali, amid rolling hills of banana and coffee fields. As *bourgmestre*, Akayesu was responsible for maintaining public order and exercised exclusive control

---

6. Through this Resolution, the Security Council expressed the finding that widespread violations of international law within the territory of Rwanda constituted a threat to international peace and security, justifying intervention under Chapter VII of the U.N. Charter. It also concluded that establishing an international criminal tribunal to prosecute individuals responsible for international crimes in Rwanda would "contribute to the process of national reconciliation and the restoration and maintenance of peace."

over the local commune police and some authority over any *gendarmes* (members of the national police force) dispatched to the area.[7] Although he originally resisted the unfolding genocide in his region, Akayesu apparently later realized his political fortunes required him to join the fray, and he changed course.[8] The evidence established at trial that Akayesu presided over a meeting in which he urged the local population to eliminate accomplices of the rebel RPF, which—according to the indictment—"was understood by those present to mean Tutsis," and named three prominent Tutsi individuals to be killed. Akayesu also traveled throughout his region ordering particular "accomplices of the RPF" to be abused or killed, and he permitted numerous acts of violence to occur in his presence. The Prosecutor alleged that, all told, at least 2,000 murders took place in Taba Commune and that Akayesu did nothing to prevent them or punish the perpetrators.[9]

Akayesu had not originally been on the ICTR's radar until his name appeared on a list of individuals the government of Rwanda was seeking. When Akayesu surfaced in 1995, Goldstone hastily indicted him for his role in inciting and enabling violence against Tutsi individuals in his commune. In particular, Goldstone charged Akayesu with direct responsibility for genocide, complicity in genocide, incitement to genocide, crimes against humanity (extermination and murder), and war crimes (murder).

The Tribunal determined that Akayesu was indigent—despite the fact that he had been one of the most prominent figures in his community—and so counsel was appointed for him at the Tribunal's expense. The prosecution team included Yacob Haile-Mariam (Ethiopia), Pierre-Richard Prosper (United States), Mohamed Chande Othman (Tanzania), and others. During the course of the trial, jurist Louise Arbour (Canada) succeeded Justice Goldstone as the Chief Prosecutor for both the ICTR and the ICTY.

The Trial

Akayesu's trial commenced on January 9, 1997 before Trial Chamber I of the ICTR composed of Judge Laïty Kama (Senegal), presiding alongside Judge Lennart ASPERGEN (Sweden) and Judge Navanethem Pillay (South Africa). At the time, Judge Pillay was the only female judge on the Tribunal. After a number of witnesses testified to violence against

---

7. As the Trial Chamber noted, Akayesu "was in charge of the total life of the commune in terms of the economy, infrastructure, markets, medical care and the overall social life.... The *bourgmestre* was ... commonly treated with great respect and deference by the population." *Akayesu*, Case No. ICTR-96-4-T, at para. 54.

8. *Id.* at paras. 187-193.

9. *Id.* at para. 12.

the Tutsi population in Taba Commune, Witness J[10] was called to the stand on January 27, 1997. A resident of Taba Commune, J was six months pregnant when the genocide erupted. Most members of her family were killed by a group of militia that came to their home. J and her six-year-old daughter managed to escape this fate by hiding in a tree and scavenging for food. In response to questioning from a prosecutor, J mentioned, in an almost offhand way, that her six-year-old daughter had been raped.[11] J confirmed that she had never been questioned about this

---

10. Pursuant to Article 21 of the ICTR Statute and Rule 75 of the Rules of Procedure and Evidence ("RPE"), the Prosecutor in the *Akayesu* case requested, as a protective measure, that witness identities not be disclosed to the public. *Akayesu*, Case No. ICTR–96–4–T, Motion on Behalf of Prosecutors for Orders for Protective Measures for Witnesses to Crimes Alleged in Counts 1 Through 12 of the Indictment (Aug. 16, 1996). In connection with the motion, the Prosecutor submitted a Declaration of Ian Martin, the Chief of Mission for the United Nations High Commissioner for Human Rights Field Operation in Rwanda (HRFOR), which detailed attacks on survivors of and witnesses to the 1994 genocide. Virtually all eyewitnesses called on behalf of either party received protective measures.

11. J testified as follows on direct examination and in response to questions from the bench:

BY MR. HAILE–MARIAM: . . .
A. After that I went to Kabgaye.
Q. Did anybody go with you?
A. I was with my daughter, who had been raped.
Q. When was she raped?
A. They raped her when they had come to kill my father.
Q. How many men did rape your daughter?
A. Three men.
Q. Was this question ever put to you by the investigators of the Tribunal?
A. No, they did not ask me this question. . . .
Q. I would like to ask you one question, which I skipped when I was asking concerning the rape of your daughter. How old was your daughter?
A. She was six years old.
Q. I don't have any more questions, Mr. President. Thank you.
MR. PRESIDENT: Your daughter was raped by three men you say? Do you know these three men or some of the three men?
THE WITNESS: Yes, I know them.

Akayesu, Case No. ICTR–96–4–T, Transcript, at pp. 00101–00102 (Jan. 27, 1997).

Later, a different judge returned to the topic:

JUSTICE ASPERGEN: To your knowledge were there any other incidents of rape in Taba?
THE WITNESS: I heard it said that there were young girls who were at the *bureau communal* [the office of the commune] who were raped. I heard that, but I did not see it.
JUSTICE ASPERGEN: Thank you very much, Madame.

Id. at p. 00137.

by any investigators of the Tribunal. The President of the Tribunal and then Judge Aspergen returned to this line of questioning, and J testified further that she had heard that other girls had been raped in Akayesu's *bureau communal*, but she had not seen it herself.

In March 1997, Witness H—the last of the Prosecution's witnesses—was called to the stand. H testified that her house had been attacked as well and her family had fled into nearby bushes. Eventually she was discovered, raped, and abandoned. Her father found her and brought her to the *bureau communal* where he had heard people were taking refuge. By her account, most of the people there were women and children; members of the communal police and Interahamwe were also present with weapons, but did nothing to stop the violence. H testified that Akayesu was present while these abuses were occurring.

On cross examination, the defense did not take up the issue of the rapes, but Judges Pillay and then Aspergen did, asking H to elaborate upon where Akayesu was and what he was doing while women were being raped at or near the *bureau communal*. Accounts of this trial credit Judge Pillay with bringing the issue of sexual violence in Taba Commune to the attention of the prosecution.[12] The transcript reveals, however, that all members of the bench pursued this line of questioning in the face of virtual silence from the parties.[13] The transcript also suggests that the key testimony emerged somewhat randomly. If J had not offered the fact that her six-year-old daughter had been raped, the existence of sexual violence in Taba Commune might never have made it into the formal record. In addition, it is noteworthy how few details were solicited from the witnesses, almost as if no one wanted to touch the material or failed to immediately recognize its significance. That said,

---

12. *See, e.g.,* Rhonda Copelon, *Gender Crimes as War Crimes: Integrating Crimes Against Women into International Criminal Law,* 46 McGill L.J. 217, 225 (2000).

13. This is not the only case in which the judges intervened to raise the issue of gender violence. In the Decision confirming the *Prosecutor v. Nikolić* Indictment, the ICTY Trial Chamber exhorted the Prosecutor to include gender crimes in the Indictment:

> It appears that women and girls were subjected to rape and other forms of sexual assault during their detention.... Dragan Nikolić and other persons connected with the camp are related to have been directly involved in some of those rapes and sexual assaults. These allegations do not seem to relate solely to isolated incidents. The Trial Chamber feels that the prosecutor may be well advised to review these statements carefully with a view to ascertaining whether to charge Dragan Nikolić with rapes and other forms of sexual assault, either as a crime against humanity or as grave breach or war crimes.

Prosecutor v. Nikolić, Case No. IT-94-2-R61, Review of Indictment Pursuant to Rule 61 of the Rules of Procedure and Evidence, at para. 33 (Oct. 20, 1995). The Prosecutor did amend the indictment several years later to include rape charges. *Nikolić,* Case No. IT-01-46-I, First Amended Indictment, at paras. 44–59 (Feb. 12, 1999), *available at* http://www.un.org/icty/indictment/english/nik-1ai990212e.htm.

prosecutors working on the case had apparently been aware of the existence of sexual violence in Taba, through the testimony of witness H and others, but had been unable to link it to the accused sufficiently as required by principles of individual criminal responsibility.[14]

At the close of H's testimony, trial was adjourned until May 12, 1997. Trial observers brought the testimony of J and H to the attention of women's groups active in Rwanda and elsewhere. At this time, the issue of gender justice had been on the agenda of many human rights organizations. Accounts of rape in Rwanda had appeared in the press and elsewhere. Human Rights Watch, for example, issued a comprehensive report in 1996 on sexual violence during the Rwandan genocide that drew in part on interviews with women in Taba Commune.[15] The report called upon the ICTR to fully and fairly investigate and prosecute acts of sexual violence as war crimes, crimes against humanity, and genocide, where appropriate; integrate a gender perspective into investigations by, among other things, hiring more women investigators; treat sex crimes against women with the same gravity as other crimes; amend existing indictments to ensure that sexual violence charges were brought, where appropriate; and strengthen and expand the Witness Protection Unit to protect witnesses and prepare them for testifying. Mobilizing around these concerns, feminist activists formed a non-governmental organization ("NGO"), the Coalition for Women's Human Rights in Conflict Situations ("Coalition"), in 1996 specifically to monitor the ICTR and ensure that it protected the rights and interests of women appearing before the Tribunal.[16]

In light of J and H's testimony, the Coalition[17] submitted an amicus curiae brief[18] ("Coalition Brief") on behalf of over forty other NGOs and

---

14. Email from Patricia Viseur–Sellers to author (Feb. 2, 2008) (on file with author). Viseur–Sellers indicated that various amended indictments were drafted during April and May, but that these remained confidential at the time. Other accounts suggest that the Prosecutor's office in The Hague was supportive of pursuing these investigations, but that the office in Kigali, Rwanda was pursuing rape investigations less earnestly, due to lack of expertise, interest, or resolve. At the time, genocide was largely considered to be the equivalent of mass and discriminatory killings, and so prosecutors may have overlooked the potential for acts of sexual violence to serve as predicate acts for genocide. This does not explain, however, why these acts were not charged as crimes against humanity. Email from Rhonda Copelon to author (June 18, 2008) (on file with author).

15. HUMAN RIGHTS WATCH, SHATTERED LIVES: SEXUAL VIOLENCE DURING THE RWANDAN GENOCIDE AND ITS AFTERMATH (1996) [hereinafter HUMAN RIGHTS WATCH, SHATTERED LIVES], available at http://www.hrw.org/reports/1996/Rwanda.htm.

16. The Coalition continues to promote the prosecution of perpetrators of gender violence in transitional justice systems based in Africa in order to create precedents that recognize violence against women in conflict situations and to obtain justice for women survivors of sexual violence. See http://www.womensrightscoalition.org/site/main_en.php.

17. The brief was not the Coalition's first communication with the Tribunal over the dearth of indictments addressing gender violence in Rwanda. On August 7, 1996, the Coalition wrote to then Chief Prosecutor Richard Goldstone urging him to include gender

18. See note 18 on page 202.

law clinics to the ICTR on May 27, 1997.[19] The Coalition Brief called upon the Trial Chamber to exercise its inherent supervisory authority to invite the Prosecutor to amend the indictment against Akayesu to charge rape and other serious acts of sexual violence. It also urged the Trial Chamber to expand the investigation to inquire into the prevalence of sexual violence in Rwanda, and to examine why none of the indictments issued up until that point had included charges of rape or sexual assault, despite the existence of probative evidence in the record,[20] and in the

---

crimes in his Rwandan indictments and to undertake a number of reforms to ensure that such crimes were fully and effectively investigated. Letter from Coalition for Women's Human Rights in Conflict Situations to Chief Prosecutor Richard Goldstone (Aug. 7, 1996) (on file with the author).

18. Amicus Brief Respecting Amendment of the Indictment and Supplementation of the Evidence to Ensure the Prosecution of Rape and Other Sexual Violence within the Competence of the Tribunal, Coalition for Women's Human Rights in Conflict Situations, *available at* http://www.womensrightscoalition.org/site/advocacyDossiers/rwanda/Akayesu/amicusbrief_en.php [hereinafter Coalition Brief].

19. The Brief is not part of the official online record of the case, for reasons that are not entirely clear. The speculation is that there were procedural errors in its filing, perhaps because the Coalition did not seek leave of the Tribunal to appear as amicus in advance of its submission (the brief itself includes a prefatory motion under Rule 74). In any case, it is not clear if leave was strictly necessary; an ICTY document entitled "Information Concerning the Submission of Amicus Curiae Briefs" (IT/122), dated March 27, 1997, indicated that "amicus briefs may be submitted unsolicited or in response to a general invitation from a Trial Chamber." A subsequent letter from the President of the ICTR to the Coalition acknowledged receipt of the Brief and indicated that it was placed in the official case file and served on all parties. *See* Letter from Laïty Kama to Coalition for Women's Human Rights in Conflict Situations (June 4, 1998) (on file with the author). The Coalition also received letters from the Registrar and the Office of the Prosecutor acknowledging receipt. Indeed, on July 7, 1997, after the indictment had been amended, the Coalition received a letter inviting its members to seek leave to present arguments concerning the Brief. The Coalition declined, as the indictment had already been amended. Email from Rhonda Copelon to author (June 18, 2008) (on file with author). The Judgment refers to the Coalition Brief in this passage:

> The Chamber notes that the Defence in its closing statement questioned whether the Indictment was amended in response to public pressure concerning the prosecution of sexual violence. The Chamber understands that the amendment of the Indictment resulted from the spontaneous testimony of sexual violence by Witness J and Witness H during the course of this trial and the subsequent investigation of the Prosecution, rather than from public pressure. Nevertheless, the Chamber takes note of the interest shown in this issue by non-governmental organizations, which it considers as indicative of public concern over the historical exclusion of rape and other forms of sexual violence from the investigation and prosecution of war crimes. The investigation and presentation of evidence relating to sexual violence is in the interest of justice.

Akayesu, Case No. ICTR–96–4–T, at para. 417.

20. At the time the brief was filed, amici were unable to obtain a full transcript of the trial because it was not yet publicly available. They were, thus, relying upon unofficial public reports of the trial.

public domain, supporting such charges. The Coalition Brief argued further that the Tribunal, in the civil law tradition, had the authority to issue orders as necessary for the purposes of investigation, the conduct of the trial, and the production of additional evidence or the summoning of witnesses. Without an amendment to the indictment, the Coalition Brief argued, Akayesu would be granted immunity for rapes committed within his commune, the women of Taba would be denied justice, and the Tribunal would send a message that sexual violence is not as serious as other forms of assault. The Coalition Brief argued that the indictment should be amended to charge rape and sexual mutilation as crimes against humanity (torture, rape, and persecution on political, racial or religious grounds) and war crimes (violence to life, health and physical or mental well-being; outrages upon human dignity, in particular humiliating and degrading treatment, rape, and any form of indecent assault; and threats to commit same). The Coalition Brief also suggested that the Prosecutor consider charging rape as genocide, arguing that rape and sexual violence were an integral and pervasive part of the Hutu genocidal campaign designed "to destroy a woman from a physical, mental or social perspective and [to destroy] her capacity to participate in the reproduction and production of the community."[21]

On June 17, 1997, the Prosecution sought a hearing before the Trial Chamber. During this hearing, Prosper and his co-counsel, Sara Darehshori (United States), made an oral motion to amend the indictment in light of the testimony about sexual violence that had emerged during the trial. Prosper argued that he had been aware of the acts of rape and sexual violence in Taba Commune, but had been unable to connect these crimes to the defendant until hearing the testimony of J and H. He explained:

> I think it's safe to say that the issue of sexual violence is of great importance to the Office of the Prosecutor and we take this issue very, very seriously. We feel that sexual violence being used as a weapon or as a tool is deplorable and cannot be accepted. In this case it is clear throughout the testimony that there had been hints that there were acts of sexual violence occurring in the Taba Commune. It came up not only in the testimony of Witness J or Witness H but I have to say it also came up in prior investigations, but the ... information we received before, in our opinion, was not enough to link the accused to the acts of sexual violence. We continued to look into it.... After receiving [additional witness statements], we as the Office of the Prosecutor feel that we are duty bound to come here today and make this request....[22]

---

21. Coalition Brief, *supra* note 18, at para. 19.

22. *Akayesu*, Case No. ICTR–96–4–T, Transcript, at p. 6 (June 17, 1997).

Addressing the absence of allegations concerning sexual violence in the first indictment, Prosper explained: "Maybe because the shame that sometimes accompanies these acts prevented the women from testifying or declaring what occurred to them or also I'm ready to admit, maybe sometimes we were not as sensitive as we should have been on the issue."[23] He denied that the Prosecution was motivated by the Coalition Brief. "I would like to say to this Chamber right now and make it perfectly clear that the amicus curiae is not motivating us today. It is not motivating us today and, in fact, it can only be considered as a factor. And I say this as a factor because what it does is it reminds us of the importance of the issue of sexual violence."[24] The prosecution proposed to amend the indictment to charge the crime against humanity of rape, the crime against humanity of inhumane acts, and the war crime of outrages upon personal dignity, including rape and indecent assault, under Common Article 3 and Additional Protocol II.[25] Prosper did not propose to amend the genocide counts to specifically include reference to sexual violence as predicate acts of genocide. Not surprisingly, Akayesu's counsel opposed the proposed amendments, arguing that the timing was improvident and that the defense had been given no time to consider the supporting materials, having been provided copies of witness statements—most of which were dated June 12, 1997—over the preceding weekend and an English translation of the proposed Amended Indictment that morning.

After deliberating for ten minutes, the Chamber granted leave to amend and postponed the trial until October 22, 1997. The following three paragraphs concerned with sexual violence in Taba were then added to the amended indictment:

> 10A. In this indictment, acts of sexual violence include forcible sexual penetration of the vagina, anus or oral cavity by a penis and/or of the vagina or anus by some other object, and sexual abuse, such as forced nudity....
>
> 12A. Between April 7 and the end of June, 1994, hundreds of civilians (hereinafter "displaced civilians") sought refuge at the *bureau communal*. The majority of these displaced civilians were Tutsi. While seeking refuge at the *bureau communal*, female displaced civilians were regularly taken by armed local militia and/or communal police and subjected to sexual violence, and/or beaten on or near the *bureau communal* premises. Displaced civilians were also murdered frequently on or near the *bureau communal* premises. Many women were forced to endure multiple acts of sexual violence

---

23. *Id.* at 7.
24. *Id.* at 8.
25. *Id.* at 18.

which were at times committed by more than one assailant. These acts of sexual violence were generally accompanied by explicit threats of death or bodily harm. The female displaced civilians lived in constant fear and their physical and psychological health deteriorated as a result of the sexual violence and beatings and killings.

12B. Jean Paul Akayesu knew that the acts of sexual violence, beatings and murders were being committed and was at times present during their commission. Jean Paul Akayesu facilitated the commission of the sexual violence, beatings and murders by allowing the sexual violence and beatings and murders to occur on or near the *bureau communal* premises. By virtue of his presence during the commission of the sexual violence, beatings and murders and by failing to prevent the sexual violence, beatings and murders, Jean Paul Akayesu encouraged these activities.[26]

The Prosecution also added three additional counts, charging Akayesu with the crimes against humanity of rape and "other inhumane acts" as well as the war crime of committing "outrages upon personal dignity, in particular rape, degrading and humiliating treatment and indecent assault."[27] The genocide counts were textually unchanged. Due to the placement of the new factual allegations immediately after paragraph 12 as set forth above, however, the alleged acts of sexual violence were incorporated by reference into the original genocide counts of the indictment. So, in essence, the Prosecution also charged sexual violence as a predicate act of genocide, although it had not expressly sought, or received, leave to do so.[28]

Testimony of Sexual Violence

The trial recommenced on October 23, 1997 pursuant to the amended indictment. Akayesu again pled not guilty. The Prosecution presented six new witnesses, five of whom (JJ, OO, KK, NN, and PP) testified to being raped repeatedly and/or to seeing other women and girls being raped, humiliated, or sexually abused. All testified that Akayesu was either present or nearby when the abuses occurred and that he was often supervising, encouraging, or ordering the direct perpetrators. The harrowing testimony of Witness JJ about the prevalence of rape in the *bureau communal*, as summarized by the Trial Chamber, is emblematic of what transpired in Taba Commune on that day.

---

26. *Akayesu*, Case No. ICTR–96–4–I, Amended Indictment (June 17, 1997).

27. *Id.*

28. According to Patricia Viseur–Sellers, it was not necessary to amend the genocide counts specifically, because the definition of genocide, and particularly the actus reus of causing serious bodily or mental harm, covered the new evidence of sexual violence. Adding the new allegations was sufficient to charge genocidal rape. Viseur–Sellers Email, *supra* note 14.

421. ... Witness JJ testified that this happened to her—that she was stripped of her clothing and raped in front of other people. At the request of the Prosecutor and with great embarrassment, she explicitly specified that the rapist, a young man armed with an axe and a long knife, penetrated her vagina with his penis. She stated that on this occasion she was raped twice. Subsequently, she told the Chamber, on a day when it was raining, she was taken by force from near the *bureau communal* into the cultural center within the compound of the *bureau communal*, in a group of approximately fifteen girls and women. In the cultural center, according to Witness JJ, they were raped. She was raped twice by one man. Then another man came to where she was lying and he also raped her. A third man then raped her, she said, at which point she described herself as feeling near dead. Witness JJ testified that she was at a later time dragged back to the cultural center in a group of approximately ten girls and women and they were raped. She was raped again, two times. Witness JJ testified that she could not count the total number of times she was raped. She said, "each time you encountered attackers they would rape you,"—in the forest, in the sorghum fields. Witness JJ related to the Chamber the experience of finding her sister before she died, having been raped and cut with a machete.

422. Witness JJ testified that when they arrived at the *bureau communal* the women were hoping the authorities would defend them but she was surprised to the contrary.... On the way to the cultural center the first time she was raped there, Witness JJ said that she and the others were taken past the Accused and that he was looking at them. The second time she was taken to the cultural center to be raped, Witness JJ recalled seeing the Accused standing at the entrance of the cultural center and hearing him say loudly to the Interahamwe, "Never ask me again what a Tutsi woman tastes like," and "Tomorrow they will be killed." According to Witness JJ, most of the girls and women were subsequently killed, either brought to the river and killed there, after having returned to their houses, or killed at the *bureau communal*. Witness JJ testified that she never saw the Accused rape anyone, but she, like Witness H, believed that he had the means to prevent the rapes from taking place and never even tried to do so.[29]

A number of defense witnesses—many of whom were in detention in Rwanda—testified that they did not see any rapes in the *bureau communal*.[30] Several also testified that Akayesu attempted to help Tutsi individuals, by issuing *laissez-passers* and holding off the *Interahamwe*. Defense

---

29. *Akayesu*, Case No. ICTR–96–4–T, at paras. 421–22.
30. *Id.* at paras. 439–45.

witness Matata, called as an expert, expressed the opinion that "rapists were more interested in satisfying their physical needs, that there were spontaneous acts of desire even in the context of killing [and] that Tutsi women, in general, are quite beautiful and that raping them is not necessarily intended to destroy an ethnic group, but rather to have a beautiful woman."[31] Akayesu also secured the testimony of Major-General Roméo Dallaire, former force commander of UNAMIR, in an effort to prove that if Dallaire could not stop the abuses, Akayesu could not have been expected to do so.

This was Akayesu's defense when he finally took the stand on March 12, 1998. Akayesu tried to refashion the facts to show he was a figurehead under the control of the *Interahamwe* and that he did all he could to reduce the violence in his commune. On direct examination, Akayesu conceded that genocide occurred in Rwanda and that acts of violence, including killings, occurred in Taba Commune. He denied, however, that any acts of rape or other sexual violence took place in his *bureau communal*, while he was present or otherwise.[32] Prosper, the lead prosecutor, did not pursue the issue on cross examination, focusing instead on the meeting in Gishyeshye sector in which the incitement to genocide allegedly occurred.[33] Judge Pillay raised the issue of sexual violence, after Prosper announced he had no more questions, by asking Akayesu for his reaction to the testimony on rape that he had heard. Akayesu again denied that he had witnessed acts of rape in his Commune.[34] He also questioned why evidence of rape had not been in the initial witness statements procured by the Prosecution. He suggested that the indictment had been amended because of pressure from the women's movement and that the testimony was fabricated: "There have been some amicus curiae. There have been activities. Akayesu must be accused of rape. People, women are agitated in Rwanda. They are

---

31. *Id.* at para. 442.

32. *Akayesu*, Case No. ICTR-96-4-T, Transcript (Direct Examination) (Mar. 12, 1998). In its Judgment, the Trial Chamber noted "the Accused's emphatic denial of facts which are not entirely within his knowledge." *Akayesu*, Case No. ICTR-96-4-T, at para. 32. One observer has noted that defendants almost always deny responsibility for acts of sexual violence, even when they acknowledge their involvement in other crimes. GAËLLE BRETON-LE GOFF *on behalf of the* COALITION FOR WOMEN'S HUMAN RIGHTS IN CONFLICT SITUATIONS, ANALYSIS OF TRENDS IN SEXUAL VIOLENCE PROSECUTIONS IN INDICTMENTS BY THE INTERNATIONAL CRIMINAL TRIBUNAL FOR RWANDA (ICTR) FROM NOVEMBER 1995 TO NOVEMBER 2002 (Nov. 28, 2002), *available at* http://www.womensrightscoalition.org/site/advocacyDossiers/rwanda/rapeVictimssDeniedJustice/analysisoftrends_en.php.

33. *Akayesu*, Case No. ICTR-96-4-T, Transcript (Cross Examination), at pp. 189-92 (Mar. 13, 1998).

34. In particular, Akayesu testified: "nobody ever reported to me that it had taken place, that we had rape in my commune, and certainly nothing, to the best of my knowledge, was done in the *bureau communal* and I never saw with my eyes anybody being raped in the *bureau communal*." *Id.* at p. 190.

awakened. They are worked up to agree that they have been raped. So there is a change in my indictment."[35]

In closing arguments, the Prosecution focused more actively on the acts of sexual violence in the record, arguing that they constituted "serious bodily and mental harm" and "conditions of life calculated" to destroy the group within the meaning of the genocide definition.[36] In their closing, defense counsel attacked the testimony of various witnesses on the ground that they lacked credibility and accuracy, arguing, for example, that it was incredible that J—being six months pregnant—would have been able to climb a tree. The defense also argued that the rape allegations were a reaction to "public pressure" without basis in reality and that a syndicate of informers had procured the testimony against his client in an effort to misappropriate his property, notwithstanding that Akayesu had been found indigent.[37] All told, the trial proceedings consumed about sixty days—over fourteen months. The Chamber retired for their deliberations.

Genocidal Rape in Theory

Women experience armed conflict and repression in ways that are different from men. In particular, "[w]omen are violated in ways that men are not, or rarely are."[38] Rape and other forms of sexual violence against women have long been employed as weapons of war and as tools to subjugate entire communities.[39] The 1863 Lieber Code, one of the first efforts to codify the laws of war, designated rape as a war crime,[40]

---

35. *Id.* at p. 192. *See also Akayesu*, Case No. ICTR–96–4–T, at para. 448.

36. *Akayesu*, Case No. ICTR–96–4–T, Transcript (Closing Arguments), at pp. 14–19 (Mar. 23, 1998).

37. *Akayesu*, Case No. ICTR–96–4–T, Transcript, at pp. 54–55 (Mar. 26, 1998). *See also Akayesu*, Case No. ICTR–96–4–T, at paras. 44–47 (ruling that such allegations should be put to particular witnesses on cross examination rather than raised with respect to all witnesses).

38. Catherine A. MacKinnon, *Crimes of War, Crimes of Peace*, in ON HUMAN RIGHTS: THE OXFORD AMNESTY LECTURES 1993 83, 85 (Stephen Shute and Susan Hurley eds., 1993).

39. As Susan Brownmiller has written about rape in wartime:

Rape of a doubly dehumanized object—as woman, as enemy—carries its own terrible logic. In one act of aggression, the collective spirit of women and of the nation is broken, leaving a reminder long after the troops depart. And if she survives the assault, what does the victim of wartime rape become to her people? Evidence of the enemy's bestiality. Symbol of her nation's defeat. A pariah. Damaged property. A pawn in the subtle wars of international propaganda.

Susan Brownmiller, *Making Female Bodies the Battlefield*, NEWSWEEK, Jan. 4, 1993, at 37. *See also* SUSAN BROWNMILLER, AGAINST OUR WILL: MEN, WOMEN AND RAPE 31–113 (1975) (discussing rape and war).

40. *See* Francis Lieber, Instructions for the Government of Armies of the United States in the Field, art. 47 (Apr. 24, 1863) ("Crimes punishable by all penal codes, such as

rejecting the customary view that the rape of women associated with the enemy was an expected spoil, inevitable byproduct, or legitimate tactic of war. Despite this promising beginning, many modern international humanitarian law treaties euphemistically condemn sexual violence as a violation of dignity or honor rather than as crime of assault against the physical integrity of the victim. Even when positive law recognizes rape as an international crime, prosecutions may be sparse when the commission of rape is invisible, considered inevitable, or trivialized. For example, the World War II Nuremberg indictment and Judgment did not mention rape, although evidence of rape was entered into the record. The contemporaneous Tokyo Tribunal did hold Japanese officials liable for failing to control their troops, including during the literal and metaphorical "Rape of Nanking"; however, the proceedings were entirely silent as to the sexual slavery suffered by the so-called "comfort women," and victims continue to seek justice today. Modern definitions of international crimes now routinely include rape and other forms of sexual violence as enumerated acts. The crime of genocide, which anchored the indictment against Akayesu, has not been amended since its inception. The definition of genocide does not mention sexual violence per se, but it does encompass various acts involving the commission of serious bodily and mental harm.

The term genocide "is a modern word for an old crime."[41] When the Allies unveiled the Nazi concentration camps, revealing the horrific full scope of the Nazi "Final Solution," the world community was faced with the challenge of how to understand and explain the enormity of the Holocaust. As an initial response, and in reply to Winston Churchill's portrayal of the entirety of Nazi violence as a "crime without a name,"[42] the Polish scholar and jurist Raphaël Lemkin coined the term "genocide" from the Greek word *genos* (race, tribe) and the Latin word *caedere* (to kill). For Lemkin, who had fled Poland upon the German invasion, the critical elements of genocide were not the individual acts, though they may be crimes in themselves, but the broader aim to destroy entire human collectivities.[43] On Lemkin's urging, the General Assembly even-

---

arson, murder, maiming, assaults, highway robbery, theft, burglary, fraud, forgery, and rape, if committed by an American soldier in a hostile country against its inhabitants, are not only punishable as at home, but in all cases in which death is not inflicted, the severer punishment shall be preferred."). President Abraham Lincoln promulgated the Lieber Code to govern Union forces during the United States Civil War.

41. Louis René Beres, *Justice and Realpolitik: International Law and the Prevention of Genocide*, 33 AM. J. JURIS. 123, 124 (1988).

42. WINSTON S. CHURCHILL III, THE CHURCHILL WAR PAPERS: THE EVER-WIDENING WAR 1099–1106 (Martin Gilbert ed. 2000), *available at* http://ibiblio.org/pha/policy/1941/410824a.html.

43. *See* RAPHAËL LEMKIN, AXIS RULE IN OCCUPIED EUROPE: LAWS OF OCCUPATION, ANALYSIS OF GOVERNMENT, PROPOSALS FOR REDRESS 79 (1944).

tually promulgated a multilateral treaty defining the crime of genocide (Article II) as follows:

In the present Convention, genocide means any of the following acts committed with intent to destroy, in whole or in part, a national, ethnical, racial or religious group, as such:

(a) Killing members of the group;

(b) Causing serious bodily or mental harm to members of the group;

(c) Deliberately inflicting on the group conditions of life calculated to bring about its physical destruction in whole or in part;

(d) Imposing measures intended to prevent births within the group;

(e) Forcibly transferring children of the group to another group.[44]

This definition has been incorporated verbatim into the statutes of the ad hoc criminal tribunals and the permanent International Criminal Court (ICC). While there have been some prosecutions for genocide before the ICTY, all the defendants before the ICTR have been prosecuted with participation of one sort or another in this "crime of crimes."[45] Akayesu was the first.

The idea that acts of rape and other forms of sexual violence could be charged as acts of genocide—as well as crimes against humanity and war crimes—was first debated in connection with the violence in the former Yugoslavia. As that war broke out, reports by journalists and women's groups surfaced that Bosnian Muslim, and to a lesser extent Croat, women were being detained in a network of rape camps or were being forcibly impregnated by Serbian aggressors intent on propagating more Serb children.[46] Evidence emerged that Bosnian Serb soldiers had been instructed to employ rape to demoralize the Muslim forces and maximize the shame and humiliation experienced by the Muslim commu-

---

44. Convention on the Prevention and Punishment of the Crime of Genocide, Dec. 9, 1948, 78 U.N.T.S. 277 (entered into force Jan. 12, 1951) [hereinafter Genocide Convention].

45. *Akayesu*, Case No. ICTR-96-4-T, Sentencing Hearing (Oct. 2, 1998).

46. Most importantly, a Special Rapporteur appointed by the U.N. Commission on Human Rights highlighted the deliberate and extensive use of rape in the former Yugoslavia as an attack on an individual victim and also as a method of ethnic cleansing "intended to humiliate, shame, degrade and terrify the entire ethnic group." Tadeusz Mazowiecki, *Report on the Situation of Human Rights in the Territory of the former Yugoslavia*, Annex at 57, U.N. Doc. A/48/92–S/25341 (Feb. 10, 1993). *See also* Final Report of the Commission of Experts Established Pursuant to S.C. Res. 780 (1992), U.N. Doc. S/1994/674 (May 27, 1994) (also detailing systemic practice of rape).

nity.[47] There was also evidence that Serbian soldiers were attempting to alter the demographic profile of the country by forcing women to carry babies born of rape to term. The first legal cases to plead rape as genocide were a pair of Alien Tort Statute cases brought in New York against Radovan Karadžić, the self-proclaimed President of Republika Srpska (the Serbian enclave in Bosnia–Herzegovina), in which both sets of plaintiffs won default judgments against the defendant.[48]

The allegations of widespread sexual violence in the former Yugoslavia mobilized the feminist community globally, but especially in the United States, to advocate the creation of a vigorous system of international justice to prosecute such crimes.[49] Scholars and activists conceptualized the crime of genocidal rape as a way to physically and psychologically harm individual victims while at the same time undermining and denigrating the group or community to which the women belonged.[50] A new concept was needed, feminist academics and advocates argued, to counter the tendency within international criminal law to either characterize acts of rape as isolated war crimes or to overlook them as incidental to issues of real international concern: the perpetration of aggressive war, ethnic cleansing, or genocide.[51]

As multiple sources have now revealed, rape in Rwanda was committed on a massive scale. Although accurate statistics are impossible to gather,[52] estimates range from 250,000 to 500,000 rapes during the

---

47. See Richard P. Barrett & Laura E. Little, *Lessons of Yugoslav Rape Trials: A Role for Conspiracy Law in International Tribunals*, 88 MINN. L. REV. 30, 69–72 (2003).

48. See Kadić v. Karadžić, 70 F.3d 232, 236–37 (2d Cir. 1995) (reinstating claims alleging "various atrocities, including brutal acts of rape, forced prostitution, forced impregnation, torture, and summary execution, carried out by Bosnian–Serb military forces as part of a genocidal campaign conducted in the course of the Bosnian war."). Karadžić has been indicted by the ICTY and was only recently brought into custody to stand trial.

49. ARYEH NEIER, WAR CRIMES: BRUTALITY, GENOCIDE, TERROR, AND THE STRUGGLE FOR JUSTICE 178 (1998) (noting that gender crimes abroad became a domestic political issue for United States women). See also Symposium: *Rape as a Weapon of War in the Former Yugoslavia*, 5 HASTINGS WOMEN'S L.J. 1, 1–315 (1994).

50. CHRISTOPHER C. TAYLOR, SACRIFICE AS TERROR: THE RWANDAN GENOCIDE OF 1994 151–79 (1999).

51. MacKinnon, *supra* note 38, at 88 (noting that violations are seen "either as genocide or as rape, or as femicide but not genocide, but not as rape as a form of genocide specifically directed at women. [An act of rape] is seen either as part of a campaign of Serbia against non-Serbia or an onslaught by combatants against civilians, but not an attack by men against women. Or, in the feminist whitewash, it becomes just another instance of aggression by all men against all women all the time, rather than what it is, which is rape by certain men against certain women.").

52. Alex Obote–Odora, *Rape and Sexual Violence in International Law: ICTR Contributions*, 12 NEW ENG. J. INT'L. & COMP. L. 135, 141 (2005) ("Sex-based crimes are not easily identifiable, like gunshot wounds or amputated limbs. This is because these crimes inflict physical and psychological wounds, which women can conceal to avoid further emotional

period of the genocide.[53] Rape in Rwanda was also accompanied by sexual mutilation and torture. Women and girls were often literally raped to death by perpetrators wielding machetes, sharpened sticks, broken bottles, and other implements. Major Brent Beardsley, the assistant to Major–General Dallaire, was once asked before the ICTR to describe the female corpses he saw. He responded:

> [W]hen they killed women it appeared that the blows that had killed them were aimed at sexual organs, either breasts or vagina; they had been deliberately swiped or slashed in those areas.... [G]irls as young as six, seven years of age, their vaginas would be split and swollen from obviously multiple gang rape, and they would have been killed in that position.[54]

Other women were held as "wives" in a form of sexual slavery. Many women were rendered infertile or HIV-positive by this sexual violence. In the former Yugoslavia, forced impregnation was a hallmark of sexual violence and a key proof point for rape as genocide.[55] In the Rwandan context, the emphasis on the reproductive consequences of rape was less salient; most women were killed or left for dead after they were raped. Many of the women who survived their rapes did end up pregnant. The lack of available abortion in the largely Catholic country of Rwanda resulted in the births of innumerable *enfants de mauvais souvenir*—"children of bad memories."[56]

The evidence presented before the ICTR revealed that Hutu Power adherents targeted women victims on the basis of both their gender and their ethnicity. This intersection is highlighted by the explicitly gendered hate propaganda employed by Hutu Power adherents in the months leading up to the genocide.[57] This propaganda vilified Tutsi women as

---

anguish, ostracization, and retaliation from perpetrators who may live nearby. [Estimates based on pregnancies] do not account for the women whose injuries prevented them from conceiving a child, or the number of women who experienced multiple rapes and gang rapes.").

53. *See* U.N. Special Rapporteur of the Commission on Human Rights under para. 20 of S.C. Res. S–3/1, *Report on the Situation of Human Rights in Rwanda*, para. 16, U.N. Doc. E/CN.4/1996/68 (Jan. 29, 1996), *available at* http://www1.umn.edu/humanrts/commission/country52/68–rwa.htm ("rape was the rule and its absence the exception").

54. Binaifer Nowrojee, *"Your Justice is Too Slow": Will the ICTR Fail Rwanda's Rape Victims?*, 1 (United Nations Research Institute for Social Development Occasional Paper 10, Nov. 15, 2005), *available at*: http://www.unrisd.org/80256B3C005BCCF9/(http Publications)/56FE32D5C0F6DCE9C125710F0045D89F?OpenDocument.

55. *See* R. Charli Carpenter, *Surfacing Children: Limitations of Genocidal Rape Discourse*, 22 Hum. Rts. Q. 428, 437–39 (2000).

56. Emily Wax, *Rwandans Are Struggling to Love Children of Hate*, Wash. Post, Mar. 28, 2004, at A01, *available at* http://www.genocidewatch.org/RwandanAreStrugglingToLovChildreno%20Hate.htm.

57. *See generally* Llezlie L. Green, *Gender Hate Propaganda and Sexual Violence in the Rwandan Genocide: An Argument for Intersectionality in International Law*, 33 Colum. Hum. Rts. L. Rev. 733 (2002).

emblematic of Tutsi hegemony and invited the abuse of Tutsi women as a way to destroy the Tutsi community. The *Ten Commandments of the Hutu*, an extremist ideological tract published in *Kangura*, contained four commandments denigrating Tutsi women, one of which warned that "A Tutsi woman ... works for the interests of her Tutsi ethnic group. As a result, we shall consider a traitor any Hutu who marries a Tutsi woman, befriends a Tutsi woman, or employs a Tutsi woman as a secretary or concubine."[58] *Kangura* also warned that the Tutsi "will not hesitate to transform their sisters, wives and mothers into pistols" to conquer Rwanda.[59] In the iconography and rhetoric of Hutu propaganda, Tutsi women were demonized as sexual "infiltrators" intent on undermining Hutu Power. In a case against the editor-in-chief of *Kangura*, the Trial Chamber noted that this saturation propaganda created a "framework" that "made the sexual attack of Tutsi women a foreseeable consequence."[60] This propaganda confirms that acts of rape and other sexual violence were not a mere "side effect" of the armed conflict between the Rwandan Army and the RPF but were instead "an integral part of a genocidal campaign."[61]

The sudden focus on genocidal rape raised concerns among members of the feminist legal community. Some objected to the notion that there is something more egregious about genocidal rape than "ordinary" rape or even rape committed in wartime. The concern was that acknowledging and penalizing rape only when it is a form of genocide risks "rendering rape invisible once again."[62] Some emphasized that the fixation on the ethnic element of the crime would obscure the gendered nature of the genocidal rape, which represents an intersection between

---

58. SAMANTHA POWER, A PROBLEM FROM HELL: AMERICA AND THE AGE OF GENOCIDE 338 (2002).

59. HUMAN RIGHTS WATCH, SHATTERED LIVES, *supra* note 15.

60. Prosecutor v. Nahimana, Barayagwiza, and Ngeze, Case No. ICTR-99-52-T, Judgment, at para. 118 (Dec. 3, 2003) ("The Chamber notes that Tutsi women, in particular, were targeted for persecution. The portrayal of the Tutsi woman as a *femme fatale*, and the message that Tutsi women were seductive agents of the enemy was conveyed repeatedly by RTLM and *Kangura*."). Like *Akayesu*, *Nahimana* was heard by Trial Chamber I with Judge Pillay presiding, now joined by Judges Erik Mse (Norway) and Asoka de Zoysa Gunawardana (Sri Lanka).

61. Green, *supra* note 57, at 734.

62. Rhonda Copelon, *Gendered War Crimes: Reconceptualizing Rape in a Time of War*, *in* WOMEN'S RIGHTS, HUMAN RIGHTS: INTERNATIONAL FEMINIST PERSPECTIVES 197, 204 (Julie S. Peters & Andrea Wolper eds., 1995) ("[W]e must surface gender in the midst of genocide at the same time that we avoid dualistic thinking. We must examine critically the claim that rape as a tool of 'ethnic cleansing' is unique, worse than, or incomparable to other forms of rape in war or in peace—even while we recognize that rape coupled with genocide inflicts multiple, intersectional harms.... To exaggerate the distinctiveness of genocidal rape obviates the atrocity of common rape.").

ethnic violence and sexualized violence.[63] Adherents of this view also sought to avoid "privileging" some victims of rape over others by conceptualizing them as victims of genocide—the crime at the pinnacle of international criminal law.[64]

In contrast, proponents of the recognition of genocidal rape argued that viewing sex/gender as the only vector upon which violence may be committed in an act of rape ignores the intersectionality of women's identities.[65] It accordingly overlooks the fact that women may be seen, and may see themselves, more saliently as members of a besieged ethnic group than as bearers of a particular sex/gender, especially in the context of inter-ethnic warfare. While rape happens "on all sides" in war as in peace, genocidal rape is more often unidirectional, committed by the aggressor group against the victim group. This asymmetry belies laying blame solely along gender lines and thus equalizing the responsibility of all sides in a conflict.[66] The exploitation of the intersectionality of women's identity in a multiethnic society thus provides a key factor differentiating genocidal rape from "ordinary" rape in war or peace.[67] Furthermore, proponents of the concept argued that genocidal rape is almost inevitably the result of a policy or deliberate strategy of a perpetrator group[68] to effectuate the destruction—in whole or in part—of a protected group through attacks on women as a vulnerable and discrete segment of a community. A single act of rape may implicate multiple international criminal law prohibitions, but it is this surplus of intent inherent to the crime of genocide that also distinguishes genocidal rape from rape perpetrated as a war crime or a crime against humanity, or rape committed as an act of gender persecution.

---

63. Rhonda Copelon, *Surfacing Gender: Re-Engraving Crimes Against Women in Humanitarian Law*, 5 HASTINGS WOMEN'S L.J. 243, 246 (1994).

64. *See also* Neier, *supra* note 49, at 186 (arguing that focusing on genocidal rape "distorted the reality of the harm done to women and men").

65. For more on intersectionality, *see generally* Kimberlé Crenshaw, *Mapping the Margins: Intersectionality, Identity Politics, and Violence Against Women of Color*, 43 STAN. L. REV. 1241 (1991).

66. The debate over whether women should advance gender solidarity over nationalism with respect to the rapes in the former Yugoslavia seriously split the feminist community in that region. *See* Jelena Batinic, *Feminism, Nationalism, and War: The 'Yugoslav Case' in Feminist Texts*, 3 J. INT'L WOMEN'S STUD. 2 (2001).

67. *See* BEVERLY ALLEN, RAPE WARFARE: THE HIDDEN GENOCIDE IN BOSNIA-HERZEGOVINA AND CROATIA 39, 62, 75 (1996).

68. MacKinnon, *supra* note 38, at 89 (writing of the use of rape in the former Yugoslavia, "[t]his is ethnic rape as an official policy of war.... It is rape under orders.... It is rape as an instrument of forced exile.... It is rape to be seen and heard by others, rape as spectacle. It is rape to shatter a people, drive a wedge through a community. It is the rape of misogyny liberated by xenophobia and unleashed by official command.").

The notion of genocidal rape was of thus of great concern to feminist academics and activists. It was not until *Akayesu* that the idea was first litigated and ultimately grounded in the jurisprudence of international criminal law. The opinion is chilling in its ability to demonstrate the lived experience of women during a genocide.

The Judgment: Prosecutor v. Akayesu

In its 169–page Judgment, the Tribunal found Akayesu liable for inciting, ordering, and causing harm to Tutsi individuals seeking refuge in the *bureau communal*. For this, he was convicted of murder, extermination, and torture as crimes against humanity. Akayesu was acquitted on the war crimes counts, including the new Count 15 concerning outrages upon dignity under Protocol II to the Geneva Conventions, based on the Trial Chamber's ruling that the Prosecutor had failed to demonstrate that the events in Taba Commune were sufficiently connected to the armed conflict between the Rwandan government and the RPF being fought elsewhere in the country.[69]

When it turned to the allegations of Akayesu's involvement in acts of sexual violence in the record, the Chamber limited its inquiry to several incidents that occurred in the *bureau communal*: the rape of a number of girls and women (including Witness JJ and OO) and the forced undressing of several women, who were then forced to perform "gymnastics" in public. The victims of several of these events did not testify at trial, although the incidents were recounted by other eyewitnesses. The Chamber disregarded the evidence in the record concerned with sexual assaults committed outside the *bureau communal* on the ground that the indictment alleged only Akayesu's responsibility for acts "on or near" the compound.

Through ordering, instigating or aiding and abetting these acts, Akayesu was found guilty of the crimes against humanity of rape and "other inhumane acts."[70] In so holding, the Chamber, for the first time in history, defined rape and sexual violence under international law:

---

69. The Prosecution had presented evidence that Akayesu wore a military jacket, carried a weapon, and assisted the members of the military upon their arrival in Taba Commune; however, this was deemed insufficient to trigger the applicability of the war crimes prohibitions in the ICTR Statute. *Akayesu*, Case No. ICTR–96–4–T, at paras. 641–44. The Prosecution successfully appealed the legal standard employed by the Trial Chamber when it held that the defendant must be shown to be a commander, combatant, or other member of the armed forces; however, the Appeals Chamber left the verdict on the war crimes counts untouched. *Akayesu*, Case No. ICTR–96–4–A, Judgment of the Appeals Chamber, at paras. 425–46 (June 1, 2001) [hereinafter, *Akayesu* Appeals Judgment].

70. *Akayesu*, Case No. ICTR–96–4–T, at paras. 696–7. Specifically, the Chamber held that Akayesu was responsible for these acts "by allowing them to take place on or near the premises of the *bureau communal* and by facilitating the commission of such sexual violence through his words of encouragement in other acts of sexual violence which, by

The Tribunal considers that rape is a form of aggression and that the central elements of the crime of rape cannot be captured in a mechanical description of objects and body parts. The Tribunal also notes the cultural sensitivities involved in public discussion of intimate matters and recalls the painful reluctance and inability of witnesses to disclose graphic anatomical details of sexual violence they endured.... The Tribunal defines rape as a physical invasion of a sexual nature, committed on a person under circumstances which are coercive. The Tribunal considers sexual violence, which includes rape, as any act of a sexual nature which is committed on a person under circumstances which are coercive. Sexual violence is not limited to physical invasion of the human body and may include acts which do not involve penetration or even physical contact.... The Tribunal notes in this context that coercive circumstances need not be evidenced by a show of physical force. Threats, intimidation, extortion and other forms of duress which prey on fear or desperation may constitute coercion, and coercion may be inherent in certain circumstances, such as armed conflict or the military presence of *Interahamwe* among refugee Tutsi women at the *bureau communal*.[71]

In crafting these open-textured, holistic and explicitly ungendered definitions of rape and sexual violence,[72] the Chamber invoked the Convention Against Torture and Other Cruel, Inhuman and Degrading Treatment or Punishment, which does not "catalogue specific acts in its definition of torture, focusing rather on the conceptual framework of state-sanctioned violence."[73] The Chamber furthered the analogy when it noted that "[l]ike torture, rape is used for such purposes as intimidation, degradation, humiliation, discrimination, punishment, and the control or destruction of a person. Like torture, rape is a violation of personal dignity, and rape in fact constitutes torture when it is inflicted by or at the

---

virtue of his authority, sent a clear signal of official tolerance for sexual violence, without which these acts would not have taken place." *Id*. at para. 694.

71. *Id*. at paras. 687–88.

72. For a discussion of these definitions and alternative definitions employed in the international criminal law jurisprudence, *see generally* Catharine A. MacKinnon, *Defining Rape Internationally: A Comment on Akayesu*, 44 COLUM. J. TRANSNAT'L L. 940 (2006). Professor MacKinnon lauds the Trial Chamber for defining rape as a crime of coercion rather than with reference to non-consent, which she argues is inapposite in the context of war or a widespread and systematic attack against the civilian population. *Id*. at 942. Other Trial Chambers did not adopt this approach. *See generally* Adrienne Kalosieh, Note, *Consent to Genocide? The ICTY's Improper Use of the Consent Paradigm to Prosecute Genocidal Rape in Foča*, 24 WOMEN'S RTS. L. REP. 121 (2003).

73. *Akayesu*, Case No. ICTR–96–4–T, at para. 687.

instigation of or with the consent or acquiescence of a public official or other person acting in an official capacity."[74]

On the genocide counts, the Tribunal—after devising a flexible, subjective view of ethnicity—had little trouble finding that Akayesu acted with genocidal intent,[75] and that genocide had occurred in Rwanda. The Trial Chamber also explicitly recognized the concept of genocidal rape when it ruled that the acts of rape and sexual violence in the record could serve as the predicate acts of genocide along with the other murders and assaults on members of the Tutsi group.

> With regard, particularly, to the acts described in paragraphs 12(A) and 12(B) of the Indictment, that is, rape and sexual violence, the Chamber wishes to underscore the fact that in its opinion, they constitute genocide in the same way as any other act as long as they were committed with the specific intent to destroy, in whole or in part, a particular group, targeted as such. Indeed, rape and sexual violence certainly constitute infliction of serious bodily and mental harm on the victims and are even, according to the Chamber, one of the worst ways of [inflicting] harm on the victim as he or she suffers both bodily and mental harm.... These rapes resulted in physical and psychological destruction of Tutsi women, their families and their communities. Sexual violence was an integral part of the process of destruction, specifically targeting Tutsi women and specifically contributing to their destruction and to the destruction of the Tutsi group as a whole.[76]

The Tribunal concluded that even those rapes that do not result in the death of the victim could constitute genocide where "[s]exual violence was a step in the process of destruction of the Tutsi group—destruction of the spirit, of the will to live, and of life itself." At the same time, it recognized that the goal of many acts of sexual violence was to make Tutsi women suffer and to mutilate them even before killing them, the intent being to destroy the Tutsi group while inflicting acute suffering on its members in the process.[77] In this way, the Tribunal emphasized that both the mental and physical harm associated with rape satisfied

---

74. *Id.*

75. *Id.* at para. 729 ("regarding Akayesu's acts and utterances during the period relating to the acts alleged in the Indictment, the Chamber is satisfied beyond reasonable doubt, on the basis of all evidence brought to its attention during the trial, that on several occasions the accused made speeches calling, more or less explicitly, for the commission of genocide.").

76. *Id.* at 731.

77. Notably, unlike other depictions of genocidal rape, this account of murderous genocidal rape does not depend upon rapes happening in a "traditional" or patriarchal cultural milieu that values women's chastity or fidelity. *Cf.* Kalosieh, *supra* note 72, at 132 (emphasizing the religious and cultural characteristics of Bosnian Muslim society in describing genocidal impact of rape).

the actus reus of the crime of genocide.[78] Akayesu was thus convicted of genocide.[79]

Prior to his pre-sentencing hearing, Akayesu dismissed his trial lawyers and spoke in his own defense. He was sentenced to life imprisonment, with multiple sentences to be served concurrently for offenses arising from the same acts.[80] After he staged an eight-day hunger strike that was joined by twenty-five other defendants, the Tribunal awarded Akayesu his choice of new counsel for his appeal—Canadians John Philpot and André Tremblay. One argument central to Akayesu's appeal was that he had been prejudiced by the amendment of his indictment to include the rape charges. The Appeals Chamber—composed of Judges Claude Jorda (France), Lal Chand Vohrah (Malaysia), Mohamed Shahabuddeen (Guyana), Rafael Nieto–Navia (Colombia) and Fausto Pocar (Italy)—ruled that the scope of the amendments proposed did not amount to a "new indictment" that prejudiced Akayesu, and that he was given reasonable and adequate time to prepare his defense.[81] His appeal rejected, Akayesu with several other defendants was transported to Mali where he is serving his life sentence pursuant to an agreement between that country and the Tribunal.

The Akayesu Legacy

The Judgment against Akayesu was a significant development for gender justice and suggested an enhanced role for advocates to play in influencing the work of the ad hoc tribunals. In the end, however, the case did not necessarily herald a sea change within the jurisprudence of the ICTR. The case concerning abuses in the prefecture of Cyangugu presents a telling counterpoint. No sexual violence charges were included in the original indictments against defendants André Ntagerura, Emmanuel Bagambiki and Samuel Imanishimwe, all of whom were government and military officials in Cyangugu.[82] The local Association of Widows of the Genocide of April 1994 (AVEGA) organized themselves to help investigators find witnesses who would testify to sexual violence in

---

78. In this way, the Tribunal's reasoning also tracked cases before regional human rights institutions that have found acts of rape to constitute physical and mental torture. *See* Raquel Martí de Mejía v. Perú, Case 10.970, Inter–Am.C.H.R., Report No. 5/96, OEA/Ser.L/V/II.91, doc. 7, at 157 (1996); Aydín v. Turkey, 25 Eur. Ct. H.R. 251 (1997).

79. He was also convicted of incitement to commit genocide. *Akayesu*, Case No. ICTR–96–4–T, at paras. 672–75. The complicity in the genocide count was dismissed on the ground that charges of committing and being complicit in genocide were mutually exclusive. *Id.* at paras. 723–30, 734.

80. *Akayesu*, Case No. ICTR–96–4–T, Sentencing Hearing (Oct. 2, 1998).

81. *Akayesu* Appeals Judgment, Case No. ICTR–96–4–A, at paras. 102–23.

82. Prosecutor v. Ntagerura, Case No. ICTR–96–10–I, Indictment (Jan. 29, 1998); Prosecutor v. Bagambiki, Case No. 97–36–I, Indictment (Oct. 13, 1997).

the prefecture.[83] In response, the Prosecution announced that it intended to amend the indictment against accused Bagambiki and Imanishimwe "as soon as possible" to include new rape charges, but took months to do so.

After finally filing the motion, Chief Prosecutor Del Ponte was called before the Trial Chamber. She subsequently withdrew the motion to amend.[84] As happened in the *Akayesu* case, female witnesses began giving evidence about sexual violence they experienced in the prefecture during the trial. Once again, as in the *Akayesu* case, the Coalition moved to appear as amicus, urging the Tribunal to call upon the Prosecution to amend the indictment to include sexual violence charges. This time, however, the Prosecution opposed the Coalition's motion, arguing that the choice of what charges to bring was within prosecutorial discretion. The Chamber denied the Coalition's motion, siding with the Prosecution.[85] In addition, upon defense motion, the Trial Chamber excluded evidence of uncharged crimes, such as sexual violence, fearing prejudice to the accused. The Tribunal ultimately acquitted Ntagerura and Bagambiki for lack of evidence; it convicted Imanishimwe.[86] The verdict was upheld on appeal.[87] Rwanda later announced that it would try defendant Bagambiki, once the Cyangugu prefect, for sexual violence, even though the ICTR had ruled that he was not responsible for the prefecture massacres in which the alleged sexual violence occurred. Because no rape charges were pursued before the ICTR, there was no double jeopardy bar. Rwanda sought his extradition from Tanzania and eventually tried and convicted him of rape in absentia in October 2007. Bagambiki eventually received political asylum in Belgium, which is considering an extradition request from Rwanda, although there is no extradition treaty in place between the two.[88]

Other cases before the ICTR have met similar fates. At one point, more than half of the ICTR indictments included charges of rape and

---

83. Human Rights Watch, Shattered Lives, *supra* note 15, at 14.

84. This incident is recounted in Human Rights Watch, Shattered Lives, *supra* note 15, at 15. Del Ponte reportedly stated, "I can do this because I am a woman. If I were a man, there would be a fuss." *Id.*

85. Prosecutor v. Ntagerura, Bagambiki & Imanishimwe, Case No. ICTR–99–46–T, Decision on the Application to File an Amicus Curiae Brief According to Rule 74 of the Rules of Procedure and Evidence Filed on Behalf of the NGO Coalition for Women's Human Rights in Conflict Situations (May 24, 2001).

86. Prosecutor v. Ntagerura, Bagambiki & Imanishimwe, Case No. ICTR–99–46–T, Judgment (Feb. 25, 2004).

87. Prosecutor v. Ntagerura, Bagambiki & Imanishimwe, Case No. ICTR–99–46–A, Judgment (July 7, 2006).

88. *See* Kevin Jon Heller, *What Happens to the Acquitted?*, 21 Leiden J. of Int'l L. 663 (2008).

other sexual violence (many involving counts added by amendment). Many cases, however, have ended in acquittal on the rape and sexual violence counts. For example, *Prosecutor v. Musema* resulted in a conviction for rape as genocide and as a crime against humanity before the same Trial Chamber that heard the *Akayesu* case.[89] Musema was accused of personally raping a Tutsi woman in May 1994. On appeal, however, new evidence emerged that controverted the testimony presented at trial. The Appeals Chamber ruled that a miscarriage of justice had occurred and quashed the rape conviction.[90]

In *Prosecutor v. Kajelijeli*, the defendant was acquitted of rape (charged as a crime against humanity), because two of the judges found the key witness lacked credibility due to inconsistencies in her testimony at trial and statements to investigators. The Trial Chamber acquitted the defendant of rapes that were proven to have occurred.[91] In a strong dissent, Judge Arlette Ramaroson (Madagascar) argued that the inconsistencies were not due to a lack of credibility but to an incompetent investigation.[92] Later, the Prosecution missed a deadline to appeal the acquittal, and was chastised for prosecutorial negligence by the judges.

Other acquittals for rape occurred in the cases against Niyitegeka,[93] Muvunyi,[94] and Kamuhanda[95]—primarily because the prosecutor failed to meet the required burden of proof. The Prosecution did not appeal these acquittals. In other cases, such as with respect to defendants Ndindabah-

---

89. Prosecutor v. Musema, Case No. ICTR–96–13–A, Judgment and Sentence, at para. 933 (Jan. 27, 2000) ("acts of serious bodily and mental harm, including rape and other forms of sexual violence, were often accompanied by humiliating utterances, which clearly indicated that the intention underlying each specific act was to destroy the Tutsi group as a whole. The Chamber notes, for example, that during the rape of Nyiramusugi, Musema declared: 'The pride of the Tutsis will end today.' In this context, the acts of rape and sexual violence were an integral part of the plan conceived to destroy the Tutsi group. Such acts targeted Tutsi women, in particular, and specifically contributed to their destruction and therefore that of the Tutsi group as such. Witness N testified before the Chamber that Nyiramusugi, who was left for dead by those who raped her, had indeed been killed in a way. Indeed, the Witness specified that 'what they did to her is worse than death.' ").

90. *Musema*, Case No. ICTR–96–13–A, Judgment, at paras. 172–194 (Nov. 6, 2001).

91. Prosecutor v. Kajelijeli, Case No. 98–44A–T, Judgment, at paras. 908–925 (Dec. 1, 2003).

92. *Kajelijeli*, Case No. 98–44A–T, Dissenting Opinion of Judge Arlette Ramaroson, at paras. 26–28, 36 (Dec. 1, 2003).

93. Prosecutor v. Niyitegeka, Case No. 96–14–T, Judgment (May 16, 2003) (acquitting defendant of rape charges (pled as a crime against humanity) for insufficient evidence).

94. Prosecutor v. Muvunyi, Case No. 00–55A–T, Judgment (Sept. 12, 2006) (finding prosecutor failed to prove rapes were committed by the subordinates alleged in the indictment).

95. Prosecutor v. Kamuhanda, Case No. 95–54A–T, Judgment (Jan. 22, 2004).

izi,[96] Nzabirinda,[97] Serushago,[98] and Bisengimana,[99] the Prosecution withdrew sexual violence counts. Since the establishment of the Tribunal, only a handful of defendants had been found guilty of gender crimes, including Akayesu, Gacumbitsi,[100] Semanza,[101] and Muhimana.[102] One is left with the impression that the *Akayesu* case is a mere anomaly.

How to explain the apparent *volte face* within the organs of the ICTR when confronted with crimes of gender violence? A number of potential explanations come to mind. It is tempting to look to the composition of the bench and the presence of female judges. Judge Pillay has observed that, "Who interprets the law is at least as important as who makes the law, if not more so.... I cannot stress how critical I consider it to be that women are represented and a gender perspective integrated at all levels of the investigation, prosecution, defense, witness protection and judiciary."[103] The *Akayesu* transcript, however, reveals that all the judges participated in the process of surfacing indictable gender crimes, and the *Cyangugu* narrative reveals that placing a woman in charge of prosecutions will not necessarily ensure that gender justice is aggressively pursued. Alternatively, the Tribunal may simply have been exhausted with prosecutorial mishandling of cases generally. Finally, the relentless Completion Strategy mandated by the U.N. Security Council is no doubt weighing against the expansion of proceedings in any fashion.

Most critics of this apparent trend against gender justice take aim at the ICTR Office of the Prosecution, and in particular with then-Chief

---

96. Prosecutor v. Ndindabahizi, Case No. 01–71–I, Judgment, at para. 13 (July 15, 2004) (recounting the granting of a motion to withdraw counts that had been added through amendment of the indictment).

97. Prosecutor v. Nzabirinda, Case No. 01–77–T, Judgment, at paras. 3, 4, 44 (Feb. 23, 2007) (discussing withdrawal of counts "because the evidence was not there.").

98. Prosecutor v. Serushago, Case No. 98–39–S, Judgment, at para. 4 (Feb. 5, 1999) (noting that defendant pled guilty to four out of five counts, but pled not guilty to the rape count; prosecutor subsequently withdrew the rape charge).

99. Prosecutor v. Bisengimana, Case No. 00–60–T, Judgment, at paras. 7, 12 (Apr. 13, 2006) (noting that prosecution withdrew rape and other charges; defendant later pled guilty to remaining counts of murder and extermination).

100. Prosecutor v. Gacumbitsi, Case No. 01–64–T, Judgment (June 17, 2004).

101. Prosecutor v. Semanza, Case No. ICTR–97–20–T, Judgment (May 15, 2003).

102. Prosecutor v. Muhimana, Case No. ICTR–95–1B–T, Judgment (Apr. 28, 2005). In *Muhimana*, the Appeals Chamber affirmed a genocide acquittal, reversed a finding of criminal responsibility for two specific rapes, and affirmed a finding of guilt for crimes against humanity with respect to other acts of rape.

103. U.N. DIVISION FOR THE ADVANCEMENT OF WOMEN & CENTRE FOR REFUGEE STUDIES, YORK UNIVERSITY, CANADA, GENDER-BASED PERSECUTION: REPORT OF THE EXPERT GROUP MEETING, at 33, U.N. Doc. EGM/GBP/1997/Report (Nov. 9–12, 1997), *available at* http://www.un.org/documents/ecosoc/cn6/1998/armedcon/egmgbp1997–rep.htm.

Prosecutor Del Ponte.[104] Advocates of gender justice have accused Del Ponte and the Office of the Prosecution in Kigali of neglecting the prosecution of crimes of sexual violence committed in Rwanda. After the Prosecution failed to amend the Cyangugu indictment, for example, the Coalition sought a meeting with Del Ponte. Their concerns are memorialized in a letter sent to the Chief Prosecutor after the meeting. The letter accuses Del Ponte of neglecting gender justice:

> [W]e believe that your four-year record as ICTR prosecutor shows no concrete commitment to effectively developing evidence to bring such charges, despite the longstanding and overwhelming proof of sexual violence during the 1994 Rwandan genocide.[105]

The Coalition expressed similar concerns in a letter to then-Secretary General of the United Nations Kofi Annan, who was at the time considering Del Ponte's renewal.[106] Several days later, Annan announced the appointment of Hassan Bubacar Jallow (Gambia) to replace Del Ponte[107] as Chief Prosecutor for the ICTR. Del Ponte stepped down from

---

104. As he was leaving office as Chief Prosecutor, Justice Goldstone created a sexual violence investigations team and appointed Patricia Viseur–Sellers as a Legal Officer on Gender Issues for the Office of the Prosecutor to direct the indictment of individuals responsible for such crimes in Yugoslavia and Rwanda. Hon. Richard J. Goldstone, *Prosecuting Rape as a War Crime*, 34 CASE W. RES. J. INT'L L. 277, 280 (2002) (noting that soon after he "arrived as the Chief Prosecutor in The Hague on August 15, 1994, [he] was inundated with letters and petitions from women and men in the United States, Canada, and many of the western European nations. [These letters implored him] to give adequate attention to gender-related crimes."). Prosecutor Arbour continued this work, earning praise from gender advocates for her comprehensive approach to gender justice. HUMAN RIGHTS WATCH, SHATTERED LIVES, *supra* note 15, at 10.

105. Letter from the Coalition for Women's Human Rights in Conflict Situations to Carla Del Ponte, Prosecutor, International Criminal Tribunal for Rwanda (Mar. 12, 2003), *available at* http://www.womensrightscoalition.org/site/advocacyDossiers/rwanda/rape VictimssDeniedJustice/lettertoprosecutor_en.php.

106. Letter from the Coalition for Women's Human Rights in Conflict Situations to Kofi Annan, Secretary General of the United Nations (July 24, 2003), *available at* http://www.womensrightscoalition.org/site/advocacyDossiers/rwanda/rapeVictimssDeniedJustice/lettrekofiannan_en.php.

107. From the Tribunals' beginning, observers expressed concern that the Rwandan prosecutions were not getting the Chief Prosecutor's full attention. *The Economist*, for example, reported that Del Ponte spent only thirty-five days in Africa. Simultaneous with the adoption of the Completion Strategy, the Security Council by Resolution 1503 (2003) split the Office of the Prosecutor into two positions over the objections of Del Ponte. S.C. Res. 1503, Annex I, U.N. Doc. S/RES/1503/Annex I (Aug. 28, 2003). Although the Security Council ostensibly bifurcated this position to facilitate the completion of investigations and trials, it has been argued that the real reason stemmed from dissatisfaction with Del Ponte's articulated intentions to prosecute high level members of the Tutsi-dominated RPF for massacres of Hutus during the war in Rwanda. Rwandan President Paul Kagame, the founder of the RPF and a strong ally of the West, allegedly obstructed these investigations and complained about Del Ponte to the Security Council and the U.N. Secretary General.

her ICTY post in December 2007 and was replaced by Belgian Serge Brammertz.

Several policies and practices of the Office of the Prosecutor are specifically singled out for criticism. The failure of early investigations to surface allegations of sexual violence is blamed on the fact that the majority of investigators were men, having been drawn from national police forces, with little experience or training in taking rape testimony from women victims and making it trial ready. Critics also point to the original lack of expertise in gender justice in the Office of the Prosecutor; the 2000 decision to disband the sexual assault investigative team formed in 1997;[108] the lack of coordination between the Office of the Prosecution and the Victims and Witnesses Unit (housed in the Registry); the failure to add sexual violence counts to new indictments despite available evidence; the pursuit of sexual violence claims with inadequate evidence; and the failure to fully and consistently incorporate investigations of sexual violence into the investigative or prosecutorial strategy.[109] After repeated frustrating experiences with the Tribunal,[110] several victims' groups in Rwanda eventually cut off all cooperation with the Tribunal. One report indicated that the overwhelming sentiments expressed by rape survivors in Rwanda about their experience with the ICTR were "burning anger, deep frustration, dashed hopes, indignation and even resignation."[111] Overall, it appears that the Office of the Prosecution proceeded without a coherent strategy for investigating sexual violence or a theory of how sexual violence fit into the way in which genocide was committed in Rwanda. Where rape allegations are not central to a prosecutorial strategy, they become dispensable.

The record of other international and quasi-international tribunals in prosecuting gender crimes is perhaps somewhat better, although none of these tribunals has yet adjudicated charges of genocidal rape.[112] Prior to the *Akayesu* case, Justice Goldstone issued from the ICTY the first international indictment focused exclusively on sexual violence committed in the town of Foča. Defendants were convicted of rape and sexual

---

108. Amid complaints that sexual violence was not receiving the attention it deserved, Del Ponte reinstated the sexual violence investigations unit in 2003.

109. *See, e.g.*, HUMAN RIGHTS WATCH, SHATTERED LIVES, *supra* note 15, at 10–13.

110. Nowrojee, *supra* note 54, at 3 (interviewing victims about what they hoped the ICTR would achieve).

111. *Id.* at 4.

112. The current indictments against Karadžić and Mladić before the ICTY plead sexual violence as a predicate act of genocide. *See, e.g.*, Prosecutor v. Karadžić, Case No. IT-95-5/18, Amended Indictment, at para. 17 (Apr. 28, 2000). The original indictments against both men had specifically mentioned the rape of women in the recitation of genocidal crimes. *See* Prosecutor v. Karadžić & Mladić, Case No. IT-95-5-I, Indictment, at para. 19 (May 24, 1995).

slavery as crimes against humanity.[113] Likewise, *Prosecutor v. Furundžija* exclusively involved sexual violence claims. After an eleven day trial—the Tribunal's shortest—the defendant was convicted of rape as a form of torture, a conviction upheld on appeal despite a challenge to the Judge's impartiality.[114] The ICTY has generally taken a conservative approach to convicting defendants of the crime of genocide. It has ruled that the massacre at Srebrenica constituted genocide,[115] but so far has not found a policy on the part of the Serbian political leadership to commit genocide in Bosnia–Herzegovina writ large.[116] Where most charges for sexual violence are brought, they are charged as crimes against humanity or war crimes, not as genocide. Before the Special Court for Sierra Leone, the former Chief Prosecutor integrated charges of sexual violence into virtually all indictments, although genocide is not implicated in the violence there. In addition, he successfully charged individuals with forced marriage, which is not specifically enumerated in the Statute of the Special Court.[117]

The Coalition's Amicus Brief recently made a cameo appearance before the ICTY. In June 2008, the Prosecution moved to amend the indictment against cousins Milan and Sredoje Lukić to include crimes of sexual violence—including rape, enslavement, and torture—arising out of their establishment of a rape camp in Višegrad.[118] In support of his motion, the Prosecutor argued that the acts of sexual violence were an intrinsic part of the crimes committed in Višegrad. Moreover, the Prosecutor argued, it would be in the interests of justice to permit the amendments in order to allow the witnesses, most of whom had already been disclosed, to testify fully about the harm they suffered at the hands of the defendants and to establish the full truth of the defendants' crimes. The Prosecutor cited *Akayesu* and the Coalition's Brief for the authority to belatedly amend the indictment, as the deadline to amend

---

113. Prosecutor v. Kunarac, Case No. IT–96–23 & 23/1–T, Judgment (Feb. 22, 2001).

114. Prosecutor v. Furundžija, Case No. IT–95–17/1, Judgment, at paras. 199–200 (July 21, 2000) ("[E]ven if it were established that Judge [Florence] Mumba expressly shared the goals and objectives of the U.N. [Commission on the Status of Women] and the Platform for Action in promoting and protecting the human rights of women, that inclination, being of a general nature, is distinguishable from an inclination to implement those goals and objectives as a Judge in a particular case. It follows that she could still sit on a case and impartially decide upon issues affecting women.").

115. Prosecutor v. Krstić, Case No. IT–98–33–A, Judgment, at para. 599 (Apr. 19, 2004).

116. *See* Prosecutor v. Krajišnik, Case No: IT–00–39–T, Judgment, at paras. 857–69, 1091–94 (Sept. 27, 2006) (acquitting Serbian political leader of genocide).

117. Prosecutor v. Alex Tamba Brima et al., Case No. SCSL–2004–16–A, Judgment, at paras. 175–203 (Feb. 22, 2008).

118. Prosecutor v. Lukić, Case. No. IT–98–32/1–PT, Prosecutor's Motion Seeking Leave to Amend Second Amended Complaint (June 16, 2008).

the indictment had passed during Del Ponte's tenure as Chief Prosecutor.[119] The ICTY, however, declined the motion on the ground that the granting the motion after the Prosecutor's unjustified delay would unduly prejudice the accused.[120]

Although the outcomes of the cases are mixed, much of this jurisprudence served as a foundation for the gender violence provisions in the Rome Statute creating a permanent International Criminal Court ("ICC"). As a result of the comprehensive work of advocates for gender justice during the multilateral drafting of the ICC Statute, that treaty is not only characterized by gender inclusiveness in its substantive law, but also in its structures and procedures.[121] In particular, the ICC Statute contains an expansive list of gender crimes in the war crimes and crimes against humanity provisions.[122] Gender is listed as a ground—like ethnicity or race—on which an individual or collective may be persecuted.[123] With respect to the possibility of charging genocidal rape, the definition of genocide in Article 6 mirrors that of the Genocide Convention. However, the Elements of Crimes—drafted to assist the ICC in interpreting its substantive offenses—note that "serious bodily or mental harm" "may include, but is not necessarily restricted to, acts of torture, rape, sexual violence or inhuman or degrading treatment,"[124] thus laying the foundation for future prosecutions of genocidal rape before the ICC. In

---

119. *Id.* at paras. 49–51.

120. *Prosecution v. Lukić*, Case No. IT–98–32/1–PT, Decision on Prosecution Motion Seeking Leave to Amend the Second Amended Indictment and on Prosecution Motion to Include U.N. Security Council Resolution 1820 (2008) as Additional Supporting Material to Proposed Third Amended Indictment as Well as on Milan Lukić's Request for Reconsideration or Certification of the Pretrial Judge's Order of 19 June 2008, at paras. 62–3 (July 8, 2008).

121. This reflects calls by NGOs and the United Nations for the integration of a gender perspective into all aspects of the human rights system and for a focus on accountability for violence against women. *See* World Conference on Human Rights, General Assembly, *Vienna Declaration and Program of Action*, U.N. Doc. A/Conf. 157/23 (July 12, 1993), *available at* http://www.unhchr.ch/huridocda/huridoca.nsf/(Symbol)/A.CONF.157.23.En; World Conference on Human Rights, General Assembly, *Declaration on the Elimination of Violence Against Women*, 48th Sess., U./N. Doc. A/Res/48/104 (Feb. 23, 1994).

122. Arts. 8(2)(b)(xxii) and (e)(vi) of the Rome Statute specifically enumerate the crimes of rape, sexual slavery, enforced prostitution, forced pregnancy, enforced sterilization, and other forms of sexual violence as war crimes whether committed in international or non-international armed conflict. The same crimes are listed as crimes against humanity in Art. 7(1)(g). Enslavement as a crime against humanity is also defined with reference to the trafficking of women and children. Art. 7(2)(c). *See* Rome Statute of the International Criminal Court, July 1, 2002, 2187 U.N.T.S. 90 [hereinafter Rome Statute].

123. Rome Statute, Art. 7(1)(h).

124. International Criminal Court, Elements of Crimes, U.N. Doc. PCNICC/2000/1/Add.2 (2000).

terms of personnel, the Statute requires the state parties to choose judges and other staff with experience with "violence against women or children"[125] and calls for "fair representation of female and male judges."[126] Of the eighteen ICC judges, eight are now women. This compares favorably with other international courts, whose composition is dominated by men.[127] The ICC Statute also contains a non-discrimination provision stating that the ICC's application and interpretation of the law must be consistent with internationally recognized human rights and be without adverse distinction founded on, inter alia, gender.[128]

Many of these provisions in the Rome Statute are the result of the work of another coalition of women's groups, then called the Women's Caucus for Gender Justice ("Caucus"), which was active during the drafting of the Rome Statute.[129] The Caucus formed in 1997 to infuse a gender perspective in the negotiations surrounding the establishment of the ICC. To achieve these provisions, the Caucus had to overcome significant resistance from certain states and delegations to the Rome Conference—including the Vatican, several anti-choice organizations, and a core of Islamic states—that were less sympathetic to the concerns of gender justice. The Caucus, reorganized in 2004 as the Women's Initiative for Gender Justice,[130] is now focused on monitoring the Court's implementation of the gender provisions of the Rome Statute and channeling the concerns of women in the regions in which the ICC is working. These achievements may prove to be the most enduring legacy of the *Akayesu* case as the ICC begins work.

Conclusion

Every once in a while, a case comes along that, for the first time, firmly embeds legal theory into positive law. The case against Akayesu is one such jurisprudential pioneer. The case is also often cited as a promising example of successful feminist advocacy. Advocacy did produce

---

125. Rome Statute, Arts. 36(8) (Judges), 42(9) (Office of the Prosecution), and 43(6) (Victims and Witnesses Unit).

126. *Id.* at Art. 36(8).

127. A study conducted of international courts (of which there are now over thirty) revealed that the vast majority of international judges are male. Cherie Booth, *Prospects and Issues for the International Criminal Court: Lessons From Yugoslavia and Rwanda*, in From Nuremberg to The Hague: The Future of International Criminal Justice 157, 162 (Philippe Sands ed., 2003) (citing study).

128. Rome Statute, Art. 21(3).

129. For a discussion of the contributions of the Caucus and others, *see* Barbara Bedont & Katherine Hall Martinez, *Ending Impunity for Gender Crimes under the International Criminal Court*, 6 Brown J. World Aff. 65 (1999), *available at* http://www.crlp.org/pub_art_icc.html.

130. *See* http://www.iccwomen.org/.

important concrete results in the *Akayesu* case. It situated the concept of genocidal rape within the international criminal law framework, despite the Prosecutor's claim that he was not motivated by the Coalition's work. Placed in a larger context, the case better exemplifies the difficulty activists face in influencing the prosecutorial and adjudicative process, where prosecutorial discretion is paramount, and tribunals may only rule on the evidence that properly appears before them. It is tempting to credit much of the story about the progress of gender justice before the international tribunals to the presence of key women involved in the international criminal law process. The stories recounted above, however, reveal that male judges and prosecutors were at times equally as enlightened to issues of gender justice as their female counterparts and that the presence of women in leadership roles does not always translate into feminist policies.

Subsequent cases—at least before the ICTR—have not, by and large, built on the *Akayesu* precedent. If anything, the cause of gender justice seems to have been subject to backsliding. As the two ad hoc tribunals wind down under their Completion Strategies, the story of *Akayesu* is likely to become a mere introduction to further developments in gender justice achieved before the International Criminal Court. For now, *Akayesu* stands alone in recognizing rape as a form of genocide.

*

7

The Story of *Samuel Hinga Norman* in Sierra Leone: Can Truth Commissions and Criminal Prosecutions Coexist After Conflict?

Ari S. Bassin & Paul van Zyl

Introduction

In the wake of a ten-year civil war, Sierra Leone, like many other transitional societies, set up both a truth and reconciliation commission ("TRC") and special criminal prosecutions to address the abuses that occurred during the conflict. Yet the creation of—and the relationship between—these two overlapping and potentially complementary institutions generated tension. This tension came to a head in late 2003 when, in an unforeseen move, one of the Special Court's key indictees, Samuel Hinga Norman, petitioned to testify publicly before the TRC. What ensued illustrated the potential for conflict between TRCs and court prosecutions. It was also entirely avoidable. Since both TRCs and criminal prosecutions will often be necessary in transitional societies, this Chapter examines the political and legal questions that arise when considering the optimal relationship between courts and truth commissions. It also tells the story of some of the personal and institutional dynamics that shaped this relationship in Sierra Leone. By telling the story from both a policy and a personal perspective, we hope to offer insights to help avoid unnecessary tensions in the future and to confront those that are inescapable with clarity and integrity.

The Conflict in Sierra Leone and Its Immediate Aftermath

The Horrors of the Conflict in Sierra Leone

By all accounts, the civil war in Sierra Leone from 1991 through 2001 was filled with some of the most horrendous atrocities in modern history. Though the fighting was technically between groups seeking political control over the country, in practice civilians bore the brunt of much of the conflict's brutality, which tore the country apart from its very foundations.

Brothers and sisters as well as children and their parents were forced to have sex with each other at gunpoint. Thousands of people's limbs were cut off (and many were forced to eat their own amputated body parts). Women and girls were abducted, raped, gang raped, forced into sexual slavery and married off to militia members. Children were taken from their families and communities and forced to become child soldiers, committing horrendous atrocities themselves under the influence of specially concocted drug cocktails. As one civilian victim told the TRC:

> They cut my son in pieces alive. I was under gun point and all actors were in uniform and caps [which] were very low over their eyes, I did not detect anybody. They cut him in pieces with a knife and when they opened his chest, they took out his heart and cut a piece of it and pushed it into my mouth, saying you first eat of it, but then when they have cut his head, they laid it in my hand saying go and breast feed your son and they started dancing.[1]

The scope of these atrocities was as immense as their nature was horrific. They dominated life for over ten years and engulfed every person and region of the country. These atrocities were perpetrated, to varying degrees, by each of the fighting factions, even those claiming to fight for the protection of the Sierra Leonean people. The number of perpetrators likely rose into the thousands or tens of thousands and the number of victims was even higher.[2]

The Search for Justice: The Creation of the Sierra Leone TRC and the Special Court

In July 1999 the Government of Sierra Leone came together with the Revolutionary United Front ("RUF") to sign the Lomé Peace Accord, in an attempt to end Sierra Leone's civil war. In addition to declaring an official ceasefire, the parties included an absolute pardon and amnesty provision for "all combatants and collaborators in respect of anything done by them in pursuit of their objectives," up to the signing of the peace agreement.[3] In order to offset this amnesty, but not

---

1. 3A SIERRA LEONE TRUTH AND RECONCILIATION COMM'N, WITNESS TO TRUTH: REPORT OF THE SIERRA LEONE TRUTH AND RECONCILIATION COMMISSION (2004), *available at* http://www.trcsierraleone.org, [hereinafter TRC REPORT], ch. 4, para. 43 (testimony to the TRC from Cecilia Caulker, a civilian victim of the conflict in Sierra Leone).

2. For more information about the conflict in Sierra Leone, *see generally* TRC REPORT, *id.*

3. Peace Agreement Between the Government of Sierra Leone and the Rebel United Front of Sierra Leone, July 7, 1999, U.N. Doc. S/1999/777, annex art. 9, *available at* http://www.sierra-leone.org/lomeaccord.html [hereinafter Lomé Peace Accord].

alter its legal effect, the Lomé Peace Accord called for the establishment of a truth and reconciliation commission to address the human rights violations which occurred since the initial outbreak of violence in 1991.[4]

The Sierra Leonean Parliament adopted official legislation establishing the Sierra Leone Truth and Reconciliation Commission in February of 2000,[5] but unfortunately the ceasefire did not hold. Hostilities broke out again between the parties, culminating in the RUF taking 500 U.N. Peacekeepers hostage and a violent political crisis in Freetown. In the end, the RUF leaders were captured and arrested. Sensing a change in leverage, Sierra Leone's President Kabbah officially requested that the U.N. Security Council establish an international criminal tribunal to prosecute members of the RUF for their crimes against the people of Sierra Leone and the U.N. Peacekeepers.[6] The U.N. Security Council responded, passing Resolution 1315, in August of 2000, which instructed the U.N. Secretary–General to come to an agreement with the Government of Sierra Leone regarding the establishment of a special court.[7] However, contrary to President Kabbah's initial request, the resolution clarified that this special court should have jurisdiction to prosecute *all* persons bearing the greatest responsibility for the commission of serious crimes threatening the establishment and implementation of the peace process in Sierra Leone, not just members of the RUF.[8] Subsequent negotiations between the U.N. Secretary–General and the Government of Sierra Leone led to the creation of the Special Court for Sierra Leone ("SCSL"), with a governing Statute agreed upon by the U.N. Security Council in January 2002.[9] The result was a "hybrid" court with both national and international actors, and based on both national and international law.[10]

The SCSL was given jurisdiction to look into crimes against humanity, war crimes and other serious violations of international humanitarian

---

4. See Lomé Peace Accord, *supra* note 3, art. 26.

5. Truth and Reconciliation Commission Act 2000, Supp. to the Sierra Leone Gazette, Vol. CXXXI, No. 9 (Feb. 10, 2000), *available at* http://www.usip.org/library/tc/doc/charters/tc_sierra_leone_02102000.html [hereinafter TRC Act 2000].

6. See William A. Schabas, *A Synergystic Relationship: The Sierra Leone Truth and Reconciliation Commission and the Special Court for Sierra Leone*, 15 CRIM. L.F. 3, 15 n. 36 (2004).

7. S.C. Res. 1315, U.N. Doc. S/RES/1315 (Aug. 14, 2000).

8. *Id.* ¶ 3.

9. Agreement on the Establishment of a Special Court for Sierra Leone, Jan. 16, 2002, U.N.–Sierra Leone, *available at* http://www.sc-sl.org/Documents/scsl-agreement.html.

10. Unlike the International Criminal Tribunals for Yugoslavia and Rwanda, its authority was based on a treaty agreement between Sierra Leone and the U.N., rather than on a Security Council resolution.

law in Sierra Leone starting as far back as 1996.[11] This created a significant overlap between the jurisdiction of the SCSL and the scope of the Sierra Leone TRC created under the Lomé Peace Accord, for crimes and activities that took place between 1996 and 1999.[12] It also meant that the SCSL, in effect, overturned the absolute amnesty granted under the Lomé Peace Accord.[13] The U.N. and the Government of Sierra Leone asserted that "an amnesty granted to any person falling within the jurisdiction of the Special Court in respect to crimes referred to in articles 2 to 4 of the present Statute [Crimes Against Humanity, War Crimes, and other serious violations of international humanitarian law] shall not be a bar to prosecution."[14] They defended this move by noting that, under international law, it was illegal to grant amnesties for such crimes, and thus the amnesties granted at Lomé in respect to these crimes lacked legal effect.[15]

Despite the overlap between the jurisdiction of the SCSL and the subject matter of the TRC there was no officially recognized agreement delineating the relationship between the two institutions. The TRC was created before the SCSL with the understanding that there would be general amnesties. As a result, it did not foresee having to work alongside any court with overlapping jurisdiction, and did not include guidelines regarding how it would do so in its founding documents. The SCSL, on the other hand, had notice that it would be working alongside the Sierra Leone TRC, yet its establishing Statute and its Rules of Evidence and Procedure made no specific reference to the TRC nor did it provide specific guidelines regarding how the two institutions would interact.

---

11. The U.N.'s report stated that it limited the SCSL's temporal jurisdiction to 1996 rather than to the beginning of the conflict in 1991, in order to make it more realistic that it could complete its mission within a three-year period. However, some have suggested that the 1996 date was chosen because the Abidjan peace agreement was signed in 1996. Unlike at the Lomé Peace Accord negotiations, at the negotiations of the Abidjan peace agreement—which also guaranteed general amnesties—the U.N. Special Representative of the Secretary–General appended his signature with a statement that effectively limited its understanding of the amnesty provisions. However, the U.N. Special Representative of the Secretary–General did append his signature on the Lomé Peace Accord with the statement that the U.N. understands that the Agreement's amnesty provisions do not apply to the international crimes of genocide, crimes against humanity, war crimes and other serious violations of humanitarian law. *See* Schabas, *supra* note 6, at 21–22.

12. Given the language of the statutes governing each institution, there are uncertainties about whether their temporal scope may overlap even outside those dates.

13. Prosecutor v. Kallon, Kamara, Decision on Challenge to Jurisdiction, Nos. SCSL–2004–15–AR72(E), SCSL–2004–16–AR72(E), ¶ 71 (Mar. 13, 2004).

14. The Secretary–General, *Report of the Secretary–General on the Establishment of a Special Court for Sierra Leone*, ¶ 24, U.N. Doc. S/2000/915 (brackets added) [hereinafter SG Report].

15. *Id. See also* 3B TRC Report, *supra* note 1, ch. 6, para. 20.

Despite this, or perhaps because of it, there has been considerable discussion and confusion regarding the relationship between the two institutions. Many argued that the SCSL had primacy over the TRC. The Statute of the SCSL included a clause stating that "[t]he Special Court shall have primacy over the national courts of Sierra Leone. At any stage of the procedure, the Special Court may formally request a national court to defer to its competence in accordance with the present Statute and the Rules of Procedure and Evidence."[16] While not specifically referencing the TRC, some argued that this clause defined the relationship between the SCSL and TRC and gave the SCSL primacy over the TRC, which was a national body of Sierra Leone.[17] Others argued that Article 17 of the agreement between Sierra Leone and the U.N. with respect to establishment of the Special Court, which bound the "Government" of Sierra Leone to co-operate with and comply with the requests of the Special Court, established the SCSL's primacy over the TRC.[18] And many referenced the *Special Court Agreement (Ratification) Act 2002*, between the government of Sierra Leone and the Special Court, which stated "[n]otwithstanding any other law, every natural person, corporation, or other body created by or under Sierra Leone law shall comply with any direction specified in an order from the Special Court,"[19] in their conclusion that the SCSL had primacy over the TRC, "because the TRC was created under Sierra Leone law."[20]

Others have challenged these assertions that the SCSL had primacy over the TRC.[21] They pointed to the fact that the clause in the Statute of the Special Court referred only to national courts and did not specifically

---

16. Statute of the Special Court for Sierra Leone, annex to Agreement on the Establishment of a Special Court for Sierra Leone, *supra* note 9, art. 8(2), *available at* http://www.sc-sl.org/Documents/scsl-statute.html.

17. *See, e.g.,* Prosecutor v. Norman, Case No. SCSL–03–08–PT, Decision on Appeal by the Truth and Reconciliation Commission for Sierra Leone ("TRC" or "Commission") and Chief Samuel Hinga Norman JP against the decision of His Lordship, Mr. Justice Bankole Thompson delivered on 30 October, 2003 to deny the TRC's request to hold a public hearing with Chief Samuel Hinga Normal JP, ¶ 4 (Nov. 28, 2003), *available at* http://www.sc-sl.org/CDF-appealdecisions.html [hereinafter Robertson Decision].

18. *See* January 2002 discussion paper prepared by the Office of the Attorney General and Ministry of Justice of Sierra Leone (cited in TRC Report, *supra* note 1, paras. 62–3).

19. Special Court Agreement, 2002 (Ratification) Act § 21(2), Supp. to the Sierra Leone Gazette, Vol. CXXXIII, No. 22 (Apr. 25, 2002), *available at* http://www.sc-sl.org/Documents/SCSL-ratificationact.pdf.

20. *See* Human Rights Watch, Policy Paper on the Interrelationship Between the Sierra Leone Special Court and the Truth and Reconciliation Commission 1–2 (2002); Marieke Wierda, Priscilla Hayner & Paul van Zyl, *Exploring the Relationship Between the Special Court and the Truth and Reconciliation Commission of Sierra Leone* 5 (Int'l Ctr. for Transitional Justice, 2002), *available at* http://www.ictj.org/images/content/0/8/084.pdf

21. *See, e.g.,* U.N. Doc. E/CN.4/2002/3, ¶ 70(ii); Schabas, *supra* note 6, at 35–36.

refer to the TRC.[22] They asserted that the agreement between Sierra Leone and the U.N. with regard to the SCSL did not cover the TRC either, because the TRC, while being established under domestic law, was "a body independent of the Government of Sierra Leone."[23] The Truth Commission also involved international participation in the form of non-Sierra Leonean Commissioners appointed by the U.N. These commissioners, together with their national counterparts, benefited from immunities conferred upon them by the legislation establishing the TRC[24] and it was therefore difficult to see how they could be held liable criminally or otherwise for failing to comply with an order issued by the SCSL. Moreover, those claiming that the SCSL lacked primacy over the TRC note that the aforementioned clause of the *Special Court Agreement (Ratification) Act 2002*, if understood literally, would result in absurd conclusions, giving the SCSL complete power to rewrite all the laws of Sierra Leone. Therefore, the Sierra Leonean Parliament could never have intended for it to be understood literally.[25]

In addition to disputing various clauses suggesting the primacy of the SCSL, those who argued that there was no hierarchy between the SCSL and the TRC often pointed to the U.N. Secretary–General's January 2001 letter to the Security Council to show that the U.N. intended both institutions to be equal. The letter noted that "care must be taken to ensure that the Special Court for Sierra Leone and the Truth and Reconciliation Commission will operate in a complementary and mutually supportive manner, fully respectful of their distinct but related functions."[26]

The lack of a specified relationship between the SCSL and the Sierra Leone TRC created concern in the international community. Many transitional justice specialists within NGO and the U.N. communities came together to discuss the issue on several occasions.[27] The various meetings and working groups resulted in an array of recommendations for how to design the working relationship between the SCSL and the TRC. Regardless of the substance of their recommendations, they were all unanimous in their call for the two institutions to come together, before either began its work, to discuss and create an official agreement

---

22. 3B TRC REPORT, *supra* note 1, ch. 6, paras. 60–61.

23. *Id.*, para. 63.b.

24. TRC Act 2000, art. 143(4), *supra* note 5.

25. Schabas, *supra* note 6, at 37–8.

26. Letter, Secretary–General to the President of the Security Council, ¶ 9, U.N. Doc. S/2001/40 (Jan. 12, 2001) (*cited in* Schabas, *supra* note 6, at n. 7).

27. In particular, an Expert Group was convened by the U.N. Office of Legal Affairs on Dec. 20–21, 2001. Legal experts and representatives of human rights organizations met to try to develop a common approach on the optimal relationship between the SCSL and the TRC. Paul van Zyl made a presentation at this meeting.

on how they would interact and share information.[28] Despite this almost universal recommendation by international experts, the SCSL and the Sierra Leone TRC never formed a signed, written agreement concerning how they would interact and share information. Leaders of both institutions came together to discuss this issue, but conversations regarding this issue came to an end (somewhat prematurely) when SCSL Prosecutor David Crane indicated in September 2002, that, for its part, the SCSL Prosecutor would only use information from its own investigations and would not rely on or use any information presented before the TRC.[29]

While some—including apparently, the leaders of the SCSL and the TRC—believed that this solved the issue of the relationship between the two institutions, in fact it only resolved one aspect of the relationship. Among other things, it left unresolved whether and how the judges at the SCSL could take judicial notice of evidence presented at the TRC; whether and how defense teams at the SCSL could seek to use information from the TRC; whether and how the TRC commissioners could request or use information in the possession of the SCSL; and importantly, whether those indicted by the SCSL could, before the resolution of their trial, testify before the TRC.

The Case of Samuel Hinga Norman

The Indictment of Samuel Hinga Norman and his Request to Testify before the TRC

During the Sierra Leone conflict, Chief Samuel Hinga Norman was the National Coordinator of the Civil Defense Force ("CDF") and the leader and commander of a CDF sub-faction, the Kamajors. The CDF was a pro-government militia that played an active role in the conflict. On 10 March 2003, Norman was arrested while serving as a Cabinet member in the Sierra Leonean government. He was indicted by the

---

28. *See, e.g.*, SG Report, *supra* note 14, ¶ 8. For a further outline of these many meetings, *see* Schabas, *supra* note 6, at 25–29. It is interesting to note that despite the intellectual muscle present at many of these meetings, unfortunately, they lacked adequate consultation with members of the Sierra Leone TRC or the SCSL.

29. *See, e.g.*, Schabas, *supra* note 6, at 29; TRC REPORT, *supra* note 1, paras. 51, 67. *See also* 3B TRC REPORT, *supra* note 1, ch. 6, para. 51 (quoting November 2002 interview with OTP Chief Investigator Allan White: "We strongly support the TRC. We are on record saying that we do not plan to use any information at all from the TRC. We do want to encourage people to come and tell their story so the nation can begin the healing process.... We will not concern ourselves if you come before the TRC. Nor do we necessarily want to know who comes before the TRC. It is a separate and distinct operation, and it should be. We do not plan on asking the TRC for any information whatsoever....").

SCSL for crimes against humanity, war crimes, and other serious violations of international humanitarian law in reference to his role in the CDF and Kaymajors, who, according to the SCSL indictment, were responsible for many atrocities, including forced cannibalism as well as recruiting and using child soldiers.

As a member of the Sierra Leonean government at the time of his arrest, Norman had recently attended the opening of the TRC headquarters and agreed to an informal interview with the TRC.[30] After his arrest, under the advice of his legal counsel, Norman reconsidered and refused the TRC's official request for his testimony.[31] Yet only a few months later, while in custody and awaiting his trial, Norman heard President Kabbah provide dramatic public testimony in front of the TRC referencing Norman's role in running the CDF,[32] and decided that he too desired to testify publicly before the TRC. In a letter to his attorney on 26 August 2003, Norman declared:

> I have long been in receipt of copy of your letter ... expressing the inappropriateness for me (your client) to appear before the Truth and Reconciliation Commission while I remain an indictee before the Special Court.
>
> Well, I was arrested, charged and detained on the 10th March 2003, thinking that by now, 25th August 2003, my trial would have started long ago; but I thought wrongly. Since there is no news about the start of the trial and there are signs that the TRC may soon close its sittings, I would prefer to be heard by the people of Sierra Leone and also be recorded for posterity especially where my boss, The President of Sierra Leone, who appointed me and under whom I served as the Deputy Minister of Defence and National Coordinator of the Civil Defense Force (CDF/SL), has already testified before the Commission.
>
> As my SOLICITOR, I am applying through you and requesting you as a matter of urgency to please inform the necessary parties of my willingness to appear and testify before the TRC without any further delay.

The response to this unforeseen request led to an unprecedented escalation of tension between the TRC and the SCSL as these two theoretically complementary institutions working on behalf of the Sierra Leonean people and the international community to bring peace, securi-

---

30. Schabas, *supra* note 6, at 43.

31. The letter sent from Norman's attorney to the TRC said that he believed it would be inappropriate for his client to testify before the TRC while he was indicted by the SCSL. Schabas, *supra* note 6, at 43 n. 107 and accompanying text.

32. Telephonic interview with Robin Vincent, SCSL Registrar (Mar. 16, 2007).

ty, and democracy to Sierra Leone, argued over whether and how Norman, as an indictee of the SCSL, should be able to testify before the TRC.

The TRC received Norman's request to testify publicly before them in late August 2003, just four months before the TRC was set to close its operations. According to the TRC, the Commission sent a letter to the Registrar of the SCSL, Robin Vincent, requesting that he facilitate an interview between TRC representatives and Norman on 4 September 2003.[33] Mr. Vincent said that he never received this request. Despite the fact that the TRC received no reply from the SCSL, on September 4, TRC representatives went to the SCSL to speak with Norman. Upon their arrival, instead of going to speak with the Registrar to request access to Norman, TRC representatives went through SCSL security and headed directly to the detention facilities to access Norman. Before they could reach him, however, they were stopped and diverted to the Registrar's office. Mr. Vincent explained to these TRC representatives that there was no official policy in place for how or whether members of the TRC could access detainees of the SCSL. He also recognized that there were potential legal concerns over providing the TRC access to SCSL indictees. As a result, Mr. Vincent denied the TRC representatives immediate access to Norman, but recommended that an official protocol be immediately developed so that the issue of TRC access to SCSL indictees could be fully considered and the proper safeguards be put in place.[34]

The TRC's disappointment (and frustration) over not being given immediate access to Norman escalated when the SCSL issued its protocol regarding TRC access to SCSL detainees. The provision, entitled "Practice Direction on the procedure following a request by a National Authority or Truth and Reconciliation Commission to take a statement from a person in the custody of the Special Court for Sierra Leone," required any requesting authority to make an official application to a justice of the SCSL, including a list of the specific questions that would be asked to the detainee. If the interview was granted it would be supervised by a legal officer from the SCSL who would have the authority to intervene regarding specific questions and even stop the interview. The Practice Direction also required that all interviews be recorded and the transcripts handed over to the Prosecutor for use in trial.[35]

---

33. 3B TRC REPORT, *supra* note 1, ch. 6, para. 81.

34. Telephonic interview with Robin Vincent, SCSL Registrar (Mar. 16, 2007); TRC REPORT, *supra* note 1, para. 81.

35. Practice Direction on the Procedure Following a Request by a National Authority or Truth and Reconciliation Commission to Take a Statement from a Person in the

The TRC fundamentally disagreed with the Practice Direction's conditions of access and automatic information-sharing. But, its disappointment was compounded by the fact that the SCSL neglected to consult them during the process of developing the protocol.[36] They responded by way of a letter to the Registrar of the SCSL stating that they believed that the monitoring requirement was an "outrage" and a denial of an accused's right not to incriminate himself. Furthermore, "[t]he Direction is dismissive of the spirit and purpose behind the Truth and Reconciliation Commission . . . [and] would be a highly regrettable development between our two important institutions."[37] The TRC was particularly upset by the Practice Direction's infringement on their ability to take confidential statements. However, in practice, this issue was not relevant to the testimony of Norman, who specifically wished to testify publicly.

In response to the TRC's concerns, the SCSL reconsidered and amended their Practice Direction on 4 October 2003. The revised Practice Direction called for the interview transcript to be filed with the SCSL Registrar, instead of automatically transferring it to the Prosecutor. The transcripts could then be made available to either party in the proceedings upon the order of the Presiding Judge.[38] The revised direction also used language that implied there would be a presumption in favor of granting requests for interviews with detainees, and that such requests "will only be rejected if the Presiding Judge is satisfied that a refusal is necessary in the interests of justice or to maintain the integrity of the proceedings of the Special Court."[39]

With the balance of the Practice Direction remaining the same, and another month gone, the TRC was still unhappy, and tensions between the two institutions continued. The TRC wrote another letter to the SCSL Registrar on 8 October 2003, expressing its concerns about the direction's violation of the TRC's authority to "guarantee strict confidentiality."[40] In his responding correspondence, SCSL Registrar Vincent stated that he was "disappointed that so much of the correspondence with the Commission on this issue ha[d] been couched in somewhat

---

Custody of the Special Court for Sierra Leone (Sept. 9, 2003), *available at* http://www.sc-sl.org/Documents/practicedirection–090903.html.

36. 3B TRC REPORT, *supra* note 1, ch. 6, para. 83.

37. *Id.*, para. 87.

38. Revised Practice Direction on the Procedure following a Request by a National Authority or Truth and Reconciliation Commission to Take a Statement from a Person in the Custody of the Special Court for Sierra Leone, ¶ 4(b)–(c) (Oct. 4, 2003), *available at* http://www.sc-sl.org/Documents/practicedirection–090903.html [hereinafter Revised Practice Direction].

39. *Id.*, ¶ 5.

40. 3B TRC REPORT, *supra* note 1, ch. 6, para. 101.

aggressive language which could be seen to both inappropriate and counter productive, given that both institutions have difficult tasks to perform and expectations to meet."[41]

Luckily, Norman had specifically requested to testify publicly before the TRC—not confidentially—so despite the growing tensions about the Practice Direction's effect on confidential testimony, the TRC made an application to Judge Bankole Thompson, the judge presiding over Norman's case, for his testimony before the TRC. The official application of the TRC echoed the demands of Norman himself who asked to provide his testimony before the TRC in a public forum so that the people of Sierra Leone could hear it. The TRC's application requested that this public hearing take place within the SCSL courthouse, and that it be broadcast live to the nation, as public TRC hearings normally were.[42] When informed of this request, Prosecutor David Crane, in contrast to his earlier statement about not using any information from the TRC in his investigations, responded that if such testimony was given, he would feel free to use any information provided against Norman.

Judge Bankole Thompson's Ruling

Judge Bankole Thompson's 29 October 2003 ruling on the TRC's application to hear Norman's testimony did nothing to allay the tensions between the SCSL and the TRC. In a ruling that was unconvincing and rather poorly reasoned, Judge Thompson decided to refuse the TRC's request for Norman's testimony. He based this decision mostly on what he referred to as a "super due process" rationale. Despite the fact that Norman himself requested to testify before the TRC, Judge Thompson asserted that allowing him to do so would violate his right to a presumption of innocence, his privilege against self-incrimination, and his right to remain silent.[43]

In fact, allowing Norman to testify before the TRC would not have violated any of these rights.

In his decision, Judge Thompson noted that the *Truth and Reconciliation Commission Act 2000* gave the TRC the authority to hear testimony from three groups of people: (1) victims of abuses and violations, (2) perpetrators of abuses and violations, and (3) other interested parties. The TRC's assertion in their application that Norman played a central

---

41. *Id.*, para. 103.

42. Robertson Decision, *supra* note 17, ¶ 24.

43. Prosecutor v. Norman, Case No. SCSL–03–08–PT, Decision on the Request by the Truth and Reconciliation Commission of Sierra Leone to Conduct a Public Hearing with Samuel Hinga Norman, ¶¶ 10–16 (Oct. 29, 2003), *available at* http://www.sc-sl.org/CDF-trialchamberdecisions.html [hereinafter Thompson Decision].

role in the conflict in Sierra Leone indicated, according to Judge Thompson, that he was being invited to testify as a perpetrator of abuses and violations. As a result, granting such a request would amount to a determination of Norman's guilt, and was therefore inconsistent with a presumption of innocence.[44]

The fact that the TRC regarded Norman a central player in the Sierra Leone conflict and therefore wished to hear from him clearly did not constitute a violation of his presumption of innocence. There was no way to factually determine the precise basis upon which the TRC called Norman to testify. The TRC may have invited Norman to testify as an interested party, rather than as a perpetrator of abuses. Judge Thompson dismissed this possibility with the assertion that "[i]t seems disingenuous to suggest that the Accused ... is being invited to testify as an 'interested party;'" but he never explained why this was necessarily the case.[45] Even if the TRC had invited Norman to testify as a "perpetrator",[46] the abuses the TRC thought Norman might have committed might not have fallen under the limited jurisdiction of the Special Court or the purview of Norman's indictment.[47] Moreover, even if the abuses did correspond, the TRC was simply extending an invitation and had not made any factual determinations that Norman was a perpetrator based on consideration of the evidence.

Even assuming, *arguendo*, that all the following had been true—the TRC invited Norman to testify as a "perpetrator" and had made factual determinations that Norman was a "perpetrator" of abuses included in his SCSL indictment based on a presentation of evidence—allowing him to testify before the TRC still would not have been a violation of Norman's presumption of innocence before the SCSL. The presumption of innocence is a doctrine holding that a mere accusation of wrongdoing is not enough to convict. At the opening of a trial, the accused is always assumed innocent, and the burden of proving guilt lies with the prosecution. The accused has no burden to provide evidence to prove his innocence unless the prosecution presents sufficient evidence to meets its burden of proof that the accused is guilty of the charged crimes.[48]

---

44. *Id.*, ¶ 11–12

45. *Id.*, ¶ 12.

46. *See* Request SHN 001, submitted on Oct. 7, 2003 by the TRC to conduct a public hearing with Chief Samuel Hinga Norman. (Document on file with authors.)

47. For example, the abuses might have constituted domestic crimes that were not violations of the Geneva Conventions or crimes against humanity, i.e., because they were not systematic in nature.

48. Burdens of proof for criminal offenses differ between many adversarial and inquisitorial systems. Traditional adversarial systems generally use the "beyond a reasonable doubt" standard. Traditional inquisitorial systems often rely on a more subjective *"intime conviction du juge"* (intimate conviction of the judge) standard.

As a result, even if the TRC made determinations about a person indicted by the SCSL, these determinations would not shift the burden of proof to the accused in his trial before the SCSL. The prosecution would still have the burden of proving Norman's guilt and, as a result, Norman would still have the presumption of innocence.[49] The same dynamic is seen in many domestic jurisdictions where people may be tried in both a civil action and a criminal action on the same set of facts. In such circumstances, a person may testify, and even be found liable for their actions in a civil case, without violating the presumption of innocence for the criminal charge based on the same set of facts. In the end, Justice Thompson appears to have misconstrued the presumption of innocence doctrine and inappropriately used it to bar Norman's testimony before the TRC.

Judge Thompson's next argument, that allowing Norman to testify before the TRC would violate his due process rights against self-incrimination and remaining silent, was equally problematic. As long as a person is given proper notice of his rights and has the opportunity to obtain advice from qualified legal counsel, he should have the right to voluntarily waive these rights. This is the case in most domestic legal systems. The Practice Direction issued by the SCSL ensured that when a request to testify in front of the TRC was made, the accused would be both given notice of his rights and "ample opportunity to take legal advice before deciding whether or not to agree to the questioning."[50] It was clear that Norman was both informed of his rights and had received ample legal advice by his attorneys; and he decided to voluntarily waive his rights. With knowledge to this effect, Judge Thompson's ruling and declaration of a "super due process right" amounted not to the protection of Norman's rights, but rather a decision that Norman was not entitled to waive his rights. While in many cases remaining silent may be the best strategic legal advice, allowing voluntary waiver is not a violation of an accused's due process rights.[51]

---

49. Such findings by the TRC may be more problematic if the SCSL held jury trials, as public findings by the TRC might taint the jury pool or inappropriately bias the jury. But this is not a presumption of innocence issue, rather it is an issue of prejudicing the jury. Yet, even in domestic jurisdictions where criminal trials involve a jury, holding a civil trial based on the same set of facts does not itself inappropriately prejudice the jury.

50. Revised Practice Direction, *supra* note 38, ¶ 4.

51. In fact, denying the ability to waive one's right to silence may be considered a violation of the freedom of expression enshrined in Article 19 of the Universal Declaration of Human Rights and Article 19 of the International Covenant on Civil and Political Rights. While this right is not absolute, it is important to note that Judge Thompson made no reference to the enumerated limitations to this right, but rather referred only to his "super due process" argument. *See* Thompson Decision, *supra* note 43; 3B TRC REPORT, *supra* note 1, ch. 6, para. 134.

In the end, Judge Thompson's judgment was so poorly reasoned that it could lead one to the conclusion that the Court was only interested in defending its turf and insulating the decision to prosecute Norman from public scrutiny. Unlike the prosecution of Foday Sankoh, the decision to indict Norman was regarded as controversial by a significant number of Sierra Leoneans. Key TRC staffers thought that the SCSL should not be entitled to prevent them from discharging a vital part of their mandate because of an unwillingness to weather the criticism that Norman might direct at them if given a public platform. Some also argued that the Thompson judgment reflected a judicial arrogance that dismissed the importance of another transitional justice mechanism, or at least subordinated it to the prerogatives of the court.

Disquiet about the Thompson judgment was not confined to the TRC. Judge Geoffrey Robertson, President of the SCSL, felt compelled to arrange a further hearing in an effort to resolve the issue or, at least, present a more cogent and defensible ruling if he was unable to broker an agreement. Robertson was at pains not to characterize his ruling as an appeal and sought to schedule proceedings at the Bintumani Hotel that were more akin to an informal discussion between all parties than a formal hearing. Nevertheless, his decision effectively to overturn Judge Thompson's ruling was deeply unpopular with his fellow judges, who felt that the needs and interests of the TRC should not be allowed to intrude into an arena that they regarded as their sole preserve.

Judge Robertson's Unorthodox Appeals Process

On 4 November 2003, the TRC and Samuel Hinga Norman filed for an appeal of Judge Thompson's ruling, as per their right under the Practice Direction.[52] Instead of hearing the appeal in a formal and official manner, President Robertson invited the parties to an informal discussion/hearing at the Bintumani Hotel in Freetown. Judge Robertson claimed that Rule 5 of the Practice Direction provided the authority to conduct such an informal appeal because its intent was "to allow the President to take a broader view about an indictee's contacts with third parties and institutions, a role he is in any event given by the Rules of Detention."[53] Nevertheless, it is unclear whether he really had such authority, as the informal process was highly unusual. Yet neither party objected. This may have been because, just before the informal appeal discussion/hearing, President Robertson informed Norman's SCSL de-

---

52. Revised Practice Direction, *supra* note 38, ¶ 5 ("An appeal against rejection shall be decided by the President if it is made expeditiously and jointly by the detainee and the requesting authority.").

53. Robertson Decision, *supra* note 17, ¶ 3.

fense team (who in turn informed TRC representatives) that there would be no need to present arguments, as he was inclined to let Norman's hearing before the TRC proceed, and was merely interested in working out the details of the TRC hearing.[54] As a result of receiving this information, the TRC and defense team did not raise any objections to the informal nature of the proceedings.[55] When Judge Robertson's initial overview of the issue included a declaration that his "main concern is not to inhibit anyone from giving testimony in any form but to let them know what they are letting themselves in for; particularly if [it is] going on public record," it appeared as if he was indeed planning on allowing Norman to testify publicly before the TRC.[56]

The rest of the informal discussion, which was plagued by interjections and seemingly incongruous changes of topic, however, found Judge Robertson swinging from this permissive position to one that seemed more wary and suspicious. Judge Robertson began his questioning by asking the parties about the background details of Norman's indictment, whether Norman had been acting under the "approval of Government," and whether that would be part of his defense. When the final two questions were answered in the affirmative, Judge Robertson clarified that if a *prima facie* case were established against President Kabbah, who had heretofore not been indicted by the SCSL, then President Kabbah would have to appear before the SCSL as a witness.[57] He then moved on to ask the TRC representatives about the specifics of the proposed hearing, including the location, which media would be present, how the proceeding would be organized, whether the testimony would be under oath, whether there would be cross-examination, etc. When the Commission's representative, Howard Varney, stressed that such details had yet to be determined because they would rely on an agreement between the TRC and Norman's defense team, the Judge moved on to inquire about whether the TRC would be making judgments.[58] To this, Mr. Varney stated that the TRC is not a court and explained the nature of a TRC's findings.[59]

The discussion then jumped to the issue of the prosecution's general fears concerning witness intimidation and the incitement of Norman's supporters, some of whom, the prosecution claimed, were still armed.[60] This appears to have been the turning point. From this point on, the

---

54. 3B TRC Report, *supra* note 1, ch. 6, para. 145.
55. *Id.*, para. 147.
56. *Id.*, paras. 149–50.
57. *Id.*, para. 150.
58. *Id.*, paras. 151–54.
59. *Id.*, para. 154.
60. *Id.*, paras. 156–57.

Judge clarified his view that "rights are amenable to dilution," and that a public hearing before the TRC would be tantamount to a "party political broadcast."[61] Judge Robertson then suggested that the TRC might suspend its proceedings until after all the trials at the SCSL were complete, after which time it could use the Court's findings and be free to talk with any indictees who had been convicted or acquitted.[62] When Mr. Varney informed Judge Robertson that such a suspension was not possible under the TRC's mandate, Judge Robertson concluded the "appeals process" by noting that he would allow subsequent submissions. Mr. Varney reminded him of the Commission's tight time constraints, to which Judge Robertson replied that his final decision would be issued within a week.[63] Instead, it was more than three weeks before the decision was released.

The "Appeals" Decision

In his official ruling delivered on 28 November 2003, just one month before the scheduled closing of the TRC, Judge Robertson allowed the application in part. He agreed that Norman should be able to provide testimony to the TRC, but that such testimony could not be given in a public hearing. In his ruling, Judge Robertson generally refused to comment on Judge Thompson's initial decision, claiming that "[i]t is not normally appropriate for one judge to review another's discretion," and as a result he has "not treated this appeal as a judicial review of the decision of Judge Thompson or strictly as an appeal from his decision, but rather as a fresh hearing in a context where, as President, I have the flexibility to explore alternative solutions."[64] In the end, Judge Robertson appears to have based his decision on four main rationales: (1) public confusion, (2) fear of incongruous findings of fact, (3) witness intimidation and national security, and (4) the rights of other indictees. While his ruling may have attempted to provide a compromise between the parties, Judge Robertson's rationales for rejecting the TRC and Norman's joint application for a public hearing before the TRC were, on balance, unpersuasive.

Before examining each of these arguments, it is important to understand the various sources of pressure Judge Robertson was under. As stated earlier, his fellow judges, with whom he had to work on a daily basis, were angry that he had intervened in the matter. In addition, both the Prosecutor and the Registrar were firmly opposed to granting the

---

61. *Id.*, paras. 158–59.
62. *Id.*, para. 160.
63. *Id.*, paras. 161–62.
64. Robertson Decision, *supra* note 17, ¶ 3.

hearing. In other words, there was almost complete unanimity from all organs of the SCSL—the judges, the prosecutors and the registry—that Norman should not be granted a public hearing. There are a number of different reasons why such opposition existed: a fear of violence; a reluctance to grant Norman a public platform to criticize the SCSL or bolster his legitimacy; concerns about due process; and a sense amongst certain judges that courts should have primacy and should not have their work jeopardized by other institutions. To be fair, Judge Robertson was not comfortable with simply asserting the primacy of the Court. Both publicly and privately he recognized that the TRC had an important and complementary role to play. However, he was not fully able to step outside his legal and judicial world-view. Perhaps the most telling indication of his view that the interests of courts should in the final instance prevail is contained in the first few paragraphs of his discussion of the issues:

> Let me return to first principles. Truth Commissions and International Courts are both instruments for effectuating the promise made by states that victims of human rights violations shall have an effective remedy. Criminal courts offer *the most effective remedy*—a trial, followed by punishment of those found guilty, in this case of those who bear the greatest responsibility.[65]

Once you have taken the position that criminal courts offer *the most effective remedy* in dealing with mass atrocity—rather than a view which holds that courts, TRCs, reparations programs, and vetting mechanisms, are all important parts of a holistic response to human rights violations—then it is likely that your judgment will be an exercise in defending institutional prerogatives rather than carefully weighing equally legitimate institutional interests.

Other parts of Judge Robertson's decision also reveal a pro-court prejudice. He was clearly uncomfortable at the prospect of a "Bishop, rather than a presiding judge" chairing a highly charged political "spectacle" with no rules or procedures to maintain order. He referred disparagingly to TRC proceedings as having "the appearance of a sort of trial familiar from centuries past" despite the fact that half a dozen truth commissions had held precisely these sorts of hearings in other countries, without evidencing any unfair or medieval qualities.[66]

An additional factor that influenced the settlement of this dispute was the fact that by the time Judge Robertson intervened, relations between key staffers at the TRC and the SCSL had soured. The Judge's attempt to broker a compromise occurred in an atmosphere in which

---

65. *Id.*, para. 33 (emphasis added).
66. *Id.*, para. 30.

both sides lacked the rapport conducive to negotiating a mutually satisfactory solution.

Having provided some of the personal and institutional context, we can turn to an analysis of the judgment itself. Judge Robertson's first reason for denying the TRC's application for a public hearing was that such a hearing would have led to public confusion between the roles of the two institutions. He seemed particularly concerned that the TRC had requested that its hearing take place in SCSL courthouse. Moreover, in the TRC proceedings, Norman would have been questioned by a barrister, and then by a Bishop and five or six Commissioners sitting at the judges' bench. Such an event, Judge Robertson declared, "will have the appearance of a trial and may set up public expectation that it will indeed pass judgment on indictees thus confronted and questioned, whose guilt or innocence it is the special duty of the Special Court to determine."[67] While Judge Robertson's concern that such a proceeding would cause public confusion over the roles and responsibilities of the TRC and SCSL was valid, it could have been addressed less restrictively than denying Norman the right to testify publicly before the TRC. One option would have been to offer an alternative location for the TRC's public hearing to avoid justifiable misconceptions that the two institutions were connected. Another would have been to distinguish the physical configuration of the room where TRC testimony would be given from that of a courtroom, so that people would not think that the TRC used a similar set of procedures and participants to make judgments about the guilt or innocence of people involved. Any remaining confusion could have been less restrictively addressed by outreach efforts to educate the public about the differences between the TRC and the SCSL.

Judge Robertson also never explained why concerns about public confusion between the roles of the TRC and SCSL were more problematic when an indictee, like Norman, publicly testified before the TRC, than when witnesses and victims publicly testified before both institutions. Both could cause potential (although addressable) confusion, but witnesses and victims were permitted to publicly testify in front of both while, in this case, Judge Robertson held that Norman could not. Singling out and excluding persons from testifying at the TRC on the basis that the SCSL had accused/indicted them as the "most responsible" for serious crimes was not only irrational, but also seriously and unnecessarily hampered the TRC's goal of obtaining a full and impartial account of the conflict.

Related to the concern about public confusion was Judge Robertson's apprehension about having two official institutions making two potentially incongruous findings of fact about abuses that took place

---

67. *Id.*

during the conflict in Sierra Leone and responsibility for them. Judge Robertson revealed his concern over the TRC's determinations and the resultant public confusion should those findings conflict with those of the SCSL during the informal appeal hearing at the Bintumani Hotel as well as in his ruling. As noted above, during the Bintumani session, Judge Robertson specifically asked TRC representatives whether the TRC would "make a determination on the guilt or innocence of certain individuals," and whether "the Commission addressed the issue of making judgments on people?"[68] These questions revealed a misunderstanding of the nature of TRCs and the determinations that they make. TRCs do not issue judgments. Furthermore, governments are seldom obliged to implement TRC recommendations, and even when they are so obligated—as they were in the case of Sierra Leone[69]—their determinations about individuals' roles in conflict have no direct legal effect.[70] Yet, despite the TRC's representatives' response to that effect, Judge Robertson remained concerned that the TRC would make judgments about the accused. He was also worried that those judgments, which would be reported before the SCSL had a chance to issue its own judgments, could put pressure on the SCSL to comply with TRC findings or risk public confusion.

Of course, the same factual circumstances might result in different and even incongruous findings regardless of whether indictees were permitted to testify publicly at the TRC. Each institution had different sources of evidence and information in its possession. Even when evidence was about the same occurrences and came from the same sources, there was still a chance that the TRC and the SCSL could make incongruous findings because more information could have been considered by the TRC, as it was not bound by judicial rules of evidence or the same burdens of proof as the SCSL.

Judge Robertson's ruling also appears to have been based on concerns raised by the prosecutor regarding national security and witness intimidation. Judge Robertson noted that while Norman still retained his right to free speech, because of his status as an indictee who pled "not guilty," this right might be restricted "in the interest of security," as well as to ensure "fairness to the Prosecutor and its witnesses," and

---

68. 3B TRC REPORT, *supra* note 1, ch. 6, para. 154.

69. In fact, Sierra Leone is one of the few countries where the legislation establishing the TRC requires the government to report on the progress it has made in implementing the TRC's recommendations.

70. When TRCs are empowered to grant amnesty (such as in South Africa) or preside over quasi-judicial "plea-bargaining" arrangements (such as in Timor Leste) then their findings do have direct legal consequences. But this is not the case in Sierra Leone, where the TRC's findings had no direct legal consequences.

"other indictees who face trial."[71] Thus, "[h]is testimony must ... be provided in a manner that reduces to an acceptable level any danger that it will influence witnesses (whether favourably or adversely) or affect the integrity of court proceedings or unreasonably affect co-defendants and other indictees."[72] The implication was that, should Norman be allowed to testify before the TRC with his testimony broadcast via television and radio, there would be a risk that he might use the opportunity to intimidate witnesses and rally dormant forces.[73]

Concerns about national security and witness protection were unquestionably serious in Sierra Leone, as they are in many transitional societies. However, these security concerns would remain even if Norman did not testify publicly in front of a TRC because accused are given the opportunity to make public statements during their trials.[74] Moreover, precisely because security concerns are easy to assert in transitional societies, where fear and instability linger—especially in the minds of the people—such claims, which can hamper legitimate desires to speak publicly, should be subject to a specific pleading requirement, to establish more than a mere conjecture that such incitement or intimidation is likely to occur.

Judge Robertson's concern about the rights of, and fairness to, other indictees seems similarly misplaced. While permitting Norman to testify publicly before a TRC *might* pressure other indictees to testify before the TRC to tell their side of the story and defend themselves in the court of public opinion, it is unclear how this violates their rights. Judge Robertson seemed to believe that any pressure on indictees to testify at the TRC unduly infringing on their right to remain silent. However, the pressure created by indictees testifying before the TRC would be no different than the pressure created by non-indictees testifying publicly in front of the TRC. Both may create pressure for those who are already indicted to testify before the TRC. In fact, President Kabbah's testimony before the TRC was a major factor behind Norman's desire to testify before the TRC. It is therefore unclear why, if such testimony infringes on an indictee's right to remain silent, why Norman should have been prohibited from publicly testifying for this reason while others, like President Kabbah, were not.

---

71. Robertson Decision, *supra* note 17, ¶¶ 39–40.

72. *Id.*, para. 41.

73. *Id.*, paras. 30, 41.

74. For example, consider many of the public statements made by Saddam Hussein or Slobodan Milošević attempting to incite public unrest during their trials at the Iraqi High Tribunal and the International Criminal Tribunal for the Former Yugoslavia. *See* Michael P. Scharf, *Lessons from the Saddam Trial: Article: Chaos in the Courtroom: Controlling Disruptive Defendants and Contumacious Counsel in War Crimes Trials*, 39 Case W. Res. J. Int'l L. 155, 161–64 (2006).

In the end, Judge Robertson's attempt to find a compromise so that each institution could "accommodate the existence of the other"[75] held that Norman be allowed to testify before the TRC, but he could not do so in a public hearing. In order to balance Norman's interest in testifying before the TRC with the public interests discussed above, Norman could either provide written testimony, or, if another application were submitted, he could testify privately before the TRC.[76]

Dueling Press Releases

Tension between the two institutions continued to escalate after Judge Robertson's ruling. The growing discomfort was expressed in dueling press releases. The SCSL's press release in the wake of Judge Robertson's ruling touted that the decision opened the way for Norman to "testify before the TRC."[77] The TRC responded on 1 December 2003 with a press release titled, "Special Court Denies Hinga Norman's Right (and that of the other detainees) to Appear Publicly before the TRC." The release, in no uncertain terms, attacked the SCSL, claiming that:

> the Special Court has closed the door on any meaningful participation [in the TRC] by all detainees in its custody, [and the ruling of Judge Robertson] rejected the right of the detainees to testify before the TRC; denied the freedom of expression of detainees to appear openly and publicly before the TRC; denied the right of the Sierra Leonean people to see the process of truth and reconciliation done in relation to the detainees.[78]

In a radio interview and a corresponding press release, the SCSL responded that it stood by its original statement that the ruling had cleared Norman to testify before the TRC, and "claimed that the TRC had corrected 'certain inaccuracies'" in its 1 December press release. The TRC, countered with another press release on 3 December, "TRC Stands by its Statement on Hinga Norman." This statement emphasized that the TRC had neither retracted nor corrected its earlier press releases, and condemned the SCSL's media office for its attempts "to mislead the public in this regard."[79] Even Norman's defense team got into the fray, issuing a press release expressing their frustration with the SCSL's ruling and noting Norman's disappointment that this "head-on clash between the TRC and the Special Court has done much to obstruct the course of peace and reconciliation in Sierra Leone."[80]

---

75. Robertson Decision, *supra* note 17, ¶ 44.
76. *Id.*, para. 41.
77. 3B TRC REPORT, *supra* note 1, ch. 6, para. 171.
78. *Id.*, para. 172.
79. *Id.*, para. 173.
80. *Id.*, para. 174.

At the end of the day, all of this was left unresolved and Norman declined the opportunity to give written or "private" testimony to the TRC. The TRC was left with no other option than to tell its story and vent its frustration in its final report, in which it attacks the entire process and findings of the SCSL in relation to this issue.

Criminal Prosecutions and TRCs in Transitional Societies
Complementary Functions

While the tensions between the SCSL and the Sierra Leone TRC were based on particular circumstances, there is a risk of repeating these harmful and unnecessary tensions in other transitional societies, as criminal prosecutions and TRCs continue to work side-by-side as fundamental components of a holistic transitional justice agenda.

Transitional societies like Sierra Leone face the challenge of moving out of armed conflict into a peaceful and stable democracy. To consolidate this transition, parties must not only stop fighting, but the country must confront human rights abuses and atrocities that occurred during conflict. There are a wide range of activities that a society can undertake to address this legacy of abuse. These include prosecuting perpetrators, organizing truth-telling initiatives, providing reparations, creating memorials, and promoting institutional reform. Not all of these activities are needed to the same degree in each transitional situation, but they represent the basic tools available to help come to terms with a violent past. As we have seen, two of the most prominent transitional justice activities have been criminal prosecutions—domestic, international, or hybrid—and truth and reconciliation commissions.

In general, criminal prosecutions serve several important functions. By publicly demonstrating that those who do break the law will be punished, they support and strengthen the rule of law. Punishment can also serve as a potential deterrent to those who consider breaking the law, and can satisfy society's and victims' desire for retribution. In addition to their punitive role, criminal prosecutions, and the criminal justice system more generally, can also play a rehabilitative role, giving those who have committed wrongs a chance and a space to atone and change their ways. And, in a broader societal sense, criminal prosecutions convey norms about what acts and activities society finds acceptable and strengthen social solidarity behind common values.[81]

---

81. *See* Miriam J. Aukerman, *Extraordinary Evil, Ordinary Crime: A Framework for Understanding Transitional Justice*, 15 HARV. HUM. RTS. J. 39 (2002).

TRCs can also serve to strengthen democracy and a commitment to human rights. By providing a forum for airing grievances and collecting broad accounts of activities that occurred during conflict, they can play a vital fact-finding, punitive, and therapeutic role. The broad fact-finding function of TRCs is critical to setting up appropriate and comprehensive reparations programs and delineating areas in need of institutional reform. The public airing of abuses that occurred during conflict and the identification of those responsible publicly shames and stigmatizes perpetrators. And providing a safe and controlled forum to air grievances and address one's abusers or victims is often essential to post-conflict reconciliation.

While TRCs and criminal prosecutions serve different functions, they share many overarching goals. Both seek to establish the truth, and to determine criminal responsibility for the various atrocities that have taken place. Both impose a measure of punishment in the form of shaming and stigmatization, although only courts can order imprisonment. Courts and truth commissions can compensate victims for the harm they have suffered, through either reparation payments or damages awards, although only courts can actually order payment through damages awards. They can both catalyze institutional reform to help prevent future abuse. Courts do this by physically removing people from society and demanding change through legal orders. TRCs do the this by helping to consolidate a moral consensus that reform is necessary and making official recommendations, which, depending on their founding statute, may be binding on the government.[82]

Though many of the overarching goals are the same, their disparate functions mean TRCs and criminal prosecutions go about achieving these goals differently. Courts must adhere to more stringent due process requirements and their rules of evidence and procedure are more elaborate and demanding because the consequences of an adverse finding are more severe. Moreover, criminal trials are ultimately concerned with establishing the guilt or innocence of specific individuals, so the determination of political or moral responsibility for the crimes in question is of secondary importance. As a result, a court's scope of inquiry is considerably narrower than that of a TRC, which is generally concerned with creating an impartial account of an entire conflict.[83] The combination of a broader truth-seeking mandate and less stringent procedures enables

---

82. *See, e.g.*, TRC Act 2000, art. 17, *supra* note 24.

83. However, the trials of those who bear the greatest responsibility for mass atrocity often involve a much broader examination of the historical context and root causes of the conflict in which the atrocities occurred. Nevertheless, even trials that assume this broader truth-telling function still have a much narrower focus and more rigid set of procedures than do truth commissions.

TRCs to adopt a less restrictive approach to evidence gathering and to accept information from a far wider set of sources.

The Need for Both Criminal Prosecutions and TRCs

Given their different functions and limitations, neither criminal prosecutions nor TRCs on their own can comprehensively address the causes and consequences of mass atrocity. Yet, by adopting both criminal prosecutions and a TRC, transitional countries can offset many of the inherent limitations of each institution alone. They can also realize gains as TRCs are able to affirmatively assist court prosecutions and vice versa.

The scope of modern conflicts and resulting atrocities often makes it impossible to prosecute everyone responsible for crimes and human rights violations. Trials are designed for societies in which violation of the law is the exception and not the rule. In many post-conflict settings, including Sierra Leone, Rwanda, Guatemala, Timor Leste, Peru, Cambodia and the former Yugoslavia, there have been thousands, if not tens of thousands, of perpetrators. When the violation of the law is the rule rather than the exception—as it is during these periods of mass atrocity or systemic abuse—then, criminal justice systems simply cannot cope. Criminal trials, in general, require a significant investment of both financial and human resources. Criminal trials for war crimes, crimes against humanity, and/or genocide consume even more time and resources because of the evidence needed to prove a large number of crimes over a long period of time, the systematic nature of the crimes, systems of authorization, command and control, and the linkages between those who physically committed the crimes and those who organized and planned them (often referred to as the "material authors").

Yet, the resources necessary to conduct trials are even more scarce in transitional societies. Criminal justice institutions in these settings are often weak and dysfunctional. The result is that national investigators, prosecutors and judges required to pursue accountability for mass atrocity are generally unable to do so effectively. Transitional societies, moreover, are generally plagued by weak economies, the result of long periods of conflict or extortion by ruling elites, and an increased demand for social programs needed to rebuild the society and help those most affected by war and oppression. Consequently, no more than a small percentage of perpetrators has ever been held criminally responsible following the commission of tens of thousands of crimes. Thus, while criminal prosecutions are unquestionably necessary and generally beneficial to the transitioning society, they should be supplemented by TRCs, which are designed to address the broad range of abuses and large number of victims and perpetrators.

The stigma and severe punishments that accompany criminal prosecution also may not be the most appropriate means of dealing with all types of perpetrators. In Sierra Leone, thousands of young children were abducted from their homes, forced into military groups, and compelled to commit atrocities against innocent civilians, often members of their own families and villages. Child soldiers committed heinous crimes and clearly bear some responsibility for their actions; but, in a very real way, they were also victims of the conflict. In a context where limited resources means that only a small number of perpetrators can be prosecuted, it is not clear that child soldiers are the most appropriate criminal defendants. An absence of criminal liability for child soldiers however, increases the need for an alternative set of strategies to deal with their crimes and the suffering and resentment felt by their victims. Truth commissions can make an important contribution to dealing with the crimes committed by child soldiers.[84]

Criminal prosecutions are also limited by their focus on the guilt or innocence of persons accused of serious crimes. They do not concern themselves with the full range of needs and interests of the victims of the crimes. In adversarial judicial systems, victims may only participate in criminal trials at the request of the state or the defendant. If they participate in trials, they do so as conveyors of evidence; and the judicial process is not specifically geared towards addressing or acknowledging their suffering. In inquisitorial systems, victims may often initiate a civil claim against a defendant and join it with the criminal prosecution, and thus play a greater role in the criminal proceedings. However, even in inquisitorial systems, the perpetrator must be available to be tried in order for the victims to be able to address their needs publicly. The result is that criminal prosecutions alone do not address victims' need to tell their stories, and to confront those who were responsible for their abuses.

TRCs, on the other hand, are victim-focused. They provide a space for victims to recount their abuses and have them recognized in an official historical record, regardless of whether theirs is an adversarial or inquisitorial legal system, and regardless of whether the person who abused them is available to appear or not. Moreover, TRCs may provide an opportunity for victims to confront their abusers, ask for explanations and apologies, and offer forgiveness, possibilities which are not available in court prosecutions.

---

84. The U.N. Secretary–General made this point in a 2000 report stating that "relationship and cooperation arrangements would be required between the Prosecutor and the National Truth and Reconciliation Commission, including using the Commission as an alternative to prosecution, and the prosecution of juveniles, in particular." SG Report, *supra* note 14, ¶ 8.

TRCs not only offset various limitations of criminal prosecutions, they also affirmatively assist criminal prosecutions. Even before criminal prosecutions are under way, truth-seeking initiatives can provide a less threatening way to begin uncovering the past, and in doing so, help create a political consensus that criminal justice is necessary.[85] TRCs compile a broad range of evidence, which can be used to identify potential criminal defendants and various forms of criminal responsibility. Furthermore, by highlighting broad patterns of abuse, TRCs facilitate the prosecution of international crimes, which often requires evidence that the attacks were widespread and systematic. These patterns also help prove liability under command responsibility, because the systematic nature of abuse means it was likely ordered, or that those in positions of authority at least should have had knowledge of the abuse and intervened to prevent it or punish those who committed it. Lastly, TRCs may further ease burdens on the court's evidence-gathering resources, since courts often may take judicial notice of TRC findings.

While TRCs can serve as an effective complement to prosecutions, and may even significantly bolster criminal prosecutions, they have their own limitations and should not be established as a substitute for criminal accountability. They can help narrow the range of "permissible lies"[86] about a conflict and end denial about abuses; but they do not always produce a social consensus or a shared view of history. TRCs may prove therapeutic for victims, providing a process for airing their abuses and addressing perpetrators, which can help provide closure and be healing in itself. But it is not always the case that "revealing is healing" and, in fact, victims may be re-traumatized by testifying if proper precautions are not taken and support systems are not included to help with the long-term healing process.[87] TRCs also risk framing human rights abuses too narrowly by focusing only on civil and political rights and paying less attention to economic, social and cultural rights. If TRCs view victims of a conflict as only those who were tortured and assassinated rather than those who died of "war-related" causes, such as malnutrition or preventable disease, then they can paint an inaccurate picture of the conflict, its causes, and its remedies.

Another significant limitation of TRCs is their ability to punish. While TRCs may provide shaming and stigmatization, they do not have

---

85. In both Argentina and Chile, truth commissions served as a prelude to and helped facilitate justice efforts. In South Africa, on the other hand, the TRC process significantly delayed post-Apartheid prosecutions. These delays, combined with an absence of political will on the part of the South Africa government, have substantially undermined the prospects for justice for apartheid-era crimes.

86. Michael Ignatieff, *Articles of Faith*, 25 INDEX ON CENSORSHIP, 5, 113 (1996).

87. *See* Office of the U.N. High Comm'r for Human Rights [OHCHR], *Rule-of-Law Tools for Post Conflict States: Truth Commissions*, 23, U.N. Doc. HR/PUB/06/1 (2006).

the authority to imprison, or restrict the freedoms of perpetrators. Those most responsible for mass atrocities like the crimes that occurred in Sierra Leone deserve a more severe punishment than shame and stigma. They also need to be removed from society, so that they cannot continue to pose a threat to peace and stability. A TRC cannot accomplish this on its own. Criminal prosecutions are needed to reestablish the rule of law, convey a clear and proportionate condemnation of past crimes, and deter future criminal conduct.

Criminal prosecutions can also affirmatively assist TRCs. Because they have the power to compel testimony and provide plea deals, prosecutions may have access to otherwise unavailable information, and can provide more in-depth accounts of the activities of essential actors and key atrocities. Additionally, by offering more severe punishments for those most responsible for atrocities, they help distinguish these actors from those who may be less morally culpable, thereby strengthening reconciliation efforts.

While it is true that having both a TRC and criminal prosecutions creates a risk establishing multiple official versions of "the facts," incongruous findings of fact between various official institutions is not unique to the relationship between courts and TRCs. Rather it is a common feature in complex societies and justice systems throughout the world. In many systems, those found personally liable for injury in a civil trial may be found not guilty in a criminal trial based on the exact same set of facts. Public reports and findings by official, but non-judicial, entities are commonly examined and contradicted by judicial institutions. For example, in its final report, the South African Truth Commission made a series of findings holding cabinet-level members of various apartheid governments criminally responsible for authorizing assassinations and disappearances of anti-apartheid activists. Notwithstanding these findings, no prosecutor chose to initiate prosecutions against individuals implicated in the TRC's final report in the immediate aftermath of its issuance. While this was certainly unsatisfactory from the perspective of the TRC and many others, it did not lead to a constitutional crisis or produce conflict or widespread confusion. Most citizens understand that there may be a difference between the findings of a commission and the decision of a prosecutor or judiciary to initiate criminal proceedings.

It is also important to realize that incongruous findings of fact by different transitional justice institutions are just one—and by no means the most serious—of many potential flashpoints created by transitional justice mechanisms. Disarmament, demobilization and reintegration ("DDR") programs may allow lower-level perpetrators to get away with past abuses in exchange for their agreement to cooperate with the program. Reparations programs often inadequately address the harms victims suffered, are administered only after a significant delay, or are not introduced at all. Those most responsible for serious crimes may be acquitted for lack of admissible evidence, or may receive light sentences for agreeing to help prosecutors convict other defendants. With all of these conceivable "injustices," it is highly unlikely that incongruous findings of fact between a TRC and a criminal prosecution would be the tipping point to destabilize peace, especially since such concerns could be addressed, at least in part, through public outreach and education.

In the end, any confusion and dissatisfaction concerning potentially contradictory findings made by TRCs and courts also needs to be weighed against the realistic alternatives. The development of a "perfect" division of labor between courts and commissions such that they will never deal with the same subject matter and thereby avoid the potential for incompatible findings would significantly undermine the functioning of one—if not both—institutions. The kinds of cases that special courts prosecute following mass atrocity typically involve those who bear greatest responsibility for the crimes and/or the most notorious or heinous crimes. A truth commission report would be fundamentally incomplete if it did not deal with the perpetrators or victims of these crimes. If one accepts that courts and commissions are autonomous and independent institutions that cannot realistically avoid dealing with the same subject matter, then the potential for incompatible findings in unavoidable. The focus should therefore be on how to ameliorate the undesirable consequences of such findings, rather than seeking to avoid them altogether.

Criminal prosecutions and TRCs are two important components of a comprehensive transitional justice strategy. Though there are some challenges to conducting both for a single conflict, it is clear that when both are used, they are greater than the sum of their parts. Moreover, international law requires states to both punish perpetrators and establish the truth,[88] in response to gross violations of human rights. We should therefore regard both strategies as necessary to helping nations come to terms with their past.

Lessons Learned from Sierra Leone

TRCs and court prosecutions are integral to establishing a stable and peaceful democracy in transitional societies dealing with a legacy of abuse. Yet, as we have seen in the case of Sierra Leone, even though these potentially complementary institutions share common goals, considerable tensions can erupt between them that hamper their ability to

---

88. *See* Velasquez Rodriguez Case, 1988 Inter–Am. Ct. H.R. (ser. C) No. 4, at 172 (July 29, 1988); Mahmut Kaya v. Turkey, 2000–III Eur. Ct. H.R. 149; Barbato v. Uruguay, U.N. Doc. CCPR/C/17/D/84/1981 (U.N. Human Rights Comm., Oct. 21, 1982).

achieve optimal results. It is therefore critical that we learn from this experience to prevent these tensions in future transitional environments. The following are some conclusions and recommendations gleaned from the Sierra Leone experience.

No Hierarchy

TRCs and criminal prosecutions each play an important and complementary role in transitional societies. Both are needed to help society promote accountability for past abuses, create a historical record, and move forward into a more stable peace based on democracy, human rights and the rule of law. Since both TRCs and criminal prosecutions are necessary to complete this task, there should be no hierarchy establishing one as more important than the other.

A Mutually Reinforcing Relationship

TRCs and courts should cooperate with each other to complement and buttress their own work. Not only are both institutions necessary to complete the overall goals of transitional society, each helps the other achieve its mission. TRCs can help mobilize support for criminal prosecutions. They can also bring together information that will help identify perpetrators, outline elements of criminal responsibility, and illuminate patterns of abuse needed to prosecute international system crimes. Court prosecutions provide more in-depth accounts of key atrocities, and the actions of key actors. They can facilitate eventual reconciliation by punishing those most responsible and distinguishing them from those with lesser criminal and moral responsibility.

Information–Sharing

The goal of an agreement creating an official relationship between a TRC and a court is to encourage the greatest possible participation in the TRC (both publicly and privately), while ensuring that those accused of being most responsible for grave abuses can be vigorously prosecuted without infringing on their rights to due process and a fair trial. There are three basic approaches that can be taken to information-sharing between a court and a TRC: the "firewall" model, the "free access" model, and the "conditional sharing" model.[89]

The "firewall" model mandates no information-sharing between a TRC and a court. This model helps allay concerns of those who fear that evidence provided to a TRC may be used against them or their accom-

---

89. *See* Wierda et al., *supra* note 20, at 8–11.

plices in a criminal prosecution, and thus increases the number of people willing to testify before a TRC. Prosecutor David Crane's assertion that he would not rely on information presented to the TRC for his prosecutions, combined with the lack of any further formal information-sharing agreement between the TRC and SCSL, suggests that this was the model (unofficially) agreed to by the SCSL and the Sierra Leone TRC. This model, however, is not practical. Defendants in court prosecutions will always have an argument that they should have access to any exculpatory information held by the TRC, especially regarding charges as grave as genocide, war crimes, and crimes against humanity. A TRC itself will not want to withhold information that is indispensable to determining the guilt or innocence of a person standing trial. Similarly, prosecutors and the international community will want access to "smoking gun" evidence provided at a TRC, to ensure that those most responsible for such heinous international crimes are appropriately held to account. And, as was the case with Norman, the TRC may strongly desire access to indictees and information in the possession of the court.

The "free access" model allows all information to be continually shared between the two institutions. While potentially ideal for helping the TRC and courts to work cooperatively, such unconditional information-sharing would be problematic. Prosecutors will not want to give the TRC unconditional access to all their evidence, as such public disclosure will undermine their investigation and prosecution strategy. Conversely, the TRC will not want to provide prosecutors with free access to all information it gathers, as this will dissuade perpetrators from cooperating with the TRC. It might cause the TRC to be perceived as an investigative branch of the court, and thus create powerful disincentives for people to testify before the TRC. Valuable information would be lost, and the TRC may not be able to function effectively as a venue for truth-seeking or reconciliation.

"Conditional sharing" may provide the best compromise between the need for certain types of information-sharing and preserving the autonomy and individual goals of each institution. This model permits certain information to be shared between the TRC and court, but only if specified conditions are met. What information should be shared and under what conditions will be context specific, as every transitional situation is different, and the mandates and rules of each court and truth-seeking mechanism may vary considerably. However, in every situation the specific conditions of information-sharing should be determined in consultation with both institutions. They must also be transparent and set out beforehand. If such conditions are met, this model may provide the greatest overall benefit to both institutions.

Confidential Evidence–Gathering by a TRC

Truth commissions can make an important contribution to establishing the causes, nature, and effect of gross violations of human rights, as well as revealing the fate and whereabouts of victims, by receiving evidence from perpetrators on a confidential basis. In most instances, perpetrators will only be prepared to furnish this information if they receive assurance that it will not be used against them. One of the deep frustrations of the Sierra Leone TRC staff was that, not only were they denied the opportunity to obtain information from Norman via public testimony, but the nature of both Practice Directions meant that any information that Norman gave to the TRC might be used by the SCSL prosecution. Commissions and courts should come to some arrangement early in their mandates that clarify whether and in what way commissions will be able to gather confidential information from perpetrators and what assurances they can and will be given regarding its use.

Dispute Resolution Mechanism

TRCs and courts need to agree on a dispute resolution mechanism to resolve disputes between them regarding information-sharing should unforeseen, unaccounted for, or specific situations arise. As evidenced by the Norman case, the SCSL unilaterally decided it had the authority to resolve the dispute between itself and the TRC. A dispute resolution agreement would go a long way towards alleviating unnecessary tension and animosity between institutions that are supposed to be working toward the same goal. Many examples of appropriate dispute resolution mechanisms may be found in the well-established fields of mediation and arbitration.[90] Whatever mechanism is chosen, it must be specified and clearly agreed to before any conflict between the institutions arise. In the end, procedural fairness is as important as substantive fairness.

Allay Public Confusion

When a TRC and courts operate at the same time and address the same general set of facts and abuses, there is a real concern about public confusion over their respective roles. The confusion can be addressed without unnecessarily limiting either institution by developing sophisticated and pro-active outreach campaigns to carefully explain and differ-

---

90. For example, the parties could agree to use a neutral mediator to help them reach an agreement. Or the parties could agree to create a three-person panel to make a binding determination, based on mutually agreed-to rules of procedure. To determine the members of the panel, each party may choose one person and together those two people agree on a third.

entiate the role and mandate of each institution. The SCSL's claim that Norman's public testimony before the TRC would result in public confusion may have been accurate. Yet, barring Norman's public testimony before the TRC was not necessary to address this issue. There were many less restrictive alternatives—moving the testimony out of the SCSL courtroom, reconfiguring the room where the testimony would take place, increasing public outreach, and promoting public education about the differences between the TRC and SCSL—that could have addressed potential public confusion concerns, while permitting Norman's public testimony.

Incongruous Findings

The substantive overlap between a TRC and criminal prosecutions creates the potential for incongruous findings of fact. As both of these processes are tasked with establishing facts regarding the same events using different methodologies and standards of proof, the possibility that they may result in inconsistent findings is a legitimate concern. This is unavoidable in complex societies and legal systems; and it is not unique to the relationship between TRCs and courts. It is, in fact, fairly commonplace: criminal courts and civil courts make their own judgments of liability based on the same set of facts; and non-judicial bodies write official reports about their findings that judicial bodies may take into account or disregard. The public is used to incongruous official findings; and in many cases, the public reconciles these differences by understanding the reasons behind them. Consequently, possible incongruous findings between a TRC and courts should not be a significant cause for concern.

National Security and Witness Protection Programs

Concerns about national security and witness safety are very real in transitional societies. Such concerns are particularly pertinent where, for example, criminal defendants are often former high-ranking members of government or the military with considerable resources and continuing influence. These security concerns exist even if indictees do not testify publicly before a TRC, because the accused generally have the opportunity to make public statements during trial.[91]

Given the risks associated with these threats, arguments that public hearings could jeopardize witness safety or national security should be

---

91. As an example, consider statements made by Saddam Hussein or Slobodan Milošević attempting to incite public unrest during their trials at the Iraqi High Tribunal and the International Criminal Tribunal for the Former Yugoslavia. *See* Scharf, *supra* note 74, at 161–64.

taken seriously and investigated thoroughly. What's more, precisely because such security issues are easy to assert in the context of transition, where fear and instability linger—especially in the minds of the people, rules must be in place to ensure that any claims about witness safety or national security are made with due cause and subject to specific pleading requirements. Such requirements would not be too onerous, as safety concerns for victims or witnesses could be minimized with less restrictive means than barring public testimony at a TRC. For example, there might be a minimal delay on the broadcast of live testimony in order to give the broadcasters time to censor threats or incitements to violence before they are aired.

Once security concerns are deemed legitimate by a court or the relevant dispute resolution mechanism, they should not automatically result in the barring of testimony. Rather, if possible, the witness should be allowed to testify and the court or TRC should use a less restrictive alternative to avoid undesirable consequences. First allow the testimony to be given publicly so long as there is a mechanism for delaying and censoring any public broadcast. If this is not possible, permit the testimony to be given privately or confidentially just to the requisite members of the TRC and a special representative of the court.[92] These steps would allow for a greater degree of security without sacrificing potentially important testimony or unnecessarily curtailing free speech.

Conclusion: The Real Issues

The confrontation between the SCSL and the Sierra Leone TRC might not have happened at all were it not for two factors. First, the TRC chose *public* hearings as a central strategy to engage citizens regarding the conflicts of the past. Second, these public hearings were broadcast on national television. The combination of public hearings and widespread television coverage has transformed truth commissions from virtually invisible institutions that gather information behind closed doors and only attract attention upon the issuance of their final reports into bodies that function in the public realm and whose processes are, in many respects, more important than their final reports. This transformation occurred because of the massive publicity generated, both nationally and internationally, by the South African Truth and Reconciliation Commission, and it is no coincidence that every significant truth commission since—in Peru, Ghana, Sierra Leone, Timor Leste, Liberia and Morocco—has held televised public hearings.

---

92. Although Judge Robertson gave the TRC this option, it was not preceded by the pleadings and the requisite finding by a court or dispute resolution mechanism regarding witness safety or national security, nor was there any consideration of the possibility of broadcasting the testimony with a delay to avoid any potential incitements to violence.

TRCs should be entitled to provide a public platform to those wishing to testify before them, as this is essential to their fact-finding and therapeutic functions.[93] TRCs catalyze public discussion about the past, determine who the victims are and what happened to them, establish responsibility for past abuse, prompt the delivery of reparations and promote institutional reform. According to the Attorney General of Sierra Leone, the role of the Sierra Leone TRC was "to serve as the most legitimate and credible forum for victims to reclaim their human worth; and a channel for the perpetrators of atrocities to expiate their guilt, and chasten their consciences. The process has been likened to a national catharsis, involving truth telling, respectful listening and above all, compensation for victims in deserving cases."[94] This understanding was supported by the *Truth and Reconciliation Act 2000*, which noted that the object of the TRC was "to create an impartial historical record of violations and abuses of human rights and international humanitarian law related to the armed conflict in Sierra Leone . . . ; to address impunity, to respond to the needs of victims, to promote healing and reconciliation and to prevent repetition of the violations and abuses suffered."[95] Thus, the TRC's role was not only to gather information and create an impartial historical record, but also to respond to the needs of victims, catalyze national discussion, and promote reconciliation.[96]

In many TRCs, the public aspects of the truth-seeking process (public hearings at which victims, perpetrators and other interested parties testified) generate far more public interest, attention and discussion than the compilation and issuance of a final report as an official historical record of the conflict. An important dimension of this process is giving the key protagonists an opportunity to publicly testify as to their versions of what happened during the conflict, as this prompts nationwide discussion about the causes, nature and extent of human rights abuse. Public testimony also engages citizens far more effectively than the formal process of writing and releasing a final report, especially in a country like Sierra Leone, where a large portion of the population is illiterate. The fact that the TRC's public hearings held throughout Sierra Leone were well attended[97] suggests that people valued the public nature

---

93. *But see supra* note 87 and accompanying text.

94. Solomon Berewa, *Addressing Impunity Using Divergent Approaches: The Truth and Reconciliation Commission and the Special Court, in* TRUTH AND RECONCILIATION IN SIERRA LEONE 59 (U.N. Mission in Sierra Leone 2001).

95. Article 6(1).

96. Textually, it is unclear whether the clause of objectives after the semicolon were separate and equal goals to the creation of the historical record, or merely an enumeration of what the creation of the historical record was meant to achieve. However, by virtue of their specific enumeration, they explain the role of the TRC as envisaged by its creators.

97. *See* Beth K. Dougherty, *Searching for Answers: Sierra Leone's Truth & Reconciliation Commission*, 8 AFR. STUD. Q. 39, 48–49 (2004), *available at* http://www.africa.ufl.edu/

of the hearings, and that such hearings were a valuable way of reaching the local population. With this understanding of the role that public TRC hearings play in helping nations, communities and individuals grapple with the past, it appears that, in general, a TRC should be entitled to give a public platform to a person in custody awaiting trial.

This seems to have been understood by the Parliament of Sierra Leone, which passed the *Truth and Reconciliation Act 2000*. The Act declared that "[t]he Commission shall ... solely determine its operating procedures and mode of work with regard to its functions, which shall include ... holding sessions, some of which may be public, to hear from the victims and perpetrators of any abuses or violations or from other interested parties."[98] This gave the TRC explicit authorization to hold public hearings, as well as the sole discretion to determine when such hearings were necessary or prudent in order to achieve its broader mandate.

While clearly there may be important competing reasons for not holding a public hearing, these issues can often be dealt with using less restrictive means than barring them, as discussed above. Judge Robertson failed to attach sufficient importance to the value of *public* testimony before TRCs, but rather assumed that allowing non-public testimony was an ample and sufficient alternative. This view was not based on a detailed analysis of the respective roles of TRCs and courts in responding to mass atrocity.

Perhaps more important than the public nature of the TRC hearings is the fact that they are often televised. Precisely because of the power and reach of the media, evidence presented at truth commission hearings has the potential for major political, social and legal impact before any formal conclusions are drawn at the end of their mandate periods. In a recent discussion on the relationship between courts and commissions, Judge Geoffrey Robertson reflected on the impact of the media in post-conflict settings.[99] Judge Robertson indicated that he would have allowed Norman to convey his views on the conflict to a print journalist while he was awaiting trial, even if this meant that Norman's opinions received front page coverage the following day. However, he would not have allowed Norman to be interviewed on camera if that resulted in his views being broadcast on television. Robertson defended this distinction

---

asq/v8/v8i1a3.pdf. The only public hearings that were not particularly well attended were those in Freetown. However, since the hearings in Freetown were well covered in the media and included in a nightly television broadcast, this was not necessarily an indication of disinterest. *Id.*

98. Article 7(1).

99. Telephonic interview with Geoffrey Robertson, President of the SCSL (Feb. 22, 2008).

by acknowledging the power of television and noting that "a picture is worth a thousand words." Implicit in Judge Robertson's argument is the belief that televised coverage of truth commission hearings has the potential to subvert criminal proceedings in a way that written coverage will not.

While human rights trials in international courts are often filmed and broadcast on television, they are usually subject to careful judicial oversight. It is clear from Judge Robertson's decision in the Norman case that he is not confident that the TRC could or would have offered the kind of oversight that would be necessary. Herein lies a great irony. While judicial oversight certainly regulates the nature and extent of evidence presented during human rights trials, the panoply of rights granted to the accused gives them ample opportunity to attempt to publicly subvert and undermine the court in the eyes of their supporters and the public at large. Because truth commissions lack the power to punish, they are not required to grant those who appear before them as many due process rights and, therefore, offer greater latitude in controlling their testimony. Nevertheless, in the age of television it is possible—perhaps even likely—that perpetrators may seek to use the broadcast hearings of truth commissions to subvert the courts where they are simultaneously facing trial. But, sophisticated perpetrators will surely know that televised trials offer them a powerful public platform to broadcast to their supporters and to seek to undermine the legitimacy of the entire endeavor.

Preventing an important figure in pre-trial detention from appearing publicly before a truth commission will not prevent him/her from criticizing both the trial and the court itself. In fact it may result in the worst of both worlds: undermining a truth commission's ability to offer the public a comprehensive account of the conflicts of the past, while failing to prevent a notorious indictee from using his fair trial rights to attack the legitimacy of his trial and the pursuit of justice itself.

Yet the reason the tension between SCSL and the Sierra Leone TRC got so heated had as much to do with the perceived fairness and consideration of the procedures used to resolve the dispute as with the substance of the disagreement than. The TRC expressed considerable frustration with the SCSL for taking the time it did to decide whether or not Norman could testify before them. The TRC was required to complete its mandate by the end of 2003, and it was rapidly running out of time to arrange a hearing for Norman. This meant that it had to hear all the relevant testimony several weeks before the end of 2003, in order for the data to be analyzed and incorporated into a report due by the end of 2003. The amount of time it took the SCSL to come to a final decision about Norman's testimony, including the need to create two Practice Directions, as well as the hearings before both Judge Thompson and

Judge Robertson, meant that alternative strategies for gathering evidence from Norman or allowing him to convey his views to the public in some way became effectively impossible to implement.

This raises a larger and more fundamental point about the need for commissions and courts to develop a detailed understanding regarding how they will relate to each other, thus allowing the institutions to anticipate and minimize conflict before it arises. Had the TRC and SCSL recognized this, they might have spent more time and given more consideration to these (and other potential) issues before either institution began its operations. Instead, the TRC was satisfied with Prosecutor Crane's assurance that he would not use their information in his investigations, as the only (informal) agreement it needed with the Special Court. Better forethought and planning might have eliminated or significantly reduced the amount of time required to resolve this issue.

Unfortunately, Norman died before the completion of his trial. As a result, the people of Sierra Leone and the international community were deprived of the opportunity to obtain a full account of the role this central figure played in the conflict from *both* the SCSL and the Sierra Leone TRC.

*

8

Universal Jurisdiction and the Dilemmas of International Criminal Justice: The Sabra and Shatila Case in Belgium

Deena R. Hurwitz[*]

Those in Sabra and Shatila ... were the victims of a massacre, and it is as though such deaths are two rather than one. The first death is death itself. The second is the denial that death ever occurred; it lies in the search for a lost victim, and in the attempt to establish a number of lost rights for that victim—

---

[*] I worked with the plaintiffs' attorneys on this case while a teaching fellow in the Allard K. Lowenstein International Human Rights Law Clinic at Yale Law School and acknowledge the outstanding contribution of Lowenstein Clinic graduates Jessica Clarke, Greg Khalil, Elizabeth Maxwell, Fadia Rafeedie, Brent Wible and of my colleague, Professor Jim Silk. I offer my deepest appreciation and esteem to Chibli Mallat, Luc Walleyn, and Michael Verhaeghe for their dedication and assistance with the many facets of telling this story, and to Mohammad Abu Rdaini for his strength of spirit. Thanks, too, to the Belgian parliamentarians and human rights advocates who met with me in Brussels in March 2007; and to University of Virginia (UVA) Law students Katy Caouette, Jason Curtin, Mai–Linh Hong, Alexandre Lamy, Alaa Mahajna, Amy Schuller, and Olivier Winants for their assistance. An early version of this chapter was presented at the Junior International Law Scholars Workshop (Feb. 2008), and I am grateful for the feedback I received from colleagues there. Research for the chapter was supported by grants from the Dean and Foundation of UVA School of Law. Special appreciation is due the magnificent reference librarians at the UVA School of Law Library. Finally, I respectfully acknowledge the survivors of the Sabra and Shatila massacres.

The record of the Sharon case is crucial to the unfinished history of the massacre, and it must offer, for the sake of the victims, an impeccable record. There is no place for half truths, mistakes, or lies: such would ruin the memory of the massacre, and the victims' right not to be forgotten or manacled by history.

CHIBLI MALLAT, *Judicial Redress in Palestine*, in PRESIDENTIAL TALK/PROPOS PRÉSIDENTIELS 404, 409 (2007), *available at* http://www.mallatforpresident.com/books/prestalk.php. Any errors or transgressions are mine alone.

including the right to die, and finally, to have a death certificate issued.[1]

* * *

I was at home with my father, my mother, and my sister. When the shelling started, we were at the home of my father's uncle.... Then we went to a neighbour's house. There were about 25 or more of us. A little while later, we heard the cries of a girl who had been injured in the back. Armed men had stationed themselves in the area. Then we heard shooting, screams and strange voices. Aida, my cousin, went up to the shop and turned on the light. A man slit her throat and they dragged her by her hair. She started screaming "Daddy!" then her voice went dead. Her father went to follow her. They killed him immediately. That's how they realised that we were in the house. They came down to the floor above us, where they broke and ransacked everything and we heard them calling out to each other, "George, Tony...." When we heard them breaking everything our voices rose, and that's how they knew that we were on the floor below. One of them came down and saw us. He immediately told the others, and they all came down. My father was sitting on a chair, and as soon as he saw them, he kissed me, put some cologne on me and told my mother to take good care of the children. My father's cousin said to his wife, "The children are your responsibility."

I will never forget. The image of that day is engraved in my memory. They ordered the men to stand against the wall. They made us go out behind them into the road. When I got to the door, I looked up at the red sky, red streaked with flare grenades. Once we arrived at the beginning of the road, we heard the shots fired at my father and my uncle, as well as some shouting. We walked several metres, flanked by armed men.... I saw my father's car, which they had opened and were sitting in. That image is also engraved in my memory, because I asked my mother what they were doing with my father's car but she didn't reply. As we walked along we saw the dead people.

Mohammad Shawkat Abu Rdaini, who lost his father, his (pregnant) sister, his brother-in-law and three other members of his family[2]

* * *

---

1. Bayan Nuwayhed al-Hout, Sabra and Shatila September 1982 256–57 (2004). Al-Hout began an Oral History Project in November 1982 to document and preserve the names and testimonies of survivors of the massacre. The study contains conclusions regarding the events leading up to, during, and in the aftermath of the massacres, as well as statistical tables on the victims.

2. Complaint Lodged by Survivors Against Israeli Prime Minister Ariel Sharon, Director General of the Defense Ministry Amos Yaron and Other Israelis and Lebanese

In September 1982, Mohammad Abu Rdaini was four years old, and living in the Shatila "district"[3] of Beirut, the son of Palestinian refugees who fled Haifa in 1948. Chibli Mallat, an LLM candidate from Beirut, was studying international and comparative law at Georgetown Law Center. He remembers the moment he learned about the assassination of Bashir Gemayyel, leader of the Christian Phalange Party, and Lebanon's president-elect. It was September 14, and he was in a car in Washington D.C. with a Lebanese friend who let go of the steering wheel when the radio announced the news. They nearly had an accident. Not until a few days later when news started trickling down did he begin to grasp the magnitude of what had transpired in the camps.

In 1982, Luc Walleyn had already been an attorney for ten years, working with the anti-racism movement in Brussels, predominantly in local Arab and Turkish communities. As a member of a left-wing Belgian political party that supported the Palestinians, he closely followed the war in Lebanon and the siege of Beirut. The massacres provoked outrage from him and his friends and associates. Michael Verhaeghe recalls the images on the news ("just like I clearly remember the images about the Rwandan massacres"). In 1982, he was nineteen and had just finished his first year at the university, studying law. "In our family we had more than the average interest in Lebanon, since my aunt is Lebanese."[4]

Nineteen years later, the lives of these four men intersected in one of the first criminal actions brought on behalf of the victims of Sabra and Shatila.[5] Abu Rdaini and twenty-two[6] other Palestinians and Leba-

---

Responsible for the Sabra and Shatila Massacre, filed in the Brussels (Belgium) Criminal Court 18 June, 2001, 12 PAL. Y.B. INT'L. L., 219–232 (2005) [hereinafter *Complaint*]. Given transliteration of Arabic to English, Mohammad's name is also spelled "Muhammad Shawkat Abu Roudeina" (in the Complaint) and "Abu Rudaineh."

3. Sabra and Shatila are two of sixteen refugee camps in Beirut at the time (now there are twelve official camps). In 1982, there were some 400,000 Palestinian refugees in Lebanon, the majority of whom had fled Israel during the wars of 1947–48 and 1967. THE BEIRUT MASSACRE, THE COMPLETE KAHAN COMMISSION REPORT 7 (1983) [hereinafter, *Kahan Commission Report*], *citing* UNRWA. The camps of Burj-el-Burajneh, Fakahani, Sabra and Shatila had a combined population of 85,000, of which 56,000 lived in Sabra alone. *Id.* at 15. *See also* Lebanon Refugee Camp Profiles, http://www.un.org/unrwa/refugees/lebanon.html. Al–Hout notes that the dominant designation of these latter "two" refugee camps or districts as the site of the massacres is flawed. By generalizing the true location, it obscures the full geographic area it encompassed. AL-HOUT, *supra* note 1, at 42–44.

4. Michael Verhaeghe, Email correspondence with Deena Hurwitz, Sept. 30, 2008.

5. Other legal actions in connection with the events include a suit in U.S. federal court by Ariel Sharon against *Time* magazine for libel over an article written by an Israeli journalist suggesting he was directly responsible for the massacres. Sharon v. *Time*, 599 F.Supp. 538 (S.D.N.Y. 1984). Both sides claimed victory in the jury verdict, which didn't even deal with the issue of Sharon's responsibility. In 1987, the District Court of the District of Columbia ruled that, as Israel's Military Attaché to the U.S. and Canada since August 1986, Amos Yaron had immunity from civil suit brought by relatives of victims of

6. See note 6 on page 270.

nese individuals who were personally injured and/or lost close family members or property as a result of the events of September 16–18, 1982 filed a complaint as *parties civiles*[7] in the Brussels Criminal Court on June 18, 2001. The Complaint named "Ariel Sharon, Amos Yaron, and other Israeli and Lebanese leaders responsible for the massacre, killing, rape, and disappearance of civilians that took place in Beirut between Thursday 16 and Saturday 18 September, 1982 in the camps of Sabra and Shatila and the surrounding area."

Filed under Belgium's broad universal jurisdiction statute—the 1993 Act Concerning the Punishment of Grave Breaches of the Geneva Conventions, as amended by the 1999 Act Concerning the Punishment of Grave Breaches of International Humanitarian Law ("the 1993/1999 Law" or "the Law")[8]—the allegations of acts of genocide, crimes against humanity, and war crimes were "founded on international customary law and on '*ius cogens*' which relate to these crimes."[9]

This chapter recounts the story of a remarkable case, and it also illustrates the limits of justice when politics stake a claim.[10] While Belgium might seem an unlikely forum for such a momentous and complex legal initiative, such a landmark statute did not seem unusual

---

the Sabra and Shatila massacres. Aidi v. Yaron, 672 F.Supp. 516 (D.D.C. 1987). However, Israel recalled Yaron around the time of the court case, apparently under pressure from the Reagan administration. *See* Victor Kattan, *From Beirut to Brussels: Universal Jurisdiction, Statelessness and the Sabra and Shatila Massacres,* 11 Y.B. OF ISLAMIC & MIDDLE E.L. 32, 33 n. 26 (2004–2005).

6. There were twenty-eight original plaintiffs, but for reasons of Belgian procedure allowing more detailed testimony, five plaintiffs were listed in the complaint as "witnesses." One survivor, a resident of Belgium, joined the plaintiffs subsequently, while one of the original plaintiffs abruptly distanced herself from the case. As of 2004, one of the plaintiffs had died. Chibli Mallat, *Accountability in the Middle East: The Sharon Case Polysemy,* in THE CASE OF ARIEL SHARON AND THE FATE OF UNIVERSAL JURISDICTION 40, n. 8 (John Borneman ed., 2004) [hereinafter Borneman].

7. Private parties may initiate a criminal case claiming damages in some civil code systems.

8. The Act of 16 June, 1993 Concerning the Punishment of Grave Breaches of the Geneva Conventions of 12 August 1949 and their Additional Protocols I and II of 18 June 1977 (MONITEUR BELGE [M.B.], Aug. 5, 1993), as amended by the Act of February 10, 1999 Concerning the Punishment of Grave Breaches of International Humanitarian Law, 38 I.L.M. 921 (1999) (M.B., Mar. 23, 1999); *see also* 12 PAL. Y.B. INT'L L. (2005), 191 (Act of 16 June 1993, at 194) [hereafter, the Law or the Act].

9. Complaint, *supra* note 2 at 221. The law, officially titled the "Act providing for the punishment of serious violations of international humanitarian law of 1993," belatedly incorporated the 1949 Geneva Conventions into the Belgian legal system, and provided for universal jurisdiction as applied to war crimes only. In 1999, the law was amended to include crimes against humanity and genocide.

10. For a thoughtful series of discussions on the issues of politics and legality in the case, *see* Borneman, *supra* note 6.

to many Belgians. The country has a tradition of open-mindedness toward international law.[11] Since the 1970s, the Belgian Supreme Court has considered international treaty law to have supremacy over national law. What's more, as the victims'/plaintiffs' attorney Luc Walleyn noted, where social and economic law are in large part determined by regulations of the European Union, and penal and family law are substantially influenced by the European Convention of Human Rights and the jurisprudence of the Strasbourg Court, implementing international law is considered a natural process.[12] Thus, when asked to reflect on the choice of venue, plaintiffs' attorney Chibli Mallat said, "Why not Belgium?"[13]

In reality, Mallat opted to file the case in Belgium for reasons of complementarity[14] rather than convenience. "If our clients could have sued Sharon in Israel and had any opportunity for justice, it would have been better," Mallat remarked. "But, not only could they not get standing in Israel, as Palestinian refugees (technically 'absentees' under Israeli law) they could not even legally enter Israel in the first place."[15] Nor was Lebanon an option, having passed an amnesty law in 1990 that reaches back to 1975 for acts committed during the country's civil war.

Universal Jurisdiction, Aut Dedere Aut Judicare, *and Immunity*

The principle of universal jurisdiction allows states to investigate and prosecute in their domestic courts certain grave violations of international law, namely genocide, torture, war crimes and crimes against humanity, that have occurred extraterritorially even when there is no link (nexus) with the perpetrator, victims or location of the crime.[16] A

---

11. Luc Walleyn, *The Sabra and Shatila Massacre and Belgian Universal Jurisdiction, in* Borneman, *supra* note 6, at 59 [hereinafter Walleyn, *The Sabra and Shatila Massacre*].

12. *Id.*

13. Interviews with Chibli Mallat, Charlottesville, Virginia, November 2 and 4, 2006. *See also* Mallat *in* Borneman, *supra* note 6 at 37–41.

14. Complementarity refers to the principle that states (and the ICC) should defer to the state with the narrowest (most direct) basis for jurisdiction that is willing and able to initiate investigation and undertake prosecution. The ICC may only exercise jurisdiction where national legal systems fail to do so, including where they purport to act but in reality are unwilling or unable to genuinely carry out proceedings. The complementarity principle has been codified in Article 17 of the Rome Statute for the International Criminal Court. Belgium signed the Rome Statute on Sept. 10, 1998, and ratified it on June 28, 2000.

15. Telephonic interview with Chibli Mallat (Sept. 15, 2008). Mallat referred to the Absentees' Property Law, 5710–1950 (initially passed by the Knesset March 14, 1950 and amended numerous times since).

16. *See e.g.,* LUC REYDAMS, UNIVERSAL JURISDICTION, INTERNATIONAL AND MUNICIPAL LEGAL PERSPECTIVES (2003).

related rule, *aut dedere aut judicare*, stems from the principle that states may not shield a person suspected of certain categories of crimes, and that they have an obligation to prosecute or facilitate the extradition of a perpetrator found within their territory to a country or tribunal willing or able to prosecute.[17] This principle is well established as a matter of international treaty law, though its status as customary international law is contentious.[18]

Does universal jurisdiction obligate the state to *search* for an alleged perpetrator wherever he/she may be, or does it merely require that the state take steps to initiate prosecution or extradite an alleged perpetrator to a country willing and able to do so, when the person is found within their territory? Depending on how it is carried out, actively searching beyond a state's territory may conflict with the principle of sovereignty. On the other hand, as some argue, the principle of universal jurisdiction (as set out in the Genocide Convention, the Geneva Conventions, and the Torture Convention, among other treaties) and the customary law prohibition against war crimes, crimes against humanity and genocide would lose its substance if perpetrators could find refuge in a country unwilling to abide by the principles of *aut dedere aut judicare*.

Thus, legislation in some countries—such as Belgium prior to 2003—allow for absolute universal jurisdiction, grounded in the state's obligations under international law and the principle *of jus cogens*.[19] Other countries' statutes include conditions on the exercise of universal jurisdiction, notably, that the accused be present in the country in order

---

17. Zdzislaw Galicki, Special Rapporteur, *Preliminary report on the obligation to extradite or prosecute (*"aut dedere aut judicare"*)*, International Law Commission, U.N. Doc. A/CN.4/571 (7 June 2006), para. 31.

18. *Id.* at para. 32. *See also* Report of the International Law Commission on the work of its fifty-seventh session (2005), ¶ 243, U.N. Doc. A/CN.4/560 (Jan. 13, 2006); M. Cherif Bassiouni & E. M. Wise, Aut Dedere Aut Judicare: The Duty to Extradite or Prosecute in International Law 43 (1995).

19. The principle of *jus cogens* evolved out of the recognition that certain values and interests are common to and affect the international community as a whole, and that their violation threatens peace, security and world order. *Jus cogens* norms have a peremptory status under international law, i.e., they are by their nature superior to other rules of international law and cannot be changed or derogated through agreement or custom. Although *jus cogens* norms have an independent validity and status, separate from the consent and practice of states, their enforcement of course depends on the will of states. And, though the concept of *jus cogens* is accepted, its content is still hotly debated. However, it is generally agreed that the prohibition of torture, genocide, slave trade and slavery, apartheid, and other gross violations of human rights are *jus cogens* norms. Lorna McGregor, *Addressing the Relationship between State Immunity and* Jus Cogens *Norms: A Comparative Assessment*, in International Prosecution of Human Rights Crimes 70–72 (Wolfgang Kaleck et al., eds. 2007). *See also* Restatement (Third) of Foreign Relations Law § 102 (1987).

for the case to go forward.[20] The presence requirement has been a major controversy. Undoubtedly, the question of how to "navigate presence" varies depending on whether it is viewed as a jurisdictional requirement or a fair trial right.[21] The controversy over trial *in absentia* has overtaken its reality, perhaps because safeguards exist in countries that allow such trials—such as the right to a trial *de novo* once the accused is arrested—and states may be reluctant to incur the costs of such proceedings. The key question is whether the law allows for investigation to commence in the absence of the accused in order to proceed with an extradition request, with the judicial phase taking place after the individual's extradition to the particular country.[22]

While the primary duty to fight impunity rests with the state in which a crime is committed and the state of nationality of the accused, unfortunately, officials in many such countries are unwilling or unable to bring perpetrators to justice. Historically, universal jurisdiction is a tool of last resort in the wake of large scale atrocities.

The Rome Statute of the International Criminal Court ("ICC") included the principle of *aut dedere aut judicare* as a measure of subsidiarity and complementarity. Under this principle, the ICC defers to any state willing and able to prosecute the crimes under its jurisdiction (Article 17). For this principle of complementarity to work and for State Parties to meet their obligations as a practical matter, State Parties are expected to implement all of the crimes under the Rome Statute into domestic legislation.[23]

Immunity is another highly contested issue with respect to violations of international law. Under a traditional application of immunity, a current head of state or high government official accused of war crimes might be protected from prosecution and possibly even indictment while in office, based on the individual's status (immunity *rationae personae*) and not the acts themselves. While officials often have immunity before the courts of foreign states under doctrines like diplomatic immunity, human rights treaties and the statutes of international criminal tribunals reject such immunities.[24] Further, not all officials can benefit from

---

20. This is also the form of universal jurisdiction that is included in the Convention Against Torture. *See* Jayne Huckerby & Sir Nigel Rodley, *Outlawing Torture: The Story of Amnesty International's Efforts to Shape the U.N. Convention against Torture*, Chapter 1 in this volume.

21. E-mail from Bruce Broomhall, Professor, University of Quebec, to author (Sept. 29, 2006) (on file with author).

22. According to Professor Broomhall, how the procedural steps are sequenced varies widely from one jurisdiction to another. *Id.*

23. *See* Coalition for the International Criminal Court, Ratification and Implementation, *available at*: http://www.iccnow.org/?mod=ratimp.

24. For example, the Convention against Torture makes the participation, consent or acquiescence of a state official or another person acting in an official capacity an element of

diplomatic immunity. A former head of state enjoys immunity for *official* acts committed in his function as head of state (immunity *rationae materiae*). The House of Lords in the *Pinochet* case considered the question whether torture could be considered an official act or part of the functions of a ruler. In their final decision (No. 3), the Law Lords concluded that immunity *rationae personae* applied to a very limited category of persons, such as heads of state, but only while they remain in office. Once out of office, immunity *rationae materiae* could apply, but only to official acts; and they concluded that torture could not be such an official act.[25] The Rome Statute of the ICC codified this principle in Article 27: official capacity as a head of state or government neither exempts a person from criminal responsibility, nor bars the Court from jurisdiction over him. One of the signature aspects of the Belgian statute was its rejection of all forms of immunity. Certain crimes, including genocide, torture and other atrocities can never be deemed official acts and therefore merit no immunity, leaving officials subject to prosecution.[26]

Belgium's Procedural Particularities

In synergy with the 1993/1999 Law, three particularities of the Belgian legal system accounted for its allure, according to Eric David, Professor of Public International Law at the Université Libre de Bruxelles.[27] One was the victim-friendly *partie civile* process, which allowed private individuals to lodge a complaint directly before an investigating judge "who was obliged to take cognizance of the complaint. [Second], Belgium was the only state in the world that expressly rejected the idea that immunity could be an obstacle to criminal process. And [third], Belgium, like many other states, accepted the idea of prosecution *in absentia*."[28]

---

the crime of torture. HUMAN RIGHTS WATCH, THE PINOCHET PRECEDENT, HOW VICTIMS CAN PURSUE HUMAN RIGHTS CRIMINALS ABROAD, *available at* http://www.hrw.org/campaigns/chile98/precedent.htm [hereinafter HRW, THE PINOCHET PRECEDENT].

25. *R. v. Bow Street Metropolitan Stipendary Magistrate ex parte Pinochet Ugarte* (3) (1999), 2 WLR 827.

26. It is worth noting that Israel has a genocide law that excludes immunity based on official capacity and provides for universal jurisdiction. REYDAMS, *supra* note 16, at 117.

27. Professor David has been called the "father of the Belgian Law." Chibli Mallat, *Introduction: New Lights on the Sharon Case, Special Dossier on the "Sabra and Shatila" Case in Belgium*, 12 PAL. Y.B. INT'L L. 183, 184 (2005).

28. Interview with Eric David, Professor, Université Libre de Bruxelles (Mar. 12, 2007). Prosecution *in absentia* is relatively common in civil law countries (e.g., France, Switzerland, Spain). The European Court of Human Rights has stated that prosecution *in absentia* is not a violation of the European Convention provided certain guarantees are

At the time of the Sabra and Shatila case, when a *partie civile* complaint was filed in Belgium, an investigating judge was assigned by turn. Under Belgian procedural law, if a case involving serious violations of international law was brought directly to a public prosecutor (*procureur*), the prosecutor could refuse to take it. However, when such a complaint was filed by private persons, it went to an investigating magistrate (*juge d'instruction*), who determined whether there was sufficient evidence for the complaint to be admissible. As a threshold matter, the investigating magistrate was required to first determine whether he/she had jurisdiction over the offenses. If so, he/she could not refuse the case, but had to investigate to ascertain if the complaint was legally well-founded and the evidence sufficient to proceed with the prosecution. On a parallel track, the prosecutor acting for the state had the discretion to submit the complaint to the indictment chamber (*chambre des mises en accusation*) of the Court of Appeals (*Cours d'Appel de Bruxelles*) where it was vetted for any legal issues that might have a bearing on admissibility.[29]

Thus, fundamentally, the investigating judge was acting on behalf of the *parties civiles*. Even if the public prosecutor did not request the case, the investigating judge made a jurisdictional decision according to his or her own sense of the case. Having significant authority; the judge could initiate inquiries and fact-finding, even issuing an arrest warrant without having to wait for a special request from the public prosecutor.[30]

Universal Jurisdiction in Practice: The Belgian Legal Context

The government first drafted a bill in 1989 to implement the Geneva Conventions, which it had ratified in 1952. The bill was submitted to Parliament in 1991, and debated while the atrocities in the former Yugoslavia raged. In May 1993, the U.N. Security Council passed Resolution 827 establishing the International Criminal Tribunal for the Former

---

recognized for the accused. *See, e.g.,* Krombach v. France, 2001–II Eur. Ct. H.R. 35; Colozza v. Italy, 89 Eur. Ct. H.R. (ser. A) (1985).

29. The primary objective is to free an investigation from any legal discussions that might otherwise slow or complicate the judicial process once trial has begun. Consequently, decisions taken following pre-trial hearings are considered final. Court Diary, Outline and Explanation of Court Hearings during the Pre-trial Procedure, June 2001—January 2002, Michael Verhaeghe and Laurie King–Irani, www.indictsharon.net (follow "The Case Against the Accused" hyperlink; then follow "Court Diary" hyperlink) [hereinafter Court Diary]. *See also* Damien Vandermeersch, *Prosecuting International Crimes in Belgium,* 3 J. INT'L CRIM. JUST. 400 (2005).

30. That is what happened with the *Arrest Warrant (Yerodia)* case, which ended up at the International Court of Justice. It was not because of a request from the public prosecutor; it was an investigating judge on his own examination of the whole dossier who issued the arrest warrant. E. David interview, *supra* note 28.

Yugoslavia, with jurisdiction to prosecute grave breaches of the 1949 Geneva Conventions, violations of the laws or customs of war, genocide, and crimes against humanity. The debates in the Belgian Parliament reflected concern over the grave violations of humanitarian law witnessed in the Iraq–Kuwait war, the former Yugoslavia and Somalia. A Senate proposal to include violations of Protocol II to the Geneva Conventions was easily accepted, criminalizing war crimes and torture.[31] The Act was passed unanimously in June 1993.

Between the passage of the Act in 1993 and its amendment in 1999, nine other European countries passed universal jurisdiction laws.[32] Six completed trials resulted in four convictions and two acquittals.[33]

Concern over mass atrocities characterized the policies of Belgian Foreign Minister Louis Michel, and he enjoyed significant support for much of the latter part of the 1990s. Given the country's colonial legacy in Rwanda and the Democratic Republic of the Congo, Belgians were particularly attentive to the events in those countries during the 1990s. Senator Alain Destexhe described the broad support that existed among lawmakers, human rights advocates and academics for widening the Act beyond grave breaches of the Geneva Conventions (war crimes). "Because of the genocide in Rwanda we thought . . . it made more sense to get a clear law punishing [crimes against humanity and genocide]."[34] On behalf of their party, the Groupe liberal francophone du Sénat (PRL FDF), Destexhe and the PRL FDF president Senator Michel Foret organized a 1996 symposium in the Senate to explore possibilities for modifying the Law, titled "From Nuremberg to the Hague."[35] After the symposium, "we moved to change the Law. We got signatures from all the political parties. I think it went quite fast for this kind of work. . . . We had already a few high profile Rwandan cases in Belgium of people

---

31. Walleyn, *The Sabra and Shatila Massacre, supra* note 11 at 56.

32. REDRESS, UNIVERSAL JURISDICTION IN EUROPE, CRIMINAL PROSECUTIONS IN EUROPE SINCE 1990 FOR WAR CRIMES, CRIMES AGAINST HUMANITY, TORTURE AND GENOCIDE (1999), at 9, *available at* http://www.redress.org/documents/unijeur.html [hereinafter REDRESS, UJ IN EUROPE]. In addition to Belgium, the other countries with such statutes at that time included Austria, Denmark, France, Germany, Italy, the Netherlands, Spain, Switzerland and the United Kingdom.

33. *Id.*

34. Interview with Alain Destexhe, Senator of Belgium (Groupe liberal francophone du Sénat. PRL FDF), Brussels (Mar. 12, 2007). Destexhe had an earlier career as a field doctor and was Secretary General of Médecins Sans Frontières International from 1991–1995.

35. The proceedings are published in ALAIN DESTEXHE AND MICHEL FORET, DE NUREMBERG À LA HAYE ET ARUSHA (Alain Destexhe and Michel Foret, eds. 1997). The colloquium was organized on September 26, 1996, the day that the International Criminal Tribunal for Rwanda opened its first session in Arusha, Tanzania, and the fiftieth anniversary to the day of the final session of the Nuremberg Tribunal. *Id.* at 13.

who had committed genocide, who were under investigation by the criminal law system." Once again, it passed unanimously in both chambers of Parliament.

When the statute was amended in 1999, there was also near unanimity among Belgian lawmakers that Article 5(3) prohibiting immunity reflected customary international law concerning breaches of international humanitarian law. Thus, legislators felt comfortable taking an extremely wide approach to this issue.[36] Commentators referred to international law provisions such as Article 27 of the Rome Statute for the ICC, the Convention on the Prevention and Suppression of the Crime of Genocide, and the Statutes of the International Criminal Tribunals for both the former Yugoslavia and Rwanda, to support the provision abrogating immunities.

The first complaints utilizing the Act were brought by victims of the Rwandan genocide against perpetrators who were living in Belgium.[37] The country became very politically active in relation to the events in Rwanda, from victims rights groups clear up to the executive, supporting the creation of the International Criminal Tribunal for Rwanda, sponsoring the rebuilding of the Rwandan judiciary, assisting in organizing defense attorneys for the Rwandan cases. International humanitarian law emerged as a major political issue when, under the presidency of Prime Minister Guy Verhofstadt, the Senate established a commission to investigate Belgian involvement in the events in Rwanda.[38]

In 1998, Belgium joined Spain in requesting that Britain extradite former Chilean dictator Augusto Pinochet to face charges of torture and other atrocities carried out during his rule. Investigating Judge Damien Vandermeersch handed down the first procedural decision applying the universal jurisdiction statute in November 1998, ruling that he had

---

36. Alain Winants, *The Yerodia Ruling of the International Court of Justice and the 1993/1999 Belgian Law on Universal Jurisdiction*, 16 Leiden J. Int'l. L. 491, 496 (2003). Some did express the view that the rejection of immunities was limited to prosecutions before international courts.

37. The *Butare Four* Case was the first case concluded under the universal jurisdiction statute. Public Prosecutor v. Higaniro et al. (the Butare Four Case), Ass. 8 Juin 2001 [Court of Assizes] (Belg.) (detailed English summary available at Luc Reydams, *Belgium's First Application of Universal Jurisdiction: The Butare Four Case*, 1 J. Int'l Crim. Just. 428 (2003)). Although it took five years to investigate, the trial was swift (eight weeks) and ended with a clear conviction. Between May and December 1995, one investigating magistrate (Damien Vandenmeersch) and five investigators worked full time on the Rwandan cases, which in the main had some link to Belgium. (The Butare Four were found in Belgium.) Another case involved the murder of ten Belgian members of the U.N. peacekeeping force; and the infamous RTLM Radio Milles Collines incitement to genocide case involved a Belgian citizen, Georges Ruggiu. Ten files were opened, involving twenty-one individuals. Reydams, *supra* note 16 at 109–111.

38. Walleyn, *The Sabra and Shatila Massacre*, *supra* note 11 at 56–57.

jurisdiction to conduct a criminal investigation of Pinochet, who was then under house arrest in London.[39]

By 2000, some twenty-four states had universal jurisdiction laws of various form, (including incidentally, Israel),[40] but Belgium's was the most far-reaching. As amended in 1999, the Belgian Law was a model of pure universal jurisdiction, covering genocide, war crimes and crimes against humanity and requiring no nexus whatsoever between the acts, the accused and the state of Belgium. Inspired by the Pinochet ruling in the British House of Lords,[41] the 1999 Law also included the principle that "immunity attaching to the official capacity of a person" should not be a bar to prosecution.[42] Under Belgian law an individual charged with

---

39. Michael Verhaeghe, *The Political Funeral Procession for the Belgian UJ Statute*, *in* INTERNATIONAL PROSECUTION OF HUMAN RIGHTS CRIMES 139 (Wolfgang Kaleck, Michael Ratner, Tobias Singelnstein, Peter Weiss, eds., 2007). The case, *Aguilar Diaz et al. v. Pinochet*, was brought by Chilean exiles living in Belgium. Aguilar Diaz et al. v. Pinochet, Tribunal de Premiére Instance de Bruxelles [Court of First Instance of Brussels], order of 6 Nov. 1998 (Belg.), 118 J. des Tribunaux 308 (1999), *also available at* http://www.hague justiceportal.net/Docs/NLP/Belgium/pinochet_mandat_arret_06-11-98.pdf.

40. *See* AMNESTY INT'L, UNIVERSAL JURISDICTION: THE DUTY OF STATES TO ENACT AND IMPLEMENT LEGISLATION (2001), *available at* http://www.amnesty.org/en/library/info/IOR53/010/2001; REDRESS, UJ IN EUROPE, *supra* note 32.

With regard to Israel, *see* Israel's Penal Code, Article 16(a), which enables Israeli courts to exercise universal jurisdiction over torture and grave breaches of the Geneva Conventions; the Nazi and Nazi Collaborators (Punishment) Law 1950 and the Crime of Genocide (Prevention and Punishment) Law 1950. *C.f.* REYDAMS, *supra* note 16 at 158–160.

Concerning universal jurisdiction legislation in the U.S., *see, e.g.*, Alien Tort Statute, 28 U.S.C. § 1350 [hereinafter ATS]. Although not a criminal statute, the ATS is an important analog; it grants federal courts jurisdiction over "any civil action by an alien for a tort only, committed in violation of the law of nations or a treaty of the United States." While the claim itself need not have links to the U.S., in order for the lawsuit to proceed beyond filing, one must be able to effectuate service over the defendant. Under most circumstances, physical presence in the U.S. is required (however brief) for personal jurisdiction. Personal jurisdiction may also be obtained over an individual, organization, or corporation not physically present based on long-arm jurisdiction. *See* BETH STEPHENS, ET AL., INTERNATIONAL HUMAN RIGHTS LITIGATION IN U.S. COURTS (2nd ed. 2008). *See also*, Katie Redford & Beth Stephens, *The Story of* Doe v. Unocal: *Justice Delayed But Not Denied*, Chapter 11 in this volume.

41. Stefaan Smis & Kim Van der Borght, *Introductory Note to Belgium: Act Concerning the Punishment of Grave Breaches of International Humanitarian Law*, 38 I.L.M. 918, 918 (1999); Interview with Senator Josy Dubié, (Ecolo/Green Party), in Brussels (Mar. 12, 2007). A former United Nations journalist, Dubié was elected in 1999 after the Law was amended; he became president of the Justice Committee, which handled challenges in the application of the Law.

42. Article 5 § 3. Article 7 of the Law provides that "Belgian courts shall have jurisdiction in respect of the offences provided for in the present Law, wherever they may have been committed." Following as it did the passage of the Rome Statute for the ICC, the Belgian Law of 1993/1999 also incorporated the criminal definition of crimes against humanity from that instrument. Several other important principles were included in the

committing such violations of international law could be indicted, investigated, and tried *in absentia*, without ever setting foot on Belgian soil.[43]

The Belgian populace was familiar with the Law, and a 2001 poll organized by the Belgian newspaper, *Le Soir*, showed that those who favored the Law were in the majority. Eighty-two percent knew about the Rwandan genocide proceedings in Belgian courts, and seventy percent believed that Belgium should take the initiative to prosecute perpetrators of crimes against humanity or acts of genocide. Nearly nine out of ten respondents felt that the fight against impunity for crimes against humanity should be a part of Belgian foreign policy.[44] Green Party Senator Josy Dubié, former president of the Senate Justice Committee who supported the Law and the Sabra and Shatila case, explained that the Belgian public was very concerned about the genocide in Rwanda. "First, because Rwanda had been a former Belgian colony. Secondly, almost a million people were killed. And ten Belgian blue helmets were also killed. It's the reason why this Law was accepted almost with no discussion.... Everybody said we must do something."[45]

But even before the Sabra and Shatila case was filed, red flags were being raised over the newly amended Law. Belgian international law scholar Luc Reydams admonished, "Belgium was taking the lead again, albeit in a rash and haphazard way, in the development of international criminal law by establishing universal jurisdiction over the three 'core' international crimes: war crimes, crimes against humanity and genocide."[46] Reydams sounded more than a note of caution about the consequences of a trial *in absentia*, suggesting that "human rights lawyers might find themselves torn between advocating universal jurisdiction to prevent impunity and condemning a completely arbitrary determination of the forum and the applicable law."[47] Observing that litigators from Cambodia and the Congo to Iran and Iraq had discovered Belgium "as an avenue for criminal class actions," he warned that "[a]lthough such actions will for the most part produce symbolic actions, they may push the matter too far. An adverse international ruling on jurisdiction could

---

amended Law. Procedurally, the 1999 Law retained the abolition of statutes of limitation for offences under the 1993 Act (Article 8). Smis & Van der Borght, *id.* at 919.

[43]. The defendant's fair trial rights would be protected because the law requires a trial *de novo* once he/she is arrested.

[44]. Colette Braeckman & Martine Dubuisson, *Sondage exclusif, Les Belges plébiscitent la diplomatie éthique Contre l'oubli et pour l'ingérence: Survey & Action montre un pays qui a choisi son camp*, LE SOIR, June 2, 2001. The results of the poll were touted as a plebiscite for Foreign Minister Louis Michel's policies.

[45]. Dubié interview, *supra* note 41.

[46]. Luc Reydams, *Universal Criminal Jurisdiction: The Belgian State of Affairs*, 11 CRIM. L. F. 183, 214 (2000).

[47]. *Id.* at 216.

turn the clock back. It may, therefore, be wiser to select cases carefully in order to lay more solid foundations for an effective and durable system of universal jurisdiction."[48]

In April 2000, the Law was applied against Abdulaye Yerodia Ndombasi, foreign minister of the Democratic Republic of the Congo (DRC). An arrest warrant was issued *in absentia* charging Yerodia with war crimes stemming from speeches he made in the DRC during August 1998 inciting racial hatred, allegedly resulting in the massacre of several hundred Tutsis. The DRC responded by instituting proceedings in October 2000 in the International Court of Justice on the basis that the Law violated the principles of state sovereignty and diplomatic immunity.[49]

Despite this challenge, complaints continued to be filed under the Law. None was as well documented and well-pled, nor as critically important, as the Sabra and Shatila case.

The Sabra and Shatila Massacres[50]

Political events leading up to the massacres began with the June 3 1982 attempted assassination of Israeli Ambassador Shlomo Argov in London. A U.S.-brokered ceasefire in Lebanon had held since July 1981 among Syria, the Palestinian Liberation Organization (PLO), and Israel. The PLO had been based in Lebanon since 1970 when they were driven out of Jordan in the events known as "Black September." Their military command bases as well as an elaborate political, social and economic infrastructure were located in and around Sabra and Shatila.[51] Since 1976 and the Lebanese civil war, Syria had maintained a presence in the country.[52] A major aspect of this long presence was Syria's backing of political parties and partisan militias, including most importantly for this story, the Lebanese Christian Phalange militia, whose chief of intelligence was Elie Hobeika.

The PLO denied responsibility for the shooting of Argov.[53] On June 4, 1982 Israel launched a major retaliatory attack against West Beirut

---

48. *Id.*

49. *Arrest Warrant of 11 April 2000 (Democratic Republic of the Congo v. Belgium), Judgment*, 2002 I.C.J. 3 (Feb. 14) [hereinafter, ICJ *Arrest Warrant Case*].

50. *See* Complaint, *supra* note 2, at 222–225.

51. *See e.g.*, Rashid Khalidi, Under Siege: P.L.O. Decisionmaking During the 1982 War 28–33, 100 (1986).

52. The Syrians left Lebanon in 2005 in the aftermath of the assassination of former Prime Minister Rafiq Hariri.

53. *See* Complaint, *supra* note 2, at 222, n. 1. Though the extremist, Iraqi-backed, Abu Nidal faction claimed responsibility, it was a cover for Saddam Hussein. According to Chibli Mallat, Saddam needed to deflect the pressure on the Iran–Iraq war front, which he was losing. Scotland Yard's investigation into Argov's assassination attempt yielded the

and South Lebanon. In the following days, Israel and PLO forces traded attacks, with significant casualties among Palestinian and Lebanese inhabitants in Lebanon, and Israel succeeded in advancing twenty-five miles into the country. Despite a 2000-strong protest in Tel Aviv against Israeli military actions, a unanimous call for ceasefire by the U.N. Security Council (Resolution 508), and the United States' dispatch of Special Envoy Philip Habib to restore the July 1981 ceasefire—all on June 5—on June 6, Israel launched a full-scale invasion of Lebanon.[54] The Israeli Defense Forces (IDF) called it "Operation Peace for Galilee," aiming to establish a deeper security zone by ridding Southern Lebanon of Palestinians so the PLO would not have a base there, and pushing Syrian troops out of Lebanon, ultimately paving the way for an Israeli-Lebanese peace agreement.[55] The Israeli government and Lebanese militias shared the objective of routing the PLO from Lebanon.

Much has been written on the Israeli invasion of Lebanon, the war that summer and events prior to September 16. For the purpose of this story, however, only a few points need to be highlighted. Israel claimed to have targeted the camps for harboring Palestinian fighters and weapons. Among the main objectives of the August 11 Cease-fire Agreement brokered by Habib was the safe departure of Palestinian forces from Lebanon. The governments of Lebanon and the United States pledged to "provide appropriate guarantees of the safety ... of law-abiding Palestinian non-combatants left in Beirut, including the families of those who have departed. The United States [provided] its guarantees on the basis of assurances received from the government of Israel and from the leaders of certain Lebanese groups with which it has been in contact."[56]

On August 21, the very day the Agreement was implemented, the Palestinian fighters began to leave the country. On September 1, 8,300

---

name of an Iraqi official who was working in the Iraqi embassy in London at the time. Email from Chibli Mallat to the author (Oct. 6, 2008), on file with author.

54. *See* REASON NOT THE NEED: EYEWITNESS CHRONICLES OF ISRAEL'S WAR IN LEBANON (Franklin P. Lamb ed., 1984), and ZE'EV SCHIFF & EHUD YA'ARI, ISRAEL'S LEBANON WAR (2d ed., 1986).

55. SCHIFF & YA'ARI, *supra* note 54, at 105–106, 240; *see also* U.S. Department of State, Bureau of Near Eastern Affairs, Background Note: Lebanon (Nov. 2007), *available at:* http://www.state.gov/r/pa/ei/bgn/35833.htm.

56. AL-HOUT, *supra* note 1, at 301. SEÁN MACBRIDE, ISRAEL IN LEBANON: REPORT OF THE INTERNATIONAL COMMISSION TO ENQUIRE INTO REPORTED VIOLATIONS OF INTERNATIONAL LAW BY ISRAEL DURING ITS INVASION OF THE LEBANON, 28 AUGUST 1982–29 NOVEMBER 1982, vii (1983) [hereinafter, MACBRIDE REPORT], "Certain Lebanese groups" refers to the Phalange (Lebanese Forces) and the Israeli-backed Southern Lebanese Army militia of Sa'ad Haddad. *Id. See also Hearings Before the Subcommittee on Europe and the Middle East of the House Committee on Foreign Affairs*, 97th Cong. 2d Sess., Sept. 22–29, 1982 [hereinafter House Subcomm. Hearings].

PLO guerillas and 3,600 Palestinian and Syrian Liberation Army troops were evacuated from Beirut.[57] Israel, however, claimed that over 2,000 fighters remained behind in the camps. The implausibility of this charge could be presumed by the early departure on September 10 of the U.S. troops that had come to supervise the Palestinian forces' exodus,[58] followed by the Italian and French forces over the next two days. Thus, the camps were left unprotected.

On Tuesday, September 14, Phalange/Lebanese Forces leader and president-elect Bashir Gemayyel was assassinated at the Phalange headquarters in East Beirut. Claiming that they would "forestall the danger of violence, bloodshed and chaos" from the alleged 2000–plus remaining Palestinian fighters, as well as protect Muslims against Christians,[59] Israeli Defense Forces (IDF) General and Defense Minister Ariel Sharon and Prime Minister Menachem Begin made the decision to move into West Beirut, without consulting the Israeli Cabinet. That night, Sharon and IDF Chief of Staff Rafael Eitan met with Phalange leaders and finalized the plan to send the Phalange militia into the camps.

The next day—Wednesday September 15—Sharon installed himself in the general army area at the Kuwait embassy junction a few hundred yards from the edge of Shatila camp. From the roof of this six-story building, it was possible to observe the town and the camps of Sabra and Shatila clearly and Sharon was able to personally direct the Israeli invasion.[60] The IDF began shelling West Beirut and the camps, and electricity was cut in West Beirut. An IDF soldier later testified that he received orders Wednesday night to begin firing flares over Sabra and Shatila camps.[61]

By late morning on Thursday, September 16, IDF General Amir Drori met at the Beirut office of IDF commander General Amos Yaron with Hobeika and other Phalangist commanders "to coordinate the entrance of the Phalange units into the Shatila camp."[62] The camps were

---

57. MacBride Report, *supra* note 56, at 164; *see also* Lamb, *supra* note 54, at 95–97. According to Schiff & Ya'ari, over twelve days, 14,398 Palestinian and Syrian fighters were evacuated from Beirut. Schiff & Ya'ari, *supra* note 54, at 228.

58. According to the Agreement they were to stay until September 21. *See* House Subcommittee Hearings, *supra* note 56, at 27.

59. Kahan Commission Report, *supra* note 3, at 28; *see also* House Subcomm. Hearings, *supra* note 56, at 17–18; Al-Hout, *supra* note 1, at 304, n. 40.

60. Complaint, *supra* note 2, at 223.

61. Lamb, *supra* note 54, at 101–102.

62. *Id.* at 102. *See also* House Subcomm. Hearings, *supra* note 56, at 32; Kahan Commission Report, *supra* note 3. Thomas Friedman reported in 1982 that "Mr. Sharon does not say who the Phalangist commander was, but it is believed to have been the Phalangist chief of staff, Fadi Ephram." Thomas Friedman, *The Beirut Massacre: The Four Days*, N.Y. Times, Sept. 26, 1982.

barricaded and nearby residents and journalists in the area that afternoon reported seeing convoys of Phalange military police and soldiers of Major Sa'ad Haddad's Israeli-backed Southern Lebanese Army forces moving into the area.

The events of the forty-plus hours between late afternoon Thursday, September 16 and mid-morning Saturday, September 18 were not disputed in the Belgian case. What was and still is disputed—as explored below—was the extent of Israeli and Lebanese responsibility and the level of impunity for the massacres. Their involvement has been well documented in photographs and survivor testimonies; journalistic reports; television documentaries; legal analyses; official governmental, international and NGO reports; academic, historical and advocacy books and articles.[63] Painstakingly researched accounts compiled by Franklin Lamb and Bayan Nuwayhad al-Hout provide details down to the hour.[64] The Complaint filed in the Brussels Court summarized the massacre:

> For the next 40 hours, the Phalangist militia raped, killed, and injured a large number of unarmed civilians, mostly children, women and elderly people inside the "encircled and sealed" camps. These actions, accompanied or followed by systematic roundups, backed or reinforced by the Israeli army, resulted in dozens of disappearances.
>
> The Israeli army had full knowledge of what was going on in the camps right up until the morning of Saturday, 18 September 1982, and its leaders were in continuous contact with the militia leaders who perpetrated the massacre. Yet they never intervened. Instead, they prevented civilians from escaping the camps and arranged for the camps to be illuminated throughout the night by flares launched into the sky from helicopters and mortars.
>
> The count of victims varies between 700 (the official Israeli figure) and 3,500 (in the inquiry launched by the Israeli journalist [Amnon] Kapeliouk). The exact figure can never be determined because, in addition to the approximately 1,000 people who were buried in communal graves by the International Committee of the Red Cross (ICRC) or in the cemeteries of Beirut by members of their families, a large number of corpses were buried beneath bulldozed buildings by the militia members themselves. Also, particularly on 17 and 18

---

63. *See generally,* AL-HOUT, *supra* note 1, at 301 (and Bibliography at 435–451); LAMB, *supra* note 54; Kahan Commission Report, *supra* note 3; SCHIFF & YA'ARI, *supra* note 54; Complaint, *supra* note 2; AMNON KAPELIOUK, ENQUÊTE SUR UN MASSACRE: SABRA ET CHATILA (1982). For a detailed catalogue of the violations of the Geneva Conventions with regard to the civilian population, *see* the MACBRIDE REPORT, *supra* note 56, at 187–192 (Conclusions).

64. LAMB, *supra* note 54, AL-HOUT, *supra* note 1.

September, hundreds of people were carried away alive in trucks towards unknown destinations, never to return.[65]

At the start of the siege and again on Thursday, September 16, Samiha Abbas Hijazi, the first named plaintiff in the Complaint and a Lebanese woman married to a Palestinian man, went to the home of her newly-wed, pregnant daughter Zainab, to persuade her to stay with her in al-Horsh, in the heart of Shatila, where Samiha thought she would be safer. Zainab and her husband, Fahd, lived with Fahd's mother on the edge of the district, under the Sports City near where the Israelis had positioned themselves. The first time Samiha went (on Wednesday), Zainab's mother-in-law would not let her leave. On Thursday, her mother-in-law allowed Zainab to go, but not Fahd, so Zainab stayed. Samiha spent that night in the shelter of a nearby school. The next morning, she left the shelter very early intending to hurry back to her daughter's home.[66]

> *I looked over the first part of the street and saw the piled up bodies. Some still had heads, some didn't. The men were all on top of each other. Suddenly, I heard someone moaning, saying: "I beg you, for your children's sake, come and help me." I went up to him, and I recognized Mustafa ... straight away, and I found his wife and children killed on their doorstep, not far from where he was. I started screaming.... I thought, maybe if I save this man, God will send me someone to save my daughter. I went and picked the man up, with a Syrian and a Lebanese helping me ... and we all went to the Gaza Hospital.*[67]

Samiha searched for her daughter for over a week, enlisting the help of the Civil Defense whenever she learned of the existence of a pit. Finally, in a pit near the Sports City, accessible only after the removal of mines, she found Zainab's body.

> *There were 21 in the pit. I found another three in a pit in the military camp [the former training camp], and I found another two at the side of the camp, killed near the shelter, making five altogether.... Some people told me later how my daughter's mother-in-law came out with other women, carrying a white flag. They thought the ones who'd come were Israelis, who wouldn't kill women. My son-in-law, Fahd, came out along with his mother, and ended up being one of the first killed. The killers had hit him and cut him in three pieces. He still had his [identity] card in his pocket.... Hana' Wahbeh said they laid the victims down, then booby-trapped them. That was why the*

---

65. Complaint, *supra* note 2, at 224.
66. AL-HOUT, *supra* note 1, at 139.
67. *Id.* at 230.

expert wouldn't go and search with me.... They defused the booby-traps under the bodies, then they brought the bulldozers and started digging with them, and straight away the corpses appeared.[68]

Accountability dispersed

What transpired in Sabra and Shatila has been exhaustively documented, but the victims' right to a remedy had never been vindicated. Despite multiple commissions of inquiry, official reports, and international outcry, the victims had no legal judgment, no compensation, no reparations—not even an apology.

The Lebanese government officially denied all Lebanese culpability, and a Lebanese report was hastily completed on September 29, 1982. The Jermanos Report, named for the president of the Commission, military prosecutor Ass'ad Jermanos, was never published and remained entirely confidential, in part because the Phalangists had assumed control of the government.[69] Only extracts were summarized and published in the Lebanese and Israeli press, stating that the report acquitted the Phalangists, and "inasmuch as there was no distinction to be made between war-related acts and those individual acts leading to the massacre," it demanded that prosecution be postponed until the judicial system was functional.[70] In 1991, Lebanon officially granted amnesty to participants in the civil war (1975–1990), which benefitted Hobeika and all other Lebanese involved in the events of Sabra and Shatila.[71]

Although no charges of war crimes or genocide had been filed anywhere before the complaint in Belgium, allegations were certainly manifest. The U.N. Security Council condemned the massacres as "criminal"; the U.N. General Assembly described it as an "act of genocide."[72] In hearings convened by the U.S. House of Representatives Foreign Affairs Subcommittee, Representative Tom Lantos called it "a large-scale butchery of innocent civilians by military units."[73] It was noted for the record that the Israelis were "well aware of their responsibility under the Fourth Geneva Convention for the safety of inhabitants of the camps,"[74] and that what transpired by letting in the Phalangists was foreseeable.

---

68. *Id.*

69. *Id.* at 316.

70. *Id.*

71. General Amnesty Law No. 84 of 26 August 1991.

72. U.N. Security Council, U.N. Doc. S/RES/521, 19 September 1982; General Assembly, U.N. Doc. A/RES/ 37/123D, 16 December 1982.

73. House Subcomm. Hearings, *supra* note 56, at 14.

74. *Id.* at 38.

In the absence of an official U.N. investigation into the massacres (in part because Lebanon refused to allow any commissions of inquiry[75]), an independent commission, chaired by 1974 Nobel Peace Prize laureate and Ireland's former Minister for External Affairs, Seán MacBride, convened to "enquire into reported violations of international law by Israel during its invasion of Lebanon,"[76] including the events at Sabra and Shatila.

The MacBride Report, released November 29, 1982, concluded that Israel shared responsibility with the Lebanese militias for the massacres, because Israel was the occupying power of the camps from when the IDF entered West Beirut on September 15 until its withdrawal on September 26.[77] As the MacBride Report noted, the Fourth Geneva Convention sets out the duties and responsibilities of an Occupying Power with respect to all civilians who find themselves under occupation. These include responsibility for the actions of agents of the Occupying Power towards "protected persons" (Article 29), which legally characterized the civilians in West Beirut, including Sabra and Shatila.[78] "Article 32 comprehensively prohibits any measure which is of a character such as '... to cause the physical suffering or extermination of protected persons ...' Article 147 indicates that breaches of the above cited Articles would be regarded as 'grave breaches' of the Convention."[79] The MacBride Commission concluded that grave breaches were committed by Israel during the Lebanon War, and recommended that

> all Parties to the Geneva Conventions carry out their legal obligation to prosecute individuals guilty of grave breaches of the laws of war, ... particularly ... the apprehension of Israeli and Lebanese political and military leaders and participants involved in the massacres at Chatila and Sabra. The Geneva Conventions require the

---

75. AL-HOUT, *supra* note 1, at 317.

76. MACBRIDE REPORT, *supra* note 56, at vii. The members of the Commission were influential academics; five were lawyers from the United States, Canada, France, South Africa and Ireland. The sixth was a professor of Semitic Languages and Islamic Studies at the University of Bonn. *Id.* Israel declined to cooperate with the Commission, which it viewed as "one-sided" (letter to Commission sent on 26 August 1982, *id.*).

77. *Id.* at 163, 169, 212 (Chronology).

78. *Id.* at 169 ("The reports of witnesses to the events of 14–18 September confirm the Commission in its opinion that Sabra and Chatila were neither centres of military resistance nor hiding places for large numbers of fighters. The fact that there may have been small arms in the camps and that inevitably many people present in the camps had 'links with the PLO' does not deprive the camps of their general civilian character.") Israel has been a party to the four Geneva Conventions since 1951. In 1983, the Israeli Supreme Court held that the Fourth Geneva Convention was applicable to southern Lebanon in the context of Israel's Ansar detention camp. HCJ 593/82 *Tsemel v. Minister of Def.* [1983], *translated in* 1 PAL. Y.B. INT'L. L. 164 (1984).

79. MACBRIDE REPORT, *supra* note 56, at 169.

Parties to use their national courts to carry out this responsibility and the Commission recommends that this requirement be honoured in the present instance.[80]

In the immediate aftermath of the massacres on September 25, approximately 400,000 Israelis took to the streets in Tel Aviv calling for an independent inquiry into Israel's role.[81] The government responded by forming an investigative commission named for its chair, Yitzhak Kahan.[82] Yet, the Israeli "body politic" seemed mainly concerned with releasing Israel from complicity, not with facilitating justice for what Israeli statesman and former ambassador to the U.N. Abba Eban called "the terrifying ordeals of the victims, of the Nazi-like sadism with which the Phalangists did their work."[83] In his Introduction to the official published version of the Kahan Commission Report, Eban wrote:

> It was later published in many Israeli newspapers and speeches that the media had ignored the fact that the actual killing had been done by Lebanese Phalangists, not by Israelis. This is not accurate. I have not seen a single report that failed to attribute the slaughter to the Lebanese Phalangists. But they are a vague, new, unfamiliar concept to world opinion: they have never sought or obtained the legitimacy or sanction of the outside world. They have not been actors in the universal drama, and their very obscurity and irrelevance gave them shelter from the censure of the world. Most of the immense eruption of public comment and argument centered on Israel's role. Were the Israel soldiers in the vicinity merely by chance or were they, inconceivably, in liaison or contact with the Phalangists or even in some posture of command? The question gnawed at the very roots of Israel's conscience, and within a few days it was plain that without some great cathartic release the question would have a stifling

---

80. *Id.* at 192. Other recommendations included the immediate withdrawal of all armed forces present in Lebanon without the government's consent, to be replaced by a U.N. multilateral force with authority to protect the refugee camps; that Israel pay reparations and indemnity to the victims and survivors, to the Government of Lebanon, to the ICRC and other voluntary bodies who had responded to the invasion; that the U.N. set up a special tribunal to investigate and prosecute individuals charged with crimes of state; that a competent international body be established to clarify the conception of genocide in relation to Israeli policies and practices towards the Palestinian people; and that financial and military sanctions be enacted on Israel until the Government complied with the Commission's recommendations. *Id.* at 192–193.

81. Schiff & Ya'ari, *supra* note 54, at 281.

82. In addition to Kahan, who was President of the Supreme Court, the Commission was presided over by Supreme Court Justice Aharon Barak and Maj. General (Res.) of the IDF Yona Efrat. The Commission held sixty sessions, heard fifty-eight witnesses, and reviewed scores of documents, statements collected from witnesses (though none were victims). Kahan Commission Report, *supra* note 3, at 1.

83. *Id.* at XIII.

effect. Israeli life simply could not go on unless the release was sought.... It was vital to cleanse the army of any doubt, whether by confession, by acquittal, by inquiry, or by the clear attribution of responsibility. It was in that atmosphere that the inquiry commission was born.[84]

The Kahan Commission was not a court of law, nor did it recommend legal action. In its report, issued on February 8, 1983, the Israeli Commission of Inquiry concluded that Israel or those acting in its behalf bore "absolutely no direct responsibility" for the atrocities, which had been perpetrated by the Phalangists. At the same time, the Commission found indirect responsibility for the failure to "foresee as probable" and to act to prevent the danger that "the Phalangists would commit massacres and pogroms against the inhabitants of the camps."[85] What is more, indirect responsibility could be assigned for the failure to respond, restrain and stop the Phalangists once reports of what was happening began to come in.[86]

The Commission found Sharon "personally responsible" for "non-fulfillment of a duty" and recommended that he be removed from office.[87] He was forced to resign as Minister of Defense, but remained a minister without portfolio. Yaron was found "personally responsible" for committing a "grave error" and making a "thoroughly mistaken judgment" in his inaction with respect to what he knew was likely the Phalangists would do, and then with respect to the reports of actual killings.[88] He was relieved of his command position for three years, but promoted to major general over a year later. The Commission found that Director of Military Intelligence, Maj. Gen. Yehoshua Saguy, Maj. Gen. Amir Drori, and Brig. Gen. Amos Yaron had "committed a breach of the duty incumbent upon them." Saguy was relieved of his position and he retired from the army. Regarding Drori and others deemed indirectly responsible, including IDF Chief of Staff Lt. Gen. Rafael Eitan, the

---

84. *Id.* at XIII–XIV.

85. *Id.* at 63.

86. *Id.*

87. *Id.* at 73, 104 ("It is our view that responsibility is to be imputed to the Minister of Defense for having disregarded the danger of acts of vengeance and bloodshed by the Phalangists against the population of the refugee camps, and having failed to take this danger into account when *he decided to have the Phalangists enter the camps*.") (emphasis added). *Id.* at 73. The Commission further remarked that it is "ostensibly puzzling that the Defense Minister did not in any way make the Prime Minister privy to the decision on having the Phalangists enter the camps." *Id.*

88. *Id.* at 96. Yaron "testified that he was aware that the Phalangists' norms of behavior during wartime are different from those of the IDF and that there is no sense in arguing with them to change their combat ethics...." *Id.* at 93.

Commission decided it was "sufficient to determine responsibility without making any further recommendation."[89]

Beyond noting the political and military links between Israel and the "Christian forces,"[90] the Kahan Commission did not examine the implications of those links for Israeli accountability, particularly with the Southern Lebanese Army militia (Sa'ad Haddad's forces), which it absolved of any responsibility. Nor did it mention the presence or participation by Haddad's forces in the massacres. The Commission specifically stated that, "[p]ursuant to I.D.F. orders, Haddad's army did not proceed north of the Awali River,"[91] a claim that was contradicted by many who spoke of seeing Haddad himself and men bearing uniforms with the insignia of his militia in and around the camps.[92]

None of the Israeli leaders who were found "personally responsible" suffered any real repercussions with respect to personal or public liability.[93] Sharon continued to serve in high government positions, and was appointed Foreign Minister in 1998. In February 2001, Sharon was elected Prime Minister of Israel.[94] This reopened wounds and inflamed the indignation that he had avoided any real responsibility for the massacres.

So it was that twenty-three victims of massacres that took place over three days in 1982 in the largely Palestinian refugee camps of Sabra and Shatila in Beirut saw a chance for redress in Belgium in 2001. Nearly twenty years after the Israeli Kahan Commission found Sharon indirectly, though personally, responsible for the massacres; ten years after a Lebanese amnesty law had pardoned all participants in the civil war (which had benefited at least one of the defendants—Phalange militia leader Elie Hobeika); there had still been no judicial accountability or restitution. There would be no civil or criminal action in Israel or Lebanon—that much was clear.

---

89. *Id.* at 104–105. The Commission "arrived at grave conclusions regarding the acts and omissions of the chief of staff," but since his term was about to expire, they let the matter drop. SCHIFF & YA'ARI, *supra* note 54, at 283.

90. Kahan Commission Report, *supra* note 3, at 7–8.

91. *Id.* at 8.

92. Friedman, *The Beirut Massacre, supra* note 62; *see also,* AL-HOUT, *supra* note 1, at 319.

93. Notwithstanding the inconvenience and expense of defending against the U.S. civil suits. *See* cases discussed *supra* note 5.

94. Even before that, in 1999, Amos Yaron became Secretary General of the Ministry of Defense, a position he held until September 2005. After establishing the right-wing Tsomet party before the 1984 elections, Rafael Eitan was elected to the Knesset and went on to become Minister of Agriculture in the Likud government in 1990–91. He was also Minister of Agriculture and the Environment and deputy Prime Minister in the Netanyahu government in 1996.

The Dilemmas of Rendering the Victims Visible

Impact litigation depends to a large degree on civil society: national and international activists—both legal and non-legal—who coordinate, organize, and communicate technical legal processes to the public. They may coordinate *amicus curiae* submissions, provide analyses of the issues and proceedings in the case, help to direct media response and guide public opinion to support the case. Civil society activists also can create a more effective platform for the victims/plaintiffs, whose voices are often muted as they are channeled through the legal process.

Rendering the "cause" or the case into public discourse or the mainstream media was not difficult with the Rwanda and the Congo cases, because the stories involved Belgium's colonial past intertwined with current events. Rwandan and Congolese refugees were living in Belgium and could add their voices to explanations of the cases. Nor was such translation required with the Pinochet case; the crimes of his reign had long been infamous worldwide. The Israeli and Palestinian narratives, on the other hand, were far more complicated and contested.

The fact that there were no Sabra and Shatila victims' groups in Belgium and no victims living there at all was a disadvantage not only in the eyes of the court, but also for the public eye. The Palestine Liberation Organization ("PLO") was ambivalent and stayed more or less out of the picture, to the relief of the legal team, who sought to avoid politics as much as possible. Thus, the image of the plaintiffs was rendered mainly through the ghastly photographs of the massacres, or through solidarity groups, who the public tended to view—whether correctly or not—as anti-Israel.

While civil society plays a role vis à vis the public, plaintiffs' attorneys have a professional responsibility to assist victims in telling their story to the court and a moral responsibility to help victims make their stories known to the public in their own words. This is especially so for human rights lawyers, who understand better than most the dehumanization that their clients have suffered. And, while victims of a massacre normally elicit great sympathy, it was not so for the victims of Sabra and Shatila. This may have been due to the language barrier, or to cultural differences, or perhaps to anti-Arab discrimination that intensified after September 11 (recall that the Sabra and Shatila case was filed less than three months earlier).[95]

The inability of the support committees and the legal team to create a groundswell of public empathy in Belgium for the victims might also be

---

95. Mohammad Abu Rdaini told Mallat, "That night [September 11, 2001], I knew you had lost the case. How much is jeopardized by extreme violence." Mallat interview, *supra* note 13.

attributed to Israel's capacity for casting itself as a victim. In one of many ironies of the Sabra and Shatila case, Israel hired a well-known victims' lawyer, Michèle Hirsch, as its defense attorney. A colleague of Walleyn and other human rights attorneys, Hirsch had represented the Rwandan victims in the successful *Butare Four* case (among others). After working on behalf of many victims seeking redress under the Law, Hirsch dismissed universal jurisdiction in the Sabra and Shatila case, saying, "Belgium is a small country. We cannot be the judge of the world."[96]

An international solidarity coalition focused on the survivors and their stories, and maintained a website with photos of the plaintiffs, their brief statements, commentary and regular updates on the case.[97] Belgian and European human rights organizations devoted considerable energy to the legal dimensions of the case. Israeli attorney Lea Tsemel sent reports to Walleyn about Israeli legal issues in the early stages. Both the International Secretariat and the Belgian section of Amnesty International as well as the Fédération Internationale des Droits de l'Homme (FIDH), among others, provided support to the attorneys and the case. They published press releases detailing the process and reports analyzing the convoluted legal proceedings and the universal jurisdiction Law. They issued public calls for accountability from the Belgian legal system and the government. Human Rights Watch (HRW)—in particular, Reed Brody, Brussels-based International Justice Program director—was involved with the Law. He had been centrally involved with the Pinochet case in the U.K., and in November 2000 he initiated a case with a group of Chadians living in Belgium as *parties civiles* against the former dictator of Chad, Hissène Habré. Brody had misgivings about the Sabra and Shatila case, which he discussed privately with Walleyn and Verhaeghe, as he recounted:

> I had this image of the guy in *The Old Man and the Sea*—he finally catches the shark or whatever fish it was and he's dragging it back, but he can do nothing to protect it from getting eaten by all these

---

96. Daphne Eviatar, *Debating Belgium's War Crime Jurisdiction*, N.Y. TIMES, Jan. 25 2003.

97. The International Campaign for Justice for the Victims of Sabra and Shatila was coordinated by Laurie King–Irani, a Canadian anthropologist from the University of Victoria, *see* www.indictsharon.net. A number of Sabra and Shatila committees emerged, including in Belgium; but the most important were in Beirut. Headed by Rifaat Nimr and Jaber Sleiman, they performed all the critical non-legal work, e.g., keeping the victims informed, organizing travel of witnesses to Spain, Norway and elsewhere. All financial expenses went through this committee, allowing Mallat to avoid having money "sully the case." In Italy, Stefano Chiarini arranged international visits to the camps on the anniversary of the massacres (which he had begun before the case). "The larger than life Leila Shahid, PLO ambassador in Paris, was extremely supportive and thanks to her, *Le Monde* carefully covered the developments in Belgium." Email from Mallat, *supra* note 53.

other fish. I felt that way about the Law because it was there and it said you could bring any lawsuit in the world, and the only limitation was self-restraint. And, you know, human rights activists and particularly lawyers and political dissidents are not known for self-restraint. So people kept filing cases.... We would not have brought the Sharon case, but once it was brought, we were behind it because it was meritorious. And I think Belgium weathered Sharon. If it weren't for the United States, for the Bush cases and all that, [Belgium] would have gotten away with it.[98]

Thus, despite initial reluctance, HRW supported the case publically with reports, press releases and statements. Reed Brody and Geraldine Mattioli helped set up the human rights NGO Platform and played an important role working with key Belgian parliamentarians when the law was being overhauled in 2002–2003.

A paradox of litigation is that it often gets mired down in procedural minutiae and may never get to the merits where the stories lie. Such was the situation with this case. For the most part, the case stayed at a very technical legal level; the international support coalition did not have a base in Belgium, and the NGO Platform was working full throttle trying to explain—and then retain—the Law. Could the legal team have done more to get the victims seen and heard by the Belgian public? Perhaps—but in reality the moment wasn't theirs; all attention was on the Law and legal procedure. Under normal circumstances, the investigation should have taken one to three years. Thus, rather than bringing the plaintiffs to Belgium, their lawyers expected that as the case proceeded the investigating magistrate would undertake rogatory missions to obtain depositions in Beirut, as was done in Rwanda, for instance.[99] They were more focused on preparing the groundwork in Lebanon "to show that there was a real case behind the investigation, to show the judge and prosecutor that there was real evidence."[100] They worked conscientiously with the victims making sure they understood what to expect, and to keep their expectations in check.

---

98. Interview with Reed Brody, Human Rights Watch International Justice Advocacy Director, in Brussels (March 13, 2007).

99. Extraterritorial investigation is handled through implementation of a rogatory letter and commission. A rogatory letter is executed by the local authorities in the presence of the Belgian team. In Rwanda, for instance, it was a Rwandan representative of the judiciary who conducted the interviews. The team investigating in the context of a rogatory mission abroad includes one investigative judge, a prosecutor and investigators, and often a registrar and a translator. HUMAN RIGHTS WATCH, UNIVERSAL JURISDICTION IN EUROPE, THE STATE OF THE ART, section B.3.b, *available at:* http://www.hrw.org/reports/2006/ij0606/6.htm#_Toc 137876513 [hereinafter HRW, UJ IN EUROPE]

100. Interview with Luc Walleyn, Brussels, March 14 2007 [hereinafter, Walleyn interview March 14].

When they realized that the investigating judge was not going to collect evidence from the plaintiffs, Walleyn, Verhaeghe and Mallat knew they had to bring the victims to Brussels. Walleyn noted, "We wanted to show the public that these are real people, with a story. It was important in a symbolic sense also for the Court. But we didn't do it every time; it's not easy to bring someone over. Because they're stateless, most of these people don't have passports; they need a *laissez passer*, permission from the Lebanese authorities, a visa for Belgium, and so on." Considering the logistics and expense, they focused on important hearings where the press could be expected to show up, and where a representative would have something to report to the group back in Lebanon.

Three of the victims came to Brussels in connection with the case: Samiha Hijazi Abbas, Mohammad Abu Rdaini, and Souad Srour. Mohammad was the only one who spoke English (he worked with CNN, and was able to engage with the legal team and others). Souad and Samiha spoke only Arabic.[101] Souad was selected to come in part because she already had travel documents. She was also familiar with the foreign press, having given a number of interviews. Souad lost her father, three brothers, (ages eleven, six and three) and two sisters (eighteen months and nine months). Mallat brought her to Brussels when they filed the complaint, in which Souad described in part her ordeal.

Unfortunately, Souad overstayed her visa and dropped out of the case. She was influenced and encouraged to do so by members of the European Arab League, an organization headed by a Belgian of Lebanese origin that tried to get control over the case. They attacked the legal team for their relationships with Jewish Israeli lawyers and because Walleyn travelled to Israel. Mallat was criticized for his Christian origin and accused of having a hidden agenda. The League used Souad to try to enhance themselves; but ultimately, Mallat said, "we contained their mischief rather well." Of greatest consequence, Souad's action made it much more difficult to obtain visas for others. Still, the logistical challenges were worthwhile for the case and for the individual plaintiffs themselves.

> They gave interviews; and, for instance, Samiha came with large photos of her husband and children, which she put beside her at the entrance of the court. It was very important also for them. Some of these elderly people were born in what is now Israel, and are really refugees from the first generation [who fled in 1948]. None of them—at least the older generation—had gone out of Lebanon since they had arrived there. Some had never even gone out of Beirut. So,

---

101. *Id*. For Mohammad's testimony, *see supra* text accompanying note 2. For Samiha's testimony, *see supra* text accompanying notes 66–68.

it was of such importance to come to Europe, to go into the court—this palace.[102]

Law, Politics, and Many Twists of Fate

Some questioned why Mallat was undertaking this case now—why not before? It was, to some degree, purely serendipitous. In 1996, Mallat had helped set up INDICT, a U.K.-based campaign that focused on the international crimes of the former Iraqi regime.[103] Bolstered by the Pinochet case, in August 1999 they filed a complaint against deputy chief of the Iraqi armed forces Izzat Ibrahim al-Duri in Vienna, where he had gone for medical treatment.[104] Al–Duri had a brutal reputation. Among other things, he was accused of directing the 1988 Anfal campaign against the Kurds in Halabja, during which between 3200–5000 people were killed. The complaint was brought under the Austrian Criminal Code's extraterritorial jurisdiction provision (Article 64), the Convention Against Torture, and the Genocide Convention. Mallat was appalled when the Austrian government let al-Duri slip quietly out of the country rather than face prosecution.[105] "These cases told me something important: when you have someone in place, it's much easier to effectuate the case."[106]

Just over one year later in September 2000, an incident in Jerusalem sparked Mallat's sense of outrage and started him thinking about Sabra and Shatila.

> Something I never forgave Sharon for: he started the [second] *intifada* by going to the Haram-al-Sharif [Temple Mount] on September 28 in order to destabilize [Prime Minister Ehud] Barak, to embarrass [Benjamin] Netanyahu and to provoke Palestinians in

---

102. *Id.*

103. "INDICT was established to campaign for the creation of an ad hoc international criminal tribunal—similar to those established for the former Yugoslavia and Rwanda— to try leading members of the former Iraqi regime on charges of war crimes and crimes against humanity, including genocide and torture. The campaign was launched in the House of Commons and in the U.S. Senate, and remained dependent on voluntary donations and assistance until it was awarded a financial grant through the Iraq Liberation Act, passed by the U.S. Congress in December 1998, which allocated funds to various Iraqi opposition groups and specifically allocated money for war crimes issues." *About INDICT*, http://www.indict.org.uk/about.php.

104. Barbara Crossette, *The World; Dictators Face the Pinochet Syndrome*, N.Y. TIMES, Aug. 22, 1999. *See also* Human Rights Watch, press release, Prosecution of Iraqi in Austria Urged, Saddam Hussein Aide Accused of Genocide, Murder and Torture (Feb. 17, 1999), *available at:* http://www.hrw.org/english/docs/1999/02/17/austri1053.htm.

105. Human Rights Watch, press release, Austria Blasted for Release of Iraqi, Jordan Urged to Arrest Saddam Hussein Aide Accused of Genocide (Aug. 18, 1999), *available at:* http://hrw.org/english/docs/1999/08/18/austri1052.htm.

106. Mallat Interview, *supra* note 13.

their most sacred symbolic site. That angered me and made me think of the murders, and remedies that might be possible.[107]

Mallat had read every book that was written on Sabra and Shatila. From working with INDICT, and from closely watching the Pinochet case and other cases, he had a deep sense of the importance that the complaint be professionally executed.

> I knew also that I had to collect serious evidence, and serious evidence would come only from the victims. At the time, I had never set foot in a Palestinian camp because, well ... they were too miserable. But also, Sabra and Shatila were off-bounds—they were completely dominated by Syrian intelligence. What would a Maronite lawyer be doing in Sabra and Shatila? There was no way I could do anything directly myself. So I did a [very basic] questionnaire with [some interns].... I knew of Rosemary [Sayegh], because she has written beautiful books about the Palestinians, and I knew her husband.... I called her and ... she was very excited; she told me of a sociologist from the camps, not a victim but very good. We wanted straightforward testimony, not inflated or exaggerated.[108]

Thus, in Beirut, from January 2001, Mallat and a small team headed by Professor Rosemary Sayegh and researcher Sana Husein had been identifying Palestinian and Lebanese victims of the massacres and collecting testimonies in the camps for some six months before the complaint was filed. From numerous questionnaires and interviews, the team selected thirty potential plaintiffs. Two declined, not wanting to revisit the psychological trauma. A few whose stories were especially powerful were asked to serve as witnesses rather than plaintiffs, so that they might be brought into the proceeding in a more public manner. In the end, there were twenty-three plaintiffs.

Mallat researched various universal jurisdiction statutes before deciding on Belgium. In choosing the venue, he knew that several threshold legal elements had to be in place. Even if the statute provided jurisdiction, the country also had to be willing to exercise jurisdiction in *this* case. Given the date of the events, Mallat looked for countries whose statutes of limitations would not bar the claims. And, considering the defendants, Mallat looked for laws in which head of state or other official immunities were rejected. Recognizing that the Belgian statute was fully aligned with the Rome Statute and met all of the key legal elements,

---

107. *Id.* Sharon was a vociferous critic of Barak's decision to negotiate with the Palestinians. *See*, e.g., MERIP Primer on the Uprising in Palestine, *available at* http://www.merip.org/new_uprising_primer/primer_all_text.html; BBC News, *On this day: 28 September, 2000: "Provocative" mosque visit sparks riots*, *available at* http://news.bbc.co.uk/onthisday/hi/dates/stories/september/28/newsid_3687000/3687762.stm.

108. Telephonic interview with Mallat, *supra* note 15.

Mallat concluded that Belgium had "the most sophisticated and remarkable law, with the greatest chance for justice."

In May 2001, Sharon announced that he was going to visit Belgium. This might have had no bearing on Mallat's case, but it forced him to act before he had been planning to file. On June 4, Mallat read in the Lebanese daily newspaper, *Hayat*, that a case had been filed in Belgium against Ariel Sharon. At that point, he had had only initial contact with Luc Walleyn and Michael Verhaeghe, but they had not met. Mallat had little time to make a critical decision. The complaint that had been filed was a few pages at most; those who filed it had no connection with Sabra and Shatila nor with specific victims. Mallat thus concluded that it was an ideological exploit of the universal jurisdiction law and not a serious complaint. The situation with the Law and the nature of a case such as this was sensitive and vulnerable. Concerned that their painstakingly documented evidence would be compromised by such a flawed complaint, Mallat announced plans to file his case, hoping that real victims and the thoroughness of their report would prevent a publicly derisive dismissal of the earlier complaint. For their part, Walleyn and Verhaeghe made sure that the judiciary would not move to dismiss the case for lack of standing, which also bought them a little more time to work with the victims and refine the complaint. Their case would essentially be joined with and envelope the defective one.

On June 18, just before Belgium assumed the presidency of the European Union, the seventy-page victims' complaint was submitted to the office of the public prosecutor, where it was assigned to an investigating magistrate of the Brussels Court of First Instance. The case was immediate front page news in Europe and the Middle East. Sharon cancelled his trip to Belgium. Mallat reflected on this. "Tactically, had I known as I do now—that you do it all in great silence, you give the complaint to the investigating judge and quietly ask for investigation— we could have gone to one of the Pinochet judges...."[109] That is, had Sharon come to Belgium after the complaint had been filed and the case was opened, the investigating judge could have quietly issued a warrant for Sharon's arrest, and—perhaps—the story might have unfolded like that of Pinochet in England.

The Legal Proceedings, The Political Heat

Fate had dealt the Pinochet plaintiffs a sympathetic and uniquely well-qualified investigating judge. Indeed, Damien Vandermeersch, an expert in international criminal and humanitarian law, was already

---

109. Mallat interview, *supra* note 13.

involved in some of the Rwanda cases.[110] The Sabra and Shatila plaintiffs drew a very different card. The investigating judge assigned to their case, Patrick Collignon, was reluctant about the complaint, raising questions of admissibility and procedure, in effect challenging the jurisdictional scope of the Law itself.

A week after the victims' complaint was filed, Philippe Meire, Acting Deputy Prosecutor of Brussels responsible for international investigations (*premier substitut du procureur du roi de Bruxelles*) had exercised his discretion to join the case and submitted to Collignon his motion of indictment (*requisitoire de mise à l'instruction*) against "X" and the named defendants, as per the complaint. The prosecutor's indictment has the same legal effect as that of the investigating judge, but, as the prosecutor represents the state, his support carries considerably greater weight. Thus, Meire's support for the complaint strengthened the case, effectively doubling the indictment against Sharon, Yaron, and the others. If the Law was not later amended, it also should have allowed the case to proceed, Collignon's decision notwithstanding.[111] Almost simultaneously, the plaintiffs' attorneys submitted under seal a list of names identifying the "X" defendants to Collignon.

Normally, an investigating judge faced with the amount of information and the level of specificity contained in the Sabra and Shatila complaint would have indicted (*inculpé*)[112] the defendants. For reasons

---

110. NAOMI ROHT-ARRIAZA, THE PINOCHET EFFECT: TRANSNATIONAL JUSTICE IN THE AGE OF HUMAN RIGHTS 119 (2005). Until around spring of 2001, all international cases filed with the investigating magistrates were handled by Vandermeersch, but he was overwhelmed. Dean of the investigating magistrates, Bruno Bulthé asked for volunteers to be appointed in such cases, and some judges took part in a special training. Among them was Patrick Collignon.

111. E-mail from Luc Walleyn, to author (Sept. 20, 2008) (on file with author). Oddly, Meire's motion was based on war crimes only, and not on crimes against humanity and genocide as were alleged in the complaint. Walleyn believes Meire wanted to be consistent with the position of his office in the Rwanda cases, although the 1999 law made it possible to broaden the indictment to include genocide and crimes against humanity.

112. Where the common law system has only suspects and accused, a defendant in the Belgian legal system can be any of the following:

(1) "*une personne contre laquelle l'action publique est engagée*"—term used for someone against whom an individual party complaint has been filed (*constitution de partie civile*) and who is the subject of an investigation by the investigating magistrate or indictment by the public prosecutor.

(2) "*inculpé*"—charged or indicted; term applied when the investigating magistrate proceeds to formally charge a person "against whom serious evidence of culpability exists" ("*toute personne contre laquelle existent des indices sérieux de culpabilité*"). This must be done through a formal proceeding (in the Indictment Chamber) or by official notification of the defendant. It is possible to issue an international warrant of arrest before the person has been formally designated "*inculpé*," but he becomes officially so upon his arrest.

that remain unclear, Collignon did not indict the defendants; instead, he contested the admissibility of the case. This challenge was not based on any inadequacies with the Complaint itself; indeed he had not even begun to investigate the allegations or their factual basis. Further, Collignon didn't oppose the complaint on immunity grounds, since the Law was very clear on that issue. Instead, he made two assertions, both of which were ultimately shown to be incorrect, but which threw the case and the Law into a legal and political morass. Collignon asserted that the Law conflicted with Article 12 of the Preliminary Title of the Code of Criminal Procedure of 1878, which requires that a criminal prosecution take place only if the suspect is found on Belgian soil. And, secondly, he claimed that the case was precluded by the 1991 Lebanese amnesty that covered the events of the Lebanese civil war from 1975.

Michèle Hirsch, counsel for the state of Israel, claimed to Collignon and the media that Sharon had immunity as a head of state; that the case was barred by the principle of *ne bis in idem,* since the crimes had already been considered in Israel by the Kahan Commission, which she maintained was a judicial commission; that the Law could not be used retroactively; and that the case had no connection with Belgium.[113] As the state of Israel was not a defendant in the case, however, Hirsch could not appear before the Indictment Chamber for the accused. Thus, Sharon and Yaron retained Adrien Masset, Professor of Criminal Procedure at the University of Liège.

On September 7, 2001, Collignon suspended the investigation and handed his decision to the office of the prosecutor. Because of the unusual legal issues, Meire submitted the case to the *chambre des mises en accusation* ("indictment chamber," located within the Brussels Court of Appeals). The prosecutor "strongly contested" Collignon's decision, which he believed was based on an error of law, and argued that the Code of Criminal Procedure is not applicable to special laws providing extraterritorial jurisdiction, such as the 1993/1999 statute.

Between October 23, 2001 and January 23, 2002, the Indictment Chamber convened four pre-trial hearings on these questions. During the proceedings, Masset objected that his clients had not been officially notified to appear. The case was postponed in order to do so, but the Israeli Ministry of Foreign Affairs refused to transmit to the Israeli

---

(3) *"accusé"*—term used for a person whose case is submitted to the Criminal Court (Cour d'Assises) by the Indictment Chamber of the Court of Appeals. At this stage, the court considers that the charges are sufficient to justify a trial.

There is no legal difference between a person indicted (*"inculpé"*) by *constitution de partie civile* or by the prosecutor; both initiatives trigger an investigation. But the practical difference is significant, as the latter involves the state apparatus. *Id.*

113. Amnesty Int'l press release, Amnesty International urges investigation of Ariel Sharon (Oct. 3, 2001).

judiciary the notice presented by the Belgian embassy. To resolve this problem, Masset was forced to appear on behalf of his clients as *"personnes contre laquelle l'action publique est engagée."*[114] Thus, though they still contested jurisdiction, by formally appearing in court the defendants became a party in the procedure. Masset was furious that the prosecutor had joined the case, adding the weight of his office to the *constitution parties civiles*.[115]

The president of the Indictment Chamber finally requested all evidence, notes and submissions be filed by January 30, 2002, and the final pre-trial admissibility hearing was set for March 6. Two dramatic events then significantly impacted the case, at least one of which postponed the March hearing.

Assassination

Almost immediately after the complaint was filed, former Phalange head of intelligence Elie Hobeika called a televised press conference in Beirut to applaud the Belgian initiative and declare his willingness to assist with the investigation and clear his name. Hobeika long harbored bitterness that he had been named by the Kahan Commission and others as having ordered the massacres.[116] Unaware that he was already named as a defendant (under seal) in the Belgian case, he tried to present himself as a witness and probably thought he could negotiate testifying in exchange for assurances that he would not be arrested.[117] Through their pleadings, the plaintiffs' lawyers had been urging Collignon to meet with Hobeika formally, and they were laying the groundwork in Lebanon so that Collignon could make a rogatory mission to collect evidence. Walleyn sent the investigating judge a letter in early August noting

---

114. See *supra* note 112.
115. Email from Mallet, *supra* note 53.
116. Kahan Commission Report, *supra* note 3, at 20–22, 55–56.
117. No Lebanese were directly named as defendants as a precaution that proved wise, given the fate of Hobeika. Saad Haddad died in 1984 and, of course, Gemayyel had been assassinated. That Hobeika was not a named defendant in the case was calculated; Mallat had a "strong hunch" that Hobeika would come forward to clear his name. "Although he had a reputation for being ruthless, he was only twenty-five or twenty-six in 1982, and probably didn't have a commanding role in the massacres. Hobeika was not present at a meeting that took place between Mossad and commanders of the Lebanese Forces shortly afterwards, and this is when it was decided that Hobeika would be the main scapegoat. Not being from the Gemayyel background, and not from a rich Beiruti Christian family, he was an easy target." Telephonic interview with Mallat, *supra* note 15. Evidence in Appendix B of the Kahan Commission Report—the secret documents, never released to the public, but obtained by the plaintiffs' attorneys—confirmed this. One day while the case was going on, a large packet of documents arrived "anonymously" at Walleyn's office—included was a copy of the secret Appendix B.

Hobeika's readiness to come to Brussels, formally providing Hobeika's address and urging Collignon to invite him. Collignon did not respond. Walleyn recalled,

> That was our big disappointment, of course. Had he started the investigation it would have been possible to complete it very quickly, because a lot of investigative work on the role of the IDF, for example, had been done by the Kahan Commission. Eyewitnesses and also former militia leaders could be interviewed by the investigators and probably we could have had some archives from the Phalange. At least it was our expectation that sooner or later that could come up. And, the victims were still there. From the point of practicability, it was an easy investigation.[118]

Instead they waited, expecting that Collignon would do his job without further prodding.

The legal team submitted the formal complaint (under seal) against Hobeika in October 2001, and they referred to him as an *"inculpé"* in their submissions to the court in December. (The attorneys used this term for the suspects, although Collignon never recognized them as such.) A discussion ensued at the hearings of November 28 and December 26 as to whether the case against Hobeika was the "same case" or a "distinct case" from the one against Sharon and Yaron, and whether Hobeika had to be notified of the court proceedings, as were the Israelis. Pierre Morlet, Attorney General (*premier avocat general près de la cour d'appel*) who represented the prosecution in the proceedings before the indictment chamber, considered it unnecessary to officially notify him. Hobeika always had the opportunity to intervene of his own free will. The final pleadings took place on January 23, 2002. That same day, Hobeika met in East Beirut with Belgian senators Josy Dubié and Vincent Van Quickenborne, to whom he reiterated his willingness to come to Brussels. Hobeika told the senators that he had new taped evidence on the massacres that would implicate Sharon.[119] Dubié tried to get him to say more, but Hobeika just said that he would "keep that for the court."[120]

Hobeika was never interviewed, and the taped evidence he referred to never surfaced. On January 24, 2002, Hobeika was assassinated in Beirut in a massive car bombing. Although no one claimed responsibility, many, including the victims and their attorneys, are convinced that the murder was directly tied to their case.[121] In addition to ensuring that

---

118. Walleyn interview March 14, *supra* note 100.

119. *Hobeika taped "evidence" against Sharon before assassination: Beirut press*, AGENCE FRANCE PRESSE, Jan. 2002.

120. Dubié interview, *supra* note 41.

121. *Id.; see also* Robert Fisk, *"The man who would testify against Ariel Sharon is blown up. Was this another targeted killing?"* THE INDEPENDENT, Jan. 25, 2002.

crucial evidence would have been collected, had Hobeika come to Belgium, his presence almost certainly would have undermined Collignon's opposition and the defense's main argument that no suspect was in Belgium.

The ICJ's Decision in Yerodia, and Its Limits

On February 14, 2002, the ICJ handed Belgium a reality check on the Law's broad bar to immunity. The Court held in *Democratic Republic of the Congo v. Belgium (Arrest Warrant of Abdulaye Yerodia Ndombasi)* that Belgium had violated the immunity of the DRC's foreign minister in issuing an arrest warrant related to charges while he was in office. Since it was not plainly asked to rule on the issue of universal jurisdiction, the ICJ refrained from doing so.[122]

The ICJ decision was a setback for the Law and for victims' rights. Morlet and the plaintiffs' lawyers in the Sabra and Shatila case asked to re-open the proceedings in order to enter a plea that the ICJ judgment had no bearing on the investigating judge's jurisdiction to conduct a criminal investigation of the 1982 killings. The Indictment Chamber agreed to this request and scheduled the final pre-trial admissibility hearing for May 15. In the meantime, on April 16 the Court of Appeals in the remanded *Yerodia* case held that the 1878 Code of Criminal Procedure limiting criminal investigations to situations in which the suspect is on Belgian territory was fully applicable to the 1993/1999 statute.

At the May hearing, Attorney–General Morlet rejected this interpretation of the presence requirement. While he acknowledged immunity for Sharon as a sitting prime minister, Morlet confirmed that immunity did not apply against the others, and the investigation should proceed. The plaintiffs' attorneys argued that the Sabra and Shatila case had not gone beyond a preliminary criminal investigation. It was premature to determine that the decision meant no indictment could be issued when the case had not yet been determined to be admissible. Even if the ICJ decision were to be applied, only Sharon would have immunity, and only for the duration of his term in office. Furthermore, they could distinguish the *Yerodia* case because the Sabra and Shatila complaint alleged acts of genocide. Article IV of the Genocide Convention expressly denies

---

122. ICJ *Arrest Warrant* Case, *supra* note 49. Alain Winants, prosecutor at the Brussels Court of Appeals (who prosecuted the successful *Butare Four* case) and professor at the Université Libre de Bruxelles, noted the opinions of the particular judges on the issue. "Four judges are clearly against the exercise of universal jurisdiction *in absentia* [see the Opinions of Judges Guillaume, Ranjeva, Rezek, and Bula–Bula], while the other seven hold it permissible [see the Opinions of Judges Higgins, Kooijmans, Buergenthal, Koroma, Oda, Al–Khasawneh and Van Den Wijngaert]." Winants, *supra* note 36, at 500.

immunity for acts of genocide and ancillary crimes, without regard to the status of perpetrator. The legal team argued that the ICJ judgment on immunity should be narrowly construed as applying to the simple issuance and delivery of an arrest warrant.[123]

Notwithstanding the support of the deputy Attorney–General, on June 26 the Brussels Court of Appeals reached the same ruling in the Sabra and Shatila case with respect to the presence requirement. The Court then dismissed the case because none of the accused were present in Belgian territory. Profoundly disappointed, the legal team issued a press statement expressing their concern that the judicial process,

> far removed from violence, [was] interrupted on the grounds of narrow procedure at a time when the law was clear.... This absence of judicial recourse cannot continue. We should also recall that Mr. Sharon and his main aide, Mr. Yaron, have been charged twice (*"mis en cause"*) by the prosecution in Belgium: in the first instance for war crimes, in the second by the Attorney–General for war crimes, crimes against humanity and genocide. This is an historic benchmark in the Sabra and Shatila massacres victims' search for justice in a neutral forum of law.[124]

A week later, on July 3, 2002, they appealed the case to the Supreme Court (*Cour de Cassation*).

The NGO Platform and the Interpretive Law

According to Luc Walleyn, "many thought this would be the end of the Belgian universal jurisdiction law."[125] But, not yet—it was time for politics. Following an intensive lobbying campaign by victims' rights groups, human rights NGOs and academics, a group of Belgian parliamentarians submitted a proposal for an "interpretive law" to clarify and reconfirm the intent and meaning of the 1993/1999 Law. This was linked to a second, more general proposal to take account of the international law developments from the ICJ's decision in *Yerodia* and the Rome Statute of the ICC, which came into effect July 1, 2002. This second bill included some significant restrictions on the rights of individuals to initiate an investigation, and provided for a more consistent role for the

---

123. In a comprehensive report just before the hearing, Amnesty International analyzed these legal issues and stated the organization's position that the ICJ decision could not deprive the Belgian prosecutor of jurisdiction to conduct a criminal investigation in the Sabra and Shatila case. AMNESTY INT'L, UNIVERSAL JURISDICTION: BELGIAN COURT HAS JURISDICTION IN SHARON CASE TO INVESTIGATE 1982 SABRA AND CHATILA KILLINGS (2002).

124. Court Diary: Statement by the lawyers of the victims of Sabra and Shatila on the decision of the Court of Appeals in Brussels, 26 June 2002, *supra* note 29.

125. Walleyn, *The Sabra and Shatila Massacre*, *supra* note 11, at 61.

federal prosecutor in cases lacking any nexus with Belgium. Both bills were negotiated with the significant involvement of human rights NGOs.[126]

Belgian civil society played a critical role in the drafting and passage of the original laws, and again with the 2003 Interpretive Law and amended Law. In the wake of the ICJ *Yerodia* decision, Montserrat Carreras, Amnesty International staff in the Francophone Belgian section responsible for government relations, spearheaded an NGO Platform. Carreras and others organized a colloquium in March 2002 under the auspices of the Belgian Ministry of Foreign Affairs and the Coalition for the International Criminal Court. Out of this colloquium came the Brussels Principles Against Impunity and for International Justice.[127] The Principles were, in effect, a trial run for the interpretive law.

The Platform galvanized around saving the Law. Geraldine Mattioli represented HRW in the Platform; she explained that they "came together as a group knowing that each of us had stronger interest in certain cases, and we would work together to ensure that the Law went forward."[128] The Platform coordinated relations with a core group of parliamentarians from all the main political groups "who could be called upon and would be ready to move forward with the Law."[129] They also met with opponents of the Law to whom, according to Michael Verhaeghe, Israel was providing legal advice.[130] The members of the NGO Platform immersed themselves in the process at a technical level, discussing the amendments, language, and consequences of various proposals. Mattioli recalled the extraordinary level of access and influence that they developed with parliamentarians.

> It seemed crazy to me, because I was young and I didn't think democracies worked in that way. I was thrown into the lobbying world and I had no idea. In some of the debates in the Chamber, . . . I was just sitting in the back of the room and someone would propose an amendment. Karine Lalieux was there sitting in the front and she would call me and ask me, "How does that sound?" Because it turned so technical. But the new Law is a *casse-tête*

---

126. *Id.* at 62; Verhaeghe, *The Political Funeral Procession*, *supra* note 39, at 140.

127. Preamble, *available at:* http://www.iccnow.org/documents/BrusselsPrinciples6Nov02.pdf, at 2. Inspired by the Princeton Principles on Universal Jurisdiction (2001), *available at* http://lapa.princeton.edu/hosteddocs/unive_jur.pdf, the Colloquium resulted in the creation of the Brussels Group for International Justice.

128. Interview with Human Rights Watch counsel, Geraldine Mattioli, Brussels, March 14, 2007.

129. *Id.*

130. Verhaeghe, *Political Funeral Procession*, *supra* note 39, at 140.

(headache). It's really complicated; it was so intensely negotiated that it became some kind of monstrous result.[131]

An advisory opinion from the Council of State found both bills legally solid, and the government was favorably disposed. But, outside pressure—specifically from the United States and Israel—had been growing. In early January 2003, the Belgian newspaper *La Libre Belgique* reported that the United States was pressuring the Belgian government, including the Justice Commission that was reviewing the laws.[132] (During this period the Bush Administration was actively lobbying against the ICC, fearing it would become a forum for politically motivated prosecutions against U.S. soldiers and officials). Senator Clothilde Nyssens (Social Christian Party) recalled the intense political pressure in the period when the interpretive law was being discussed.

> I think that [Prime Minister] Verhofstadt had to abandon [his support of the main important points of this law] quickly at a certain moment, only because the Americans [said]: "If you don't, there will be negative effects towards Belgium. You have to listen to us." That was the end of the story. I heard there were conversations with government about cutting transports through the Antwerp port—economic reaction. I am sure that our discussion here, which was very, very interesting for human rights lawyers, at a certain point was abandoned only for economic reasons.
>
> The American embassy, the Consul, came here, very naïve, very ingenious. He gave me a bottle of whiskey I think. In Belgium, that just isn't done. In America, it's normal to do that, to come and visit Parliament, to lobby. For Belgium, it doesn't work like this. I remember, I told a journalist only to have a laugh, and he wrote about it. And so, there was a reaction. It was a mistake of the American embassy.... Anyway, the government took their [position], and Parliament had nothing to say anymore. I think it was decided with diplomatic relations—that was my impression.[133]

---

131. Mattioli interview, *supra* note 128.

132. *La Libre Belgique* newspaper reported that U.S. Attorney General John Ashcroft expressed "concern" in talks with Belgian Justice Minister Marc Verwilghen on January 6 over the "universal competence" law. *U.S. presses Belgium over law on pursuing foreigners: report*, AGENCE FRANCE-PRESSE, Jan. 11, 2003; *see also Belgian justice minister denies U.S. pressure regarding genocide law*, BBC MONITORING, Jan. 13, 2003.

133. Interview with Senator Clothilde Nyssens, Brussels, March 13, 2007. *See also* Vandermeersch, *supra* note 29, at n. 9. ("During the parliamentary debates, reference was made several times to the substantial deterioration of relations with the United States and namely to the latter's threat to remove the headquarters of NATO from Brussels" (*citing Report of the Justice Commission of the Chamber of Representatives, Documents parlementaires, Chambre*, S.E. 2003, doc. 51/0103/003, at 14, 27, 28, 30 and 50).)

Victory, short-lived—where politics and law intersect

All in all, there had been an extraordinary level of debate over procedural technicalities of international law without rejecting the application of international law altogether. On January 29, 2003, the Justice Commission of the Belgian Senate adopted the two proposed bills.

And then, on February 12, 2003 in a remarkable decision that "completely reversed the situation,"[134] the Supreme Court ruled that the Sabra and Shatila case could proceed. Rejecting the reasoning of the Court of Appeals and the prosecutor with respect to trial *in absentia*,[135] the Court held that the Law encompassed no restrictions on the exercise of universal jurisdiction, and that prosecution does not require the presence of the accused on Belgian soil. Further, the Court held that the rules of the general Code of Criminal Procedure (i.e., Article 12) did not apply to the universal jurisdiction statute because of its specific nature. However, the Court also ruled that customary international law grants current heads of states and governments immunity, and that no international convention provides for an exception to that principle in prosecution before national courts for international crimes. As Sharon was prime minister when the complaint was lodged and still incumbent, the Supreme Court declared his prosecution inadmissible for so long as he remained head of state. However, the decision enabled the prosecution to proceed against Yaron and other Israelis and Lebanese involved.[136]

Israel reacted to the Supreme Court decision by recalling its ambassador for almost three months. Israeli Foreign Minister Benjamin

---

134. "It took some time before the political world grasped the consequences of this ruling, which completely reversed the situation." Verhaeghe, *Political Funeral Procession*, supra note 39, at 141.

135. In January 2003, Jean du Jardin, General Prosecutor (*Procureur Général près de la cour de cassation*) submitted his opinion to the Supreme Court that it uphold the June 2002 Appeals Court decision on the ground that universal jurisdiction *in absentia* is contrary to international customary law, and that the legislative intent was not to go beyond the international obligation of *aut dedere aut judicare*. He argued that "a trial *in absentia* would be an imperfect tool that would eventuate in a virtual rather than a real judicial process.... [It] would not further the effective prosecution of these crimes, and would do more harm than good to the Law's objective ... [and it] would raise questions as to [the trial's] legality, as it might be a violation of the defendant's right to a fair trial." Walleyn, *The Sabra and Shatila Massacre*, supra note 11, at 63. To this, the Plaintiffs' attorneys responded that Belgian law permitted both investigation and trial *in absentia*, although Walleyn pointed out that, "for serious crimes, such trials are unusual, and generally the prosecution seeks arrest and extradition of the accused before starting the trial, in order to avoid a second procedure after arrest occurs." *Id.* at n. 19.

136. Verhaeghe, *Political Funeral Procession*, supra note 39, at 141; Walleyn, *The Sabra and Shatila Massacre*, supra note 11, at 63–64. *See also* Antonio Cassese, *The Belgian Court of Cassation v. the International Court of Justice: the* Sharon and Others *Case*, 1 J. OF INT'L CRIM. JUST. 437 (2003).

Netanyahu called it a "blood libel."[137] The decision also opened the floodgates for new complaints. As Luc Walleyn put it, "a string of mostly frivolous complaints followed, ... making the situation ... more ridiculous in the eyes of the public."[138] On March 18, 2003, as the U.S. was preparing to invade Iraq, a group of Iraqi survivors of the U.S. bombing of the al-Ameri (Baghdad) bomb shelter in the first Gulf War lodged a complaint against former president George H.W. Bush. Although this "complaint" was no more than a series of letters sent to the federal prosecutor, it was treated by the media and by the U.S. and Belgian officials as a serious case.

The U.S. joined Israel's vehement opposition to the Belgian Law. U.S. Congressman Gary Ackerman (D–N.Y.) introduced the Universal Jurisdiction Rejection Act of 2003 (H.R. 2050) "to prohibit cooperation with or assistance to any investigation or prosecution under a universal jurisdiction statute."[139] The bill made no secret of being a response to Belgium's "Anti–Atrocity Law of 1993/1999," describing at length the procedure of the statute's roller-coaster ride through the courts there.

Just days before the national election (which was on May 18), Jan Fermon, a Belgian attorney who had been involved with the Rwanda cases and was running for parliament representing the far-left Resist party,[140] filed a complaint against U.S. General Tommy Franks for crimes against humanity on behalf of a group of Iraqi and Jordanian plaintiffs. But, a month earlier on April 5, 2003—just before the close of the parliamentary session, and with the government fairly split over the reform of the Law—new amendments were passed that allowed the government to transfer a case to another country if that country can prosecute war crimes, crimes against humanity and crimes of genocide, and if they can grant a fair trial. The amendments also provided that investigation could be initiated only by the federal prosecutor (and not by *parties civiles*). Without waiting for the prosecutor's decision, the government referred the case to the United States.[141] Nevertheless, the U.S. continued to react heatedly to the Law.

---

137. Laura King, *Israel Denounces Belgian Ruling*, L.A. TIMES, Feb. 14, 2003, at A–4, *available at* http://articles.latimes.com/2003/feb/14/world/fg-sharon14.

138. Walleyn, *The Sabra and Shatila Massacre, supra* note 11, at 66.

139. H.R. 2050, 101st Cong. (2003). Notably, it stated: "Implicit within the very concept of universal jurisdiction is a threat to the sovereignty of the United States." *Id*. at 7. Rep. Ackerman introduced the bill on May 9, 2003, following a trip to Israel that included a meeting with Prime Minister Sharon. *See* Prime Minister Ariel Sharon meeting with U.S Congressman Gary Ackerman at the PM's office in Jerusalem, *available at* http://www.pmo.gov.il/PMOEng/Archive/Current+Events/2003/02/Speeches7089.htm. The bill didn't get further than the House Committee on International Relations.

140. *War Crimes Complaint Targets U.S.*, CBS NEWS, May 15, 2003, *available at* http://www.cbsnews.com/stories/2003/05/14/iraq/main553783.shtml.

141. The provision was heavily criticized as "unacceptable interference of the executive in judicial affairs," particularly by the Council of State. Verhaeghe, *Political Funeral*

In that same period, there was a campaign of op-eds in newspapers, rumors that some U.S. companies would cancel investments, and even positions taken by union leaders against universal jurisdiction as a threat to the Belgian economy.[142]

On June 10, 2003, despite all the political pressure from Israel and the U.S., the Brussels Court of Appeals on remand rejected the defense's other arguments, and investigating judge Patrick Collignon announced he would re-open the investigation. But two days later, at a press conference following the NATO defense ministers meeting in Brussels, U.S. Defense Secretary Donald Rumsfeld threatened that American officials might stop attending NATO meetings in Belgium "because of a law that allows 'spurious' suits accusing American leaders of war crimes. Rumsfeld said the United States would withhold any further funding for a new NATO headquarters building until the matter is resolved."[143]

Within a month, the Belgian political parties negotiating a new government coalition agreed to withdraw the Law. The final version of the Law adopted August 5, 2003[144] annulled the 1993/1999 universal jurisdiction statute. As amended, it could more accurately be called an international crimes law, with certain limited possibilities for "universal"/extraterritorial jurisdiction. Among its provisions: (1) Belgian authorities have extraterritorial ("universal") jurisdiction over a narrow set of crimes (genocide, crimes against humanity, and war crimes) where required by treaty or customary international law; and (2) the accused or the victim is a Belgian national or resident for at least three years (determined from the date proceedings commence for the defendant, and by the date of the crime for the victim). (3) Where the victim alone has the requisite links to Belgium, only the federal prosecutor may initiate the case, even in *absentia*. He is not required to involve an investigating

---

Procession, supra note 39, at 142–143; Walleyn, *The Sabra and Shatila Massacre, supra* note 11, at 65. Dubbed "the Bush clause," it was aimed at dispensing of the case against the senior Bush. Despite pressure from Israel, Parliament adopted the view that the Bush clause could only be applied to cases lodged after the entry into force of the Rome Statute of the ICC, i.e., after July 1, 2002, which would not include the Sabra and Shatila case. Verhaeghe, *Id.* at 142.

142. E-mail from Luc Walleyn, to author (Sept. 28, 2008) (on file with author).

143. Jim Garamone, *Belgian Law May Force U.S. to Stop Attending NATO Meetings*, AM. FORCES PRESS SERV., June 12, 2003, *available at* http://www.defenselink.mil/news/Jun 2003/n06122003_200306125.html; Ian Black & Ewen MacAskill, *U.S. Threatens NATO Boycott over Belgium War Crimes Law*, THE GUARDIAN, June 13, 2003, *available at* http://www.guardian.co.uk/world/2003/jun/13/nato.warcrimes.

144. Loi relative aux violations graves du droit humanitaire, Aug. 5, 2003, M.B., Aug. 7, 2003, *translated as* Belgium's Amendment to the Law of June 15, 1993 (As Amended By the Law of February 10, 1999 and April 23, 2003) Concerning the Punishment of Grave Breaches of Humanitarian Law (Aug. 7, 2003), 42 I.L.M. 1258 (2003).

judge if there was no nexus to Belgium, and his decision may not be appealed. Further, the *constitution partie civile* is eliminated for these crimes. (4) The August 2003 Law further recognized functional immunity for heads of state and incumbent ministers, consistent with the ICJ *Arrest Warrant* judgment.

HRW counsel Geraldine Mattioli said that one of the biggest consequences of the 2003 amendments was the restriction of *parties civiles* for international crimes. "It's so contrary to civil law culture; it's amazing that it could have led to this kind of change. The Ligue des Droits de l'Homme filed a complaint before the Constitutional Court for discrimination, arguing: 'someone who is the victim of rape in the street in Belgium can be a *partie civile* for that crime, but someone who is gangraped in Rwanda cannot, because it's an international crime.' "

The Supreme Court ruled on September 24, 2003 that, as Belgium no longer had universal jurisdiction, all pending cases not meeting one or more of the new criteria must be dismissed. The Court held that cases in which at least one initial plaintiff was a Belgian citizen could proceed. Thus, the Sabra and Shatila case was dismissed. "Ironically," wrote Luc Walleyn,

> this ruling came from the very same chamber that had confirmed less than [seven] months earlier, on February 12, 2003, that prosecution could begin against Amos Yaron and other Israelis and Lebanese involved in the commission of these crimes.... Between rendering these two contrary decisions ... Belgium adopted two new laws and endured seven months of diplomatic incidents, economic threats, provocative complaints, and political debate associated with the country's universal jurisdiction legislation.[145]

Damien Vandermeersch later remarked, "In the absence of filtering safeguards to ascertain that those complaints were a priori founded and not frivolous, certain alleged victims gave the appearance of availing themselves of Belgian justice by abusing procedures to pursue political objectives that did not include justice."[146] Consider that, in legal terms, a "frivolous" filing is one that is manifestly unfounded or improperly prepared and can draw penalties beyond the mere dismissal of the case, though it is worth noting that in Belgium, attorneys are rarely sanctioned for legal filings. (What's more, though fines may be levied, it is hard to collect if the client is living abroad.)

There is a problem when frivolous becomes a synonym for politically-motivated. "Politically-motivated" is often used in the pejorative sense

---

145. Walleyn, *The Sabra and Shatila Massacre, supra* note 11, at 54.

146. Vandermeersch, *supra* note 29, at 410. For example, several plaintiffs declared that they were filing the complaint against Bush, Sr. preventively, in light of the build-up to the new war in Iraq. *Id.* at n. 35.

to mean ideological, biased, infused with ulterior motives. But, it can also mean simply that there exists a particular objective in filing the case larger than the specific facts or issues at hand, generally one that aims at legal or social reform (or justice). This is a common dilemma with impact litigation and one might ask, are there any universal jurisdiction cases that would not provoke the label "politically motivated"? These cases are, after all, only about international crimes. War crimes, crimes against humanity, and genocide almost by definition occur within the political realm.

Political cases themselves can be intended in various ways. One is as a tool against the Law itself, to undermine it, to make it look ridiculous. Another is to use the Law as a vehicle for direct action, to demonstrate a point—often political rather than legal. A third is to obtain justice for victims of international crimes when other options are closed to them. Cases were filed in Belgium for all three reasons. The Belgian Law, like any law, can be used ideologically. But like any legal tool, there are ways to discern when a case filed is frivolous, legally speaking, and deserves to be dismissed on legal grounds; and when it is ideological but carefully documented, with a firm basis in the law and, presumably, admissible.

Indeed, the 1993/1999 Law contained measures that under normal circumstances—i.e., absent the political stakes or where politics could be more reasonably managed—should have filtered out complaints (and generally did) that lacked a legal basis or sufficient evidence on which to proceed. One of these procedures, however weak, was the requirement that a complaint be confirmed by the court (i.e., *chambre des mises en accusation,* or indictment chamber).

The April 2003 amendments fortified these procedures in the sense that, in a complaint filed *in absentia*, only the prosecutor could initiate the investigation and prosecution (the *partie civiles* action having been eliminated for international crimes), and he/she had to do so within one month. The plaintiff could then appeal a negative decision to the *chambre des mises en accusation*. But, it was not enough for the U.S. after the complaint against Tommy Franks. Thus, the amendment of August 5, 2003 dropped the one month provision and the possibility of appeal and put the decision whether or not to go forward with the case in the sole hands of the prosecutor. The Law was further changed in 2006, and now, at the prosecutor's request, an independent judge in the indictment chamber holds this power. The victim/plaintiffs are excluded from the hearing.

Many sorely regret the loss of Belgium's exceptional universal jurisdiction statute (many more surely than those who grieve the denial of judicial recourse for the victims of Sabra and Shatila). But, it would be a mistake to conclude that the Sabra and Shatila case destroyed Belgium's Law. As Verhaeghe pointed out,

> Contrary to ... popular misunderstanding, Belgium was not swamped by hundreds of complaints. Apart from the dozen or so well known Rwandan cases, of which two have actually led to convictions, only 21 other complaints were actually introduced into the Belgian system. Considering the over one thousand complaints registered so far with the Office of the Prosecutor of the ICC, I am even surprised that the Belgian law, the possibilities of which were widely known among human rights activists, did not attract more complaints than it actually did. A possible explanation for this is that that a serious complaint with an investigating magistrate entails serious preparatory work and also forces the victims filing the complaint to relive their horrible experiences. Whatever the circumstances, I resent the idea, often portrayed in some media, that victims of serious international crimes file their complaints lightly.[147]

Rather, according to the legal team, the failure of the Law must be understood as a combination of negative forces that played each upon the other.[148] These include the panicked reaction of top Belgian politicians; the lack of respect for the rules developed in the statute, particularly by the investigating judge, and later with the April 2003 amendment;[149] definite abuses of the process in filing (which could have been mitigated had the Law been applied, i.e., had the prosecutor simply dismissed those complaints that were facially unsubstantiated); the actual or deliberate lack of understanding of the Belgian legal process by governments such as the U.S.—for example that "complaint" does not mean "indictment;"[150] and also, the effect of the ridicule to which the

---

147. Verhaeghe, *Political Funeral Procession*, *supra* note 39, at 144–145.

148. These points are developed by Verhaeghe, *id.* at 145–147.

149. This version of the statute contained rules allowing dismissal of a complaint by the federal prosecutor, e.g., if it failed to demonstrate the necessity of Belgium as the solicited forum (comparable to the *forum non conveniens* doctrine in the U.S.). "The application of these rules would indeed have entailed a judicial process, including the possibility of appeals, but they were at least not corrupted by fundamental legal shortcomings, as in the Bush clause. If the Belgian government had maintained its position on the separation of powers and the independence of the judiciary, combined with sufficient faith in the judiciary, it would have at least allowed the rules to be tested in practice." *Id.* at 145.

150. "Belgium did not even attempt to explain the precise nature of a complaint before an investigative judge.... The complaint in fact retains its private character, as the expression of the plaintiff's position, until the judge formally issues warrants for the arrest of suspects or formal notices of suspicion. Until this stage, a complaint under the UJ Statute did not differ in any fundamental way from a writ of summons filed under the Alien Torts Claims Act in the U.S." *Id.*

statute fell prey, which caused Belgian public opinion to shift from sympathy for universal jurisdiction to viewing it

> as a useless and even economically dangerous *folie*. The most devastating effect of a campaign of ridicule is not so much the content of the ridicule as the lack of space it leaves for real debate on the issue. Ridicule contaminated the very phrase universal jurisdiction to such an extent that a calm discussion of its principles became next to impossible in April, May, and June of 2003.[151]

Another factor contributed to the statute's demise; as Michael Verhaeghe expressed it: "Belgium stood alone."[152] Amnesty International's Carrerras described her disappointment "because our section didn't receive support from other sections. We felt very much that Belgium was isolated in taking the position they did, at the level of the E.U. and at the level of Amnesty International." Verhaeghe concurs: "None of its European partners, who had stood side by side in the battle for the ICC, even attempted to come to Belgium's rescue."[153]

Conclusions

Parliamentarians and human rights activists involved in drafting and amending the original statute seem to have been caught off guard by both its magnetizing appeal as well as the rancor against Belgium for its apparent hubris in taking on the world's crimes. Given the historic moment in which the story unfolded, they can be forgiven if they were focused on the righteous role that Belgium could play in deterring impunity. Indeed, Verhaeghe argues:

> Universal jurisdiction as such is not a ridiculous idea. It is the result of many years of legal evolution, propelled by a history of countless atrocities and crimes against humanity. A state exercising universal jurisdiction in a genuine manner, i.e., with the purpose of contributing to the international legal order and not of shielding national interests, is not arrogant. It does not arrogate to itself a jurisdiction to which it is not entitled, but merely tries to offer solutions to impunity. In this sense, one can say that universal jurisdiction is not a formula for *gaining* jurisdiction, but one for placing the national legal order *at the service* of the international community.[154]

Should we conclude, then, that universal jurisdiction can only succeed where it is accompanied by the political will to take on the service role Verhaeghe describes, despite the risks? One might think that other

---

151. *Id.* at 146.
152. *Id.* at 147.
153. *Id.*
154. *Id.* at 146.

countries would be chastened in the wake of Belgium's experience. To the contrary, prosecution for international law crimes under universal jurisdiction seems to be gathering steam.[155] Armed with statutes that harmonize their domestic criminal law with the Rome Treaty of the ICC, countries like Spain,[156] Germany, France, and the U.K. have continued to prosecute international crimes under universal jurisdiction (as has Belgium).

A legal action was filed in October 2008 in Spain, for example, against a group of Israeli officials, including Ariel Sharon, former Shabak head Avi Dichter, former Air Force commander Dan Halutz, and former commander of the Southern Brigade Doron Almog, for war crimes for ordering the army to shell a civilian residential building in Gaza 2002 in order to assassinate Saleh Shihada, leader of the al-Qassam Brigades. The Israeli Foreign Ministry has reportedly advised the officials not to travel to Spain. Based on the Gaza incident, among others, several years ago, Israel snuck Halutz out of the U.K. after he was informed of a warrant to arrest him. In 2005, Almog also flew to the U.K. and when he too was informed upon landing of an arrest warrant, he left the country without even disembarking from the plane.[157]

* * *

The political will to prosecute seems to be present when the cases involve rogue leaders from Chad, Uganda, Rwanda, the Democratic Republic of the Congo, the Sudan, or Guatemala, but not where the perpetrators of international crimes come from the global "north" and its democratic allies. There is no doubt that universal jurisdiction is infinitely more difficult and potentially impracticable when the defendants—and their governments—are still in power, not to mention presumptively democratic. This is, in part, because the legal systems of these countries are presumed to be "able" to prosecute those who perpetrate violations of international law. Seen in this light, universal jurisdiction appears to be a tool reserved to check the impunity of people of color, in countries of relative economic and political isolation. Colonialist overtones are hard to ignore.

Should we conclude then that universal jurisdiction is a legal tool that serves not the rights to an effective remedy, to equality before the

---

155. *Political Immunity: Pulling back the blanket,* THE ECONOMIST, July 10, 2008, *available at*: http://www.economist.com/world/international/displaystory.cfm?story_id=11707994.

156. For sources and discussion of the procedural application of these and other countries' laws, *see* HRW, UJ IN EUROPE, *supra* note 99.

157. Saed Bannoura, *Israel holding talks with Spain in an attempt to stop arrest warrants against senior officials,* INTERNATIONAL MIDDLE EAST MEDIA CENTER, Oct. 5, 2008, *available at* http://www.imemc.org/article/57212.

law, and non-discrimination in access to justice, but political and legal expediency, and power differentials? If so, what happens to the victims in the legal process? What process is available to stateless persons and others who, through no fault of their own, have no judicial system through which they may access their rights?

* * *

There is a fundamental paradox with these cases. Criminal law focuses on individual responsibility; international law focuses on state responsibility. International criminal law falls in a space between the two. War crimes, crimes against humanity and genocide are individual crimes, perpetrated by individuals—in the Sabra and Shatila case brought not against Israel or Lebanon or the Israeli or Lebanese people, but against individuals. These crimes occur and are prosecuted in the context of the public order. Yet, the very legal doctrines that establish individual responsibility do so through principles that are explicitly about larger processes—such as command responsibility, which implicates the hierarchy of a military; genocide, which implicates the motive to destroy a group; crimes against humanity, which require proof of a nexus to armed conflict or a "widespread or systematic attack" and targeting of a "civilian population"; and war crimes, which require a nexus with an armed conflict.

Chibli Mallat reflected on the importance of the careful choice of opponents—the "leitmotiv" for the plaintiffs' attorneys was that the Sabra and Shatila case was against individuals, not against societies or nation-states.[158] Still, Mallat has noted, the question of collective responsibility of the state and the government always becomes a factor in these circumstances.

> In all these large-scale massacres, the killers use the power of the state at their disposal to commit and amplify their crime. [R]ecall that the Israeli army encircled the camps for two days and three nights to allow the killers to do their sinister job.... Is there no responsibility, then, for the Israeli Ministry of Defense, for the Israeli army, in addition to the rounding up of the Palestinians after the massacres ... by the Israeli army, with so many ending up as disappeared ... ?[159]

While international law focuses on state responsibility, Mallat believes that the most difficult issue for international criminal law is the personalization of criminal responsibility. How much is the society itself responsible for what occurred? Isn't a blanket amnesty such as the one

---

158. CHIBLI MALLAT, *Judicial Redress in Palestine*, in PRESIDENTIAL TALK/PROPOS PRÉSIDENTIELS 404, 410 (2007), *available at* http://www.mallatforpresident.com/books/prestalk.php.

159. *Id.* at 410.

Lebanon passed a collective measure intended to salve a political wound so that society as a whole can "move on"? After 400,000 Israelis demanded that their government respond to the events of September 16–18, 2001, wasn't the Kahan Commission, in a sense, just that?

What happened in Belgium may well have been inevitable. Even the ICJ's immunity decision in *Yerodia* was probably inevitable. After that, it was only a matter of time before a case came along that was meritorious enough to go forward through the threshold procedural stages, but sufficiently "radioactive" to provoke oppositional political intervention. It would have been advantageous had there been a few more successful prosecutions before the Sabra and Shatila case, preferably against significant perpetrators like Pinochet, for example. But the problems of presence and immunity will always favor prosecution of "smaller fish," such as refugees, while the intellectual authors of serious crimes remain diplomatically—and politically—protected.

The legal questions in these cases are intrinsically bound to political issues. This is so not only because oppositional political intervention is inevitable, but also because the political will is required for these cases to go forward, let alone succeed. At every step—investigation, extradition, prosecution—universal jurisdiction requires an investment of political and judicial resources. At the most basic level, if a state has not provided for these aspects of implementation and enforcement, then allocation becomes a matter of political good will.[160] In Belgium, perhaps surprisingly, the Sabra and Shatila case was in many ways fast tracked, indicating there were measures of political will. Yet, Israelis and supporters of Israel viewed that will as an expression of anti-semitism, a form of collective, as opposed to individual prosecution. Where serious crimes are perpetuated from a presumptively democratic state, this issue of collective responsibility becomes a political issue that cannot be ignored.

But, such a value is fairly stymied where the victims are politically disenfranchised, or the object of racial or ethnic discrimination. Stateless persons, especially Palestinians, caught between hostile and dysfunctional host governments, are fully dependent on the political will and the courage of third parties—the most powerful of which are of course states—to defend their rights in justice.

---

160. Reydams, *Universal Criminal Jurisdiction*, supra note 46, at 197.

9

Arresting Juxtapositions: The *Story of Roper v. Simmons*

Alison J. Nathan[*]

Introduction

Among those in the overflow crowd that filled the Supreme Court on October 13, 2004 who were there to hear the oral argument in *Roper v. Simmons*[1] was Xiao Yang, the president and chief justice of the Supreme People's Court of China, and a delegation of Chinese judges.[2] The Chinese judges' presence for the argument was significant: in *Roper*, the Court ultimately would conclude that executing juvenile offenders violates the U.S. Constitution's prohibition against "cruel and unusual punishment"[3]—a decision similar to that the Chinese legal system already had reached.[4] Chief Justice Rehnquist noted the delegation's visit at the beginning of the Court session that morning. Seth Waxman, the former Clinton Administration Solicitor General and now partner at the Washington, D.C. law firm of Wilmer Cutler Pickering Hale & Dorr LLP, who was moments away from arguing the case on behalf of death row inmate Christopher Simmons, was intrigued by their presence in the courtroom and took it as a noteworthy and positive sign.[5] As Waxman recalled:

---

[*] I completed research for this Chapter while a Visiting Assistant Professor of Law at Fordham University School of Law and I am thankful to Fordham for its generous support. Margaret Satterthwaite and Danielle Spinelli provided insightful comments and suggestions. I thank Marisa Antos–Fallon and Ellyde Roko for their invaluable research assistance.

   1. 543 U.S. 551 (2005).

   2. Charlie Savage, *Justices Weigh Limit on Death Penalty*, Boston Globe, Oct. 14, 2004, at A2.

   3. U.S. Const. amend. VIII.

   4. *See* Savage, *supra* note 2.

   5. Telephonic interview with Seth P. Waxman, Partner, Wilmer Cutler Pickering Hale & Dorr LLP (Sept. 3, 2007).

We didn't have any idea that the Chinese judicial delegation would be in attendance, and I didn't alter my argument when we learned that they were there, but it was an arresting juxtaposition to be able to stand at the podium and say that essentially all other countries—including China, whom the U.S. has criticized for human rights violations and whose judges were sitting in the Supreme Court observing the case—have disavowed this practice.[6]

On October 12, 2004, the day before the *Roper* oral argument, the Justices were listening to the case of *Jama v. Immigration and Customs Enforcement*.[7] *Jama* considered the question of whether U.S. immigration law required consent from a country before an individual being removed from the United States could be sent there.[8] The INS was seeking to send Keyse Jama to Somalia, the country where he was born, following his commission of a crime.[9] The difficulty was that Somalia could not consent to Mr. Jama's removal to the country, as the U.S. removal law appeared to require, because, as Mr. Jama's lawyer argued to the Court, "Somalia has no functioning government."[10] There is no apparent connection between the argument the Court heard in *Jama* on October 12 and the one it heard the next day in the death penalty case of *Roper*. Nevertheless, Waxman reminded the Court of the *Jama* argument:

> MR. WAXMAN: We have not just a worldwide consensus that represents the better view in Europe. There are 194 countries—
>
> CHIEF JUSTICE REHNQUIST: Well, how does one—how does one determine what is the better view?
>
> MR. WAXMAN: I was—I was referring to the implication that it has often been said that because the European Union thinks something, we should, therefore, presume that the world views it that way. We're now talking about—
>
> CHIEF JUSTICE REHNQUIST: Are you suggesting that we adopt that principle?
>
> MR. WAXMAN: To the contrary. My point is we are not talking about just what a particular European treaty requires.... [T]he eight States ... that have statutes that theoretically permit execution of offenders under [eighteen] are not only alone in this country, they are alone in the world. Every country in the world, including China and Nigeria and Saudi Arabia and the—and the Democratic

---

6. *Id.*
7. 543 U.S. 335 (2005).
8. *Id.* at 337.
9. *Id.*
10. *Id.* at 338; Transcript of Oral Argument at 3, Jama, 543 U.S. 335 (No. 03–674).

Republic of the Congo, every one has agreed formally and legislatively to renounce this punishment, *and the only country besides the United States that has not is Somalia, which as this Court was reminded yesterday, has no organized government.*[11]

Waxman's invocation of the prior day's argument in the *Jama* case and Somalia's lack of functioning government was an indirect reference to the United Nations Convention on the Rights of the Child (CRC), which explicitly and categorically prohibits the execution of any person who committed their crime prior to the age of eighteen.[12] Only two countries in the world have not ratified the CRC—Somalia, because, as Waxman suggested, it has no functioning government, and the United States, at least in part, because several states, including Missouri, where Chris Simmons was sentenced to death, had executed juvenile offenders and steadfastly wished to maintain the power to do so.[13]

The issuance of the Supreme Court decision in *Roper* a little more than four months later eliminated that power. Writing for a five-four majority, Justice Kennedy held that the Eighth Amendment to the U.S. Constitution prohibits the execution of juvenile offenders.[14] In reaching this conclusion, Justice Kennedy's opinion cites an international consensus, as embodied in international law and the laws of foreign countries, firmly opposed to the practice.[15] The reaction to this portion of the *Roper* opinion has been substantial, to say the least.[16] Sitting Justices, legal

---

11. Transcript of Oral Argument at 26–27, Roper, 543 U.S. 551 (No. 03–633) (emphasis added).

12. Convention on the Rights of the Child, art. 37, Nov. 20, 1989, 1577 U.N.T.S. 3.

13. *See* Roper, 543 U.S. at 622 (Scalia, J., dissenting); Office of the U.N. High Comm'r for Human Rights, Status of Ratifications of the Principal Human Rights Treaties (June 9, 2004), *available at* http://www.unhchr.ch/pdf/report.pdf; *see also* Paul Taylor, *Senators Press President Bush to Sign U.N. Children's Rights Treaty*, Wash. Post, Apr. 19, 1991, at A21 (reporting the first Bush administration's concern about the treaty's conflict with existing state death penalty laws).

14. Roper, 543 U.S. at 578.

15. *Id.* at 576–78.

16. *See, e.g.*, Steven G. Calabresi, *The Supreme Court and Foreign Sources of Law: Two Hundred Years of Practice and the Juvenile Death Penalty Decision*, 47 Wm. & Mary L. Rev. 743 (2005) (arguing that although foreign law can be instructive in Fourth and Eighth Amendment interpretation, use of foreign law in other constitutional cases is problematic); Robert J. Delahunty & John Yoo, *Against Foreign Law*, 29 Harv. J.L. & Pub. Pol'y 291 (2005) (arguing that foreign law should not be used to interpret the Constitution because such use violates separation of powers and supremacy clause principles, as well as principles of limited judicial review); Ruth Bader Ginsburg, Assoc. Justice, U.S. Supreme Court, "A Decent Respect to the Opinions of [Human]kind": The Value of a Comparative Perspective in Constitutional Adjudication, Keynote Address Before the Ninety–Ninth Annual Meeting of the American Society of International Law (Apr. 1, 2005), *in* 99 Am. Soc'y Int'l L. Proc. 351, 355 (2005) (" 'U.S. jurists honor the framers' intent 'to create a more perfect Union,' I believe, if they read our Constitution as belonging to a global

scholars, and the media have spilled oceans of ink on the implications of the Court's use of foreign and international law in this opinion.[17] Missing from these discussions, however, is an examination of how Simmons' lawyers used international and foreign law in their Supreme Court litigation strategy. The omission is surprising because Justice Kennedy's invocation of international and foreign law in the *Roper* opinion tracks precisely the litigants' advocacy in their briefings to the Supreme Court. A full understanding of the implication of the *Roper* Court's use of foreign and international law, then, is advanced by considering the litigators' strategic deployment of it.

In this regard, these two vignettes—the visit from the Chinese delegation on the day of the *Roper* oral argument and the indirect reference to the CRC in that argument—capture and symbolize much about the state of international human rights advocacy before the U.S. Supreme Court at this historical moment. It is a story of cautious engagement, legal incrementalism, and the critical importance of human rights advocacy beyond the courtroom. And while the *Roper* Supreme Court strategy regarding international human rights law very much embodied caution and gradualism, its effectiveness holds promise and lessons for future advancement.

Background

Case Background

Trial

On September 10, 1993, seventeen-year-old Chris Simmons was arrested at his school, Fox Senior High, in Arnold, Missouri, for the murder of Mrs. Shirley Cook.[18] At approximately 2:00 a.m. the night

---

twenty-first century."); *see also* Roper, 543 U.S. at 624 (Scalia, J., dissenting) ("[T]he basic premise of the Court's argument—that American law should conform to the laws of the rest of the world—ought to be rejected out of hand."); Sarah H. Cleveland, *Is There Room for the World in Our Courts?*, WASH. POST, Mar. 20, 2005, at B4 (arguing that critics of the Court's use of international law in *Roper* fail to consider that ignoring international law impedes the United States' ability to benefit from it); Thomas P. Kilgannon, *Does the Constitution Matter?*, WASH. TIMES, Mar. 12, 2005, at A15 (criticizing the Court for being more willing to cite international treaties than the Constitution or the Federalist Papers).

17. In some discussions of *Roper*, commentators conflate foreign and international law into a single category. Throughout this Chapter, I will differentiate between foreign law, i.e., the domestic laws of other countries, and international law, i.e., the law binding on nations as a matter of treaty ratification or customary law. As discussed below, in finding an "international consensus" against the execution of juveniles, the U.S. Supreme Court in *Roper* considered both foreign and international law sources.

18. Petitioner's Statement, Brief, and Argument at 15, State *ex rel.* Simmons v. Roper, 112 S.W.3d 397 (Mo. 2003) (No. SC 84454).

before his arrest, Simmons and a fifteen-year-old friend, Charles Benjamin, had broken into Mrs. Cook's home with the pre-meditated intent to commit burglary and murder.[19] After the commotion in her home awakened Mrs. Cook, Simmons and Benjamin restrained her and used duct tape to bind her hands and cover her eyes and mouth.[20] The two forced her to leave her home in a van before leading her on foot to a railroad bridge over the Meramec River.[21] Using electrical wire, they re-bound her hands and tied her feet.[22] Upon covering her entire face with duct tape, they threw her over the bridge and into the river.[23] After her body was discovered, the coroner concluded that drowning was the immediate cause of Mrs. Cook's death.[24]

The charges against Simmons and arrest for this heinous and inexplicable murder were surprising because, although Simmons was failing badly at Fox High and had serious disciplinary problems there,[25] he had no previous criminal record.[26] Nevertheless, there was no doubt of Simmons' involvement. Within two hours after his arrest, believing it would lead to leniency in charges and potential sentence, Simmons waived his right to counsel, confessed to the murder, and agreed to perform a re-enactment of the crime, which the police videotaped.[27] With this evidence, the state of Missouri charged Simmons with burglary, kidnapping, stealing, and murder in the first degree.[28]

Approximately nine months later, and after his eighteenth birthday, Simmons was tried as an adult.[29] During the guilt phase of his trial,[30] the state presented Simmons' confession, the videotaped re-enactment, and

---

19. *Roper*, 543 U.S. at 556.

20. *Id.*

21. *Id.* at 556–57.

22. *Id.* at 557.

23. *Id.*

24. *Id.*

25. Petition for Commutation of, or Reprieve of, a Sentence of Death before the Governor of Missouri, Honorable Bob Holden at 11, *available at* http://www.internationaljusticeproject.org/pdfs/CSimmons-clemency.pdf.

26. Roper, 543 U.S. at 558.

27. *Id.* at 557.

28. *Id.*

29. Petitioner's Statement, Brief, and Argument, *supra* note 18, at 15; Roper, 543 U.S. at 557.

30. In *Gregg v. Georgia*, the Supreme Court found that, because evidence presented in the sentencing phase of a capital trial could be irrelevant and prejudicial to a jury's guilt determination, the jury should not consider sentencing evidence until a guilty verdict is reached. 428 U.S. 153, 190–91 (1976). As a result, state capital punishment statutes require bifurcated guilty and penalty proceedings. WAYNE R. LaFAVE, JEROLD H. ISRAEL, & NANCY J. KING, CRIMINAL PROCEDURE § 26.1(b) (2d ed. 2004).

testimony regarding Simmons' pre-meditation of the murder.[31] Simmons' counsel presented no witnesses in defense.[32] Following the jury's return of a guilty verdict on the murder charge, the trial moved to the penalty phase, in which the state was seeking the death penalty.[33] In support of death, the state called Mrs. Cook's husband, daughter, and two sisters to testify as to how their lives had been devastated by the murder.[34] Among the aggravating factors relied upon by the state was the claim that the crime "involved depravity of mind and was outrageously and wantonly vile, horrible, and inhuman."[35] Simmons' defense counsel argued that there were several important mitigating factors, including Simmons' lack of criminal record, his ability to form close relationships, his capacity to show love, and his willingness to care for his younger siblings. This mitigating testimony was presented by Simmons' mother, father, two younger half brothers, a neighbor, and a friend.[36]

Then, during closing argument of the penalty phase, Simmons' defense counsel honed in on the potentially mitigating significance of Simmons' youth, arguing that, based on their lack of responsibility, children of Simmons' age could not drink alcohol, serve on juries, or see certain adult-themed movies.[37] The state's rebuttal to this contention was to argue the opposite should be inferred from Simmons' young age at the time of the offense: "Age, he says. Think about age. Seventeen years old. Isn't that scary? Doesn't that scare you? Mitigating? Quite the contrary I submit. Quite the contrary."[38] The jury sentenced Simmons to death. The final order of conviction and death sentence was entered by the presiding trial court on August 19, 1994.[39]

Appeals and Post–Conviction

Following his conviction, Simmons, represented by an appointed public defender, pursued available avenues of relief in state court, including a direct appeal and a petition for state post-conviction relief.[40] The Missouri Supreme Court was unmoved, and by the fall of 1997, all options in state court had been exhausted and the U.S. Supreme Court

---

31. *Roper*, 543 U.S. at 557.
32. *Id.*
33. *Id.*
34. *Id.* at 558.
35. *Id.* at 557.
36. *Id.* at 558.
37. *Id.*
38. *Id.*
39. Petitioner's Statement, Brief, and Argument, *supra* note 18, at 15.
40. *Roper*, 543 U.S. at 559.

had denied discretionary review.[41] Seemingly, the next and last avenue of recourse for Simmons would be to pursue his claims in federal court pursuant to 28 U.S.C. § 2255, the federal habeas corpus statute. In seeking federal habeas relief, Simmons was represented by newly appointed counsel, Jennifer Herndon, a defense attorney with experience in capital litigation.[42] In Simmons' federal habeas petition filed with the Federal District Court for the Eastern District of Missouri, Herndon sought relief on multiple grounds, including challenges to the voluntariness of Simmons' confession, challenges to the victim impact testimony that the prosecution had presented at his trial, and challenges to aspects of the prosecutor's closing argument.[43] The federal district court denied relief on all grounds,[44] a ruling that was affirmed by the Eighth Circuit Court of Appeals in early 2001.[45] Soon after the U.S. Supreme Court again denied discretionary review on October 1, 2001, the state of Missouri set an execution date for June 5, 2002.[46]

In a last-ditch effort to save Chris Simmons from execution, Herndon filed a new habeas petition in Missouri state court raising an argument that had minimal chance of success in light of the existing state of the law.[47] Herndon argued for the first time that Simmons could not constitutionally be executed because he was under eighteen years old at the time he committed his offense.[48] The argument relied in part on a case that was then pending before the U.S. Supreme Court called *Atkins v. Virginia*,[49] in which the Court was considering the question of whether it was constitutional to execute people with mental retardation.[50] Eight days before he was to be put to death, the Missouri Supreme Court stayed Simmons' execution pending the U.S. Supreme Court's resolution of the *Atkins* case.[51]

---

41. Petitioner's Statement, Brief, and Argument, *supra* note 18, at 15–16.

42. Leonard Post, *'Home Run' Hitters Set Legal Milestone*, NAT'L L. J. (Jan. 2, 2006), at 14.

43. *Simmons v. Bowersox*, 235 F.3d 1124, 1130 (8th Cir. 2001).

44. *Id.* at 1129.

45. *Id.* at 1139.

46. Petitioner's Statement, Brief, and Argument, *supra* note 18, at 16.

47. Missouri does not have a bar to successive habeas petitions. *State ex rel.* Nixon v. Jaynes, 63 S.W.3d 210, 217 (Mo. 2001).

48. Petitioner's Statement, Brief, and Argument, *supra* note 18, at 16.

49. 536 U.S. 304 (2002). The author was a law clerk for Supreme Court Justice John Paul Stevens during the Term that the Court heard and decided *Atkins*. All discussion of the case in this Chapter is based on publicly available information.

50. *Id.* at 306–07.

51. Petitioner's Statement, Brief, and Argument, *supra* note 18, at 16.

Less than one month later, the Supreme Court issued its decision in *Atkins* barring the execution of persons with mental retardation,[52] and, in doing so, provided Simmons a thin sliver of hope.

Doctrinal Background: From Penry and Stanford to Atkins

Penry

In 1989, the Supreme Court decided *Penry v. Lynaugh*,[53] which held, among other things, that the Eighth Amendment's ban on "cruel and unusual punishments" did *not* categorically forbid the execution of persons with mental retardation.[54] Justice Sandra Day O'Connor wrote the fractured opinion for the Court, and she was joined by Chief Justice Rehnquist and Justices White, Scalia, and Kennedy.[55]

Justice O'Connor's opinion embodies the now-dominant structure of analysis in the Court's treatment of categorical challenges to the death penalty under the Eighth Amendment: the Court assesses whether execution is categorically prohibited because it is "excessive" or disproportionate.[56] Disproportionality or excessiveness can be based either on the offense committed (for example, the Court has held that death is not a disproportionate punishment for murder,[57] but it is a disproportionate punishment for the rape of adult women[58]); or disproportionate given the nature of the individual who committed the offense (for example, the Court has held that death is a disproportionate punishment to inflict on someone who suffers from insanity[59]). Pursuant to this jurisprudential line, the Court at a minimum would forbid the infliction of punishments prohibited at the time of the adoption of the Bill of Rights.[60] But even the most ardent of originalists—for example, Justice Scalia—have recognized that the Eighth Amendment's prohibition is not limited to those practices forbidden in 1789, but rather requires consideration of what the

---

52. *Atkins*, 536 U.S. at 320–21.
53. 492 U.S. 302 (1989).
54. *Id.* at 340.
55. *Id.* at 306.
56. This line of cases is related to the Eighth Amendment's general prohibition against "cruel and unusual punishments," which also prohibits forms or methods of punishment such as, for example, torture or "lingering death." *See* In re Kemmler, 136 U.S. 436, 447 (1890). Recent challenges to lethal injection protocols and administration are based on this line of cases. *See, e.g.* Baze v. Rees, 128 S.Ct. 1520 (2008).
57. Gregg v. Georgia, 428 U.S. 153, 187 (1976).
58. Coker v. Georgia, 433 U.S. 584, 598 (1977).
59. Ford v. Wainwright, 477 U.S. 399, 409–10 (1986).
60. Penry v. Lynaugh, 492 U.S. 302, 330 (citing Ford, 477 U.S. at 405, and Solem v. Helm, 463 U.S. 277, 285–86 (1983)).

Court in *Trop v. Dulles* described as the "evolving standards of decency that mark the progress of a maturing society."[61] This analysis, in turn, unfolds in essentially two steps.

In the first step, what I will call the consensus evaluation, the Court looks to various pieces of "objective evidence" to discern how society currently views the punishment in question.[62] Textually, this component of the jurisprudence can be tied to the Eighth Amendment's prohibition of "unusual" punishment.[63] Most consistently favored by the Court among the objective indicators of consensus is an evaluation of state legislation. For example, in *Penry*, the Court assessed how many states had legislation allowing for or disapproving of the execution of offenders with mental retardation.[64] In some instances the Court has also been willing to look to evidence of how juries actually sentence defendants[65] (for example, even if a state allows the death penalty for mentally retarded offenders, do juries rarely or frequently impose it in those instances?). Other evidence the Court has—at times, but not always—been willing to consider in this consensus-evaluation mode includes the views of "respected professional organizations," public opinion polls, and, most significantly for the purposes of this Chapter's discussion, the views of the "world community."[66] As discussed below, it is from this jurisprudential perch that litigators and Justices have engaged in analysis of foreign and international law in the context of the Eighth Amendment.

In the second step of the analysis, often called proportionality review,[67] the Justices themselves seek to assess whether, in their "own

---

61. Trop v. Dulles, 356 U.S. 86, 101 (1958). For Justice Scalia's recognition of the evolving nature of the Eighth Amendment standard *see, for example, Penry*, 492 U.S. at 351 (Scalia, J., concurring in part and dissenting in part).

62. *Penry*, 492 U.S. at 330–331.

63. Thompson v. Oklahoma, 487 U.S. 815, 823, n. 7 (1988) ("[W]hether an action is 'unusual' depends, in common usage, upon the frequency of its occurrence or the magnitude of its acceptance."); *Trop*, 356 U.S. at 101, n. 32 ("If the word 'unusual' is to have any meaning apart from the word 'cruel' ... the meaning should be the ordinary one, signifying something different from that which is generally done."). In the same *Trop* footnote, however, the court noted that "[w]hether the word 'unusual' has any qualitative meaning different from 'cruel' is not clear. On the few occasions this Court has had to consider the meaning of the phrase, precise distinctions between cruelty and unusualness do not seem to have been drawn."; *see also* Furman v. Georgia, 408 U.S. 238, 277, n. 20 (1972) (Brennan, J., concurring) (citing *Trop* for this concept).

64. *Penry*, 492 U.S. at 337–38.

65. *See, e.g.*, Coker v. Georgia, 433 U.S. 584, 597 (1977).

66. *Thompson*, 487 U.S. at 830; *see also* Atkins v. Virginia, 536 U.S. 304, 316, n. 21 (2002); *Penry*, 492 U.S. at 334–35.

67. The Court has given variant meanings to excessiveness and disproportionality. Youngjae Lee, *The Constitutional Right Against Excessive Punishment*, 91 VA. L. REV. 677, 695 (2005).

independent judgment," the imposition of the death penalty is disproportionate to the offense or the nature of the offender.[68] This typically requires the Court to assess whether the recognized and accepted penological purposes of capital punishment—retribution and deterrence—are being served by the infliction of the death penalty on individuals within the group in question.[69] If they are not, then the punishment would be disproportionate or "cruel" within the meaning of the Eighth Amendment.[70] Although the language of the Eighth Amendment appears in the conjunctive—prohibiting the infliction of "cruel *and* unusual" punishments—the Court has not consistently required that a punishment be both outside of the existing consensus (i.e., "unusual") and disproportionate (i.e., "cruel").[71] To the contrary, the weight of the Court's precedent supports a disjunctive reading of the clause.[72]

---

68. *Coker*, 433 U.S. at 597–98; *see also* Atkins, 536 U.S. at 321; *Penry*, 492 U.S. at 335; Enmund v. Florida, 458 U.S. 782, 797 (1982).

69. *Enmund*, 458 U.S. at 798–99; *Coker*, 433 U.S. at 592. In the recent cases, the Court also has included within the independent-judgment evaluation an analysis of whether there are features of the group in question that might undermine procedural protections that are heightened in the capital context. *See Atkins*, 536 U.S. at 317 ("Additionally, it suggests that some characteristics of mental retardation undermine the strength of the procedural protections that our capital jurisprudence steadfastly guards."); *see also* Roper v. Simmons, 543 U.S. 551, 573–74 (2005).

70. *See* Solem v. Helm, 463 U.S. 277, 285 (1983) (explaining the roots of Eighth Amendment language in the English Bill of Rights and noting that English legal commentators understood "cruel" to mean "severe or excessive"); Anthony F. Granucci, *"Nor Cruel and Unusual Punishments Inflicted:" The Original Meaning*, 57 CAL. L. REV. 839, 860 (1969). *But see* Trop v. Dulles, 356 U.S. 86, 100, n. 32 (1958); *see also* Furman v. Georgia, 408 U.S. 238, 277, n. 20 (1972) (Brennan, J., concurring).

71. *Thompson*, 487 U.S. at 833 (plurality opinion); *Trop*, 356 U.S. at 99. *But see* Stanford v. Kentucky, 492 U.S. 361, 378–80 (1989), *overruled by Roper*, 543 U.S. 551 ("The punishment is either 'cruel *and* unusual' (i.e., society has set its face against it) or it is not.").

72. The Supreme Court specifically found in *Roper* that the *Stanford* Court's refusal to conduct a proportionality review after finding no consensus against the juvenile death penalty was "inconsistent with prior Eighth Amendment decisions." 543 U.S. at 574–75; *see also Atkins*, 536 U.S. at 312–13, 317–21; *Enmund*, 458 U.S. at 797; *Coker*, 433 U.S. at 597 (plurality opinion); Furman v. Georgia, 408 U.S. 238, 331–32 (Marshall, J., concurring) ("[O]ne of the primary functions of the cruel and unusual punishments clause is to prevent excessive or unnecessary penalties.... [T]hese punishments are unconstitutional even though popular sentiment may favor them.... [W]here a punishment is not excessive and serves a valid legislative purpose, it still may be invalid if popular sentiment abhors it."). This understanding of the clause is equally supportable as a textual matter. *See* Tom Stacy, *Cleaning Up the Eighth Amendment Mess*, 14 WM. & MARY BILL RTS. J. 475, 503–06 (2005) (collecting evidence that the phrases "cruel and unusual punishment" and "cruel or unusual punishment" were used interchangeably at the time the Eighth Amendment was adopted and noting the implausibility of outlawing cruel punishments only if they are infrequently implemented); *see also* Hugo Adam Bedau, *Fundamental Questions, Thinking of the Death Penalty as Cruel and Unusual Punishment*, 18 U.C. DAVIS L. REV. 873, 880 (1984–1985) ("cruel and unusual punishment is not regarded as a true conjunction....

Applying this doctrine to the question in *Penry*, Justice O'Connor concluded that neither step of the analysis led to the conclusion that the Eighth Amendment prohibited the execution of people with mental retardation.[73] With respect to the consensus-evaluation analysis, Justice O'Connor was unmoved by the numbers—in 1989, only Georgia, Maryland, and the federal government had banned the execution of mentally retarded offenders.[74] Justice O'Connor wrote that "[i]n our view, the two state statutes prohibiting execution of the mentally retarded, even when added to the 14 States that have rejected capital punishment completely, do not provide sufficient evidence at present of a national consensus."[75] Given that legislative tally and the lack of other evidence, such as contrary voting patterns of juries or decisions of prosecutors, Justice O'Connor remained unmoved by either polling data suggesting a majority of Americans opposed the imposition of the death penalty on the mentally retarded or similar opposition expressed by relevant professional organizations such as the American Association on Mental Retardation.[76] Nor, in engaging in an independent-judgment evaluation, was Justice O'Connor persuaded that at least the penological goal of retribution was not appropriately served in executing people with mental retardation.[77] Because of the sufficient variance in ability among people with mental retardation, Justice O'Connor wrote, she was unpersuaded it could "be said on the record before [the Court at the time] that all mentally retarded people, by definition, can never act with the level of culpability associated with the death penalty."[78]

No litigants in the case—neither the Petitioner nor any amici—made any arguments regarding world opinion, foreign law, or international law. It is unsurprising, then, that neither the plurality opinion nor the dissent discussed these issues.

Stanford

On the same day that the Supreme Court handed down *Perry*, the Court also announced a decision in the case of *Stanford v. Kentucky*.[79] In an opinion written by Justice Scalia, *Stanford* held that the Eighth Amendment also did not prohibit the death penalty for sixteen- or

---

[T]he idea of a 'tolerably cruel punishment' verges on an oxymoron. The converse possibility, that 'cruel and unusual' means 'cruelly unusual' . . . place[s] too much emphasis on the moral justifiability of punitive practices for no other reason than their familiarity or usualness."); George Kannar, Comment, *The Constitutional Catechism of Antonin Scalia*, 99 Yale L.J. 1297, 1321, n. 127 (1990) (noting that Scalia himself has argued that "or" and "and" can be used interchangeably).

73. *Penry*, 492 U.S. at 340.
74. *Id.* at 334–35.
75. *Id.* at 334.
76. *Id.* at 334–35.
77. *Id.* at 338–39.
78. *Id.*
79. 492 U.S. 361 (1989).

seventeen-year-old offenders.[80] The Court reached this conclusion by finding the absence of a national consensus against the practice, just as it had found a consensus lacking in the context of offenders with mental retardation.[81]

In contrast to *Penry*, there was forceful advocacy in the *Stanford* case based on foreign and international law regarding the execution of juvenile offenders.[82] Although such arguments were not incorporated into the Petitioner's merits brief, three groups filed amicus briefs that focused on the relevance of foreign and international law: Amnesty International ("AI"), the Defense for Children International–USA, and the International Human Rights Law Group (now Global Rights).[83] For example, AI's brief outlined what it called the "massive evidence" that well-established international standards prohibited the execution of juvenile offenders.[84] This evidence included the 144 countries that forbade the execution of juvenile offenders at the time, the existence of three major human rights treaties that banned the practice, and the position of the United Nations opposing it.[85]

The arguments made by these international human rights advocates plainly had some impact on several of the Justices. For example, in

---

80. *Id.* at 380. A year earlier, the Court had concluded that the Eighth Amendment prohibited the execution of offenders who committed their crimes at the age of fifteen or younger. Thompson v. Oklahoma, 487 U.S. 815, 838 (1988).

81. *Stanford*, 492 U.S. at 370–73. Part V of Justice Scalia's opinion also rejected any kind of independent-judgment evaluation. *Id.* at 377–80. But on this jurisprudential point, Justice Scalia found only a plurality of support. Justice O'Connor's concurring opinion "reject[ed] the suggestion that the use of such analysis is improper as a matter of Eighth Amendment jurisprudence." *Id.* at 382. (O'Connor, J., concurring).

82. Originally, the Supreme Court agreed to hear two cases regarding the constitutionality of the death penalty for offenders between the ages of sixteen and eighteen: Wilkins v. Missouri and High v. Zant. Wilkins v. Missouri, 487 U.S. 1233 (1988) (granting certiorari and consolidating oral argument in the case with High v. Zant). Subsequently, the Court replaced the case with Stanford v. Kentucky, 488 U.S. 906 (1988). Several international organizations filed amicus curiae briefs in High v. Zant, No. 87-5666, and, therefore, these briefs were considered in *Stanford* and are cited as such.

83. Brief for Amicus Curiae Amnesty International in Support of Petitioners, Stanford, 492 U.S. 361 (1989) (Nos. 87-5765, 87-6026); Brief for Amicus Curiae Defense for Children International–USA in Support of Petitioners, Stanford, 492 U.S. 361 (1989) (Nos. 87-5765, 87-6026); Brief for Amicus Curiae International Human Rights Law Group in Support of Petitioners, Stanford, 492 U.S. 361 (1989) (Nos. 87-5765, 87-6026).

84. Brief for Amicus Curiae Amnesty International in Support of Petitioners at 5–6, *Stanford*, 492 U.S. 361 (Nos. 87-5765, 87-6026).

85. *Id.* at 17.

Justice Blackmun's file on the case, his law clerk's memo outlined the arguments contained in all of the briefs before the Court.[86] In the section on the arguments made by AI, Justice Blackmun highlighted substantial sections and commented in the margins that the argument was "interesting."[87] More significantly, in a dissent joined by Justices Blackmun, Marshall, and Stevens, Justice Brennan focused on the doctrinal significance of foreign law when he stated that "[o]ur cases recognize that objective indicators of contemporary standards of decency in the form of legislation in other countries is also of relevance to Eighth Amendment analysis."[88] Then, relying heavily on the factual evidence and arguments marshaled in AI's amicus brief in particular, Justice Blackmun documented the world community's "overwhelming[] disapprov[al]" of the application of the death penalty to juvenile offenders.[89] He also noted that "[i]n addition to national laws, three leading human rights treaties ratified or signed by the United States explicitly prohibit juvenile death penalties."[90]

This passage in the dissent provoked a footnote response from Justice Scalia in the majority opinion, rejecting the relevance of foreign law to the Eighth Amendment consensus evaluation.[91] Justice Scalia stated that "[w]e emphasize that it is *American* conceptions of decency that are dispositive, rejecting the contention of petitioners and their various *amici* (accepted by the dissent) that the sentencing practices of other countries are relevant."[92] It is clear from historical evidence that Justice Scalia's first footnote was not originally included in his opinion

---

86. Justice Harry A. Blackmun, Stanford v. Kentucky Case File, *in* The Blackmun Collection (on file with the Library of Congress).

87. *Id.*

88. *Stanford*, 492 U.S. at 389 (Blackmun, J. dissenting).

89. *Id.* at 390.

90. *Id.* at 389–90. At approximately the same time that *Stanford* was being decided, the United States was engaging in negotiations regarding the United Nations Convention on the Rights of the Child, which contains a provision prohibiting the execution of juvenile offenders. Convention on the Rights of the Child art. 37, Nov. 20, 1989, 1577 U.N.T.S. 43. In the treaty negotiations, the United States objected to the ban on juvenile executions. *See* Curtis A. Bradley, *The Juvenile Death Penalty and International Law*, 52 Duke L.J. 485, 531 (2002). Eventually the United States moved beyond the objection with the understanding that it retained a right to reserve on the point. *See id.* President Clinton signed the Convention in 1995. *Id.* In doing so he stated that he would encourage the Senate to ratify the treaty with a number of reservations, including ones relevant to the juvenile execution prohibition. *Id.* at 531–32. To this day, the Senate has not ratified the Treaty. Office of the United Nations High Comm'r for Human Rights, Ratifications of the Convention on the Rights of the Child, *available at* http://www2.ohchr.org/english/bodies/ratification/11.htm (last updated Feb. 12, 2008).

91. *Stanford*, 492 U.S. at 370, n. 1.

92. *Id.* (internal citation omitted).

but was in fact provoked by the dissent. The footnote was added after Justice Brennan circulated his dissent to the Conference on June 8, 1989 and in time for the third circulation of Justice Scalia's opinion, which occurred June 13, 1989.[93] Interestingly, Justice Kennedy, who had just joined the Court that term and would go on to author the *Roper* opinion in 2005, signed on to Justice Scalia's opinion without reservation on June 2, 1989, prior to the circulation of Justice Brennan's dissent and prior to Justice Scalia's inclusion of footnote one.[94]

Atkins

Thirteen years after deciding *Penry*, the Court agreed to consider again the permissibility of the death penalty for people with mental retardation.[95] The intervening years had witnessed several relevant developments. On the national front, since the time of the *Penry* decision, sixteen states and the federal government had addressed the issue and expressly prohibited the death penalty for offenders with mental retardation.[96] And even in states that did not formally prohibit the execution of mentally retarded offenders, the instances of such executions had become exceedingly rare in practice.[97] Based on these changes, in an opinion written by Justice Stevens, a solid six-member majority of the Court—including Justices O'Connor and Kennedy, both of whom had joined the majority opinion in *Penry*—concluded that the practice of executing people with mental retardation in the United States had "become truly unusual," leading the Court to conclude that "a national consensus [had] developed against it."[98]

On the international level, the time between *Penry* and *Atkins* saw increasing condemnation of the United States' execution of mentally retarded defendants by international organizations. In 1989, the year in which the Court decided *Penry*, the United Nations Economic and Social Council had reiterated a previous resolution safeguarding the protections of individuals facing the death penalty, which included eliminating the death penalty for persons suffering from mental retardation, whether at

---

93. The first draft of Justice Scalia's opinion is contained in the papers of both Justice Blackmun and Justice Marshall, which are maintained in the Library of Congress.

94. After a draft majority opinion has been circulated to the Court, the Justices may proceed in a number of different ways. FORREST MALTZMAN, JAMES F. SPRIGGS II & PAUL J. WAHLBECK, CRAFTING LAW ON THE SUPREME COURT 62–69 (2000). A justice may decide to join without reservation, wait to join until subsequent drafts, concurrences or dissents are circulated, suggest that the author make specific substantive changes to the opinion, or circulate a concurrence or dissent. *Id.*

95. Atkins v. Virginia, 534 U.S. 809 (2001) (granting the petition for *certiorari*).

96. Atkins v. Virginia, 536 U.S. 304, 314–15 (2002).

97. *Id.* at 316.

98. *Id.*

the sentencing stage or the execution stage.[99] In each of the three years preceding *Atkins,* the United Nations Humans Rights Commission had adopted resolutions specifically urging countries not to impose the death penalty on people with mental retardation.[100] The Human Rights Committee criticized the United States for state executions of mentally retarded inmates during its 1995 review of U.S. compliance with the International Covenant on Civil and Political Rights, finding that "in some cases, there appears to be a lack of protection from the death penalty of those mentally retarded."[101]

In sharp contrast to what occurred at the time of *Penry,* advocates in *Atkins* mounted a coordinated effort to demonstrate the illegality of the practice as a matter of foreign and international law, and this advocacy influenced the Court. Both the European Union and a group of former United States diplomats filed amicus briefs, chronicling the developments and highlighting the lonely status of the United States as one of three countries that had executed a person with mental retardation since 1995.[102]

After concluding that a national consensus had formed against the practice of executing the mentally retarded, the majority opinion in *Atkins* noted in a lengthy footnote (footnote 21) that there was "[a]dditional evidence" confirming that the judgment of state legislators was part of a broader consensus.[103] Included among this evidence was the fact that "within the world community, the imposition of the death penalty for crimes committed by mentally retarded offenders is overwhelmingly disapproved."[104] For this proposition, Justice Stevens cited the amicus brief filed by the European Union.[105]

Although this footnote reference to world opinion appears to play only a minimal (at best) role in the reasoning of the Court in *Atkins,* it provoked a high-pitched dissent from both Chief Justice Rehnquist and

---

99. Brief of Amicus Curiae by the European Union in Support of the Petitioner at 8, *Atkins,* 536 U.S. 304 (No. 00–8452) (originally filed in McCarver v. North Carolina, *cert. denied,* 533 U.S. 975 (2001) (No. 00–8727) (citing Implementation of the Safeguards Guaranteeing Protection of Rights of those Facing the Death Penalty, U.N. Economic and Social Council, ECOSOC Res. 1989/64, U.N. Doc. E/1989/91 (May 24, 1989)).

100. *Id.*

101. *Id.* at 16 (citing Concluding Observations of the Human Rights Committee: United States of America, Human Rights Committee, ¶ 281, U.N. Doc. A/50/40 (1995) (internal quotation marks omitted)).

102. *See generally id.;* Brief of Amici Curiae Diplomats Morton Abramowitz, et al. in Support of Petitioner, 536 U.S. 304 (No. 00–8452) (originally filed in *McCarver, cert. denied,* 533 U.S. 975 (No. 00–8727)).

103. *Atkins,* 536 U.S. at 316, n. 21.

104. *Id.*

105. *Id.*

Justice Scalia. Chief Justice Rehnquist argued that "the views of other countries regarding the punishment of their citizens provide [no] support for the Court's ultimate determination."[106] Citing the *Stanford* Court's emphasis on the "dispositive" nature of "*American* conceptions of decency," the Chief Justice complained that "*Stanford's* reasoning makes perfectly good sense, and the Court offers no basis to question it."[107] Justice Scalia was less kind. After awarding the reference "the Prize for the Court's Most Feeble Effort to fabricate 'national consensus,'" Justice Scalia argued that "irrelevant are the practices of the 'world community,' whose notions of justice are (thankfully) not always those of our people."[108]

Advocacy Background: From Stanford *to* Roper

Although it would be fifteen years before the Court would again consider the *Stanford* issue of whether the Constitution bars the execution of a juvenile offender, significant events occurred both inside and outside the courtroom walls during that time. Multi-layered human rights and anti-death penalty advocacy strategies set the stage for the Court's reconsideration of the juvenile execution issue and the possibility for a different outcome.

First, there was the U.N.'s adoption of the CRC and its provision prohibiting the execution of juvenile offenders in 1989—the year that *Stanford* was decided. Through relentless advocacy, nearly every country in the world ratified the treaty within five years.[109] Second, non-governmental organizations such as Amnesty International engaged in worldwide reporting on and advocacy against the execution of juvenile offenders. This work culminated in a major report by Amnesty International on the issue in 2004.[110] This report, in turn, formed the basis of significant advocacy before a number of courts in the United States, including, as discussed below, the U.S. Supreme Court in the *Roper* case.[111] During the fifteen years between *Stanford* and *Roper*, advocacy

---

106. *Id.* at 325 (Rehnquist, C.J., dissenting).

107. *Id.* (internal citation and quotation marks omitted).

108. *Id.* at 347–48 (Scalia, J., dissenting).

109. *See* STATUS OF RATIFICATIONS OF THE PRINCIPAL HUMAN RIGHTS TREATIES, *supra* note 13. At the time of this writing, every country in the world other than the United States and Somalia have ratified the treaty. *Id.*

110. *See* AMNESTY INTERNATIONAL, STOP CHILD EXECUTIONS! ENDING THE DEATH PENALTY FOR CHILD OFFENDERS (2004).

111. *See* Brief of Amici Curiae the European Union and Members of the International Community in Support of Respondent, Roper, 543 U.S. 551 (No. 03-633); Brief of Amici Curiae Former U.S. Diplomats Morton Abramowitz, et al., in Support of Respondent, Roper, 543 U.S. 551 (No. 03-633); Brief of Amici Curiae President James Earl Carter, Jr.,

efforts also focused on U.N. and other regional human rights organizations. This advocacy led to several formal statements or resolutions condemning the practice. For example, in 1997 following a mission to the United States, the U.N. Special Rapporteur on Extrajudicial, Summary or Arbitrary Executions found that the execution of juvenile offenders violated international law and called on the United States to cease the practice.[112] Third, both death penalty and human rights lawyers began forcefully litigating the issue of the execution of juvenile offenders in a variety of international fora. For example, in the case of a sixteen-year-old Nevada death row inmate, Michael Domingues, lawyers persuaded the Inter–American Commission on Human Rights (IACHR or Inter–American Commission) that the prohibition against executing juveniles had achieved *jus cogens* status.[113] In other words, the IACHR found that the prohibition against the execution of juvenile offenders was a norm that was "accepted and recognized by the international community of States as a whole as a norm from which no derogation is permitted and which can be modified only by a subsequent norm of general international law having the same character."[114]

Following in the wake of this international advocacy and litigation, U.S. lawyers filed domestic litigation that brought both constitutional and international law arguments to bear.[115] As discussed below, the lawyers for Christopher Simmons took part in this trend in the lower courts. By doing so, they created the opportunity for the Supreme Court to reconsider its *Stanford* decision. Given these cross-currents of advocacy taking place in the United States and internationally and both inside and outside the courtroom, the stage was set for the *Roper* case to become part of what Professor Harold Koh has described as the "judicial internalization" of the human rights norm barring the execution of juvenile offenders.[116]

---

et al., (Nobel Peace Prize Laureates) in Support of Respondent, Roper, 543 U.S. 551 (No. 03–633); Brief for the Human Rights Committee of the Bar of England and Wales, Human Rights Advocates, Human Rights Watch, and the World Organization for Human Rights USA as Amici Curiae in Support of Respondent, Roper, 543 U.S. 551 (No. 03–633).

112. *See* Report of the Special Rapporteur on Extradjudicial, Summary or Arbitrary Executions: Mission to the United States of America, U.N. Doc E/CN.4/1998/68/Add.3 para. 55 (Jan. 22, 1998).

113. Domingues v. United States, Case 12.285, Inter–Am. C.H.R., Report No. 62/02 (merits), OEA/Ser.L/V/II.116, Doc. 33 (Oct. 22, 2002).

114. Vienna Convention on the Law of Treaties art. 53, May 23, 1969, 1155 U.N.T.S. 331; *see also* RESTATEMENT (THIRD) OF FOREIGN RELATIONS LAW § 102 cmt. K (1990).

115. *See e.g.*, Beazley v. Johnson, 242 F.3d 248 (5th Cir. Tex. 2001); Domingues v. State of Nevada, 961 P.2d 1279 (1998).

116. Harold Hongju Koh, *Review Essay: Why Do Nations Obey International Law*, 106 YALE L.J. 2599 (1997).

Victory for Simmons at the Missouri Supreme Court and the Grant of Certiorari by the U.S. Supreme Court

When Christopher Simmons' lawyer, Jennifer Herndon, read the Supreme Court's decision in *Atkins*, she knew that in it lay the potential to turn her client's stay of execution by the Missouri Supreme Court into a more permanent reprieve.[117] After all, several of the factors relied upon by the Court in moving from the *Penry* conclusion to the *Atkins* result were strikingly similar in the juvenile context. In particular, the number of states that prohibited the execution of juvenile offenders was strikingly similar to the number of states that the Court in *Atkins* recently had credited as sufficient to establish a national consensus against the execution of the mentally retarded.[118] But Herndon's optimism was tempered as she read a footnote contained in *Atkins*. In describing the direction of state legislative change outlawing the execution of persons with mental retardation that had occurred since the Court had decided *Penry*, the majority opinion in *Atkins* dropped a footnote contrasting the trend with the lack of legislative developments regarding juvenile offenders in the same period of time since *Stanford* was decided.[119]

Despite this footnote and the existing *Stanford* Supreme Court precedent to the contrary, Simmons' post-conviction lawyers pressed the case that the Eighth Amendment prohibited the execution of Simmons to the Supreme Court of Missouri. Before that Court, Herndon and her team deployed international and foreign law arguments for two distinct purposes.[120] First, they focused on the reference in *Atkins* to the relevance of foreign and international law to establish that Simmons' late Eighth Amendment claim was not procedurally barred even though he had failed previously to raise the claim.[121] Rules of "procedural bar" operate in both state and federal post-conviction courts to preclude consideration of claims if a petitioner "failed to comply with a state procedural rule when he presented the claim to the state courts ... typically ... because of a petitioner's failure to raise a claim at the time or in the manner prescribed by state law."[122] Typically, to overcome a

---

117. Telephonic Interview with Jennifer Herndon, Attorney (Sept. 21, 2007).

118. Roper v. Simmons, 543 U.S. 551, 564 (2005).

119. *Atkins*, 536 U.S. at 316, n. 18 ("Although we decided *Stanford* on the same day as *Penry*, apparently only two state legislatures have raised the threshold age for imposition of the death penalty" during the thirteen years between the decisions in *Stanford* and *Penry* and the decision in *Atkins*).

120. *See generally* Brief on Petition for Original Writ of Habeas Corpus to the Missouri Supreme Court, Simmons v. Luebbers, 112 S.W.3d 397 (Mo. 2003) (No. SC84454).

121. *Id.* at 25.

122. RANDY HERTZ & JAMES S. LIEBMAN, FEDERAL HABEAS CORPUS PRACTICE & PROCEDURE § 26.1 (3d ed. 2007).

procedural default rule, a petitioner will have to establish "cause and prejudice."[123] To the Missouri Supreme Court, Simmons argued that, while *Stanford* had expressly rejected reference to foreign or international law, *Atkins* had considered the opinion of the world community as relevant to the analysis.[124] This change in the law, Simmons' brief argued, demonstrated cause for failure to raise the claim earlier.[125]

Second, turning to the merits of the Eighth Amendment claim, the brief argued that, in light of the Supreme Court's recent decision in *Atkins*, the Missouri Supreme Court should conclude that the Eighth Amendment now prohibited the execution of juvenile offenders.[126] On each of the steps of the analysis, Herndon contended that *Atkins* compelled the same conclusion in the juvenile context. Focusing on international and foreign law, Herndon included briefing on the world community's universal opposition to the execution of juvenile offenders.[127] Herndon made three distinct arguments that the execution of juveniles specifically violated binding international law. First, the brief contended that a customary international law prohibition against the execution of juvenile offenders existed and that this norm had achieved *jus cogens* status.[128] Interestingly, the brief did not itself provide an analysis developing this available international law argument, but instead simply cited to the *Domingues* case before the IACHR.[129] The brief urged that the Missouri Supreme Court should, at the least, consider the *Domingues* case persuasive authority on the *jus cogens* issue.[130]

Second, Herndon argued in the alternative that the Missouri Court should consider itself bound by the IACHR decision in *Domingues*.[131] Here, the brief provided a relatively extensive argument detailing why the United States, as a member of the Organization of American States ("OAS") and a party to the OAS Charter, is bound as a matter of treaty law by the *Domingues* decision.[132]

---

123. *Id.* at § 26.3(a).

124. Brief on Petition for Original Writ of Habeas Corpus to the Missouri Supreme Court, *supra* note 120, at 25.

125. *Id.* at 26–27.

126. *Id.* at 43.

127. *Id.* at 88–97

128. *Id.* at 88.

129. Domingues v. United States, Case 12.285, Inter–Am. C.H.R., Report No. 62/02 (2002).

130. Brief on Petition for Original Writ of Habeas Corpus to the Missouri Supreme Court, *supra* note 120, at 89.

131. *Id.* at 89–90.

132. *Id.* at 90–92. This argument was not without detractors. International human rights scholars are divided on this point. *See, e.g.*, Laurence E. Rothenberg, *International*

Third, the brief placed the foreign law argument more directly within the framework suggested by *Atkins*. Herndon argued that international rejection of the execution of juvenile offenders was now at a sufficiently clear and nearly universal level that it could be said that an international consensus had developed against the practice and that this "near unanimous position of the world community supports the legislative and other trends in this country showing a consensus against the execution of juveniles."[133] It was this final form of the argument that took hold in the decision issued by the Missouri Supreme Court.

On August 26, 2003, the Supreme Court of Missouri issued its controversial decision in *Simmons v. Roper*.[134] After finding that the procedural bar rule of waiver does not apply in the context of categorical exclusions to the death penalty, the Missouri Court held that "[a]pplying the approach taken in *Atkins*," the Eighth Amendment prohibited the execution of juvenile offenders.[135] Simmons was re-sentenced to life in prison.[136] The Missouri Court found that, under the framework required by *Atkins*, both the consensus evaluation and the proportionality analysis militated in favor of a constitutional bar against the execution of juvenile offenders.[137] With respect to the relevance of international or foreign law, the Missouri Court did not address the arguments for recognition of the norm as *jus cogens* or the claim that the IACHR's decision in *Domingues* was controlling as a matter of binding treaty law. Instead, in a subsection entitled "National and International Consensus," the Missouri court simply stated, along the lines of the *Atkins* footnote citing to "world opinion," that

> We also find of note that the views of the international community have consistently grown in opposition to the death penalty for

---

Law, U.S. Sovereignty, and the Death Penalty, 35 GEO. J. INT'L L. 547, 552 (2004) ("The IACHR's position on the death penalty has no legal effect, however. As a matter of both international and U.S. law, IACHR reports are considered recommendations only.").

133. Brief on Petition for Original Writ of Habeas Corpus to the Missouri Supreme Court, *supra* note 113, at 97.

134. 112 S.W.3d 397 (Mo. 2003); *see* Tim O'Neil, *Missouri's High Court Says Ruling Follows Legal Tide*, ST. LOUIS (MO.) POST-DISPATCH, Aug. 31, 2003, at B1 (noting that the decision earned justices "praise ... as bold visionaries and condemnation as brazen activists"); *see also* Joe Lambe, *High Court Overturns Capital Case: Man Who Killed at 17 Cannot Be Executed*, KANSAS CITY (MO.) STAR, Aug. 27, 2003, at A1 (discussing the party affiliations of the members of the Missouri high court and reporting the anger of the victim's family); Frank J. Murray, *State Executions Ruling Defies High Courts: Killers Under 18 at Time Can't Get Death*, WASH. TIMES, Aug. 28, 2003, at A4 (reporting various opinions as to whether the ruling was legally permissible and whether it accurately reflected "evolving standards of decency").

135. *Simmons*, 112 S.W.3d at 399.

136. *Id.* at 399–400.

137. *Id.* at 407–13.

juveniles. Article 37(a) of the United Nations Convention on the Rights of the Child and several other international treaties and agreements expressly prohibit the practice. According to Amnesty International, officially sanctioned executions of juveniles have occurred in only two other countries in the world in the last few years, Iran and The [Democratic] Republic of the Congo (DRC). Of the last seven juvenile offender executions, five occurred in the United States.[138]

Unsurprisingly, the state of Missouri sought review by the United States Supreme Court of the Missouri decision.[139] Equally unsurprisingly, particularly given the clear tension with *Stanford* as well as the different result on the same question of federal constitutional law that had been reached by a variety of state and lower federal courts,[140] the Supreme Court agreed to hear the case. The Court granted Missouri's petition for *certiorari* on January 26, 2004.[141]

The Supreme Court Strategy

Once the Court agreed to hear the case, Herndon joined efforts with an experienced team of Supreme Court litigators from the Washington, D.C. law firm of Wilmer Cutler Pickering Hale & Dorr, which took on the case *pro bono*.[142] The team was headed by the former Solicitor General of the United States, Seth Waxman, who had extensive experience arguing before the Supreme Court.[143] Herndon and the WilmerHale team quickly began developing their Supreme Court strategy. The obstacles were significant and included the fact that the Missouri Supreme Court below had ruled in seeming opposition to the directly controlling precedent of *Stanford*; that six members of the Court were on record in existing opinions indicating disagreement with the position that the execution of juvenile offenders violated the Eighth Amendment; and that a footnote in the majority opinion in *Atkins* seemingly had distinguished

---

138. *Id.* at 410–11 (internal citations omitted).

139. Petition for Writ of Certiorari, Roper v. Simmons, 540 U.S. 1160 (2004) (No. 03–633).

140. *See* Villarreal v. Cockrell, 73 Fed. Appx. 742, 743 (5th Cir. 2003); Beazley v. Johnson, 242 F.3d 248, 268–69 (5th Cir. 2001); Foster v. State, 848 So.2d 172, 175–76 (Miss. 2003); Adams v. State, 955 So.2d 1037, 1105 (Ala. Crim. App. 2003).

141. Roper v. Simmons, 540 U.S. 1160 (2004).

142. *See* Post, *supra* note 42, at 14.

143. The WilmerHale team also included two additional Supreme Court experts: David Ogden, also a partner at WilmerHale and a former Assistant Attorney General of the United States, and Danielle Spinelli, then a young and upcoming WilmerHale associate and member of the firm's Supreme Court litigation group who, three years earlier, had clerked for U.S. Supreme Court Justice Stephen Breyer.

the national consensus regarding the execution of mentally retarded defendants from that of juvenile offenders.

Despite these challenges, one thing was utterly clear—*Atkins* provided the template for litigating the case. It was a model for how to establish that between 1989, when *Penry* and *Stanford* were decided, and 2004, standards of decency could evolve away from a given punishment for Eighth Amendment purposes. The Supreme Court litigation team's task was to develop arguments demonstrating that, as a matter of both consensus and disproportionality, the juvenile context was on all fours with the evidence presented regarding the mentally retarded in *Atkins*.

As a model, however, *Atkins* sent an ambiguous message as to what extent international and foreign law arguments ought to be relied upon in litigating the juvenile case. Relegated to a footnote about "world opinion," the majority's reliance on international and foreign law was decidedly minimal. And yet, that footnote managed to provoke an impassioned dissenting response from both Chief Justice Rehnquist and Justice Scalia. If anything, the reaction of the dissent regarding the mere footnote in *Atkins* served as a caution to the Supreme Court litigators as to how much reliance ought to be placed on international and foreign law.

The Briefs

With respect to foreign and international law, the Supreme Court team quickly realized it had three critical decisions to make. First, should foreign and international law arguments be included in the merits briefing at all, or should they be raised only by relevant *amici*? Second, if such arguments should be included in the merits briefing, should the merits brief include a formal argument that execution of juvenile offenders violated international law, akin to the argument made on Simmons' behalf below? Third, if not—if instead, discussion of foreign or international law should be confined to the confirmatory Eighth Amendment factor it minimally played in *Atkins*—how much emphasis should be placed upon it?[144]

Including foreign and international law arguments in the merits briefing in some form had opponents. Some members of the anti-death penalty community with whom the Supreme Court team was consulting suggested that the international and foreign law arguments ought not be included in the merits briefing at all.[145] This view was a reaction to the vociferousness of the dissent that had been provoked by *Atkins*' mere

---

144. Interview with David W. Ogden, Partner, WilmerHale, and Danielle Spinelli, Partner, WilmerHale, Washington, D.C. (Aug. 31, 2007).

145. Telephonic Interview with Seth Waxman, *supra* note 5.

footnote reference to the "views of the world community." According to Waxman, the worry expressed to them was: "Why give that complement on the Supreme Court that views comparative law regime with derision an opportunity to caricature our overall argument in the case as 'Because other countries aren't doing this, you shouldn't'?"[146] Additionally, the concern was expressed to the team that the ability to make convincing arguments before the Court regarding international norms depended on being able to provide unassailable evidence as to actual state practice. According to Waxman, there was concern that the Court might view skeptically formal rejections of the practice if the real world application of the death penalty in those countries was not consistently open to public transparency and scrutiny.[147]

Despite these cautions, the Supreme Court team leaned decidedly toward including the line of argument in the briefing in some capacity.[148] Even if *Atkins'* reliance was minimal, footnote 21 clearly opened the door. Moreover, concerns about an anti-internationalist backlash from some members of the Court could be dealt with by including the evidence of international consensus against the practice but de-emphasizing the role the argument played in the ultimate outcome of the case. And, finally, beyond the doctrinal significance, the team strongly believed that international consensus against juvenile executions was an extremely valuable atmospheric asset. As David Ogden explained:

> We thought, perhaps there are arguments to be made by the other side about the ultimate legal relevance. But you simply can't argue the impact and optics of the point. And, even if the reliance on foreign and international law in other contexts is controversial, we had clear jurisprudential support in the Eighth Amendment cases, even if *Stanford* had backed away from that line and the dissenters in *Atkins* had stated their views against it.[149]

The decision, ultimately, was made easier by a strategy employed by the state of Missouri. As the losing party before the Supreme Court of Missouri and, therefore, as Petitioner to the U.S. Supreme Court, Missouri filed its opening merits brief first. In that brief, Missouri itself raised arguments pertaining to international and foreign law.[150] Indeed, the state referenced international and foreign law both affirmatively and defensively. Affirmatively, Missouri discussed the reservations the United States had entered when ratifying the International Convention on

---

146. *Id.*

147. *Id.*

148. *Id.*; interview with Ogden and Spinelli, *supra* note 144.

149. Interview with Ogden and Spinelli, *supra* note 144.

150. Brief for Petitioner at 27–28, 41, Roper v. Simmons, 543 U.S. 551 (2005) (No. 03–633).

Civil and Political Rights ("ICCPR"). One such reservation explicitly stated that the United States reserved the right to execute juvenile offenders.[151] Missouri also pointed to the United States' failure to ratify the CRC, which contains a provision prohibiting the execution of juvenile offenders.[152] The state argued that the ratification of the ICCPR with reservation and the failure to ratify the CRC constituted affirmative legislative evidence demonstrating a national consensus in favor of the availability of the death penalty for juvenile offenders.[153] Defensively, the state argued that the Missouri Supreme Court's reference to international and foreign law below was in error. According to the state, *Stanford*'s determination that international law is irrelevant to a determination of the "American consensus" continued to be controlling.[154]

Accordingly, the real strategic decision to be made by the Simmons team was not whether but how to make use of the available international and foreign law evidence and arguments. As a preliminary matter, the team decided that even if a formal international law argument like the one Herndon had pressed to the Supreme Court of Missouri below was available, for example that the ICCPR Reservation was invalid or that the prohibition had obtained the status of a *jus cogens* norm, it would not serve the case well to include it within the merits briefing.[155] Doing so, the team feared, would simply place too much emphasis on this aspect of the argument. Ogden explained that the strong strategic sentiment was to make plain that "we weren't resting our case on it."[156]

The strategic option, then, was for the team to follow *Atkins'* minimalist model. In their Eighth Amendment argument, the team would use evidence regarding "world opinion" about the juvenile death penalty—as embodied in formal rejections of the practice by states that ratified the CRC as well as statements and opinions from inter-governmental bodies criticizing the practice—to bolster and confirm their arguments regarding the evidence of an existing national consensus. Yet,

---

    151. *Id.* at 27; *see also* U.S. Senate Resolution of Advice and Consent to Ratification of the International Covenant on Civil and Political Rights, 138 Cong. Rec. 8070 (Apr. 2, 1992) ("[T]he United States reserves the right, subject to its Constitutional constraints, to impose capital punishment on any person (other than a pregnant woman) duly convicted under existing or future laws permitting the imposition of capital punishment, including such punishments for crimes committed by persons below eighteen years of age."). The question as to whether under international law this Reservation is valid has provoked sustained debate. *See, e.g.*, Rothenberg, *supra* note 132, at 565 (discussing the controversy of the reservation).

    152. Brief for Petitioner, *supra* note 150, at 27–28.
    153. *Id.*
    154. *Id.* at 41.
    155. Telephonic Interview with Seth Waxman, *supra* note 5.
    156. Interview with Ogden and Spinelli, *supra* note 144.

even within this Eighth Amendment doctrinal context, the team was cautious. According to Ogden: "The trick in the briefing in this area was to figure out how much emphasis to put on it and how to avoid making it appear to be a lynchpin. I think we were pretty careful not to make this one feel like it was a lynchpin."[157] As Spinelli expressed: "We wanted the point to strike the Justices *not* as a necessary element of the consensus argument, which it wasn't, but rather as an 'and indeed.' "[158]

In implementing this strategy, the team included reference to international and foreign law in a concise, final section of the brief. It followed lengthy sections arguing the disproportionality of the death penalty in light of neurological and behavioral factors affecting juvenile decision-making[159] and the existence of a national consensus against the practice that bore striking numerical similarity to the evidence that persuaded the Court in *Atkins*.[160] The section vividly captures the dynamic course of change that had occurred at the international level since *Stanford* was decided in 1989. As the brief described, it was in that very year that the United Nations adopted the CRC, including its provision barring the execution of juvenile offenders.[161] In the fifteen years following, the brief argued, every country in the world, save the United States and Somalia, had ratified the treaty and almost all had accepted the provision concerning the juvenile death penalty prohibition without reservation.[162] In addition to these formal prohibitions on the practice, the brief argued that the real world facts fully supported the rarity of the practice. Relying on the recently released report by Amnesty International, the brief argued that since 1990 only seven countries other than the United States were believed to have executed juvenile offenders.[163] Finally, the short section of the merits brief noted one important effect of the changes occurring at the international level. Over the course of fifteen years, the Inter–American Commission on Human Rights had moved from concluding in *Roach and Pinkerton v. United States*[164] that there was not yet sufficient evidence to hold that executing juvenile offenders violated international customary law, to concluding in 2002 in

---

157. *Id.*

158. *Id.*

159. Brief for Respondent at 14–27, Roper v. Simmons, 543 U.S. 551 (2005) (No. 03–633).

160. *Id.* at 39–40 (thirty-one jurisdictions prohibited the juvenile death penalty at the time of filing); *Atkins*, 536 U.S. 304, 314–15 (2002) (thirty-one jurisdictions prohibited execution of mentally retarded offenders at the time of the decision).

161. Brief for Respondent, *supra* note 159, at 48.

162. *Id.*

163. *Id.* at 49, n. 105 (citing AMNESTY INTERNATIONAL, *supra* note 110).

164. Case 9647, Inter–Am. C.H.R., Report No. 3/87, ¶ 60 (1987).

the case *Domingues v. United States*[165] that, in light of near world unanimity on the issue, a *jus cogens* norm against the practice had emerged.[166] In a final sentence that elegantly wove together the atmospheric with the doctrinal, the merits brief concluded that, "[t]he small minority of United States jurisdictions that continue to execute those under 18 now stand virtually alone—not just in this country, but in a world that has concluded that the execution of juvenile offenders is contrary to contemporary standards of decency."[167]

Four international-law-focused amicus briefs were filed in support of Simmons. They were submitted by: the European Union, former U.S. diplomats, Nobel Peace Prize Laureates, and a group of human rights organizations.[168] It was in this set of amicus briefs that the international human rights law heavy lifting was done. In varying degrees, the international amici provided for the Court the formal international law arguments from which Simmons' team had shied away. The E.U. Brief argued that an international consensus existed against the execution of juvenile offenders as evidenced by the practices of a vast majority of countries, provisions of international treaties, and the views of states as advocated before international bodies. According to that brief, the Supreme Court "may take the existence of this consensus into account in its consideration of this case."[169] Moreover, the E.U. Brief delineated with some detail the argument that the United States' reservation to Article 6(5) of the ICCPR was invalid and, therefore, that the United States was prohibited as a matter of international law from executing juvenile offenders.[170] The U.S. Diplomats, like the E.U., argued that the worldwide consensus against the practice was a relevant factor in the Court's consensus-evaluation prong of its Eighth Amendment jurisprudence. Moreover, the Diplomats Brief argued that allowing states to continue executing juvenile offenders risked harming U.S. diplomatic relations with allies and impairing U.S. foreign policy interests. The Nobel Laureates Amicus Brief advocated a much more formal reliance on

---

165. Case 12.285, Inter–Am. C.H.R., Report No. 62/02, ¶ 84 (2002).

166. Brief for Respondent, *supra* note 159, at 49–50.

167. *Id.* at 50.

168. Brief of Amici Curiae the European Union and Members of the International Community in Support of Respondent, Roper, 543 U.S. 551 (No. 03–633); Brief of Amici Curiae Former U.S. Diplomats Morton Abramowitz, et al. in Support of Respondent, Roper, 543 U.S. 551 (No. 03–633); Brief for the Human Rights Committee of the Bar of England and Wales, Human Rights Advocates, Human Rights Watch, and the World Organization for Human Rights USA as Amici Curiae in Support of Respondent, Roper, 543 U.S. 551 (No. 03–633), Brief Amici Curiae President James Earl Carter, Jr., et al., (Nobel Peace Prize Laureates), Roper, 543 U.S. 551 (No. 03–633).

169. Brief of Amici Curiae the European Union and Members of the International Community in Support of Respondent at 6, Roper, 543 U.S. 551 (No. 03–633).

170. *Id.* at 14–17.

international law. It argued that the prohibition against executing juvenile offenders was widely accepted as customary international law, noted that several bodies had found the norm to be *jus cogens*, and contended that the Court must construe domestic law to avoid violating principles of international law. Finally, the amicus brief submitted by the various human rights organizations argued directly that the prohibition against the execution of juvenile offenders had taken on the status of a nonderogable *jus cogens* norm and thus the United States was bound to refrain from the practice.

The Oral Argument

Consistent with the order of briefing, the state of Missouri as Petitioner argued first. Encouragingly for the Simmons team, Justice Kennedy, the likely swing Justice, early on asked the State Attorney General about the significance of world opinion. In doing so he placed the foreign and international law issue squarely within the textual and doctrinal structure of the Eighth Amendment:

> JUSTICE KENNEDY: [L]et's focus on the word "unusual." Forget "cruel" for the moment, although they're both obviously involved. We've seen very substantial demonstration that world opinion is—is against this, at least as interpreted by the leaders of the European Union. Does that have a bearing on what's unusual? Suppose it were shown that the United States were one of the very, very few countries that executed juveniles, and that's true. Does that have a bearing on whether or not it's unusual?[171]

Justice Kennedy thus appeared to be warm to the inclusion of arguments regarding international consensus in the Eighth Amendment analysis. The state's response was to parrot *Stanford* and the *Atkins'* dissenters, that the "decision as to the Eighth Amendment should not be based on what happens in the rest of the world. It needs to be based on the mores of—of American society."[172] Beyond this conclusory statement, the Missouri Attorney General contended that it was "unimaginable" that the Eighth Amendment analysis should include consideration of what occurs in other countries because doing so would require acceptance of the "flip side" of this argument, namely that it could be urged that the United States must engage in a cruel practice simply because other states were doing so.[173] The claim appeared to be that forcing the United States to follow international opinion and law as a *punishment* limiting principle (or rights floor) would conversely constrain the United

---

171. Transcript of Oral Argument at 14, *Roper*, 543 U.S. 551 (No. 03–633).
172. *Id.*
173. *Id.* at 15.

States to follow international opinion and law also as a *rights* limiting principle (or rights ceiling). Not only does this claim suffer from illogic, but it also is contrary to the existence in the major human rights conventions of savings clauses, which explicitly acknowledge that state parties can provide greater protection than that accorded by the treaty.[174]

In accord with the strategy of the briefing, and buoyed by the presence of the Chinese judicial delegation in the Courtroom as well as by the receptive questioning of Justice Kennedy, Waxman intended to invoke the international consensus argument in the same fashion as the team had done in the merits briefing. As is apparent in the oral argument passage quoted in the introduction to this Chapter, in doing so Waxman quickly incurred the ire of Chief Justice Rehnquist, whose disdain for international and foreign law arguments caused him to miss the sarcasm of Waxman's reference to the "better view in Europe."[175] Waxman was pushed further on the point by Justice Scalia who, like the Missouri Attorney General, concluded that, by accepting the principle that the United States should be influenced by international norms limiting the exercise of state power in inflicting certain punishments, it would necessarily follow that the United States would also be constrained in its ability to provide greater rights protections. Waxman responded by returning to his core international consensus theme and directing it to Justice Kennedy's apparent receptiveness:

> MR WAXMAN: Of course not, but this is a—this is a standard which—a constitutional test that looks to evolving standards of moral decency that go to human dignity. And in that regard, it is—it is notable that we are literally alone in the world even though 110 countries in the world permit capital punishment for one purpose—for one crime or another, and yet every one—every one formally renounces it for juvenile offenders.
>
> And, Justice Kennedy, my submission isn't that that [sic] that's set—you know, game, set, and match. It's just relevant, and I think it is relevant in terms of the existence of a consensus.[176]

The Result: Roper v. Simmons

On March 1, 2005, the Court issued its historic decision in *Roper*, holding that the Eighth Amendment prohibits states from executing

---

174. *See, e.g.*, International Covenant on Civil and Political Rights, art. 5, Dec. 16, 1966, 999 U.N.T.S. 171 ("There shall be no restriction upon or derogation from any of the fundamental human rights recognized or existing in any State Party to the present Covenant pursuant to law, conventions, regulations or custom on the pretext that the present Covenant does not recognize such rights or that it recognizes them to a lesser extent.").

175. Transcript of Oral Argument at 26, *Roper*, 543 U.S. 551 (No. 03–633).

176. *Id.* at 27–28.

individuals who were under age eighteen at the time they committed their offense.[177] The structure of the opinion largely tracks the now familiar two-step analysis regarding consensus and proportionality. The one deviation from the norm in *Roper* is its protracted defense of the appropriateness of consideration of international and foreign law. Elevated from the footnote ghetto of *Atkins* to its own Part in the opinion, *Roper* elaborated upon relevant international and foreign law sources and defended the relevance of the Court's consideration of those sources.[178]

After detailing the relevant facts and procedural posture, the Court set the general framework for its overall analysis. In framing the right at issue, the Court explained that the "Eighth Amendment guarantees individuals the right not to be subjected to excessive sanctions."[179] Then, in a reformulation of this right, the Court stated that "[b]y protecting even those convicted of heinous crimes, the Eighth Amendment reaffirms the duty of the government to respect the dignity of all persons."[180] This articulation of the Eighth Amendment protection sounds in the discourse of human rights not only because it invokes human dignity as the core, unassailable value, but also because it casts the state's obligation not as a negative restriction, but as an affirmative obligation on the part of the state to protect the human dignity of all, even those judged guilty and sentenced to death.[181]

With the framework set, the Court turned first to its consensus analysis, where the focus was entirely domestic. In calculating the number of states that bar the practice of executing juvenile offenders, the Court found the evidence of consensus "parallel" to that in *Atkins*.[182] In *Atkins*, twelve states had abandoned the death penalty outright, and an additional eighteen states that continued to maintain the death penalty specifically had excluded persons with mental retardation from its reach.[183] An identical majority consisting of thirty states precluded the execution of juvenile offenders, with twelve that rejected the death penalty in whole and eighteen additional death penalty states that prohibited the execution of juvenile offenders.[184] Moreover, as in *Atkins*, the Court described that even among the states that continue to author-

---

177. *Roper*, 543 U.S. at 578–79.

178. *Id.* at 575–78.

179. *Id.* at 560.

180. *Id.*

181. *See e.g.* Universal Declaration of Human Rights, G.A. Res. 217A(III), U.N. GAOR, 3d Sess., 1st plen. mtg., U.N. Doc. A/810 (Dec. 12, 1948).

182. *Roper*, 543 U.S. at 564.

183. *Id.*

184. *Id.*

ize the juvenile death penalty, the practice is exceedingly rare.[185] Between *Penry* and *Atkins* only five states had executed individuals with IQs in the range of mental retardation.[186] At the time the Court decided *Roper*, only six states had executed juvenile offenders since *Stanford*.[187] Finally, although the Court noted that the number of states that had moved from allowing the execution of the mentally retarded at the time of *Penry* to disallowing it by the time of *Atkins* had increased at a greater pace than that for juveniles from *Stanford* to *Roper*, the "consistency of direction of change"—from permissive to proscriptive and not vice versa—was identical.[188]

The Court concluded the national consensus section with a rebuttal of the State of Missouri's affirmative invocation of international law sources. As discussed above, Missouri contended in its briefing that the Senate's 1992 reservation regarding Article 6(5) of the ICCPR was evidence that there was not in fact a consensus against juvenile executions.[189] According to the Court, the "reservation at best provides only faint support for petitioner's argument" because, subsequent to 1992, five states outlawed juvenile executions and Congress in 1994 considered and rejected the extension of the juvenile death penalty to juvenile offenders.[190] The binding international law doctrinal arguments advanced by the amici—for example, that the reservation was invalid because it runs counter to the object and purpose of the treaty or that the prohibition had otherwise reached the status of a *jus cogens* norm— could have been considered and potentially deployed effectively by the Court as a factor. They were not. In its minimal analysis, the Court gave no consideration to these arguments.

Having found "objective indicia of consensus" in *Roper* comparable to that in *Atkins,* the Court turned to its independent proportionality analysis. Noting first that the Court's Eighth Amendment death penalty jurisprudence requires careful narrowing of the class of eligible offenders, the Court considered arguments based largely on psychological data demonstrating that juveniles as a group are less mature and more susceptible to influence and that the personality traits of juveniles are more transitory than that of adults.[191] For these reasons, the Court found that juvenile offenders were less culpable than the average adult offend-

---

185. *Id.* at 564–65.
186. *Id.* at 564.
187. *Id.* at 564–65.
188. *Id.* at 565–66.
189. *See supra* note 151 and accompanying text.
190. *Roper,* 543 U.S. at 567.
191. *Id.* at 569–70.

er and, therefore, that the penological purposes of capital punishment—retribution and deterrence—applied with less force.[192]

In concluding this core part of the opinion regarding both consensus and proportionality, the Court made clear that *Stanford* was no longer controlling—not only as to the holding that juvenile offenders may not be executed, but also as to two other aspects of the opinion.

> It should be observed, furthermore, that the *Stanford* Court should have considered those States that had abandoned the death penalty altogether as part of the consensus against the juvenile death penalty.... [T]o the extent *Stanford* was based on a rejection of the idea that this Court is required to bring its independent judgment to bear on the proportionality of the death penalty for a particular class of crimes or offenders, it suffices to note that this rejection was inconsistent with prior Eighth Amendment decisions ... [and] with the premises of our recent decision in *Atkins*.[193]

Of course, *Stanford* also had rejected any reliance on international and foreign law as part of its analysis, something also deemed "inconsistent with prior Eighth Amendment decisions." No mention was made of this here, presumably because the *Roper* opinion had not yet itself relied in any form upon international or foreign law, except to the extent that it rejected Missouri's invocation of the ICCPR reservation as counter to a consensus conclusion. Presumably, then, the Court's opinion could have ended there, as the text of the opinion had reached and justified its conclusion that the Eighth Amendment prohibits the execution of juvenile offenders. It did not. In the final Part of the opinion, much like the final section of the Simmons' merits brief, the Court engaged in a limited, but unapologetic, consideration of both international and foreign law.[194]

The Court began its international and foreign law discussion by making clear the limited doctrinal role that discussion would play. At this point in the narrative of the opinion, the Court already "determin[ed] that the death penalty is disproportionate punishment for offenders under 18."[195] The Court's determination "[found] confirmation in the stark reality that the United States is the only country in the world that continues to give official sanction to the juvenile death penalty."[196] And although this was not "controlling" in the Eighth Amendment analysis, the Court's precedent at least since *Trop v. Dulles*

---

192. *Id.* at 571.
193. *Id.* at 574–575 (internal citations omitted).
194. *Id.* at 576–78.
195. *Id.* at 575.
196. *Id.*

"ha[d] referred to the laws of other countries and to international authorities as instructive for its interpretation of the Eighth Amendment."[197]

In partaking of this instruction, the Court noted that every country in the world "save for the United States and Somalia" has ratified the CRC, which included a prohibition on the execution of juvenile offenders.[198] The Court did not mention, let alone analyze, whether this fact had significance in establishing a customary international law norm as had been pressed by several of the amici. Similarly, the Court delineated that the ICCPR and the American Convention on Human Rights contain parallel provisions.[199] The Court merely noted parenthetically that the United States ratification of the ICCPR is subject to a reservation regarding the prohibition of the execution of juveniles.[200]

Next, the Court discussed the reality that since 1990 only seven countries other than the United States—Iran, Pakistan, Saudi Arabia, Yemen, Nigeria, the DRC, and China—have executed juvenile offenders.[201] It explained that, subsequently, every one of those states formally disavowed the practice.[202] Finally, the Court outlined the U.K.'s particular and more long-standing rejection of the juvenile death penalty, noting that the U.K.'s experience was particularly instructive "in light of the historic ties between our countries and in light of the Eighth Amendment's" origin as modeled after the English Declaration of Rights of 1689.[203]

To the extent that the Court provided a justification beyond longstanding precedent for its willingness to receive instruction and confirmation of its conclusion from the world community, the Court stated only that international opinion rests "in large part on the understanding that the instability and emotional imbalance of young people may often be a factor in the crime."[204] The opinion cited the amicus brief of the

---

 197. *Id.* at 575 (citing Atkins v. Virginia, 536 U.S. 304, 317, n. 21 (2002); Thompson v. Oklahoma, 487 U.S. 815, 830–31 (1988); Enmund v. Florida, 458 U.S. 782, 796–97 (1982); Coker v. Georgia, 433 U.S. 584, 596, n. 10 (1977); Trop v. Dulles, 356 U.S. 86, 102–03 (1958)).

 198. *Roper*, 543 U.S. at 576.

 199. *Id.*

 200. *Id.*

 201. *Id.* at 577.

 202. *Id.*

 203. *Id.*

 204. *Id.* at 578. Several scholars of diverse views have criticized the Court for essentially failing to provide a theoretical justification for reference to international and foreign law. *See, e.g.,* Roger P. Alford, *Roper v. Simmons and Our Constitution in*

Human Rights Committee of the Bar of England and Wales, et al., for this proposition.[205]

Finally, the Court concluded with the following contention in support of its willingness to engage in this examination of world opinion: "It does not lessen our fidelity to the Constitution or our pride in its origins to acknowledge that the express affirmation of certain fundamental rights by other nations and peoples simply underscores the centrality of those same rights within our own heritage of freedom."[206]

Two Justices penned dissents: Justice Scalia, who was joined by then-Chief Justice Rehnquist and Justice Thomas, and Justice O'Connor. Although both Justice O'Connor and Justice Scalia disagreed vehemently with the Majority's conclusion that a national consensus had formed against the execution of juvenile offenders, the primary point of departure between the two dissents was on the pertinence of foreign and international law. As in *Atkins*, Justice Scalia vociferously admonished that "the basic premise of the Court's argument—that American law should conform to the laws of the rest of the world—ought to be rejected out of hand."[207] In contrast, Justice O'Connor insisted that in the Eighth Amendment context, reference to foreign and international law is consistent with the Court's practice.[208] Moreover, she asserted that "this Nation's evolving understanding of human dignity certainly is neither wholly isolated from, nor inherently at odds with, the values prevailing in other countries."[209]

Conclusion

Waxman's descriptive phrase, "arresting juxtaposition," elegantly captured multiple dynamics at play in the advocacy and the Court's treatment of foreign and international law in *Roper* and highlighted lessons that can be distilled from it. There is, of course, the dynamic to which Waxman was referring: that essentially every country in the world except the United States formally had eliminated the death penalty for juvenile offenders. This fact could have been deployed by the Supreme Court litigators as part of a formal international law argument regarding

---

International Equipoise, 53 UCLA L. REV. 1 (2005); Jeremy Waldron, *Foreign Law and the Modern Ius Gentium*, 119 HARV. L. REV. 129 (2005).

205. *Roper*, 543 U.S. at 578 (citing Brief for the Human Rights Committee of the Bar of England and Wales, et al. at 10–11, *Roper*, 543 U.S. 551 (No. 03–633)).

206. *Id.*

207. *Id.* at 625 (Scalia, J., dissenting).

208. *Id.* at 604–05 (O'Connor, J. dissenting) ("This inquiry reflects the special character of the Eighth Amendment, which, as the Court has long held, draws its meaning directly from the maturing values of civilized society.").

209. *Id.* at 605.

the status of the norm in customary international law, as was done by several of the international human rights amici. Instead, the litigators chose a mode of cautious engagement, primarily allowing the existence of international consensus to impact the Justices at the level of optics and atmospherics. Waxman's indirect reference to the CRC at oral argument via mention of the lack of a functioning government in Somalia symbolized the softness of the invocation. This strategic choice—one that litigators often make in the context of any constitutional litigation, or any litigation for that matter—was savvy and successful. The Court's separate discussion of international and foreign law as a confirmatory component of its already-reached conclusion regarding the Eighth Amendment question suggests that the foreign and international law arguments had precisely the impact intended by the Simmons' team.

Another arresting juxtaposition is that between *Stanford's* explicit rejection of the relevance of foreign and international law and *Roper's* forceful statement of acceptance. Recall further that Justice Kennedy, newly appointed to the Court in 1989, had joined Justice Scalia's opinion in *Stanford*. The change in the fifteen years separating the two cases was not a relevant change in members of the Court, but rather a change that can be attributed to the international human rights advocacy and scholarship that had taken place outside of the courtroom walls. The widespread ratification of the CRC, the meticulous reporting and advocacy of NGOs such as the heavily relied-upon 2004 Amnesty International report on juvenile executions, the domestic and international litigation of the issue, and the filing of sophisticated international human rights briefs by a wealth of respected international institutions and players, were all factors that moved the Justices from noting the "interesting" nature of international law arguments, as Justice Blackmun did in reading the briefs in *Stanford*, to a meaningful, if cautious, engagement with those materials by Justice Kennedy writing for the Court in *Roper*. As these trends continue, surely the Court will increase its understanding and "internalization" of international human rights law arguments.

Finally, the presence of the Chinese judicial delegation at the Supreme Court on the day of the *Roper* arguments wonderfully symbolized the "rich dialogue between international and constitutional norms."[210] The final Part of the *Roper* opinion on international and foreign law can be read, in part, as a statement to the world that the United States, which speaks often to other countries about the necessity of human rights standards, also is capable of listening.

---

210. Sarah H. Cleveland, *Our International Constitution*, 31 YALE J. INT'L L. 1, 124–125 (2006).

Part Four

Globalization, Foreign Policy and the Economy

*

10

The Story of Narmada Bachao Andolan: Human Rights in the Global Economy and the Struggle Against the World Bank

Smita Narula[*]

India's first Prime Minister, Jawaharlal Nehru, once called dams the "temples of modern India."[1] His quixotic analogy is often invoked to support the view that building large dams is essential to meeting India's myriad development needs.[2] Though he later retracted his statement and called large dams "a disease of gigantism" that India must abandon,[3] the drive to build large dams for the sake of building large dams continues to blind the government to their human and environmental costs. Nowhere has this rung more true than along the banks of the Narmada River.

The Narmada River traverses three of India's northwestern states: Gujarat, Madhya Pradesh, and Maharashtra. In 1978, the Indian government sought the World Bank's assistance to build a complex of dams along the river as part of the Narmada Valley Development Project ("Narmada Project"). The Narmada Project envisioned the creation of thirty large dams, 135 medium dams, and 3,000 small dams.[4] The Indian

---

[*] Work on this Chapter was supported by the Filomen D'Agostino Research Fund at New York University School of Law. The author thanks Jane Pek, Tara Mikkilineni, Jonathan Horne, Dennis Hermreck, and Nishanth Chari for their invaluable research assistance.

1. Jawaharlal Nehru, Prime Minister of India, Speech at the Opening of the Nangal Canal (July 8, 1954).

2. Balakrishnan Rajagopal, *The Role of Law in Counter-hegemonic Globalization and Global Legal Pluralism: Lessons from the Narmada Valley Struggle in India*, 18 LEIDEN J. INT'L L. 345, 355 (2005).

3. Jawaharlal Nehru, Prime Minister of India, Address at the 29th Annual Meeting of the Central Bureau of Irrigation and Power (Nov. 17, 1958).

4. Supriya Garikipati, *Consulting the Development–Displaced Regarding Their Settlement: Is There a Way?*, 18 J. REFUGEE STUD. 340, 341 (2005).

government promised that the dams would help provide potable water for almost forty million people, irrigation for over six million hectares of land, and hydroelectric power for the entire region.[5] Central to the claim that the dams were essential for India's economic development was the assertion that these benefits, which would purportedly accrue to millions of people living in the Narmada River valley, outweighed any potential human or environmental costs. The narrative of the "common good" has been emblematic of the government's stance throughout the many controversies generated by the project and reflects the dominance of a "balancing" or "cost-benefit" approach to development over an approach that puts human rights at the center of the debate.[6]

The Sardar Sarovar Project ("SSP") in the state of Gujarat includes the most controversial large dam. The government claimed that the Sardar Sarovar dam alone would irrigate almost 1.8 million hectares of land in Gujarat and an additional 73,000 hectares in the dry neighboring state of Rajasthan, in addition to providing potable water to over 8,000 Gujarati villages and 135 urban centers.[7] The ostensible benefits, however, would come at a high cost, including the displacement of tens of thousands of individuals and considerable environmental damage. Despite these foreseeable consequences, and in the absence of consultation with indigenous communities that would experience the environmental impact and involuntary displacement, in 1985 the World Bank agreed to finance the Sardar Sarovar dam to the tune of $450 million, approximately 10% of the total cost of the project.[8]

In response, local opponents, environmental activists, and professionals from the academic, scientific, and cultural worlds founded a cluster of non-governmental organizations ("NGOs"). These NGOs gained strength in the late 1980s when they allied to form the Narmada Bachao Andolan ("NBA"), or the Save Narmada Movement. Led by the legendary activist Medha Patkar, the NBA employed creative means of resistance to mobilize opposition to the Sardar Sarovar Project. On the national front, the NBA opposed the dam and proposed various development alternatives, including decentralized methods of water harvesting. Internationally, the NBA led the charge to demand World Bank accountability for its involvement in a project that threatened to harm millions. Their campaign led to the creation of a Bank commission in 1991 to

---

5. Rajagopal, *supra* note 2, at 358.

6. *See* Benedict Kingsbury & Doreen Lustig, *Displacement and Relocation from Protected Areas: International Law Perspectives on Rights, Risks and Resistance*, 4 CONSERVATION AND SOC'Y 404, 411 (2006).

7. Rajagopal, *supra* note 2, at 358.

8. HUMAN RIGHTS WATCH & NATURAL RES. DEF. COUNCIL, DEFENDING THE EARTH: ABUSES OF HUMAN RIGHTS AND THE ENVIRONMENT 24 (1992), *available at* http://www.hrw.org/reports/pdfs/g/general/general2926.pdf [hereinafter HUMAN RIGHTS WATCH].

independently review the project, which ultimately recommended the Bank's withdrawal.

Citing human rights concerns that reached far beyond the Sardar Sarovar dam, and focusing on the participation of those most directly affected, the review concluded that "unless a project can be carried out in accordance with existing norms of human rights—norms espoused and endorsed by the Bank and many borrower countries—the project ought not to proceed."[9] The Bank ceased to support the project the following year. Furthermore, the controversy surrounding the dam led directly to the creation of the World Bank Inspection Panel in 1993. It was a milestone for the human rights movement and the first mechanism established to enable local groups to challenge World Bank projects.

Prior to the Panel's creation, local groups had no formal way of challenging development schemes conceived and financed in faraway national and international capitals where their voices were seldom heard. Fifteen years after its creation, and despite its mixed record, the Panel represents a major milestone in integrating international human rights norms into the practice of development aid.

However, the Bank's withdrawal may have been a pyrrhic victory for the Narmada campaign. Though a triumphant symbol of the power of mass mobilization, the withdrawal reduced the Indian government's accountability to the outside world. It also removed a body that had the obligation and ability to hold the project to a higher set of standards than the Indian government would have adhered to on its own. Ironically and unwittingly, the NBA's transformative impact on the World Bank helped others find their forum even as it lost its own. The Narmada struggle remains unceasing and increasingly urgent.

The Narmada Valley Dam Project

The idea of building dams in the Narmada river basin predates independent India. In 1946, India's Central Waterways, Irrigation, and Navigation Commission constituted a committee to study the feasibility of such a project.[10] Fifteen years later, Prime Minister Nehru inaugurated the Narmada Valley Development Project. The Narmada Project's costs have been both human and environmental though the foremost issue remains the displacement of the Narmada basin's inhabitants.[11]

---

9. BRADFORD MORSE ET AL., SARDAR SAROVAR: THE REPORT OF THE INDEPENDENT REVIEW 358 (1992).

10. Rajagopal, *supra* note 2, at 356.

11. *See* Balakrishan Rajagopal, *From Resistance to Renewal: The Third World, Social Movements, and the Expansion of International Institutions*, 41 HARV. INT'L L.J. 529, 566 (2000).

The Narmada basin is almost 100,000 square kilometers in size and is home to twenty-one million people.[12] The Sardar Sarovar dam's impounding of water in a 455–foot–high reservoir would ultimately submerge 37,000 hectares of land in Gujarat, Maharashtra, and Madhya Pradesh, and divert 9.5 million acre feet of water into a canal and irrigation system.[13] According to unofficial estimates, the Sardar Sarovar dam alone has displaced 320,000 people.[14] Added to these human costs is the considerable environmental damage to a valley teeming with plant and animal life.[15] Tellingly, the Indian government has not reported official statistics on the number of displaced individuals,[16] reflecting a level of disregard for the seriousness of the problem that continues to date.

Narmada Water Disputes Tribunal

The Narmada Water Disputes Tribunal ("Narmada Tribunal") was set up in 1969 to resolve the river water sharing dispute between Madhya Pradesh, Gujarat, and Maharashtra. Additionally, the Narmada Tribunal aimed to set out conditions regarding the resettlement and rehabilitation of those displaced by the dams.[17] Chaired by then-sitting Supreme Court Justice V. Ramaswami, the Tribunal was assisted by technical experts. Notably absent from this team of experts were any sociologists, anthropologists or environmental engineers.[18]

In 1978, the Narmada Tribunal approved the Narmada Project and final planning and work commenced.[19] With regard to the treatment of the displaced population, the Narmada Tribunal mandated that the state

---

12. Armin Rosencranz & Kathleen D. Yurchak, *Progress on the Environmental Front: The Regulation of Industry and Development in India*, 19 HASTINGS INT'L & COMP. L. REV. 489, 512 (1996).

13. *Id.* at 513. In addition, it was estimated that the canal and irrigation system would adversely affect 140,000 farmers and thousands of additional individuals who live downstream. *Id.* at 513–14. Rajagopal argues that the SSP dam "would alone potentially affect 25–40 million people, whereas the canal to be built would have displaced 68,000 households." Rajagopal, *supra* note 11, at 566.

14. *See* Friends of River Narmada, *available at* http://www.narmada.org/sardarsarovar.html.

15. *See* Rajagopal, *supra* note 11, at 566.

16. *See* Internal Displacement Monitoring Center, *available at* http://www.internaldisplacement.org/idmc/website/countries.nsf/(httpEnvelopes)/017EF48C508340A1802570B8005A7175?OpenDocument.

17. Rosencranz & Yurchak, *supra* note 12, at 512–13. The Narmada Tribunal was established under India's Interstate Water Disputes Act of 1956. *Id.*

18. Rajagopal, *supra* note 2, at 356.

19. Rosencranz & Yurchak, *supra* note 12, at 512–13.

of Gujarat, as the primary beneficiary of the project, provide "land for land" to those displaced by the Sardar Sarovar dam.[20] While the Narmada Tribunal's Final Order aimed to alleviate displacement, commentators have critiqued both the judgment and its implementation by the government of Gujarat. The judgment, for instance, only guaranteed compensation for legal landowners even though many dam-affected villages kept poor land records.[21] In addition, many displaced persons were tribal community members who lacked formal land ownership rights under Indian law.[22] A more general indictment suggested that "the [Narmada] Tribunal was itself a creature of politics that was incapable, *ab initio*, of delivering justice."[23] First, the Narmada Tribunal focused on the interstate dispute between riparian states and insufficiently considered the affected communities themselves.[24] Second, political deal-making between the states limited the Narmada Tribunal's terms of reference, including consideration of whether alternatives existed to achieve the project's objectives.[25]

In December 1979, the Narmada Tribunal's final award came into effect,[26] and in 1987 construction began on the Sardar Sarovar dam.[27] Problems soon emerged with Gujarat's resettlement policy,[28] which formally sought to award each eligible family settling there at least five irrigable acres, housing, and various entitlements to facilities.[29] In reality, there was not enough land available for distribution; amenities were substandard; and settlers had difficulty integrating with host communities.[30] As a result, though 196 families had accepted the resettlement

---

20. Garikipati, *supra* note 4, at 341–42; John R. Wood, *India's Narmada River Dams: Sardar Sarovar under Siege*, 33 ASIAN SURV. 968, 975 (1993). Specifically, the Narmada Tribunal guaranteed every displaced family five acres of irrigable land at least one year prior to submergence, required that villages be resettled as units, qualified adult male children of affected families for individual rehabilitation as distinct from their families, and emphasized timely and appropriate resettlement. Komala Ramachandra, *Sardar Sarovar: An Experience Retained?*, 19 HARV. HUM. RTS. J. 275, 276 (2006).

21. Garikipati, *supra* note 4, at 342.

22. Rajagopal, *supra* note 2, at 357–58.

23. *Id.* at 356.

24. *Id.*

25. *Id.* at 357. Rajagopal adds a third point: that the act granting the Narmada Tribunal jurisdiction lacked any appeals process by which an ordinary court might examine its conformity to evolving legal standards—although this did not in fact prevent the Indian Supreme Court from subsequently admitting petitions from the NBA. *Id.*

26. *Id.* at 356.

27. Garikipati, *supra* note 4, at 341.

28. Chittaroopa Palit, *Monsoon Risings: Mega–Dam Resistance in the Narmada Valley*, 21 NEW LEFT REV. 81, 84 (2003), *available at* http://www.newleftreview.org/A2450.

29. Garikipati, *supra* note 4, at 342.

30. *Id.* According to Paramjit Judge, following pressure from NGOs and community leaders, the government bought land in areas preferred by those displaced by the project.

offer, many settlers ended up returning to their homes, which were already partially submerged.[31]

The World Bank's Involvement in the Sardar Sarovar Dam Project

Although the Bank had long been interested in financing the Sardar Sarovar dam, it could not do so before the Narmada Tribunal's Final Order. Once the order was issued, the Bank quickly stepped in.[32] Working closely with Indian officials, Bank staffers spent a number of years reconfiguring the Sardar Sarovar dam in order to minimize its negative side effects while maximizing its financial and technical viability.[33] Between 1979 and 1983, the Bank prepared the first-stage project. The appraisal of this phase that soon followed[34] notably did not include an assessment of social or environmental issues.[35]

In 1985 the Bank lent the three state governments a total of $200 million and gave them $250 million in credits to finance the Sardar Sarovar dam.[36] The Bank's involvement transnationalized the projects at multiple levels. First, it indicated international approval, bringing in several other foreign actors.[37] Second, it internationalized resistance to the project. Third, the Bank's internal policies provided a standard against which to judge the project's performance with regard to involuntary resettlement.[38] Despite the benefits of transnationalization, the

---

Even so, a host of problems remained, such as relocation stress, the end of descent group collectivity, kinship zone enlargement, land encumbrance, host village hostility, and bureaucratic indifference. Paramjit Judge, *Response to Dams and Displacement in Two Indian States*, 37 ASIAN SURV. 846, 847 (1997).

31. Garikipati, *supra* note 4, at 342.

32. CATHERINE CAUFIELD, MASTERS OF ILLUSION: THE WORLD BANK AND THE POVERTY OF NATIONS 11 (1997). India initially approached the Bank for funding for the SSP in 1978. Rajagopal, *supra* note 11, at 568.

33. CAUFIELD, *supra* note 32, at 11.

34. Rajagopal, *supra* note 11, at 568.

35. CAUFIELD, *supra* note 32, at 11.

36. The governments then requested $350 million more to complete the canal and $90 million for the Narmada Basin Development Project. Rosencranz & Yurchak, *supra* note 12, at 514; Stephanie C. Guyett, *Environment and Lending: Lessons of the World Bank, Hope for the European Bank for Reconstruction and Development*, 24 N.Y.U. J. INT'L L. & POL. 889, 906–07 (1992).

37. Rajagopal, *supra* note 2, at 360. These actors included the Japanese Organization for Economic Co-operation and Development, which would fund turbines provided by the Sumitomo and Hitachi corporations; Kreditanstalt für Wiederaufbau of Germany to support the development of fisheries; Canadian International Development Agency, which would conduct environmental impact studies; and Official Development Assistance of the U.K. for studies on downstream impact and environmental plans. *Id.*

38. *Id.* at 360–361.

Bank ignored shortcomings in the approval process[39] to the point of violating its own policies concerning resettlement and environmental degradation.[40]

Tension Emerges between the World Bank's Policies and its Support of the Dam

The Bank's role in the construction of the Sardar Sarovar dam must be viewed against the backdrop of various human rights-related policies adopted by the Bank in the 1980s and 1990s. The World Bank's Operational Policies and Directives developed in response to external and internal pressure to establish environmental and human rights guidelines for its lending practices.[41] The Bank's first general resettlement policy, adopted in 1980, provided that "upon resettlement, displaced persons should regain at least their previous standard of living."[42] Two years later the Bank adopted a resettlement policy specifically addressing "tribal" populations and requiring that customary usage of tribal land be respected and that tribal community members only be displaced when the borrowing country can effectively safeguard their integrity and well-being.[43]

In 1990, the Bank issued Directive 4.30 on involuntary resettlement, followed a year later by Directive 4.20 on the resettlement of indigenous peoples. These Directives, which were the result of a decade of policy deliberation, established the highest standards of any development aid or lending organization for responding to the consequences of involuntary resettlement.[44]

Under the Bank's policies on involuntary resettlement, the Bank must finalize resettlement plans prior to the loan's approval. In addition,

---

39. See Guyett, *supra* note 36, at 906–07.

40. CAUFIELD, *supra* note 32, at 12.

41. Guyett, *supra* note 36, at 895–909.

42. World Bank Operational Manual Statement No. 2.33: Social Issues Associated with Involuntary Settlement in Bank–Financed Projects, *reprinted in* SARDAR SAROVAR, THE REPORT OF THE INDEPENDENT REVIEW 23 (1992), *quoted in* Thomas R. Berger, *The World Bank's Independent Review of India's Sardar Sarovar Projects*, 9 AM. U. J. INT'L L. & POL'Y 33, 40 (1993) (internal quotation marks omitted).

43. The policy, entitled Operational Manual Statement 2.34, was later replaced by Directive 4.20 to substitute "tribal" with "indigenous," which was further modified to "indigenous peoples" under Operational Policy 4.10 in 2005. *See* Legal Note on Indigenous Peoples, World Bank, *available at* http://siteresources.worldbank.org/INTINDPEOPLE/Publications/20571167/Legal%20Note.pdf; *see also* Operational Policy 4.10, World Bank, *available at* http://web.worldbank.org/WBSITE/EXTERNAL/PROJECTS/EXTPOLICIES/EXTOPMANUAL/0,,contentMDK:20553653~menuPK:4564185~pagePK:64709096~piPK:64709108~theSitePK:502184,00.html

44. Operational Manual Statement No. 2.33, *supra* note 42, at 41.

credit agreements with the Indian states required resettlement plans that conform to these policies. Nevertheless, a comprehensive plan for the resettlement of affected individuals had not been formulated even six years after the loan's approval.[45] Although the Bank attempted to address this violation by imposing deadlines on the state governments to produce these plans, these deadlines were not enforced.[46] Nor did the Bank address the vast and foreseeable ecological consequences of the Sardar Sarovar dam; the Bank approved the project even though the Indian Ministry of Environment and Forests would not consent to the project without completed environmental impact studies, which were never performed.[47]

The Narmada Bachao Andolan Movement

Since the early 1980s, the Narmada Project has faced mounting opposition from a variety of sources. Protest groups formed in all three affected states and included or were supported by individuals facing displacement, students, social activists, Indian environmental NGOs, international NGOs, and transnational networks.[48] In Gujarat, nineteen villages, whose submersion the Sardar Sarovar dam ensured, formed the Chhatra Yuva Sangharsh Vahini, a youth protest group.[49] The group engaged in protests and initiated court actions, ultimately forcing the government of Gujarat to offer a more generous resettlement package. The group's belief that Gujarat's water needs made the dam project necessary guided its decision to focus on rehabilitation efforts and to ensure that the government adhered to its promises.[50]

In contrast, groups in Madhya Pradesh and Maharashtra opposed the dams altogether. Two such groups, the Narmada Ghati Navnirman Samiti in Madhya Pradesh and the Narmada Ghati Dharangrastha Samiti in Maharashtra, subsequently merged to form the Narmada Bachao Andolan in 1989.[51] Under the leadership of the principal figure

---

45. *Environmental, Social and Economic Concerns Related to the World Bank Financed Sardar Sarovar Dam and Power Project and Sardar Sarovar Water Delivery and Drainage Project*, Memorandum from the Environmental Defense Fund to Barber Conable, president of the World Bank (Mar. 1991) (on file with author). *See also* Guyett, *supra* note 36, at 906–907.

46. *Id.* at 907.

47. *Id.* at 906–07.

48. Benedict Kingsbury, *"Indigenous Peoples" in International Law: A Constructivist Approach to the Asian Controversy*, 92 AM. J. INT'L L. 414, 444 (1998). *See also*, Ashok Swain, *Democratic Consolidation? Environmental Movements in India*, 37 ASIAN SURV. 818, 825 (1997).

49. Wood, *supra* note 20, at 977.

50. *Id.*

51. *Id.*

associated with the movement, Medha Patkar, the NBA initially sought to verify the claims regarding the benefits that would flow from the construction of the dams. In the process, it focused on securing access to documents from the government and the World Bank to ensure greater transparency.[52]

The NBA's Methods

The success of the NBA campaign resulted from its innovative strategies of resistance that operated simultaneously at the grassroots, national, and international level. As such, the campaign's significance as a social movement extends far beyond India's national borders.[53] Balakrishnan Rajagopal—a leading scholar on development and social movements and a long-time observer and researcher of the Narmada struggle—notes that globally, the NBA is "regarded as one of the signature public contestations of the twentieth century that redefined the terms of development, democracy and accountability."[54]

While the NBA originally employed "Gandhian methods" such as peaceful marches and protests,[55] after a high-profile hunger fast in 1991 failed, the NBA announced a "noncooperation movement" in the Narmada valley. This movement campaigned against the payment of taxes and sought to deny entry to the villages to all government officials, except teachers and doctors.[56] The NBA subsequently began to consider litigation as an additional option for a variety of reasons. Their tactics up to this point had frequently drawn violent reactions from the government.[57] In addition, other disadvantaged groups had successfully moved the Supreme Court,[58] inspiring the NBA to do the same.

The NBA's Leadership

The NBA, a broad-based participatory movement, flourished under the leadership of visionary environmental champions. One of India's

---

52. Rajagopal, *supra* note 2, at 364.

53. *Id.*

54. Email interview with Balakrishnan Rajagopal, Ford Assoc. Professor of Law and Dev., M.I.T. (June 18, 2008). Rajagopal is author of INTERNATIONAL LAW FROM BELOW: DEVELOPMENT, SOCIAL MOVEMENTS AND THIRD WORLD RESISTANCE (2003), and co-editor of RESHAPING JUSTICE: INTERNATIONAL LAW AND THE THIRD WORLD (Richard Falk, Balakrishnan Rajagopal, & Jacqueline Stevens eds., 2008).

55. Jayanth K. Krishnan, *Lawyering for a Cause and Experiences from Abroad*, 94 CAL. L. REV. 575, 610 (2006).

56. Wood, *supra* note 20, at 978.

57. Krishnan, *supra* note 55, at 610.

58. *Id.*

most vibrant and best known living activists, Medha Patkar (or Medha *didi* (big sister) as she is called) has led the Narmada movement for over two decades. Her uncompromising stance against government apathy toward the human and social costs of dam construction and her ongoing efforts to ensure that transparency and accountability remain hallmark features of development projects have helped fashion the NBA into one of the most dynamic social movements of our time. A "veteran of several fasts [and] monsoon satyagrahas [civil disobedience] on the banks of the rising Narmada,"[59] she has endured police beatings and jail terms in her quest to secure the right to life and the right to livelihood for the over twenty million people whose lives would be adversely affected by the Narmada Project.

Medha Patkar's stance on the Narmada issue is emblematic of her broader political philosophy. According to Patkar:

> When the state has, under the principle of eminent domain, full right to resources, the state is expected to act in favour of the most disadvantaged communities and use the resources in such a way that the common good would be really achieved, of course, within the value frame work [sic] of equality and justice.... [Instead,] the state is using its power, its laws, ways and means, its police force, a physical brutal force, to take away the resources.... That is like a privatized state, which is privatized by those small elite sections, and this is being done more and more and more brutally and crudely, in the new context of globalization and liberalization....[60]

Other women have also played central roles in the campaign. The NBA's struggle against the Maheshwar Dam in Madhya Pradesh state,[61] for instance, has been led by the Narmada Shakti Dal, a separate women's organization within the NBA that was set up on March 8, 1988—International Women's Day—and is comprised of female villagers from Maheshwar.[62]

Alongside Medha Patkar, social activist Baba Amte provided moral leadership to the cause to preserve the Narmada River. Though renowned for his work against leprosy, beginning in the early 1980s he

---

59. South Asian Women's Network: Who's Who: Medha Paktar, *available at* http://www.sawnet.org/whoswho/?Patkar+Medha.

60. Interview by Venu Govindu with Medha Patkar, in Domkhedi, India (Aug. 7, 1999), The Face of the Narmada, *available at* http://www.indiatogether.org/interviews/iview-mpatkar.htm.

61. *See generally*, Friends of River Narmada, The Maheshwar Dam: A Brief Introduction, *available at* http://www.narmada.org/maheshwar.html.

62. Public Hearing by National Commission of Women Regarding Ongoing Struggle Against the Maheshwar Project, *available at* http://www.sandelman.ottawa.on.ca/lists/html/dam-l/2000/msg01517.htm.

involved himself in the struggle against mega dams. Amte first achieved national prominence for his work on dams with the publication of *Cry O Beloved Narmada* in 1989, an elegiac booklet that made the case for a dam-free Narmada.[63] At the end of 1989, Baba Amte moved to the banks of the Narmada, stating that "[t]he struggle for a New India is taking place in the Narmada valley. Today the Narmada valley has become the arena for a new imagination and creativity, for a society in which there must be sufficiency for all before there is superfluity for some."[64]

The NBA has continually sought to encourage people-centered and environmentally sound alternatives to mega dams,[65] even as critics target opponents of the dams as "eco-romantic activists."[66] The NBA has, for instance, identified decentralized methods of water harvesting as a viable alternative in Gujarat that could be achieved for a fraction of the over $4 billion price tag attached to the Sardar Sarovar dam alone.[67] According to Indian environmental historian Mahesh Rangarajan, Gujarat's political clout and the framing of the issue as one of "water versus displacement" made it difficult for the NBA to make much headway on the issue.[68] Still, the NBA attempted to expose contradictions and fallacies in governmental claims about the benefits of dam construction. For instance, contrary to the Gujarat government's assertion that the Sardar Sarovar dam would satisfy the water needs of the arid regions of Kutch and Saurashtra in northern Gujarat, the NBA found that water would reach only 1.5% of Kutch's total cultivable area, and only 7% of that of Saurashtra. Most would serve the politically influential, already water-rich central Gujarat.[69] Before the NBA forced them to do so, the government had never performed a proper cost-benefit analysis. This review led the government to admit that it had both exaggerated benefits and underes-

---

63. Narmada Bachao!, *available at* http://mss.niya.org/people/baba8_amte.php.

64. *Id.*

65. Z Magazine Online, Interview by Robert Jensen with Medha Patkar (Apr. 1, 2004), *available at* http://www.zmag.org/zmag/viewArticle/13856.

66. Jay Narayan Vyas, *Water and Energy for Development in Gujarat with Special Focus on the Sardar Sarovar Project*, 17 INT'L J. OF WATER RES. DEV. 37, 51 (2001). *See also* Jay Narayan Vyas, *Large Dams and Sustainable Development: A Case Study of the Sardar Sarovar Project, India*, 17 INT'L J. OF WATER RES. DEV. 601, 605 (2007); B. G. Verghese, *Sardar Sarovar Project Revalidated by Supreme Court*, 17 INT'L J. OF WATER RES. DEV. 79, 79 (2001).

67. Palit, *supra* note 28.

68. Email interview with Mahesh Rangarajan, Professor of Modern Indian History, University of Delhi (June 14, 2008). Rangarajan has authored and edited numerous books on conservation and the environment. He is, for example, editor of ENVIRONMENTAL ISSUES IN INDIA: A READER (Mahesh Rangarajan ed., 2007), and co-editor of BATTLES OVER NATURE, SCIENCE AND THE POLITICS OF CONSERVATION (Vasant Kabir Saberwal & Mahesh Rangarajan eds., 2003).

69. Palit, *supra* note 28.

timated costs. The NBA pushed the government to admit, for example, that the Sardar Sarovar Project would displace over 100,000 people and affect over 900,000 more, contrary to its initial estimate that only 7,000 families would be affected.[70]

Direct Action

Together, Patkar and Amte led a number of high-profile protests,[71] only some of which met with success due to the repressive tactics mounted by the government in response. In September 1989, Amte led[72] a 60,000-person anti-dam NBA rally in Harsud—a town of 20,000 people in Madhya Pradesh that faced submersion.[73] In May 1990, a massive NBA five-day *dharna* (sit-in) at then-Prime Minister V. P. Singh's residence in New Delhi forced the Prime Minister to agree to "reconsider" the project.[74] In December 1990, Amte, along with 5,000 protestors, began the *Narmada Jan Vikas Sangharsh Yatra* (Narmada people's progress struggle march), marching over a hundred kilometers from Amte's headquarters near Barwani in Madhya Pradesh to Ferkuva on the Madhya Pradesh–Gujarat border. The government reacted by deploying the Gujarati police force and by bussing in thousands of government-supported pro-dam demonstrators from urban centers in Gujarat.[75]

Following the government's announcement that rising waters from the dam would begin to submerge villages, domestic protest intensified and with it the resulting backlash from the state. On January 5, 1991, Amte began a *"dharna* [sit-in] unto death." Two days later, seven other activists were led by Patkar on a separate hunger strike that lasted twenty-one days before the NBA called off both protests given that no compromise could be reached. While many observers considered the annulment of Amte's and Patkar's protests a sign of the Gujarat government's victory, NBA protesters subsequently declared that they would refuse to move even if this meant being drowned by waters from the Sardar Sarovar reservoir.[76]

---

70. Interview by Govindu, *supra* note 60.

71. Caufield, *supra* note 32, at 15.

72. Wood, *supra* note 20, at 977.

73. *Id.*; *see* Caufield, *supra* note 32, at 14. In January 1990, a 5,000–strong march forced the closure of the Narmada Valley Development Authority offices. *Id.* Two months later, another large-scale protest in Madhya Pradesh blocked the Delhi–Bombay highway bridge for two days. Wood, *supra* note 20, at 978.

74. *Id.* This led to a robust response from the Gujarat Chief Minister, who led an equally large pro-dam demonstration in Delhi shortly thereafter, followed by a massive 100,000–person march in Bombay. *Id.*

75. *Id.*

76. *Id.*

The NBA's slogans—such as *Vikas Chahiye, vinash nahin!* ("We want development, not destruction")[77] and *Koi nahi hatega, bandh nahi banega!* ("No one will move, the dam will not be built")[78]—directly challenged the project's purported benefits and defied the conventional wisdom that the tribal community members would simply cede to government plans. Staying true to their words, during numerous monsoon *satyagrahas* (acts of civil disobedience) hundreds of individuals refused to budge as rising water entered their fields and their homes. According to one NBA activist:

> [S]atyagraha is ... a way of bearing witness to what the state is doing to the people. It affirms the existence of the Valley inhabitants and shows our solidarity. It makes a moral point, contrasting the violence of the development project with the determination of those who stand in its path. In most of the monsoon satyagrahas where the waters have actually flooded the houses ... police have physically dragged people out of the areas being inundated, in an attempt to rob the agitation of its symbolic power.[79]

A less common and much criticized practice—including from within the NBA—is the practice of *jal samarpan* (sacrifice by drowning), wherein protestors prepare to give their lives to the cause. Manibeli, a village in Maharashtra near the Gujarat border, was among the first to be flooded and was therefore the site of numerous demonstrations and concomitant police abuse.[80] During a *satyagraha* launched at Manibeli in 1992, the inhabitants of the valley declared their readiness for *jal samarpan*. As waters rose, the affected people of the lower hamlets stood knee-deep, refusing to move.[81] The state reacted with force, undertaking a number of arrests, beatings and detentions in Maharashtra and Madhya Pradesh between 1992 and 1993.[82] The image of Valley inhabitants, standing motionless and defiant in the face of rising waters ready to sacrifice their lives, is perhaps the most haunting of the movement.

On occasion, direct action proved effective, as when the NBA's new *satyagraha* at Manibeli in 1993 forced a federal government review of the project.[83] It was, however, unable to bring about any meaningful change—the panel appointed by the government to review the project

---

77. Rajagopal, *supra* note 2, at 365–366.
78. *Id.* at 366.
79. Palit, *supra* note 28.
80. HUMAN RIGHTS WATCH, *supra* note 8, at 25.
81. Rajagopal, *supra* note 2, at 367–68.
82. *Id.*
83. *Id.* at 368.

had no power to revisit the project's viability and state police forces continued their repression of the villages in Maharashtra and Gujarat.[84]

International Interventions and Coalition Building

Large-scale protests at home were complemented by international interventions abroad. Lori Udall, then with the Environmental Defense Fund, led the international campaign against the Sardar Sarovar dam and implemented a "multi-pronged strategy of public pressure, organizing, media outreach, and lobbying."[85] In 1987, Patkar met with World Bank officials in Washington, D.C. and questioned their 1985 loan agreement in light of the fact that the Indian Ministry of Environment and Forests had not granted environmental clearance to the project, as required by Indian law.[86] In 1989, Udall worked with a U.S. Congressional Committee that held an oversight hearing on Sardar Sarovar at which Patkar testified, detailing the dams' social and environmental impact.[87]

In addition to working with the Environmental Defense Fund, the NBA partnered with numerous other human rights, environmental, and solidarity organizations overseas.[88] A Narmada International Action Committee—consisting of NGOs from India, the United States, Canada, Europe, Australia, and Japan—lobbied against the Narmada Project in several investing countries,[89] which helped focus international and national attention on the Narmada issue. Most notably, the Japanese branch of the international NGO Friends of the Earth conducted a field visit in Narmada pursuant to which it held the first International Narmada Symposium in Tokyo. The Symposium, greeted with great fanfare by the press, led—within weeks—to the withdrawal of Japan's Overseas Economic Cooperation Fund from the Narmada Project. Soon

---

84. *Id.*

85. Email interview with Lori Udall, Senior Advisor, Bank Info. Ctr. (June 24, 2008). Udall's efforts included lobbying executive directors at the World Bank, the U.S. Congress and Treasury, meeting with affected individuals in the Narmada Valley, and writing and submitting reports to the Bank's U.S. executive director, Bank management, and Congress. Udall additionally lobbied the Japanese government and went on a speaking tour in Japan. For more on Japan, *see infra* text accompanying notes 89–90. Additionally, she networked with activists in all of the Bank's major shareholder countries who in turn lobbied their own governments. Udall worked with the Environmental Defense Fund from 1985 to 1994 and was Washington Director of the International Rivers Network from 1994 to 1997. Since 2000, she has managed her own international consulting business. *Id.*

86. Rajagopal, *supra* note 2, at 364.

87. Udall interview, *supra* note 85; Rajagopal, *supra* note 2, at 364–65.

88. *See, e.g.*, Friends of River Narmada, *available at* http://www.narmada.org and International Rivers Network, *available at* http://www.irn.org/index.php?id=basics/about.html.

89. Rajagopal, *supra* note 2, at 365.

thereafter, Japanese Diet members began pressuring the World Bank president to stop financing the Sardar Sarovar dam.[90] Japan's withdrawal from the project bolstered the case of the environmental activist groups supporting the struggle against the Narmada Project, and pressure mounted on the World Bank to cease its support.

As protests intensified, so too did the backlash from the state; international human rights NGOs began documenting abuses against NBA activists. A June 1992 report by Human Rights Watch noted increases in arbitrary arrests, illegal detentions, beatings, and other forms of physical abuse of NBA activists.[91] That same month, the findings of the report were featured as one of nine country studies in a joint report issued by Human Rights Watch and the Natural Resources Defense Council entitled *Defending the Earth: Abuses of Human Rights and the Environment*.[92] The report was issued at the time of the Earth Summit in Rio de Janeiro, as its authors hoped that it would help focus attention on causal relationships between human rights and environmental abuses and foster greater collaboration and exchanges between human rights and environmental advocates.[93]

The Environmental Defense Fund and the Bank Information Center, both U.S.-based NGOs, led the formation of the Narmada International Human Rights Panel, which garnered the support of forty-two environmental and human rights NGOs representing sixteen countries. The Panel, funded in part by the World Bank until 1993 and assisted by the NBA, sought "to document ongoing violations of political, economic, social and cultural rights of the people of the Narmada Valley."[94] An interim report issued by the Panel in October 1992 also detailed rights violations in the Narmada Valley, which was followed in 1993 by a report of the U.S.-based Lawyers Committee for Human Rights (now Human Rights First).[95]

The World Bank Withdraws

In response to a tide of mounting pressure, the World Bank announced in June 1991 that it would commission a team of independent

---

90. *Id.*

91. *See generally* ASIA WATCH, BEFORE THE DELUGE: HUMAN RIGHTS ABUSES AT INDIA'S NARMADA DAM (1992).

92. HUMAN RIGHTS WATCH, *supra* note 8.

93. *Id.* at iii.

94. Narmada International Human Rights Panel, THE NARMADA SARDAR SAROVAR PROJECT, MASS ARRESTS AND EXCESSIVE USE OF POLICE FORCE AGAINST ACTIVISTS IN CENTRAL INDIA 28 (1993), *available at* http://www.narmada.org/sardar-sarovar/hrreport9310.html.

95. LAWYERS COMMITTEE FOR HUMAN RIGHTS, UNACCEPTABLE MEANS: INDIA'S SARDAR SAROVAR PROJECT AND VIOLATIONS OF HUMAN RIGHTS, OCTOBER 1992 THROUGH FEBRUARY 1993 (1993).

experts, known as the Morse Commission, to reexamine the Sardar Sarovar Project.[96] The Commission's independent review had two aims: to assess steps taken to resettle those affected by the Sardar Sarovar dam, and to assess the efficacy of measures aimed at diminishing the project's environmental impact.[97] It was chaired by Bradford Morse, the former head of the UN Development Programme, and Thomas Berger, a former British Columbia Supreme Court judge, neither of whom had ever been Bank employees.[98] The Commission had unprecedented responsibilities. According to Berger, "[a]n international aid organization [had] never before established an investigatory body with a mandate as sweeping."[99] To carry out this mandate, the Commission visited sixty-five villages throughout the Narmada valley, met frequently with both Indian governmental officials and NGOs, including the NBA, and received full informational and financial support from the Bank.[100]

Though the Bank's president set out the Commission's terms of reference, the Commission retained its full independence and editorial control over the final report.[101] The 357-page report, issued on June 18, 1992, documented the Bank's disregard for its own involuntary resettlement and environmental assessment policies. The report also found that the Bank had tolerated violations of these policies by its borrower and recorded in great detail the resulting environmental and human rights consequences.[102] In one notable passage, the report clearly accused the Bank:

> We think the Sardar Sarovar Projects as they stand are flawed, that resettlement and rehabilitation of all those displaced by the Projects is not possible under prevailing circumstances, and that environmental impacts of the Projects have not been properly considered or adequately addressed. Moreover we believe that the Bank shares responsibility with the borrower for the situation that has developed.... We have decided that it would be irresponsible for us to patch together a series of recommendations on implementation when the flaws in the Projects are as obvious as they seem to us. As a result, we think that the wisest course would be for the Bank to

---

96. Rosencranz & Yurchak, *supra* note 12, at 515.

97. Berger, *supra* note 42, at 34.

98. *Id.* at 33, 37.

99. *Id.* at 37.

100. *Id.* at 37–39.

101. *Id.* at 37.

102. Dana L. Clark, *The World Bank and Human Rights: The Need for Greater Accountability*, 15 Harv. Hum. Rts. J. 205, 217 (2002).

step back from the Projects and consider them afresh. The failure of the Bank's incremental strategy should be acknowledged.[103]

Despite the Commission's unequivocal condemnation, the Bank was quick to reassure the Indian government that it would continue support to the Narmada projects.[104] A World Bank team traveled to India to assess the resettlement and environmental issues for the World Bank's executive board and dismissed the Morse Commission's environmental and health warnings. However, the team affirmed the report's concern for the displaced and urged the Bank to push the Indian government on compensation packages for the resettled.[105] Such a conclusion presented the Bank with a difficult decision—it had already invested a great deal of money into the Sardar Sarovar Project, and withdrawing altogether would prevent it from being able to influence policies towards the displaced and the environment, as the Gujarat government had privately indicated that construction of the dam would go forward with or without the Bank's aid.[106] On the other hand, several of the Bank's donor countries were unhappy with the developing image of the Bank as a human rights violator, and a significant number of directors became vocally opposed to continued funding of the project.[107]

Ultimately, on the strength of a compromise brokered by the Western European directors,[108] the Bank narrowly voted in October 1992 to continue funding the Sardar Sarovar Project,[109] but also gave India six months to comply with certain environmental and rehabilitative "benchmarks."[110] Moreover, in February 1993 the Bank's directors proposed to establish an internal inspection mechanism for ongoing projects.[111] And in March 1993, in a "face-saving formula" for the World Bank,[112] the government of India announced that it was cancelling the remaining $170 million Bank loan—what many regarded as an admission that the government could not meet the new "benchmark" conditions demanded in return for continued assistance.[113] In September that same year, the

---

103. MORSE ET AL., *supra* note 9, at xii, xxv.

104. Wood, *supra* note 20, at 981–82.

105. Id.

106. Id.

107. Id.

108. Id.

109. Rosencranz & Yurchak, *supra* note 12, at 515.

110. Wood, *supra* note 20, at 982.

111. Sabine Schlemmer–Schulte, *The Impact of Civil Society on the World Bank, the International Monetary Fund and the World Trade Organization: The Case of the World Bank*, 7 ILSA J. INT'L & COMP. L. 399, 414 (2001).

112. Rajagopal, *supra* note 2, at 366–367.

113. Rosencranz & Yurchak, *supra* note 12, at 515.

Bank adopted a resolution authorizing the creation of an Inspection Panel.

The Broader Impact of the NBA on the World Bank

The NBA's success in compelling action from the World Bank depended on its ability to force the Bank to acknowledge the Indian government's disregard for the Narmada Project's consequences.[114] Nationally, amidst increasing consciousness about environmental issues among India's urban middle classes and rural lower classes, Narmada became a symbol of the debate over the place of the most vulnerable members of Indian society in the country's political and economic order.[115] Internationally, the Narmada Project was seen as an effective hook for campaigning against the social and environmental impact of Bank projects.[116]

The controversy generated by the Sardar Sarovar dam represented a "historical watershed for the World Bank and an important landmark in the struggle for accountability."[117] In addition to establishing an independent commission to review a Bank-funded project, a first in the Bank's history,[118] the Bank subsequently established a quasi-independent Inspection Panel that would allow those affected by Bank policies to complain about violations.[119] The Inspection Panel was "the first forum in which private actors [could] hold an international organization directly accountable for the consequences of its failure to follow its own rules and procedures"[120] and was the first institution to legally recognize the relationship between international organizations and non-state actors.[121] The Bank's procedures were opened to the public, its guidelines on funding were rewritten, and its currently funded projects were reexamined.[122] The Sardar Sarovar Project experience also had a more general transformative effect on the Bank in bringing environmental concerns

---

114. Guyett, *supra* note 36, at 906.
115. Rajagopal, *supra* note 11, at 566.
116. *Id.* at 567.
117. Clark, *supra* note 102, at 216.
118. Andres Rigo Sureda, *Informality and Effectiveness in the Operation of the International Bank for Reconstruction and Development*, 6 J. INT'L ECON. L. 565, 586 (2003).
119. Clark, *supra* note 102, at 217.
120. *Id.*; Daniel B. Bradlow, *International Organizations and Private Complaints: The Case of the World Bank Inspection Panel*, 34 VA. J. INT'L L. 553, 555 (1994).
121. *Id.* at 553.
122. Rosencranz & Yurchak, *supra* note 12, at 514.

into mainstream development discourse and in compelling the Bank to see NGOs as partners in development.[123]

The World Bank Inspection Panel

The Bank's Executive Board faced increasing pressure to authorize the creation of the Inspection Panel because of "[e]vidence of mismanagement and poor governance from both internal and external reviews [which] galvanized criticism of the Bank's accountability failures."[124] A report by former Bank vice president, Willi Wapenhans, critiqued what it deemed the Bank's sweeping "culture of approval."[125] The Wapenhans report claimed that the Bank did not impose 78% of its negotiated loan conditions and that by the Bank's own criteria over one-third of its projects were unsatisfactory.[126] Non-governmental groups and member countries who were sizeable lenders to the Bank also levied general criticisms against the Bank.[127] Its reluctance to suspend loans to India in the wake of the independent review fueled further criticism[128] and brought the Bank under even greater pressure to respond. The World Bank Inspection Panel was established as a direct response to these criticisms and various NGO proposals.[129]

According to Udall, who helped spearhead the creation of the Inspection Panel, the NBA "was the main coalition behind the grassroots movement opposing the dams. Because the crisis around Narmada was at the forefront of the battle for more public accountability at the Bank ... without Narmada and the Morse Commission ... we would not have an inspection panel."[130]

---

123. Rajagopal, *supra* note 11, at 565.

124. Clark, *supra* note 102, at 217.

125. *Id.* at 216–17.

126. Kristine J. Dunkerton, *The World Bank Panel and Its Effect on Lending Accountability to Citizens of Borrowing Nations*, 5 U. BALT. J. ENVTL. L. 226, 235 (1995).

127. Schlemmer–Schulte, *supra* note 111, at 413.

128. *See* Sureda, *supra* note 118, at 586.

129. *See* Schlemmer–Schulte, *supra* note 111, at 414.

130. Udall interview, *supra* note 85. Referring to her work spearheading the creation of the Panel, Udall notes that after the Morse Commission submitted its report, "we called on the Bank to establish a 'Permanent Appeals Mechanism' so that adversely affected people could appeal to have projects investigated. We drafted a resolution and circulated it in Congress and among the Board of Executive Directors and legal counsel at the Bank. We worked with [U.S. Representative] Barney Frank's committee to pressure the Bank to establish this accountability mechanism." *Id.* After the United States Congress required an independent oversight system as a condition of payment, the Bank finally authorized the creation of the Inspection Panel. Dunkerton, *supra* note 126, at 236. For a brief history of the creation of the Panel, *see* LORI UDALL, BANK INFO. CTR., THE WORLD BANK INSPECTION PANEL: A THREE YEAR REVIEW 5–15 (1997). *See also* DEMANDING ACCOUNTABILITY: CIVIL SOCIETY CLAIMS AND THE WORLD BANK INSPECTION PANEL 258–266 (Dana Clark, Jonathan Fox, Kay Treakle eds., 2003).

The Structure and Processes of the Inspection Panel

The Inspection Panel was established in September 1993 to "provid[e] people directly and adversely affected by a Bank-financed project with an independent forum through which they can request the Bank to act in accordance with its own policies and procedures."[131] The Inspection Panel consists of three members, appointed by the Board for non-renewable five-year terms.[132] It is a forum of last resort, which requires affected individuals to exhaust local remedies prior to filing a claim.[133] The claim itself must allege that the actions or omissions of the Bank, and not the borrower, have caused or may cause material harm in violation of the Bank's policy.[134]

After the Panel is satisfied that the claim fits within its jurisdiction, Bank Management prepares a response to the allegations. The merits of the response are then assessed by the Panel, which then issues a recommendation to the Board of Directors on whether the claims merit further investigation. Preliminary investigation often involves an on-site visit to the country in which the project is based. After this, and subject to the board's approval, the Panel investigates the claim. Finally, the Panel prepares a report on its findings, which it sends to both the Board of Directors and the Bank Management.[135]

After this point, the matter is largely out of the Panel's hands. The Board first attempts to resolve any conflicts that may arise between the Panel's reports and the response of Bank staff, pursuant to which the Bank Management recommends actions to be taken in response to the Panel's findings. The Board subsequently investigates whether the problems identified by the Panel need to be remedied and what steps might be taken in order to do so. While some investigations have led to outright cancellation of Bank involvement, the overall record is mixed.[136]

---

131. World Bank Inspection Panel Operating Procedures, Introduction, Purpose, *available at* http://www.worldbank.org/inspectionpanel (follow "Policies and Procedures" to "Panel Operating Procedures").

132. *Id.*

133. Clark, *supra* note 102, at 218.

134. *Id.*

135. *See* World Bank Inspection Panel Operating Procedure, IV, V, and VII, *available at* http://www.worldbank.org/inspectionpanel (follow "Policies and Procedures" to "Panel Operating Procedures").

136. Clark, *supra* note 102, at 218–219.

The Record of the Inspection Panel

The Inspection Panel has been subject to critique since its creation.[137] Perhaps the biggest concern is the Panel's "lack of independent oversight" in two key areas: the implementation of the remedial measures decided upon by the Board and the Bank Management's response plan.[138] When the Board decided to exclude the Panel from supervision of remedial measures, it failed to set up an alternative mechanism for ensuring that plans for bringing projects into compliance with Bank policies were successful.[139] The Bank appears to be responding to these criticisms; in a 2004 decision (Paraguay–Argentina: Reform Project for the Water and Telecommunications Sectors, SEGBA V Power Distribution Project) the Board granted the Panel power to oversee the implementation of its recommendations.[140]

The Panel has also been criticized for its narrow focus on procedural issues. Since the Panel's mandate is limited to examination of the Bank's compliance with the Bank's operational guidelines, there is limited leeway for bringing in human rights concerns.[141] The Panel's primary focus on shortcomings in the implementation of the Bank's own criteria in the projects that it funds also limits the participation of outside actors to procedural rather than substantive issues and renders advocacy efforts to being "'reactive' rather than 'proactive' to policy choices."[142]

Rajagopal sees the Panel as diminishing in importance, both because World Bank financing for infrastructure projects is less important for developing countries that have access to private capital or other sovereign funds[143] and because the Panel "shot itself in the foot by not being activist enough [to] win a constituency outside of the Bank for its legitimacy." At the same time, the Panel was "not entirely pliable in the

---

137. *Id.* at 217.

138. *See id.* at 219.

139. *Id.* Clark sees a number of problems with putting the Bank's Board of Directors in charge of remedial measures—first, the Board "is overwhelmed with information and quickly loses focus on past cases;" second, it "does not have a standing committee to track the implementation of action plans or to evaluate the effectiveness of remedial measures in Inspection Panel cases;" third, it "largely accepts Management's word on the status of a project without independently verifying the facts on the ground or surveying the opinions of claimants." *Id.* at 220.

140. Mariarita Circi, *The World Bank Inspection Panel: Is It Really Effective?*, 6 GLOBAL JURIST ADVANCES 1, 15 (2006).

141. James Thuo Gathii, *Good Governance as a Counter Insurgency Agenda to Oppositional and Transformative Social Projects in International Law*, 5 BUFF. HUM. RTS. L. REV. 107, 166 (1999).

142. *Id.* at 167–68.

143. Rajagopal adds that Bank funding increasingly supports institution-building and rule of law projects. Rajagopal interview, *supra* note 54.

hands of Bank management thereby losing the Bank's support as well."[144]

Other commentators, however, have responded with guarded enthusiasm to the Panel's effect, noting that the Panel "play[s] a significant role in bringing local concerns and complaints to the attention of decision makers at the bank"[145] but also adding that in 2003, only eleven out of twenty-eight claims[146] (twenty-eight out of thirty-seven claims as of January 2006[147]) had resulted in positive change. Interestingly, commentators note that the Panel's record appears to be improving: from 2000–2005, the Board approved nine inspections of seventeen recorded requests, whereas from 1993–1999 it only authorized four of eighteen.[148] In 2005–06 the Panel registered four new claims and investigated five, while in 2006–07 the Panel registered six new claims, completed two, and undertook three new investigations.[149] In its fifteen years of operation, and at this writing, the Panel had processed fifty-two claims. Those that met with positive outcomes for claimants included the following results: compensation for claimants; mitigation of environmental impacts; release of project information; improvements in resettlement packages for affected people; cessation of evictions; and project suspension, cancellation or redesign.[150]

In her June 2008 testimony before the U.S. House of Representatives Committee on Financial Services, Udall underscored the impact of the Bank's Inspection Panel on other International Financial Institutions (IFIs). Since the Panel's establishment, a number of other IFIs have followed suit and have each set up accountability mechanisms to address complaints from adversely affected individuals.[151] Udall, speaking

---

144. *Id.*

145. Kay Treakle et al., *Lessons Learned*, in DEMANDING ACCOUNTABILITY, *supra* note 130, at 247, 267 (2004).

146. *Id.* at 258.

147. *See generally* Circi, *supra* note 140, at 16–26.

148. *Id.* at 11.

149. The Inspection Panel, ANNUAL REPORT, JULY 1, 2006–JUNE 30, 2007 13 (2007).

150. DEMANDING ACCOUNTABILITY, *supra* note 130, at 258–266. An internal Bank study also suggests that the Panel has had a deterrent effect; risky infrastructure projects have been forestalled early in the process because of the Panel's existence. WORLD BANK, INFRASTRUCTURE AT THE CROSSROADS: LESSONS FOR 20 YEARS OF WORLD BANK EXPERIENCE 68–71 (2006), *cited in* Regarding the World Bank Inspection Panel: Update and Recommendations for Reform in the Context of the Fifteenth Replenishment of the International Development Association, Before the H. Comm. on Fin. Servs., 110th Cong. 2, at 4 (2008) (statement of Lori L. Udall, Senior Advisor, Bank Info. Ctr.).

151. Udall, *supra* note 150, at 4. The Asian Development Bank, the Inter–American Development Bank, the African Development Bank, the European Bank for Reconstruction and Development, and the International Monetary Fund have all created accountability

on behalf of a number of NGOs, also offered recommendations for strengthening the Panel process.[152] The recommendations focused, *inter alia*, on: providing stakeholders greater access to the Panel process; involving them in the design of project remedies; and increasing the authority of the Panel to monitor project compliance with remedies and conduct post-inspection follow ups.[153]

NBA Developments Post–Bank Withdrawal

Ironically, the Bank's withdrawal from the Sardor Saravor Project in 1993 reduced the accountability of the Indian government to the outside world. Consequently, while the NBA's actions may have made the Bank more accountable, its withdrawal was a mixed blessing for the NBA.[154] Three important developments occurred in the wake of the Bank's withdrawal. First, the withdrawal itself greatly reduced the international dimension of the Narmada struggle.[155] Second, the NBA decided to pursue an additional avenue for change—appeal to the Supreme Court of India. Third, the government's continued construction raised the stakes of the struggle for both sides—more and more villages faced submergence, and the government's commitment to the Narmada Project deepened as the project progressed, and continues to this day.[156]

The NBA and the Supreme Court

The NBA approached the Supreme Court of India in May 1994 out of a sense of urgency and following significant internal discussion.[157] The decision of Sardar Sarovar Narmada Nigam Ltd ("SSNL," the corporation responsible for the Sardar Sarovar dam) to close the sluice gates of the dam meant water was rising in the valley.[158] Rajagopal characterizes

---

mechanisms. The Inter–American Development Bank has proposed an Independent Investigation Mechanism that is still awaiting approval by the IDB Board. *Id.*

152. Udall testified on behalf of the Bank Information Center, the Center for International Environmental Law, the Environmental Defense Fund, the International Accountability Project, the National Wildlife Federation, Oxfam America, and the World Wildlife Fund. *Id.* at 1.

153. *Id.* at 7–13.

154. *See* Rajagopal, *supra* note 2, at 386.

155. *See id.* at 371.

156. The Sardar Sarovar Narmada Nigam Limited (SSNL) stated in June 2008 that the entire project will be completed by 2009–10. *See Narmada dam to be completed by 2010,* THE PENINSULA, June 4, 2008, *available at* http://www.thepeninsulaqatar.com/Display_news.asp?section=World_News&subsection=India&month=June2008&file=World_News20080 6057732.xml.

157. Rajagopal, *supra* note 2, at 368.

158. *Id.*

the NBA's overall legal strategy as "schizophrenic" and notes that "its decision to avoid the Court until its back was against the wall in 1994 did not help, as Gujarat created a *fait accompli* with regard to the dam construction and then was able to argue that [it would] be too costly to reverse."[159]

Ultimately, the NBA's decision to petition the Supreme Court may have been inspired by the Court's activist record; it had liberally interpreted the Constitution to allow social action groups to bring claims. In *Maneka Gandhi v. India*, the Court broadly interpreted Article 21's guarantees of the right to life, the right to personal liberty, and the right not to be deprived of either of these rights except by procedure established by law.[160] Namely, the Court saw these rights as including the right to livelihood, potable drinking water, fresh air, health care, and clean environment.[161] This laid the foundation for the NBA to seek a similarly broad interpretation.

The NBA's lawyers began to push three novel legal arguments—one, that the project was an unconstitutional taking; two, that it violated the equal protection clause of the Indian Constitution; and three, that the government had infringed on their right to reside and settle in any part of India.[162] The NBA's petition to the Supreme Court called for a comprehensive review of the Sardar Sarovar Project and for a court order to stop all construction and displacement until the review's completion.[163] Initially it seemed as if the Court might grant the petition—it admitted the petition despite constitutional barriers; it ordered the government to release a previously conducted expert review of the project (the review had confirmed the negative findings of the Bank's Independent Review); it issued a stay on further construction of the dam; and it conducted numerous hearings on the matter.[164]

In December 1994, the Narmada Control Authority formally suspended riverbed construction of the dam. The suspension resulted from several actions: direct action in the valley; the actions of the new Chief Minister of Madhya Pradesh who petitioned to lower the height of the dam from 136.5 to 130.8 meters in order to save 30,000 people and 6,500 hectares of land from submergence; and the proceedings of the Supreme Court.[165] In May 1995 the Court issued a stay on further construction of

---

159. Rajagopal interview, *supra* note 54.
160. INDIA CONST. art. 21, § 1.
161. A.I.R. 1978 S.C. 597.
162. Writ Petition No. 319 of 1994, Narmada Bachao Andolan v. Union of India.
163. Rajagopal, *supra* note 2, at 368.
164. *Id.* at 369–70.
165. *Id.* at 369.

the dam.[166] But both the Narmada Control Authority and Supreme Court orders to suspend riverbed construction on the dam were disregarded on the ground. In late 1995, the NBA's march on Delhi resulted in a halting of the construction work. Direct action had succeeded where the Narmada Control Authority and Supreme Court orders did not.[167]

The suspension of construction between 1995 and 1999 allowed the NBA to focus on protecting the environment rather than opposing its destruction, both nationally and internationally.[168] On the national front, the NBA helped establish the National Alliance of Peoples' Movements ("NAPM")—a collective of likeminded organizations striving against injustice, exploitation and discrimination on the basis of ethnicity, caste and gender.[169] Among its major campaigns, the NAPM scrutinized the activities of multinationals in India, led an anti-nuclear movement, formed the People's Political Front to challenge politics' criminal and communal culture, and campaigned against slum demolitions in Mumbai.[170]

Internationally, the NBA participated in two conferences in 1997 on issues relating to dams—the first, in Brazil, was the first international conference against large-scale dams; the second, organized by the World Conservation Union and the World Bank, brought together various peoples' movements and non-governmental groups alongside bilaterals and companies that built dams.[171] The latter led the Bank to found its World Commission on Dams ("WCD") in 1998, an oversight group made up of both civil society actors and dam builders.[172] Medha Patkar was selected to be a Commissioner of this body.[173]

---

166. Order of 5 May, 1995, Narmada Bachao Andolan v. Union of India, *available at* http://www.ielrc.org/content/c9501.pdf.

167. Rajagopal, *supra* note 2, at 369–70.

168. *Id.*, at 371. According to Rajagopal, the NBA did so with a view to "reclaim[ing]" the international aspects of the struggle which "[t]he World Bank's pullout from the project in 1993 had effectively removed." *Id.*

169. *See generally* National Alliance of Peoples' Movements, *available at* http://www.proxsa.org/politics/napm.html.

170. *See id.*; Praful Bidwai, *Crisis India–Pakistan: No Nukes for Peace*, THE TIMES OF INDIA (Aug. 9, 2007), *available at* http://www.indianet.nl/indpk207.html; Kalpana Sharma, *Medha Patkar Forms Political Front*, THE HINDU, Mar. 18, 2004, *available at* http://www.hinduonnet.com/2004/03/18/stories/20040318.03371400.htm; *Activists Protest Slum Demolition*, THE TIMES OF INDIA, Dec. 27, 2007, *available at* http://timesofindia.indiatimes.com/Cities/Activists_protest_slum_demolition/rssarticleshow/2654080.cms.

171. Rajagopal, *supra* note 2, at 371.

172. *Id.*

173. *See* World Commission on Dams, *available at* http://www.dams.org//docs/overview/wcd_overview.pdf. The WCD disbanded after it released its final report in 2000. *Id.*

After 1997, the Court's approach to the Narmada Project shifted dramatically. Instead of undertaking a comprehensive review of the entire project, the Court decided in February 1999 to vacate the stay on construction work on the Sardar Sarovar dam[174] and to limit itself to the question of resettlement and rehabilitation.[175] In April 1999, Booker Prize winning author and activist Arundhati Roy penned her oft-cited essay, *The Greater Common Good*, in which she criticized the Supreme Court's decision.[176] Her essay lyrically rejected the theory that large-scale dams were good for development:

> Big Dams are to a Nation's 'Development' what Nuclear Bombs are to its Military Arsenal. They're both weapons of mass destruction. They're both weapons Governments use to control their own people. Both Twentieth Century emblems that mark a point in time when human intelligence has outstripped its own instinct for survival. They're both malignant indications of civilisation turning upon itself. They represent the severing of the link, not just the link—the *understanding*—between human beings and the planet they live on. They scramble the intelligence that connects eggs to hens, milk to cows, food to forests, water to rivers, air to life and the earth to human existence.[177]

Roy scathingly critiqued the government's rationale for the dam—that it would reorient resources so as to deliver the benefits of economic development to rich and poor alike and was therefore worth the marginal human and environmental costs of its implementation. Conversely, Roy's reasoning typified the perspective that human rights trump all other considerations;[178] a perspective that refuses to regard displacement as legitimately out-balanced by the competing public interests furthered by the Sardar Sarovar Project. As Roy wrote, "[r]esettling 200,000 people in order to take (or pretend to take) drinking water to forty million—there's something very wrong with the scale of operations here. This is Fascist maths. It strangles stories. Bludgeons details. And manages to blind perfectly reasonable people with its spurious, shining vision."[179] But even as Roy was caricatured by dam supporters as "anti-development" for espousing this view, she continued pointing out that

---

174. Narmada Bachao Andolan v. Union of India, A.I.R. 2000 S.C. 3751.
175. Id.
176. ARUNDHATI ROY, THE GREATER COMMON GOOD (1999), *available at* http://www.narmada.org/gcg/gcg.html.
177. Id.
178. See Kingsbury & Lustig, *supra* note 6, at 410–11.
179. Roy, *supra* note 176.

the alleged economic benefits of the dam never materialized—rendering the "common good" reasoning essentially meaningless.[180]

Roy's public criticism and activism in opposition to the construction project and the Court's orders ultimately may have backfired. In June 1999, the Supreme Court contemplated trying the NBA for contempt of court for its media advocacy tactics and direct political action, as well as Roy's writings.[181] The Court ultimately found Roy guilty of contempt, but imposed a symbolic punishment of imprisonment for one day and a fine of Rs. 2,000.[182] The case may have helped to cement the Court's image as immoderate towards its critics.[183]

The Supreme Court's final order in 2000[184] authorized the construction of the dam to proceed up to ninety meters and, in a dramatic move, stated that the completion of the construction of the dam was a matter of priority.[185] Among the reasons offered for the Court's about-face, despite auspicious beginnings, are the Court's change in membership[186] and the ensuing pro-development and anti-traditional point of view adopted by the new Court that "delegitimiz[ed] the human suffering" of local populations and supported the government's version of the facts.[187]

The NBA's response to the Court's decision decried what it saw as the Court's "complete and unjustified faith in the Government's machinery and assurances." In particular, the NBA was critical of the judgment's placement of oversight authority in the Narmada Control Authority—a body the NBA argued had already proven itself as overly protective of government power and the status quo. According to the

---

180. *Id.*
181. Rajagopal, *supra* note 2, at 372–73.
182. *See* In Re: Arundhati Roy, A.I.R. 2002 S.C. 1375, ¶ 76.
183. Rajagopal, *supra* note 2, at 383.
184. Andolan v. Union of India, A.I.R. 2000 S.C. 3751.
185. *Id.* at ¶ 57–58. In addition, it ordered the "monitor[ing] and review[ing] of resettlement and rehabilitation programmes *pari passu* with the raising of the dam height" and required clearance by "the Relief and Rehabilitation Sub-group and the Environmental Sub-group" of the Narmada Control Authority. *Id.* at ¶¶ 205, 280. It additionally ordered the states concerned to "comply with the decisions of the [Narmada Control Authority]," particularly relating to "the acquisition of land for the purpose of relief and rehabilitation," and dictated that the Narmada Control Authority "will within four weeks . . . draw up an action plan in relation to further construction and the relief and rehabilitation to be undertaken." *Id.* at ¶ 280. Finally, the Court declared that if the Review Committee of the Narmada Control Authority is unable to decide any issue, "the Committee may refer the same to the Prime Minister whose decision, in respect thereof, shall be final and binding on all concerned." *Id.* According to Rajagopal, this "seal of approval for the project [by the nation's highest adjudicative tribunal], as well as [the Court's] criticisms of the NBA, dealt major blows to the NBA's legitimacy and moral capital." Rajagopal, *supra* note 2, at 374.
186. Rajagopal, *supra* note 2, at 374.
187. *Id.* at 375.

NBA, the Court's ruling was yet another example of the government's fetish with large dams.[188]

But the NBA did not give up on legal action altogether. When the Narmada Control Authority raised the maximum height of the Sardar Sarovar dam to ninety-five meters in 2002, the NBA filed a new petition, claiming that resettlement and rehabilitation on the ground was not in fact proceeding alongside dam construction.[189] The Court dismissed the petition, claiming that any person with a grievance must first address the independent Grievance Redressal Authority—an administrative body with enforcement powers that was set up in each of the affected states— and only after failing there could they access the Court.[190]

In 2005, the Court consented to hear two interlocutory applications in the NBA's petition after twenty-seven villagers affected by submergence received a favorable judgment from the Grievance Redressal Authority of Madhya Pradesh that the state rebuffed.[191] In directing Madhya Pradesh to procure and allot suitable land to the applicants as soon as possible, the Court emphasized two principles governing the dam's construction: first, that the "complete resettlement and rehabilitation of oustees was a condition precedent for submergence" and second, that "relief and rehabilitation measures must be undertaken as and when the height of the dam is further raised."[192]

In 2006, the Court once again issued a judgment concerning the decision to raise the height of the Sardar Sarovar dam. The Court stressed that "all relief and rehabilitation measures have to be provided to the oustees in letter and spirit of the [Narmada Tribunal] Award and decisions of this Court,"[193] told the state governments to respond to allegations of failure of resettlement and rehabilitation, and gave the NBA time to file a rejoinder.[194] Meanwhile, the federal government

---

188. See Friends of River Narmada, The Order of the Supreme Court in the Narmada Case: Highlights, Comments, and Analysis, available at http://www.narmada.org/sardar-sarovar/sc.ruling/nba.comments.html.

189. See International Law Research Center, Order of the Grievance Redressal Authority, Madhya Pradesh, at ¶ 6, available at http://www.ielrc.org/content/c0409.pdf (saying the NBA filed petition because it was "[a]ggrieved" by Narmada Control Authority's decision to raise height of dam); Order of 9 September 2002, Narmada Bachao Andolan v. Union of India, available at http://www.ielrc.org/content/c0202.pdf (noting NBA's "conten[tion] that land for land has not been given.").

190. Order of 9 September 2002, Narmada Bachao Andolan v. Union of India, available at http://www.ielrc.org/content/c0202.pdf.

191. Narmada Bachao Andolan v. Union of India, 4 S.C.C. 32, 3–4 (2005).

192. Id. at 12–13.

193. Order of 17 April 2006, Narmada Bachao Andolan v. Union of India, available at http://www.ielrc.org/content/c0604.pdf.

194. Id.

constituted the Sardar Sarovar Project Relief & Rehabilitation Oversight Group "to report on the status of rehabilitation in the State of Madhya Pradesh of the Project Affected Families ... to the Prime Minister through the Minister of Water Resources" by the end of June.[195] As a result, the Court refused to stop the height of the dam from being raised.[196]

Reflecting its decision in 2000 to leave ultimate authority regarding the Narmada Project in the hands of political actors, the Court directed the Prime Minister, once in receipt of the Oversight Group report, to make a decision by July 6, 2006.[197] The Court's July 10 order accepted the Prime Minister's conclusion that since shortcomings in the relief and rehabilitation work could be remedied during the monsoon season, when construction on the dam would have to be stopped, "it would not be appropriate ... to pass any direction or orders at this stage stopping the construction of the dam which is designed to serve [sic] larger public interest."[198] The Court permitted the NBA and the government to file responses to the report and set a hearing for September.[199] The hearing ended up taking place on October 16, with the NBA arguing: first, that resettlement and rehabilitation had not in fact been completed during the monsoon season; and second, that there had been no monitoring of the rehabilitation group by the R & R Sub-group of the Narmada Control Authority.[200] The NBA pointed out that the land in the land bank was uncultivable and non-irrigable and that thousands of project-affected families had yet to be rehabilitated.[201] The Court directed the federal and state governments to file responses and listed the matter for December 2006.[202]

On March 10, 2008, the Supreme Court finally heard the Sardar Sarovar case.[203] Counsel on behalf of the farmers alleged that the Madhya Pradesh government's policy of paying cash and creating fake

---

195. Order of 8 May 2006, Narmada Bachao Andolan v. Union of India, *available at* http://www.ielrc.org/content/c0606.pdf.

196. *Id.*

197. *Id.*

198. Order of 10 July 2006, Narmada Bachao Andolan v. Union of India, *available at* http://www.ielrc.org/content/c0609.pdf.

199. *Id.*

200. Narmada Bachao Andolan, Press Release, No Compliance on Rehabilitation; Dam Remains Stalled (Oct. 16, 2006), *available at* http://www.narmada.org/nba-press-releases/october–2006/16Oct.html.

201. *Id.*

202. *Id.*

203. *See* Narmada Bachao Andolan, Press Release, Supreme Court Hears the Sardar Sarovar Case (Mar. 10, 2008), *available at* http://www.narmada.org/nba-press-releases/march–2008/March10.html.

land registries was in violation of the Narmada Tribunal Award's directives and the constitutional right to life under Article 21.[204] The Court directed the Madhya Pradesh government to file an affidavit response to the Narmada Control Authority's suggestions on relief compliance and allotted both parties eight weeks to file written arguments.[205] At this writing, the government had yet to submit its counter-affidavit in what appears to be an effort to buy time.[206] The NBA, for its part, continues to actively protest the Sardar Sarovar Project as well as other dams.

The Sardar Sarovar Project Today

Construction of the Sardar Sarovar dam proceeded uninterrupted after the suspension on construction was lifted in 1999.[207] On December 31, 2006 Gujarat Chief Minister Narendra Modi announced the completion of the Sardar Sarovar dam and symbolically poured the last bucket of concrete. Construction was halted at 121.92 meters and experts associated with the project announced they would install only thirty gates of fifty feet [15.24 m] each within three years.[208] As noted above, according to unofficial estimates, approximately 320,000 people have been displaced by the Sardar Sarovar dam and as many as one million may be affected due to related displacements by the canal system and other allied projects.[209]

The NBA has continued to engage in various forms of direct action even as it pursued its legal remedies. While the case stagnated in the Court system, NBA activists organized and participated in public meetings, rallies, marches, demonstrations, fasts, *dharnas*, and *satyagrahas*. These activities have had three overlapping aims: first, to call for rehabilitation work to take place at the same time as the raising of the dam as ordered by the Supreme Court; second, to demand the termination of the project altogether; and third, to protest the series of Supreme Court orders declining to suspend construction.[210] The struggle of the NBA has also fired the imagination of some of India's most

---

204. *Id.*
205. Order of March, 10, 2008, Narmada Bachao Andolan v. Union of India and Ors.
206. Email interview with Medha Patkar's representative (June 29, 2008).
207. Rajagopal, *supra* note 2, at 370.
208. *See* Work on Narmada Dam Complete, THE TIMES OF INDIA (Jan. 1, 2007), *available at* http://timesofindia.indiatimes.com/articleshow/1002183.cms.
209. The Sardar Sarovar Dam: A Brief Introduction, *available at* http://www.narmada.org/sardarsarovar.html.
210. *See generally* Narmada Bachao Andolan Press Releases, *available at* http://www.narmada.org/nba-press-releases/.

prominent citizens who have, along the way, acted as interlocutors for the movement.[211]

As for the movement's leaders, each won countless human rights awards in recognition of their contributions.[212] In 2000, Amte returned to his community development project at Anandwan (Forest of Bliss) near Nagpur in Maharashtra,[213] where he passed away in February 2008 at the age of ninety-four. Upon his death, the Dalai Lama lamented, "[h]is demise is a great loss to all of us. I am an admirer of Baba Amte.... [H]is [compassion] shone through everything he did, including his work for creating greater awareness about the protection of our environment."[214] Patkar continues to protest against the Narmada Project.[215] While she has abandoned efforts to pressure the government to forsake the dam, she continues to fight for the rights of displaced persons in Madhya Pradesh to receive the compensation that the Narmada Tribunal determined they were owed.

Conclusion

According to one NBA partner, the campaign against the construction of dams on the Narmada River is "symbolic of a global struggle for social and environmental justice," while the NBA itself is a "symbol of hope for people's movements all over the world that are fighting for just, equitable, and participatory development."[216] Though the NBA has yet to achieve the goals for which it has so tirelessly fought, its victories in the face of seemingly insurmountable odds have earned it the reputation of

---

211. In April 2006, for instance, Bollywood leading man Aamir Khan, accompanied by other members of the film industry, sat with NBA protesters during their hunger strike in Delhi to demand that the height of the dam not be raised, and offered to discuss his concerns about the lack of rehabilitation of those displaced directly with the Prime Minister. Aamir lends support to Narmada campaign, *available at* http://in.rediff.com/cms/print.jsp?docpath=//news/2006/apr/14nba.htm. *See also* text accompanying *supra* notes 176–183 for the activism of Arundhati Roy.

212. In 1991, Patkar and Amte received the Right Livelihood Award for their work with the NBA. *See* Right Livelihood Award Laureates, Medha Patkar and Baba Amte/Narmada Bachao Andolan (India) (1999), *available at* http://www.rightlivelihood.org/recip/narmada.htm. Amongst other awards, Baba Amte also received the Templeton Prize for Religion in 1990 and the Gandhi Peace Prize in 1999. Patkar, amongst other honors, received the Human Rights Defender's Award from Amnesty International as well as the Goldman Environmental Prize.

213. Neeta Deshpande, *A Life of Conviction*, India Together (Oct. 24, 2006), *available at* http://www.indiatogether.org/2006/oct/rvw-babaamte.htm.

214. His Holiness the Dalai Lama mourns the demise of Baba Amte, TibetNet (Feb. 11, 2008), *available at* http://www.phayul.com/news/article.aspx?id=19218&article=His+Holiness+the+Dalai+Lama+mourns+the+demise+of+Baba+Amte.

215. *See, e.g.*, Narmada Bachao Andolan Press Release, Medha Patkar and Others Arrested While Seeking Appointment with UPA Chairperson Sonia Gandhi (June 19, 2006), *available at* http://www.narmada.org/nba-press-releases/june-2006/June19.html.

216. Friends of River Narmada, *available at* http://www.narmada.org/about-us.html.

being one of the most dynamic social movements of our time and one that the government continues to expend considerable resources to fight against. As noted by Medha Patkar upon her release from jail on August 6, 2007: "It's obvious that the Government [of Madhya Pradesh] is all out to kill our right to land and also [our] right to agitate."[217]

According to Rangarajan, "the NBA put the issues of displacement on the agenda in India and at the global level." Specifically, it forced consideration of the ecological viability and social impacts of large-scale projects. Rangarajan adds that while "there is little doubt that the NBA failed in its immediate objectives and the Sardar Sarovar dam got built, and built bigger" the movement "has left a strong legacy" which is evident in the manner in which issues initially raised by the NBA have surfaced in other anti-dam struggles.[218] Rajagopal agrees, noting that the NBA's greatest domestic achievement was to "put the costs of the development agenda under the microscope" in a manner that "will continue to have a major impact on public culture."[219]

Ultimately, the Sardar Sarovar dam is symbolic of a larger struggle over the discourse of human rights and development in India. Even now, history repeats itself as the Indian government establishes "Special Economic Zones"—tax-free trade zones designed to attract foreign investment. While the Indian government argues that these zones will create jobs for India's millions of unemployed, thousands of farmers whose land is being "acquired" for the purpose of developing the zones have risen up in protest.[220] They challenge the assumption that they stand to directly benefit from the projects, and more fundamentally, that such human cost is a *sine qua non* of economic development. In the face of the resurgent rationale that the supposed "benefits" of the zones outweigh the costs of displacement,[221] the groundwork laid by movements such as the NBA has created an uncontestable space for the voices of India's faceless and nameless displaced—voices that will continue to influence the course of India's paramount task of achieving equitable development alongside economic growth.

---

217. Press Release, Fast by Medha Patkar Ends on Release from Jail: The Dharna Continues in Badwani for the 6th day (Aug. 5, 2007), *available at* http://www.narmada.org/nba-press-releases/august–2007/Aug05.html.

218. Rangarajan interview, *supra* note 68.

219. Rajagopal interview, *supra* note 54.

220. Sanjay Sangvai et al., *Farmers Rally Against Special Economic Zones*, THE SOUTH ASIAN (Oct. 1, 2006), *available at* http://www.thesouthasian.org/archives/2006/farmers_rally_against_special.html.

221. Karishma Vaswani, *Anger over India's Special Economic Zones*, BBC NEWS (Oct. 18, 2006), *available at* http://news.bbc.co.uk/2/hi/business/6054754.stm.

In addition to ensuring greater transparency and accountability in World Bank projects, the NBA has contributed to an awareness of the need to approach environmental and human rights issues in tandem—a lesson long known to Indian activists and one that is increasingly apparent to actors on the international scene who urgently battle environmental degradation and its acute impact on marginalized populations.

*

11

The Story of *Sale v. Haitian Centers Council*: Guantánamo and *Refoulement*

Harold Hongju Koh & Michael J. Wishnie*

Nearly two decades before September 11, 2001, thousands of foreign nationals were detained without due process at the U.S. Naval Base at Guantánamo Bay, Cuba. More than 300 refugees were held in the world's first offshore HIV-positive detention camp. Despite the mandate of the 1951 U.N. Refugee Convention, the United States—a land founded by refugees—returned bona fide refugees to territory where their lives and freedom would be threatened on account of their political opinion. A new model of human rights litigation and important innovations in clinical legal education emerged. And it all happened in a single lawsuit: *Sale v. Haitian Centers Council* ("the *HCC* case").[1]

When a 1991 military coup in Haiti overthrew the nation's first democratically-elected president, tens of thousands of Haitians fled the ensuing reign of terror on small boats pointed toward Florida. The United States responded by dispatching Coast Guard ships to interdict the fleeing Haitians and to destroy their boats. Initially, the United States conducted brief interviews with the Haitians, first on board the

---

* The authors were members of the Yale Law School litigation team that represented Haitian refugees in the *Haitian Centers Council* case. We are grateful to our courageous clients; to Yale Law students Brittan Heller, Kate Desormeau, Garth Schofield, and Michael Tan and Georgetown Law student Devon Chaffee for excellent research assistance; to Wanda Martinson, Sarah Cleveland, Brandt Goldstein and Gerry Neuman for their abiding friendship and support. We also thank Eric Schwartz for his historical recollections and our co-counsel in the case: Michael Ratner, Lucas Guttentag, Joseph Tringali, Robert Rubin, Susan Sawyer, Jennifer Klein, Ignatius Bau and the Yale law student litigators whose stories are told and whose names are listed in BRANDT GOLDSTEIN, STORMING THE COURT: HOW A BAND OF YALE LAW STUDENTS FOUGHT THE PRESIDENT AND WON 313 (2005) and Victoria Clawson, Elizabeth Detweiler, & Laura Ho, *Litigating as Law Students: An Inside Look at Haitian Centers Council*, 103 YALE L.J. 2337, 2337 (1994) [hereinafter *Litigating as Law Students*]. We dedicate this story to Mary–Christy Fisher and Cathy Edwards, for living these cases, and our careers, with us.

1. 509 U.S. 155 (1993).

Coast Guard ships and later at Guantánamo, in a cursory effort to determine which Haitians had a credible fear of political persecution in Haiti and which could be treated as economic migrants. The government forcibly returned to Haiti the vast majority of Haitians it had "screened out" as lacking a credible fear of political persecution.[2] The government "screened in" a second group of Haitians whom it deemed to have a credible fear of persecution, subjected them to medical testing, and if no issue arose, allowed them to enter the United States to apply for political asylum.[3] In fact, however, many of these "screened-in" Haitians were held on Guantánamo for months, and some were returned despite their credible claims to refugee status. A third group of Haitian interdictees comprised screened-in Haitians who were found to have medical conditions, such as HIV, that rendered them excludable under the immigration statutes. The government chose to detain these "HIV-positive screened-out" detainees at Guantánamo indefinitely.[4]

In spring 1992, more than six months after the coup in Haiti, the first Bush Administration abandoned its program of interdicting and screening all fleeing Haitians to determine who had a credible fear of persecution. Instead, the Administration began simply interdicting all Haitians and summarily returning them to Haiti, without any individualized inquiry into each person's potential refugee status.

The *HCC* case, brought in March 1992, lasted sixteen months and bifurcated around two core human rights issues. What we call here "*HCC-I*" or "the Guantánamo case" was the first federal lawsuit by non-citizen detainees raising a constitutional challenge to their indefinite detention on Guantánamo, an issue that arose again repeatedly after September 11, 2001. In *HCC-I*, all Haitians who had been or would be "screened in"—i.e., found by the U.S. government to possess a credible fear of persecution—brought a class action against their denial of access to counsel and their illegal detention at Guantánamo. In time, that half of the case went to a federal trial that freed about 300 HIV-positive, screened-in Haitians being held on Guantánamo, based on a finding that,

---

2. As discussed below, lawyers in Florida sued on behalf of the "screened out" Haitians, seeking to enjoin their forcible return to Haiti without fuller hearings, access to counsel, and other procedural protections. This suit was ultimately unsuccessful. *See* Haitian Refugee Ctr., Inc. v. Baker, 953 F.2d 1498 (11th Cir. 1992).

3. To secure asylum, an applicant is required to make a higher evidentiary showing, establishing that one has not only a "credible" fear of persecution, but a "well-founded" fear. 8 U.S.C. §§ 1158(b)(1), 1101(a)(42)(A).

4. Eventually, the government forced the screened-in HIV-positive refugees to undergo a second interview to prove not only a "credible," but also a "well-founded" fear of persecution. *See supra* note 2. The government forcibly returned to Haiti those screened-in Haitians who refused to submit to a second interview, or whom the government determined lacked a well-founded fear of persecution.

even on Guantánamo, these detainees should be accorded due process rights.

What we call "*HCC–II*" or "the Direct Return case" was a challenge brought within the same lawsuit by Haitians who should have been screened in but were instead summarily and forcibly returned to Haiti. In *HCC–II*, these Haitians argued all the way to the U.S. Supreme Court that two U.S. administrations had violated the international human rights proscription against *refoulement*, the direct return of refugees to their persecutors.[5]

Remarkably, after months of intensive litigation, both halves of the case were resolved on the same day. In *HCC–I*, the Eastern District's Judge Sterling Johnson, Jr. ruled, *inter alia*, that the government had violated the HIV-positive, screened-in Haitians' due process rights by denying them the procedures available to asylum applicants in the United States, by showing deliberate indifference to their medical needs, and by subjecting them to informal disciplinary procedures and indefinite detention.[6] On June 21, 1993, in *HCC–I*,[7] the Clinton Administration brought to the United States the last of the approximately 300 HIV-positive Haitians and their family members being held in Guantánamo, pursuant to a permanent injunction issued by the U.S. District Court for the Eastern District of New York. Yet even as the airplane carrying the Haitians approached New York, in *HCC–II*, the U.S. Supreme Court held, over Justice Harry Blackmun's sole dissent, that neither Article 33 of the U.N. Refugee Convention nor Section 243(h) of the Immigration and Nationality Act (INA) applied to refugees apprehended on the high seas.[8]

This complex story raises three questions: How did the *Haitian Centers Council* case evolve?[9] What was its aftermath? And what is its human rights legacy?

---

5. The rule against *refoulement* holds that no nation may return a foreign national directly to her persecutors, whether she has fled as a refugee or otherwise. Convention Against Torture and Other Cruel, Inhuman or Degrading Treatment or Punishment art. 3, Dec. 10, 1984, S. Treaty Doc. No. 100–20, 1465 U.N.T.S. 85.

6. Haitian Ctrs. Council, Inc. v. Sale, 823 F.Supp. 1028, 1041–45 (E.D.N.Y. 1993) [hereinafter *HCC–I*].

7. *Id.* at 1041–45.

8. Sale v. Haitian Ctrs. Council, Inc., 509 U.S. 155, 177, 187 (1993) [hereinafter *HCC–II*].

9. The legal history of these cases is recounted in many places, including BRANDT GOLDSTEIN, STORMING THE COURT: HOW A BAND OF YALE LAW STUDENTS FOUGHT THE PRESIDENT AND WON (2005); and Victoria Clawson, Elizabeth Detweiler & Laura Ho, *Litigating as Law Students: An Inside Look at* Haitian Centers Council, 103 YALE L.J. 2337 (1994). For a documentary history collecting litigation documents in the case, which has been designed for use in first-year Procedure courses, *see* BRANDT GOLDSTEIN, RODGER CITRON, & MOLLY

The Evolution of the Haitian Refugee Litigation

The *HCC* story began in September 1981, when the governments of the United States and Haiti entered a unique bilateral agreement "for the establishment of a cooperative program of interdiction and *selective return* to Haiti of certain Haitian migrants and vessels involved in illegal transport of persons coming from Haiti."[10] Pursuant to that agreement and its implementing executive order, the U.S. Coast Guard began "interdicting" fleeing Haitians on the high seas and "screening" (i.e. summarily interviewing) them, bringing to the United States only those few "screened-in" Haitians found to have "credible fears" of political persecution.

To the extent that the interdiction program tolerated the return of de facto political refugees, it appeared to violate the *nonrefoulement* requirement of Article 33 of the 1951 United Nations Convention Relating to the Status of Refugees.[11] That provision mandated that "[n]o Contracting State shall expel or return (*'refouler'*) a refugee *in any manner whatsoever* to the frontiers of territories where his life or freedom would be threatened on account of his ... political opinion" (emphasis added). Although an early judicial challenge to the interdiction program foundered for lack of standing,[12] various contemporaneous government documents and instruments implementing the interdiction program seemed to confirm that this obligation of non-return applied even to refugees taken on the high seas.[13]

BEUTZ, STORMING THE COURT: A DOCUMENTARY COMPANION (forthcoming 2009). For law journal accounts by the authors, from which much of the story that follows is drawn, *see, e.g.*, Harold Hongju Koh, *The "Haiti Paradigm" in United States Human Rights Policy*, 103 YALE L.J. 2391 (1994); Harold Hongju Koh, *America's Offshore Refugee Camps*, 29 U. RICH. L. REV. 139 (1994); The Lowenstein International Human Rights Clinic (including Koh & Wishnie), *Aliens and the Duty of* Nonrefoulement: Haitian Centers Council v. McNary, 6 HARV. HUM. RTS. J. 1 (1993); Harold Hongju Koh, *Reflections on* Refoulement *and* Haitian Centers Council, 35 HARV. INT'L L.J. 1 (1994) [hereinafter *Reflections*]; Harold Hongju Koh, *The Human Face of the Haitian Interdiction Program*, 33 VA. J. INT'L L. 483 (1993).

10. Agreement Effected by Exchange of Notes, U.S.–Haiti, Sept. 23, 1981, 33 U.S.T. 3559 [hereinafter 1981 U.S.–Haiti Agreement] (emphasis added). The Agreement was implemented by Exec. Order No. 12,324, 46 Fed. Reg. 48,109 (Sept. 29, 1981).

11. July 28, 1951, 19 U.S.T. 6259, 6276, 189 U.N.T.S. 150, 176 [hereinafter Refugee Convention] (emphasis added). The United States became party to the Refugee Convention when it acceded to the Protocol Relating to the Status of Refugees, Jan. 31, 1967, 19 U.S.T. 6223, 606 U.N.T.S. 267.

12. Haitian Refugee Ctr., Inc. v. Gracey, 809 F.2d 794 (D.C. Cir. 1987).

13. For a critique of the Haitian interdiction program, *see* Stephen H. Legomsky, *The Haitian Interdiction Programme, Human Rights and the Role of Judicial Protection*, 2 INT'L J. REFUGEE L. (SPECIAL ISSUE) 181 (1990). For discussion of the numerous judicial rulings against Haitians, *see, e.g.*, Cheryl Little, *United States Haitian Policy: A History of Discrimination*, 10 N.Y.L. SCH. J. HUM. RTS. 269 (1993); Kevin R. Johnson, *Judicial*

In a 1990 United Nations-monitored election, more than sixty-seven percent of the voters elected Jean–Bertrand Aristide as president of the first freely elected democratic government of Haiti. After a brief and troubled presidency, Aristide was overthrown by military coup in September 1991 and fled to the United States. Pursuant to the Santiago Commitment to Democracy, and with the support of officials of the George H.W. Bush Administration, the Organization of American States (OAS) adopted sanctions programs and issued resolutions urging the restoration of the constitutional government in Haiti. But as boatloads of refugees began fleeing Haiti, the Bush Administration directed the Coast Guard to bring screened-in Haitians not to the United States, but rather, to the U.S. Naval Base in Guantánamo Bay, Cuba, where they were detained behind razor-barbed wire in makeshift military camps without due process rights. This policy soon triggered litigation by Haitian refugee advocates before two circuits.

The Eleventh Circuit Litigation: Haitian Refugee Center v. Baker

In November 1991, the Haitian Refugee Center (HRC) sued Secretary of State James Baker and other government officials in the Southern District of Florida, challenging, *inter alia*, the practice of returning screened-out Haitians without sufficient process. HRC won several initial victories in the Southern District of Florida, but on expedited appeal, the Eleventh Circuit twice reversed, bringing the Haitian refugee crisis before the U.S. Supreme Court for the first time around Christmastime 1991.

As the Florida lawsuit volleyed rapidly between the District Court in Miami and the U.S. Court of Appeals for the Eleventh Circuit in Atlanta,

---

Acquiescence to the Executive Branch's Pursuit of Foreign Policy and Domestic Agendas in Immigration Matters: The Case of the Haitian Asylum–Seekers, 7 GEO. IMMIGR. L.J. 1 (1993).

President Reagan effectively acknowledged that the *nonrefoulement* obligations of Article 33 applied to interdicted Haitians when he issued Exec. Order No. 12,324, 46 Fed. Reg. 48,109, 48,109 (Sept. 29, 1981) (guaranteeing "that no person who is a refugee will be returned without his consent"); *see also* IMMIGRATION & NATURALIZATION SERVICE, INS ROLE IN AND GUIDELINES FOR INTERDICTION AT SEA (Oct. 6, 1981) (directing that INS personnel "be constantly watchful for any indication (including bare claims) that a person or persons on board the interdicted vessel may qualify as refugees under the United Nations Convention and Protocol"), quoted in Haitian Refugee Ctr., Inc., 953 F.2d at 1502; Proposed Interdiction of Haitian Flag Vessels, 5 Op. Off. Legal Counsel 242, 248 (1981) (reasoning that interdicted Haitians "who claim that they will be persecuted ... must be given an opportunity to substantiate their claims"); Memorandum from Larry L. Simms, Deputy Assistant Att'y Gen., Off. Legal Counsel, to the Assoc. Att'y Gen. (Aug. 5, 1981) ("Those who claim to be refugees must be given a chance to substantiate their claims [under Article 33]."), quoted in Joint Appendix at 222, Sale v. Haitian Ctrs. Council, Inc., 509 U.S. 155 (1993) (No. 92–344).

Circuit Justice Anthony Kennedy circulated an unusual memorandum to the Supreme Court on December 20, 1991: unusual, because as Justice Kennedy himself observed, "no papers have been filed here yet."[14] Nevertheless, Justice Kennedy set out to introduce the lower court litigation to his colleagues in anticipation of an imminent filing.

Justice Kennedy's initial framing of the matter placed unusual emphasis on the interests of the U.S. government, as opposed to the individual human rights claims of the refugees. This framing both shaped and foreshadowed the Court's approach to the multiple applications and petitions arising from the refugee crisis that it would face over the next eighteen months. "This case involves the efforts by the United States Coast Guard," began the Justice, "to repatriate individuals who fled Haiti in small vessels in the last several weeks."[15] In effect, Justice Kennedy advised his fellow justices, *HRC v. Baker* was not so much a human rights story as it was a case about the challenges facing the Coast Guard. Although the refugees and their counsel could not know it at the time, this framing of the case, soon widely accepted among the Justices, ultimately doomed all human rights arguments on behalf of the Haitians that would eventually come to the Court.

When the U.S. Supreme Court first ruled on an application from the Florida litigation, in early 1992, it stayed the District Court's injunction, with Justices Blackmun, Stevens, and Thomas dissenting.[16] But the HRC

---

14. Memorandum from Justice Anthony M. Kennedy, Supreme Court of the United States, to the Conference 1 (Dec. 20, 1991) [hereinafter 1991 Kennedy Memo] (on file with authors). For the inside story of how the Justices decided the Haitian refugee cases, we examined the extensive case files in Box 623 of the collected papers of the late Justice Harry Blackmun, in the Library of Congress. For a description of how those papers were bequeathed to the Library of Congress, *see* Harold Hongju Koh, *Unveiling Justice Blackmun*, 72 BROOK. L. REV. 9, 16–23 (2006).

15. 1991 Kennedy Memo, *supra* note 14, at 1. The memo concluded with Justice Kennedy's statement that if the Eleventh Circuit were to deny relief to the refugees, and if the Florida plaintiffs were to seek emergency relief from the Supreme Court, "my present inclination is to grant a stay for the sole purpose of referring the matter to the conference." *Id.* at 3. Later that same day, Justice Stevens seized on the suggestion to grant a stay, writing "I think there is a real danger that the majority in the Eleventh Circuit has acted with undue haste. I strongly support your proposed grant of a stay...." Memorandum from Justice John Paul Stevens, Supreme Court of the United States, to Justice Anthony M. Kennedy and the Conference, (Dec. 20, 1991) (on file with authors).

16. *See* Baker v. Haitian Refugee Ctr., Inc., 502 U.S. 1083 (1992) (ordering stay of District Court order pending disposition of appeal by Eleventh Circuit); *Id.* (Blackmun, Stevens, and Thomas, JJ., dissenting from entry of stay). Justice Thomas later explained, in a draft portion of his subsequent statement respecting denial of *certiorari* in *HRC* that he did not publish, that "I voted to deny the government's application ... because, in my view, the petitioners deserved the additional twenty-four hours they had requested for the purpose of taking depositions and filing a response." Draft Statement of Justice Clarence Thomas Respecting Denial of Certiorari, Haitian Refugee Ctr., Inc. v. Baker, 502 U.S. 1122

suit ended suddenly in February 1992, when the Supreme Court denied HRC's petition for *certiorari*, over Justice Blackmun's sole dissent.[17] In his memorandum to the Conference recommending denial of *certiorari*, Justice Kennedy expressed a view that would carry the day more than a year later in *Haitian Centers Council*: that "the INA [Immigration and Nationality Act] does not have extraterritorial application."[18] By contrast, throughout the various *HRC v. Baker* applications, Justices Blackmun and Stevens previewed their later positions in *HCC*, consistently displaying a respect for the legal claims and humanitarian concerns of the refugees not shared by the rest of the Court.[19] As Justice Blackmun wrote in dissent from denial of *certiorari*,

> A quick glance at this Court's docket reveals not only that we have room to consider these issues, but that they are at least as significant as any we have chosen to review today. If indeed the Haitians are to be returned to an uncertain future in their strife-torn homeland, that ruling should come from this Court, after full and careful consideration of the merits of their claims.[20]

By contrast, Justice Kennedy's memorandum to the Conference reflected the government's view that "to grant the writ and a stay only later to deny relief . . . would encourage numerous additional Haitians to flee in the interim. And if returned Haitians do indeed face greater risks than those who have not fled, our action could result in more persecution rather than less."[21] Justice Kennedy's arguments seem to have persuaded Justice Thomas, who had initially voted to deny the government's stay application. A journalistic account of the Court's deliberations (based on confidential interviews) later suggested that Justice Thomas, as the only African–American member of the Court, experienced deep inner turmoil over the Haitians' plight. But in time, Justice Thomas came to view the issue as a political, not a legal, question and

---

(1992) (No. 91–1292) (on file with authors); *but see* 502 U.S. 1122, 1122 (1992) (Thomas, J., statement respecting denial of *certiorari*) (omitting explanation).

17. Haitian Refugee Ctr., Inc. v. Baker, 949 F.2d 1109 (11th Cir. 1991); Haitian Refugee Ctr., Inc., 953 F.2d 1498, *cert. denied*, 502 U.S. 1122 (1992) (denying application for stay of mandate and petition for *certiorari*).

18. Memorandum from Justice Anthony M. Kennedy, Supreme Court of the United States, to the Conference 1 (Feb. 10, 1992) (on file with authors) [hereinafter 1992 Kennedy Memo].

19. *See* Haitian Refugee Ctr., Inc. v. Baker, 502 U.S. 1122, 1122 (1992) (Stevens, J., statement respecting denial of *certiorari*) ("It is important to emphasize that the denial of the petition for writ of *certiorari* is not a ruling on any of the unsettled and important questions of law presented in the petition.").

20. *Id.* (Blackmun, J., dissenting from denial of *certiorari*).

21. 1992 Kennedy Memo, *supra* note 18, at 2.

for the rest of the refugee crisis, never again cast a vote in the Haitians' favor.[22]

The Second Circuit Litigation: Haitian Centers Council v. Sale (HCC)

When the Supreme Court finally denied *certiorari* in *HRC*, ending that litigation, the U.S. government held some 3,000 Haitians incommunicado at Guantánamo, virtually all of whom the government had already found to have credible fears of political persecution. In March 1992, notwithstanding prior contrary representations to the Supreme Court, the Immigration and Naturalization Service (INS) determined to re-interview the Haitians held at Guantánamo without lawyers present and to send those who failed the test of political asylum back to Haiti to face possible persecution and death.[23]

Galvanized by this news, Yale Law School's Allard K. Lowenstein International Human Rights Clinic sued an array of U.S. government officials in Brooklyn federal court, asserting that lawyers and clients have a right to communicate with one another before the clients are returned to political persecution.[24] The suit invoked statutes, treaties,

---

22. *See* JAN CRAWFORD GREENBURG, SUPREME CONFLICT: THE INSIDE STORY OF THE STRUGGLE FOR CONTROL OF THE UNITED STATES SUPREME COURT 16 (2007):

> [T]he new justice was ... anguished. He sympathized with the Haitians. He called Rehnquist for advice, and the chief referred Thomas to a favorite poem by Arthur Hugh Clough. "Say not the struggle naught availeth," the poem begins, urging fortitude in the face of battle. It then ends on a hopeful note: "Westward look, the land is bright." Thomas made a copy of the poem and slid it under the glass top of his desk, where he's kept it. He joined seven other justices and declined to intervene in the plight of the Haitian boat people. "I am deeply concerned about these allegations" of mistreatment in Haiti, Thomas wrote in a separate opinion explaining why the Court would not step in. "However, this matter must be addressed by the political branches, for our role is limited to questions of law."

23. Urging denial of *certiorari* in *HRC*, the Solicitor General had represented to the Supreme Court that the INS would bring all screened-in Haitians to the United States. But an internal INS memorandum by the General Counsel for the INS, written only five days after the Court denied cert. indicated that, in fact, HIV-positive screened-in refugees would be interviewed at Guantánamo without attorneys present, in interviews that were supposedly "identical in form and substance, or as nearly so as possible" to asylum interviews in the United States. Memorandum from Grover J. Rees, General Counsel, INS, to John Cummings, Acting Assistant Commissioner for Refugees, Asylum, and Parole, INS (Feb. 29, 1992) (on file with authors).

24. The internal clinic deliberations that led to the filing of the *HCC* case complaint are recounted in GOLDSTEIN, STORMING THE COURT: HOW A BAND OF YALE LAW STUDENTS FOUGHT THE PRESIDENT AND WON *supra*, note 9, at 36–43, 45–59, and Clawson et al., *supra*, note 9, at 2350–54. The Allard K. Lowenstein International Human Rights Clinic was founded in 1991 as a clinical course at Yale Law School by Professor Harold Hongju Koh, Attorney Michael Ratner of the Center for Constitutional Rights, and a group of Yale law students.

and constitutional norms on behalf of a plaintiff class of screened-in Haitian refugees and several service organizations who sought to give the refugees legal advice: Haitian Centers Council, Inc., a Brooklyn Haitian service organization; New York's National Coalition for Haitian Refugees (now the National Coalition for Haitian Rights); and the Immigration Clinic of the Jerome N. Frank Legal Services Organization of the Yale Law School, all public service organizations that asserted First Amendment rights of access to the Guantánamo Haitians in order to give them legal counsel.

Remarkably, in the next fifteen months, the case went to the Second Circuit five times and the Supreme Court eight times. The suit evolved through three distinct phases: what we will call (1) an "access to counsel" phase of the Guantánamo case (*HCC–I*), which focused primarily on the clients' claimed constitutional right to speak to their lawyers before being returned to possible death or persecution; (2) a *"refoulement"* phase (the Direct Return case, *HCC–II*), where the refugees protested their direct return to their persecutors in the face of the proscriptions of the 1951 Refugee Convention; and (3) an "illegal detention" phase, also a part of *HCC–I,* the Guantánamo case, in which the refugees directly challenged on constitutional grounds their prolonged confinement in America's first HIV-concentration camp.

The Access to Counsel Phase (HCC–I)

In the first phase of the Guantánamo case, in March–April 1992, the plaintiffs won a temporary restraining order (TRO) and preliminary injunction before the district court, requiring that the Haitians detained at Guantánamo be afforded counsel before repatriation to Haiti. The Second Circuit denied the government's requests to stay these prelimi-

---

Its founding goal was to provide students with training in human rights lawyering by engaging in "transnational public law litigation," which seeks to challenge human rights abuses by securing the interpretation and enforcement of internationally recognized human rights standards in U.S. courts. See Harold Hongju Koh, *Transnational Public Law Litigation*, 100 YALE L.J. 2347 (1991). The Clinic originated, by student request, as an arm of the Allard K. Lowenstein International Human Rights Project, a student-run organization founded at Yale Law School in 1981 to educate and inspire law students, scholars, practicing attorneys, and policymakers in the defense of international human rights. Both the Clinic and Project took their name from Allard Lowenstein, the political activist and Yale Law graduate who had served as U.S. Ambassador to the U.N. Human Rights Commission in the Carter Administration. *See generally* WILLIAM H. CHAFE, NEVER STOP RUNNING: ALLARD LOWENSTEIN AND THE STRUGGLE TO SAVE AMERICAN LIBERALISM (1993). For an early account of the Clinic's work, *see* Thomas Scheffey, *Yale Project: Making Sure Torture Doesn't Pay,* CONN. L. TRIB., Mar. 11, 1991, at 1. The Lowenstein Clinic pioneered the growth of international human rights clinics around the country. *See generally* Deena R. Hurwitz, *Lawyering for Justice and the Inevitability of International Human Rights Clinics*, 28 YALE J. INT'L L. 505 (2003).

nary rulings and ultimately upheld them on appeal on the merits.[25] But the government was unwilling to abide by either the District Court's preliminary injunction, or the Second Circuit's refusal to stay it. Instead, claiming that the injunction represented extreme interference with a military operation outside United States territory, Justice Department lawyers took the extraordinary step of petitioning directly to the Supreme Court for an emergency stay of Judge Johnson's ruling.

Justice Thomas, as Circuit Justice for the Second Circuit, referred the government's application to stay the preliminary injunction to the full Court. The Court swiftly entered a stay, by a 5–4 vote. Justices Blackmun, Stevens, O'Connor, and Souter dissented,[26] but the Haitian refugees never again came so close to prevailing in any part of the case.

The Refoulement *Phase (HCC–II)*

Lower Court Proceedings

Even while the *HCC–I* appeal was pending before the Second Circuit, on Memorial Day of 1992, President Bush abruptly changed course and issued an executive order from his Kennebunkport vacation home, authorizing the Coast Guard to return all fleeing Haitians to Haiti without any process whatsoever.[27] Bush's "Kennebunkport Order" appeared to be a textbook case of *refoulement,* for it effectively erected a "floating Berlin Wall" around Haiti that prevented Haitians from fleeing anywhere, not just to the United States. The *HCC* plaintiffs invoked several counts in their existing complaint to return to Judge Johnson for a new TRO, now challenging the Kennebunkport Order as violating three inter-connected legal prohibitions: Article 33 of the Refugee Convention; Article 33's domestic statutory analogue, 8 U.S.C. § 1253(h) of the Immigration and Nationality Act (INA);[28] and the 1981 executive agreement between the United States and Haiti. These laws, the plaintiffs argued, imposed upon the U.S. government a unified mandate of *nonrefoulement:* executive officials shall not return political refugees with colorable asylum claims forcibly and summarily to a country where they will face political persecution.

Judge Johnson denied the plaintiffs' request for a TRO on the ground that Article 33 was not self-executing. But in an unusually

---

25. Haitian Ctrs. Council, Inc. v. McNary, 969 F.2d 1326 (2d Cir. 1992), *vacated as moot sub nom.* Sale v. Haitian Ctrs. Council, Inc., 509 U.S. 918 (1993).

26. McNary v. Haitian Ctrs. Council, Inc., 503 U.S. 1000 (1992) (entering stay pending disposition of government appeal to Second Circuit).

27. Exec. Order No. 12,807, 57 Fed. Reg. 23,133 (May 24, 1992).

28. 8 U.S.C. § 1253(h)(1) (1988) ("The Attorney General shall not deport or return any alien . . . to a country if the Attorney General determines that such alien's life or freedom would be threatened in such country on account of [his] . . . political opinion.").

candid statement, he added, "[i]t is unconscionable that the United States should accede to the Protocol and later claim that it is not bound by it. This court is astonished that the United States would return Haitian refugees to the jaws of political persecution, terror, death and uncertainty when it has contracted not to do so."[29] On expedited appeal, the Second Circuit adopted the Haitians' argument and declared the *refoulement* policy illegal, finding that the new Bush "direct return" policy violated the plain language of 8 U.S.C. § 1253(h)(1).[30]

In July 1992, for the third time in seven months, the government sought and won an emergency stay of a lower court order restricting its repatriation program. On July 31, 1992, just two days after the Second Circuit entered judgment enjoining the summary repatriation of refugees called for in the Kennebunkport Order, Justice Thomas advised the Court that the Solicitor General had requested an emergency stay.[31] Echoing Justice Kennedy's earlier memos in the Florida litigation, Justice Thomas framed the case from the government's perspective, emphasizing not human rights, but themes of law and order, foreign policy, and military affairs.[32] He emphasized the similarity of the New York and Florida cases and characterized the plaintiffs in *HCC–II* as "raising claims virtually identical to those raised and rejected in *HRC v. Baker*."[33] Given the disagreement between the Second and Eleventh Circuits regarding the applicability of the INA to refugees on the high seas, Justice Thomas concluded that "[t]here can be little doubt the present case is cert-worthy." Moreover, Justice Thomas suggested, the Second Circuit had likely erred in its analysis of 8 U.S.C. § 1253 by concluding that the *HCC–II* plaintiffs had a right to judicial review and were not collaterally estopped by the *HRC* litigation. His memo ended by returning to themes of "foreign policy and other national interests;" he dismissed the balance of equities between the Haitians and the government as "probably about equal," and declared: "I expect to vote to grant the application."[34]

---

29. Haitian Ctrs. Council Inc. v. McNary, No. 92 CV 1258, 1992 WL 155853, at *12 (E.D.N.Y. 1992).

30. Haitian Ctrs. Council, Inc. v. McNary, 969 F.2d 1350, 1360–63 (2d Cir. 1992), *rev'd sub nom*. Sale v. Haitian Ctrs. Council, Inc., 509 U.S. 155 (1993).

31. Memorandum from Justice Clarence Thomas, Supreme Court of the United States, to the Conference 1 (July 31, 1992) (on file with authors).

32. Justice Thomas began his analysis, "[p]ursuant to a proclamation and executive order issued by President Reagan in 1981, the Coast Guard has been intercepting vessels on the high seas suspected of transporting migrants for illegal entry into the United States and has repatriated such aliens to their home countries." *Id*.

33. *Id*. at 2.

34. *Id*. at 3–5.

The full Court quickly agreed with Justice Thomas, staying the Second Circuit's order by a vote of 7–2 and setting an expedited schedule for the government to file a petition for *certiorari*.[35] As in the Florida litigation, it was Justice Blackmun, joined by Justice Stevens, who viewed the case through a different lens. In his dissent from entry of the stay, Justice Blackmun questioned the government's likelihood of success on the merits, given that eight federal judges (one District Court and three Court of Appeals judges each in the Second and Eleventh Circuits) had now divided 4–4 on the applicability of § 1253 on the high seas. As a human rights matter, Justice Blackmun noted, "the plaintiffs in this case face the real and immediate prospect of persecution, terror, and possibly even death at the hands of those to whom they are being forcibly returned."[36]

The *HCC–II* plaintiffs well understood that the Court, having now granted a stay, would almost surely also grant *certiorari*. Hoping to expedite consideration, they asked the Court to treat the government's stay application as a petition for *certiorari*, to grant it, and to expedite briefing and argument on the merits. But this time, Circuit Justice Thomas circulated a memo opposing this motion and advocating "full briefing on the question of *certiorari*;" he reasoned that the plaintiffs had identified only the extraterritorial application of § 1253 as worthy of *certiorari*, whereas his prior memorandum had noted that the Court might also wish to grant review on the questions of collateral estoppel and the right to judicial review.[37] The Court agreed and deferred a vote on *certiorari* until October 1992.[38]

The parties' chief struggle in briefing the petition for *certiorari* concerned the questions for review. The government asked the Court to grant review on three additional issues: (1) whether judicial review was available to the refugees pursuant to the INA, the Administrative Procedure Act, or otherwise; (2) whether the *HCC–II* plaintiffs were collaterally estopped[39] by the Eleventh Circuit's decisions in *HRC*; and (3) whether equitable considerations, including separation of powers concerns and respect for the President's control of foreign affairs and military policy, required that the Second Circuit deny relief. Counsel for

---

35. McNary v. Haitian Centers Council, Inc., 505 U.S. 1234 (1992).

36. *Id.* (Blackmun, J., joined by Stevens, J., dissenting).

37. Memorandum from Justice Clarence Thomas, Supreme Court of the United States, to the Conference 1 (Aug. 4, 1992) (on file with authors).

38. McNary v. Haitian Centers Council, Inc., 505 U.S. 1236 (1992).

39. Collateral estoppel is a legal principle holding that a party who has actually litigated a necessarily decided issue, in a judgment which is final, and on the merits, may not attempt to re-litigate the same issue by refiling his case a second time. It was the government's view that the claims of the Haitian plaintiffs in HCC–II impermissibly overlapped with the failed claims of the plaintiffs in *HRC v. Baker* and thus were collaterally estopped.

the refugees, by contrast, emphasized that only the issue regarding the interpretation of § 1253 had divided the Second and Eleventh Circuits. The cert pool memo, by a law clerk to Chief Justice Rehnquist, recommended granting the government's petition.[40]

While the Court was deciding whether to review the Haitian refugee case during the summer and early fall of 1992 opinion, the refugee crisis also emerged as a major issue in the presidential campaign between George H.W. Bush and Bill Clinton. Shortly after the Second Circuit's July 1992 opinion, candidate Bill Clinton had praised the court for making the "right decision in overturning the Bush administration's cruel policy of returning Haitian refugees to a brutal dictatorship without an asylum hearing."[41] In October 1992, the Court unanimously granted the government's petition for *certiorari* and soon set an expedited briefing schedule.[42] The government filed its opening brief on November 9, 1992. Three days later, at a press conference, now President-elect Bill Clinton reiterated his campaign criticism of the summary repatriation of Haitian refugees, declaring, "I think that the blanket sending [of the Haitians] back to Haiti under the circumstances which have prevailed for the last year was an error and so I will modify that process."[43] Taking the President-elect at his word, counsel for the refugees immediately moved to suspend briefing at the Supreme Court until one month after Clinton's inauguration. They hoped to moot the case, thereby avoiding an adverse ruling, once Clinton took office and made good on his repeated promises to change the direct return policy. With Justices Blackmun and Souter dissenting, however, the Court denied the motion to suspend briefing.[44] This ruling forced the refugee advocates to finalize their own merits briefs and a dozen amicus briefs elaborating upon each element of their position.[45]

---

40. Preliminary Memorandum from Celestine Richards, Law Clerk, to the Conference (Sept. 14, 1992) (on file with authors); *see also* Supplemental Memorandum from Celestine Richards, Law Clerk, to the Conference (Sept. 19, 1992) (on file with authors).

41. *Clinton Statement on Appeals Court Ruling on Haitian Repatriation*, U.S. NEWSWIRE, July 29, 1992. This statement echoed remarks Governor Clinton had made only three days after the Kennebunkport Order had been issued. *See Statement by Gov. Clinton on Haitian Refugees*, U.S. NEWSWIRE, May 27, 1992 ("I am appalled by the decision of the Bush administration to pick up fleeing Haitians on the high seas and forcibly return them to Haiti before considering their claim to political asylum.... This policy must not stand."). For an extensive listing of candidate Clinton's statements, *see* Clawson et al., *supra* note 9, at nn. 61–63.

42. McNary v. Haitian Centers Council, Inc., 506 U.S. 814 (1992).

43. *The Transition: Excerpts from President–Elect's News Conference in Arkansas,* N.Y. TIMES, Nov. 13, 1992, at A18.

44. McNary v. Haitian Centers Council, Inc., 506 U.S. 996 (1992).

45. Amicus briefs were filed in support of the Haitians by three former Attorney Generals, the U.N. High Commissioner for Refugees, the Congressional sponsors of the

The Court did, however, delay calendaring oral argument until March 1993, de facto granting the refugees the time they had sought. But shortly before he took office, President-elect Clinton reversed course, abandoned his repeated pledge to rescind the Kennebunkport Order, and endorsed the Bush policy.[46] As a result, the Clinton Justice Department set about defending both the summary return policy and the legality of the Guantánamo internment before the courts.

The Supreme Court's Deliberations[47]

Shortly before the Court held argument in *Sale* on March 2, 1993, Justice Blackmun's law clerk concluded his bench memo with the words: "It is very hard to predict what the Court will do with this case. Every day a different clerk suggests that a different issue is central to his or her justice. I imagine this one will generate ten opinions."[48]

At the Court's conference that Friday, as usual, the Chief Justice spoke first, followed by each Associate Justice, speaking in order of seniority. Because the Justices had communicated many of their substantive views on the legal issues during the extensive sparring over the 1992 stay motions, there may not have been much suspense. On the other hand, the Court had not previously benefited from full briefing and argument on the merits, so the outcome could not have been entirely free of doubt. As it turned out, however, the vote was not close. At Conference, the most significant division concerned the collateral estoppel argument,[49] which remained ancillary to the case, but whose disposition proved enormously consequential to the *HCC–I* half of the litigation.

Chief Justice Rehnquist began by expressing his view that the Haitians' claims were collaterally estopped by the Eleventh Circuit's prior decision in *HRC*. Should the Court reach the merits, he believed the President's actions were fully authorized and not barred by statute. Nor was the Chief Justice persuaded by what he perceived as the Second

---

Refugee Act, Americas Watch, Amnesty International, the NAACP, the Association of the Bar of the City of New York, the Lawyers' Committee for Human Rights, the American Immigration Lawyers Association, the International Human Rights Law Group, the American Jewish Committee, and various Haitian service organizations. For a description of how this "pyramidal briefing structure" came to be, *see* Koh, *Reflections, supra* note 9, at 10–11.

46. *Clinton Warns Haitians Not to Flee to U.S.*, L.A. TIMES, January 15, 1993, at A1 (justifying the decision on the grounds that "Boat departures in the near future would result in further tragic losses of life....")

47. This discussion is based on Justice Blackmun's detailed notes of the oral argument and the March 5, 1993 Conference, contained in Box 623 of the Blackmun Papers.

48. Bench Memorandum from Andrew Schapiro, Law Clerk to Justice Harry A. Blackmun, Supreme Court of the United States 40 (Feb. 27, 1993) (on file with authors).

49. *See* note 39, *supra.*

Circuit's "policy" arguments, which he characterized as "extremely weak." Speaking next, the senior Associate Justice, Byron White, expressed uncertainty about the collateral estoppel argument, but agreed that the President had authority to issue the Kennebunkport Order. Next came Justice Blackmun. His notes of the Conference are silent as to his own remarks, except to record that his was the sole vote to affirm the Second Circuit.[50]

If there was any suspense at the Conference, it probably peaked during the pause after Justice Blackmun finished speaking and before Justice Stevens began. Justice Stevens, after all, was the Court's only member consistently to have voted with Blackmun on the various stay motions and prior petitions for *certiorari*. Under any scenario, the Haitians could not prevail without Justice Stevens' vote. Justice Stevens began by agreeing that the Eleventh Circuit decision did not estop the Haitians from pursuing their claims, which were indeed subject to judicial review. On the merits, however, Justice Stevens disagreed with Justice Blackmun. Foreshadowing his eventual opinion for the Court, he observed that the Kennebunkport Order addressed not only the Attorney General, who was constrained by the immigration statutes, but the Coast Guard as well. Conceding that the plain language of § 1253(h) was "strong in favor" of the Haitians, Stevens nevertheless concluded that, in light of the Executive Branch's long-standing application of the statute only within the United States, the lack of clarifying legislative history, and practical concerns about the consequence of holding that the treaty restricted the President's power, the United States possessed the power to prevent mass immigration. Expressing an uneasiness that would later pervade his majority opinion, Justice Stevens closed by voting "with difficulty" to reverse the Second Circuit on the merits.[51]

Speaking in turn, Justices O'Connor and Scalia also voted to reverse. Justice Scalia opined that the case was more easily disposed of on the merits than on estoppel grounds and, according to Blackmun's notes,

---

50. Justice Blackmun's Conference notes are blank with respect to his own remarks, but his notes composed on March 1, 1993, the day of oral argument, make plain his view that the Haitians' "case on t[he] merits is very strong. Nothing ambig[uous] [about] t[he] lang[uage] or t[he] st[andar]d forbids [the] U.S. from returning any alien to his persecutor." Notes of Justice Harry A. Blackmun on Oral Argument, Sale v. Haitian Ctrs. Council, Inc., 509 U.S. 155 (1993) (No. 92-344) (on file with authors). Nor was he persuaded that the respondents were collaterally estopped, because the "Fl[orid]a class ... did n[ot] include t[he] 'screened-in.' " *Id.*

51. Justice Blackmun's notes summarizing Justice Stevens's statement at Conference are far longer than those for any other justice. *See* Notes of Justice Harry A. Blackmun on Conference, Sale v. Haitian Ctrs. Council, Inc., 509 U.S. 155 (1993) (No. 92-344) (on file with authors). It is not possible to know whether this reflects the duration of Justice Stevens's comments, or merely the close scrutiny that Justice Blackmun paid to them.

"t[ook] a shot" at the Second Circuit.[52] Like Justice Stevens, Justice O'Connor acknowledged the force of the Haitians' plain language argument, but found it overcome by legislative history and the presumption against extraterritoriality, as well as by the government's argument that § 1253(h) restricted only the Attorney General, not the President. Justices Kennedy, Souter, and Thomas all preferred the disposition first presented by Justice Stevens: reversing the Second Circuit on the merits rather than on the government's estoppel argument, for, as Kennedy observed (in Justice Blackmun's notes), the "case is too imp[ortan]t"[53] to be ducked on procedural grounds.

Justice Stevens circulated his first draft of the *Sale* majority opinion on Friday, May 14, 1993. Although Justice Blackmun advised the Conference the following Monday, May 17, that he would be circulating a dissent, the other Justices did not wait. The very next day, May 18, the Chief Justice and Justices O'Connor, Thomas, and Kennedy all joined Justice Stevens, giving him a majority within two business days after circulation. One day later, Justice White added a sixth vote.[54]

The most extensive comments on the Stevens draft came in a detailed memorandum from Justice Scalia, who "seriously object[ed] to the District Court's extensive criticism of U.S. policy" toward the Haitian refugees, which the Stevens draft had quoted at length.[55] "We should not be seen to approve such an extravagant incursion into political matters that were none of the judge's business," continued Scalia. "I would prefer that this note be deleted ..."[56] Stevens agreed and deleted the challenged language.[57] Justice Scalia further requested a

---

52. *Id.*

53. *Id.*

54. Justice Kennedy included two suggestions for slight revisions to the Stevens draft, the first a clarification of the discussion of the treaty and the Supremacy Clause, and the second explaining that "I am a bit uneasy about putting presidential press releases into the *U.S. Reports*, in particular as aids to understanding formal Executive Orders.... The White House gets enough ink in other places." Memorandum from Justice Anthony M. Kennedy, Supreme Court of the United States, to Justice John Paul Stevens and the Conference (May 18, 1993) (on file with authors).

55. Draft Opinion of Justice John Paul Stevens at 11, n. 14, Sale v. Haitian Ctrs. Council, 509 U.S. 155 (1993) (No. 92–344) [hereinafter Stevens Draft] (on file with authors).

56. Memorandum from Justice Antonin Scalia, Supreme Court of the United States, to Justice John Paul Stevens and the Conference 1 (May 20, 1993) [hereinafter Scalia Memorandum] (on file with authors).

57. Letter from Justice John Paul Stevens, Supreme Court of the United States, to Justice Antonin Scalia 1 (May 20, 1993) [hereinafter Stevens Memorandum] (copies forwarded to the Conference). Justice Stevens agreed to remove the District Court's statement that "[i]t is unconscionable that the United States should accede to the Protocol and later claim that it is not bound by it.... The Government's conduct is particularly

rephrasing of the reliance on legislative history regarding the 1980 amendments and seconded Justice Kennedy's request for clarification of the discussion of the treaty and the Supremacy Clause. Finally, Justice Scalia made two suggestions that he termed "minor:" first, he expressed reservations about describing Jean–Bertrand Aristide as "the first democratically elected president" of Haiti. "Twenty years from now, when it turns out he was Fidel Castro with a Roman collar, it may look strange in our opinion."[58] Second, Justice Scalia objected to the draft's mere mention of the "moral weight" of the Haitians' claim. "For my taste, that comes too close to acknowledging that it is morally wrong to return these refugees to Haiti, which I do not believe."[59]

Justice Stevens accommodated many of Scalia's requests, but not these last two. That same day, he replied, "[e]ven if Aristide turns out to be another Castro, the statement in the opinion is nevertheless accurate and I think appropriate because of the claim that the exodus has been motivated by the political turmoil in Haiti."[60] Justice Stevens also declined to ignore the "moral weight" of the Haitians' argument. "I think it is undeniable that it has *some* moral weight and I think it would be unfortunate for us to imply that we think it may have none."[61] Justice Scalia acceded and joined the majority that day. A week later, Justice Souter joined without comment.

Justice Blackmun circulated his lengthy dissent on Thursday, June 17, 1993, but Justice Stevens neither cited the dissent, nor revised his opinion in response. The following Monday, the Court handed down its opinion in *Sale*. Even with Justice Scalia's edits, the opinion is striking for its obvious discomfort with the policy it upheld. Cautioning that "[t]he wisdom of the policy choices made by Presidents Reagan, Bush, and Clinton is not a matter for our consideration,"[62] the Court held that neither the *nonrefoulement* obligations of § 1253(h) of the INA, nor Article 33 of the Refugee Convention applied to Haitians apprehended on the high seas. Justice Stevens acknowledged the "moral weight" of the refugees' argument "that the Protocol's broad remedial goals require that a nation be prevented from repatriating refugees to their potential oppressors whether or not the refugees are within that nation's bor-

---

hypocritical given its condemnation of other countries who have refused to abide by the principle of non-refoulement. As it stands now, Article 33 is a cruel hoax and not worth the paper it is printed on...." Stevens Draft, *supra* note 55, at 11, n. 14 (quoting Haitian Ctrs. Council v. McNary, No. 92–1258, 1992 WL 155853, at *12 (E.D.N.Y. 1992)).

58. Scalia Memorandum, *supra* note 56, at 2.
59. *Id.*
60. Stevens Draft, *supra* note 55, at 1–2.
61. *Id.* at 2.
62. HCC–II, 509 U.S. at 165 (internal citation and quotation marks omitted).

ders."[63] The Court closed by "by find[ing] ourselves in agreement" with the view that "[t]his case presents a painfully common situation in which desperate people, convinced that they can no longer remain in their homeland, take desperate measures to escape. Although the human crisis is compelling, there is no solution to be found in a judicial remedy."[64]

The Supreme Court's Decision

On close examination, the Court's opinion flouts all traditional rules of legal interpretation. As Justice Blackmun's dissent cogently observed, the Court's opinion in HCC–II rested on three implausible assertions: (1) that "the word 'return' does not mean return . . . [(2) that] the opposite of 'within the United States' is not outside the United States, and . . . [(3) that] the official charged with controlling immigration has no role in enforcing an order to control immigration."[65]

Justice Stevens's opinion first engaged in a long exegesis of the meanings of "*refouler*" and "return" in the statute and treaty and concluded that the legal prohibition on returning non-citizens somehow did not apply to this kind of return. But the Kennebunkport Order itself expressly authorized the Coast Guard "[t]o return" Haitian vessels and their passengers to Haiti, which was precisely the act that the law forbade. Justice Stevens never explained why the plain meaning of the French word "*refouler*" did not apply to the Haitian situation, especially when French newspapers were contemporaneously reporting that "Les États–Unis ont décidé de *refouler* directement les réfugiés recueillis par la garde côtière" ("the United States has decided to directly *return* the refugees picked up by the Coast Guard.").[66]

Justice Stevens next reasoned that in 1980, Congress had extended the Refugee Act's protection from "any alien within the United States" to "any alien" without geographical limit, with the express intent of extending statutory protection only to foreign nationals physically, but not legally, present within the United States.[67] But if Congress meant to protect only noncitizens "physically present in the United States," why

---

63. *Id.* at 178–79.

64. *Id.* at 188 (Edwards, J., concurring in part and dissenting in part) (quoting Haitian Refugee Ctr., Inc. v. Gracey, 809 F.2d 794, 841 (D.C. Cir. 1987).).

65. *Id.* at 189 (Blackmun, J., dissenting) (internal citations omitted).

66. *Le bourbier haïtien,* LE MONDE, May 31–June 1, 1992, *quoted in* HCC–II, 509 U.S. at 192 (Blackmun, J., dissenting) (emphasis added). *But see* Exec. Order No. 12,807, 57 Fed. Reg. 23,133, 23,133–34 (May 24, 1992) (appropriate directives will be issued "providing for the Coast Guard . . . to *return* the vessel and its passengers to the country from which it came." (emphasis added)).

67. Refugee Act of 1980, Pub. L. No. 96–212 § 202(e), 94 Stat. 102 (1980) (codified as amendment to 8 U.S.C. 1253(h).).

would it not use those exact words, as it did in numerous other places in the statute?[68] The fairest reading of Congress's decision to bar the return of "any alien" seemed to be that it meant to address all noncitizens, wherever they might be located—even outside U.S. territory. Invoking the so-called "presumption against extraterritoriality," however, Justice Stevens decided against the application of section 1253(h) to noncitizens stopped on the high seas.[69] But as Justice Blackmun pointed out, that presumption was designed primarily to avoid judicial interpretations of a statute that infringes upon the rights of another sovereign.[70] Logically, the presumption should have had no force or relevance on the high seas, where no possibility exists for conflicts with other jurisdictions.

Nor did it make sense to presume that Congress legislated with exclusively territorial intent when enacting a law governing a distinctively international subject matter—the transborder movement of refugees—to enforce an international human rights obligation embodied in a multilateral convention. Whether or not the Court properly applied the presumption against extraterritorial application to the statute, it should not have applied it to presume that the United States' obligations under Article 33 of the *Refugee Convention* are territorial.[71] To "presume" that parties to human rights treaties contract solely for domestic effect would have permitted the United States to commit genocide or torture on the high seas, notwithstanding the universal, peremptory prohibitions of the Genocide and Torture Conventions.

Even more bizarre, the Court chose to invoke the presumption against extraterritoriality in a case where the executive branch itself cited the statute as the basis for its very authority to act extraterritorially. If, as the Court concluded, the presumption operated to deny the Haitians extraterritorial statutory protection, *a fortiori* it should also have operated to deny the President extraterritorial authority to stop the Haitians in the first place. Indeed, just a week after applying the presumption in *HCC–II,* the Court *permitted* extraterritorial application of the Sherman Act to foreign conduct that produced a substantial anticompetitive effect in the United States, without invoking the presumption against extraterritoriality or explaining how that presumption had been overcome.[72]

---

68. *Compare* HCC–II, 509 U.S. at 175–80 *with* provisions cited in *id.* at 202–06, n. 15 (Blackmun, J., dissenting).

69. HCC–II, 509 U.S. at 173.

70. *Id.* at 205–07 (Blackmun, J., dissenting).

71. *See id.* at 183 ("[A] treaty cannot impose uncontemplated extraterritorial obligations on those who ratify it through no more than its general humanitarian intent.").

72. Hartford Fire Ins. Co. v. California, 509 U.S. 764, 795–96 (1993) ("Although the proposition was perhaps not always free from doubt, . . . it is well established by now that

Finally, the Court's decision triply misconstrued the Refugee Convention as a part of international human rights law. First, the Court read unambiguous treaty language to be ambiguous. Although both the statute and the treaty clearly mandated the mutually reinforcing requirement that the United States shall not return or *"refoule"* "any alien" or "refugee" to his persecutors, the Court denied that either "return" or *"refouler"* meant "return" in this context and re-construed "any alien" to mean "any alien physically present in the United States."[73]

Second, the Court declined to construe the contested language in light of the treaty's object and purpose. Justice Stevens expressly recognized that the drafters of the Refugee Convention "may not have contemplated that any nation would gather fleeing refugees and return them to the one country they had desperately sought to escape; *such actions may even violate the spirit of Article 33.*"[74] Nevertheless, he construed the statute's words deliberately to offend the object and purpose of the treaty and the statute. As Justice Blackmun recalled, the

---

the Sherman Act applies" to certain extraterritorial conduct. (citation omitted)). Significantly, Justice Scalia's partial dissent for himself and three others who had joined the *HCC* majority invoked the canon that statutes should not be interpreted to conflict with international law. *See id.* at 814–15 (Scalia, J., dissenting). Yet if properly applied in *HCC–II*, that canon would have militated for, not against, extraterritorial application of the *nonrefoulement* provision of the INA. *See* HCC–II, 509 U.S. at 203, n. 13 (Blackmun, J., dissenting) (noting how the Court, erroneously "reasoning backwards, . . . actually looks to the *American* scheme to illuminate the *treaty*" (emphasis in original)).

73. In arguing that Article 33 did not apply on the high seas, the Government further claimed that the term *"refouler"* meant to "expel," not to "return," and hence, barred only the forced expulsion of Haitian refugees who had already landed in the United States, not the forced return of those refugees intercepted en route. The government's reading of *"refouler"* as to "expel" created a pointless redundancy in Article 33: "no Contracting State shall expel *or expel* a refugee" to conditions of persecution. The government's interpretation also relied on a subsidiary definition of *"refouler"* in *Cassell's*, a non-authoritative French dictionary, not the definitions "to repulse . . . drive back . . . repel" provided in the authoritative *Dictionnaire Larousse* 631 (1981) (Francais, Anglais). When the meaning of French terms in a treaty is an issue, the Supreme Court has traditionally "relied on . . . French dictionaries as a primary method for defining terms. . . ." Eastern Airlines, Inc. v. Floyd, 499 U.S. 530, 537 (1991). The Court had used *Dictionnaire Larousse* as its authoritative French dictionary for more than a century, while never citing *Cassell's* (until its decision in *Sale v. Haitian Centers Council*). *See* Brief for Respondents at 15–16, nn. 21, 23, Sale v. Haitian Ctrs. Council, Inc., 509 U.S. 155 (1993) (No. 92–344). Ordinary usage, as reflected in French newspapers, also confirmed that *"refouler"* accurately described the U.S. government's actions against the Haitian refugees. *See, e.g.*, Jean-Michel Caroit, *L'exode continue*, Le Monde, May 29, 1992, at 4 ("La décision du président Bush d'ordonner a la garde côtière americaine de refouler les boat-people haïtiens vers leur le pour tenter de mettre fin à un veritable exode a suscite. [President Bush's decision to order the U.S. Coast Guard to return the Haitian boat people to their island was an attempt to put an end to a genuine exodus.]" (emphasis added))

74. HCC–II, 509 U.S. at 183 (emphasis added).

refugee treaty's purpose was to extend international protections to those who, having fled persecution in their own country, could no longer invoke that government's legal protection.[75] He found it "extraordinary ... that the Executive, in disregard of the law, would take to the seas to intercept fleeing refugees and force them back to their persecutors—and that the Court would strain to sanction that conduct."[76] Although the Convention was drafted to prevent a replay of the forced return of Jewish refugees to Europe, *HCC–II* would permit such a replay, so long as fleeing refugees were intercepted on the high seas.

Third, the Court not only subordinated text, but also elevated snippets of negotiating history into definitive interpretive guides. The Vienna Convention on the Law of Treaties directs that reliance on a treaty's negotiating history is the alternative of last, not first, resort.[77] Elsewhere, Justice Scalia had specifically argued that if "the Treaty's language resolves the issue presented, there is no necessity of looking further to discover 'the intent of the parties.' "[78] Yet, in *HCC–II,* the Court reversed a decades-old interpretation of a multilateral treaty—the Refugee Convention—by relying on statements of two foreign delegates that were never commented or voted upon by the United States; that were never presented to or considered by the Senate during its ratification of the Refugee Protocol; and that were explicitly rebutted by a sworn affidavit submitted by the U.S. government official who negotiated the treaty.[79]

In short, the *HCC–II* Court ignored the plain meaning of statute and treaty to articulate an unprecedented domestic rule of "territorial *nonrefoulement.*" Remarkably, the majority assumed that Congress did not mean what it said when it ratified a mutually reinforcing statute and treaty: that the negotiating parties intended, through floor debate, to undercut the treaty's explicit object and purpose and that Congress had enacted universal human rights obligations governing trans-border activ-

75. *Id.* at 207 (Blackmun, J., dissenting).

76. *Id.* at 189 (Blackmun, J., dissenting).

77. Vienna Convention on the Law of Treaties, May 23, 1969, 1155 U.N.T.S. 331. Article 32 permits use of the negotiating history in treaty construction only as a last resort, and even then, only if a plain language analysis "leaves the meaning ambiguous or obscure" or leads to a "manifestly absurd or unreasonable result."

78. United States v. Stuart, 489 U.S. 353, 371 (1989) (Scalia, J., concurring) (quoting majority opinion, *id.* at 366).

79. *See* Affidavit of Louis Henkin, appended to Brief for the Respondents at 63, Sale v. Haitian Ctrs. Council, Inc., 509 U.S. 155 (1993) (No. 92–344), *excerpts appended to* Koh, *Reflections, supra* note 9, at 44–47. Article 31 of the Vienna Convention on the Law of Treaties instructs courts to rely primarily on a treaty's language and purpose. Vienna Convention on the Law of Treaties, *supra* note 77, at 340.

ities with an exclusively territorial focus. As Justice Blackmun's law clerk wrote in his pre-argument bench memo:

> The longer I work on this case, the more convinced I become that the Gov[ernment's] statutory interpretation argument may not even pass the "straight-face" test.... There is nothing at all ambiguous about the [statutory] language: it clearly and explicitly forbids the Gov[ernmen]t from returning any alien to his persecutors. Is that what the Gov[ernmen]t is doing here? Unquestionably. That should be the end of the case, on the merits.[80]

Why the Haitian Boat People Lost

If the majority's decision was so implausible, why was the vote so lopsided? In retrospect, the Supreme Court's ruling should have come as no surprise. The Court had foreshadowed its voting alignment more than a year earlier, when it denied *certiorari* to the Haitian Refugee Center's petition regarding the screened-out Haitians' due process rights, with only Justice Blackmun dissenting. The Court's internal memoranda from that period reveal that many justices appear already to have concluded that the INA did not apply beyond the territorial borders of the United States. Indeed, during the previous two years, the full Court had voted against the Haitians no less than eight times.[81] Most crucially, nearly a year before the opinion issued, by a 7–2 vote, the Court had stayed the Second Circuit's ruling blocking the Bush policy of summary return, thereby ensuring that the policy would continue for at least eleven months before plenary Supreme Court argument and decision.[82] Having tipped its hand by these acts, and effectively sanctioned *refoulement* in the interim, the Justices could now hardly turn around and declare the same policy illegal.

---

80. Bench Memorandum from Andrew Schapiro, Law Clerk to Justice Harry A. Blackmun, Supreme Court of the United States 35 (Feb. 27, 1993) (on file with authors).

81. The Court had thrice intervened to stay lower court rulings favoring the Haitians. *See* Baker v. Haitian Refugee Ctr., Inc., 502 U.S. 1083 (1992); McNary v. Haitian Ctrs. Council, Inc., 503 U.S. 1000 (1992); McNary v. Haitian Ctrs. Council, Inc., 505 U.S. 1234 (1992). Moreover, the Court had twice denied stay requests from Haitian refugee groups, Haitian Refugee Ctr., Inc. v. Baker, 502 U.S. 1084 (1992); Haitian Refugee Ctr., Inc. v. Baker, 502 U.S. 1122 (1992); had granted *certiorari* over the Haitians' opposition, McNary v. Haitian Ctrs. Council, Inc., 506 U.S. 814 (1992); and had denied their motions both to expedite briefing, McNary v. Haitian Ctrs. Council, Inc., 505 U.S. 1236 (1992), and to suspend briefing until after Inauguration Day, McNary v. Haitian Ctrs. Council, Inc., 506 U.S. 996 (1992).

82. McNary v. Haitian Ctrs. Council, Inc., 505 U.S. 1236 (1992). In addition, during the October 1992 Term, the Supreme Court had vacated or reversed the judgment of the Second Circuit in all but one of the eleven decisions for which it granted review. *See* Martin Flumenbaum & Brad S. Karp, *Second Circuit Review: Performance in the U.S. Supreme Court,* N.Y.L.J. at 3 (Sept. 22, 1993).

On reflection, the pivotal decision was not the Court's, but the President's. President Bush's issuance of the Kennebunkport Order was prompted at least in part by an election-year desire to avoid a replay of the Cuban Marielito boat crisis that had plagued the Carter presidency.[83] Bill Clinton's decision to maintain the Bush policy seems best ascribed to his desire, on the one hand, to avoid a replay of the "Fort Chaffee incident"—when Mariel Cubans seized an Arkansas penitentiary and doomed Clinton's first Governorship; and on the other, to avoid a refugee inflow that might distract attention from his ambitious domestic policy agenda.[84]

Once President Clinton had acted and Congress stood by, it became almost inevitable that the Supreme Court would validate the President's actions. For as soon as the Clinton Administration played the "presidential card" before the Supreme Court, adopting the Bush policy as well as its briefs, the handwriting was on the wall. After President Clinton had changed his position, Justices Kennedy, O'Connor, Souter, and Stevens—the potential swing votes—could only wonder, "[i]f two presidents can live with *refoulement* (including one who had repeatedly condemned it), why can't we?"

Thus, the *HCC–II* case is best remembered as part of a long line of Supreme Court precedents favoring presidential power in foreign affairs.[85] When *HCC–II* was decided, no president had lost a major foreign affairs case before the Court since the *Steel Seizure* case,[86] and presidents

---

83. *See, e.g.,* JIMMY CARTER, KEEPING FAITH: MEMOIRS OF A PRESIDENT 533–34 (1982).

84. *See* DAVID MARANISS, FIRST IN HIS CLASS: A BIOGRAPHY OF BILL CLINTON 377 (1995) (The Fort Chaffee refugee uprising "was used to great advantage by [successful Arkansas] Republican [gubernatorial] challenger Frank White and his handlers, who replayed footage of the Fort Chaffee riot to associate Clinton with images of disorder and bad times."). In addition, the group that helped Clinton make the decision—a group that reportedly included the incoming Secretary of State, National Security Advisor and Deputy, and Secretary of Defense—included no one from Congress, the Justice Department, or with bureaucratic responsibility for the promotion and protection of human rights or refugees. Moreover, the incoming Clinton administration closely coordinated its Haitian policy with officials of the departing Bush administration, some of whom stayed on well into the early months of the Clinton administration specifically to handle Haiti policy. *See* Steven A. Holmes, *Bush and Clinton Aides Link Policies on Haiti,* N.Y. TIMES, Jan. 7, 1993, at A10; Thomas L. Friedman, *Clinton Rounds Out State Dept. Team,* N.Y. TIMES, Jan. 20, 1993, at A12.

85. *See generally* cases cited in HAROLD HONGJU KOH, THE NATIONAL SECURITY CONSTITUTION: SHARING POWER AFTER THE IRAN-CONTRA AFFAIR 134–49 (1990). In at least one of these cases, Justice Stevens provided the President with the decisive vote on the merits. *See* Regan v. Wald, 468 U.S. 222 (1984) (upholding Reagan administration's authority to regulate travel to Cuba). Significantly, in *HCC–II* the Court refused to credit the Government's various claims of non-reviewability, thus avoiding broad future insulation of parallel executive conduct from judicial examination.

86. Youngstown Sheet & Tube Co. v. Sawyer, 343 U.S. 579 (1952).

had won many by asserting assorted justiciability defenses. Still, *HCC–II* added a new and surprising gloss to existing presidential power precedents. The Court docilely accepted the government's claim, newly minted for oral argument, that the case "concern[ed] the scope of the *President's* emergency powers to adopt measures that he deems to be necessary to prevent a mass migration of aliens across the high seas."[87] Yet the plaintiffs never challenged the President's constitutional authority to direct foreign and military policy. Neither President Bush nor President Clinton issued a new proclamation nor declared a national emergency to deal with the refugee problem. President George H.W. Bush's Executive Order did not even mandate that the Attorney General or Coast Guard return interdicted Haitians to Haiti. Instead, the President ordered only that "appropriate instructions" be issued, "provided . . . that the [A]ttorney [G]eneral, in his unreviewable discretion, may decide that a person who is a refugee will not be returned without his consent."[88] The plaintiffs argued that the President's Order could not grant the Attorney General such unreviewable discretion to return possible refugees, because the statute, treaty, and executive agreement had all *removed* that discretion from the President. Even on the high seas, they argued, the President's word is not the only law. Just as the Taft–Hartley Act had removed the Commerce Secretary's discretion to seize Youngstown's steel mills during the Korean War, section 1253(h) of the INA, Article 33 of the Refugee Convention, and the 1981 U.S.–Haiti Accord together removed the Attorney General's discretion to return fleeing refugees in far less emergent circumstances. Thus, properly understood, *HCC* fell within Category III of Justice Jackson's famous concurrence in *Youngstown,* in which the executive's "power is at its lowest ebb." Here, executive officials arguably acted in a manner "incompatible with the express or implied will of Congress,"[89] expressed in the statutory and treaty mandates that "[v]ulnerable refugees shall not be returned" to their persecutors.[90]

    Curiously, the Court concluded that the statute's directive to the "Attorney General" did not intend to limit the president and the Coast Guard. This argument recalled the Reagan Administration's claim dur-

---

    87. Transcript of Oral Argument (Deputy Solicitor General Maureen Mahoney) at 1 (emphasis added), Sale v. Haitian Ctrs. Council, Inc., 509 U.S. 155 (1993) (No. 92–344); *cf.* HCC–II, 509 U.S. at 187 ("[W]e are not persuaded that either [treaty or statute] places any limit on the president's authority to repatriate aliens interdicted beyond the territorial seas of the United States.").

    88. Exec. Order 12,807, 57 Fed. Reg. 23,133, 23,134 (May 24, 1992).

    89. Youngstown, 343 U.S. at 637 (Jackson, J., concurring). Indeed, *HCC* arguably presented an even less compelling case than *Youngstown,* inasmuch as the Taft–Hartley Act, unlike 8 U.S.C. 1253(h), did not expressly remove the lower executive official's discretion to perform the challenged act.

    90. HCC–II, 509 U.S. at 190 (Blackmun, J., dissenting).

ing the Iran–Contra Affair that the Boland Amendments' restriction upon United States agencies "involved in intelligence activities" somehow did not bind the National Security Council, even when it engaged in intelligence activities.[91] Yet here, Congress had carefully exercised its plenary power over immigration and directed that "the Attorney General . . . shall have the power and duty to control and guard the boundaries and borders of the United States against the illegal entry of aliens."[92] By mandating in 1980 that the Attorney General "shall not . . . return any alien" to conditions of persecution, Congress had carefully removed the discretion of the Attorney General *and any of her agents*—including the Coast Guard—to respond to perceived crises with summary return of refugees.

In dictum, the Court also cited the infamous *Curtiss–Wright* case to suggest that the statutory presumption against extraterritoriality has "special" force when courts construe "statutory provisions that may involve foreign and military affairs for which the President has unique responsibility."[93] But as Justice Blackmun correctly noted, "[t]he presumption that Congress did not intend to legislate extraterritorially has *less* force—perhaps, indeed, no force at all—when a statute on its face relates to foreign affairs."[94] In such circumstances, the presumption should have, in fact, run the other way, i.e., to favor extraterritorial application of United States law unless Congress otherwise indicated.

By overemphasizing the President's struggle to deal with the modest Haitian refugee outflow, the Court necessarily undervalued the human plight of the refugees themselves. Only Justice Blackmun, long a guardian of human rights, international law, and noncitizens, heard the Haitians' "modest plea, vindicated by the treaty and the statute," that

---

91. *Compare* HCC–II, 509 U.S. at 171–73 *with* Harold Hongju Koh, *Boland Amendments, in* 1 ENCYCLOPEDIA OF THE AMERICAN PRESIDENCY 111 (Leonard Levy & Louis Fisher eds., 1994).

92. *See* 8 U.S.C. § 1103(a) (1988), *cited in* HCC–II, 509 U.S. at 201 (Blackmun, J., dissenting); *see also* HCC–II, 509 U.S. at 201 (Blackmun, J., dissenting) ("Even the challenged Executive Order places the Attorney General 'on the boat' with the Coast Guard."). As the statute notes, "The officers of the Coast Guard insofar as they are engaged . . . in enforcing any law of the United States shall . . . be deemed to be acting as agents of the particular executive department . . . charged with the administration of the particular law . . . and . . . be subject to all the rules and regulations promulgated by such department . . . with respect to the enforcement of that law." 14 U.S.C. § 89(b) (2007).

93. *See* HCC–II, 509 U.S. at 188 (*citing* United States v. Curtiss–Wright Export Corp., 299 U.S. 304 (1936)); *see also* KOH, *supra* note 85, at 94 ("Among government attorneys, Justice Sutherland's lavish description of the president's powers is so often quoted that it has come to be known as the 'Curtiss–Wright, so I'm right' cite. . . .").

94. HCC–II, 509 U.S. at 206–07.

"the United States, land of refugees and guardian of freedom, cease forcibly driving them back to detention, abuse, and death."[95]

The Illegal Detention Phase: HCC–I

Even while the Supreme Court litigation raged in the Direct Return portion of the case, about 300 Haitian men, women, and children remained interned at Guantánamo. All had credible claims of political persecution, and many had already established full-fledged claims of political asylum. Nevertheless, they were barred from entering the United States, because most had the HIV virus.[96] When the Guantánamo phase of the case returned to Brooklyn federal court for consideration of permanent relief, the plaintiffs amended the complaint to challenge directly the legality of their confinement in America's first HIV concentration camp.

Following a two-week bench trial, Judge Johnson ordered the Guantánamo Haitians immediately released.[97] "If the Due Process Clause does not apply to the detainees at Guantánamo," Judge Johnson wrote, the government "would have discretion deliberately to starve or beat them, to deprive them of medical attention, to return them without process to their persecutors, or to discriminate among them based on the color of their skin."[98] The court also held that the U.S. Government had violated American lawyers' First Amendment rights by denying them access to the Haitians for the purpose of counseling, advocacy, and representation and that the defendants had abused their statutory authority under the Administrative Procedure Act by conducting unauthorized asylum interviews at Guantánamo and denying parole to the screened-in Haitians.[99]

The Clinton Administration chose not to seek a stay of that order, and after filing a notice of appeal, settled the case.[100] The plaintiffs ultimately agreed that Judge Johnson's orders (but not his opinions) could be vacated on the ground that defendants had fully complied with those orders, in exchange for the defendants' agreement to dismiss their appeal and to pay an award of fees and costs totaling $634,100. Just thirteen days after Judge Johnson issued his post-trial decision granting permanent injunctive relief to the Haitian refugees still on Guantánamo,

---

95. *Id.* at 208 (Blackmun, J., dissenting).

96. *See* 8 U.S.C. § 1182(a)(1)(A)(i) (1993) (excluding from admission into the United States persons "determined ... to have a communicable disease of public health significance").

97. HCC–I, 823 F.Supp. 1028.

98. *Id.* at 1042.

99. *Id.* at 1040–41, 1045–49.

100. *See* Stipulated Order Approving Class Action Settlement Agreement, Haitian Ctrs. Council, Inc. v. McNary, No. 92–1258 (E.D.N.Y. Feb. 22, 1994).

the government defendants finally released the last of the Guantánamo Haitians into the United States.

Although the Guantánamo portion of the case had been moving toward trial for months in the district court, it was very nearly derailed by the Supreme Court's actions in *HCC–II*. When the Justices met in Conference on March 5, 1993 to cast votes on *HCC–II*, Justice Blackmun's notes do not indicate that any Justice spoke to the potential impact that an estoppel ruling in *HCC–II* might have on the impending trial in *HCC–I*.[101] One cannot know how the Court would have ruled had it reached the estoppel issue, but Justice Blackmun's notes from Conference suggest the vote would certainly have been close.[102] The strong sentiment to reach the merits in *HCC–II*, however, and Justice Stevens's decision not to address the estoppel argument in his majority opinion, likely had momentous consequences for *HCC–I*. For had the Court agreed with the government that the issues and plaintiffs in *HCC–II* impermissibly overlapped with those in the Eleventh Circuit litigation, *HRC v. Baker*, (as Chief Justice Rehnquist began the Conference by suggesting), this decision would have precluded the district court from granting relief to the Haitians still at Guantánamo in *HCC–I* and denied the Clinton Administration the political option of accepting a trial defeat to allow the Guantánamo refugees to enter the United States.[103]

The Supreme Court's last brush with *HCC–I* came on June 21, 1993, the same day that the Court handed down its opinion in *HCC–II*. Justice Stevens circulated a "hold memo" to the Conference regarding the government's petition for *certiorari* to review the Second Circuit decision in *HCC–I*, which had affirmed a preliminary injunction in favor of the Haitians at Guantánamo. In light of the government's decision to comply with the district court's June 8 decision entering a *permanent* injunction in *HCC–I*, both sides advised the Court that the petition for *certiorari* to

---

101. *See* HCC–I, 823 F.Supp. at 1034 (noting that trial began March 8, 1993).

102. Justice Blackmun's notes indicate that Chief Justice Rehnquist argued most directly that the Haitians' claims were estopped, with Justices Scalia and Thomas agreeing the estoppel arguments were difficult. Justices Blackmun and Stevens stated their view that the claims were not estopped, with, apparently, both Justices Souter and Kennedy expressing sympathy for this position. Justice White was uncertain, and Justice Blackmun's notes on Justice O'Connor's view are unclear. *See* Notes of Justice Harry A. Blackmun on Conference, Sale v. Haitian Ctrs. Council, Inc., 509 U.S. 155 (1993) (No. 92–344) (on file with authors).

103. President Clinton's then-Deputy National Security Adviser, Sandy Berger, later recalled, "A lot of people [in the Clinton Administration] were happy when we lost. The President was glad. I was glad." Eric Schwartz, a National Security Council staffer, explained, after the District Court's ruling, "We didn't have to take any affirmative action anymore. . . . In a political world it's very different to make an affirmative decision than to say you're complying with a court order." GOLDSTEIN, HOW A BAND OF YALE LAW STUDENTS FOUGHT THE PRESIDENT AND WON, *supra* note 9, at 290.

review the *HCC I preliminary* injunction was now moot. In a memorandum to the Conference, Justice Stevens agreed and recommended that the Court grant the *HCC–I* petition for *certiorari* and vacate the Second Circuit decision as moot. He noted that Judge Johnson had held the Haitians' claims were not collaterally estopped, "an issue presented but left undecided in [*HCC–II*]."[104] Without amendment or dissent, on June 28 the Court entered the order that Justice Stevens proposed.[105]

But the end of the *HCC* litigation marked only a pause in the broader Haitian political crisis. As the Clinton Administration maintained its policy of direct return, domestic political pressure began to build. After months of silence, exiled President Aristide finally condemned the summary repatriation policy and announced that he would terminate the 1981 U.S.–Haiti Agreement as of October 1994.[106] The African–American community began drawing attention to the gross inconsistency of the Haiti policy with the U.S.'s international obligations and the discriminatory treatment of Haitians vis-à-vis Cubans and other immigrant groups. TransAfrica leader Randall Robinson undertook a hunger strike to publicize the Haitians' plight, personalizing the issue and becoming a focal point for media attention. The African–American community magnified its voice through the increasingly powerful forty-member Congressional Black Caucus (CBC), which in March 1994 sent President Clinton a letter announcing that "the United States' Haiti policy must be scrapped."[107]

In May 1994, President Clinton finally agreed. He appointed former Congressman William H. Gray, an African–American and former CBC member, as his new special envoy to Haiti, apparently acceding to Gray's demands that the Administration abandon its direct return policy. Finally, the U.S. encouraged the United Nations Security Council to adopt a "Desert Storm"-type resolution, authorizing member-states "to form a multinational force under unified command and control and, in this framework, to use all necessary means [including a military invasion] to facilitate the departure from Haiti of the military leadership" and to restore Aristide's government.[108] Four days later, American soldiers began landing in Haiti and, within days, numbered in the tens of thousands. Within a month, amid continuing street violence, the Haitian

---

104. Memorandum from Justice John Paul Stevens, Supreme Court of the United States, to the Conference 1 (June 21, 1993).

105. Sale v. Haitian Centers Council, Inc., 509 U.S. 918 (1993).

106. *See Aristide Ends Refugee Pact*, INT'L HERALD TRIB., Apr. 8, 1994.

107. Peter J. Boyer, *The Rise of Kweisi Mfume*, NEW YORKER, Aug. 1, 1994, at 34.

108. *U.N. Resolution for Invasion of Haiti*, N.Y. TIMES, Aug. 1, 1994, at A6; Richard D. Lyons, *U.N. Authorizes Invasion of Haiti To Be Led by U.S.*, N.Y. TIMES, Aug. 1, 1994, at A1.

Parliament had granted a limited amnesty, the coup leaders had resigned, and President Aristide had returned to Haiti in triumph.[109]

Why the Guantánamo Haitians Won

Why did the Guantánamo Haitians win, while the Haitian boat people lost? On balance, the *HCC* litigation demonstrates the human rights impact of what one of us has called "transnational public law litigation."[110] As the case unfolded, *HCC* developed a sprawling transnational party structure. In addition to the U.S. government officials, Haitian refugees, and humanitarian service organizations who comprised the original party set, the amici curiae supporting the plaintiffs came to embrace a broad array of intergovernmental organizations, international human rights nongovernmental organizations (NGOs), domestic civil rights groups, "rule of law" proponents, refugee advocates, and members of Congress. The elaborate transnational claim structure intertwined statutory claims, constitutional claims, and claims based on both bilateral and multilateral agreements. These claims not only interlocked but also evolved, the "lead claim" shifting as the case moved from forum to forum.

Like all transnational public law litigation, the suit's focus was never backward-looking, but always prospective, evolving, and expanding. The plaintiffs began with a relatively modest aim: securing the right to counsel for Haitians being subjected to de facto asylum interviews on Guantánamo. But over time, the narrow right-to-counsel case *(HCC–I)* expanded into a broad legal challenge against most aspects of the U.S. government's policy toward Haitian refugees, ranging from the extraterritorial *refoulement* of Haitians fleeing Haiti *(HCC–II)* to the sustained offshore detention of HIV-positive Haitians on Guantánamo.

---

109. *See* Larry Rohter, *Haitian Bill Doesn't Exempt Military from Prosecution*, N.Y. Times, Oct. 8, 1994, at A4. In the years that followed, Aristide went on to complete a troubled presidency, marked by continued controversy, and Haiti remains a deeply troubled country today.

110. Transnational public lawsuits exhibit five distinctive features:

a *transnational party structure,* in which states and nonstate entities equally participate; (2) a *transnational claim structure,* in which violations of domestic and international, private and public law are all alleged in a single action; (3) a *prospective focus,* fixed as much upon obtaining judicial declaration of transnational norms as upon resolving past disputes; (4) the litigants' strategic awareness of the *transportability of those norms* to other domestic and international fora for use in judicial interpretation or political bargaining; and (5) a subsequent process of *institutional dialogue* among various domestic and international, judicial and political fora to achieve ultimate settlement.

Koh, *supra* note 24, at 2371.

From the start, the plaintiffs and their counsel recognized that the chances of ultimate success before the Supreme Court were slim. For that reason, their governing strategy was to provoke the articulation of norms by sympathetic judicial fora—the Eastern District of New York and the Second Circuit—and then to transport those norms to other fora for use in political bargaining. Once won, the lower court victories were used to focus press attention, to score points in Congress,[111] to influence the Clinton campaign and transition teams, and ultimately to bargain for the clients' interests in negotiations with the Justice Department.

In the early phases of the suit, the goal of plaintiffs and their counsel was simply to keep the refugee issue politically alive until Bill Clinton could be elected President and undo the Bush Administration's Haitian policies. As in memorable domestic public law cases involving such thorny public issues as prison reform[112] and school busing,[113] the judicial decisions in *HCC* set the bounds and allocated bargaining chips for a process of institutional dialogue among a number of fora and players concerned with different dimensions of the larger Haitian problem. Like other institutional reform litigants, upon winning injunctive relief from the district court, the plaintiffs in *HCC* pursued a strategy of "complex enforcement" in which court orders formed a relatively minor part of the overall remedy.[114] Most notably, the plaintiffs became de facto partners with the district judge and government in the running of the Guantánamo camp. Although the government consistently denied plaintiffs' right-to-counsel claim, arguing that the presence of counsel would disrupt the operation of the naval base, during the last nine months of the case the defendants acquiesced in the nearly continuous presence at Guantánamo of plaintiffs' lawyers, who frequently helped to mediate disputes between the military and the refugees.[115] Over time, it became apparent that defendants' right-to-counsel violations stood at the tip of

---

111. *See, e.g., U.S. Human Rights Policy Toward Haiti: Hearing Before the Subcomm. on Legislation and National Security of the House Comm. on Government Operations*, 102d Cong. 98–99 (1992) [hereinafter *Hearing on U.S. Human Rights Policy Toward Haiti*] (statement of Harold Hongju Koh) (urging House Committee to investigate abuses on Guantánamo by citing district court preliminary injunction opinion); *U.S. Policy Toward Haitian Refugees: Joint Hearing and Markup on H.R. 5360 Before the Subcomm. on Int'l Operations and the Subcomm. on Western Hemisphere Affairs of the House Comm. on Foreign Affairs*, 102d Cong. (1992) [hereinafter *Hearing on U.S. Policy Toward Haitian Refugees*].

112. *See, e.g.*, Holt v. Sarver, 309 F.Supp. 362 (E.D. Ark. 1970), *aff'd*, 442 F.2d 304 (8th Cir. 1971).

113. *See, e.g.*, Swann v. Charlotte–Mecklenburg Bd. of Educ., 402 U.S. 1 (1971).

114. Note, *Complex Enforcement: Unconstitutional Prison Conditions*, 94 HARV. L. REV. 626 (1981) (describing judicial intervention in systemic enforcement of the Eighth Amendment).

115. *See* Clawson et al., *supra* note 9, at 2375–76.

the iceberg, as "[t]he desire to bring ongoing violation[s] to an immediate halt propel[led the] court inexorably to search for and eliminate their causes."[116] Bargaining in the shadow of the district court's injunctive orders, the plaintiffs, the INS, Justice Department officials, and various refugee resettlement groups engaged in an ongoing dialogue that led to the piecemeal parole of scores of refugees into the United States for health and humanitarian reasons, before final class-wide relief was judicially granted. In the endgame, the plaintiffs bartered *vacatur* of the district court's trial orders for the freedom of the Haitians held at Guantánamo, a governmental decision not to pursue one final appeal, and a compensatory award of fees and costs.[117]

In retrospect, the *HCC* suit won lower court declarations of illegality regarding both the policy of interdiction and prolonged detention and, during the year that appeals were pending, restored pressure on the executive branch to deal with the underlying political crisis. During the presidential campaign, candidate Bill Clinton used the court decisions as part of a broader attack on Bush's foreign policy. After Clinton took office and reversed course, the plight of the Haitian refugees became a grassroots political issue on which ordinary citizens began to take a stand, which by 1994 meant widespread dissatisfaction with the Administration's Haitian policy. Had the case simply died in the courts in February 1992, there would have been no similar focal point around which such political pressure could coalesce. Furthermore, the public outcry against the Supreme Court's decision arguably hastened the ultimate political decision to restore Aristide by military intervention.

In terms of precedent and human impact, the Guantánamo phase of the case alone vindicated the decision to bring the transnational lawsuit. On the precedential ledger, the plaintiffs won judicial enunciation of due process norms: both a ruling by a court of appeals (*HCC–I*) and a permanent injunction from the district court declaring that "aliens"—even those held outside the United States—have due process rights. These rights include decent medical care, freedom from arbitrary discipline, humane living conditions, and assistance of counsel in asylum hearings, which were violated by indefinite incommunicado detention in an HIV-internment camp.[118] Most concretely, the suit won the release

---

116. Note, *supra* note 114, at 630 (citation omitted); *see also id.* ("As the causes identified reveal deeper systemic deficiencies, they too must be addressed through increasingly expansive remedies.").

117. *See* Stipulated Order Approving Class Action Settlement Agreement, *supra* note 100.

118. HCC–I, 823 F.Supp. 1028. The Haitians also won a preliminary injunction to the same effect, later affirmed by the Second Circuit, which was vacated by the Supreme Court on other grounds. *See* Haitian Centers Council, Inc. v. McNary, 969 F.2d 1326 (2d Cir. 1992), *vacated as moot*, 509 U.S. 918 (1993).

and parole of some 310 Haitians held on Guantánamo, who began new lives in America.

Reflecting on Human Rights Practice and Pedagogy: The Lessons of HCC

As time has passed, the Haitian refugee litigation has emerged as an important landmark for the law of detention at Guantánamo, for refugee law, and for human rights litigation and clinical legal education.

HCC and the Law of Detention on Guantánamo

The Haitian crisis helped to publicize Guantánamo, which has today become a household word. When the crisis began in the 1990s, few Americans had ever heard of Guantánamo, apart from those who knew the song "Guantanamera"[119] or had seen the movie "A Few Good Men."[120] Since 1902, the United States has occupied the forty-seven-square-mile U.S. Naval Base in Guantánamo Bay under a unique, perpetual lease agreement entered between the United States and Cuba, which provides that "the United States shall exercise complete jurisdiction and control over and within such areas."[121] Thirty-one square miles of that base are on land, an area larger than Manhattan and nearly half the size of the District of Columbia.[122] The Haitian litigation joined a line of historical precedent strongly suggesting that fundamental constitutional rights and limitations on governmental authority apply to all persons detained at Guantánamo.[123] HCC–I then triggered years of intense litigation about the scope of the constitutional rights of foreign nationals detained there.

---

119. The 1929 tune "Guantanamera" ("girl from Guantánamo"), with lyrics attributed to Jose Marti and music by Jose Fernandez Diaz, popularized by American singer Pete Seeger, ranks among Cuba's best known patriotic songs. *See* La guantanamera: historia ¿conclusa?, http://www.juventudrebelde.cu/2004/julio-septiembre/sep–7/laguantanamera.html.

120. The 1992 Academy Award-nominated Rob Reiner film featured Jack Nicholson and Tom Cruise in a movie about a court-martial for acts at U.S. Naval Base Guantánamo Bay. *See* A FEW GOOD MEN (Castle Rock Entertainment 1992)

121. Agreement for the Lease to the United States of Lands in Cuba for Coaling and Naval Stations, Feb. 23, 1903, U.S.–Cuba, T.S. No. 418.

122. *See* Navy Office of Information, Statistical Information, U.S. Naval Base, Guantánamo Bay, Cuba (1985); Wayne S. Smith, *The Base from the U.S. Perspective*, in SUBJECT TO SOLUTION: PROBLEMS IN CUBAN-U.S. RELATIONS 97, 98 (Wayne S. Smith & Esteban Morales Dominguez, eds. 1988).

123. For a definitive account of these historical precedents, *see* Gerald L. Neuman, *Closing the Guantánamo Loophole*, 50 LOY. L. REV. 1, 15–32 (2004). We thank Professor Neuman for his scholarship and advocacy, which provided many of the examples given in this section.

As the Haitian crisis was winding down, in July 1994, about seventy Cuban refugees unsuccessfully sought to escape Castro's regime aboard the tugboat *13 de Marzo*. The survivors were forced to return to Cuba, where they were imprisoned by the Castro regime, triggering widespread protests there. In response, Fidel Castro temporarily allowed persons seeking exodus to leave Cuba, which led to more than 30,000 refugees fleeing toward Florida on makeshift rafts, relying on longstanding U.S. refugee policy granting asylum (and eventually permanent residence and citizenship) to fleeing Cubans under the Cuban Adjustment Act of 1966.[124] President Clinton "ordered that illegal refugees from Cuba will not be allowed to enter the United States [and instead] will be taken to the naval base at Guantánamo...."[125] On September 9, 1994, the U.S. and Cuban governments signed an unprecedented agreement "recogniz[ing] their common interest" in preventing Cubans from leaving by sea, confirm[ing] that the Cubans "will not be permitted to enter the United States, but instead will be taken to safe haven facilities outside the United States" for indefinite detention, and agreeing to "arrange ... the voluntary return of Cuban nationals who arrived in the United States or in safe havens outside the United States on or after August 19, 1994."[126]

A group of prominent Cuban–American attorneys, again assisted by Yale's Lowenstein International Human Rights Clinic, sued the Clinton Administration in federal court in Miami, seeking to enjoin the U.S. government from involuntarily repatriating Guantánamo detainees back to Cuba.[127] At the hearing on the TRO, a U.S. government lawyer asserted that "[t]he Cubans who are in safe haven at Guantánamo are without rights under our Constitution" or any other U.S. laws.[128] Judge Clyde Atkins, who had been the trial judge in the *HRC* case, rejected the government's claims. But on expedited appeal, in *Cuban–American Bar Ass'n (CABA) v. Christopher,* the Eleventh Circuit reversed, holding that "these [Cuban and Haitian] migrants are without legal rights that are cognizable in the courts of the United States...."[129] The Eleventh

---

124. Pub. L. No. 89–732, 80 Stat. 1161 (Nov. 2, 1966).

125. The President's News Conference, 30 WEEKLY COMP. PRES. DOC. 1682 (Aug. 19, 1994).

126. U.S. Dep't of State, *U.S.–Cuba joint communiqué on migration*, DISPATCH, Sept. 12, 1994, at 5(37) [hereinafter Clinton–Castro Communiqué].

127. One of this Chapter's co-authors (Koh) was counsel of record for the Cuban detainees in the *CABA* case.

128. Transcript of Hearing at R5:27–73, Cuban American Bar Ass'n v. Christopher, No. 94–2183 (S.D. Fla. Oct. 26, 1994).

129. Cuban American Bar Ass'n v. Christopher, 43 F.3d 1412, 1430 (11th Cir. 1995). The Eleventh Circuit expressly disagreed with Judge Johnson's view in *HCC–II,* affirmed

Circuit further held that American lawyers have no First Amendment rights to communicate with or associate with their clients on Guantánamo because the clients themselves lack underlying rights.

The Guantánamo litigation of the 1990s thus generated pointed disagreement between the Second and Eleventh Circuits regarding a novel issue that resurged into public consciousness a dozen years later: the legal rights of non-citizens detained at Guantánamo.[130] Although the Second Circuit's decision in *HCC–I* was vacated as moot, and Judge Johnson's permanent injunction ruling was vacated by settlement, those courts' position in *HCC* remains the far better-reasoned "law of Guantánamo." For read literally, the Eleventh Circuit's ruling that "the First Amendment does not apply to the migrants or to the lawyers at Guantánamo Bay" would permit the United States government to bar American citizens at Guantánamo not just from speaking to their Cuban clients, but also from speaking to other Americans there, and would free U.S. officials to punish Americans at Guantánamo for writing open letters, criticizing the President, or even engaging in religious worship.[131] Similarly, the panel's holding that Cuban refugees on Guantánamo "are without legal rights that are cognizable in the courts of the United States" would theoretically free American officials to terrorize or torture those refugees deliberately, to starve them, to subject them to forced abortions and sterilizations, or to discriminate against them based on the color of their skin.

The *HCC–I* rulings, by contrast, acknowledged that, although Guantánamo Bay Naval Base lies outside the formal borders of the United States, in all other senses, it "feels" like America.[132] The United States provides the only law and is accountable there only to itself. Of all the U.S. overseas military bases, only Guantánamo lacks a Status of Forces Agreement that defines the allocation of civil and criminal jurisdiction

---

by the Second Circuit, that Guantánamo is subject to U.S. law, by virtue of being under exclusive U.S. jurisdiction and control.

130. *Compare* Haitian Centers Council, Inc. v. McNary, 969 F.2d 1326 (2d Cir. 1992) (affirming preliminary injunction because plaintiffs were likely to succeed on their constitutional claims), *vacated as moot sub nom.* Sale v. Haitian Centers Council, Inc., 509 U.S. 918 (1993), *with* Cuban–American Bar Ass'n, 43 F.3d 1412 (denying that rights exist).

131. Cuban American Bar Ass'n, 43 F.3d at 1429. These examples are not merely hypothetical. In March 1995, for example, U.S. authorities at Guantánamo apparently excluded paintings by Cuban refugees from a Guantánamo art show because they were critical of U.S. policy. Pamela S. Falk, *Trapped in Cuba*, N.Y. TIMES, April 15, 1995, at 19.

132. *See* Matthew Hay Brown, *Oldest U.S. Base Overseas Harbors Hometown Feel*, ORLANDO SENTINEL, Dec. 22, 2003, at A1. Wayne S. Smith, *The Base from the U.S. Perspective*, *in* SUBJECT TO SOLUTION: PROBLEMS IN CUBAN–U.S. RELATIONS 97, 98 (Wayne S. Smith & Esteban Morales Dominguez, eds. 1988). In 2003, the base commander described it as "small-town America," Carol Rosenberg, *New chief brings Guantánamo up to date*, MIAMI HERALD, Oct. 25, 2003, at A15.

over military and other personnel. Over the years, thousands of foreign nationals have been employed as laborers at Guantánamo—including Cubans, Jamaicans and Filipinos—whom the Eleventh Circuit's ruling would leave without legal recourse.[133] Historically, the parallel judicial treatment of the Panama Canal Zone and the Trust Territory of the Pacific Islands—both non-sovereign territories under the complete jurisdiction and control of the United States—also recognized the application of fundamental constitutional rights to foreign nationals within those territories.[134] Finally, given that all manner of federal law applies at Guantánamo—from environmental regulation of iguanas to the federal Anti–Slot Machine Act[135]—it would be bizarre indeed if the Bill of Rights did not apply to human beings held against their will by the U.S. government in the same place.

The Eleventh Circuit's ruling in the Cuban case effectively invited the U.S. government to establish an offshore "rights-free zone" on Guantánamo. Although American detention camps were not new, especially for refugees, the *CABA* case enhanced the possibility that Guantánamo could be used as a long-term offshore detention facility.[136] Accordingly, during the 1990s, the U.S. Government repeatedly used Guantánamo as a holding center for thousands of asylum seekers captured at sea from Haiti, Cuba, and even China.[137] During the Kosovo Crisis of spring 1999, the Clinton Administration briefly considered, but ultimately withdrew, a plan to bring 20,000 Kosovar refugees to Guan-

---

133. *See* Associated Press, *In Cuba, U.S. Relies on Low–Paid Help of Non–Americans,* COMMERCIAL APPEAL (Memphis, TN), Feb. 1, 2002, at A7 (noting presence of 1000 foreign workers), *available at* 2002 WLNR 7300249; *Filipino residents register to vote,* 63(34) GUANTÁNAMO BAY GAZETTE 4 (Aug. 25, 2006), *available at* https://www.cnic.navy.mil/navycni/groups/public/@pub/@southe/@guantanamobay/documents/document/cnic_048662.pdf (700 Philippine nationals on Guantánamo registered to vote in home country).

134. *See generally* Neuman, *supra* note 123.

135. *Installation of Slot Machs. on U.S. Naval Base, Guantánamo Bay,* 6 Op. Off. Legal Counsel 236, 237, 242 (1982); Transcript of Oral Argument at 43, Rasul v. Bush, 542 U.S. 466 (2004) (Nos. 03–334 & 03–343) (Justice Souter noting that "[w]e even protect the Cuban iguana"), *available at* 2004 WL 943637.

136. Such camps include those holding more than 110,000 Japanese–Americans during World War II, *see, e.g.*, PETER IRONS, JUSTICE AT WAR: THE STORY OF THE JAPANESE AMERICAN INTERNMENT CASES (1983); MANZANAR (J. Armor & P. Wright, eds., 1988); the several military bases within the United States processing thousands of refugees fleeing Vietnam in the mid–1970s; the facilities that held the 125,000 Cubans of the 1980 Mariel "Freedom Flotilla," some still lingering in detention, *see* Ronald Copeland, *The Cuban Boatlift of 1980: Strategies in Federal Crisis Management,* 467 ANNALS AM. ACAD. POL. & SOC. SCI. 138 (1983); and the thousands of Central American refugees detained in tent-shelters and various federal facilities in Arizona, California, South Texas, Louisiana and Florida, *see generally* Koh, *America's Offshore Refugee Camps, supra* note 9.

137. *See, e.g.*, United States v. Li, 206 F.3d 56, 69 n. 1 (1st Cir. 2000) (Torruella, C.J., dissenting) (noting government's use of Guantánamo as an interim detention center for interdicted Chinese in 1996).

tánamo, based in part on opposition from those familiar with the Haitian refugee debacle.[138]

Nevertheless, shortly after the terrorist attacks of September 11, 2001, President George W. Bush chose to bring more than 700 alleged Al Qaeda detainees—most apprehended in Afghanistan, but including individuals picked up in Pakistan, the United Arab Emirates, Bosnia, and the Gambia, among other countries—to Guantánamo, with no apparent exit strategy. In short order, Guantánamo became a center of intense international controversy over America's commitment to human rights.[139] Before the first 9/11 detainees were brought to Guantánamo, the Bush Justice Department's Office of Legal Counsel concluded, after a review of existing case law, that "a detainee could make a non-frivolous argument that [habeas] jurisdiction does exist over aliens detained at [Guantánamo Bay, Cuba], and we have found no decisions that clearly foreclose the existence of habeas jurisdiction there."[140] Nevertheless, in three plenary cases that went to the U.S. Supreme Court, the Bush Administration unsuccessfully argued that non-citizen detainees lacked meaningful legal rights on Guantánamo.

In *Rasul v. Bush*, the Court held that non-citizen detainees on Guantánamo have a statutory right to file petitions for a writ of habeas corpus to challenge their detention.[141] Justice Stevens, writing for the *Rasul* Court, noted that "the United States exercises exclusive jurisdiction and control" at Guantánamo.[142] Justice Kennedy agreed in concurrence that "Guantánamo Bay is in every practical respect a United

---

138. *See* Philip Shenon, *U.S. Chooses Guantánamo Bay Base in Cuba for Refugee Site*, N.Y. TIMES, April 7, 1999.

139. For critical accounts of the U.S. detention policy there, *see, e.g.*, MICHAEL RATNER & ELLEN RAY, GUANTÁNAMO: WHAT THE WORLD SHOULD KNOW (2004); JOSEPH MARGULIES, GUANTÁNAMO AND THE ABUSE OF PRESIDENTIAL POWER (2006), and DAVID ROSE, GUANTÁNAMO: THE WAR ON HUMAN RIGHTS (2004).

140. *See* Memorandum from Patrick F. Philbin & John C. Yoo, Deputy Assistant Att'y Gens., Office of Legal Counsel, to William J. Haynes, II, Gen. Counsel, Dep't of Defense, *Possible Habeas Jurisdiction over Aliens Held in Guantánamo Bay, Cuba* (Dec. 28, 2001), *available at* http://www.pegc.us/archive/DOJ/20011228_philbinmemo.pdf.

141. 542 U.S. 466 (2004). Each author of this Chapter served as counsel on an amicus brief filed in support of the detainees in *Rasul*.

142. *Id.* at 476. Although the Court's ultimate holding in *Rasul v. Bush* was statutory and jurisdictional, in a key footnote, the Court suggested that detainees at Guantánamo do have valid claims to constitutional protection, stating that "allegations that, although they have engaged neither in combat nor in acts of terrorism against the United States, they have been held in Executive detention for more than two years in territory subject to the long-term, exclusive jurisdiction and control of the United States, without access to counsel and without being charged with any wrongdoing, *unquestionably describe 'custody in violation of the Constitution or laws or treaties of the United States.'* " *Id.* at 483, n. 15 (2004) (emphasis added) (quoting 28 U.S.C. § 2241(c)(3); *see also In re*

States territory."[143] In contrast to his approach in *HCC–II*, Justice Stevens held in *Rasul v. Bush* that the presumption against extraterritoriality of U.S. law had no application at Guantánamo, because petitioners were being "detained within 'the territorial jurisdiction' of the United States."[144]

Two years later, in *Hamdan v. Rumsfeld*, the Court again ruled in favor of an alleged "enemy combatant" held at Guantánamo, both on jurisdictional grounds and on the merits.[145] Justice Stevens, now writing for a 5–3 Court, found the President's Nov. 2001 Military Commissions Order unauthorized by either his constitutional Commander-in-Chief Power or the September 2001 Authorization of Use of Military Force Resolution (AUMF) passed by Congress. The Court further ruled that the Order violated the Uniform Code of Military Justice (UCMJ), which calls for military commissions to be as much like statutory courts-martial as "practicable," and Common Article 3 of the Geneva Conventions of 1949, which set minimum universal standards for treatment of detainees, including trials before "regularly constituted courts." Calling President Bush's military commissions an "extraordinary measure raising important questions about the balance of powers in our constitutional structure,"[146] the Court roundly rejected the Administration's extreme constitutional theory of executive power and invalidated a military proceeding against a non-citizen detainee on Guantánamo as unauthorized by law.[147] The *Hamdan* Court followed its earlier insistence in *Rasul*[148] that Guantánamo be treated as a land subject to law by rejecting the Administration's attempt to depict Hamdan as a person outside the law. Even while acknowledging that Hamdan might have committed serious crimes, the Court nevertheless proclaimed that "in undertaking to try Hamdan and subject him to criminal punishment, the Executive is bound to comply with the Rule of Law that prevails in this jurisdiction."[149] By so saying, the Court rejected the Government's premise that 9/11 had created a new "crisis paradigm" that somehow required that ordinary legal rules be jettisoned in Hamdan's case.[150]

Guantánamo Detainee Cases, 355 F. Supp. 2d 443, 462 (D.D.C. 2005), *rev'd sub nom.* Boumediene v. Bush, 476 F.3d 981 (D.C. Cir. 2007).

143. *Rasul*, 542 U.S. at 487 (Kennedy, J., concurring in the judgment).

144. *Id.* at 480 (quoting Foley Bros., Inc. v. Filardo, 336 U.S. 281, 285 (1949)).

145. 548 U.S. 557 (2006).

146. *Id.* at 567.

147. *See generally* Harold Hongju Koh, *Setting the World Right*, 115 YALE L.J. 2350 (2006).

148. 542 U.S. 466 (2004).

149. *Hamdan*, 548 U.S. at 635.

150. As Justice Kennedy put it, "a case that may be of extraordinary importance is resolved by ordinary rules ... those pertaining to the authority of Congress and the

After *Hamdan*, Congress quickly passed the Military Commissions Act of 2006 (MCA), which authorized the President to try "alien unlawful combatants," including those held on Guantánamo, before military commissions.[151] In *Boumediene v. Bush*, the Bush Administration argued that Congress had constitutionally abolished Guantánamo detainees' constitutional right to a writ of habeas corpus by enacting the MCA. The D.C. Circuit agreed, reasoning that the MCA abridged no rights protected by the Suspension Clause, because "the writ in 1789 would not have been available to aliens held at an overseas military base leased from a foreign government."[152] But in June 2008, the Supreme Court reversed that ruling, holding that "aliens designated as enemy combatants" and detained at Guantánamo "have the constitutional privilege of habeas corpus" to challenge the legality of their detentions in federal court.[153]

Justice Kennedy's majority opinion for five justices emphasized that habeas corpus is "a vital instrument to secure" the fundamental "freedom from unlawful restraint," and "an essential mechanism in the separation-of-powers scheme" that undergirds the American democratic system; accordingly, he found the attempt in the Military Commissions Act to restrict that right a violation of the Suspension Clause of the Constitution.[154] In so holding, the majority specifically rejected the government's twin claims that the detainees' status as designated enemy combatants and physical location outside the territorial United States stripped them of their constitutional right to petition for the writ. Significantly, the Court rejected the Government's proposed "sovereignty" test, under which noncitizens would have a constitutional right to habeas only on the sovereign territory of the U.S., as effectively granting

---

interpretation of its enactments." Rather than embracing ad hoc, crisis solutions, he argued, "[r]espect for laws derived from the customary operation of the Executive and Legislative Branches gives some assurance of stability in time of crisis. The Constitution is best preserved by reliance on standards tested over time and insulated from the pressures of the moment." *Hamdan*, 548 U.S. at 637 (Kennedy, J., concurring in part).

151. Pub. L. No. 109–366, 120 Stat. 2600 (Oct. 17, 2006). The MCA states "No court, justice, or judge shall have jurisdiction to hear or consider an application for a writ of habeas corpus filed by or on behalf of an alien detained by the United States who has been determined by the United States to have been properly detained as an enemy combatant or is awaiting such determination." *Id*. § 7(a), as amended by Pub. L. 110–181, Div. A, § 1063(f) (codified at 28 U.S.C. § 2241(e)).

152. Boumediene v. Bush, 476 F.3d 981 at 991 (D.C. Cir. 2007). With respect to Guantánamo, the D.C. Circuit essentially reasserted its own prior analysis in *Al Odah v. United States*, 321 F.3d 1134 (D.C. Cir. 2003), which had been previously rejected by the Supreme Court in *Rasul v. Bush*, 542 U.S. 466 (2004).

153. Boumediene v. Bush, 128 S.Ct. 2229, 2240 (2008).

154. *Id*. (citing U.S. CONST. art. I, § 9, cl.2).

the political branches "the power to switch the Constitution on or off at will."[155]

Choosing instead a "functional approach," Justice Kennedy emphasized that "practical concerns, not formalism," are paramount when determining whether noncitizens detained by the U.S. have a constitutional right to challenge their detentions via habeas. The detainee's citizenship, the sovereignty of the detention site, the "status" of the detainees, "the adequacy of the process" for determining enemy combatant status, "the nature of the sites where apprehension and then detention took place," and "the practical obstacles inherent in resolving the prisoner's entitlement to the writ" all made it appropriate to extend Suspension Clause protections to Guantánamo.[156] Finally, the majority found that the Combatant Status Review Tribunal process created by the Executive Branch to determine prisoners' status fell "well short of the procedures and adversarial mechanisms that would eliminate the need for habeas corpus review."[157]

By the time *Boumediene* was decided, the costs of using Guantánamo as an offshore detention facility had become glaring. The number of detainees on the base had shrunk to 300, with only a dozen or so considered "high-value." High-security facilities had been built at a cost of $54 million and the base had an annual operating cost of $100 million. Yet for all the expenditure of time and reputation, in six years, the U.S. Guantánamo policy had yielded only one guilty plea, four suicides (out of forty-one attempts), and widespread public conviction that the offshore Guantánamo prison camp should be closed as a human rights disaster.[158]

HCC–II yielded another important legacy. Many of the lawyers involved in the 9/11 Guantánamo litigation first grappled with these issues in the original Haitian cases.[159] And when the Supreme Court finally ruled that noncitizens held on Guantánamo have a constitutional right to a writ of habeas corpus, ironically, the Justices who arrived at that conclusion—Stevens and Kennedy—were the intellectual authors of the approach that had led to the Haitians' loss in *HCC–II*. Thus, sixteen

---

155. *Id.* at 2259.

156. *Id.*

157. *Id.* at 2260.

158. David Bowker & David Kaye, *Guantánamo by the numbers*, N.Y. TIMES, Nov. 10, 2007, at A15. Those making public statements suggesting that the Guantánamo camps be closed included the Secretary of Defense, the Attorney General, eight Democratic and two Republican presidential candidates, several of America's closest allies—France, Germany, and the United Kingdom—and even President Bush himself.

159. This group includes the authors, Michael Ratner, Lucas Guttentag of the ACLU, Professors Sarah Cleveland of Columbia, Gerald Neuman of Harvard, Neal Katyal of Georgetown (who argued the *Hamdan* case), the current incarnation of Yale Law School's Lowenstein International Human Rights clinic, and many others.

years after *HCC* began, the Supreme Court finally established, once and for all, that Guantánamo is not a law-free zone.

HCC and Refugee Law

Although the Supreme Court made bad law in *HCC–II*, the limited precedential weight of the Court's ruling has minimized its impact on the development of refugee law. The Haitian interdiction program was almost uniquely discriminatory, in which the Coast Guard stopped Haitian boats on the high seas pursuant to the 1981 United States–Haiti Accord, a rare agreement that provided no general authority for the Coast Guard to intercept and return refugees from other countries for whom no such accord exists.

Nor did the Supreme Court's decision in *HCC* resolve the legality of the interdiction policy under international, as opposed to U.S. domestic, law. Other human rights groups pressed arguments similar to those urged by the *HCC* plaintiffs against the U.S. government's direct return policy before the Inter–American Commission on Human Rights, which declared "... The Commission shares the view advanced by the United Nations High Commissioner for Refugees in its amicus curiae brief before the Supreme Court, that Article 33 had no geographical limitations."[160] Immediately after *HCC–II* came down, the United Nations High Commissioner for Refugees declared that it considered the Court's decision a "setback to modern international refugee law," because the obligation not to return refugees to persecution arises irrespective of whether governments are acting within or outside their borders. More recently, in an advisory opinion issued in January 2007, the UNHCR stated that

> the purpose, intent and meaning of Article 33(1) of the 1951 Convention are unambiguous and establish an obligation not to return a refugee or asylum-seeker to a country where he or she would be at risk of persecution or other serious harm, which applies wherever a State exercises jurisdiction, including at the frontier, on the high seas or on the territory of another State.... Thus, an interpretation which would restrict the scope of application of Article 33(1) of the 1951 Convention to conduct within the territory of a State party ... would not only be contrary to the terms of the provision as well as the object and purpose of the treaty under interpretation, but it would also be inconsistent with relevant rules

---

160. *See* The Haitian Centre for Human Rights et al. v. United States, Case 10,675, Inter–Am. C.H.R., Report No. 51/96, OEA/Ser.L/V/II.95, Doc. 7 rev. at 550 (1997); *see also* discussion of Case No. 10,675 in *Petitioners Release Resolution of the Inter–American Commission on Human Rights Concerning U.S. Program of Haitian Refugee Interdiction*, 32 I.L.M. 1215 (1993).

of international human rights law. It is UNHCR's position ... that a State is bound by its obligation under Article 33(1) of the 1951 Convention not to return refugees to a risk of persecution wherever it exercises effective jurisdiction. As with *non-refoulement* obligations under international human rights law, the decisive criterion is not whether such persons are on the State's territory, but rather, whether they come within the effective control and authority of that State.[161]

In stating this conclusion, the High Commissioner expressly rejected the Supreme Court's argument in *HCC–II*, stating: "UNHCR is of the view that the majority opinion of the Supreme Court in *Sale* does not accurately reflect the scope of Article 33(1) of the 1951 Convention.[162] Instead, the High Commissioner followed the reading of the text and negotiating history of the Refugee Convention in Justice Blackmun's dissent. Significantly, in the past the Supreme Court has held that the UNHCR's interpretation of its own treaty should " 'provid[e] significant guidance in construing the [1951 Refugee] Protocol, to which Congress sought to conform. It has been widely considered useful in giving content to the obligations that the Protocol establishes.' "[163]

What these international rulings show is that adverse U.S. Supreme Court decisions are no longer final stops, but way stations, in the process of complex enforcement triggered by transnational public law litigation. However unfamiliar this argument may be to American lawyers, European human rights litigants have long understood that adverse national court decisions may be "appealed" to and even "reversed" by the European Court of Human Rights. As one of us has argued, a *transnational legal process* pressures nations who flout international law rules back into compliance with those rules.[164] Law-abiding states tend to incorporate international law into their domestic legal and political structures. Thus, when such a state violates international law, that violation creates frictions and contradictions that affect its ongoing participation in the transnational legal process. Indeed, transnational public law litigation of the "institutional reform" type aims precisely to provoke judicial action that will create such frictions, thereby helping

---

161. *See* United Nations High Commissioner for Refugees, *Advisory Opinion on the Extraterritorial Application of Non–Refoulement Obligations under the 1951 Convention relating to the Status of Refugees and its 1967 Protocol*, at ¶¶ 24 & 43 (January 26, 2007), *available at* http://www.unhcr.org/cgi-bin/texis/vtx/refworld/rwmain/opendocpdf.pdf?docid=45f17a1a4.

162. Id. at ¶ 24, n. 54.

163. INS v. Cardoza–Fonseca, 480 U.S. 421, 439 & n. 22 (1987) (discussing the UNHCR Handbook on Procedures and Criteria for Determining Refugee Status).

164. *See generally* Harold Hongju Koh, *Why Do Nations Obey International Law?*, 106 YALE L.J. 2599 (1997).

shape the normative direction of governmental policies. Even resisting nations cannot insulate themselves forever from complying with international law if they regularly participate, as all nations must, in transnational legal interactions. Through a complex process of rational self-interest and norm internalization—at times spurred by transnational litigation—international legal norms seep into and become entrenched in domestic legal and political processes. In this way, international law helps drive how national governments conduct their international relations.

Fittingly, Justice Harry Blackmun was the first to recognize this point, at a speech to the American Society of International Law shortly after his retirement in 1994. Criticizing *HCC–II,* Justice Blackmun said, "To allow nations to skirt their solemn treaty obligations and return vulnerable refugees to persecution simply by intercepting them in international waters is ... to turn the Refugee Convention into a 'cruel hoax.' ... We perhaps can take some comfort," Justice Blackmun said, "in the fact that although the Supreme Court is the highest court in the land, its rulings are not necessarily the final word on questions of international law."[165]

HCC: Beyond Litigation and Clinical Legal Education

Finally, the story of the *HCC* litigation reveals important lessons for human rights litigation and for contemporary social justice campaigns. *HCC–I,* the more successful strand of the case, resulted in the shuttering of the world's first HIV detention camp and the lawful admission of nearly 300 refugees into the United States. This outcome actually reflected two victories, each necessary, but neither alone sufficient to liberate the Haitians. In June 1993, following trial in the Eastern District of New York, Judge Johnson entered a permanent injunction ordering that the refugees "be immediately released (to anywhere but Haiti)."[166] Because no other nation would accept the refugees, this order amounted to a directive to permit the Haitians to enter the U.S. Had the Haitians failed to prevail on the myriad factual and legal disputes at trial, there seems no possibility that the government would ever have admitted them.[167] At a time when some skeptics (and even some human rights advocates) disparaged litigation as a blunt instrument for promoting social change—a time-consuming, resource-intensive, lawyer-domi-

---

165. Harry A. Blackmun, *The Supreme Court and the Law of Nations*, 104 YALE L.J. 39, 44, 42 (1994) (quotations omitted).

166. HCC–I, 823 F.Supp. at 1049.

167. Joseph Tringali of the firm of Simpson, Thacher & Bartlett, and Lucas Guttentag of the ACLU Immigrants' Rights Project, served as lead counsel at trial.

nated process played out before a conservative judiciary—the *HCC–I* trial outcome offered an important counter-example. *HCC* showed that affirmative litigation still matters, and can play a crucial role in effectuating policy change as well as delivering individual justice.

But all counsel involved also understood that the victory after trial, standing alone, could not secure the release of the Haitian refugees. The government had the right to appeal the permanent injunction to the Second Circuit and would likely have secured a stay pending appeal from either the Second Circuit or the Supreme Court. Even if the Second Circuit had affirmed the trial judgment, the Haitians' counsel understood the significant likelihood of another grant of *certiorari* and eventual reversal by the Supreme Court. Freedom for the refugees, thus, depended on a second struggle outside the courtroom, in the realm of politics and public opinion.[168] That victory arrived days after the trial decision, when the voice of Webb Hubbell, a close colleague of President Clinton and then the Associate Attorney General, came booming over a speakerphone in a conference room at Simpson Thacher to announce that the government had decided to let the Guantánamo Haitians in.[169] As described by one official involved in the decision to admit the Haitians—rather than to appeal and seek a stay—senior Clinton Administration officials had "no desire" to continue detaining the refugees on Guantánamo.[170] To the best of this official's recollection, there had been significant concern about the potential public and congressional reaction to a unilateral decision to admit the refugees, but the trial opinion by Judge Johnson supplied an opportunity to "resolve the situation in a humanitarian way."[171] Consequently, the government declined to seek an immediate stay of Judge Johnson's order and the refugees were admitted to the U.S., for resettlement in New York and southern Florida.

The presence within the Administration of senior officials eager to close the Guantánamo HIV camp helped secure the release of the Haitians and confirms the importance of an "inside" advocacy strategy pursued by counsel for the refugees and their allies.[172] But benign intervention by benevolent leaders was likely not the full story, for there

---

168. Michael Ratner, *How We Closed the Guantánamo HIV Camp: The Intersection of Politics and Litigation*, 11 Harv. Hum. Rts. J. 187, 217 (1998) ("Looking back, I believe that the political climate created by our organizing work around Guantánamo is the only thing that protected the court victory.").

169. *See* Goldstein, How a Band of Yale Law Students Fought the President and Won, *supra* note 9, at 288.

170. Telephonic interview by Michael Wishnie with Eric Schwartz, former National Security Counsel staff (Jan. 2, 2008).

171. *Id.*

172. *See* Ratner, *How We Closed*, *supra* note 168 (discussing "inside" and "outside" advocacy strategies).

had been sympathetic officials in the first Bush Administration as well.[173] From the start of the case in early 1992, counsel had actively sought to explain their cause in the media, before Congress, to other civil society institutions, and on the street. This "outside" advocacy strategy—complementary to the plaintiffs' litigation strategy—sought allies in the media and political elites, as well as among local government officials, students, and grassroots activists. Over the eighteen months of the litigation, members of the legal team worked the telephones and traveled to Washington to lobby members of Congress and their staff, to meet and strategize with influential AIDS, civil rights, and human rights NGOs; to pitch stories to the national media;[174] and to collaborate with prominent civil rights and entertainment leaders such as the Rev. Jesse Jackson, director Jonathan Demme, and actress Susan Sarandon on high-profile public events.[175] In addition, the legal team pursued a bottom-up, grassroots strategy that included engagement with local AIDS and Haitian activists in New York City, resulting in modest local protests and outreach to regional and independent media, as well as municipal officials in New York, Boston, Seattle, and elsewhere. These constituencies came to support the resettlement of the refugees and offered the Clinton Administration the local political support necessary for release after trial.[176] As condemnation of the Guantánamo camps grew, so too

---

173. *See id.* at 205 ("For months I spoke daily with Paul Capuccio, the Assistant Attorney General ... who was in charge of the case for the Justice Department.... Although I had great ideological differences with Capuccio, he wanted to deal humanely with the refugees, and we developed a warm working relationship"); GOLDSTEIN, HOW A BAND OF YALE LAW STUDENTS FOUGHT THE PRESIDENT AND WON, *supra* note 9, at 173–175, 180 (discussing Capuccio's role in securing piecemeal release of numerous refugees).

174. *See, e.g.*, Pamela Constable, *U.S. Camp for Haitians Described as Prison–Like*, WASH. POST, Sept. 19, 1992, at A1 (reporting on July 1992 detainee uprising and military retribution); *See* Anna Quindlen, *Set Her Free*, N.Y. TIMES, Nov. 18, 1992, at A27; Derrick Z. Jackson, *Judge, About those Haitians* ..., BOSTON GLOBE, June 13, 1993.

175. Ratner, *How We Closed*, *supra* note 168, at 217 (describing civil disobedience by Jackson, Demme, and Sarandon on the first day of trial, and statement by Sarandon and Tim Robbins at Academy Awards presentation).

176. *See generally* Clawson et al., *Litigating as Law Students*, *supra* note 9, at 2372. The grassroots strategy yielded other critical but unintended consequences. For instance, when the Bush Administration surprised the Haitians' counsel by releasing individual refugees with pressing medical concerns, many of the activists became essential humanitarian providers, helping to arrange the quiet resettlement of more than thirty Haitians. These activists were also responsible for developing and nurturing essential relationships with municipal agencies and political leaders who later publicly supported closure of the camp and resettlement of all refugees. When Judge Johnson ordered the release of all Haitians, large refugee resettlement agencies argued that they would need federal grants, and weeks or months to prepare, for the release of the remaining refugees. The grassroots activists and providers, especially Betty Williams and William Broberg in New York, insisted that all refugees could be accommodated, immediately, and without need for grants

did the independent efforts of numerous organizations and individuals, a point driven home when students at Yale Law School initiated a rolling campaign of campus hunger strikes, termed "Operation Harriet Tubman," that resulted in media coverage across the country.[177]

At times, this "do everything" approach strained resources and caused conflicts among co-counsel who questioned the propriety and efficacy of congressional visits, media advocacy, and grassroots organizing at different moments of the litigation, when litigation deadlines for briefs or discovery loomed.[178] But a second lesson from *HCC* is that litigation does not occur in a vacuum and that courtroom victories are rarely sufficient, standing alone, to achieve lasting change. The time-consuming, often frustrating work of engaging the public debate and attempting to make the case against the Guantánamo HIV camp from the halls of Congress to the streets of Brooklyn was what transformed the courtroom victory into meaningful relief for the refugees.

HCC–I taught a third lesson: that there remains a vital role for generalist legal practice, in human rights advocacy and otherwise, across the litigation/non-litigation divide. Many law students and young attorneys are advised to identify a practice niche, master relatively narrow areas of substantive law, procedure, and forum details, and then to excel in that specialized field. Counsel for the refugees in *HCC–I* rejected this preference for specialization, instead engaging directly and intensively in both litigation and non-litigation strategies. The legal team included experienced litigators and benefited greatly from the generous counsel of lawyers far more seasoned in legislative or agency campaigns. But in the end, the plaintiffs won because their lawyers chose not to limit themselves to courtroom work, but rather, to pursue a broad range of media, political, and grassroots efforts.

Similar practical lessons for human rights litigation emerged from *HCC–II,* the ostensibly unsuccessful effort to halt the summary repatriation of Haitian refugees. The case showed that litigation matters, although often, it is not enough to have the better legal arguments. That point emerges painfully from the numerous comments by the Supreme Court Justices at conference in *HCC–II,* which both acknowledged the force of the Haitians' plain language arguments, yet strained that language to evade an outcome perceived as politically undesirable.

---

for the administrative expenses of resettlement—an offer that resulted in the swift release of the remaining Haitians.

177. Ratner, *How We Closed, supra* note 168, at 215. The question whether students on the *HCC* legal team should join their classmates' hunger strike, even though such participation would diminish their ability to work on the suit at a crucial time, further divided counsel. See Clawson et al., *Litigating as Law Students, supra* note 9, at 2378.

178. *See, e.g.*, Ratner, *How We Closed, supra* note 168, at 208 (discussing disagreements about publicizing refugee hunger strike in early 1993).

In time, engaging the public and political debate proved vital to winning this human rights struggle as well. In 1992–93, advocates for the fleeing refugees suceeded in persuading neither the elites within the Clinton Administration and Congress, nor the wider population at a grassroots level, of the "moral weight" and practical advisability of providing sanctuary to those fleeing persecution. But by 1994, the "inside/outside advocacy" game had finally helped turn the political tide in the refugees' favor, which made a different political solution possible. This same general lesson has increasingly emerged in the post-September 11 Guantánamo advocacy, which over several years has deployed a blend of litigation, political initiatives, and public commentary to turn public opinion decisively in favor of closing the Guantánamo detention camps.[179]

Finally, the *HCC* litigation offers important lessons to clinical legal education, especially as conducted by the rapidly growing number of human rights clinics.[180] Yale's Lowenstein Clinic deliberately eschewed the "small case" approach generally favored by some contemporary clinicians, in which students take on discrete matters, such as an eviction defense or divorce, handling all court appearances and exercising professional judgment in consultation with the client and their supervising attorney. Nor was *HCC* a traditional project for a human rights clinic, which often tends to be a non-litigation matter such as an analytical report documenting human rights abuses. *HCC* was a clinical undertaking of a different magnitude, in which the enormity and velocity of the litigation did not allow for the usual degree of student responsibility or structured reflection ordinarily sought in clinical education.

Nevertheless, even as pedagogy, *HCC* accomplished many objectives. Despite its law reform nature, the case involved substantial student participation in and responsibility for all aspects of the litigation, from its inception to the final settlement. Students did not argue legal motions or appeals, but they routinely exercised delicate professional judgment. They interviewed and counseled clients; drafted countless pleadings, briefs, and discovery documents; took and defended depositions; identified, interviewed, and prepared witnesses for deposition and trial; participated in face-to-face and telephonic negotiations with opposing counsel; analyzed issues of professional ethics that arose throughout

---

179. One of us has called this a process of "social internalization," which is triggered by and often spurs political and legal internalization of international legal norms into domestic law. *See* Harold Hongju Koh, *Bringing International Law Home*, 35 HOUSTON L. REV. 623 (1998).

180. *See* Hurwitz, *Lawyering for Justice, supra* note 24; Stacy Caplow, *"Deport all the Students": Lessons Learned in an X–Treme Clinic*, 13 CLINICAL L. REV. 633 (2006) (reviewing *Storming the Court* and questioning clinical pedagogy in *HCC* litigation).

the case; and examined as many witnesses at trial as any of the lawyers but for lead counsel.[181]

The intensity of the work also provided many moments for reflection and inspired many to pursue human rights careers.[182] *HCC* thus demonstrates that reflective lawyering can be achieved in complex law reform matters. Moreover, *HCC* undeniably succeeded in inspiring and nurturing student passion for law as a force for human rights and social change.[183] In many ways, *HCC* was a throwback to the early days of clinical education, which included many complex law reform suits in the service of the civil rights movement.[184] *HCC* showed that what civil rights had been to the clinical education movement of the 1960s, international human rights could become for the clinical education movement of a new global century. And in this, the Haitian refugee litigation may have helped to renew a commitment within clinical education to the goal of achieving systemic policy reform.[185]

Conclusion

At the end of the day, the Haitian refugee litigation will be remembered for telling not one, but two human rights stories. The first was an intensely human story of refugees fleeing to freedom and the lawyers who tried to help them. The second, legal story told how a transnational lawsuit helped to resolve a foreign policy crisis, open discussion over the human rights of foreign nationals held on Guantánamo, reignite debate

---

181. See Clawson et al., *supra* note 9, at 2387–88. After internal discussions, it was agreed that any student or lawyer who wished to examine a witness at trial could examine one witness each. Ultimately, only two students elected to do so.

182. Many of those who worked intensively on the *HCC* case have gone on to pursue careers in human rights, international law, or public interest lawyering, including the authors, Michelle Anderson, Ethan Balogh, Michael Barr, Graham Boyd, Ray Brescia, Sarah Cleveland, Tory Clawson, Chris Coons, Lisa Daugaard, Liz Detweiler, Margareth Etienne, Carl Goldfarb, Adam Gutride, Laura Ho, Anthony K. (Van) Jones, Christy Lopez, Catherine Powell, Steve Roos, Veronique Sanchez, Paul Sonn, Cecillia Wang, and Jessica Weisel.

183. Clawson et al., *supra* note 9, at 2388–89.

184. Caplow, *"Deport all the Students," supra* note 180, at 643 ("In the 1970s, many clinics did handle large impact cases as a means for advancing civil rights and social justice."). This is not to suggest that *HCC* was unique as law reform litigation, even in a human rights clinic. *See, e.g., Federal Jury Finds Detention Center Liable for Mistreatment*, INT'L HERALD TRIB., Nov. 13, 2007 (reporting on successful multiyear suit by Rutgers Constitutional Litigation Clinic to hold private detention facility accountable for abuse of detained asylum-seekers).

185. Foreign clinical law professors have also seized upon the potential of the *HCC* litigation in inspiring law reform litigation in a clinical setting, as well as justifying clinical legal education itself. The Committee of Chinese Clinical Legal Educators, for instance, recently secured Ford Foundation funding to translate and publish *Storming the Court*, in part to support efforts to establish clinical legal education in the People's Republic.

over the duties of states to fleeing refugees, and pioneer a new model of human rights litigation and clinical education.[186]

---

[186]. The first of these stories is well told in GOLDSTEIN, HOW A BAND OF YALE LAW STUDENTS FOUGHT THE PRESIDENT AND WON, supra note 9; the second is well told in Hurwitz, *Lawyering for Justice and the Inevitability of International Human Rights Clinics*, supra note 24.

12

The Story of *Doe v. Unocal*: Justice Delayed But Not Denied

Katie Redford* & Beth Stephens**

The district courts shall have original jurisdiction of any civil action by an alien for a tort only, committed in violation of the law of nations or a treaty of the United States.
—Alien Tort Statute, enacted by the U.S. Congress in 1789[1]

In March 2005, survivors of human rights abuses living in bamboo huts in Burma[2] and in refugee camps on the Thai–Burmese border joined human rights activists, public interest lawyers and private lawyers scattered around the United States and Asia to celebrate the settlement of *Doe v. Unocal*, a human rights lawsuit filed almost ten years earlier under the Alien Tort Statute ("ATS").[3]

---

* I am eternally grateful to the staff and board of EarthRights International, who believed in and supported this case when others told us we were crazy. Most importantly, I would like to thank ERI's brave field staff, and our clients and witnesses, all of whom took great risks to gather the evidence and testimony for Doe v. Unocal. Their commitment to justice, and resilience in the face of oppression are inspirational.

** My thanks to the entire Unocal litigation team, and especially to Jennifer Green of the Center for Constitutional Rights for her groundbreaking work in litigation against multinational corporations and for filing *Doe v. Unocal* despite my concerns that the case was too complicated for our limited resources.

1. 28 U.S.C. § 1350 (2000).

2. In 1989, the military regime changed the name of the country from Burma to Myanmar, the historical, Burmese-language name. The name Myanmar is not accepted by most opposition groups, who believe that the regime lacks legitimacy to engage in any government function, including changing the name of the country. This opposition includes the democratically elected National League for Democracy, headed by Nobel Peace Prize winner Aung San Suu Kyi, who refers to the country as Burma. The United States refers to the country as Burma, while the United Nations refers to it as Myanmar.

3. *Doe v. Unocal* produced multiple court decisions. The key decisions are as follows: Doe v. Unocal Corp., 963 F.Supp. 880 (C.D. Cal. 1997) (denying motion to dismiss); Nat'l Coal. Gov't of Burma v. Unocal, 176 F.R.D. 329 (C.D. Cal. 1997) (denying motion to dismiss

Jane Doe I, a Burmese woman who had been in hiding for seven years after fleeing her home country, celebrated the victory. The lawsuit offered her the only chance to seek justice for the killing of her baby by Burmese soldiers working with Unocal, the U.S. oil company. The *Doe v. Unocal* settlement was equally important to the ten other Burmese co-plaintiffs. From diverse ethnic backgrounds and disparate villages, they joined Jane Doe I in the lawsuit seeking redress for forced labor, rape, torture, and other human rights violations at the hands of Burma's army as it provided "security" for Unocal's gas pipeline.

In Burma, the military government commits human rights abuses with impunity. Only by filing suit in the United States were the plaintiffs able to obtain compensation and hold accountable some of those responsible for the abuses they had endured. The lawsuit was a grueling process. The plaintiffs' participation endangered their own lives, and they suffered through bitter defeats along the way. None of them expected that the lawsuit would last so long—much less that it would end suddenly with a settlement.

Although the White House, business lobbyists, and corporate executives in the United States and around the world were equally interested in the outcome of *Unocal*, they were far less pleased with the result. In response to a series of ATS cases upholding claims for egregious human rights violations, corporations and the business-friendly U.S. government tried repeatedly to eviscerate the law. Unable to convince Congress to repeal the ATS, they challenged victims' rights to sue in the courts. The *Unocal* settlement reflected in part a recognition that efforts to block this and similar lawsuits had failed. For the first time, the statute triggered a substantial payment from a U.S. corporation to victims of human rights abuses.

How is it that a group of rural farmers and herders, mothers and grandmothers, fishermen and traders came to focus their hopes on a 200–year–old U.S. law? And how did this obscure law become the target of an attack by big business and the administration of George W. Bush?

Had they been able to choose for themselves, the *Unocal* plaintiffs would have spent their entire lives on their farms, herding cattle and planting betelnut and cashews like their ancestors. As one of the Doe plaintiffs told her lawyer during the course of the case, "All I ever wanted was to live my life, raise my children, and lay down my bones in

---

in parallel case); Doe v. Unocal Corp., 110 F. Supp. 2d 1294 (C.D. Cal. 2000) (granting defendants' motion for summary judgment), *aff'd in part, rev'd in part* by 395 F.3d 932 (9th Cir. 2002) (reversing summary judgment and remanding for trial), *vacated, reh'g en banc granted*, 395 F.3d 978 (9th Cir. 2003). *See also* Doe v. Unocal Corp., 403 F.3d 708 (9th Cir. 2005) (post-settlement order granting the parties' stipulated motion to dismiss prior to oral argument on the rehearing en banc, and vacating the district court decision on the motion for summary judgment).

the earth with my family who came before me."[4] But, their lives were transformed when Unocal joined with the Burmese military government to construct a gas pipeline through their lands. They became first victims, then survivors, and then the unlikely victors in one of the most important "David and Goliath" battles in modern legal history.

Background: Unocal, Total, SLORC and the Yadana Gas Pipeline

In the early 1990s, two multinational oil companies—Total of France and Unocal of the United States—formed a partnership with the Burmese military regime, known then as the State Law and Order Restoration Council ("SLORC"),[5] to exploit natural gas reserves in the Andaman Sea. They entered into a contract to build a natural gas pipeline, the Yadana Gas Pipeline, extending from the Andaman Sea across a narrow stretch of land in southern Burma.

The SLORC had seized power in 1988[6] and was internationally condemned for widespread human rights abuses against its own people. In particular, the military was notorious for pervasive use of forced labor on public infrastructure projects and brutal treatment of porters—civilians forcibly conscripted to carry arms, ammunition and other supplies during security operations.

Putting the fox in charge of the proverbial henhouse, the pipeline contract provided that SLORC military units would act as security agents for the consortium's executives and foreign personnel. Despite knowledge of the military's human rights abuses, including the use of forced labor on public infrastructure projects, the companies delegated to the army the responsibility to procure workers and build infrastructure for the project. The Burmese regime quickly created a highly militarized pipeline corridor in what had been a relatively peaceful area in the Tenasserim region of Burma's southern peninsula. The influx of SLORC soldiers resulted in myriad human rights abuses, including forced labor, torture, rape, extrajudicial killings, and attacks on indigenous and ethnic minority peoples.

SLORC began carrying out its contract obligations by forcing thousands of villagers to build barracks to house the soldiers pouring into the

---

   4. Jane Doe II, in conversation with Katie Redford in Kanchanaburi, Thailand (May, 2006).

   5. In 1997, the SLORC renamed itself the State Peace and Development Council ("SPDC").

   6. Burma has been under military rule since 1962, but the dictatorship renamed itself the SLORC in 1988 following a bloody crackdown that left thousands of Burmese citizens dead or in political prisons.

region for the project.[7] Likewise, villagers were taken from their homes to construct helipads and other infrastructure for the project and to porter for the military while they provided security for survey teams and other project officials. The military forced villagers to carry arms, ammunition, food and other supplies—sometimes more than their body weight—up and down the pipeline route. Those forced into this backbreaking work came to be known in the region as "pipeline porters." The widespread forced relocations and restrictions on freedom of movement led farmers and fisher folk to lose access to their livelihoods, forcing many into poverty and involuntary exile.[8] Villagers could only endure the abuse or try to escape.

For example, John Doe VIII, a farmer, lived in a rural village in Burma's Tenasserim region.[9] Along with the other plaintiffs, he remained anonymous to minimize the risks of retaliation by the SLORC for his participation in the lawsuit. His village was close to the route of the Yadana Gas Pipeline. Although "Yadana" means "treasure" in Burmese, to John Doe VIII it was anything but that. In 1995, he was taken from his village and forced to serve as a "pipeline porter." As a forced laborer, he would have been killed if he refused to work, or if he grew too weak to be useful. He explained, "[t]he loads were so heavy, that I couldn't stand on my feet. My friend helped me by holding me up from behind. The weather was so hot and humid and we were so thirsty. What I did to survive was to lick the sweat from my face."[10]

Jane Doe I lived in a different village in the Tenasserim region. The Yadana pipeline went right through the middle of her village. Her husband, John Doe I, was forced by Burmese soldiers to clear bushes,

---

7. This phenomenon of forced labor has been referred to as "corporate militarization." *See, e.g.*, Betsy Apple, *Blood on Their Hands: Corporations, Militarization, and the Alien Tort Claims Act*, 1 SEATTLE J. SOC. JUST. 127, 136 (2002).

8. While the environmental harms associated with the pipeline are beyond the scope of this article, it is not surprising that a project that benefited from slavery, rape, and torture exhibited similar disregard for the environment through which it traversed. *See* EARTHRIGHTS INT'L, TOTAL DENIAL: A REPORT ON THE YADANA PIPELINE PROJECT IN BURMA (1996), *available at* http://www.earthrights.org/files/Reports/TotalDenial96.pdf [hereinafter *Total Denial Report*]; EARTHRIGHTS INT'L, TOTAL DENIAL CONTINUES: HUMAN RIGHTS ABUSES ALONG THE YADANA AND YETAGUN PIPELINES IN BURMA (2d ed. 2003), *available at* http://www.earthrights.org/files/Reports/TotalDenialCont–2ndEdition.pdf [hereinafter *Total Denial Continues*].

9. Facts about the case and the plaintiffs' claims throughout this Chapter are drawn from the Third Amended Complaint, *Doe v. Unocal*, 963 F.Supp. 880 (C.D. Cal. 1997), *available at* www.earthrights.org. For accompanying summaries of factual allegations, see the cases cited *supra* note 3.

10. Interview transcribed by authors from TOTAL DENIAL, a film by Milena Kaneva (MK Production 2006), http://www.totaldenialfilm.com/. The film won the 2006 Vaclav Havel Human Rights Award, *see* http://www.earthrights.org/pr/totaldenial.html [hereinafter TOTAL DENIAL].

trees and brush from the pipeline route. She describes the change that occurred in her village when the foreign corporations arrived:

> 'Til the pipeline came, there were no soldiers in the area where I lived. In our village, we were planting rice. When the pipeline arrived, we had to work for the white people more and more. The soldiers were forcing us to be slaves. If we refused to work, they said they would kill us. Because of the white people, our village was destroyed and we had to flee.[11]

After working for 10 days on the pipeline route, John Doe I ran out of food. He risked his life to escape from the soldiers guarding him and the other laborers, and returned home. When the soldiers came looking for him, he was fishing at a nearby river. Jane was tending the food by the cooking fire in front of their home, nursing their two-month-old baby. The soldiers began questioning her about her husband, and when she refused to tell them his whereabouts, they began to beat and kick her with their heavy army boots. At that moment, the soldiers saw her husband approaching, and began shooting at him.

> When they shot at my husband, he ran away in the jungle. A soldier hit me with his gun. I fell and hit my head on a stone, and lost consciousness. When I woke up, I saw my baby in the fire. She couldn't even cry. Her body was so burned, and all black.[12]

Shortly thereafter, their baby died.

From the beginning, Unocal was alerted to such conditions and risks by various human rights organizations. The company was explicitly told that the military would use forced labor on the pipeline project and would commit widespread human rights abuses, including portering, while carrying out its security obligations. Plaintiffs eventually learned through discovery that Unocal's own consultants, hired to perform social impact assessments, told them the same:

> [M]y conclusion is that egregious human rights violations have occurred, and are occurring now, in southern Burma. The most common are forced relocation without compensation of families from land near/along the pipeline route; forced labor to work on infrastructure projects supporting the pipeline ...; and imprisonment and/or execution by the army of those opposing such actions.... Unocal, by seeming to have accepted [the Myanmar Military]'s version of events, appears at best naïve and at worst a willing partner in the situation.[13]

---

11. Interview with Jane Doe I, *id*.
12. *Id*.
13. Report of John Haseman, Unocal Consultant (Dec. 11, 1995) (*quoted in* Doe v. Unocal Corp., 395 F.3d at 942).

Unocal ignored these warnings, at times denying that abuses were occurring, at other times boldly announcing that human rights abuses in Burma were simply the cost of doing business there. Unocal's president, who became a defendant in the case, stated: "If forced labor goes hand and glove with the military, yes there will be more forced labor."[14]

Beginning in 1992, and increasing as the years went by, villagers from the pipeline region began leaving their ancestral lands. Many found their way to the Thai–Burmese border, where some displaced peoples lived in makeshift camps[15] and others joined the growing ranks of Burma's internally displaced peoples. While survival in the jungle and the camps was difficult, the regions to which they fled were at least beyond the reach of the Burmese military, which had made life for many unbearable in the pipeline region.

Local and international non-governmental organizations providing humanitarian relief and monitoring Burma's human rights situation, as well as representatives from the media, had some access to the border region, but the pipeline corridor was completely off limits to outside scrutiny. Many who crossed the border into Thailand began to speak about the pipeline, the arrival of the "white people," the Burmese soldiers and the attendant human rights abuses. As individuals and families slipped into Thailand, so too did their stories. Accounts of human rights abuses began to appear in local newspapers, media reports, and even U.S. Embassy and State Department cables that would later be admitted as evidence in *Doe v. Unocal*.

The conditions in the pipeline region became both a focus of the worldwide movement for divestment from Burma, and one of the world's most notorious examples of corporate complicity in human rights abuses. Partly as a result of the allegations of abuse in the pipeline region, Burma and the Yadana pipeline became a focal point in a global debate on business' role in human rights.

At the center of this debate were eleven villagers from Burma who wanted simply to obtain a modicum of justice. The villagers of Burma's Tenasserim region had no difficulty linking their suffering to the corporations that profited from it. Although they may not have known the details of the Yadana production-sharing agreement or the intricacies of the legal doctrines that govern accountability for human rights violations, they did know that they had experienced devastating abuses. And,

---

14. Statement of John Imle, Unocal President, (Jan. 4, 1995) (*quoted in* Doe v. Unocal Corp., 395 F.3d at 941).

15. Since Thailand has not signed the U.N. Convention Relating to the Status of Refugees, people from the pipeline region and other areas who fled from Burma do not enjoy legal status or protections as refugees. *See* U.N. Convention Relating to the Status of Refugees, opened for signature July 28, 1951, 189 U.N.T.S. 150.

they knew that the abuses started when the "foreigners" began arriving in their land.

Individuals like Jane Doe I and John Doe VIII did not set out to make legal history, but, after considerable risk and sacrifice, they did. Their stories, and others like them, were the subject of intense litigation, debate, and controversy for more than a decade. Lawyers and judges struggled to determine the appropriate legal standard for a corporation's complicity in the abuses perpetrated by government soldiers working on its behalf.

1994: The First Trip to Burma

In the summer of 1994, as the militarization process was well underway, Katie Redford, one of the authors of this Chapter and then a second-year law student at the University of Virginia, traveled to Thailand with two other UVA law students, Tyler Giannini and Mark Bromley[16] on a summer internship. Working with local human rights and non-governmental environmental organizations, they were assigned to document the human rights abuses associated with development projects in South East Asia. At that time, controversy swirled around issues such as Indonesia's clear-cutting of rainforest, which the Indonesian government claimed would help pull people out of poverty. Likewise, large hydropower projects, such as Thailand's Pak Mun dam, had garnered significant attention as the government displaced rural fishing villages in the effort to generate electricity for its growing urban population. The debate about sanctions against the Burmese regime was growing, with a burgeoning grassroots movement that labeled Burma the "South Africa of the '90s." Because of this, their research was driven by fundamental questions about the impact of foreign investment and development aid on human rights, the environment, and poverty. Do open markets truly lead to open societies, as the proponents of corporate and economic globalization were arguing?

In an effort to answer that question, Redford and her colleagues traveled to the Burmese border to ask about the rapid development plans in Burma. They listened in horror as victims and witnesses described in terrifying detail the rape, torture and forced labor they endured under military rule. While the students were familiar with the regime's notorious reputation, they were startled to notice the English word "pipeline" appearing in the accounts of new arrivals to the border. They quickly identified the pipeline as the Yadana pipeline—and were surprised to learn that one of the companies involved in the pipeline was Unocal, a

---

16. Also a contributor to this volume; see Mark Bromley & Kristen Walker, *"The Stories of* Dudgeon *and* Toonen*: Personal Struggles to Legalize Sexual Identities,"* see supra Chapter 3.

California corporation. Preliminary research revealed that Unocal had recently begun to sell off its operations in North America and Europe in favor of projects in Southeast Asia and the former Soviet Union. The students reviewed reports to shareholders in which Unocal set out its new business strategy: to focus on high-risk areas where other companies were reluctant to operate.[17] On the border, the students spoke to individuals from the pipeline region who expressed their dismay that a company from the United States—their ideal image of democracy, freedom, and human rights—would be involved with the brutal dictatorship that was running their country. Some such sentiments were summarized in a letter written to Unocal that summer by high school students in a refugee camp:

> You say in your report that you have visited Burma and you saw that the situation is fine and there will be no problem with human rights and logging if you build a pipeline. For sure you don't know the situation better than us. You tell things to the people in America who don't know about the situation here. But we know the real situation and we know what you say is not true. People who are living where you will make your pipeline and everywhere in Burma have to do hard labour without getting any money. We are the people who had been living in Burma for all our lives, and because of the SLORC's oppression we had to escape to the Thai border. We did not do it because we wanted to come here. It was real that we could not bear the SLORC's oppression any longer.... All in all, we want to tell you please do not help the SLORC and join your hands with theirs by making a pipeline. We are worried about you because your hands are clean at the moment but if you shake your hands with hands that are dirty with blood, then your hands will also be dirty.[18]

With no response to their reports of widespread violations and their pleas for help, people in the pipeline region began to feel more desperate. News reports began to quote ethnic rebel army leaders stating that they viewed the pipeline as a legitimate target for sabotage, threatening to attack the pipeline until nothing remained but a "snake of fire."[19]

---

17. EarthRights International lawyers recall this being in a Unocal Corporation Report to Stockholders, and on personal recollection, believe it was 1994. After Chevron purchased Unocal in 2005, however, all evidence of such activities seems to have been excised from their website.

18. 1994 Letter from Karen Refugees to Unocal (1994), *reprinted in Total Denial Report, supra* note 8, at Appendix C.

19. Brad Miller, *Burma in Chains: U.S. Companies Profit from Slavery,* THE PROGRESSIVE, Oct. 1995, at 32–35. *See also* Edith T. Mirante, *Burma's Gas Pipeline: Litmus Test for Global Boycott Movement,* JINN MAGAZINE, June 11, 1996, *available at* http://www.pacificnews.org/jinn/stories/2.12/960611–burma.html.

While simultaneously listening to desperate cries for help and increasing threats of violence, Redford, Giannini and Bromley knew that they needed to do something. At the time, sitting in thatched, candle lit huts on the banks of the Salween and Moei Rivers, they didn't know what that something was. As young, idealistic law students, however, they felt confident that there were lawful alternatives to violence and sabotage to address such human rights abuses.

They returned to their third year of law school with the goal of finding those alternatives. Before they left, they discussed strategy with a small group of grassroots human rights advocates from Burma. One of these advocates, Ka Hsaw Wa, was a young Karen man from Burma who had experienced torture at the hands of the Burmese regime.[20] At the age of 18, he was a student leader in Rangoon during Burma's 1988 pro-democracy uprising, which brought hundreds of thousands of peaceful protesters throughout the country to the streets to demand basic human rights, and an end to military rule. When the Burmese regime responded by killing thousands of demonstrators in the streets, Ka Hsaw Wa, like most of the students, fled to the jungles of the Thai–Burma border to take up arms against the Burmese military. Reasoning that violence was the very problem in his country and, therefore, it could not be his solution, Ka Hsaw Wa chose to pick up a pen instead. He began documenting the many human rights violations that had occurred, in an attempt to expose them to the international community.[21]

For this reason, the legal strategy that the law students were proposing particularly appealed to Ka Hsaw Wa. To him, the strategy amounted to combining the two necessary aspects of any legal action: getting the facts and figuring out the law. Shortly thereafter, Redford and Giannini[22] joined with Ka Hsaw Wa to establish a new organization called EarthRights International ("ERI" or "EarthRights"). Initially, the organization existed only in name, and in the dreams of these three eventual co-founders. But the idea of what could be was enough for Ka

---

20. Like the Doe plaintiffs, Ka Hsaw Wa used a pseudonym while working in Burma and Thailand to protect his true identity and to minimize the potential for retaliation against himself or his family members by the Burmese regime. He has since received numerous international awards including the 1999 Reebok Human Rights Award; the 1999 Goldman Environmental Prize (*see* www.goldmanprize.org), which has been called the Nobel Prize for the Environment; and the Sting and Trudie Styler Award for Human Rights and the Environment. He was the subject of a documentary film on *Doe v. Unocal* (TOTAL DENIAL, *supra* note 10), and has been written about in numerous books, including KERRY KENNEDY, SPEAK TRUTH TO POWER, HUMAN RIGHTS DEFENDERS WHO ARE CHANGING OUR WORLD (2000), *available at* www.speaktruthtopower.org.

21. *See* TOTAL DENIAL, *supra* note 10.

22. Tyler Giannani is now the Clinical Director of the Harvard Human Rights Program and Lecturer on Law at Harvard Law School. He was co-director of ERI until 2004.

Hsaw Wa to put together a team of human rights investigators to travel to the pipeline region, while Redford and Giannini returned to the United States to legally establish the nonprofit organization and to apply for an Echoing Green fellowship that ultimately provided the initial funding for the new organization. EarthRights eventually filed *Doe v. Unocal* along with other human rights organizations and several private attorneys.[23] Before they even graduated, the soon-to-be lawyers began researching what would become their first case, while the human rights advocates gathered the facts.

Getting the Facts

In 1994, Ka Hsaw Wa began training a team of human rights investigators for a clandestine journey across the Thai–Burmese border to the pipeline region. By this time, the companies had released the proposed pipeline route and named some of the villages that would be affected by its construction, while also acknowledging the military's role in providing security for the project. The effort to document the conditions in the pipeline corridor faced formidable challenges starting with the climate of fear throughout the country and exacerbated by the concentration of soldiers guarding the pipeline. Moreover, with one person in Burma reportedly acting as a military informer for every ten households,[24] villagers were wary of any strangers, especially those who came asking questions. Nevertheless, Ka Hsaw Wa and his team spent months building relationships with local people and village headmen in the Tenasserim region. They eventually established enough trust among enough local people to begin their listening project—sitting down with villagers who had experienced or witnessed human rights abuses at the hands of the Burmese military.

For the next two years and after, they interviewed victims and witnesses of pipeline-related human rights violations. Using pencils, small notebooks, tape recorders and disposable cameras that they could hide in their sarongs and destroy at a moment's notice, they collected first-hand testimonies from several hundred victims and witnesses who lived in the pipeline corridor, or who had recently fled to the Thai border to escape the abuse. Although ERI eventually raised funds to support the

---

23. The original legal team included Paul Hoffman of Schonbrun De Simone Seplow Harris & Hoffman; Dan Stormer and Anne Richardson of Hadsell & Stormer; Judith Chomsky, Jennifer Green and Beth Stephens (co-author of this Chapter) of the Center for Constitutional Rights; and Katie Redford (co-author of this Chapter), Tyler Giannini, Rick Herz and Marco Simons of EarthRights International.

24. *See* Christina Fink, Living Silence: Burma under Military Rule 127 (Zed Books 2001).

work in Burma and Thailand, the three young colleagues paid hundreds of dollars for these initial investigations out of their own pockets.

Inside Burma, the field investigators arranged secret meetings on the periphery of villages like Eindayaza and Michaunglaung, which appeared along corporate maps of the pipeline route and in media coverage of the project. The inhabitants described the first time the "foreigners," "Americans," and "white people" had come to their villages. They spoke of town meetings attended by white people, who, through interpreters, told the villagers that the pipeline was coming and explained how it would benefit their village. The villagers described in detail the signs the foreigners had erected—emblazoned with the names and logos of Unocal and Total. Ka Hsaw Wa and his team repeatedly heard testimony describing soldiers from specific battalions who had forced men, women, children, and the elderly to build their barracks, and to porter their supplies, while boasting that they were there to provide security for the pipeline, and for the foreigners who were building it. A new word—ironically, derived from English—appeared in local languages: the term "pipeline porter" (pronounced "pie-line po-tah"), became commonplace, marking a new, "American" manifestation of this traditionally Burmese abuse.

Hiding in the forests and fields outside the villages, using binoculars and talking to local villagers, Ka Hsaw Wa and his team observed and recorded the military presence, noting details such as battalion numbers on uniforms. They gathered documentary evidence including written military orders and village decrees. When possible, they took photographs. Speaking various local languages, including Burmese, Po Karen, Skaw Karen, Mon and Tavoyan, they chronicled the complete militarization of the pipeline region that had begun in 1991, along with the devastating impact that it had wreaked on local villagers' lives, particularly through systematic forced labor.

Gathering information was somewhat easier along the Thai-Burmese border, where scores of pipeline villagers had fled to makeshift camps and villages to escape the abuse. Some spoke freely because they felt more confident outside the borders of the military's authority. Others, however, knew that they were never going home and as such, did not fear the retaliation of the regime. Still others spoke on condition of anonymity, fearing military retaliation against the family and friends that they had left behind. These testimonies from Mon, Tavoyan, and Karen villagers were corroborated by interviews with Burmese army deserters, who described in detail the forced labor and other abuses that they had committed while carrying out security operations for the pipeline.

In 1994, we were in the pipeline area in charge of protection. It took more than 150 porters to carry food and ammunition. We were taking even old men, older than 70, to be porters because they couldn't pay 150 kyat (30 cents) to be free. Most of the porters were very skinny, as we were giving them very little food. If they would fall from exhaustion, the officer would order to shoot them. I saw 3 or 4 of them shot in front of my eyes. But I didn't shoot. I didn't want to do those things. I argued with my officer. He was drunk and took out his gun; I shot him and then had to run away. I didn't want to join the army but if you cannot pay, they take you by force.[25]

All of this evidence, which was so courageously gathered by Ka Hsaw Wa and his team despite the dangers of visiting the region, showed a pattern of human rights abuses that were a direct result of the multinational corporations' investments in the region. The evidence confirmed what the local villagers had known since the companies first arrived in their lands: the human rights abuses that they were experiencing were directly connected to the pipeline, and to the foreign companies that were building it.

The victims of the abuses ranged from newborn babies to the elderly and included individuals from diverse ethnic groups and villages who spoke various languages and practiced different religions. However, they shared a desire to be more than victims—to be survivors who would not simply sit back and accept their fate. The chorus, "What can we do?" rang in Ka Hsaw Wa's ears. "We have lost so much. Please help us do something. What can we do?"

Figuring Out the Law

While the ERI investigators documented human rights abuses in Burma, Katie Redford and Tyler Giannini returned to their third year of law school, seeking a nonviolent way to address the alarming human rights violations that were occurring in the Yadana pipeline region. They approached this daunting task with only minimal resources, including EarthRights International, the unfunded non-profit organization they set up during their third year, which at that point had no paid staff. They also had volunteer investigators in Burma and Thailand, and, of course, they had their own fledgling legal skills.

Redford and Giannini looked first to the Alien Tort Statute, which they had studied in law school courses. As applied to the situation in Burma, the elements of an ATS claim against Unocal appeared simple. The plaintiff must be an alien, alleging a tort, and the alleged tort must

---

25. Interview with unidentified Burmese military deserter, TOTAL DENIAL, *supra* note 10.

be a violation of the law of nations.[26] Certainly, the Karen, Mon and Tavoyan villagers from Burma satisfied the alien requirement, and the abuses they had suffered constituted "torts." The courts had by that time determined that a tort is in violation of the "law of nations" when it violates a universal, obligatory and definable (or specific) norm of customary international law.[27] Customary international law "results from a general and consistent practice of states followed by them from a sense of legal obligation."[28] Determining when a practice rises to that level, however, is not always simple. Moreover, the ATS had never successfully been used against a corporation. Redford and Giannini realized they needed to move beyond their initial reading of the ATS and review the case law to determine whether its use against Unocal held promise.

Originally enacted in 1789, the ATS was barely used for almost two centuries. In 1980, the Second Circuit issued a landmark decision in *Filártiga v. Peña–Irala*,[29] a case filed by the father and sister of Joelito Filártiga, a seventeen-year-old Paraguayan who had been tortured to death in Paraguay by Americo Peña–Irala, then Inspector General of Police. Joelito's family discovered to their horror that the offending police officer was residing in New York. Working with lawyers from the Center for Constitutional Rights (CCR), they sued Peña–Irala under the ATS. The Second Circuit found that the Filártigas' claim met all of the ATS's requirements: the plaintiffs were aliens and the alleged torture and murder of Joelito Filártiga constituted a tort in violation of the law of nations. This breakthrough case paved the way for contemporary human rights litigation by establishing, among other things, that "courts must interpret international law not as it was in 1789, but as it has evolved and exists among the nations of the world today."[30]

The *Filártiga* case also served as an inspiration for human rights lawyers, including Redford and Giannini, who took heart from the Filártigas' story. The lawyers from CCR had not been deterred just

---

26. 28 U.S.C. § 1350 (2000).

27. *See, e.g.*, Hilao v. Marcos, 25 F.3d 1467, 1475 (9th Cir. 1994); Kadić v. Karadžić, 70 F.3d 232, 239 (2d Cir. 1995).

28. RESTATEMENT (THIRD) OF FOREIGN RELATIONS LAW § 102(2) cmt. c (1987).

29. 630 F.2d 876 (2d Cir. 1980). For a full discussion of the *Filártiga* case, *see* Harold Hongju Koh, *Filártiga v. Peña–Irala*: Judicial Internalization into Domestic Law of the Customary International Law Norm Against Torture, *in* INT'L LAW STORIES (John E. Noyes et al. eds., 2007).

30. *Filártiga*, 630 F.2d at 881. This analysis was affirmed by the Supreme Court when it considered the ATS in Sosa v. Alvarez–Machain, 542 U.S. 692, 725 (2004) (requiring "any claim based on the present-day law of nations to rest on a norm of international character accepted by the civilized world and defined with a specificity comparable to the features of the 18th–century paradigms we have recognized.").

because the ATS had never been used in the context of human rights. Adopting a similar attitude, they decided that they would not assume that the ATS could not reach corporate human rights abusers like Unocal simply because such a case would need to break new ground.

In the years following the *Filártiga* decision, some two dozen cases focused on bringing state actors to justice for human rights violations were decided by U.S. courts. In these cases, victims sued former government officials and military officers. The courts recognized that violations of "universal, definable and obligatory" international law norms were actionable under the ATS, including genocide, war crimes and crimes against humanity, summary execution, disappearance, and cruel, inhuman, and degrading treatment.[31]

Ensuing cases forced courts to determine not only which abuses qualified as violations of the law of nations, but also which defendants could be held accountable. Although international law focuses primarily on the conduct of governments and government officials, some international law norms directly apply to private parties as well, including the prohibitions against genocide, slavery and slave trading, and war crimes.[32] In addition, private parties can be held liable for violating international norms that apply to state actors when the private parties act in concert with government officials.[33]

The ATS cases make clear that private individuals can be held liable in some situations. But what if the perpetrator is neither a government nor a private individual, but a corporation? In the era of corporate globalization, when many corporations are more powerful than many state actors, what about corporate complicity in and responsibility for human rights violations? Corporations are often treated as legal persons (and indeed demand such treatment and rights); shouldn't they too be subject to ATS jurisdiction when they are involved in violations of international law?

The World Outside the Courtroom: The Age of Globalization

In the years following *Filártiga*, while lawyers litigated the cases that developed ATS jurisprudence, the world outside the courtroom was rapidly changing: "globalization" had arrived. Globalization is "[t]he process through which an increasingly free flow of ideas, people, goods,

---

31. *See, e.g.*, Cabello v. Fernández–Larios, 402 F.3d 1148 (11th Cir. 2005) (summary execution, torture, crimes against humanity, cruel, inhuman or degrading treatment); Kadić v. Karadžić, 70 F.3d 232 (genocide, war crimes and crimes against humanity, summary execution, torture); Hilao v. Marcos, 25 F.3d 1467 (9th Cir. 1994) (summary execution, disappearance, torture); Xuncax v. Gramajo, 886 F.Supp. 162 (D. Mass. 1995).

32. *See, e.g.*, *Kadić*, 70 F.3d at 239–40.

33. *Id.* at 245.

services, and capital leads to the integration of economies and societies."[34] Corporations became larger and more influential as power began to shift from national governments to private businesses. One CEO described the era of globalization in the following terms: "[m]arket forces and large corporations in many ways have a bigger impact on people's lives than governments or regional and international institutions."[35]

This vast opening of markets, combined with an increase in corporate power, accelerated during the 1990s—the years in which the Yadana pipeline project was both conceived and implemented. As President Clinton stated in his 1998 State of the Union Address:

> Rarely have Americans lived through so much change in so many ways in so short a time. Quietly, but with gathering force, the ground has shifted beneath our feet as we have moved into an Information Age, a global economy, a truly new world.... As we enter the 21st century, the global economy requires us to seek opportunity not just at home but in all the markets of the world.[36]

As Vice President Cheney stated during his tenure at Halliburton, however, "[t]he problem is that the good Lord didn't see fit to always put oil and gas resources where there are democratic governments...."[37] As corporations like Unocal sought opportunities and resources in markets like Burma, their search was accompanied by minimal, if any, legal restrictions limiting the ways in which they functioned outside of their home countries. At the same time, smaller, developing countries, in their race to join the industrial world, experienced difficulties in attracting foreign investment unless they were willing to subvert their own human rights, labor and environmental laws. Simply put, neither international nor national legal systems kept pace with the rise of transnational corporate power.[38]

---

34. International Monetary Fund, *Glossary of Selected Financial Terms*, available at http://www.imf.org/external/np/exr/glossary/showTerm.asp#91. *See also* World Bank Group, *Globalization*, available at http://www1.worldbank.org/economicpolicy/globalization/ (defining globalization as the "growing integration of economies and societies around the world").

35. Lindahl Goran, *A New Role for Global Businesses*, TIME MAGAZINE, Jan. 31, 2000, at 52.

36. Bill Clinton, President of the United States, 1998 State of the Union Address (January 27, 1998) (transcript *available at* http://www.washingtonpost.com/wp-srv/politics/special/states/docs/sou98.htm).

37. *Halliburton's Cheney Sees Worldwide Opportunities, Blasts Sanctions,* HART'S PETROLEUM FINANCE WEEK, April 1, 1996.

38. International legal processes are inadequate to deal with the kinds of harms that were occurring not only in Burma, but in other countries in which global corporations were doing business with repressive governments. International tribunals either limit them-

This legal vacuum did nothing to deter corporations from doing business with the world's most brutal tyrants. For example, at the time of their investment in Burma, Unocal's Code of Conduct for Doing Business Internationally simply stated that the company abided by "all . . . laws of our host country."[39] Likewise, private entities like Unocal were governed by tort law, which subjected them only to the jurisdiction and venue in which the tort occurred. For companies operating in Burma, it was a legal free-for-all, given that the "host country" laws constituted nothing more than martial law. What did this mean? Two months before Total signed the production-sharing agreement for the Yadana Project, Major General Khin Nyunt, First Secretary of the SLORC and head of military intelligence, stated publicly: "Martial law is neither more or less than the will of the general who commands the army; in fact martial law means no law at all."[40] Senior General Saw Maung, SLORC Chairman at the time, reaffirmed this definition, asserting that "[m]artial law means the will of the ruler. He can do anything he wishes to do."[41]

To the people of Burma, the ATS represented a beacon of hope, inspired by *Filártiga*:

> We will not let them defeat us. We know the companies and their military partners have lots of money, guns, power, and influence. But they do not have what we have. We have the truth, we have justice, we have courage, and most importantly, we have each other to protect human rights and the environment. We will win.[42]

Putting the Facts and the Law Together: Litigating Doe v. Unocal

The adoption of this "we will win" attitude was necessary in order to face the challenging and dangerous litigation of *Doe v. Unocal*. From a legal standpoint, a case against a business enterprise for human rights

---

selves to hearing cases brought by one country on behalf of its citizens against another government, or lack the ability to render enforceable legal decisions. The United Nations and other international institutions are equally inadequate to deal with corporate abuse, not only limited by their jurisdiction, but also distrusted by many people around the world. *See, e.g.,* CorpWatch, *Alliance for a Corporate Free U.N.*, available at http://www.corpwatch.org/article.php?list=type&type=101, http://www.earthrights.org/site_blurbs/alliance_for_a_corporate-free_un.html.

39. UNOCAL CORPORATE COMMUNICATIONS DEPARTMENT, THE YADANA PROJECT 18 (Nov. 1995).

40. AMNESTY INT'L, NO LAW AT ALL: HUMAN RIGHTS VIOLATIONS UNDER MILITARY RULE (1992).

41. *Id.*

42. Ka Hsaw Wa, Acceptance Speech at Goldman Environmental Prize Ceremony (April 1999).

abuses entered uncharted territory. On the ground in Burma, Ka Hsaw Wa, his team of investigators, and the plaintiffs and witnesses were risking retaliation by the Burmese regime, including torture and death, for daring to expose the true scope of the abuses committed during the construction of the pipeline, which was the SLORC's flagship project. Institutionally, ERI was a brand new and tiny organization, consisting of a young human rights activist from Burma and two new lawyers who had never litigated a case. Their goal to help rural villagers from Burma seek justice against a powerful corporation as well as one of the world's most brutal military regimes, was certainly an undertaking of David and Goliath caliber.

Filing the Complaint

By the time Redford and Giannini graduated from law school in May of 1995 and headed to Thailand to open ERI's first office, Ka Hsaw Wa's team had gathered substantial evidence demonstrating that the Burmese military had committed extensive human rights violations in the pipeline region with the support of Unocal and Total. Based on their initial research, Redford and Giannini concluded that a U.S. lawsuit against Unocal might force the corporation to compensate those harmed by the abuses. Local people in Burma had long been accustomed to the impunity with which the Burmese military ruled. Once they learned from lawyers in the United States that they could file suit under the ATS, they were eager to proceed.

Redford and Giannini contacted lawyers at CCR, recognizing that they needed CCR's expertise, experience, and bold approach to litigation. CCR attorneys had been working for several years with Burmese activists based in the United States, and they quickly agreed to join with ERI to put together a legal team adequate for the task. By mid–1996, ERI and CCR had assembled a team of veteran ATS litigators to complement the seasoned human rights investigators from Burma.[43]

The decision that the facts supported a legal claim in U.S. federal courts, and the lawyers' commitment to proceed, however, were just the start of the daunting challenge at hand. Learning the law and researching the basic facts were the easy piece of the undertaking; transforming the facts into a legally sufficient case file, backed by evidence admissible in a U.S. lawsuit, however, was another story.

The first challenge was simply transmitting the human rights information. All of the evidence, as well as potential plaintiffs and witnesses, were located in the jungles of Thailand and Burma. At a time preceding widespread use of cell phones and e-mail, it often took days or even

---

43. *See supra* note 23.

weeks to relay information to and from the legal team in the United States, Redford and Giannini in their new ERI office in Thailand, and the plaintiffs and witnesses in rural areas of Thailand and Burma.

The human rights investigators gathering this evidence and coordinating with the people on the ground were at risk in both countries—persona non grata in Burma and illegal immigrants in Thailand. They interviewed people in Burma or on the Thai–Burmese border and sneaked back across the border and through the Thai jungle, avoiding military and border checkpoints. The interviews were translated into English, transcribed, and delivered to Redford and Giannini in Thailand.

As white foreigners, the U.S. lawyers could not regularly travel to the border area, refugee camps, or inside Burma without raising suspicion and thereby placing people in danger. They generally met with the investigators in a city, gathering the transcribed interviews to send to the legal team in the United States. Concerned that their phone lines and e-mails were monitored, they used hotel business centers to fax the texts of interviews which would form the basis of the federal complaint. To avoid suspicion on the part of hotel staff, who mostly serviced wealthy business and military clients, Redford and Giannini spent days traveling from one hotel to the next, dressed in U.S. business attire, faxing no more than twenty pages at a time from each hotel. The U.S. lawyers who reviewed the documents often asked follow-up questions, and the entire process began anew.

In October 1996, ERI, CCR, attorneys Judith Brown Chomsky and Paul Hoffman, and the law firm of Hadsell & Stormer filed a lawsuit in the Central District of California against Unocal, Total, and the State Law and Order Restoration Council ("SLORC"), seeking redress for the human rights abuses associated with the Yadana pipeline project in Burma.[44] The plaintiffs consisted of eight men and three women from various villages along the pipeline who had suffered egregious violations at the hands of Burmese army units securing the pipeline route, including forced relocation, forced labor, rape, torture and murder. In addition to the international law claims filed under the ATS, the complaint included parallel state law tort claims for wrongful death, rape, forced labor, and other injuries. Furthermore, in addition to seeking damages on behalf of the eleven individual plaintiffs, the lawsuit asked the Court, on behalf of a class of all those living in the pipeline region, to order Unocal to withdraw from the pipeline project. Almost simultaneously, a separate group of attorneys filed *Roe v. Unocal* on behalf of four different plaintiffs. The case raised similar factual and legal issues and,

---

[44]. Chomsky and Hoffman, private attorneys working out of their own law firms, were also cooperating attorneys working with CCR.

though litigated separately, proceeded simultaneously on a parallel track with *Doe v. Unocal* for the life of the lawsuits.[45]

Defending the Complaint Against Legal Challenges

The defendants immediately filed motions to dismiss the complaint, raising a long list of legal defenses. The next year of the litigation focused on legal research, brief writing and oral argument. Two of the defendants won quick victories. The claims against the SLORC were dismissed on the basis of foreign sovereign immunity, which bars lawsuits against foreign governments in most cases. The claims against Total were dismissed for lack of personal jurisdiction, applying the rule that foreign corporations cannot be sued in U.S. courts for claims that arise in another country unless they have ongoing connections to this country.

Unocal's central argument asserted that the ATS did not apply to corporate defendants accused of complicity in human rights abuses committed by the Burmese army. In a landmark decision in 1997, a U.S. federal district court in Los Angeles rejected Unocal's motion to dismiss and agreed that *Doe v. Unocal* could proceed. The Court concluded that corporations and their executive officers can be held legally responsible under the ATS for violations of international human rights norms in foreign countries, and that U.S. courts have the authority to adjudicate such claims.[46] The decision sparked tremendous interest in the United States and around the world, as human rights activists and plaintiffs' lawyers realized that they could file claims in the United States against multinational corporations for human rights abuses committed in other countries, as long as they could obtain personal jurisdiction over the defendant. Business executives and the U.S. government also took notice, however, and efforts to overturn the *Unocal* precedent, and even to amend the ATS, gathered force.

---

45. *Roe v. Unocal Corp.*, 70 F. Supp. 2d 1073 (C.D. Cal. 1999), was originally filed on behalf of the exile government, the National Coalition Government of the Union of Burma ("NCGUB") and the Federal Trade Unions of Burma ("FTUB") on the basis that these organizations could represent a larger class of affected villagers from the pipeline region. *See* NCGUB v. Unocal Corp., 176 F.R.D. 329 (C.D. Cal. 1997). The district court rejected the representational status arguments, and the case was continued on behalf of four individual Roe plaintiffs. *See* Doe v. Unocal Corp., 395 F.3d at 939, 942–43 (describing the allegations and history of the *Roe* case).

46. The case suffered a partial legal defeat on one particular claim in 1999, however, when the court refused to order Unocal to cease involvement in the pipeline project. Doe v. Unocal Corp., 67 F. Supp. 2d 1140 (C.D. Cal. 1999).

Discovery

For the *Unocal* legal team, with the crucial initial legal hurdle out of the way, the case entered yet another phase of difficult, time-consuming fact-gathering. For the next three years the parties engaged in discovery, following the format of a typical U.S. lawsuit: taking and defending depositions, serving and answering interrogatories, and consulting expert witnesses. Yet, the discovery was anything but typical.

The logistical difficulties that hampered the initial investigation of the case continued to be an ongoing obstacle. Basic communication between lawyers and clients—an important and usually simple part of any lawsuit—was often the most difficult aspect of the case. The plaintiffs and most of ERI's Burma-based field staff were all stateless people who had no passports or identification papers, and no legal status in Thailand. Those who lived in Burma had been displaced from their villages, and were living in makeshift homes and temporary settlements. Because they had no electricity or telephones, communication between lawyers and clients took days or even weeks. ERI's legal workers traveled by bus, truck, and even by foot to where they were living. During the monsoon season, it was sometimes impossible to reach the clients at all, with dirt roads washed out and rivers too high and wide to cross safely. Even those living in marginally better conditions in refugee camps in Thailand had no way to communicate, except in person. Moreover, the camps were under heavy security by the Thai army, and access to the camps by outsiders was extremely limited.

One particularly painful challenge arose out of a communication nightmare that led to the accidental filing of unsigned declarations. In an emergency effort to obtain the signatures before the court ruled the declarations inadmissible, ERI sent fieldworkers into Burma during a military offensive. In the midst of flying bullets, exploding bombs, and victims running in fear, the fieldworkers spent days tracking down clients as they hid in the jungle. Finally, they located all of the plaintiffs and affirmed the information in the original, unsigned documents.

New challenges arose when Unocal's lawyers scheduled depositions of the plaintiffs. It was difficult to communicate with the plaintiffs in their own homes, much less to bring them out of their villages into Thailand for their depositions. The Court ordered the first round of discovery depositions to take place in Bangkok (as opposed to the United States, as Unocal had requested). For this, the plaintiffs had to sneak across borders or leave heavily secured refugee camps and then travel over 200 miles through border and military checkpoints to Thailand's capital. Those who were living in refugee camps had to either account for their absences, or face the prospect of losing their ability to return—they were often subject to daily head counts by Thai authorities. In 1997, during the first round of depositions, a group of six plaintiffs were stopped at a checkpoint, arrested, and held for a week in jail at the Burmese border for "illegal immigration" into Thailand. As though preparing the plaintiffs for the completely alien and intimidating deposition process was not already a stressful enough endeavor, ERI lawyers and field staff were simultaneously engaged in delicate negotiations to secure their clients' release.

The legal team also spent many months negotiating confidentiality agreements to protect the clients against retaliation for their participation in the lawsuit. The lawyers, arguing for their clients' right to proceed anonymously as John and Jane Does, presented significant evidence as to the dangers of perceived or actual criticism of the Burmese regime. Unocal argued that their researchers should be allowed to know, and to reveal the identities of the clients as they conducted factual investigations inside Burma. Perhaps more important than any other administrative issue in the proceedings, the protective order was a "make or break" hurdle for the clients. Had the court allowed Unocal to reveal the plaintiffs' identities to their SLORC counterparts while investigating their claims in Burma, many of the plaintiffs might have been too frightened to proceed. Ultimately, the Court fashioned a complex protective order governing everything from the logistics of the depositions to the treatment of the plaintiffs' testimony to the ways in which Unocal would conduct its own fact-finding inside Burma. The order balanced the plaintiffs' legitimate interests in their personal security with Unocal's equally legitimate interests in being able to examine the truth and accuracy of their allegations.

The increasing costs of the discovery put an additional toll on the legal team. Each of the law offices involved in the case paid some of the mounting bills, while ERI and CCR worked frantically to secure donations and foundation funding. Complex negotiations within the team about who would pay for what added yet another layer of stress to the litigation. Meanwhile, the clients back in Thailand and Burma were struggling for their very survival. Their participation in the lawsuit required that they remain available, both to their own, and to Unocal's lawyers, as well as to the Court, throughout the course of the case. Thus, returning to Burma, where communication with their lawyers was risky and complicated, was not a good option. Likewise, they were reluctant to enter the heavily guarded refugee camps on the border as the Thai military prohibited access to all outsiders except relief organizations. Thus, most of the clients lived in hiding with their families in various temporary situations, unable to work or farm or otherwise earn the resources they would need for their basic survival such as food, shelter, or medicine. Considerations like schooling for their children, which would require more permanent situations, were impossible.

Compounding the challenges associated with just surviving day to day, once the depositions actually began, the lawyers faced new challenges associated with the cross-cultural nature of this litigation. For example, different cultural approaches to issues such as time, dates and distance led to repeated confusion. In its effort to establish that the alleged abuses happened prior to Unocal's contract or outside of the official pipeline area, Unocal grilled the plaintiffs on the details of place and dates. When asked questions like "What date did you work on the helipad," plaintiffs often gave answers such as "during the dry season after the birth of my second child." When pressed on details like a specific month, date, or year, many of the clients who don't use or understand western calendars had difficulty nailing down consistent answers. Such challenges were later addressed with expert testimony from cultural anthropologists who explained that the plaintiffs were not lying or forgetting when their suffering occurred, but rather that they were describing time in a way that was appropriate to their culture.

Cultural taboos were also a hurdle when developing the facts related to the rape and sexual assault claims of Jane Does II and III. Jane Doe II, an elderly woman, alleged at various points in the litigation that she had either been raped or had endured an unsuccessful attempted rape by a soldier guarding the Yadana pipeline. Unocal lawyers pointed to the inconsistency in her testimony in the effort to cast doubt on either her credibility or her memory of what did or, according to them, did not happen to her. After long and delicate discussions with Jane, however, the plaintiffs' lawyers were able to determine that she had, in fact, been raped by the soldiers. She described the rape consistently, in great detail, each time that she told the full story. When she sat in the deposition room, however, with a court reporter typing every word and numerous strangers seated around a formal table, she was at times simply too ashamed to talk about the incident. Shame of this nature is, of course, common to rape survivors of every cultural background; for a Karen woman from Burma, though, the desire for secrecy is compounded by a strict cultural taboo on sex outside of marriage. Although many women have been raped by the Burmese military,[47] often the women feel pressure to keep their ordeal secret.

A Devastating Loss: The Motion for Summary Judgment

After three years of discovery, Unocal filed a motion for summary judgment arguing that the plaintiffs could not prove that the corporation was liable for the abuses that they had suffered. Plaintiffs presented

---

47. *See* BETSY APPLE, SCHOOL FOR RAPE: THE BURMESE MILITARY AND SEXUAL VIOLENCE (EarthRights International 1998); BETSY APPLE & VERONIKA MARTIN, NO SAFE PLACE: BURMA'S ARMY AND THE RAPE OF ETHNIC WOMEN (Refugees International 2003).

extensive evidence of the widespread human rights abuses and Unocal's knowledge of the tactics used by the military government in the course of the joint project. In a ruling on the motion for summary judgment in 2000, the Court held:

> Unocal knew that the military had a record of committing human rights abuses; that the Project hired the military to provide security for the Project, a military that forced villagers to work and entire villages to relocate for the benefit of the Project; that the military, while forcing villagers to work and relocate, committed numerous acts of violence; and ... Unocal knew or should have known that the military did commit, was committing, and would continue to commit these tortious acts.[48]

The Court also concluded, "the evidence does suggest that Unocal knew that forced labor was being utilized and that the Joint Ventures [Unocal and Total] benefited from the practice."[49] Finally, the court recognized that "[t]he violence perpetrated against Plaintiffs is well documented in the deposition testimony filed under seal with the Court."[50]

Despite these strong factual findings, in August of 2000, the federal district court granted Unocal's motion for summary judgment and dismissed the case, holding that Unocal could not be held liable unless it both intended that the military commit abuses and exercised control over the abuses. The Court concluded that plaintiffs had not made this showing. Furthermore, the judge dismissed the state law claims for lack of federal subject matter jurisdiction. The plaintiffs took some comfort from the fact that the Court's decision detailed the evidence of Unocal's complicity in the abuses, thus lending some legitimacy to the plaintiffs' experience. Indeed, the case had already given them a forum in which to detail the abuses committed against them, which was far more than they could have hoped for in Burma. The litigation contributed to the global effort to expose human rights abuses in Burma.

Nevertheless, the case had been dismissed. The young lawyers were devastated. Ka Hsaw Wa was devastated. How could they tell their clients, whose hopes were riding on this one case, that they had lost? The more experienced lawyers tried to console them, pointing out that this lower court loss provided a golden opportunity to appeal the decision, thus potentially setting an even more powerful precedent in the appellate court. This was the best possible case to go to the Ninth Circuit, they said; you cannot make law unless you lose. For the plaintiffs, however, the loss was a vicious blow. They had already faced

---

48. Doe v. Unocal, 110 F. Supp. 2d at 1306.
49. *Id.* at 1310.
50. *Id.* at 1298 n. 3.

hardship, endangering themselves and their families in order to participate in the lawsuit—even if the dismissal were to be reversed on appeal, the setback would nevertheless mean that the case would drag on for several more years.

The Successful Appeal

The legal team responded with a two-pronged strategy. First, they appealed the federal court dismissal with high hopes of success, given the unreasonable standard that the lower court had imposed, as well as its strained reading of the facts presented by the plaintiffs. Second, they re-filed the state claims in California state court. Although Unocal tried to remove those state claims to federal court, the federal district court rejected the maneuver and remanded the case back to state court. The state court litigation continued over the next four years, while the appeal of the federal court dismissal was pending.

As predicted by the legal team, the moral validation of their claims was followed by legal validation. On September 18, 2002, the U.S. Court of Appeals for the Ninth Circuit reversed the district court's dismissal, thereby allowing the lawsuit against Unocal to go forward. A three-judge panel held that the district court was wrong in determining that the plaintiffs had to show that Unocal controlled the Burmese military's actions in order to establish Unocal's liability. The Ninth Circuit also held that the plaintiffs need only demonstrate that Unocal knowingly assisted the military in perpetrating the abuses, not that they intended to assist the abuses. Under this standard, the Court determined that the plaintiffs had presented enough evidence to go to trial. In its reasoning, the Ninth Circuit court made clear that the imposition of aiding and abetting liability on corporations was appropriate, and defined the appropriate legal standard as "knowing practical assistance or encouragement that has a substantial effect on the perpetration of the crime."[51]

Just as important for the plaintiffs, the Ninth Circuit decision lent legitimacy to both their claims and their suffering:

> Unocal's weak protestations notwithstanding, there is little doubt that the record contains substantial evidence creating a material question of fact as to whether forced labor was used in connection with the construction of the pipeline. Numerous witnesses, including

---

51. Doe v. Unocal, 395 F.3d at 947. An aiding and abetting standard of liability for corporations and other non-state actors has been upheld in subsequent ATS cases against corporate defendants. *See, e.g.*, Khulumani v. Barclay Nat. Bank Ltd., 504 F.3d 254 (2d Cir. 2007); Aldana v. Del Monte Fresh Produce, N.A., Inc., 416 F.3d 1242; Cabello v. Fernández–Larios, 402 F.3d 1148. The U.S. standard mirrors well-established international law norms, as reflected in the statutes of the International Criminal Court and the International Criminal Tribunals for Rwanda and the former Yugoslavia.

a number of Plaintiffs, testified that they were forced to clear the right of way for the pipeline and to build helipads for the project before construction of the pipeline began. For instance, John Doe IX testified that he was forced to build a helipad near the pipeline site in 1994 that was then used by Unocal and Total officials who visited the pipeline during its planning stages. Other Plaintiffs and witnesses, including John Doe VII ... described construction of helipads at Eindayaza and Po Pah Pta, both of which were near the pipeline site, were used to ferry Total/Unocal executives and materials to the construction site, and were constructed using the forced labor of local villagers, including Plaintiffs. Other Plaintiffs, such as ... John Does I, VIII, and IX, testified that they were forced to work on building roads leading to the pipeline construction area. Finally, yet other Plaintiffs, such as John Does V and IX, testified that they were required to serve as "pipeline porters"—workers who performed menial tasks such as hauling materials and cleaning the army camps for the soldiers guarding the pipeline construction. These serious allegations create triable questions of fact as to whether the Myanmar Military implemented a policy of forced labor in connection with its work on the pipeline.[52]

[....]

Jane Doe I testified that after her husband, John Doe I, attempted to escape the forced labor program, he was shot at by soldiers, and in retaliation for his attempted escape, that she and her baby were thrown into a fire, resulting in injuries to her and the death of the child. Other witnesses described the summary execution of villagers who refused to participate in the forced labor program, or who grew too weak to work effectively. Several Plaintiffs testified that rapes occurred as part of the forced labor program. For instance, both Jane Does II and III testified that, while conscripted to work on pipeline-related construction projects, they were raped at knife-point by Myanmar soldiers who were members of a battalion that was supervising the work.[53]

Never again could Unocal deny that its project was built with the blood and tears of innocent people. No longer could there be any doubt that Unocal's involvement in Burma was morally reprehensible. The victims' voices had finally been heard. That was an enormous victory for a group of people who had literally risked their lives to tell their stories to the world, and who had been labeled as liars, simpletons and rebel insurgents in the process.

---

52. Doe v. Unocal, 395 F.3d at 952.
53. Id. at 939–40.

Unocal petitioned for rehearing en banc, and in February 2003, the Ninth Circuit decided to rehear the appeal before an eleven-judge panel. In this proceeding, the U.S. Justice Department, joined by the State Department, submitted a brief urging the court to reject *Filártiga* and subsequent ATS cases and to interpret the ATS as a purely jurisdictional statute that did not provide victims with a right to sue.[54] This brief became the template for the Justice Department's argument before the U.S. Supreme Court in *Sosa v. Alvarez–Machain*, the case in which the administration of President George W. Bush and its corporate allies argued for total eradication of twenty-three years of ATS case law.[55]

The Supreme Court's Decision in Sosa v. Alvarez–Machain

For over two decades after the *Filártiga* decision, the Supreme Court repeatedly rejected petitions to review lower court cases applying the ATS to human rights claims. By the time the Court agreed to hear *Sosa* in the fall of 2003, opposition to the modern application of the statute had intensified, led by the Bush administration and by corporations fearful of the *Unocal* precedent. The Ninth Circuit postponed oral arguments in the en banc review of *Unocal*, awaiting the Supreme Court's decision.

On June 29, 2004, the Doe plaintiffs and their lawyers waited in nervous suspense: it was the final day of the Supreme Court term, and *Sosa* was the only remaining undecided case. The result of the *Sosa* case was anxiously anticipated not only by the *Doe v. Unocal* team, but also by plaintiffs, lawyers, and activists—and corporations and politicians—around the world. In bamboo huts in Burma, K Street offices in Washington D.C., oilfields in Nigeria, corporate boardrooms, and the White House, people from all walks of life recognized that the future of two decades of human rights litigation in U.S. courts was at stake.

In a crucial victory for human rights advocates, the Supreme Court held that the ATS permits victims to sue in U.S. courts for the most serious human rights abuses. In *Sosa*, the Court addressed the question of whether the ATS allows federal courts to hear human rights claims without additional authorizing legislation from Congress—the Court answered, "Yes."

The Jane and John Does and their legal allies in *Doe v. Unocal* breathed tremendous sighs of relief upon learning that the *Sosa* decision would permit their lawsuit to continue. For nearly two years, the

---

54. *See* Brief for the United States of America as *Amicus Curiae*, Doe v. Unocal, 403 F.3d 708.

55. *See* Brief for the United States as Respondent Supporting Petitioner, Sosa v. Alvarez–Machain, 542 U.S. 692 (2004) (No. 03–339).

corporate lobby and its allies in the Bush administration had engaged in a crusade to overturn plaintiffs' victory in *Doe v. Unocal*, and managed to stall their ability to enforce their rights in the court of law. The *Sosa* ruling and the ATS renewed their hope that justice delayed would not mean justice denied.

With the Supreme Court's clarification of the ATS as a legitimate tool for human rights enforcement, the Doe plaintiffs and their lawyers were confident that the en banc panel would soon rule in their favor. Meanwhile, as the federal case was bouncing between courts, the Doe plaintiffs and their lawyers continued to litigate the state claims in California state court. In August 2001, Unocal's motion to dismiss the case from state court was rejected,[56] and in June 2002, the case survived Unocal's motion for summary judgment. The California trial court held that the plaintiffs had presented evidence indicating that they could show that Unocal was liable for the military's human rights abuses. The court set a June 2005 date for a jury trial on the plaintiffs' claims of murder, rape, and forced labor.

The Historic Unocal Settlement

The federal en banc appeals court then set a date for a post-*Sosa* oral argument. In late 2004, with the state trial date approaching and the argument in the federal case pending, Unocal for the first time engaged in serious settlement negotiations with the plaintiffs. Both sides agreed to postpone the oral argument while they attempted to reach an agreement. Finally, in March of 2005, Unocal agreed, in a historic settlement, to compensate the plaintiffs and thus end the lawsuit.

Defendants and plaintiffs issued the following statement:

> The parties to several lawsuits related to Unocal's energy investment in the Yadana gas pipeline project in Myanmar/Burma announced today that they have settled their suits. Although the terms are confidential, the settlement will compensate plaintiffs and provide funds enabling plaintiffs and their representatives to develop programs to improve living conditions, health care and education and protect the rights of people from the pipeline region. These initiatives will provide substantial assistance to people who may have suffered hardships in the region. Unocal reaffirms its principle that the company respects human rights in all of its activities and commits to enhance its educational programs to further this princi-

---

[56]. The state court rejected all of Unocal's arguments, including, for example, that the state claims were barred by the earlier decision in the federal cases and that state court resolution of the case would intrude upon the federal government's foreign affairs powers.

ple. Plaintiffs and their representatives reaffirm their commitment to protecting human rights.[57]

The settlement was hailed by the public and the press as "a big win for human rights."[58] Analysts surmised that the deal might "spur better corporate conduct."[59] The business community viewed the settlement as a wake-up call for corporations, a "milestone for human rights."[60] *Business Week* magazine stated, in an editorial, "[t]he fact that Unocal has apparently agreed to cough up such a large sum after adamantly denying responsibility strengthens a major strategy of human rights groups.... "[61] Until the settlement, corporations were able to say with a straight face that no company had ever been forced to pay for its complicity in human rights abuses. Importantly, the agreement put corporations on notice that human rights do, in fact, matter, and that even in remote, closed off countries like Burma, they cannot hide from their legal responsibilities to uphold fundamental human rights. As John Doe IX stated following the settlement: "I don't care about the money. Most of all I wanted the world to know what Unocal did. Now you know."[62]

The business risks associated with complicity in human rights abuses soon became even more evident. Two days after the settlement was announced, Unocal announced that it would be acquired by ChevronTexaco. Although neither corporation publicly admitted that the resolution of the litigation was a sticking point for any deal between the companies, the timing of the announcement certainly indicated that it had been a key factor. Chevron and its shareholders had clearly been concerned about the significant risk that the case posed to the corporation.

The settlement agreement was a difficult step for the plaintiffs and their allies, who worried that they had allowed Unocal to buy its way out of the problem. What is more, the system of justice provided by the U.S. legal system is imperfect to address harms such as those detailed in this case. Nothing, of course, can compensate for rape, torture, and death of family members. As Jane Doe I stated:

---

57. *See* EarthRights Int'l, *Final Settlement Reached in Doe v. Unocal*, 21 March 2005, available at http://www.earthrights.Forg/legalfeature/final_settlement_reached_in_doe_v._unocal.html.

58. Daphne Eviatar, *A Big Win for Human Rights*, THE NATION, May 9, 2005, at 20–22.

59. *Id.*

60. Editorial, BUS. WEEK, Jan. 24, 2005, at 63.

61. *Id.*

62. Interview with John Doe IX, TOTAL DENIAL, *supra* note 10.

> Our village was destroyed. Everything that I had from my parents and my ancestors, I'll never get them back. All my family is left behind. If I think about that, it breaks my heart.[63]

Despite all they had been through, the settlement represented a clear victory for the plaintiffs and the movement to hold corporations accountable for human rights abuses. The John and Jane Does, living in abject poverty and hiding for some ten years, were finally able to begin the process of rebuilding their shattered lives. No longer do they wonder if there will be food for themselves and their families. They have the means to send their children to school. If someone in the family gets sick, they can afford medical treatment. Many have launched small development projects in their villages, funding humanitarian and educational efforts. Most importantly, perhaps, corporate business as usual is no longer able to operate completely outside the reach of human rights laws.

Conclusion

Doe v. Unocal was a first, extraordinarily necessary step towards ending impunity for corporate violators of human rights. Companies like Unocal and Total have now posted the Universal Declaration of Human Rights on their websites. Their representatives speak of involving all of the relevant "stakeholders" in their business decisions, claiming that they are responsible members of the international community. In Burma, though, their business model included torture, forced labor, massive forced relocations and theft. The *Unocal* litigation exposed the shocking reality of corporate involvement in Burma and forced the corporation to provide some compensation to those injured by its actions. However, the final chapters of the Yadana pipeline story have yet to be written. Construction of the pipeline is complete, and gas is flowing—but human rights abuses, while curtailed, will continue as long as the companies use the Burmese army for security.[64]

For the eleven Doe plaintiffs, a modicum of justice has been served. The lawsuit was one step of many on their journey from the war-torn jungles of Burma to the jungles of Thailand, through military checkpoints and Bangkok traffic jams to deposition rooms in Thailand and, through their lawyers, to Los Angeles courtrooms. The settlement represented just one more installment in a story that began over a decade earlier in a remote region of Burma, which today remains one of the most isolated, repressive nations in the world. But, tragically, the plain-

---

63. Interview with Jane Doe I, ABC News Nightline (May 5, 2005).

64. *See* THE HUMAN COST OF EARTH RIGHTS INT'L, ENERGY: CHEVRON'S CONTINUING ROLE IN FINANCING OPPRESSION AND PROFITTING FROM HUMAN RIGHT ABUSES IN MILITARY-RULED BURMA (MYANMAR) (April 2008).

tiffs cannot go home and they cannot openly enjoy their newly acquired wealth. They cannot replace the children and family members that they lost through death and exile and they cannot forget the indignities they suffered or the freedom they lost during forced labor.

The ATS is still the subject of litigation and controversy. The business lobby and the Bush administration have continued to urge the courts to reject the statute completely or to refuse to apply it to corporations—even to those that are alleged to be complicit in genocide.[65]

Why does this case matter? Terms like "corporate accountability," "economic globalization," and "justice" conjure up theoretical frameworks and complicated legal analyses. Cases like *Doe v. Unocal* are, broadly speaking, about the relationship between transnational corporations and local regimes, as well as about what happens when domestic and international laws fail to check global corporate power. More important, however, are the implications of this case for ordinary people. The plaintiffs in *Doe v. Unocal* are representative of countless otherwise unexceptional individuals whose lives, dignity, and homelands have been devastated by corporations. Their lawyers sought to expose the effects of globalization by giving victims a forum in which to recount and redress their losses. The ATS offered this forum, by giving the plaintiffs a chance to tell their stories. The court rulings throughout the course of the litigation lent legitimacy to their experience. Most importantly for the plaintiffs, the case forced those who perpetrated and benefited from its worst abuses to listen. As Ka Hsaw Wa explained:

> [We] helped eleven villagers in the pipeline region to sue Unocal. A U.S. court agreed with what my people have known for a long time—that corporations can commit human rights abuses too. This case is so important because these kinds of atrocities are happening all over the world. In many countries, transnational corporations are involved in earth rights violations.... [Corporations] have so much power to lobby against human rights and environmental protection. With so much power, corporations *could* have a positive impact on the people and the environments in which they live. Unfortunately, not enough companies choose to do the right thing. In Burma, for example, the right thing is to refuse to participate in the kinds of abuses of the pipeline region. Unocal refused to make that choice. So *we* have no choice but to try to make them behave, using every nonviolent tool at our disposal.[66]

---

65. *See, e.g.*, Statement of Interest of the United States of America, Presbyterian Church of Sudan v. Talisman Energy Inc., Civ. No. 01–9882 (S.D.N.Y. Mar. 15, 2005) (arguing that human rights litigation seeking to hold Talisman liable for assisting in genocide and other abuses in Sudan would undermine U.S. foreign policy).

66. Ka Hsaw Wa, *Forward to* Betsy Apple, *Blood on Their Hands: Corporations, Militarization, and the Alien Tort Statute*, 1 SEATTLE J. SOC. JUST. 127, 128–129 (2002).

Part Five
Human Rights in a World at War

*

13

Inspiring and Inadequate: the *Krstić* Genocide Conviction through the Eyes of a Srebrenica Survivor

Doug Ford[*]

When does genocide begin? Mirsada Malagić, a survivor of the Srebrenica genocide, does not know. But she knows when her own world in eastern Bosnia began to unravel. It was the day her plant closed without further notice in April 1992, and the commuter buses inexplicably stopped running, forcing her to walk home. For the first time, she saw Yugoslav National Army units monitoring traffic and was required to pass through a checkpoint of Serb police reserves where a red-faced Serb colleague was embarrassed to ask her for her identification.

Mirsada was born on January 10, 1959 and grew up in Srebrenica municipality[1] in Yugoslavia.[2] Mirsada worked much of her adult life in Potočari, a village next to the town of Srebrenica, both in Srebrenica

---

[*] I am most grateful to Mirsada Malagić and the dignity and patience she shared with me. I thank all the families of the missing I had the privilege to meet over the years. I am indebted to Bosnian colleagues in various agencies who have dedicated years to unraveling the pain and injustice of Srebrenica. I benefitted greatly from colleagues at Physicians for Human Rights, the International Commission for Missing Persons and the International Criminal Tribunal for the former Yugoslavia who shared innumerable insights, especially Mary Ellen Keough, Kathryne Bomberger and Caitriona Palmer. Thanks are due to past and present University of Virginia Law students for valuable research assistance, including: Veronica Hart, Daniel Sullivan, Suzanne Libby, Homin Lee, Elena Sauber, Alice Beauheim, and Alexandre Lamy. Thanks also to Veronica and Dan for writing fine draft sections and Sue for deft editing. Also, I thank Peter Orner and my co-editors.

[1]. Srebrenica is a municipality, similar to a county in the United States, and inside the municipality was the town of Srebrenica, the town of Potočari and a series of surrounding villages and towns. Voljavica was a village in the Bratunac municipality, the municipality neighboring Srebrenica to the north.

[2]. Mirsada Malagić gave approximately twelve hours of interviews in Sarajevo, Bosnia and Herzegovina to the author in January and February 2007 [hereinafter Malagić interviews]. Unless otherwise noted, these interviews are the sources for subsections detailing her story.

municipality. It would also be the pivotal scene of the Srebrenica genocide and would forever mark her great sadness. She and her husband Salko both worked in accounting in the mining company, which extracted zinc and lead in the Srebrenica region. Mirsada, Salko and their three children lived in a house in the village of Voljavica in the vicinity of Srebrenica. Their daily life was simple but exhausting; she and Salko got up early to get the kids to school and get to work. Mirsada rose by 4 a.m., taking her youngest, Adnan, to her aunt's and getting on the bus around 5 a.m. to arrive at 6 a.m. at the company plant in Potočari. Mirsada and Salko both worked because they needed the money, "to build the house and then plan for their children's education." She had gone to high school, but not to university, because her father could not afford it.

Both Serbs and Muslims worked at the mining company where Mirsada had Serb and Muslim friends. They would visit each other on weekends and for special occasions. The local villages were mixed: some like Voljavica were largely Muslim, others more Serb and others more evenly split. Mirsada's experience was one of simple coexistence with Serbs. However, her mother had witnessed massacres during World War II and insisted that Serbs could not be trusted. When Milošević rose to power, Mirsada and her family heard about him and then about the conflict in Croatia. They had a television, but Mirsada never paid much mind to the news and "never cared about politics."

When is there justice? Mirsada does not know the answer to this question either. Yet she quietly explained in a 2007 interview why bringing General Radislav Krstić to justice was vital—she had testified in his trial—despite her sense that very little justice had been obtained. This is the story of the genocide at Srebrenica. It is the story of Mirsada, which is like far too many others of the thousands of survivors. Still, it is her individual story with a particular world lost and her own fragmented, fragile possibilities for the future.

It is also the story of the myriad failed efforts of the international community to forestall atrocities in Bosnia and their culmination in Srebrenica—leading the chief negotiator of the peace deal ending the war to refer to the former Yugoslavia as "the greatest collective security failure of the West since the 1930s."[3] It is also the story of the resulting criminal convictions of some Serb leaders, which has proven to be oxygen both to the survivors and to the international movement for accountability for human rights atrocities. Yet, these convictions and the others from the International Criminal Tribunal for the former Yugoslavia ("ICTY") have revealed that—in the eyes of many victims and experts—

---

3. Richard Holbrooke, *America, A European Power*, FOREIGN AFFAIRS, March–April 1995, at 40.

criminal prosecution is insufficient for a robust sense of justice and for laying the foundation for social renewal following mass atrocity.[4]

Background

The area of the former Republic of Yugoslavia has been a multi-ethnic, multi-religious region for centuries.[5] The three core religious identities roughly correspond with the three dominant ethnicities of the area: Croats, who are predominantly Catholic; Bosniaks, who are predominantly Muslim[6]; and Serbs, who are predominantly Orthodox Christians. The control of the region by the Habsburg and Ottoman Empires and their alteration of the social fabric gave rise to many of the historical grievances perceived today. With the collapse of both empires at the end of World War I, the triumphant nations forged the unification of the Balkan entities into the first Yugoslavia.

In World War II, Yugoslavia was dismembered, leaving three main groups: the Axis protectorate, called the Independent State of Croatia headed by the fascist Ustae (*Nezavisna Drava Hrvatska*, or NDH), the Četnik movement with officers loyal to the Serbian monarchy and the government in exile, and Josip Broz Tito's communist-led Partisan movement uniting Serbs, Croats, Bosnian Muslims, and other ethnic groups. All three groups fought each other as well as their occupiers. Out of this strife, Tito managed to cobble together a state, and the multi-ethnic Partisan movement was raised to the level of myth, with the war cast as struggles against outside fascists. The government punished those who advocated ethnic consciousness and steady economic gains helped Tito suppress ethnic identification.

---

4. For a discussion of the interplay between criminal prosecutions and other forms of transitional justice after mass atrocity, see Ari S. Bassin & Paul Van Zyl, *The Story of Samuel Hinga Norman in Sierra Leone: Can Truth Commissions and Criminal Prosecutions Coexist After Conflict?*, supra Chapter 7.

5. Sources for background include: The Secretary General, *Report of the Secretary General Pursuant to General Assembly Resolution 53/35 The Fall of Srebrenica*, ¶ 12, delivered to the General Assembly, U.N. Doc. A/54/549 (November 15, 1999), available at http://www.un.org/peace/srebrenica.pdf [hereinafter U.N.S.G. Report Fall of Srebrenica]; Ilana Bet–El, *Unimagined Communities: the Power of Memory and the Conflict in the former Yugoslavia*, in MEMORY AND POWER IN POST-WAR EUROPE: STUDIES OF THE PRESENT AND THE PAST 208 (Jan–Warner Müller ed., 2002); SABRINA RAMET, BALKAN BABEL: THE DISINTEGRATION OF YUGOSLAVIA FROM THE DEATH OF TITO TO ETHNIC WAR 10–11 (1996); *Bosnian Timeline 1914–1995*, TIME, available at http://www.time.com/time/daily/bosnia/bosniatimeline.html; S.C. Res. 743, U.N. Doc. S/RES/743 (Feb. 21, 1992), available at http://daccessdds.un.org/doc/RESOLUTION/GEN/NR0/011/02/IMG/NR001102.pdf?OpenElement.

6. Since the ICTY in the *Krstić* cases uses the term Bosnian Muslim and not Bosniak, that is the term used here. There is dispute about the Bosniak ethnicity; see Joshua Project, *Bosniak of Bosnia*, available at http://www.joshuaproject.net/peopctry.php?rop3=101629&rog3=BK.

When he died in 1980 after thirty-five years of rule, Tito left a cumbersome political system that owed too much to his personality and was compounded by economic problems in the 1980s. Into this uneasy setting stepped Slobodan Milošević, a lawyer and communist bureaucrat. Moderate politicians sought reform. Nationalists, in turn, saw opportunity. Milošević began to employ Serbian nationalist rhetoric, summoning specters of long-ago Ottomans and the more recent chaos of World War II, winning support from many dissatisfied Serbs. Alarmed, Slovenia and Croatia began to take steps to safeguard their own national interests, envisioning a future beyond Yugoslavia. Thus, instead of the common Yugoslav identity, ethnic and religious groups began to brand each other as enemies, with violence resulting.

In 1991, Slovenia voted to secede from the Socialist Federal Republic of Yugoslavia. Croatia soon followed suit, and the disintegration of Yugoslavia had begun. Milošević responded by mobilizing the Yugoslav National Army (*Jugoslovenska Narodna Armija*, or "JNA") to stop the breakaway republics, despite the fact that soldiers and officers from those republics overwhelmingly chose their seceding nations over their army and deserted. It took Slovenia only ten days of fighting to gain its independence.

There was limited international response to the rising violence in early 1991. The United States did not respond with any major diplomatic effort, only recognizing the newly declared republics of Slovenia and Croatia. Unfortunately for Croatia, ethnic Serbs comprised some twelve percent of the pre-war population, and the Croats faced the JNA, now a de facto Serb fighting force. The ferocity of the war in Croatia—especially the devastation of Vukovar, a stark scene reminiscent of destroyed cities in World War II—contrasted with the euphoria at the peaceful evolution in most of eastern Europe, symbolized by the crumbling of the Berlin Wall. The war required a response from Europe and, by extension, the international community. The latter half of 1991 saw a spate of United Nations resolutions, including Security Council resolution 743, which established a U.N. Protection Force ("UNPROFOR") to help keep the peace in Croatia and later Bosnia and Herzegovina. U.N. officials hoped the insertion of the UNPROFOR Force would bring some order to the tumult that threatened to rip apart the Balkans. In another resolution in September 1991, the Security Council enacted a general arms embargo on the former Yugoslavia. This embargo did little to reduce violence and had the unfortunate result of crystallizing the inequality of military power between, on one side, the pre-existing strength of the JNA—and the Bosnian Serb Army formed from it—and on the other side, the weak, new Bosnian government army ("BiH Army").

* * *

Srebrenica was an eastern Bosnian municipality of roughly 37,000 residents about ten miles from the Serbian border. Prior to the war, Srebrenica had been an ordinary municipality, where a Muslim majority lived peaceably alongside their Serb neighbors.[7]

In the shadow of the war in Croatia and rising tension between Bosnian Muslims and Serbs, Mirsada's Serb friends were saying to her that if there was a vote for independence, there would be war. But, "I didn't know why they would say that," she said in 2007. The initial divisions between ethnic groups were most visible to Mirsada at work. She was the first one to arrive in her part of the office in the morning. She would prepare the coffee for Serbs and Muslims, and then everybody would have coffee together. But in the months before the war Serbs and Muslims began to drink coffee in separate groups and Serb friends would not sit with her and share coffee. Also, a number of Serb employees, not Muslims, in a relatively stable workforce, were leaving the company, taking two years of severance pay and going to Serbia in Yugoslavia. Now, she says, "I refused to understand" what was happening then.

Bosnia Ignites

Bosnia observed with alarm the dissolution of Yugoslavia and the vicious war in Croatia. As the situation unraveled, political parties coalesced around different leaders and ideologies. Alija Izetbegović's Party of Democratic Action (SDA in the local language) was distinctly Muslim in character; with Bosnian Muslims making up the largest ethnic group in Bosnia, it had control of the government. It led support for a declaration of sovereignty, a precursor to independence, issued in late 1991.[8] Radovan Karadžić's Serbian Democratic Party (SDS in the

---

7. Prosecutor v. Krstić, Case No. ICTY 98-33-T, Trial Judgment, ¶ 11, 2 August, 2001, citing U.N.S.G. Report Fall of Srebrenica, *supra* note 5, at ¶ 33.

8. Sources for *Bosnia Ignites* include: Prosecutor v. Krstić, Case No. ICTY–98–33–A, Appeal Judgment, ¶ 15, 19 April, 2004); Prosecutor v. Krajišnik, Case No. ICTY–00–39–T, Trial Judgment, ¶ 104, ¶¶ 792, 794, 805, 809, 810, 813, 817, 839, 849, 1000, 1034, 1090, 1126, Case Information Sheet, 27 September 2006, *available at* http://www.un.org/icty/krajisnik/trialc/judgement/kra-jud060927e.pdf. From 18 March 1992 onwards, there was an attack directed against the Bosnian–Muslim and Bosnian–Croat civilian population. Persecution against Bosnian Muslims and Bosnian Croats as a crime against humanity was committed in all thirty-five indictment municipalities, including Bratunac municipality where Mirsada's village of Voljavica was located, with extermination or at least murder and forcible transfer as crimes against humanity committed in most of these municipalities; Prosecutor v. Deronjić, Case No. IT–02–61–PT, Plea Agreement and Factual Basis (29, Sept. 2003) *available at* http://www.un.org/icty/deronjic/trialc/plea/facts–030923–e.htm (*Deronjić* describes the attack on the village of Glogova, like Voljavica, a predominantly Muslim village in Bratunac Municipality, where the attack and persecutions were a precursor to a similar attack on Voljavica); SAMANTHA POWER, A PROBLEM FROM HELL: AMERICA IN THE AGE OF GENOCIDE 248–249 (2002); RICHARD HOLBROOKE, TO END A WAR 130–131, 135 (1998); Holbrooke *supra* note 3, at 34; CHUCK SUDETIC, BLOOD AND VENGEANCE 149 (1998); Malagić interviews.

local language) was Serb to the point of excluding other ethnicities. In late October 1991, ethnic Serbs in Bosnia held a referendum in which they overwhelmingly voted to become a part of Serbia and Montenegro and the SDS began planning shadow military and political structures.

Diplomats from Western countries had advised leaders from Bosnia to hold a referendum on independence. Ninety-nine percent of voters chose secession in the vote in early March 1992. Almost all Bosnian Serbs abstained from the vote, following the lead of the SDS. Nevertheless, the European Community and the United States gave diplomatic recognition to the new, independent Bosnia and Herzegovina [Bosnia] under the leadership of Izetbegović and SDA. Many diplomats and U.S. State Department officials hoped that this recognition would serve as a bulwark against reactive military measures from Milošević, who backed his Serb brethren in Bosnia.[9] Following a similar logic, the agreement that halted open war in Croatia had headquartered the U.N. monitoring force UNPROFOR in Sarajevo, reasoning the city was neutral to Croats and Serbs and at the same time placed a stabilizing U.N. military presence in Bosnia.

However, within days of the referendum, Serbs in Bosnia defied the central government in Sarajevo and the U.S. and Europeans, erecting a parallel government, Republika Srpska, led by the SDS. Local Bosnian Serb officials began to assert control of local governments backed by the JNA. They began ethnic cleansing, and, although varying from town to town, the campaign evolved rapidly into mass atrocities. Bosnian Serbs began rounding up Muslim and Croat intellectuals, professionals and musicians, beating them and often "disappearing" them, with later evidence showing their execution. Bosnian Serbs also began a pattern of destruction of Muslim and Croat homes as well as their cultural and religious sites, seeking to expunge the signs of their presence in Republika Srpska. The campaign's reliance on local Bosnian Serb officials and plethora of militias, in addition to the JNA, gave the early days a chaotic quality, especially for the victims, with random acts of particular brutality. In conjunction with the campaign of terror, Bosnian Serb officials, usually SDS officials in conjunction with Serb leaders in local government, made "requests" for roundups of Croats and Muslims for detention and/or expulsion to other parts of Bosnia or Croatia. Muslims and Croats were forced to comply with these, especially if they had no place to flee. Consequently, Bosnian Serb military and political officials expelled hundreds of thousands of people from their homes and pushed them to other parts of Bosnia or to Croatia.

Srebrenica was a focal point of the bitterly contested struggle for domination of Bosnia. As part of their ethnic cleansing campaign in

---

9. POWER, *supra* note 8, at 248–249.

March and April 1992, Serb paramilitaries and JNA units took control of Srebrenica, Bratunac and many other villages and municipalities in the area. However, Srebrenica broke apart into distinctly partisan sides, and the police forces splintered into Serb and Muslim factions. Whereas there was little organized resistance fighting the Serbs in Bratunac, there was a force of Muslim fighters led by commander Naser Orić in Srebrenica. In May, they seized much of the municipality.

* * *

After Mirsada walked home on her last day of work in April 1992, the uncertainty ratcheted up into terror. Mirsada described the detention and disappearance of prominent residents in Voljavica, demands for weapons, and the looting of houses. Some Muslim miners were called back to the local mine, but learned from a Serb that there was a plan to massacre them. Serb officials came to Mirsada's home and said her husband had a legal obligation to return to his job at the same mining company. He, like the other miners, went into hiding. Their family began to sleep with neighbors up on the outer slopes of the village away from the village center. She could speak by telephone with her two brothers in Potočari and they urged her and the children, Elvir, Admir and Adnan, to leave. But where to go, Mirsada asked. Her brothers had sent their own families out on a bus, but neither they nor anybody else knew where, exactly, the bus was going.

Then the phones went dead. They learned of Serb executions of Muslim civilians. Mirsada and her family saw villages, predominantly Muslim, like theirs, in flames on the hills. On May 12, the local political leader, a Serb from the neighboring mixed village, came and told everybody to surrender the next day in the schoolyard. They would be taken somewhere, maybe Tuzla, a city known for its mixed ethnic population and tolerance that stayed under Bosnian Muslim control throughout the war. People had no clear rationale for deciding what to do. Mirsada wondered why they had to surrender, as they were neither criminals nor soldiers.

She and Salko wanted to keep the family together. Some families did go to the schoolyard and some families sent only the women and children, with the men staying in the hills. On May 13, Mirsada and her family along with about 100 neighbors decided to walk through the forest up the mountains to Muslim-dominated villages that lay between them and Srebrenica. Though fellow Muslims, the villagers wanted the refugees to move on. They feared their presence would draw attack, an example of times when Bosnians would be forced to choose survival over solidarity. The moment Mirsada and her family had looked back at the house for the last time, she did not feel too bad; she thought it would not be long until they returned. But some ten days later when they descended into the deep valley holding Srebrenica after learning the Muslims controlled it, she saw the devastation from just the first days of the war and felt isolated and violated. Would they ever return? She was angry with herself for not heeding the call to women and children to surrender in the schoolyard and be expelled.

That sense of violation would not be legally vindicated until years later by the ICTY, when, for example, in the *Krajišnik* judgment of 2006, the Court found that the systematic ethnic cleansing in her home municipality and elsewhere constituted persecution and other crimes against humanity.[10]

War, Ethnic Cleansing and International Responses

The Bosnian Serbs' ethnic cleansing campaign drove out swaths of Croats and Muslims from areas they claimed as Serb territory. According to UN reports, ethnic cleansing meant "rendering an area ethnically homogeneous by using force or intimidation to remove persons of given groups from the area."[11] The phrase had a chillingly antiseptic undertone, and served to describe an entire spectrum of methods used to affect the goal of homogeneity, ranging from prejudicial hiring methods to rape and massacres. It was journalistic evidence (not governmental or transnational action) that brought the international public's attention to the crimes and atrocities ravaging Bosnia, especially the Bosnian Serb concentration camps reminiscent of Nazi times, and pushed governments and international organizations to start a peace process.

Throughout the conflict there were multiple international efforts to achieve both ceasefires and a lasting peace, such as the London Conference in August 1992.[12] The conference and its successive efforts, such as the so-called Contact Group, represented a combined effort by the European Community and the United Nations. It initially presented the position that, due to the inextricable linkages between the three principal constituent ethnicities of the former Yugoslavia, there could be no solution that attempted to forge ethnically homogeneous States. This position proceeded from the stance that any effort to create ethnic homogeneity and coherent boundaries would involve enforced population transfer. These efforts met with varying levels of failure.

---

10. Krajišnik, Case No. ICTY–00–39–T; *see* note 8 for more details.

11. Sources for para. include: U.N. Comm'n of Experts Final Report [U.N. Comm'n of Experts Report] (S/1994/674), Part III to IV.D., *available at* http://www.ess.uwe.ac.uk/comexpert/III–IV_D.htm#III.B; Roy Gutman, A Witness to Genocide: The 1993 Pulitzer Prize-Winning Dispatches on the "Ethnic Cleansing" of Bosnia (1993).

12. Sources for para. include: U.N.S.G. Report Fall of Srebrenica, *supra* note 5, at ¶¶ 29–30, 153.

After the first months, the international community did not lack public information on ethnic cleansing and related atrocities.[13] In 1992 the U.N. Security Council established a Special Rapporteur on Human Rights for the Territory of the former Yugoslavia, naming Tadeusz Mazowiecki, a former Polish Prime Minister, to the post. Mazowiecki's reports of widespread abuses were a primary catalyst in the Security Council's creation of the United Nations Commission of Experts established pursuant to Security Council Resolution 780 (1992) to investigate violations of international humanitarian law in the former Yugoslavia. Hampered by a shortage of funds, the Commission still carried out a series of some thirty investigatory missions and rigorously demonstrated widespread atrocities. Although none of the three belligerent groups, Bosnian Muslims, Croats and Serbs, were innocent of human rights abuses, the Bosnian Muslims and to a lesser extent the Croats were the major victims. In February 1993, the Commission recommended an international tribunal. The U.N. Security Council heeded this recommendation, establishing the International Criminal Tribunal for the former Yugoslavia [ICTY] in May 1993.

Among the international efforts to salvage a mixed yet united Bosnia, and characteristic of their general ineffectiveness, was the Vance–Owen peace plan, finalized in early 1993.[14] The plan was designed to reflect the areas in which the three communities had lived before the conflict. The design yielded a map effectively fragmenting each community and would have ended any possibility of Serbian secession from Bosnia. It required the Republika Srpska and its Army (essentially the JNA in Bosnia had simply switched uniforms into the RS Army) to cede over one-third of the land they held at that time—a concession strongly opposed by Serbs—and would have provided for the return of hundreds of thousands of forcibly removed Bosnian Muslims to their homes. Yet, it also would have left the Republika Srpska in control of 43% of the land area in Bosnia. This would have meant an internationally-sanctioned violent land grab unpalatable to the Bosnian government—dominated by Bosnian Muslims—which believed it had scrupulously followed the international community's requirements for independence. Thus, it was op-

---

13. Sources for para. include: Tadeusz Mazowiecki, *Report on the Situation of Human Rights in the Territory of the former Yugoslavia*, U.N. Doc. A/48/92–S/25341 (Feb. 10, 1993); TADEUSZ MAZOWIECKI, THE MAZOWIECKI REPORTS (Michael Sells ed., Haverford College), *available at* http://www.haverford.edu/relg/sells/reports/mazowiecki.html; S.C. Res. 780, ¶ 2, U.N. Doc. S/RES/780 (October 6, 1992); U.N. Comm'n of Experts Report (S/1994/674), Part III to IV.D, *supra* note 11; S.C. Res. 827, ¶ 2, U.N. Doc. S/RES/827 (May 25, 1993).

14. Sources for para. include: S.C. Res. 827, ¶ 2, U.N. Doc. S/RES/827 (May 25, 1993); Chuck Sudetic, *Leader of Bosnia Denounces New Allied Plan to Limit Fighting*, N.Y. TIMES, May 24, 1993, *available at* http://query.nytimes.com/gst/fullpage.html?res=9F0CEEDD1E3 DF937A15756C0A965958260&sec=&spon=&pagewanted=all [hereinafter Sudetic, *Leader Denounces*]; U.N.S.G. Report Fall of Srebrenica, *supra* note 5, at ¶ 41.

posed by both sides, despite international arm-twisting. Meanwhile, the war continued and the situation on the ground in Bosnia deteriorated throughout the fall of 1992 and into 1993, with the U.N. Security Council adopting forty-seven resolutions on the conflicts in the former Yugoslavia and most of those specifically on Bosnia.

After seizing Srebrenica, the ragtag force under commander Naser Orić, a unit of the BiH Army, sought to expand the enclave, with Orić's unit and the Srpska forces trading raids and counter-raids in and around Srebrenica in 1992.[15] Orić's forces retained Srebrenica and initially expanded the area they controlled, while other towns in the region fell to the Serbs. Orić became a hero to Muslims and was despised by Serbs. Orić's forces were not above reproach, according to the U.N., as their actions included terrorizing Serb civilians. Such actions led, years later, to Orić's indictment, conviction and reversal on appeal at the ICTY.

* * *

Mirsada and her family's existence in 1992 became a struggle for food, shelter and safety from shooting and violence. They stayed in the Srebrenica apartment of a colleague, but they brought their simple peacetime human values with them and felt uncomfortable in someone else's property. They moved that summer into the home of one of Mirsada's brothers in Potočari. There was practically nothing to eat and the constant shelling made it impossible to tend even a garden to grow food. However, the family had succeeded in planting back in Voljavica. The people of the enclave organized groups to scout for food, slipping through the Serb lines and returning to home villages to gather any food left in homes or growing in gardens. However, homes were often booby-trapped. Mirsada found out her house had been looted.

Her children were confined mainly to her brother's house. Her main goal was to provide each child one slice of bread. The oldest, Elvir, helped scouting locally at night for food. The middle child, Admir, would fetch water under cover of the morning fog. Adnan was too little to really help. The kids were mad because they were practically the only kids there; they wanted to know why they had not been sent away. Mirsada tried to explain they wanted all the family to be together. Her brother's home was hit several times by shelling and the family returned to Srebrenica late in the year, living in a room that would eventually hold twenty-one people. In the winter, in the snow, they were hunting for edible leaves and grinding corn cobs to make "flour." Mirsada would go days without food, giving what she had to the children.

---

15. Sources for para. include: U.N.S.G. Report Fall of Srebrenica, *supra* note 5, at ¶¶ 35–37; Sudetic, *Leader Denounces, supra* note 14; *Krstić*, Case No. ICTY–98–33–T at ¶ 14; Prosecutor v. Naser Orić, Case No. ICTY–03–68–A, Appeal Judgment (July 3, 2008).

"We were dying starving," Mirsada said. So she and a mass of civilians chose to risk a bullet rather than starve and, unarmed, they accompanied Orić's forces for an attack on Kravica. She emphasized that the attack on Kravica was an act of desperation for food. It was timed for the Orthodox Christmas of January 1993, when the Serbs would have food in their homes. She trudged back with bacon, when as Muslims, they otherwise would not eat pork. A car battery provided infrequent radio broadcasts and thus they had little news and no real knowledge of any of the early international initiatives in 1992. That winter they felt forgotten.

The Making and Reality of a U.N. Safe Area

The Srpska Army successfully counter-attacked in the winter of 1992–1993, taking back territory Orić's forces had gained, and squeezing the Srebrenica enclave.[16] Muslim refugees converged on Srebrenica, almost doubling its population and draining what emergency supplies the municipality had, leaving the people desperate. The situation in March of 1993 was sufficiently dire to warrant a fact-finding expedition from the commander of the U.N. Protection Force (UNPROFOR), General Philippe Morillon of France. His visit to Srebrenica was not pleasant. Terrified townspeople initially did not allow Morillon to leave the enclave, and before finally leaving he addressed a public gathering of Srebrenica residents. Vowing he would never abandon them, Morillon pledged U.N. protection for the enclave.

When Morillon made this extemporaneous pledge, the U.N. had not decided how to confront the Srspka Army's tightening siege.[17] Several international governments and high-ranking U.N. officers were reportedly angered by Morillon's stand. After intense debate about the wisdom and viability of safe areas and of vigorous intervention, the Security Council enacted Resolution 819 on April 16, 1993 demanding "that all parties and others concerned treat Srebrenica and its surroundings as a safe area which should be free from any armed attack or any other hostile act."[18] The Security Council ostensibly gave UNPROFOR the power to use military force. Yet Resolution 819's ambiguity and

---

16. Sources for para. include: Malagić interviews; John F. Burns, *U.N. General to Stay in Bosnian Town*, N.Y. TIMES, Mar. 17, 1993, *available at* http://query.nytimes.com/gst/fullpage.html?res=9F0CE2D81639F934A25750C0A965958260; John F. Burns, *Aid Trucks Arrive in a Bosnian Town after Serbs Yield*, N.Y. TIMES, Mar. 20, 1993, *available at* http://query.nytimes.com/gst/fullpage.html?res=9F0CE4D71F3FF933A15750C0A965958260.

17. Sources for para. include: Burns, *supra* note 16; U.N.S.G. Report Fall of Srebrenica, *supra* note 5, at ¶¶ 56, 64, 105, 226.

18. S.C. Res. 819, U.N. Doc. S/RES/819, 16 April,, 1993, *available at* http://daccessdds.un.org/doc/UNDOC/GEN/N93/221/90/IMG/N9322190.pdf?OpenElement.

lack of funding led the U.N. Secretariat to advise the UNPROFOR force commander that Resolution 819 created "no military obligations for UNPROFOR to establish or protect such a safe area,"[19] nor should demilitarization be pursued with undue zeal. Even after a further disarmament was negotiated for Srebrenica, neither the Srpska Army nor the BiH Army fully complied with disarmament or Resolution 819's safe area designation. Nevertheless, mid–1993 to early 1995 saw relative stability in Srebrenica and UNPROFOR maintained an average presence of two to three infantry companies with about 600 deployed there in the spring of 1995.

In contrast, conflict continued across much of Bosnia, including the Croat vs. Muslim mini-war which ended in the Croat–Muslim Federation uniting against the Bosnian Serbs.[20] The U.N. Security Council passed Resolution 836, which gave UNPROFOR authority to use armed force, "in self-defence," against bombardment or against obstruction of humanitarian convoys and authorized NATO bombing "to deter" attacks. Nevertheless, the Srpska Army continued to bomb safe areas. For example, until August 1995, Srpska Army shells landed in the Sarajevo safe area at the rate of 1000 per day, usually in civilian areas and seldom for military purpose, with some lulls. In one meeting, the representative of Bosnia argued to the Council that the continuing resolutions were little more than "diplomatic cover... to mitigate the need for more resolute and comprehensive measures."[21]

At the same time, peace plans came and went.[22] Although the Muslim-dominated Bosnian government had accepted the Vance–Owen plan, it was rejected by the Republika Srpska Assembly in May 1993. Another peace process convened in 1993 where Serb officials proposed exchanging Srebrenica and other enclaves for Serb held territory around Sarajevo. The Bosnian government rejected this plan. The Contact Group developed a peace plan in 1994 that was rejected by the Bosnian Serbs.

* * *

In the winter of 1993, Mirsada saw that Srpska Army attacks had pushed refugees into Srebrenica and every school, every building and every basement was full. People were living in the streets. When the first

---

19. U.N.S.G. Report Fall of Srebrenica, supra note 5, at ¶ 62.

20. Sources for para. include: S.C. Res. 836, ¶ 5, U.N. Doc. S/RES/836 (June 4, 1993); U.N.S.G. Report Fall of Srebrenica, supra note 5, at ¶ 93.

21. U.N.S.G. Report Fall of Srebrenica, supra note 5, at ¶ 81.

22. See generally for this paragraph, Sudetic, Leader Denounces, supra note 14; U.N.S.G. Report Fall of Srebrenica, supra note 5, at ¶¶ 31–32, 114–116, 153–155; Yugoslavia, HUMAN RIGHTS WATCH, 2006, available at http://www.hrw.org/reports/1994/WR94/Helsinki–25.htm.

convoy of UNHCR[23] entered Srebrenica that winter, "tears came to my eyes, it meant people remembered us." When Morillon arrived, a spontaneous mass of people surrounded him; they wanted help. The word amongst the refugees was that Morillon would leave and Srpska Army General Ratko Mladić would come in.[24] They were determined not to be forgotten. Mirsada and her sister rotated turns in the protest. Finally, Morillon addressed the crowd from the post office saying he was not running away; they would be protected; Mladić would not come into Srebrenica; a U.N. battalion would arrive; and humanitarian aid would get in.

The other promise made was that everybody who wanted to could leave with the aid convoys. It was chaotic and many left. Although Mirsada wanted to leave, she was sick, the men were not leaving—fearing that Serbs would pull them off at checkpoints—and she decided not to go because she couldn't go with her family. Her husband and brothers left the decision to her. "I just wanted us to go through that chaos together," she said.

Mirsada didn't know why the evacuations stopped. But life improved and somewhat "normalized." With regular humanitarian aid, they were not hungry. The U.N. battalion arrived. The shelling stopped. They started to cultivate the land. The U.N. restarted periodic water supply. Though her sons had to erase paper and reuse it, a school opened. Some washing machine motors were rigged to generate power and a loudspeaker broadcast the radio news. Communications through radio amateurs improved and people could finally find out about their family outside the enclave. Occasionally the BiH Army walked aid and military supplies in through Serb lines.

While living under that siege, Mirsada basically knew nothing of the atrocity documentation, of Mazowiecki, the U.N. Commission of Inquiry, the ICTY or its early investigations. Mirsada knew that the U.N. had declared Srebrenica a safe area. They would not face death under this designation, she believed at the time. The atrocities of the first year of the war would not happen again. There would be some negotiation. She remembered some Srebrenica representatives went to Sarajevo for a peace consultation in the second half of 1993, where a proposal for swapping territory around Sarajevo for Srebrenica was under consideration. The enclave was divided. She did not remember whether the Bosnian Muslims decided to support the plan or not, but she did know a peace agreement did not result. She was not aware of the specifics of other peace proposals, such as Vance–Owen, only that there were re-

---

23. UNHCR is the United Nations High Commission for Refugees.

24. Mladić was the former JNA officer who became the General leading the Republika Srpska Army throughout much of the war, including the genocide at Srebrenica.

peated negotiations and always a reason why they failed. Given all that the Serbs had done to normal people like them, she felt then and still feels now, not enough pressure and penalty was placed on the Serb side in these negotiations.

Instability and Tension

Despite relative quiet across Bosnia in late 1994, in Srebrenica, instability had crept in under the calm.[25] The safe areas, including Srebrenica, suffered from the unwillingness of Security Council members to implement Resolution 836 with their own forces and suffered from the U.N.'s reluctance to actually call for NATO bombing. The Srpska Army slowly tightened their chokehold on humanitarian convoys and UNPROFOR reinforcements into Srebrenica. Heightened tension and hunger resulted. Spats between locals and UNPROFOR troops became more common. In one instance, members of the UNPROFOR Dutch battalion were taken hostage by local BiH Army forces over a disputed patrol area.

By the time the Secretary–General gave his report to the Security Council on May 30, 1995, crisis reigned across Bosnia.[26] More than 400 U.N. personnel had been taken hostage by the Srpska Army in retaliation when UNPROFOR had finally called in airstrikes after a Srpska Army attack. The warring sides were gearing themselves up for major offensives. Yet the Secretary–General's report advocated against the use of force by international forces, and again urged de-militarization of the safe areas as a means of attaining peace. Nevertheless, UNPROFOR and the major troop contributors France and the United Kingdom began the process of establishing a rapid reaction force. Although the Serbs released the U.N. hostages and U.N. leaders asserted there was no deal made for their release, there was public confusion about whether hostages were released in return for suspending air strikes.

* * *

Mirsada recalled that in 1995 humanitarian aid diminished. Tension rose amongst the community and with the U.N. Yet, they never thought that they would face death, or the chaos and privation of early 1993 before Morillon arrived. They believed NATO would bomb if required.

Yet, when they learned of the Srpska Army holding U.N. hostages, Mirsada began to question what the U.N. would or wouldn't do. In addition, the Bosnian government issued a "strange" call for Orić and other leading officers to leave the enclave for unspecified consultations.

---

25. Sources for para. include: U.N.S.G. Report Fall of Srebrenica, *supra* note 5, at ¶¶ 103, 163, 178–180.

26. Sources for para. include: U.N.S.G. Report Fall of Srebrenica, *supra* note 5, at ¶¶ 190, 213; The Secretary–General, *Report on Bosnia and Herzegovina*, ¶ 47, *delivered* to the U.N.S.C., U.N. Doc. S/1995/444 (May 30, 1995).

Combined with the signs of U.N. weakness, Mirsada was worried. She and others had felt reassured when Orić was present. He didn't sit in an office, but he walked among the people and the front lines. With the departure of Orić and the other officers, she felt deserted.[27]

Attack and Atrocity

In March 1995, Republika Srpska President Karadžić secretly issued an order to "create an unbearable situation of total insecurity with no hope of further survival or life"[28] in Srebrenica, leading the army to plan an attack. On July 6, the Srpska Army rolled in and encountered little resistance from the BiH Army unit or U.N. forces, taking Srebrenica town on July 11. Then it planned the expulsion, designing the shelling of Srebrenica on July 10–11, 1995 to terrorize and push the civilian population toward Potočari. The civilians were not given any choice; the choice was to leave or die. An intercepted conversation found Mladić saying, "They've all capitulated and surrendered and we'll evacuate them all—those who want to and those who don't want to."

Beginning on July 12, 1995, the civilians in Potočari were subjected to a terror campaign comprised of threats, insults, looting and burning of nearby houses, beatings, rapes, and murders. The men were then isolated from the general population, with evidence of multiple executions taking place shortly thereafter. Those men who were spared in Potočari were later mingled in Bratunac with men captured from the "column" in the woods. They were held in an abandoned warehouse, an old school, and in trucks and buses. Most were slaughtered.

The Srpska military forces' take-over of Srebrenica was followed by the planned execution of Bosnian Muslim men, euphemistically labeled "military-aged"—a group that actually included early teenage boys and elderly men in their 60s. Overwhelming evidence showed the Srpska forces executed 7,000–8,000 Bosnian Muslim men in July 1995. After these executions and initial burials, Bosnian Serb officials had machines gruesomely re-excavate the graves and dump the bodies into other mass graves.

* * *

The collapse of Muslim and U.N. defenses forced Mirsada and her family into flight. Worse than in 1992, they had to separate. Srebrenica's

---

27. Some have alleged a deal took place between the Bosnian government and Serb officials brokering an exchange of territory around Sarajevo for Srebrenica, but the allegation remains "hotly contested," and unproven; *see* Krstić, Case No. ICTY 98–33–T at ¶ 35.

28. Sources for *Attack and Atrocity* include: Krstić, Case No. ICTY 98–33–T, at ¶¶ 28–35, 52–53, 58, 66–67, 120, 125, 147, 150, 425–428; ¶ 28 for Karadžić quote; ¶ 147, for the Mladić quote.

political and military leaders had decided on a desperate plan for the men to walk out of the enclave through Srpska territory. They would try to reach Bosnian government territory, with the soldiers heading a narrow column followed by the civilians. Given the years of Serb atrocities, only the oldest and youngest males stayed behind with the women. Amidst regularly exploding shells, it was a tense and chaotic parting by the long-closed gas station that Tuesday, July 11. Salko, their two older sons and Mirsada's brother left. Elvir was about twenty-one years old. Admir was only fifteen, but well developed so they were afraid that the Serb soldiers would not let him pass to wherever the women, children and elderly were going to end up. The men were worried about her—Mirsada was pregnant. But the U.N. soldiers said NATO would be bombing, so it was safe to leave. Within minutes the men were gone, and a grenade exploded, wounding Mirsada in the collarbone and leaving her thinking Adnan, age eleven, had been killed. Luckily her injury was minor and Adnan was okay.

She, Adnan, her father-in-law and thousands of others walked under a rain of shells the four or five kilometers to Potočari. At one point, a truck moved through the crowd and she could see Elvir and a friend. He saw her and smiled and waved. But what was he doing if he was supposed to be with his father and family walking out through the forest? She learned these trucks were transporting wounded men to the U.N. base. She figured he was safe in the U.N. compound. She never saw him again.

Mirsada was surprised and worried that she, Adnan and her father-in-law were not let into the U.N. base, because the word was that people inside were being registered and thus protected. Most people didn't get into the U.N. compound and were sleeping in the open or, like them, in some corner of one of the buildings in the area. Though she, Adnan and her father-in-law spent Tuesday night in the nearby zinc factory, she felt like the U.N. was still protecting them. But, already from the behavior of the soldiers, she was worried that the U.N. wasn't going to help. She heard Mladić address the crowd saying they would be evacuated, which brought relief and applause from many in the crowd. Yet, Wednesday descended into palpable terror. She realized the U.N. couldn't protect them when she saw one U.N. soldier tied up by Serb soldiers and later, Serb soldiers dressed in U.N. uniforms. Men and some young women were taken away, some who she knew were taken to a nearby house, and there were horrible screams. She never heard from them again. Some people were so terrified, they hung themselves.

On Wednesday and Thursday, she exchanged looks with several local armed Serbs, including a Serb policeman whom she had considered a friend. They didn't acknowledge her. On Thursday, they were led to buses. "All of the men, my father-in-law and a number of my neighbours whose names I can tell you, were being put aside, on the left-hand side from us."[29] Most terrible, a man she knew was pulled aside, with his baby in his arms. The Serb soldiers made him give the baby away to a woman who happened to be boarding the bus; the white fear on his face haunts her to this day. Neither her father-in-law, this man nor other men she knew who were separated have ever appeared again.

On the buses, they passed columns of men. She recognized several men and realized they were from Srebrenica. She saw a large crowd of men in a meadow. She saw men dead along the road. Mirsada and those on the buses were taken to the line between Bosnian government and Republika Srpska territory, where they walked across to Bosnian territory. There they met U.N., Red Cross and other officials and were taken to a military base near Tuzla. A sister-in-law met her there and took her to a town nearby.

Aftermath and Peace

A tumultuous series of events unfolded after the Srebrenica tragedy.[30] The U.S. became fully engaged in the crisis. A rearmed Croatia mounted Operation Storm and the Serb separatist state in Croatia collapsed within days. Bosnian and Croatian forces linked up and pressed on against Republika Srpska territory. The head of the Srebrenica column had successfully fought its way to government territory, but thousands did not make it. Reports from the U.N., journalists, and U.S. satellite photographs indicated possible massacres of the men from Srebrenica. The Serbs denied a massacre. But neither the U.N. or Red Cross[31] was able to visit any location revealing prisoners or missing men from Srebrenica.

In late July 1995, the ICTY issued its indictment of Republika Srpska President Radovan Karadžić and General Ratko Mladić, for genocide across Bosnia and other crimes (not for events in Srebrenica).[32] Many hailed the investigation and courage of the Prosecutor, Justice Richard Goldstone, in issuing the indictment. However, some U.S. diplomats were upset and feared it would jeopardize a peace agreement, an ironic turn since arguably the United States had used its support of the

---

29. Krstić, Case No. ICTY 98–33–T at ¶ 53.

30. Sources for para. include: U.N.S.G. Report Fall of Srebrenica, *supra* note 5, at ¶¶ 85, 88–90, 93–94.

31. When referring to the Red Cross in this chapter, it is the International Committee of the Red Cross.

32. Sources for para. include: Prosecutor v. Radovan Karadžić, Ratko Mladić, Case No. IT–95–5–I, Initial Indictment (July 24, 1995), *available at* http://www.un.org/icty/indictment/english/kar-ii950724e.htm; John Cerone, *Dynamic Equilibrium: The Evolution of US Attitudes Toward International Criminal Courts and Tribunals*, 18 Eur. J. Int'l L. 277, 290 (April 2007).

ICTY as a cover for the fact it would not put troops on the ground like the Europeans, or otherwise act to prevent atrocities.

In the aftermath of the Srpska Army mortaring of a Sarajevo marketplace that killed thirty-seven civilians—the site of a previous massacre in 1994—the U.N. called in NATO airstrikes and the heavy guns of the rapid reaction force.[33] This began Operation Deliberate Force, which destroyed Serb weapons across much of Bosnia over about three weeks. Despite belligerence from Srpska officials such as Karadžić and Mladić, the U.S.-led peace effort yielded three key agreements: a) Srpska officials agreed Milošević and the Federal Republic of Yugoslavia could negotiate for them, b) a cessation of hostilities, and c) an agreement on basic principles that Bosnia would continue to exist with the internationally-recognized border, but the Bosnian government and Serb side would use a 51%–49% territory split, originally from the peace proposals of 1994, as a starting point.

Soon a full ceasefire was brokered, which held.[34] Croatia, the Bosnian government and the Federal Republic of Yugoslavia hammered out the "Dayton" peace agreement in Dayton, Ohio with the agreement formally signed and endorsed by the U.N. Security Council on December 14 and 15, 1995. It created a unified Bosnia formed by two entities—the Muslim–Croatian Federation and the Republika Srpska—with each side retaining its military. UNPROFOR was replaced by a NATO-led peace implementation force, IFOR, that later became SFOR (stabilization force). The agreement included a Constitution and extensive human rights protections, modeled on the European human rights system. Remarkably, considering how often peace agreements have had amnesty provisions, leaders of all sides were still subject to the mandate of the ICTY, a reflection of the integrity of the early ICTY work and the support of Europe and the United States.

The silencing of the guns was an achievement, and the peace agreement had strong anti-discrimination protection and an explicit right of return for the displaced.[35] But elections generally returned to

---

33. Sources for para. include: U.N.S.G. Report Fall of Srebrenica, *supra* note 5, at ¶¶ 438–439, 441–444, 446.

34. Sources for para. include: U.N.S.G. Report Fall of Srebrenica, *supra* note 5, at ¶ 466; The General Framework Agreement for Peace in Bosnia and Herzegovina, signed in Dayton, Ohio, Dec. 14, 1995, *available at* http://www.ohr.int/print/?content_id=379 [hereinafter DPA].

35. Sources for para. include: U.N. REFUGEE AGENCY, UPDATE ON CONDITIONS FOR RETURN TO BOSNIA AND HERZEGOVINA 1 (Jan. 2005), *available at* http://www.unhcr.ba/publications/B&HRET0105.pdf [hereinafter UNHCR Update on Conditions]; DPA, *supra* note 34, at Article VII, Agreement on Refugees and Displaced Persons, art. II; INT'L CRISIS GROUP, THE CONTINUING CHALLENGE OF REFUGEE RETURN IN BOSNIA & HERZEGOVINA, Europe Report No. 137, 7 (Dec. 13, 2002), *available at* http://www.crisisgroup.org/home/index.cfm?id=1473&l=1

power ethnic nationalist parties from the war, such as the SDA and SDS. Especially in the Republika Srpska, officials resisted much of the peace agreement. Violence against minorities continued and minority returns were minimal.

Yet at the same time, the displaced, with their needs for housing and public benefits, were a problem for their own governmental authorities and were resented at times by the communities hosting them.[36] The survivors from Srebrenica faced further obstacles and a distinct sense of ambivalence about the peace. The government could not work out pensions for families of the missing. Nobody could satisfactorily explain where their men were, though survivors and international agencies talked of mounting evidence of massive slaughter. The Red Cross had survivors initially register their family members as prisoners. But the Red Cross could not locate them and Srpska officials alternated between denial of a massacre and claims of a large battlefield death toll. The Red Cross frustrated the families by making them come in and re-register them as missing, instead of simply converting the prisoners list to a list of missing persons. Moreover, despite previous atrocities, survivors could not believe Serb forces had committed such a crime and vainly chased malicious rumors of survivors, such as forced laborers in Serbian mines, which preyed on the instinct to hope. These took years to put to rest.

Within a year of the peace, the ICTY had exhumed hundreds of bodies from execution sites that presumably contained the corpses of men from Srebrenica. Yet the Serbs had stripped valuables and identification from the executed and three years of siege meant basically no medical and dental records commonly used in forensic identification were available. So from 1996 on, the survivors were confronted with hundreds, and then thousands, of bodies. Despite an increasingly sophisticated international and domestic forensic identification operation, few women received the body of a husband or son to allow them to close the chapter. Culturally and psychically they could not give up hope.

The unidentified bodies became a further symbol of failure for the women. They were often just bones or bodies in gruesome states of decay and neither the ICTY nor any international or local authority had a plan to care for them. Forensic science dictated a temporary burial for later

---

[hereinafter ICG Balkans Report]; Amnesty Int'l, Waiting on the Doorstep: Minority Returns to Eastern Republika Srpska (July 1, 2000), *available at* http://www.unhcr.org/refworld/topic,4565c2254d,4565c25f5c9,3b83b6dc7,0.html.

36. Sources for remainder of section include: Author's work as Deputy Director of the Bosnia Projects of Physicians for Human Rights with families of the missing, exhumations, and identifications (1996–1999) and files maintained from this time (on file with the author) [hereinafter Author's Bosnia work]; Interviews with several officials of the International Commission on Missing Persons, in Bosnia (Feb. 2007) [hereinafter, ICMP interviews].

re-exhumation when proper identification and burial was feasible. For Srebrenica survivors, burial in any place but Srebrenica was a further injustice and symbol that ethnic cleansing had succeeded.

* * *

After evacuation, Mirsada lived in a displaced persons collective center, then a room in a private house near Tuzla. Her brothers made it through and from other relatives she learned that her husband and son were seen captured. She harbored some belief that the Serb forces, populated as they were by former neighbors, had some "humanity" and would not kill all the men captured and separated out in Potočari like her father-in-law. Thus, she and the other survivors hoped their men were still alive. If alive, she had every reason to fear that her husband, sons and father-in-law were being beaten, forced to work and abused. Mirsada's own hope perversely left her in anguish. This was yet another crime. She felt guilty for surviving, and guilty because she couldn't do anything about what her men might be suffering.

Mirsada despaired at the living situation, felt generally depressed, and thought of killing herself. She gave birth to her baby, Amela. The owner of the room always wanted her to leave. By 1997 she moved to a Sarajevo suburb in formerly Srspka territory turned over to the Federation with the peace, which thus had some abandoned housing. Based on her residence in Bratunac and Srebrenica municipalities, some small amount of funds were available for those who had been forced out of these municipalities, but, painfully, no formal pension. To obtain a government pension, she had to declare her husband dead. She initially refused, like many survivors of Srebrenica. After two years, she was fed up with the lack of money. Having to declare her husband dead and navigate the cumbersome process was another blow dealt her by her government. Given this mistrust of her own government, she understood why the women refused to have some temporary memorial or burial of the bodies. That had to take place in Srebrenica.

Krstić: Making the Case and the Power of Witnesses

While Mirsada suffered through post-war Bosnia, Radislav Krstić continued as a general commanding the Srpska Army Fifth Corps. Meanwhile, the ICTY Office of the Prosecutor ("Prosecution" or "Prosecutor") delved into the putrid earth of the mass graves, the reams of intercepts and other documents from military sources, and the tragic stories of witnesses. Seeking to prove the scope of the carnage, the prosecution intensively pursued crime-based evidence in the Republika Srpska, but first had complicated negotiations with NATO commanders of IFOR seeking security for investigators and mass graves.[37] The excru-

---

37. Author's Bosnia work, *supra* note 36.

ciatingly detailed history of the genocide resulting from this evidence is one of the sterling legacies of these cases and of the ICTY.

With the already indicted Karadžić and Mladić defying arrest, at first openly and later in hiding, the Tribunal began issuing sealed indictments, unknown to the public. The Krstić indictment of October 1998 was released after the warrant was served and Krstić was captured by SFOR troops on December 2, 1998.[38] Prosecutors charged him with genocide (or alternatively, complicity to commit genocide), crimes against humanity, including extermination, murder, persecution and deportation (or alternatively, inhumane acts of forcible transfer) and murder, as a violation of the laws or customs of war, both as an individual and under the doctrine of command responsibility.[39] Krstić faced ninety-eight days of trial during 2000–2001. The 118 witnesses were crucial to proving the crimes and especially genocide's special intent to destroy.[40] Fifty-eight witnesses sought some form of protected status, with many remaining anonymous. ICTY witnesses have faced retaliatory violence. This, combined with the fact that the Srpska Army protected Mladić until at least 2004, illustrate that testifying could be dangerous for some witnesses.[41]

The *Krstić* judgments are cornerstones in the foundation of international criminal justice. For the victims, the factual and legal establishment of genocide in Srebrenica, the conviction of Krstić and the sentencing were key results. For international lawyers, Krstić set a number of other crucial precedents. A key issue in finding genocide in Srebrenica and convicting Krstić was how to define the group and the "part" that was targeted in Srebrenica. To meet the legal standard, an intent to destroy only part of the group must concern a substantial part thereof, either numerically or qualitatively, and the accused must view the group as a distinct entity, with the total context of the physical destruction considered.[42] Despite the fact that the trial Court found the prosecution shifting its formulations, the Court decided that the protected group was

---

38. ICTY Press Release, The Hague, Statement by the Prosecutor Regarding the Detention of Radislav Krstić (December 2, 1998), *available at* www.un.org/icty/pressreal/p 368–e.htm.

39. *Krstić*, Case No. ICTY 98–33–T, at ¶ 3.

40. Special intent, specific intent and *dolus specialis* are all used to describe the heightened intent required for genocide by different sources. This chapter uses special intent, unless a quote uses a different term.

41. U.N. High Comm'r for Refugees, Update on Conditions for Return to Bosnia and Herzegovina (1 Jan. 2005), *available at* http://www.unhcr.ba/publications/B&HRET0105.pdf.

42. Krstić, Case No. ICTY 98–33–T, at ¶¶ 581, 590; *see also* ¶ 552 (outlining various sources of definitions of "human group", including the U.N. General Assembly, the International Law Commission, ICTR cases such as *Akayesu*; *Kayishema*; *Ruzindana*); Krstić, Case No. ICTY-98–33–A, [Appeal] ¶¶ 8–11 (referring to similar sources).

defined as the Bosnian Muslims, with the Bosnian Muslims of Srebrenica constituting a part of the protected group.[43] The prosecution and Court agreed that the "in whole or in part" clause modified intent, rather than the actual destruction.[44] This meant that the evidence had to establish that Serb officials and Krstić intended, but did not necessarily have to have succeeded in, the destruction of the "part"—Bosnian Muslims of Srebrenica.

Witness after witness, many cited by the Court in its judgment, gave descriptions of the terror of the civilians, forcible expulsion of the women and young children, separation of men, stripping of captured men of their personal belongings, random executions and massive killing operations.[45] Corroboration came from the immense amount of forensic evidence, counting at least 2,000 found in mass graves.[46] The trial Court concluded there was "overwhelming evidence showing that the Bosnian Serb forces went to great lengths to seize Bosnian Muslim men at virtually every opportunity, whether or not they posed a military threat, collected them together in detention centres and subsequently executed them."[47]

Despite the proof of a massive, organized massacre, the prosecution's genocide theory needed further development to show the special, complicated intent to destroy.[48] It needed to overcome a tendency of the Tribunal to easily see the guilt of trigger pullers, but have exacting standards to prove the guilt of masterminds who did not walk the actual killing fields. At the outset of its investigation, the prosecution was slow to pursue linkage evidence, crucial in connecting Srpska officials and commanders to the crimes and in gaining individual convictions. For example, with the arrival of peace, work began immediately on exhumations, while subpoenas on Srpska military facilities would be a couple of years away. The prosecution ultimately secured significant linkage evidence such as Srpska official documents, military orders and intercepted conversations and convinced the Court that Sprska Army Main Staff possessed the special genocidal intent.

---

43. Krstić, Case No. ICTY 98–33–T, at ¶ 560–561. *See also* Krstić, Case No. ICTY–98–33–A, [Appeal] at ¶ 15.

44. *Id.* at ¶ 584.

45. *Id.* at ¶ 63. *See also* Transcript at 9947, Krstić, Case No. ICTY–98–33–T (Witness O); *id.* at 3018 (Witness Q); *id.* at 2957 (Witness P); *id.* at 2634–2635 (Husic).

46. Krstić, Case No. ICTY 98–33–T, at ¶¶ 73, 222, 257; *see Bosnian Reform and Justice Efforts* below where current figures give more than 5600 identified from the mass graves.

47. *Id.* at ¶ 86.

48. Sources for para. include: Krstić, Case No. ICTY 98–33–T, at ¶ 102; Author's Bosnia work, *supra* note 36.

Furthermore, the concept of physical destruction was expanded beyond just death. The prosecution initially aimed much of the surviving women's testimony at victim impact and sentencing, but their eloquent expression of profound loss later became a central feature of the argument portraying destruction. The women were waiting for their men to come out of the forest, not marrying, and dying in squalor as refugees. Local experts testified to the trauma throughout the community and the women and children's inability to restart lives and to support themselves. The Court summarized the impact on the community as "catastrophic."[49] The "evacuation" of the women and children was not done to protect the civilians, nor was it an imperative military necessity.[50] The prosecution showed, and the Court found, that the survivors' experience of separation from the men, forcible transfer, specific acts of cruelty during the process and their traumatic inability to restart any semblance of normal life afterwards constituted serious harm and inhumane treatment as constituent acts of genocide, extermination, and other crimes against humanity.[51] Moreover, the survivors' experience of these serious inhumane harms evidenced the intent to physically destroy the Bosnian Muslims of Srebrenica.[52] Thus, the prosecution ultimately convinced the court of this more holistic understanding of physical destruction.

* * *

Mirsada and other survivors demonstrated their inner strength in the courtroom. Their vivid description of events proved critical in proving several key elements of the case. For example, the grisly testimony of the men who survived the executions took the court to the scene and showed the massive organization of the executions. Witness N described:

> I was the last one in the truck, so I was taken out first. And they showed me where I was supposed to stand, next to some dead bodies. And everybody was lined up like that, in several rows, with their backs facing them. The tamic (a small truck) left immediately, and immediately after it had left, we heard automatic rifles being fired. Everybody fell down at that point, and those who were not killed, who were still giving some signs of life, were shot at individually, were killed individually. I didn't dare move ... they kept killing men. And this continued until they finished off everyone. And when

---

49. Krstić, Case No. ICTY 98–33–T, at ¶¶ 90–93.

50. *Id.* at ¶ 527.

51. *Id.*at ¶¶ 513, 516, 518, 523, 530. *See Attack and Atrocity* and *Aftermath and Peace* sections above for Mirsada's account related to these issues.

52. *Id. at* ¶ 543, referring by implication to ¶¶ 516–519, which in turn refer to 506–515; *see* ¶¶ 568, 595.

the last tamic arrived, somebody said, 'That's it, there's no one left.'[53]

Mirsada's testimony stirred the court and her descriptions of the separations and seeing the men captured, recounted in the *Attack and Atrocity* section above, as well as the ongoing grief and survivors' guilt, recounted in the *Aftermath and Peace* section above, were emblematic of that given by survivors. The Court quoted Mirsada in its judgment to summarize the tragic reality:

> "... from the face of the earth were wiped off three generations of men in the cruelest way possible. I can corroborate it by a fresh example from my family ... [listing seven members of her family] ... There are hundreds of such families in Srebrenica ..."[54]

The surviving women, such as the witness DD, powerfully articulated the catastrophic trauma, verifying the prosecution's theory concerning the concept of destruction. She captured the horror and the resulting trauma and heartbreak:

> [Soldiers pulled her son aside] And then I begged them, I pleaded with them. Why are you taking him? He was born in 1981 [making him thirteen years old]. But he repeated his order. And I held him so hard, but he grabbed him ... [A]nd he took my son's hand, and he dragged him to the left side. And he turned around, and then he told me, "Mommy, please, can you get that bag for me? Could you please get it for me? ... That was the last time I heard his voice.[55]

DD then painted the picture of simultaneous hope and despair:

> "I dream of him bringing flowers and saying, 'Mother, I've come,' I hug him and say, 'Where have you been, my son?' and he says, 'I've been in Vlasenica all this time ... sometimes I also think it would be better if none of us had survived. I would prefer it."[56]

Guilt and Sentencing

The further difficulty for the trial Court was finding the specific knowledge and intent of Krstić. General Krstić played a critical role in the terrorizing of the civilian population and in the criminal forcible transfer of the civilians during July 10–13, as chief of the Drina Corps.[57]

---

53. Transcript at 2824–2825, 2827, Krstić, Case No. ICTY–98–33–T (Witness N).

54. Krstić, Case No. ICTY 98–33–T, at ¶ 90; Malagić T. at pp. 1983–84; Witness DD's son was not yet fourteen, *see* Transcript at 5764, Krstić, Case No. ICTY–98–33–T.

55. Krstić, Case No. ICTY 98–33–T, at ¶ 55, citing Transcript at 5754–55, Krstić, Case No. ICTY–98–33–T.

56. Krstić, Case No. ICTY 98–33–T, at ¶ 91 citing Transcript at 5761, Krstić, Case No. ICTY–98–33–T.

57. Krstić, Case No. ICTY 98–33–T, at ¶¶ 155, 335, 337, 340, 354, 367, 443, 464–465.

However, it was not proven that the original attack plan called for mass execution or mass expulsion.[58] The Court could not find proof of the genocidal plan, or at least proof of Krstić's knowledge of it, before July 13, 1995.[59]

In finding intent for genocide the trial Court clarified that: 1) the accused must intend the genocidal acts, in this case the mass executions and/or the serious physical and mental harm—such as the forcible transfer; 2) the overall criminal enterprise must intend to destroy the group (or part of the group), not just to commit widespread atrocities; and 3) the accused must share the intent to destroy.[60] On appeal, the Chamber further clarified that the "proof of the mental state with respect to the commission of the underlying act can serve as evidence from which the fact-finder may draw the further inference that the accused possessed the specific intent to destroy."[61] Although such inferences can be risky, concrete evidence of direct orders to murder will not exist or will be nearly impossible to obtain, as *Krstić* illustrates, given the nature of contemporary crimes.[62] Based on the magnitude of killing, along with the Main Staff's knowledge of the effects the killing would have on the Srebrenica Muslim community, the Chamber found a "sufficient factual basis" for the special intent to destroy.[63]

However, the Chamber concluded that the prosecution and trial Court did not establish that Krstić shared the genocidal intent.[64] His contacts with General Mladić, clear knowledge of the killings, and the fact that units from his Corps were involved in the killing were not enough to support the inference of Krstić's genocidal intent as a principal perpetrator.[65] He remained, however, guilty as an aider and abettor

---

58. *Id.* at ¶ 120.

59. *Id.* at ¶ 295.

60. *Id.* at ¶¶ 549, 561, 571. This interpretation is echoed by the ICJ and ICTR so that genocide can only apply to acts that are committed with the special intent or purpose to destroy all or part of the group.

61. Krstić, Case No. ICTY 98–33–A [Appeal], at ¶ 20; *see also id.* at ¶ 33 ("genocidal intent may be inferred, among other facts, from evidence of 'other culpable acts systematically directed against the same group' " [e.g. transfer]); ¶ 34 ("Where direct evidence of genocidal intent is absent, the intent may still be inferred from the factual circumstances of the crime.").

62. Patricia Wald, *General Radislav Krstić: A War Crimes Case Study*, 16 Geo. J. Legal Ethics 445, 463, 468–69 (2003).

63. Krstić, Case No. ICTY–98–33–A, [Appeal] at ¶ 35.

64. Krstić, Case No. ICTY 98–33–A [Appeal], at ¶¶ 98–100.

65. *Id.* at ¶¶ 76, 98, 100, 104, 121, 129; *see* ¶ 133 (Krstić had specific intent toward a forcible transfer, not to complete genocide); *and see* ¶¶ 68–78 (no direct evidence that establishes the Corps' involvement in the executions themselves, however evidence of the facilitation of those executions has been established).

of genocide, since he knew that the criminal enterprise had the special genocidal intent to destroy Srebrenica's Bosnian Muslim community.[66] Following similar reasoning, the Chamber lowered Krstić's liability from that of a principal co-perpetrator to aiding and abetting the murders, extermination, and persecution.[67] On the one hand, the decision upheld the heightened standard for special intent for finding genocide. On the other hand, the decision could be labeled another example of the Court's more stringent culpability standard for high officials, the white collar war criminals, in contrast to the lower standard for soldiers, those pulling the triggers.

In sentencing, the seriousness of the crimes is a central factor, with potential aggravating factors being the premeditation, any abuse of power, the motive of the convicted person and direct participation, such as ordering or inciting.[68] Common mitigating factors can be cooperation with the prosecution, other positive behavior, and more indirect participation, such as aiding and abetting.

At trial, Krstić was sentenced to forty-six years of imprisonment, with prominent sentencing factors being the sheer scale and gravity of the crime—organization, speed, and the suffering inflicted on the victims—and Krstić's role as a one of the highest ranking officers involved.[69] On Appeal, the Chamber found that his reduced role in aiding and abetting and other factors, such as his order to treat Muslims humanely, mitigated his sentence.[70] Still the Chamber sentenced him to thirty-five years.[71] The sentence for Krstić, even with the reduction, was one of the longer given by the ICTY. Despite this, the prosecution was not satisfied. In fact, the prosecutor for the Krstić trial has written that "it is impossible to make the punishment proportional to the seriousness of the crime."[72]

Despite the detail described above, the sentencing scheme has inherent problems. Yet, because sentencing is discretionary based on rather

---

66. *Id.* At ¶¶ 129, 134, 137; *see* ¶ 140 ("an individual who aids and abets a specific intent offense may be held responsible if he assists the commission of the crime knowing the intent behind the crime").

67. *Id.* at ¶ 144.

68. Sources for para.: Krstić, Case No. ICTY 98–33–T, at ¶¶ 704–705, 708–709, 714–715.

69. Krstić, Case No. ICTY 98–33–T, at ¶¶ 720, 721,726.

70. Krstić, Case No. ICTY 98–33–A [Appeal], at ¶ 272. The original trial court sentence was consistent with ICTR sentencing practice, and properly reflected the sheer gravity of the crimes involved. *Id.* at ¶ 249

71. *Id.* at ¶ 275.

72. Mark Harmon, Fergal Gaynor, *Ordinary Sentences for Extraordinary Crimes*, 5 J. INT'L CRIM. JUST. 683, 692.

vague factors,[73] the ICTY is influenced by modest European sentencing practice, in contrast to the harsher sentences supported by Mirsada, other survivor groups and many ordinary Bosnians. For example, Krstić's sentence is fewer years than that of the lower level officers just convicted for Srebrenica crimes in the Court of Bosnia and Herzegovina, see *Bosnian Reform and Justice Efforts* section below.

* * *

Survivors such as Mirsada clearly shared the prosecution's conviction that Krstić was a primary perpetrator and disagreed with any "reduction" in the level of culpability. The survivors agreed that the sentences did not fit the crimes, repeatedly citing specific sentence terms in relation to those convicted, such as Krstić, Nikolić and Deronjić.[74] They did not understand why Krstić did not get life. Mirsada said Krstić's years in a British prison will never be as harsh as what they endured in Srebrenica.

The survivors saw such findings as an illustration of the myriad due process rights benefiting perpetrators, while they ponder the limited rights that victims like themselves have.[75] They had hoped the Krstić trial and conviction would lead to many things: more locations of mass graves, more captures and trials of other perpetrators, possibly some shift in official and popular Serb attitudes—only some of which resulted.[76] They also did not see Krstić showing remorse, a fact noted as well by the court.[77] One leader of a Srebrenica family group said she would have been happy if he said, "I committed these crimes and I would never do it again."[78] For this reason, Momir Nikolić's confession and apology in pleading guilty to persecutions in Srebrenica was a more emotionally satisfying outcome for many, even though there was no conviction for genocide and his sentence was much less than that of Krstić.

The Resonance of the Krstić Decisions

The *Krstić* decisions have stood up to repeated scrutiny as some of Krstić's fellow perpetrators have come to trial and been convicted. The most important finding of the Court, from the perspective of Mirsada and many survivors, was that there was a plan by Serb officials to destroy Srebrenica's Muslim community through the gruesome mass

---

73. Patricia Wald, Symposium on 'The ICTY 10 Years On: The View from Inside,' IV. The Judiciary, *ICTY Judicial Proceedings*, 2 J. INT'L CRIM. JUST. 466, 472–473 (2004).

74. Interview with Munira Subašić, a leader of Mothers of Srebrenica and Žepa Enclaves, in Sarajevo (February 2007); Interview with Nura Begović, a leader of Women of Srebrenica, in Potočari (February 2007).

75. Subašić Interview, *supra* note 74; Begović Interview, *supra* note 74.

76. Subašić Interview, *supra* note 74; Begović Interview, *supra* note 74.

77. Interview with Subašić, *supra* note 74.

78. *Id.*

executions of 7000 plus men accompanied by the forcible expulsion of about 25,000 others. This finding has been repeatedly upheld.[79] The *Krstić* precedent will face further scrutiny with the arrest of war-time Srpska President Radovan Karadžić and his transfer to the ICTY to face charges, including charges of genocide for the events in Srebrenica. In addition, nine defendants in three ongoing cases face genocide and other Srebrenica-related charges.[80] The *Krstić* Trial and Appeals Chambers decisions have become precedent on a variety of other substantive and procedural questions besides genocide, such as the displacement of civilians,[81] complicity in crimes,[82] evidence issues—notably the standard for permissible inferences,[83] and sentencing.[84]

In other cases, the ICTY has upheld other major portions of the *Krstić* genocide analysis, such as the use of quantitative and qualitative factors to demonstrate that the Bosnian Muslims of Srebrenica were a significant "part" of the Bosnian Muslim group. They also have found, as in *Krstić,* the combination of the execution of a significant minority of

---

79. Prosecutor v. Vidoje Blagojević, Dragan Jokić, Case No. ICTY IT–02–60–T, Sentencing Judgment, (Jan. 17, 2005); Prosecutor v. Momir Nikolić, IT–02–60/1–S, Sentencing Judgment, (Dec. 2, 2003); Prosecutor v. Dragan Obrenović, IT–02–60/2–S, Sentencing Judgment, (Dec. 10, 2003).

80. Prosecutor v. Popović et al., IT–02–57–AR65.1, Decision on Interlocutory Appeal (Oct. 28, 2005), involves seven defendants and includes charges for genocide, conspiracy to commit genocide, aiding and abetting genocide, extermination, murder, persecutions, forcible transfer, and deportation. Zdravko Tolimir, IT–04–80–AR65.1, Decision on Interlocutory Appeal (October 19, 2005), was indicted for genocide, conspiracy to commit genocide, extermination, murder, persecutions, forcible transfer, deportation. Milorad Trbić, IT–05–88/1–PT (July 20, 2007), is in proceedings after indictment for genocide, conspiracy to commit genocide, extermination, murder, persecutions, and forcible transfer.

81. Krajišnik, Case No. ICTY IT–00–39–T, at ¶ 725 ("limited circumstances under which the displacement of civilians during armed conflict is allowed"); Prosecutor v. Mladen Naletilić and Vinko Martinović, "Tuta and Stela," ICTY Case IT–98–34–A, Appeals Chamber, Judgment, 3 May 2006, ¶ 4.

82. Krajišnik, Case No. ICTY IT–00–39–T, Judgment, 27 September 2006, ¶¶ 864–65, FN 1706–07 (discussing complicity in genocide); Prosecutor v. Naser Orić, Case No. ICTY IT–03–68–T, Trial Chamber II, Judgment, 30 June 2006, FN 776, 841, citing Krstić, Case No. ICTY 98–33–T, at ¶¶ 601, 604 ("aiding and abetting" as a singular legal concept).

83. Krajišnik, Case No. ICTY IT–00–39–T, at ¶ 1196, citing Krstić, Case No. ICTY 98–33–T, at ¶ 708 (standard for making inferences); Prosecutor v. Milomir Stakić, Case No. ICTY IT–97–24–A, Appeals Chamber, Judgment, 22 March 2006, ¶¶ 186, 188, citing Krstić, Case No. ICTY–98–33–A, [Appeal], at ¶¶ 215, 180, 153 (strict compliance standard with Tribunal rules).

84. Prosecutor v. Biljana Plavšić, ICTY Case IT–00–39 & 40/1–S, Sentencing Judgment, 27 February 2003, ¶¶ 54, 56, citing Krstić, Case No. ICTY 98–33–T, at ¶ 709 (leadership is an aggravating factor, with direct participation as an aggravating circumstance); Prosecutor v. Milan Babić, Case No. ICTY IT–03–72–A, Appeals Chamber, Judgment on Sentencing Appeal, 18 July 2005, ¶¶ 40, 80, citing Krstić, Case No. ICTY–98–33–A, [Appeal] at ¶ 242 (indirect participation may result in a lower sentence).

this "part," the forcible expulsion of the majority of the "part" and other inhumane acts, amounted to physical destruction.[85] Yet, courts have had doubts about the proof of genocidal intent for other officers and about which acts can be ascribed to officers' units. The ICTY has convicted other Serb officers for extermination, persecution, and murder—or aiding and abetting these crimes—not genocide.[86] Moreover, the overall reasoning of these cases when examining genocidal intent, even when not directly citing *Krstić,* have implicitly bolstered the rigorous genocidal intent standard required by the *Krstić* decisions.

Arguably, the rigor of the *Krstić* case obliged the ICJ in the *Bosnia v. Serbia* judgment to find genocide in Srebrenica, since on the other key elements of the case, Bosnia lost its genocide case against Serbia. The ICJ gave substantial regard to the factual findings in *Krstić,* in its own assessment of the facts, including that fact that the military plan to reduce the Srebrenica enclave converted into a genocidal plan to eliminate Srebrenica's Bosnian Muslims only after the physical takeover on July 12 or 13.[87] This factual finding was "decisive" in the ICJ's conclusion that it was not proven that Serbia and Montenegro ordered or even knew about the genocidal plan. Thus, it was not responsible for genocide.[88] With other atrocities, such as the widespread and systematic abuses of 1992, the Court said the plan for a greater Serbia involved dissolution of a community, but not the special intent to destroy for genocide.[89]

The ICJ based much of its analysis of the key element—special intent to destroy a part of the group—on the *Krstić* decisions.[90] The ICJ ratified the trial Court and Appeals Chamber's findings of genocidal acts

---

85. Prosecutor v. Vidoje Blagojević and Dragan Jokić, Case No. ICTY IT–02–60–T, 23 April, 2004, at ¶ 666.

86. Jokić was found guilty of aiding and abetting extermination and persecutions on political, racial, and religious grounds (crimes against humanity), and aiding and abetting murder (violations of the laws or customs of war) and sentenced to nine years. Vidoje Blagojević and Dragan Jokić, Case No. ICTY IT–02–60–T. Momir Nikolić pleaded guilty to persecutions (crimes against humanity) and was sentenced to twenty years imprisonment. Case No. IT–02–60/1–S. Obrenović pleaded guilty to persecutions (crimes against humanity), and was sentenced to seventeen years in prison. IT–02–60/2, Sentencing Judgment (Dec. 10, 2003).

87. Int'l Court Case Concerning the Application of the Convention on the Prevention and Punishment of the Crime of Genocide *(Bosn. & Herz. v. Serb. & Mont.)* 2007 I.C.J. General List No. 91 (Feb. 26), [hereinafter ICJ *Bosnia v. Serbia*], at Chapter VI "The Facts Invoked by the Applicant, in relation to Article II," section (5) "The Massacre at Srebrenica," paras. 278, 281, 292–297, citing Krstić, Case No. ICTY 98–33–T and Case No. ICTY–98–33–A, [Appeal].

88. ICJ *Bosnia v. Serbia, supra* note 87, at paras. 295, 423.

89. ICJ *Bosnia v. Serbia, supra* note 87, at paras. 372, 376.

90. ICJ *Bosnia v. Serbia, supra* note 87, at para. 693.

of killing and serious harm in Srebrenica, coupled with solid evidence of the special intent to destroy by the Srpska army central command.[91] Like the *Krstić* Appeals Chamber, the ICJ accepted a geographic limitation as a factor in defining a "part" of a group and wanted a quantitative component to go with the qualitative evaluation of the "part."[92]

The *Krstić* case has set key precedents in the analysis of genocide and crimes against humanity cited in other international fora, including decisions of the International Criminal Tribunal for Rwanda. The *Krstić* trial court itself relied on the seminal ICTR *Akayesu* judgment the first case to enforce genocide after the 1948 Genocide Convention.[93] ICTR judgments have turned to the reasoning in *Krstić* on several issues, such as the key element of special intent to destroy a part of the group. The *Mpambara* decision employed the *Krstić* approach in stating that victims of genocide must be specifically targeted because of their membership in the protected group, which can be shown by evidence that the perpetrator intended to destroy a substantial part of the protected group.[94] The *Ndindabahizi* Trial Chamber cited the *Krstić* holding that special intent to destroy can be properly inferred from circumstantial evidence and from the actual destruction of a substantial part of the group.[95] Nevertheless, in some other key respects, the showing of special intent had a divergent meaning in the judgments of the ICTR and the ICTY.[96] Factually, the *Krstić* treatment of genocide differed from the Rwandan because there had been no public calls in Bosnia for the killing of any group. Thus, legally, the ICTY had to infer the required genocidal intent from the pattern of executions and deportations.[97]

---

91. ICJ *Bosnia v. Serbia*, supra note 87, at paras. 292–295; Andrew B. Loewenstein and Stephen A. Kostas, *Divergent Approaches to Determining Responsibility for Genocide, The Darfur Commission of Inquiry and the ICJ's Judgment in the Genocide Case*, 5 J. INT'L CRIM. JUST. 839, 854 (2007).

92. ICJ *Bosnia v. Serbia*, at Chapter VI; David Scheffer, *Genocide and Atrocity Crimes*, Vol. 1, No. 3, GENOCIDE STUD. & PREVENTION, 229, 240 (2006); David Turns, *Application of the Convention on the Prevention and Punishment of the Crime of Genocide: Bosnia and Herzegovina v. Serbia and Montenegro*, MELB. J. INT'L L. (8.2), 413 (2007).

93. Krstić, Case No. ICTY 98–33–T, at ¶¶ 484, 492; see Beth Van Schaack, *Engendering Genocide: The Akayesu Case Before the International Criminal Tribunal for Rwanda*, supra Chapter 6.

94. Prosecutor v. Jean Mpambara, Case No. ICTR–01–65–T, Judgment, 11 September 2006, ¶¶ 8–9; see also Prosecutor v. Emmanuel Ndindabahizi, Case No. ICTR–2001–71–I, Judgment and Sentence, 15 July 2004, ¶ 454.

95. *Ndindabahizi*, ¶ 454, 460; see also *Muvunyi*, ¶ 480, FN 685.

96. International Center for Transitional Justice, *Applicability of the U.N. Convention on the Prevention & Punishment of the Crime of Genocide to Events which Occurred during the Early Twentieth Century*, at 16, available at http://groong.usc.edu/ICTJ-analysis.pdf.

97. Wald, *Case Study*, supra note 62 at 463, 468–69.

In Darfur, the *Krstić* decisions were primary analytical tools for the U.N. Commission of Inquiry, led by former ICTY Chief Judge, Antonio Cassese.[98] In a fact situation with parallels to Bosnia and Srebrenica, the Commission found extensive evidence of crimes against humanity, including extermination. However, despite employing the *Krstić* standards on several points, including aspects of special intent and the "part" of the targeted group,[99] the Commission concluded it could not label the atrocities genocide because the special intent was not proven.[100] The Commission's analysis has generated criticism and support. Arguably, the Commission ignored key aspects of the *Krstić* decisions in analyzing intent and failed to appreciate the significance of the "cluster of abuses," including forcible displacement. These abuses amount to serious harm that not only count as genocidal acts, but are evidence of intent.[101] In contrast, the Commission has been lauded for not taking the "quantum leap" made by the *Krstić* court in its analysis combining the massacre of rebels and forced expulsion of women and children to find special intent.[102]

* * *

In addition to its far-flung legal impact, Mirsada found that the *Krstić* verdict had a concrete impact on her life, especially her ability to travel to her house in Voljavica and the Srebrenica area. It also had a noticeable impact on the attitude of some Serbs. Mirsada has had to go occasionally to her home municipality, Bratunac, for official paperwork. Before *Krstić*, she and others would go with a police escort to the municipal offices and police would wait and then accompany them on any other business they had. After the verdict, the Serb officials made her feel welcome, almost as if nothing happened.[103]

Yet, to this day, Mirsada retains a distinct feeling of powerlessness and lost identity. Although not afraid to go back to Bratunac, Mirsada does not feel she can return to her house there. She cannot make her children confront the discriminatory schools and the omnipresent picture

---

98. *Report of the International Commission of Inquiry on Darfur to the United Nations Secretary General*, U.N. Doc. S/2005/60 (Jan. 25, 2005), *available at* http://www.un.org/News/dh/sudan/com_inq_darfur.pdf.

99. *Id.* at 124, 128; Claus Kreb, *The International Court of Justice and the Elements of the Crime of Genocide*, 18 EUR. J. INT'L L. 619, 624 (2007).

100. David Luban, *Calling Genocide by Its Rightful Name: Lemkin's Word, Darfur and the U.N. Report*, 7 CHI. J. INT'L L. 303, 314–316 (Summer 2006).

101. Beth Van Schaack, *Darfur and the Rhetoric of Genocide*, 26 WHITTIER L. REV. 1101, 1131–1134 (Summer 2005); Luban, *supra* note 100, at 314–316

102. William A. Schabas, *Genocide, Crimes against Humanity, and Darfur: The Commission of Inquiry's Findings on Genocide*, 27 CARDOZO L. REV. 1703, 1715–16 (2006).

103. Other developments likely also had an impact, *see Bosnian Reform and Justice Efforts infra*, but this is the way Mirsada expressed it in the interviews.

of Karadžić. Admir would not be able to find work and Republika Srpska officials have made it difficult for Bosnian Muslims, such as Mirsada, returning to Srpska to maintain the public benefits they have received elsewhere in Bosnia. Mirsada trusted the police in 1992, yet they helped ethnically cleanse them, leading her to question how she can possibly trust them now, especially given that some Serbs she saw at Potočari during those fateful days are now in official positions, including the police. Reforming these unacceptable conditions would be more important than the guilty verdict against Krstić in weighing the possibility of return.

Bosnian Reform and Justice Efforts

Despite the ICTY's conviction of Krstić and others, many lower-level war criminals remain at large—10,000 by one estimate in 2005—with some participating in public life.[104] This combined with policing failures and discrimination, especially in socio-economic spheres, compromised public trust, especially of returnees. Moreover, while international intervention in the property return process led to resolution of the vast majority of claims, the overall trend was for minorities to sell repossessed or rebuilt property in order to live in new areas where they are not ethnic minorities. This toxic mix depressed minority returns in Srebrenica and elsewhere and meant the peace had not reversed ethnic cleansing. In the years since the peace agreement, less than half, 1.03 million of the 2.2 million refugees and displaced persons, have returned to their communities in Bosnia. Of these 1.03 million returnees, according to UNHCR, less than half, 466,000, of the returnees were minority returns by June 2008. About 125,000 displaced persons remained in Bosnia.

But the peace agreement has offered survivors of Srebrenica other mechanisms to pursue those responsible.[105] The *Krstić* decision helped

---

104. Sources for para. include: U.N. High Comm'r for Refugees Representation in Bosnia and Herzegovina, *Statistical Package* (June 30, 2005), *available at:* http://www.unhcr.ba/updatejune08/SP_06_2008.pdf; Office of High Representative, *33rd Report of the High Representative for Implementation of the Peace Agreement on Bosnia and Herzegovina*, ¶ 45 (May 13, 2008), *available at* http://www.ohr.int/print/?content_id=41694; ICG Refugee Return, *supra* note 35 at 9; Rhodri C. Williams, *Post–Conflict Property Restitution and Refugee Return in Bosnia and Herzegovina: Implications for International Standard–Setting and Practice*, 37 N.Y.U. J. INT'L L. & POL. 441, 486–91 (2005).

105. Sources for para. include: Interview with Amor Mašović, Co–Director of the Missing Persons Institute in Sarajevo (Feb. 2007); Ferida Selimović, et al. v. Republika Srpska, CH01–8365, Decision on Admissibility and Merits (Mar. 3, 2003), ¶¶ 40, 220; Constitutional Court of Bosnia and Herzegovina, Decision on Admissibility and Merits, Appeal of Ms. Muniba Hadza, *et al.*, AP_129/04, ¶ 68 (May 27, 2005). The Chamber found that, even though its jurisdiction commenced after the war, the disappearance of those from Srebrenica constituted a continuing crime over which it had jurisdiction. Created by the Dayton Peace Agreement, the Human Rights Chamber was later folded into the

pave the way for the Bosnia Human Rights Chamber, a court created by the Dayton Peace Agreement, to grant some redress to survivors through a novel series of cases known as the "Srebrenica cases," where the disappearance of men from Srebrenica was viewed as a continuing crime since Srpska authorities had not clarified what happened to the missing. The lead case, *Selimović*, essentially mandated that the Republika Srpska disclose information on the applicants' missing family members, produce comprehensive findings on the events occurring during July 1995 in Srebrenica, and pay as reparation approximately two million Euros to benefit the families of Srebrenica victims. The Republika Srpska investigation that resulted finally and startingly yielded official admissions, such as the conclusion "that between 10 and 19 July 1995, several thousands of Bosniaks were liquidated, in a manner that represents severe violation of International Humanitarian Law and that the perpetrators, among the others, undertook measures to cover up the crime by reallocating the bodies."[106] It also revealed previously unknown locations of mass graves and led to a list of war crimes suspects still holding official Srpska positions. In 2007, Srpska began to restrict the travel of some 100 of them.

In another forum, the Court of Bosnia and Herzegovina (BiH Court) issued its first convictions in July 2008 for genocide in Srebrenica, the work of a special branch staffed with local and international lawyers with dozens of war crimes cases.[107] The BiH Court convicted seven former Serb officials for the massacre of 1,000 plus men from Srebrenica at a warehouse in Kravica on July 13, 1995, and acquitted four others. The successful prosecution of such cases in Bosnia, where the lower and mid-level planners and perpetrators have their international due process rights, is clearly one of the valuable legacies of the ICTY. The prosecution team in the Chamber noted that building a specific case for an individual's conviction remained a substantial task, even with the factual and legal precedent of ICTY cases such as *Krstić*. One leader of a Srebrenica survivors group highlighted the challenge facing the prosecu-

---

Constitutional Court of Bosnia; Bosnia and Herzegovina, Republika Srpska, Government, The Commission for Investigation of the Events, in and around Srebrenica between 10 and 19 July 1995, June 2004, at 40; *available at* http://www.ikv.nl/docs/200406151734116442.pdf?&username=gast@ikv.nl&password=9999&groups=IKV, [hereinafter RS Report]; Associated Press, *30,000 Gather to Rebury Srebrenica Massacre Victims on Anniversary of Killings*, July 11, 2007, *available at* http://www.foxnews.com/story/0,2933,288945,00.html.

106. RS Report *supra* note 105, at 40.

107. Sources for para. include: Court of Bosnia and Herzegovina, Press Release, *Verdicts Announced in the cases against Miloš Stupar et al., Petar Mitrović and Miladin Stevanović (Kravica Cases)*, (29.07.2008), *available at* http://www.sudbih.gov.ba/?id=959&jezik=e; Gabrielle Kirk McDonald, *Problems, Obstacles and Achievements of the ICTY*, 2 J. INT'L CRIM. JUST., 558, 568–69 (2004); author interviews in February, 2007 in Sarajevo with prosecution lawyers in the war crimes branch of the Court of Bosnia and Herzegovina.

tion by pointing to the continuing injustice of seeing in public in Srebrenica the man who pulled her son from her during the tragedy. The potential of such prosecutions to pull from the streets perpetrators the victims personally know could address an injustice that the ICTY was institutionally not set up to address.

Even before the latest decision from the BiH Court, several thousand people had returned to the Srebrenica area, many in Potočari.[108] A complex mix of factors—the admissions by Republika Srpska authorities, incipient steps at identifying serving officials who participated in atrocities, the *Krstić* and other Srebrenica decisions, the economic and housing difficulties facing Srebrenica survivors—contributed to the phenomenon.

Another of the major injustices facing Mirsada and the other survivors is being revealed and resolved, thanks to the International Commission on Missing Persons and some other groups.[109] Within months of the end of the war, the ICTY undertook a massive effort to exhume many of the mass graves with Srebrenica victims. In a parallel process coordinated with the ICTY, that marked one of the first signs of official cooperation, Bosnian Muslim officials went into Republika Srpska to recover bodies under the watch of RS authorities, and RS authorities did the same on Federation territory under the watch of Federation Bosnian Muslim officials.

While the recovery of remains moved ahead, the identification of the bodies proved to be a point of friction. The ICTY did not need to identify hundreds, much less thousands of bodies, to prove their cases. The local authorities did not have the resources and a complicated mix of international, intergovernmental and non-governmental organizations attempted to respond. An extensive effort to reach the families and enlist their participation and understanding of the forensic exhumation and identification process had a real impact. It simply acknowledged the families' loss while sharing evidence of massacres, when the families were hoping that the missing were alive. But the families' main desire for identification of bodies could not be met early on with standard forensic technology. Eventually, ICMP assumed leadership of the process and pushed the DNA technology to develop a process which led to thousands of identifications. The identification of more than 5,600 of the estimated 8,100 Srebrenica missing and the dignity of the cemetery and memorial in Potočari are repeatedly cited by survivors such as Mirsada as a tangible benefit and source of comfort. In the process, ICMP built on its outreach to form a network of survivor (families of the missing) groups, not only

---

[108]. Sources for para. include: Subašić interview, *supra* note 74; Begović interview *supra* note 74; ICMP interviews, *supra* note 36.

[109]. Sources for this para. and next include: ICMP interviews *supra* note 36; Author's Bosnia work, *supra* note 36.

among Srebrenica survivors, but across the former Yugoslavia. The effort has not only given voice to a disempowered sector of these societies, but their voices—more frequently than other sectors of society—call for understanding and reconciliation across the ethnic divide.

* * *

Mirsada, like many of the survivors, is gratified with and takes solace from the memorial cemetery established in Potočari and she goes to the commemorative events. She is glad to see all the identifications and families burying their sons, husbands and fathers. The day in July 1995 she rode the bus out of Srebrenica and saw the captured men and the men separated in Potočari getting on buses going in a different direction, a part of her had realized they were going to be killed. There had been many exchanges of those captured during the war between the Muslims and Serbs, but she couldn't imagine how the Bosnian government could have anything to exchange for all these men. And how could the Serbs put them all to work? Now more than ten years later, it makes more complete sense that they are dead. However, her husband and sons have not been identified and she is deprived of their burial and a proper place for grieving.

In 2007, some twelve years after the genocide and the peace, Mirsada lived on 500 KM/month,[110] basically from her pension, in an apartment in Sarajevo. Her son Adnan was finishing school with little job prospects. Her daughter Amela, born just after the genocide, was physically handicapped with one leg shorter than the other and required weekly hospital visits. Mirsada could work, but what she would earn wouldn't cover the cost of the care for Amela.

She occasionally goes back to her home village of Voljavica, but only for holidays or during the summer. She has had her home repaired with aid money, but even that process brought indignities. The Serb workmen—intentionally, she believed—worked on the house on a major Muslim holiday. She planned to keep the house, explaining that "I will never give them the pleasure that the land that was ours would become theirs." The land is a symbol that the Srebrenica Muslims were not defeated. She keeps the land in honor of her family and the thousands buried at the Memorial Cemetery.

Krstić's Impact on Accountability and Responsibility

The genocide carried out within a U.N. safe area shattered any myth of safety that came from blue helmets and U.N. Security Council proclamations. In a thorough searching report, the U.N. Secretary General, Kofi Annan, detailed the blow-by-blow development of the Srebreni-

---

110. KM are the official Bosnian currency (symbolized as BAM): 500 KM was worth U.S. $281.67 in February 2007.

ca tragedy and the critical gaps between U.N. field command, U.N. staff leadership and the Security Council. The reluctance of senior U.N. staff, including Annan himself, to use their heaviest weapon—NATO air power—was wrong, Annan concluded, despite the sound reasons for their reluctance. Many of these reasons had their root in the politics in the Security Council, European capitals and Washington D.C., and the fact they could not muster political consensus and the will to act. In their absence, the major powers and the Security Council issued ambiguous resolutions creating unsafe safe areas and a limited peacekeeping force with no peace to keep. Other experts agree that the Srebrenica genocide has shown that the international community needs to intervene more quickly when confronted with confirmed atrocities.[111] The "cardinal lesson" for Annan was there exists a moral duty to confront "with all necessary means"—i.e., with military force as a humanitarian intervention—a deliberate and systematic attempt to kill, expel or otherwise terrorize a civilian population.[112]

Annan's findings and the concept of humanitarian intervention were arguably a revolutionary sentiment for an organization built upon the sovereign stones of each individual member. Yet, despite the powerful lessons of Srebrenica and other such tragedies, the U.N. has not operationalized the doctrine of humanitarian intervention, for example in Darfur, and the Bush Administration has muddled the concept with double-standards. Nevertheless, these tragedies have catalyzed a movement for new standards, and one arguable result is the Responsibility to Protect. The U.N. General Assembly unanimously adopted the norm in a Resolution in 2005. It restates the sovereign's existing responsibility to its own people and innovates in establishing the outlines for the international community's responsibility to intervene, possibly with military force, in fulfilling its responsibility to protect.

While beginning with legitimate grounds for military response to September 11, 2001, the Bush Administration over-reached by belatedly folding a humanitarian rationale into its shifting justification for the war in Iraq. The double standard is highlighted by the fact the United States has labeled Darfur genocide and done nothing militarily to confront Sudan. Moreover, caution in the use of humanitarian intervention comes also from competing human rights concerns, since the law of armed conflict tolerates actions, such as civilian killings and detention without

---

111. David Scheffer, *Genocide and Atrocity Crimes*, Vol. 1, No. 3, GENOCIDE STUD. & PREVENTION 229, 229 (2006); Ralph Wilde, *Enhancing Accountability at the International Level: The Tension Between International Organization and Member State Responsibility and the Underlying Issues at Stake*, 12 ILSA J. INT'L & COMP. L. 395, 397 (2006); Patricia M. Wald, Symposium: *Judgment at Nuremberg, Genocide and Crimes against Humanity*, 6 WASH. U. GLOBAL STUD. L. REV. 621, 625–26 (2007).

112. U.N.S.G. Report Fall of Srebrenica, *supra* 5, at ¶ 502.

trial, that would otherwise violate human rights. The U.S. military interventions show the facility with which the powerful can co-opt the moral imperative and legal arguments for humanitarian intervention to cloak its political motives for war. The challenge of initiatives such as the Responsibility to Protect will be, like many a human rights norm, to limit such government abuse. Nevertheless, no short-term fix appears on the horizon for this paradox—of the need for, and easy corruption of, humanitarian intervention.

The Srebrenica genocide, the *Krstić* case and the ICTY generally have a more specific, instructive legacy for international tribunals. The ICTY shows the U.N. and international community can conduct fair trials, provide accountability and enrich the jurisprudence of international law.[113] The ICTY provides an authoritative history based on its "detailed contextualization of criminal acts and extensive historical interpretation" required by the systemic and collective nature of crimes such as genocide and crimes against humanity.[114] Society attempts to bring accountability and punishment to the perpetrators through official channels to help heal victims and prevent further violence.[115] The prosecution of an official like Krstić helps avoid vigilantism, provides an impartial forum, and contributes to the restoration of order and peace.[116]

Further, the *Krstić* case and ICTY generally, have developed a substantial body of international humanitarian and criminal law and precedent for future courts, such as the ICC.[117] The "real work," of the ICTY for many, "is to secure the foundation of an international jurisprudence on war crimes and crimes against humanity which can be brought to bear globally."[118] While justifiable, this emphasis reveals a key tension. Focusing on a global goal can lead a tribunal to be inattentive and even insensitive to the local people and their society. Moreover, this compounds

---

113. McDonald, *supra* note 107 at 568–569; John Hagan & Sanja Kutnjak Ivkovic, *The Politics of Punishment and the Siege of Sarajevo: Toward a Conflict Theory of Perceived International (In)Justice*, 40 LAW & SOC'Y REV. 369, 374, 385 (2006).

114. Richard A. Wilson, *Judging History: The Historical Record of the International Criminal Tribunal for the Former Yugoslavia*, 27 HUM. RTS. Q. 908 (Aug. 2005); Claude Jorda, *The Major Hurdles and Accomplishments of the ICTY*, 2 J. INT'L CRIM. JUST. 572, 577 (2004).

115. Leila Nadya Sadat, *Exile, Amnesty and International Law*, 81 NOTRE DAME L. REV. 955, 983–84 (2006).

116. Eric Markusen and Martin Mennecke, Chapter XIV, *Genocidal Violence in Bosnia and Herzegovina Eyewitness Accounts,* A CENTURY OF GENOCIDE: CRITICAL ESSAYS AND EYEWITNESS ACCOUNTS 425 (2004); Christine Van den Wyngaert, *International Criminal Courts as Fact (and Truth) Finders in Post–Conflict Societies: Can Disparities with Ordinary International Courts be Avoided?*, 100 AM. SOC'Y INT'L L. PROC. 63, 65 (2006).

117. David Wippman, Comment, *The Costs of International Justice*, 100 AM. J. INT'L L. 861, 878 (2006); Wald, *ICTY 10 Years On*, *supra* note 73, at 471–73; Jorda *supra* note 114, at 578.

118. Wald, *Case Study*, *supra* note 62, at 451.

the flaws of a court like the ICTY, located hundreds of kilometers from the Balkans and lacking, at least initially, an adequate outreach effort.[119] Sentencing at the ICTY, with victims decrying the short sentences, illustrates the global vs local tension. "Sentencing is an important component in any potential deterrent value of the ICTY and, certainly, is looked to by the victims as a signal of how seriously the crimes are viewed by the international community."[120] But, if international standards preclude sentences more in line with local sentiment, then the ICTY and similar tribunals need to at least develop a communication strategy so the victims, if not the entire society, have some rudimentary respect for the sentencing logic. Otherwise, such flaws can leave survivors with a sense of injustice, as Mirsada articulated, or, worse, society can sideline the Tribunal and consign it to the dustbin of irrelevance.

In the maelstrom of post-conflict societies, such tribunals must focus on integrating international law and process into the local society, and they must not be afraid to weather storms of vitriol by extremists. Mechanisms were developed to coordinate the ICTY and domestic prosecutions, such as the creation of the aforementioned Bosnian war crimes branch of the BiH Court, and a referral mechanism where the ICTY passed lesser cases to Bosnia for prosecution. In the future, however, those setting up Tribunals should consider such explicit linkages from the outset. Tribunals could have an appellate role in reviewing domestic prosecutions. Broadly, such tribunals should be cautious about emphasizing the pursuit of global agendas of justice and instead focus on the facilitation of the particular society's pursuit of justice. They should highlight their role as practitioners who can help build local capacity. In conclusion, tribunals like the ICTY need a vision of integration to overcome the inevitable gaps separating the society and the tribunal.

* * *

In the first years after the genocide and the war, Mirsada expected that the Serb leaders would be captured and that all mass graves would be opened and at least the missing would be found. She was disappointed. Yet, Mirsada testified at the ICTY because, "[p]eople needed to know what happened," and the guilty needed to be punished. Mirsada is satisfied in knowing that Krstić was convicted and will spend decades in prison. She believes that Serbs must get some message from this.[121]

---

119. McDonald, *supra* note 107, at 569; Jane Stromseth, *Pursuing Accountability for Atrocities after Conflict: What Impact on Building the Rule of Law?*, 38 GEO. J. INT'L L. 251, 268–69, 322 (2007).

120. Wald, *ICTY 10 Years On, supra* note 73, at 473.

121. *See*, Eric Stover, THE WITNESSES, Conclusion (2005), which summarizes a study of some ninety ICTY witnesses and the main reasons they testified; Mirsada's reasons for testifying echo several of the main rationales.

Yet, after testifying at The Hague, she said, "I realized that everybody knows what happened in Srebrenica and that nobody feels sorry for us; nobody pays attention to us." She does not see much support from her government or the international community that would enable her to put her family's life back together. She sees herself as having few real choices in struggling to get by on her pensioner's paltry income and believes the privation she suffered during the war is worse than what Krstić endures in his "comfortable" British Prison. Mirsada is resentful of the delay in ICTY justice, especially after the futility of international responses prior to the genocide, of the lack of concrete social achievements from the peace, and of the ICTY's marginal relevance to what social reconstruction she observes. Thus, she does not see justice.[122]

Mirsada clearly expressed her support for the idea behind humanitarian intervention. In fact, she did not see it as revolutionary. She thought and expected that people the world over had long understood the concept, and therefore the international community would intervene in Bosnia and Srebrenica. Mirsada's tragedy and her bitter conviction that military intervention could have prevented Srebrenica and saved her family is shared by other survivors. This illustrates the intuitive popular appeal of humanitarian intervention in the face of mass atrocity. It signals that an enduring constituency exists supporting the concept, and future mass atrocities will only increase support for humanitarian intervention.

Conclusion

The ICTY's trials, especially the exhaustive proof of crimes such as genocide in Srebrenica and convictions of leaders like Krstić, give a fair, irrefutable version of history. While neither the first or last draft of history, this is the most renowned version in the region, even if hailed in some corners and reviled in others. The ICTY has put a "complete stop to false, fabricated denials" of crimes, said Justice Goldstone commenting in the wake of Karadžić's arrest in July 2008, a violent protest in Belgrade and renewed allegations of ICTY bias against Serbs.[123] But this modest achievement is not the end of the story. The history lives, witness that the government of Serbia, not some international agents, captured Karadžić. Still the ambivalence of Mirsada and other survivors

---

122. *See*, Eric Stover, Harvey Weinstein, *Conclusion: A Common Objective, A Universe of Alternatives*, MY NEIGHBOR, MY ENEMY, JUSTICE AND COMMUNITY IN THE AFTERMATH OF MASS ATROCITY, (Stover, Weinstein eds., 2004); what Mirsada sees lacking in her life are major components of what the authors see as required for social reconstruction.

123. Interview with Justice Richard Goldstone, by Morning Edition, National Public Radio, *Ex–U.N. Prosecutor: Linking Karadžić to War Crimes*, broadcast July 31, 2008, *available at* http://www.npr.org/templates/player/mediaPlayer.html?action=1&t=1&islist=false&id=93111071&m=93111041.

runs deep. The tortured and twisted history of international efforts and mechanisms in Bosnia before and after the genocide leave Mirsada and other survivors with a profound wound of injustice. Their ability to move on and lead a new life is crippled in so many ways. The justice delayed is unacceptable to them and suggests there may be a validity to the victims' having some claim to a right in a speedy trial.

Yet Mirsada and other survivors applauded the convictions, if not the sentences, of Krstić and other perpetrators at the ICTY. She acknowledged that, though it is justice much delayed, the conviction did have an impact, including in that it appears to have contributed to a revised understanding on the part of some Serbs.

The survivors' perhaps instinctual understanding of basic human values lead them to simply articulate the fundamental sentiments at the heart of the justice process and do so in words that echo past their particular roles and place. One survivor captured the basic sense of justice sought and the capacity for the society to move on. He was a survivor of a mass execution, and sat in the trial court giving wrenching testimony of Serb soldiers mowing down his fellow Srebrenica Muslims; at one point he turned to face Krstić and said,

> From all of whatever I have said and what I saw, I could come to the conclusion that this was extremely well organised. It was systematic killing. And that the organisers of that do not deserve to be at liberty. And if I had the right and courage, in the name of all those innocents and all those victims, I would forgive the actual perpetrators of the executions, because they were misled.[124]

Mirsada, when asked by the judge for any final comments, offered up a gem that captured the loss of so many and left people in the courtroom with tears in their eyes. She had walked around The Hague where the ICTY is located and stated that:

> "what caught my eye, was ... a monument to women, that is, women awaiting sailors who never come back. And the monument to those wives touched me profoundly.... Perhaps it could be likened to mothers and wives of Srebrenica who have been waiting and hoping for all those years, except that we followed different roads. We could turn to our empty forests. We saw our sons and husbands off to those woods and never found out anything about them again, whether they are alive or dead, where are their bones lying. Many mothers have died hoping against hope...."[125]

---

124. Transcript at 2936, Krstić, Case No. ICTY–98–33–T.
125. Transcript at 1995, Krstić, Case No. ICTY–98–33–T.

14

The Story of Hamid Karzai: The Paradoxes of State-building and Human Rights

Aziz Z. Huq*

... there is no place for Industry; because the fruit thereof is uncertain; and consequently no Culture of the Earth; no Navigation; nor use of the commodities that may be imported by Sea; no commodious Building; no Instruments of moving, and removing such things as require much force; no Knowledge of the face of the Earth; no account of Time; no Arts; no Letters; no Society; and, what is worst of all, continuall feare, and danger of violent death.[1]

Kabul by Night

On December 13, 2001, Afghanistan's future president took a night flight into Kabul. Hamid Karzai would have seen little of the city as he descended into the new U.S. military base at Bagram.[2] Twenty years of war had savaged the country's physical infrastructure, leaving essential transport, sanitation, and electricity networks in tatters. Swathes of the country were inaccessible due to land-mines. The wars' human toll had been enormous. One million dead; six million more refugees, mostly in Pakistan and Iran.[3] Emerging from the jagged folds of the Hindu Kush to the high plain on which Kabul lay, Karzai might have spied a scattering of dim lights, but little else to distinguish the capital from the barren plains and mountains beyond. But on the darkling plain below, a country with no apparatus to defend or achieve its citizens' human rights shivered in winter frost.

---

* The author thanks Margaret C. Ladner and Deena R. Hurwitz, Margaret L. Satterthwaite and Doug Ford for their insightful help and editing. All errors are the author's alone.

1. THOMAS HOBBES, LEVIATHAN 186 (C.B. Macpherson, ed. 1981).

2. Peter Baker, *Quietly, in Dark, Karzai Arrives in Kabul*, WASH. POST, Dec. 14, 2001, at A29.

3. INTERNATIONAL CRISIS GROUP, REBUILDING THE AFGHAN STATE: THE EUROPEAN UNION'S ROLE 3 (2005).

Driving into Kabul, the immensity of the task of leading Afghanistan might have hit Karzai. Once Kabul had been a lively modern metropolis with "a steady stream of new multi-story buildings in which men and women labour[ed] together."[4] But Karzai drove into a shattered and ruined city. A city of mortar-cratered roads, walls blistered by bullet holes, buildings with their frontage blown clean off, huddled figures collapsed beside open sewers, and fragile shacks woven out of corrugated aluminum, cardboard and U.N. grain sacks. The wars flayed the city, laying waste to a proud people and a country that once boasted state-of-the-art airports, roads, and institutions.[5]

Hamid Karzai returned to Kabul that night to rebuild a state and fashion an environment that could sustain Afghans' basic human rights—thanks to another war. And another *foreigners'* war—devastating, brutal, and cynical in the way war almost always is—but a war that nonetheless marked a new path for human rights in Afghanistan. In an unstable global environment, where sometimes military force alone can secure space for human rights, Afghanistan's post-invasion story assumes wider significance. What prospect is there for crafting new rights-respecting entities by military force from the rubble of failed states? Can rights, and not just power, ever come from the barrel of a gun? How are rights best embedded into a new state? What undermines that goal? What role can human rights advocates play? This Chapter uses Karzai's return and the ensuing events as a lens to examine these questions, which arise in any effort to incorporate human rights into state-rebuilding as violent conflict either winds down, or—more commonly—takes new forms.

The U.S.-led Operation Enduring Freedom found its primary justification in the presence of al Qaeda in Afghanistan after the September 11, 2001, attacks. But American and British governments also invoked human rights as supernumerary justification for war. Perhaps suggestive of human rights norms' status in North American and European chancelleries, it was the spouses of U.S. and U.K. executives, Laura Bush and Cherie Blair, who invoked the Taliban's destructive approach to women's rights as license for the regime's overthrow.[6]

But in this regard, Afghanistan was not exceptional: many contemporary military interventions have been justified publicly in terms of human rights and humanitarian norms even as *realpolitik* looms in the

---

4. NANCY DUPREE, AN HISTORICAL GUIDE TO KABUL 61 (2d ed. 1972). It is sad and strange to take Dupree's marvelous guide to modern Kabul in the 1970s and to trace what fragments remain across the savaged and ruined city today.

5. *Id.* at 62.

6. Alice Thompson, *Lifting the Veil on What Afghan Women Want*, DAILY TELEGRAPH, Nov. 23, 2001.

background.[7] Spurred by the failure to prevent large-scale human rights abuses in Rwanda and the former Yugoslavia, American and European policy-makers took an assertive stance to humanitarian intervention in the mid– to late–1990s.[8] Failed or failing states of the Balkans, and Somalia, Haiti, and East Timor, precipitated international intervention with the blessing of the United Nations ("U.N."). Despite the breakdown of post-intervention regimes in Haiti and East Timor, today's regional instability and the specter of transnational violence from terrorism, organized crime, and predatory armed forces furnish ample future incentives to intervene when a state fails. With the ascendance of this "new imperialism" of humanitarian intervention,[9] "the ability to shore up or create from whole cloth missing state capabilities and institutions has risen to the top of the global agenda."[10] In recognition of the trend, a high-level U.N. panel in 2004 suggested a novel international law concept of a "responsibility to protect" that extended authority for military intervention to instances of humanitarian need.[11]

But in an age when human rights organizations' yearbooks approach phone-book size, does such a "responsibility" invite abuse by global super-powers? Is there a risk—perhaps illustrated by the 2003 Iraq

---

7. MICHAEL BYERS, WAR LAW: UNDERSTANDING INTERNATIONAL LAW AND ARMED CONFLICT 92–103 (2005).

8. Tony Judt's magisterial history of postwar Europe brings into sharp focus the surprising, and largely forgotten, violence and insurgency prevalent through post-war Europe. See TONY JUDT, POSTWAR: A HISTORY OF EUROPE SINCE 1945 13–62 (2005). See also Ulrich K. Preuss, *Perspectives on Post–Conflict Constitutionalism: Reflections on Regime Change Through External Constitutionalization*, 51 N.Y. SCH. L. REV. 467, 474–81 (2006–07) (discussing efforts to impose a new constitution on Germany after World War II).

9. JANE STROMSETH, DAVID WIPPMAN & ROSA BROOKS, CAN MIGHT MAKE RIGHTS? BUILDING THE RULE OF LAW AFTER MILITARY INTERVENTIONS 1–8 (2006).

10. Francis Fukuyama, *The Imperative of Statebuilding*, 15 J. DEMOCRACY 17, 18 (2004).

11. The idea of a "responsibility to protect" was first developed by a Canadian-sponsored expert panel, and subsequently was adopted by the United Nations. See International Commission of Intervention and State Sovereignty, *The Responsibility to Protect: Report of the International Commission on Intervention and State Sovereignty* (2001); *Report of the Secretary–General's High Level Panel on Threats, Challenges and Change, A More Secure World: Our Shared Responsibility* (2004). The idea of a "responsibility to protect" that shaped national sovereignty and that could license intervention evolved from frustration about the United Nation's failure to intervene in either Rwanda or Kosovo. See Gareth Evans, *From Humanitarian Intervention to the Responsibility to Protect*, 24 WISC. J. INT'L L. 703, 707–08 (2006). It evolved into the wider notion that "to be sovereign means both to be responsible to one's own citizens and to the wider international community." *Id.* at 709. See also Christopher C. Joyner, *"The Responsibility to Protect": Humanitarian Concern and the Lawfulness of Armed Intervention*, 47 VA. J. INT'L L. 693 (2007) (canvassing debate in terms of U.N. Charter and in terms of sovereignty with attention to humanitarian concerns).

adventure[12]—that concerns about human rights will merely serve as justificatory veneer for super-power politics? Arguably, the manifest abuse of human rights language risks devaluing its coin. But is there any general framework for international intervention that can contain and address cases as divergent as Rwanda in 1994 and Iraq in 2003?[13] This larger question of legitimacy necessarily lurks in the shadows of any consideration of Afghanistan's story.

Yet for a bright moment in late 2001, it seemed that human rights and international security goals could happily converge in the project of building Afghanistan anew. International conferences in Bonn and Tokyo in 2001 and 2002 yielded diplomatic support and multi-billion dollar commitments to recreate an Afghan state that would not only prevent fresh terrorist plots but also yield good governance under the rule of law. International aid agencies and the U.N. flocked to Karzai's side in Kabul. And international human rights advocacy groups struggled to secure tickets on cramped and wobbly U.N. flights from Dubai.

For Karzai and for the human rights advocates on these flights, Afghanistan embodied the moral dilemmas of the new imperialism. First of all, the exercise of state-building raises fundamental questions about the relation between the state and human rights norms. The Afghan experience illustrates how rights violations cannot be addressed without re-constituting the state. But that new state in turn can quickly become a violator of rights itself.

Second, great powers spearheading interventions often have divergent priorities from local actors, leading to conflicts that can complicate efforts to ameliorate or institutionalize human rights. This proved repeatedly the case in Afghanistan, where great power decisions often had more influence on events than local actors' concerns. Karzai is the focus of this Chapter, but in fact he played only a bit part. Most critical decisions occurred outside Afghanistan, leaving Karzai scant leeway for maneuver. Nevertheless, Karzai singularly failed to seize residual opportunities to promote rights, spurning even fleeting opportunities to work in tandem with rights groups.

Third, human rights can be promoted outside the framework of representative government, and imposed on a new state. But what costs, denominated in legitimacy, public acceptance, and durability, does circumvention of representative democratic institutions impose? Can circumvention be justified in terms of the need to restrain the state? There

---

12. *See, e.g.,* Thomas E. Ricks, Fiasco: The American Military Adventure in Iraq 3–4 (U.K. ed. 2006) (explaining why the 2003 Iraq invasion is properly characterized as an "adventure" in the "critical sense of adventurism").

13. For an elegant survey of the issues, *see* Jonathan Moore, *Deciding Humanitarian Intervention*, 74 Soc. Res. 169 (2007).

remain practical disagreements as to when human rights should supersede commitments to democracy, and when emerging states should be able to exercise the same authority, which more established states do wield, to decide what rights commitments they will respect, at least within the bounds of customary international law.

Finally, problems arise in implementing rights. Most obviously, human rights standards may be in tension with local cultural norms, leading to possible trade-offs between the achievement of short-term goals through compliance with those norms, and the longer-term aim of re-constituting norms in a more rights-respecting manner. And the actions of human rights NGOs in post-invasion contexts also implicate hard ethical questions related to who human rights groups properly answer to, and how their actions affect local actors.

Roads to Kabul

Karzai came back to a country, like any other, with specific cultural and historical traditions that inflected the ways human rights policies could be implemented. Lying at the crossroads of subcontinental South Asia and Central Asia, Afghanistan is a patchwork of fifty-five ethnic groups,[14] most importantly Pashtuns in the south and east, Tajiks and Uzbeks in the north and west, and Hazaras in the west and center.[15] Ethnic cohorts in Afghanistan generally articulate and value cultural norms highly, claiming deep historical anchors for them. These norms, however, may also reflect and protect contemporary privileges and imbalances of power—between men and women, or between ethnic groups—that are selfishly, but zealously, defended.[16] Practices such as child marriage and the exchange of women to settle inter-clan feuds thus have long proved resilient to regulation by law—especially when that law arrives with foreign imprimatur.

At the same time, the nationalist solidarities that Karzai could invoke against such local practices remained weak. The idea of a geographic entity called "Afghanistan" emerged only in the 1740s and 1750s as the Pashtun commander Ahmed Shah Durrani carved out a new kingdom between the Safavid and Moghul empires. Like his succes-

---

14. Nigel J.R. Allen, *Defining Place and People in Afghanistan*, 42 POST-SOVIET GEOGRAPHY & ECON. 545 (2001); BARNETT R. RUBIN, THE FRAGMENTATION OF AFGHANISTAN: STATE FORMATION AND COLLAPSE IN THE INTERNATIONAL SYSTEM 38–42 (1995) [hereinafter B. RUBIN, THE FRAGMENTATION OF AFGHANISTAN].

15. There are strong continuities between historical ethnic categories and today's cultural norms. A traveler carrying the British explorer Mountstuart Elphinstone's 1808 "Account of the Kingdom of Caubal" finds that the cultural and tribal variances of the early nineteenth century are still recognizable two centuries later. 1 & 2 MOUNTSTUART ELPHINSTONE, AN ACCOUNT OF THE KINGDOM OF CAUBUL (1992).

16. B. RUBIN, THE FRAGMENTATION OF AFGHANISTAN, *supra* note 14, at 22–37.

sor Hamid Karzai, Durrani was a Pashtun of the Popalzai tribe in the south of Afghanistan.[17] From its inception, the Afghan state has been aligned with one of the nation's several competing ethnic groups. (Tellingly, "Afghan" is a self-assigned ethnonym for "Pashtun.")[18] A theme of Karzai's presidency, therefore, was a constant jockeying between ethnic leaderships for power in Kabul—often at the cost of equitable or necessary distributions of basic state services. Failure to accommodate competing demands would have collapsed state-building into anarchy and war. Peace, therefore, was a product of historically situated compromises in power-sharing.

State-building in Afghanistan, moreover, has always been entangled in great power politics. Afghanistan only developed a state (i.e., a centralized bureaucracy capable of predictable exercises of power) at the turn of the twentieth century, when Emir Abdul Rahman Khan fashioned the first national civil administration.[19] Known as the "Iron Emir," Abdul Rahman built his state with the aid of British subsidies and guns.[20] The latter found employ in brutal campaigns of murder, terror, and forced population transfers.[21] Like the Iron Emir, Karzai relied on foreign aid to govern domestically. Unlike Abdul Rahman, however, Karzai tried using diplomacy and compromise to win over his domestic adversaries rather than state terror—and by and large failed. The contrast suggests one paradox in state-building: If states are generally built out of blood, how can a state ever be an unsullied tool for promoting human rights?[22]

In the 1970s, the Afghan king was deposed by a republican regime, which in turn was overthrown by a Communist regime that promoted modernization by sidelining religious leaders and supporting female emancipation.[23] Its efforts to promote women's rights ran straight into

---

17. INTERNATIONAL CRISIS GROUP, AFGHANISTAN: THE PROBLEM OF PASHTUN ALIENATION, 3, n. 16 (2003), *available at* www.crisisweb.org.

18. MICHAEL BARRY, LE ROYAUME DE L'INSOLENCE: L'AFGHANISTAN 1504–2001 at 91 (1984).

19. VARTAN GREGORIAN, THE EMERGENCE OF THE MODERN AFGHANISTAN: POLITICS OF REFORM AND MODERNIZATION, 1880–1946 134–51 (1969); GILLES DORRONSORO, LA REVOLUTION AFGHANE: DES COMMUNISTS AUX TÂLEBÂN 40–44 (2000); *cf.* 2 MOUNTSTUART ELPHINSTONE, *supra* note 15, at 41 (noting the central government's weakness).

20. B. RUBIN, THE FRAGMENTATION OF AFGHANISTAN, *supra* note 14, at 48–49. At the same time, Abdul Rahman skillfully resisted the tentacles of British imperialism, refusing, for instance, the extension of rail links from the Punjab.

21. RALPH H. MAGNUS & EDEN NABY, AFGHANISTAN: MULLAH, MARX AND MUJAHID 36–38 (2000).

22. Sociologist Charles Tilly has famously argued that there is a close connection between state-building and militarism. *See* CHARLES TILLY, *War Making and State Making as Organized Crime*, *in* BRINGING THE STATE BACK IN 169 (Peter B. Evans et al. eds., 1985).

23. ANTONIO GIUTOZZI, WAR, POLITICS AND SOCIETY IN AFGHANISTAN 1978–1992 20–32 (2000) (describing policies); DORRONSORO, *supra* note 19, at 114–15 (linking the 1979 Herat revolt

enduring customary practices such as child marriage and bride exchange in rural communities—and there provoked violent resistance. In 1979, the Soviet Union invaded, hoping to prop up its client regime. After the Soviet retreat of 1989, the Communist regime lasted three years. In 1992, Afghanistan dissolved into a bloody, internecine conflict, with the country scissored up by competing warlords, all former *mujahideen* who had fought the Soviets.[24]

Another Pashtun force united Afghanistan. The Taliban, religious leaders and *madrassa* students, emerged from the southern city of Kandahar in 1994 with support and training from Pakistan's intelligence service, and captured Kabul by September 1996.[25] Like Abdul Rahman, the Taliban spared no brutality in building their version of a state. Of their 1998 capture of the northern city Mazar-i-Sharif, one eyewitness reported: "the streets were covered with dead bodies and blood. No one was allowed to bury the corpses for the first six days. Dogs were eating human flesh and going mad and soon the smell became intolerable."[26] The Taliban also brought social policies, particularly with respect to women, that earned world calumny. Taliban edicts required women to wear cumbersome head-to-toe coverings, and drastically limited female employment, access to public services, and general mobility. These policies impacted metropolitan Kabul more profoundly than rural Afghanistan, where women were already largely excluded from public life.[27]

Afghan state-building, in sum, has long been a matter of brute, brutal force. Because the state historically was a vehicle for Pashtun advancement at the expense of other ethnic groups, creating a new state, whether under a Pashtun such as Karzai or another ethnic leader, inexorably produced sectarian tension. Yet the experience of Mazar-i-Sharif in 1998 suggests that a sturdy state with mechanisms to manage inter-group conflict is a pre-condition for human rights in Afghanistan. Further, state attempts to "modernize" social relations, including the promotion of women's rights to education, work, and political access,

---

to the Communist attempt to reduce religious leaders' power); B. RUBIN, THE FRAGMENTATION OF AFGHANISTAN, *supra* note 14, at 118–20 (pointing to lack of alternatives to violence as means for political expression).

24. Competing *mujahideen* factions turned their rockets on Kabul, which had until then been spared, shelling quarters of the city into smoldering wreckage. *See generally* WILLIAM MALEY, THE AFGHANISTAN WARS (2002).

25. PETER MARSDEN, THE TALIBAN: WAR, RELIGION AND THE NEW ORDER IN AFGHANISTAN 43–56 (1998).

26. Quoted in AHMED RASHID, TALIBAN: MILITANT ISLAM, OIL AND FUNDAMENTALISM IN CENTRAL ASIA 73 (2000). The *mujahideen*, incidentally, were and are equally brutal.

27. NANCY HATCH DUPREE, *Afghan Women Under the Taliban*, in FUNDAMENTALISM REBORN? AFGHANISTAN AND THE TALIBAN 151–59 (William Maley ed., 1998); INTERNATIONAL CRISIS GROUP, WOMEN AND RECONSTRUCTION 8–10 (2003), *available at* www.crisisgroup.org.

generally have met fierce resistance to the point of insurrection.[28] The failures of post–2001 state-building and promotion of human rights reflect, in one respect, an inability to reckon successfully with this complex historical legacy.

Why State Building?

The Afghanistan that Karzai came into would have been darkly familiar to the English political philosopher Thomas Hobbes, who hypothesized that in the absence of a state, people live in "continuall feare, and danger of violent death."[29] Like many other successors to post-intervention states, Karzai inherited a frayed patchwork of fragmented and localized state institutions and a national army of barely a few thousand troops. Outside the capital, warlords seized patches of a country balkanized by military competition.[30] In the western city of Herat, the warlord Ismael Khan monopolized customs revenues from the Iranian border to fund his own *de facto* independent entity, virtually independent of Kabul.[31] In the south, tribal institutions balanced in precarious equilibrium against emerging opium magnates. Under these circumstances, the most basic human rights lost meaning among random violence or arbitrary power. As Hobbes' dictum suggests, a state for Afghanistan was *sine qua non* protection against private violence and for human rights in 2001.

Beyond restraining violence, the state is needed for human rights in other ways. Most obviously, many associational and speech rights, as well as any emerging right to democratic governance,[32] depend on there being a representative process in which to participate, and a state to manage this process.[33] To protect and promote civil or socio-economic rights, moreover, is costly. Fair courts require trained judges and lawyers, just as housing, health systems and basic services such as water and sanitation demand fiscal outlays. Sustainable state support for

---

28. The Communists' fate echoed that of reformist King Amanullah, who was toppled by a rural revolt in 1928.

29. HOBBES, *supra* note 1, at 186; MARK KISHLANSKY, A MONARCHY TRANSFORMED: BRITAIN 1603–1714 189 (1996).

30. INTERNATIONAL CRISIS GROUP, SECURING AFGHANISTAN: THE NEED FOR MORE INTERNATIONAL ACTION (2002).

31. Doug Struck, *A Self–Styled Emir Wins Loyalty, Power; Local Autonomy Challenges Afghan Leader*, WASH. POST, Feb. 2, 2002, at A15.

32. Thomas Franck, *The Emerging Right to Democratic Governance*, 86 AM. J. INT'L L. 46 (1992).

33. Indeed, there is a challenging paradox to be faced in constitution-making processes, where the exercise of those very rights can diminish other human rights protections because the people choose not to entrench rights in an organic document.

human rights requires predictable sources of income, generally in the form of taxation.[34]

Karzai, however, inherited a state with virtually no fiscal or service-delivery infrastructure. Afghanistan always had a weak economy dependent on external aid. But civil war destroyed its local agrarian economies, precipitating crises in food supply, income, and housing stock.[35] For Afghanistan's new order to become viable, Karzai also would have to rebuild the tattered skein of government offices in provincial centers and the accompanying apparatus of regulation and taxation. Creation of a licit, taxable economy was vital not only to fund the state, but to eliminate rights-corroding alternate economies, such as poppy cultivation.[36] Protecting human rights, in short, demanded a state not only with a monopoly on violence, but also with a rooted fiscal infrastructure. This meant Karzai had to negotiate with those who had power and who controlled resources—local warlords whose power had been consolidated via alliances with the United States. And his tools for doing so were largely determined by the roadmap and resources provided by international actors in late 2001.

Maps for Lost Rights

Karzai had to operate within parameters and against benchmarks set by the international community in the form of an international framework agreement describing a process for Afghanistan to emerge from violent conflict. The Bonn Agreement, endorsed by the U.N. Security Council on December 7, 2001, is typical of international agreements used in recent years to structure putative transitions from war to democratic governance. Such agreements are moments when human rights norms can be entrenched before domestic politics has really come into play, and when international attention is at its zenith.[37] Importantly, such agreements also channel transitional processes, and create

---

34. "All rights make claims upon the public treasury." STEPHEN HOLMES & CASS SUNSTEIN, THE COST OF RIGHTS: WHY LIBERTY DEPENDS ON TAXES 15 (1999).

35. AMALENDU MISRA, AFGHANISTAN: THE LABYRINTH OF VIOLENCE 57 (2004).

36. Elizabeth Rubin, *In the Land of the Taliban*, N.Y. TIMES (Magazine), Oct. 22, 2006, at 86, 91–92 [hereinafter E. Rubin, *In the Land of the Taliban*].

37. SIMON CHESTERMAN, YOU, THE PEOPLE: THE UNITED NATIONS, TRANSITIONAL ADMINISTRATION, AND STATE-BUILDING 175–76 (2004). On the one hand, human rights advocates might have seized the Bonn Agreement as an opportunity to push ratification of new treaties. On the other hand, what popular or political legitimacy would new treaty commitments have had if enacted at a transitional time in the absence of any elected or representative government? This dilemma raises a larger question of the relation between domestic political processes and human rights norms, and the degree to which domestic legitimacy matters for human rights norms—either a pragmatic matter (i.e., will imposed norms be unstable?) or in normative terms (i.e., should sovereign states be bound only by those norms that are accepted by those states?).

openings for the exercise of political rights, determining a future state's character (including whether it will be, for example, rights-respecting or not).

The Bonn Agreement created a thirty-member executive council headed by Karzai. This council would rule until the convening of a non-elected national assembly, the "Emergency Loya Jirga." This body was named after a traditional kind of Pashtun tribal council, but in fact was an ungainly mix of long-standing tribal forms and modern democratic impulses. The Loya Jirga met in June 2002 to select a transitional administration. The transitional administration's most important task—addressed below—was drafting a new constitution, which would be debated nationally and then voted on by a second "Constitutional Loya Jirga." Elections for a new government would follow.

Karzai did not attend the Bonn Conference of December 2001.[38] While the internal debates at Bonn remain undisclosed, it is safe to infer that Karzai's candidacy was not proffered by any of the four Afghan factions attending, each of whom had their own favored candidates. Instead, Karzai became the first transitional (and later the first elected) president of the new "democratic" Afghanistan thanks to U.N. and U.S. backing. Since 1999, Karzai had led the Popolzai tribe of Durrani Pashtuns. Initially a Taliban supporter, he broke with them and later became known and respected in Washington, where his eloquence and fluent English commanded entrées to the Rand Corporation, the State Department, and the National Security Council.[39] While Karzai was a Pashtun, the United States' military allies in the Northern Alliance were primarily Tajik and Uzbek. Given the Taliban's Pashtun roots, and Afghanistan's history as a Pashtun political project, the United States and its allies likely believed they needed a Pashtun leader if the country was not to fly apart.[40] Compromising on Karzai was a way to defer ethnic divisions. Paradoxically, it deepened those fissures.

International framework agreements are also opportunities for incorporating or institutionalizing human rights. But, absent from Bonn, the new Afghan president could have no voice as to which human rights treaties "his" country would respect. With domestic input minimal, what legitimacy would such rights commitments have? Were the international sponsors of the new Afghanistan right to bind President Karzai's hand

---

38. *See* Barnett R. Rubin, *Crafting a Constitution for Afghanistan*, 15 J. DEMOCRACY, 16–17 (2004).

39. Marc Kaufman, *Karzai's Ties to U.S. are a Mixed Blessing*, WASH. POST, Dec. 22, 2001, at A16.

40. *See* CHRIS JOHNSON & JOLYON LESLIE, AFGHANISTAN: THE MIRAGE OF PEACE 160–61 (2004) (discussing the options for a new Afghan state); *accord* Amy Waldman, *Afghan Vote is a Referendum on Karzai*, N.Y. TIMES, Oct. 8, 2004, at A8.

when it came to Afghan rights before they handed him the awesome instruments of the state? The Bonn Agreement addressed these questions in three ways. First, unlike similar agreements for Bosnia, Kosovo, and East Timor, the Bonn Agreement did not incorporate the whole corpus of international human rights instruments, but only the more limited set that previous Afghan governments had signed and ratified—a markedly cautious approach in a country where rights have historically been a point of social conflict. In effect, Bonn deferred hard questions of rights to the moment at which a new constitution would be written. Second, the Bonn Agreement stipulated creation of an "Independent Human Rights Commission" tasked with "human rights monitoring, investigation of violations of human rights, and development of domestic human rights institutions."[41] Finally, Bonn authorized a political mission with a human-rights component named the U.N. Assistance Mission for Afghanistan, or UNAMA, to aid in that process.[42]

But legal frameworks are only part of the background that determines the scope of human rights protection in a new state like Karzai's. Military and political decisions by the international coalition also torqued Karzai's efforts in pivotal ways.

Paradoxes of State–Building, Kabul Style

Arriving in Kabul, Karzai had scant internal political support and many enemies eager for his downfall.[43] Mere days after his arrival, Karzai found himself desperately brokering between warring factions in Kandahar for fear of renewed conflict.[44] But in three important ways, Karzai's international allies failed to resolve contradictions in their own approaches to state-building. First, the U.S.-led military coalition did not align its military strategy with its political goals in state-building. A disabling security vacuum ensued, undercutting efforts to promote human rights. Second, external actors undermined their own efforts to promote the rule of law through malfeasance and corruption. Finally, international actors did not take the time or pay the attention necessary to build institutions that could protect human rights. Aiming for a quick

---

41. *See Agreement on Provisional Arrangements in Afghanistan Pending the Re-Establishment of Permanent Government Institutions*, Dec. 7, 2001, *available at* http://www.reliefweb.int/rw/RWB.NSF/db900SID/SNAO–63DPZB?OpenDocument.

42. The U.N. mission was originally named the U.N. Special Mission for Afghanistan, or UNSMA. INTERNATIONAL CRISIS GROUP, *supra* note 30, at 1.

43. Pamela Constable, *Behind Confident Front, Karzai's Control Often Illusory*, WASH. POST, Feb. 22, 2002, at A16. *See also* Kenneth Katzman, CONGRESSIONAL RESEARCH SERVICE, *Afghanistan: Post–War Governance, Security, and U.S. Policy* 11–12 (2007) (listing warlord enemies).

44. John Pomfret, *Afghanistan's Next Leader: Karzai Warns U.S. Not to Walk Away, Pledges Friendship*, WASH. POST, Dec. 11, 2001, at A1.

public triumph, the international community (here, including more than just the United States) poured money into projects that had scant hope of succeeding in Afghanistan's political and social context. These three external constraints drastically limited Karzai's room for maneuver to achieve rights. But even to the extent room remained, Karzai sought short-term political stability over rights entrenchment.

The Mixed Motives of State–Building

The first paradox of state-building arose from the United States' failure to identify contradictions between its military and political goals in Afghanistan. It had been the 9/11 attacks that primarily spurred the American intervention. U.S. armed forces thus understood their mission in counter-terrorism terms, as targeting Osama bin Laden and his co-conspirators. State-building was a second-tier goal. As a consequence, the U.S.-led invasion of Afghanistan deployed a "light footprint" of CIA operatives and Special Forces, who coordinated the anti-Taliban Afghan forces of the Northern Alliance. This also accorded with the Bush Administration's desire to avoid "nation-building" and to pivot quickly toward Iraq.[45] At the operational level, Allied commanders were fearful of being seen on a par with the Soviet invaders of 1979, and hence husbanded their troops for carefully spare use as "force multipliers" for Northern Alliance forces.[46] After the American-supported forces rapidly swept the country, the United States thus did not introduce new ground troops to secure it. Only reluctantly did America agree to the creation of the peace-keeping International Security Assistance Force (ISAF), whose writ at first covered only Kabul.[47] Although the ISAF's mandate later expanded to include Afghanistan's thirty-three other provinces, ISAF command was unable to muster sufficient troops for any meaningful operational commitment.[48]

The U.S.-driven decision to minimize troop commitments limited Karzai's options, however, and colored Afghan state-building. It is no exaggeration to call it the most important decision in terms of human rights to be made after the U.S.-led invasion. As one recent study of state-building that encompasses both lessons from Afghanistan and the 2003 Iraq invasion concluded, "the re-establishment of a secure environment is the *sine qua non* of post-conflict reconstruction."[49]

---

    45. *See* Bob Woodward, BUSH AT WAR 60–61 (2002); RICKS, *supra* note 12, at 24–25.

    46. *See* ANTHONY H. CORDESMAN, THE LESSONS OF AFGHANISTAN: WAR FIGHTING, INTELLIGENCE AND FORCE TRANSFORMATION 3–9 (2003).

    47. Barnett R. Rubin, *Saving Afghanistan*, FOREIGN AFF., Jan.–Feb. 2007.

    48. UNITED STATES INSTITUTE FOR PEACE, ESTABLISHING THE RULE OF LAW IN AFGHANISTAN 4 (2004).

    49. STROMSETH et al. *supra* note 9, at 134 (citation and quotation marks omitted).

By limiting deployment of external ground forces in Afghanistan and relying instead on Northern Alliance forces, the United States and its international allies created a security vacuum.[50] In this environment, local military commanders, or warlords, were able to operate free of Karzai's control.[51] These warlords were infamous for their brutality. Afghans tell fearful stories about the checkpoints local commanders would maintain all over the country. If travelers were lucky, they would be "taxed." Less fortunate ones, especially women and children, would face physical and sexual assault, or worse. Compounding the problem, the United States "continued to pay off and work closely with local warlords" as part of its counter-terrorism efforts.[52] Indeed, warlords who had been U.S. allies committed the most atrocious of Afghanistan's manifold rights violations.[53] Moreover, as Uzbeks and Tajiks, they were suspicious of Karzai. Thus, U.S. military policy recreated ethnic divisions that had divided Afghanistan since Abdul Rahman Khan's days and undermined Karzai's ability to monopolize coercion and collect revenues. Just as violent opposition to the Karzai regime was rising, the United States shifted resources to Iraq, leading to a lack of personnel, resources, and funds in Afghanistan to redress these imbalances.[54]

Karzai found himself in a delicate, decidedly disadvantaged, position. Perhaps unsurprisingly, he proved "reluctant to act decisively" against warlords.[55] His efforts at co-opting them by negotiation—particularly on issues of rights—yielded what Francis Fukayama has called a "neopatrimonial" regime, in which political institutions are "used to service a clientist network of supporters."[56] On issues of women's rights and human rights, for example, Karzai proved willing to compromise rather than establishing clear norms. Collaterally, he proved unwilling to col-

---

50. *See generally* Seth G. Jones, *Averting failure in Afghanistan*, 48 SURVIVAL 111 (2006); Larry Goodson, *Bullets, Ballots, and Poppies in Afghanistan*, 16 J. DEMOCRACY 24, 35 (2005).

51. JOHNSON & LESLIE, *supra* note 40, at 48–51.

52. Seymour M. Hersh, *The Other War: Why Bush's Afghanistan Problem Won't Go Away*, NEW YORKER, Apr. 12, 2004, at 40.

53. RASHID, *supra* note 26, at 55–56 (discussing the Uzbek general Rashid Dostum who controlled parts of north-eastern Afghanistan).

54. "At critical moments in the fight for Afghanistan, the Bush Administration diverted scarce intelligence and reconstruction resources to Iraq...." David Rhode & David E. Sanger, *How the "Good War" in Afghanistan Went Bad*, N.Y. TIMES, Aug. 12, 2007, at A1.

55. Marc Kaufman, *Wondering If This Man Can Pull It Off*, WASH. POST, Feb. 17, 2002, at B1; Ali Jalali, *The Future of Afghanistan*, PARAMETERS, Spring 2006, at 6. Jalali, the former interior minister, referred to "Kabul" being "reluctant to act" in a way that can only be read to refer to Karzai alone.

56. Fukuyama, supra note 10, at 26.

laborate with or even heed domestic and international human rights actors.

One early example of Karzai's unwillingness to protect human rights norms arose in the Populzai heartland of Kandahar. Despite Karzai's roots in Kandahar, the President's control was shaky because the U.S. military decided that one of its allies, Gul Agha Shirzai, should be given the governor's office—regardless of what Karzai thought.[57] To Kandahar's residents however, Shirzai was a "symbol of ... arbitrary, bloody madness."[58] Under Shirzai, humanitarian aid was diverted to provide the governor a personal powerbase. Kandahar suffered from "abusive, predatory" governance.[59] But, even with the support of civil society groups who lobbied the United States ferociously, Karzai failed to seize an opportunity that opened in 2003 to replace Shirzai. In the acrid judgment of one observer, "instead of protecting the people from the warlords, Karzai seemed to be waltzing with them."[60] Subsequently, Karzai tried the same strategy with members of the Taliban, whose war crimes and suicide bombings evinced even less compunction for human life and dignity than Shirzai's depredations.[61]

Kandahar's fate is illustrative. The International Crisis Group concluded in January 2007:

> At what should be a time of rebuilding, the violence has claimed far more than its immediate victims. Affected programs include road building; airport reconstruction; census taking; telecommunications; health; agriculture; the National Solidarity Program, the flagship program for democratization and development.[62]

Every facet of human life connected to the international human rights instruments that protect essential entitlements and liberties, in other words, faltered due to the security vacuum.

A side consequence of political fragmentation was an explosion in opium production.[63] Despite a Taliban crack-down on opium production in 2001 that almost eliminated opium production, by 2007 Afghanistan was producing ninety-three percent of the world's opium. One southern province alone, Helmand, produced more opium than any other country

---

57. SARAH CHAYES, THE PUNISHMENT OF VIRTUE: INSIDE AFGHANISTAN AFTER THE TALIBAN 170 (2006).

58. *Id.* at 75.

59. *Id.* at 170.

60. *Id.* at 219–20, 228–29, 316–18.

61. *See* Carlotta Gall, *Karzai Says He Has Met With Some Taliban Members in an Effort at Reconciliation*, N.Y. TIMES, Apr. 7, 2007, at A7.

62. INTERNATIONAL CRISIS GROUP, AFGHANISTAN'S ENDANGERED COMPACT 8 (2007).

63. The best overall account is JOHNSON & LESLIE, *supra* note 40, at 110–33.

in the world.[64] Like other black market economies, the opium trade nurtures human rights problems. Opium yields no tax revenue for the central state, and instead strengthens local warlords and deepens the security vacuum. It puts rural Afghans in the cross-hairs of violence, with Karzai's international allies pushing the new government to enforce narcotics law. And it fosters other illicit economies,[65] including the trafficking of women.[66] Rumors that Karzai's family was implicated in the drug trade also sapped the President's reputation, despite his apparent personal probity.

Instead of cementing the state together for Karzai, American strategy thus strengthened past human rights violators, deepened fissures in the new polity, and made it far more difficult for the new Afghan government to extend its writ beyond Kabul. And Karzai simply failed to push back enough against his sponsors. International rights advocates likewise were muted in their criticism of U.S. officials. Some advocates expressed alarm when *jus in bello* violations occurred, for example in the use of cluster bombs by the U.S. air force.[67] But few provided a sufficiently clear condemnation of the United States' *strategic* approach and the contradictions between its military and political goals. Only later, long after most fateful decisions were made, did several realize the importance of military strategy for securing rights.

Mismanagement and Malfeasance

The second paradox of state-building in Afghanistan arose because the United States and its allies undermined their own efforts to promote the rule of law through malfeasance and mismanagement. Consider the story of Afghanistan's new security institutions. Afghanistan in 2001, like many other post-conflict states, lacked an army or police force. The security vacuum, however, could not be filled forever by international bodies. Thus, a new police and a new army were essential.[68] To address

---

64. David Rhode, *2nd Record Level for Afghan Opium Crop*, N.Y. TIMES, Aug. 28, 2007, at A6; Goodson, *supra* note 50.

65. SARAH LISTER & ADAM PAIN, AFGHANISTAN RESEARCH AND EVALUATION UNIT, TRADING IN POWER: THE POLITICS OF 'FREE' MARKETS IN AFGHANISTAN 4–5 (2004).

66. Barnett R. Rubin & Andrea Armstrong, *Regional Issues in the Reconstruction of Afghanistan*, WORLD POL'Y. J. Spring 2003, at 31, 32.

67. *See, e.g.,* HUMAN RIGHTS WATCH, BACKGROUNDER: CLUSTER BOMBS IN AFGHANISTAN (2001), *available at* http://www.hrw.org/backgrounder/arms/cluster-bck1031.htm. Reliance on air-power had other, non-obvious consequences. The Northern Alliance used a "mercantile" approach to war-making, buying off many Taliban allies: This meant that there were far fewer pitched battles (such as the Mazar-i-Sharif battle of 1998), and consequently far fewer casualties than there would have been with a direct U.S.-led invasion. CORDESMAN, *supra* note 46, at 16.

68. *See* STROMSETH et al. *supra* note 9, at 138, 148.

insecurity, new institutions must have the capacity to use force to prevent violent crimes such as rape and murder, to suppress illegal economies such as human trafficking, and to eliminate localized military confrontations. Yet any new coercive institution also risks becoming a new source of insecurity. Indeed, Karzai's Northern Alliance cabinet colleagues were particularly eager to make the new army and police forces personal fiefdoms. Hence, external actors have a special obligation in building new security institutions to ensure they are both accountable and efficient. Karzai's international allies failed on both counts.

International efforts to rebuild the rule of law were sapped from inception by mismanagement, or worse. One essential feature of the rule of law, especially against a backdrop of widespread lawlessness, is an effective police force. The Afghan police, concluded Amnesty International, was comprised largely of former *mujahideen* with little or no professional police training. Their loyalty ran to local commanders rather than to Karzai or the communities they purported to serve.[69] Efforts to reform the police were undermined by a lack of transparency and accountability on the part of international actors and an absence of any strategic focus from Karzai. The United States funneled $1.1 billion into police training, largely through the Virginia-based DynCorp. But in June 2006, a U.S. government audit found no effective field training program for police existed. Units had less than half their authorized equipment. Auxiliary police had received only two of the necessary eight weeks training.[70] These flaws in police training risked exacerbating insecurity rather than resolving it.

Another victim of international self-dealing and mismanagement was justice sector reform, which was delegated to the Italian government. Afghanistan's judicial system stood in ruins in 2001. Those judges and prosecutors remaining in the courts were largely political appointees without legal training. Trials were infrequent and highly imperfect.[71]

For Karzai, justice reform never presented a high priority because the little-utilized and largely moribund courts contained few opportunities for patronage or horse-trading.[72] The one exception was the Supreme Court. Initially, Karzai appointed a violently conservative cleric Fazl Hadi Shinwari as Chief Justice of the Supreme Court. This was a

---

69. AMNESTY INTERNATIONAL, AFGHANISTAN: POLICE RECONSTRUCTION ESSENTIAL FOR THE PROTECTION OF HUMAN RIGHTS (2003).

70. James Glanz & David Rohde, *U.S. Report Finds Dismal Training of Afghan Police*, N.Y. TIMES, Dec. 4, 2006, at 1.

71. UNITED STATES INSTITUTE FOR PEACE, ESTABLISHING THE RULE OF LAW IN AFGHANISTAN, *supra* note 48 at 5–9; INTERNATIONAL CRISIS GROUP, AFGHANISTAN: JUDICIAL REFORM AND TRANSITIONAL JUSTICE 7–14 (2003).

72. Traditional dispute resolution occurred at the village or tribal level under longstanding tribal codes. *See, e.g.,* LOUIS DUPREE, AFGHANISTAN 126–27 (1980).

concession to conservative warlord 'Abd al-Rabb as-Rasul Sayyaf, a commander closely aligned with the Saudis and known for his advocacy of exacting forms of Salafist Islam. In exchange, Karzai got Sayyef's support in areas around Kabul.[73] Among his first decisions, Shinwari banned cable television and co-education.[74] However the complex interaction of Islam and human rights is resolved over time in Afghanistan, Shinwari's own brand of religious authoritarianism was plainly uncompelled by the dictates of faith and inconsistent with rights norms.[75]

Karzai's international counterparts did little better. The Italian government used an Italian non-governmental organization ("NGO"), the International Development Law Organization, or IDLO, to lead justice sector reform. In its first years of operation, IDLO's most notable achievements were the rental of one of the largest NGO offices in Kabul and the creation of a digital compilation of Afghan laws that it declined to share.[76] As one former Afghan interior minister diplomatically put matters, "Italian-supported justice sector reform suffers from a very low level of human resources and infrastructure capacity."[77]

Mismanagement can be compounded by malfeasance. State-builders, in invading and re-constructing another country, sometimes purport to stand above the law. The United States maintained large counter-terrorism detention facilities in the southern city of Kandahar and at Bagram Airforce Base near Kabul, in addition to its detention site at the Guantánamo Bay Naval Base. American detention facilities in Afghanistan operated without oversight from the International Committee of the

---

73. BARNETT R. RUBIN, COUNCIL ON FOREIGN RELATIONS, AFGHANISTAN'S UNCERTAIN TRANSITION FROM TURMOIL TO NORMALCY 24 (2006). Subsequently, the new Afghan parliament rejected this appointment. *See* J. Alexander Thier, *Order in the Courts*, N.Y. TIMES, Aug. 28, 2006, at A15.

74. *See Afghan Justice Wants Co-ed Schools Shut*, available at http://www.hvk.org/articles/0203/256.html.

75. As Ann Elizabeth Mayer suggests, Islam is "only one factor" in a complex range of considerations that shape views on human rights in the Muslim world: there is no such thing as the Muslim view on rights. *See* ANN ELIZABETH MAYER, ISLAM AND HUMAN RIGHTS, xi (4th ed. 2007). *See generally* CARL W. ERNST, FOLLOWING MUHAMMAD: RETHINKING ISLAM IN THE CONTEMPORARY WORLD 206–07 (2003) (distinguishing the "prescriptive, normative, ideal context or religion and the descriptive, historical, and sociological accounts of religion" and pointing out that many Western representations of Islam emphasize the former and ignore the complexity of the latter); KHALED ABOU EL FADL, THE PLACE OF TOLERANCE IN ISLAM 13–22 (2002) (explicating Qur'anic basis for an ethos of tolerance). The complex relationship between variants on Islamic practice and human rights is an enormous subject, far beyond the scope of this Chapter but well addressed by Mayer, Ernst, and El Fadl. For a brief survey of Islamic approaches to human rights, *see* Aziz Huq, *Human Rights*, in ENCYCLOPEDIA OF ISLAM IN THE UNITED STATES (Joceylyne Cesari ed. 2007).

76. UNITED STATES INSTITUTE FOR PEACE, ESTABLISHING THE RULE OF LAW, *supra* note 48, at 9. UNAMA also moved slowly on judicial reform. *See* CHESTERMAN, *supra* note 37, at 178.

77. Jalali, *supra* note 55, at 10.

Red Cross. The bases became sites for prolonged detention and coercive interrogation in violation of international human rights norms.[78] Under an executive order issued by U.S. President George W. Bush on February 7, 2002, prisoners in Afghanistan did not benefit from any of the protections of international humanitarian law contained in the 1949 Geneva Conventions, including the minimum detention standards for all persons outlined in Common Article 3 of those treaties.[79] While Karzai was attempting to build the rule of law, his international allies were flouting international humanitarian law by detention without due process and brutal interrogation practices mere miles from Kabul.[80]

At a minimum, powerful actors' manifest defiance of rights norms promotes the belief that the norms are irrelevant or a fig leaf for venal interests. In Afghanistan, it also distorted the allocation of much-needed resources. Even as the judicial system struggled for money and personnel, the United States, concerned with "the future repatriation of Afghan detainees from the U.S. detention facility at Guantanamo Bay," routed resources to create a parallel system of Afghan military courts.[81] In other parts of South and Central Asia, of course, military courts are closely associated with political repression and state injustice. Yet the United States, for motives of its own, pushed the militarization of Afghanistan's judiciary at a time when the country hardly had a functioning civilian justice system.

Failed Commitments

The third paradox of state-building in Afghanistan stems from fiscal and expertise-related limitations on state-building. Karzai's sponsors never committed the finances or know-how to state-building necessary to make the project work. From the beginning, Karzai faced chronic shortfalls in aid; in 2002, for example, the government was able to collect in tax only a tenth of the national budget.[82] The January 2002 Tokyo conference provided Afghanistan with $5 billion, one-eighth of the fund-

---

78. *See, e.g.*, HUMAN RIGHTS WATCH, OPERATION ENDURING FREEDOM: ABUSES BY U.S. FORCES IN AFGHANISTAN (2004), *available at* http://hrw.org/reports/2004/afghanistan0304/; Suzanne Goldberg & James Meek, *Papers Reveal Bagram Abuse*, THE GUARDIAN, Feb. 18, 2005; James Meek, *Nobody is Talking*, THE GUARDIAN, Feb. 18, 2005.

79. *See* FREDERICK A.O. SCHWARZ & AZIZ Z. HUQ, UNCHECKED AND UNBALANCED: PRESIDENTIAL POWER IN A TIME OF TERROR 72–77 (2007).

80. For one first-hand account (with all the problems that involves), see MOAZZAM BEGG, ENEMY COMBATANT: MY IMPRISONMENT AT GUANTÁNAMO, BAGRAM, AND KANDAHAR (2006).

81. Major Sean M. Watts & Captain Christopher E. Martin, *Nation–Building in Afghanistan: Lessons Learned in Military Justice Reform*, ARMY LAWYER, May 2006.

82. Astri Suhre, *When More is Less: Aiding Statebuilding in Afghanistan*, at 4 (2006) *available at* http://www.cmi.no/publications/publication.cfm?pubid=2402.

ing Bosnia received on a per capita basis between 1996 and 1999.[83] And between 2005 and 2006, American assistance to Afghanistan dropped thirty-eight percent, from $4.3 billion to $3.1 billion.[84] On top of war damage, Afghanistan had to cope with millions of returning refugees, almost without infrastructure or an agricultural base capable of sustaining its population. Karzai thus never had the resources needed to reconstruct the state, or even to provide basic services.

In other areas, neither Karzai nor his allies invested time or effort to identify rights concerns. Prison reform was one area in which attention and investment shortages were particularly acute. Again, for Karzai there was scant political capital to be gained from addressing prison issues. As in other post-conflict situations, moreover, no international agency or donor stepped forward to address the utter disintegration of the Afghan prison system.[85] Reflecting a blindness learned at home, North American and European donors were all too willing to invest in police to arrest criminals and soldiers to fight the Taliban, but not in the prisons needed to house the resulting detainees in a secure and humane way.[86] And when investment in Afghan prisons did begin, it was directed at re-establishing a centralized facility at Pul-i-Charki, near Kabul, a prison notorious for its wretched conditions and long history of torture.[87]

Worse, the international community approached rights issues too often eager for quick results and disdainful of Afghanistan's complex historical and cultural context. The limits of social engineering became perhaps most evident in the failure to further Mrs. Blair's and Mrs. Bush's purported cause célèbre, women's rights. The revolt against the Communists of the late 1970s had been precipitated by efforts to foster greater educational and economic access for women. According to one Afghanistan scholar, men of numerous ethnic groups tended to view women as "the repository of their honor."[88] Even outside the family, political and economic life hinged on familial links, often cemented through arranged marriages. Efforts to alter the subordination of women were, in effect, efforts to rewrite rural Afghanistan's social compact. Advocates for women's rights, therefore, were faced with a paradox: Immediate improvements in women's health and education could be

---

83. J. Alexander Thier, *The Politics of Peace–Building: Year One: From Bonn to Kabul in* NATION BUILDING UNRAVELING? AID PEACE AND JUSTICE IN AFGHANISTAN, at 41 (Antonio Donini ed., 2003).

84. Rhode & Sanger, *supra* note 54, at A1.

85. STROMSETH et al., *supra* note 9, at 218–26.

86. *See generally* BRUCE WESTERN, PUNISHMENT AND INEQUALITY IN AMERICA (2006).

87. Bilal Sarwary, *Kabul's Prison of Death*, BBC NEWS, *available at* http://news.bbc.co.uk/2/hi/south_asia/4756480.stm.

88. B. RUBIN, THE FRAGMENTATION OF AFGHANISTAN, *supra* note 14, at 23–24.

secured through cooperation with existing social structures. But it was and still is precisely those structures that entrench and prolong inequalities in treatment.

Without doubt, some NGOs and international organizations crafted effective service and education delivery mechanisms with women in mind, for example, by recognizing that girls' access to education hinged not only on the existence of educational infrastructure but also on predictable physical security that enabled travel to and from schools. But they were working against the grain. In large measure, post-war efforts to promote women's rights simply failed to heed the bitter lessons of Communist efforts twenty years previously. Despite his relatively liberal personal inclinations, Karzai never invested seriously in women's rights. One early, promising sign was the ratification in March 2003 of the United Nations Convention on the Elimination of All Forms of Discrimination Against Women (CEDAW), without reservations.[89] But Karzai made no serious effort to implement any of CEDAW's commitments. Article 16's provision on the right to freedom of marital choice, for example, remains nakedly unenforced.

Unwilling to displease his conservative domestic allies, but needing to do enough to appease his international audience, Karzai made gestures in lieu of serious attempts to integrate women's rights into broader social and political planning. The result was Potemkin institutions without political capital or funds. Instead of appointing a respected leader on the issue (and such leaders indeed existed), Karzai drew on a Communist-era women's association to create a new Ministry of Women's Affairs. Wholly dependent on foreign support and lacking the skills or credibility to push for social change, the Ministry proved ineffectual. It built expensive "community centers" for women at fourteen regional capitals that were to serve as focus points for access to services and education.[90] International donor agencies thus had concrete "achievements" to trumpet, even though Afghan women hardly benefited. In 2006, an American reporter came across one of these "lovely new" buildings in the provincial capital of Lashkar Gah, "empty except for three women getting ready to leave," who explained that women in that region were too scared of being robbed or raped to travel to the center.[91]

Gender-biased deprivation and violence were not limited to the countryside. One former USAID gender advisor explained that, in 2004, "day-to-day life for women, even in Kabul, isn't any better" than under

---

[89]. Michael Schoiswohl, *The New Afghanistan Constitution and International Law: A Love–Hate Affair*, 4 INT'L J. CONST. L. 664, 672 (2004).

[90]. INTERNATIONAL CRISIS GROUP, *Women and Reconstruction*, supra note 27, at 11–14.

[91]. E. Rubin, *In the Land of the Taliban*, supra note 36, at 86.

the Taliban.[92] In September 2006, Safia Amajan, the sixty-three-year-old head of women's affairs in the southern city of Kandahar, was murdered in front of her house, steps away from her husband and son.[93] Her murder reflected the U.S.-backed warlords' continued power and was a stark reminder that international promises to protect Afghan women against entrenched fundamentalist violence were cheap talk, sacrificed quickly to political exigency or convenience.

Constitution–Making and Human Rights

Whatever the constraints imposed by foolish or compromised international efforts, Karzai preserved some room for maneuver. The constitution-making process was one such instance. But rather than using constitution-making as an opportunity for expanding civil and political rights against the warlords' arbitrary rule, or for building legitimate institutions to elaborate and implement rights norms, Karzai exploited constitution-making as a chance to co-opt warlords as allies without changing their conduct and to entrench his own power.

Often, constitution-making is viewed solely in terms of the opportunity to incorporate explicit textual commitments to rights in an organic document. But hard experience suggests that a constitution's textual commitment to rights, when examined apart from the institutions needed to implement that commitment, has only a weak connection to rights' implementation. While rights-rich Communist constitutions of the Cold War era did little good, unwritten constitutions in the United Kingdom and New Zealand have provided some shelter for rights. The relationship between constitutions and rights thus cannot be reduced to textual analysis.

A constitution matters only to the extent it has popular legitimacy and governing institutions willing to respect it. Equally, rights norms embedded in constitutional text will be accounted for and elaborated in practice only to the extent supported by popular legitimacy and institutional structure. Yet the process whereby a constitution is adopted—which is pivotal today to legitimacy—and its institutional framework too often receive insufficient attention from rights advocates. Process also matters because constitution-making is a moment for citizens to exercise core political freedoms.[94] And, the more meaningful that exercise, the more likely the outcome will respect rights. One 2006 comparative study of constitution-making processes concluded that "more representative and more inclusive constitution building processes resulted in constitu-

---

92. Hersh, *supra* note 52, at 40.

93. Robert Klujver, *Safia Amajan*, THE GUARDIAN (U.K.), Oct. 16, 2006.

94. *See* Vivien Hart, UNITED STATES INSTITUTE FOR PEACE, DEMOCRATIC CONSTITUTION-MAKING, July 2003, at 5–7.

tions favoring free and fair elections, greater political equality, more social justice provisions, human rights protections, and stronger accountability mechanisms."[95] Constitutional transparency, like any democracy-fostering process, can have costs: It can, for example, manifest or augment ethnic tensions.[96] Yet such costs may pale beside the price of an imposed constitution.

Finally, constitutions settle the rules of political competition and thereby provide non-violent alternatives to armed conflict.[97] If the rate of rights violations varies with levels of conflict—as Afghanistan's harsh experience suggests—by far the most important rights-preserving role constitutions play may be the provision of a visibly just and enduring framework for settling conflict. Yet settlement of political conflict equally may require compromises—for example, with powerful political actors who have violated human rights norms in the past—that are far from satisfactory from a human rights perspective. Complex issues thus arise around the trade-off between avenging past wrongs and providing a stable future especially, as in Afghanistan, when human rights violators retain a significant hold on power.[98]

Constitutions must also be viewed and accepted as legitimate in order to be effective. They must create institutions that have practical political power to step in when rights are violated. Whatever normative theory of rights is adopted—whether or not, for instance, rights avail as "trumps" against mundane political interests[99]—rights must still be argued for and operationalized in the course of politics.[100] Constitution-making therefore is perhaps the best evidence that the accomplishment

---

95. Kirsti Samuels, *Post–Conflict Peace–Building and Constitution–Making*, 6 Chi. J. Int'l L. 663, 668 (2005–06). *Cf.* Vivien Hart, *Constitution–Making and the Transformation of Conflict*, 26 Peace & Change 153, 168 (2001).

96. *See* Note, Alicia Bannon, *Designing a Constitution–Drafting Process: Lessons from Kenya*, 116 Yale L. J. 1824, 1853 (2006) (describing Kenyan experience). Exacerbation of ethnic tensions is a risk in any democratization process; but ethnic tensions can fester equally in non-democratic conditions.

97. In deeply divided societies, moreover, constitutions ideally furnish power-sharing mechanisms that permit cooperation and mitigate conflict. Stromseth et al. *supra* note 9, at 91–92; Yash Ghai & Guido Galli, International IDEA, Constitution Building Process and Democratization 7–8 (2006).

98. For thoughtful reviews of the hard issues thereby raised, *see* Jon Elster, Closing the Books: Transitional Justice in a Historical Perspective (2004); Ruti G. Teitel, Transitional Justice (1999).

99. For the canonical formulation, *see* Ronald Dworkin, *Taking Rights Seriously*, in Taking Rights Seriously 184–205 (1978). This chapter does not purport to wrestle with the complex issues raised by Dworkin's formulation. Suffice to say that even if rights are trumps, the game being played is still politics.

100. *See* David Kennedy, The Dark Side of Virtue 21 (2004).

of rights cannot stand *above* politics. Rights must be labored for and achieved *in* politics.

The Afghan process illustrates these subtle dynamics—and shows how parochial political calculation can sap the legitimacy of a constitution. The Bonn Agreement stipulated that Afghanistan would hold a "Constitutional *Loya Jirga*" no later than January 2004, but provided little further detail on how constitution-making was to occur.[101] The process, in fact, was largely directed by the Karzai Administration in a way that shut out popular voices, reduced democratic space, and vitiated the legitimacy of the resulting document. Preoccupied with the risks of political participation, Karzai failed to seize constitution-making as a moment when power could be shifted from the warlords to a more diffuse public.

The first step was the establishment of a drafting committee. In October 2002, Karzai announced that the commission would be led by his Vice President Neamatullah Shahrani. A religious scholar linked to one of Karzai's political allies, Shahrani was known as an ally of religiously conservative warlords. The committee's only two women were known to follow Shahrani's lead. By appointing Shahrani, Karzai failed to grasp an opportunity to partner with civil society actors more committed to human rights, and to reduce the influence of warlords who had abused human rights, all in the name of short-term political gain and a narrowly-conceived sense of stability. Working in secret, this commission produced a draft. Without sharing the draft with the public, a larger version of the commission conducted "public consultations" in the summer of 2003.[102] These "consultations" were "little more than lectures from local power-brokers, who warned the participants ... not to challenge their [i.e., the warlords'] views."[103]

The second step involved closed-door negotiations in which Karzai consolidated his political power at the cost of institutional checks on governmental power. The draft formally submitted to Karzai in September 2003 created a "mixed" system with both a prime minister and a president. But the draft released to the public in November 2003 (after

---

101. The following three paragraphs are drawn from INTERNATIONAL CRISIS GROUP, AFGHANISTAN'S FLAWED CONSTITUTIONAL PROCESS (2003), and INTERNATIONAL CRISIS GROUP, AFGHANISTAN: THE CONSTITUTIONAL LOYA JIRGA (2003).

102. Karzai dissolved the initial commission on April 26, 2003 and created a larger commission with "a broader political and ethnic spectrum than the first commission." J. Alexander Thier, *The Making of a Constitution in Afghanistan*, 51 N.Y. L. SCH. L. REV. 557, 567–58 (2006–07).

103. JOHNSON & LESLIE, *supra* note 40, at 167. *See also* Thier, *The Making of a Constitution, supra* note 102, at 568 ("Members of the Constitutional Commission traveled to provincial capitals, holding meetings with pre-selected groups [and] limited public discussion to vague principles rather than eliciting concrete views on key questions.").

the public "consultation" and only five weeks before the final *Loya Jirga*) established a system vesting almost untrammeled executive power in the president.[104]

In the third stage, the draft constitution was put before the Constitutional *Loya Jirga*, which was selected through a sequence of local meetings organized by the U.N.[105] Despite rules that formally excluded anyone who had committed war crimes and despite valiant efforts by the U.N., in practice many delegates either had blood on their hands or represented warlords. The *Loya Jirga* convened for 22 days in December 2003. Karzai himself avoided the limelight, exercising influence though closed-door negotiations and via American allies. In the public debates, women delegates who managed to raise issues of accountability for past crimes received violent threats from attending warlords.[106] Under pressure from the United States, behind-the-scenes haggling yielded "a constitution that reflected to a considerable extent the agenda shared by Karzai" and his allies in the cabinet—one with scant room for transitional justice concerns or effective rights-protecting mechanisms.[107]

The final draft preserved the presidential system, shoring up Karzai's power. Karzai also spurned the idea of a constitutional court. As a concession to religiously inclined warlord allies, he pushed for the highly conservative Supreme Court to have plenary power to decide constitutional matters.[108] More broadly, the Constitution created a weak human rights commission. It thus failed to "provide clarification or mechanisms concerning the implementation of international obligations."[109] Combined with the largely unrepresentative process whereby the draft was adopted, this meant the Constitution lacked both legitimacy and institutional armatures to implement its paper commitments to rights.

---

104. Karzai was also instrumental in choosing the electoral mechanism for national polls, the rarely used single non-transferable vote system. According to one account of the decision, Karzai alighted on this vote in an effort to ensure there was not a solid parliamentary block against him, but acted with a poor understanding of the functioning or consequences of this system. *See* Andrew Reynolds, *The Curious Case of Afghanistan*, 17 J. DEMOCRACY 104, 105–12 (2006).

105. Under a July 2003 presidential decree, 344 delegates were elected at a district level; sixty-four women were elected at the provincial level; forty-two delegates were selected from refugee, internally displaced, and other minority communities; and fifty delegates were selected by Karzai. Thier, *The Making of a Constitution*, *supra* note 102, at 569.

106. CAROLYN MCCOOL, INTERNATIONAL IDEA, THE ROLE OF CONSTITUTION-BUILDING PROCESS IN DEMOCRATIZATION: CASE STUDY AFGHANISTAN 18–19 (2004).

107. B. Rubin, *Crafting a Constitution*, *supra* note 38, at 10.

108. *See* Michael Schoiswohl, *Linking the International Legal Framework to Building the Formal Foundations of a "State at Risk": Constitution–Making and International Law in Post–Conflict Afghanistan*, 39 VAND. J. TRANSNAT'L L. 819, 838–39 (2006).

109. *Id.* at 859.

The Constitution also adopted an unstable compromise on tensions that could arise between women's rights and interpretations of Islam. Article 3 banned laws contrary to Islam, while Article 22 endorsed women's rights. Article 121, however, elevated constitutional norms, including Article 3, above Afghanistan's international commitments, such as CEDAW.[110] As a result, the highly conservative Supreme Court would decide on which international human rights laws violated Article 3.

The Constitution adopted in December 2003 did contain a "promising" list of human rights protections.[111] Whether aspirational commitments will translate into later realities—or whether their rampant abuse will undermine the Constitution's legitimacy further—remains open to question.[112] But early indications were far from promising. For example, one of Afghanistan's success stories had been a flourishing press, including six independent television channels and dozens of radio stations and newspapers. Article 34 of the new Constitution states that "Freedom of speech is inviolable." Yet in early 2007, Karzai announced the need to "curb journalists" to ensure stability, especially those who had reported on the rising fortunes of the Taliban. His administration proposed a new law that would have prohibited journalism deemed insulting to Islam, individuals, or corporations (truth being no defense), or that endangered national stability, security, or sovereignty.[113] Although the proposal was not enacted into law, it reflects the ease with which mere paper guarantees of civil and political rights could be ignored. And it underscores how even a relatively fragile and limited state such as Afghanistan's can quickly become a violator of rights itself, despite having established *de jure* rights protections.

The Role of Human Rights Advocates in State-Building

The political and historical complexity of state-building forced human rights NGOs, particularly international human rights NGOs headquartered in the United States and Europe, to make difficult judgments. Despite their high profile in the world media, international NGOs have limited resources, and only infrequently can afford to station (or hire) staff inside a country. Based in Europe or the United States and

---

110. *See* JOHNSON & LESLIE, *supra* note 40, at 168. In March 2005, one respected journalist noted that Article 3 had not been enforced. David Rohde, *A World of Ways to Say "Islamic Law"*, N.Y. TIMES, Mar. 13, 2005, at 4.

111. Chapter 2 of the 2004 Constitution contains thirty-seven articles that cover the gamut of civil, political, economic, and social rights.

112. *See* Noah Feldman, *Imposed Constitutionalism*, 37 CONN. L. REV. 857, 871–73 (2005).

113. Abdul Waheed Wafa & Carlotta Gall, *Afghan Media Face Threat of Controls*, N.Y. TIMES, May 7, 2007, at A12.

speaking to a global public, moreover, international NGOs compete with one another for funds and for a market share of scant public attention. They thus hone their message for American and European policy-makers and media. But what makes headlines in Washington may not be a priority in Kabul or Mazar-i-Sharif. In consequence, no beneficial partnership between Karzai and international NGOs developed: Karzai was too preoccupied with horse-trading his way into the warlords' good graces, while the NGOs were largely speaking to a different audience.

The research and advocacy agendas of two of the most important global human rights NGOs, Human Rights Watch (HRW) and Amnesty International (AI), illustrate different ways of responding to those pressures. After a brief field presence in early 2002, HRW's permanent non-Afghan staff began conducting missions from its office in New York. Early on, HRW tended to focus on violations involving physical violence, rather than structural and institutional flaws that allowed violence to continue. For example, it described the security vacuum and published reports on women's rights focusing on violations of physical integrity and of political rights—subjects that preoccupied external audiences and that reflected established models of human-rights reporting.[114] By contrast, AI established an office in Kabul in the year after the U.S.-led invasion and conducted research designed not merely to identify problems, but to provide durable solutions. During its presence in Kabul, AI published reports covering police, the prison system (an issue many other groups failed to address), women's access to justice, the courts, and the justice system: the core components of state-building necessary to address a security vacuum.[115] These reports not only charted physical abuse and violence, but also highlighted institutional problems with the imperfect instruments of the new Afghan state. By locating in Kabul, AI could reach different audiences, including U.N. staff, implementing agencies such as USAID, and (critically) Afghan politicians and "civil

---

114. Hence, in 2002–03, Human Rights Watch published a report on coalition use of cluster bombs (FATALLY FLAWED: CLUSTER BOMBS AND THEIR USE BY THE UNITED STATES IN AFGHANISTAN (2002)), three reports on violence in specific regions of Afghanistan (PAYING FOR THE TALIBAN'S CRIMES: ABUSES AGAINST ETHNIC PASHTUNS IN NORTHERN AFGHANISTAN (2002); ALL OUR HOPES ARE CRUSHED: VIOLENCE AND REPRESSION IN WESTERN AFGHANISTAN (2002) and KILLING YOU IS A VERY EASY THING FOR US: HUMAN RIGHTS ABUSES IN SOUTHEAST AFGHANISTAN (2003)), and one report on women's rights (WE WANT TO LIVE AS HUMANS: REPRESSION OF WOMEN AND GIRLS IN WESTERN AFGHANISTAN (2002)). All of these reports are available at http://hrw.org/doc/?t=asia_pub&c=afghan.

115. In 2003, Amnesty International published one report on prisons (AFGHANISTAN: CRUMBLING PRISON SYSTEM DESPERATELY IN NEED OF REPAIR); one on the police (AFGHANISTAN: POLICE RECONSTRUCTION ESSENTIAL FOR THE PROTECTION OF HUMAN RIGHTS); one on women, violence, and the justice system (AFGHANISTAN: 'NO-ONE LISTENS TO US AND NO-ONE TREATS US AS HUMAN BEINGS': JUSTICE DENIED TO WOMEN); and one on the courts (AFGHANISTAN: REESTABLISHING THE RULE OF LAW). These reports are available at http://web.amnesty.org/library/eng-afg/reports&start=31.

society" leaders. But AI kept its presence in Kabul for only a year, shifting focus to Iraq in 2003 with the rest of the world. By prematurely withdrawing, the organization was unable to follow through on the detailed research accomplished in the first year.

International NGOs' operation in Afghanistan illustrated other difficulties of delicate investigative work in a fragile post-conflict situation.[116] Unable to operate without the knowledge and experience of local staff, human rights groups hired Afghans, who were vulnerable to intimidation. Human rights work also posed risks to others. In mid–2003, for instance, the fact that an international human rights group was conducting investigations into a warlord's activities in an eastern province of Afghanistan became known. This not only put that NGO's staff at risk, but also imperiled the staff of humanitarian NGOs who were working in the area—a risk compounded by the fact that the human rights NGO failed to inform other NGOs of the threats made against non-Afghan staff.

Domestic human rights institutions found themselves in an even more precarious position than their international counterparts, thanks to persisting insecurity. Karzai never gave his full backing to the Afghan Human Rights Commission. The Commission's work on transitional justice, for example, stalled thanks to political resistance and mounting security risks for commissioners and their staff.[117]

At the same time, international NGOs drew talented local staff away from domestic counterparts unable to compete on salaries in a context where skilled personnel were already thin on the ground.[118] For an ambitious Afghan human rights advocate, working with an international NGO, the U.N., or a European mission provided relative security and an unmatched set of tools for change. As in other post-conflict situations, international aid thus had the unintended consequence of diluting Afghan civil society. International organizations, including NGOs, also contributed to a property bubble in Kabul that forced out local residents. Ironically, the bubble was the result of international actors paying

---

116. The examples in this paragraph are based on the author's personal experience, and have been verified with other NGO employees working in Kabul at the same time.

117. UNITED STATES INSTITUTE FOR PEACE, ESTABLISHING THE RULE OF LAW IN AFGHANISTAN 12–13 (2004).

118. The problem is endemic to transitional scenarios and is exacerbated in particular by the United Nations. *See* Richard Sannerholm, *Legal, Judicial and Administrative Reforms in Post–Conflict Societies: Beyond the Rule of Law Template*, 12 J. CONFLICT & SECURITY L. 65, 80–81 (2007); Francis Fukuyama, *"Stateness" First*, 16 J. DEMOCRACY 84, 85 (2005). Furthermore, local employees almost always receive lower salaries than ex-patriates working in the same agency or organization.

exorbitant rents largely to warlords who had seized or "bought" property, often with the acquiescence of the Karzai regime.[119]

Conclusion

On the morning of July 9, 2007, a thirteen-year-old girl called Shukria was leaving her school in the south-eastern province of Logar when two men, perhaps Taliban, rode up on a motorcycle and opened fire at the school, hitting Shukria in the arm and back. The men rode closer and emptied their weapons into Shukria's stomach and heart.[120] Shukria was a victim—one of the countless—of the international failure to provide stability and security to Afghans.

Could Shukria have been saved? Recent Afghan history provides no easy answer, no assurance that internal and external actors will avoid compromised, flawed approaches to state-building. Rather, it suggests international state-building efforts can yield successes, but more often conflicting aims will foster unsatisfying results. Too often, an invading nation's military goals or mere inattention undermine human rights and stability. Critically, in Afghanistan, the U.S. decision to rely on local warlord allies reduced Karzai's leeway to address human rights concerns. In the space remaining to him, however, Karzai compromised with human rights abusers and deeply conservative forces that opposed the spread of human rights. To consolidate political power, he engineered a constitutional process that failed to establish new democratic space, legitimate rights-protecting institutions, or provide meaningful voice to the Afghan people.

Fundamental sources of instability and rights violations in Afghanistan remained poorly addressed by both the Karzai government and the international community. These included a Taliban insurgency on the rise, abetted by Pakistani intelligence and Pashtun discontent;[121] a burgeoning narcotics economy;[122] and a state showing few signs of being

---

119. *See* Anthony Fontenot & Ajmal Maiwandi, Capital of Chaos: The New Kabul of Warlords and Infidels, in Evil Paradises: Dreamworlds of Neoliberalism 71–74 (Mike Davis & Daniel Bertrand Monk, eds. 2007). *See generally,* Mary B. Anderson, *To Work or Not to Work, in "Tainted" Circumstances: Difficult Choices for Humanitarians*, 74 Soc. Res. 201 (2007) (canvassing ethical dilemmas of humanitarian and human rights work in conflict zones).

120. Barry Bearak, *As War Enters Classroom, Fear Grips Afghans*, N.Y. Times, July 10, 2007, at A1.

121. *See, e.g.,* David Rhode, *Afghan Police Suffer Setbacks as Taliban Adapt*, N.Y. Times, Sept. 2, 2007, at A11; Carlotta Gall, *At Border, Signs of Pakistani Role in Taliban Surge*, N.Y. Times, Jan. 21, 2007, at A1. That Pakistan's involvement in the Taliban's rebirth counted as front-page news in January 2007 is some indication of the impoverished nature of U.S. debate on the Afghan situation, despite the presence of several fine reporters there.

122. *See* Goodson, *supra* note 50, at 35; Anne Applebaum, *Ending an Opium War*, Wash. Post, Jan. 16, 2007, at A19. *See also* Ahmed Rashid, Descent into Chaos: The United

able to bring security to its people.[123] Opinion surveys in 2006 thus found that two-thirds of Afghans believed that addressing insecurity—whether from insurgent attack, warlord extortion, or pervasive crime—should be Karzai's first priority.[124] International actors, particularly the United States and its allies, failed to foster the secure environment in which rights-respecting institutions could be created, let alone sustained.[125] Further, their military strategy compounded abuses: the recklessness of U.S. bombing tactics forced even the timorous Karzai, facing re-election in 2009, to condemn his international sponsors in harsh terms, lest his electoral prospects suffer.[126]

State-building's trajectory in Afghanistan thus must be understood as the nexus of complex historical, political, economic, and military forces. Effective human rights advocacy requires an understanding of all these forces, and how they constrain advocacy opportunities. To be effective, an advocate must bring to the table (or marshal in others) the skills of an historian, an anthropologist, a sociologist, an economist, a political scientist, and a constitutional lawyer. She must discern the push and pull of the transnational opiate trade, tracing its links to Afghanistan's leaders (and their relatives), and its ties to other dark economies. She must understand the weave of local culture that has resisted improvements in the legal rights and status of women. For without these skills, she will neither understand nor help those like Shukria who pay the price for international and local hypocrisies, as new states unravel into the bloody Hobbesian days of "continuall feare" and the near absolute absence of human rights.

STATES AND THE FAILURE OF NATION-BUILDING IN PAKISTAN, AFGHANISTAN, AND CENTRAL ASIA 317–37 (2008). Rashid's analysis, published after this essay was completed, and just before publication, reinforces skepticism about the Afghan state's future.

123. James Glanz & David Rhode, *U.S. Report Finds Dismal Training of Afghan Police*, N.Y. TIMES, Dec. 4, 2006, at A1.

124. Jones, *supra* note 50, at 114.

125. *See generally* Sarah Chayes, *NATO Didn't Lose Afghanistan*, N.Y. TIMES, July 10, 2007, at A21.

126. *See, e.g.*, Barry Bearak, *Karzai Calls Coalition 'Careless,'* N.Y. TIMES, June 24, 2007, at A10.

*

15

The Story of *El–Masri v. Tenet*: Human Rights and Humanitarian Law in the "War on Terror"

Margaret L. Satterthwaite*

The Apprehension and Transfer of Khaled El–Masri[1]

Khaled El–Masri had been on the bus for many hours by the time he was asked to exit at the Macedonian border. A German national, El–Masri had left his home town of Senden the day before and was heading to Skopje, Macedonia for a short vacation. Things had recently become difficult at home; El–Masri was unemployed and lived in a small apartment with his wife and four small children. He planned to get away for a bit to clear his mind, and he thought Macedonia would be an inexpensive and interesting place to visit.

---

* Certain sections of this Chapter draw significantly on a series of articles I have published on the topic of rendition, including Margaret L. Satterthwaite, *Rendered Meaningless: Extraordinary Rendition and the Rule of Law*, 75 Geo. Wash. L. Rev. 1333 (2007); Margaret Satterthwaite, *Extraordinary Rendition and Disappearances in the "War on Terror,"* 10 Gonz. J. Int'l L. 70 (2006); and Margaret Satterthwaite & Angelina Fisher, *Tortured Logic: Renditions to Justice, Extraordinary Rendition, and Human Rights Law*, 6 The Long Term View 52 (2006). Work on this Chapter was supported by the Filomen D'Agostino Research Fund at New York University School of Law. I am grateful to Alison Nathan, Steven Watt, Ben Wizner, and Maria LaHood for comments on draft versions of this Chapter, and to Tafadzwa Pasipanodya (NYU J.D. '08) and Mitra Ebadolahi (NYU J.D. '08) for their impeccable research assistance and editing suggestions. Thanks also to Shannon Kunath (NYU J.D. expected '09) and Ryan Gee (NYU J.D. expected '10) for research help.

1. Unless otherwise noted, the facts in this section are taken from: Declaration of Khaled El–Masri in Support of Plaintiff's Opposition to the United States' Motion to Dismiss or, in the Alternative, for Summary Judgment, El–Masri v. Tenet, 437 F. Supp. 2d 530 (E.D. Va. 2006) (No. 1:05cv1417), aff'd sub nom. El–Masri v. U.S., 479 F.3d 296 (4th Cir. 2007), cert. denied, 128 S.Ct. 373 (2007), available at http://www.aclu.org/pdfs/safefree/elmasri_decl_exh.pdf [hereinafter Declaration of Khaled El–Masri]. A brief note on the Arabic transliterations used in this Chapter: "El–Masri" has been adopted because this is the spelling used by Mr. El–Masri. For consistency, I capitalize "Al" and "El" in other Arabic names used in this Chapter.

The bus ride had been uneventful as it crossed through Germany, Austria, Slovenia, Croatia, and Serbia. It was about 3:00 pm when El–Masri was asked to step off the bus at the Macedonian border to talk to border officials. The officials asked what he planned to do in Macedonia, and how long he would be there. After El–Masri explained that he planned to stay about a week in Skopje, the border official allowed him to climb onto the bus again, and it headed off toward the city. After a few minutes, El–Masri asked the bus driver for his passport; the driver replied that he did not have it, and turned the bus around to allow El–Masri to retrieve it at the border crossing. The border officials told El–Masri that they could not return his passport, since there was a problem that would take some time to resolve. Unable to wait for him, the bus drove on to Skopje, leaving El–Masri behind with the border officials.

El–Masri was interrogated by Macedonian officials from about 6:00 pm until 10:00 pm that night—New Year's Eve, December 31, 2003. He was asked about his home town—whether there were mosques in his neighborhood, who attended services there, and whether he had been invited by anyone to participate in Islamic activities. El–Masri was also asked whether he belonged to any Islamic groups and whether he prayed and fasted. El–Masri explained that although he had heard of some of the organizations mentioned, he did not belong to any of them. A while later, he was taken outside. It was a dark, foggy night. Some of the border guards were drunk in anticipation of the new year.

El–Masri was driven to Skopje and taken to a hotel. At the hotel, he was interrogated until the early morning hours. Although he could not speak the language well, El–Masri's captors questioned him in English. Things continued like this for days. El–Masri was under constant surveillance; a team of nine men rotated on six-hour shifts. He was never left alone and was never allowed any privacy. Despite the fact that he obviously could not leave, when El–Masri asked if he was under arrest, the guards replied sarcastically: "Can you see handcuffs?"[2] El–Masri asked to see a lawyer, to call the German embassy, to call his family. His captors refused each of these requests. At one point El–Masri attempted to escape. One of the men forced him to stop by pointing a gun at his head.

After about a week, two officials arrived. They offered El–Masri a deal: if he admitted to being a member of Al Qaeda, they would return him to Germany. El–Masri refused. A few days later one of the officials returned to the room and told El–Masri that his case had been referred to the President of Macedonia. El–Masri again asked to see a representative of the German government. This request was again refused. A few days later, El–Masri stopped eating to protest his detention.

---

2. James Meek, *"They beat me from all sides,"* GUARDIAN (LONDON), Jan. 14, 2005.

One evening, El–Masri's captors demanded that he speak into a video camera. They told him to state his name and say that he had been treated well. El–Masri had been in the hotel room for twenty-three days. His captors told him that they were returning him to Germany, and they escorted him out of the building.

As soon as he was outside, two men approached El–Masri and grabbed his arms. Another man then handcuffed and blindfolded him. El–Masri was shoved into a vehicle and driven to a location where he was made to sit on a chair for some time.

Eventually, he was taken into a room where he was beaten, his clothes were sliced off silently, and he was thrown to the ground.[3] He was subjected to a forceful anal probe and then made to stand. The blindfold was removed for a moment and photos were taken; during this time, El–Masri was able to see seven or eight men surrounding him. These men were dressed head to toe in black, with masks covering their heads and faces, and gloves covering their hands. The men diapered El–Masri, dressed him in new clothes, and blindfolded him again. They shoved earplugs into his ears and placed a hood over his head. Headphones were placed over his ears. His cuffed hands were chained to his waist, and his feet were shackled.

El–Masri was forced aboard a plane, shoved to the floor, and his legs and arms were secured in a spread-eagle position. He received two injections—one in each arm. Something was placed over his nose. El–Masri lost consciousness at some point. Although he was not alert the entire time, he thought the flight lasted about four hours. The plane made one stop. When the plane landed for the final time, El–Masri was taken outside and forced into a vehicle. After travelling for about ten minutes, El–Masri was pulled down a flight of stairs into a building. He was led into a cell, thrown onto the floor, and was beaten and kicked. His chains were removed and his blindfold was taken off.

El–Masri was left alone in the tiny, dirty cell made of concrete. Once his eyes had adjusted to the dim light, he could see graffiti on the walls written in Arabic, Urdu, and Farsi. When he looked around he saw one blanket, a pillow, some old clothes, and a bottle of fetid water. Though he had already been detained for more than three weeks, El–Masri's ordeal had just begun.

The Development of the Extraordinary Rendition and Secret Detention Program

Although he did not know it at the time, El–Masri's apprehension, transfer, and detention was part of a secret program that was approved

---

3. *Id.*

by President George W. Bush after the attacks of September 11, 2001.[4] Aimed at taking terrorism suspects "off the streets,"[5] the extraordinary rendition and secret detention program ("the Program") reportedly[6] involves the covert approval of "kill, capture or detain" orders for specific individuals.[7] As the name implies, such "K–C–D" orders reportedly allow U.S. agents—secretly and without warning to those targeted—to apprehend, imprison, and perhaps even target for death those individuals who are determined to be eligible for the Program.

"Rendition to Justice" Becomes Extraordinary Rendition

While the term "extraordinary rendition" is newly in use, its cousin—"rendition to justice"—has been official U.S. policy for several decades. Rendition to justice was approved for use against terrorism suspects by President Ronald Reagan in 1986.[8] Rendition was apparently authorized along with a variety of other procedures in National Security Decision Directive 207, which formalized U.S. policy to fight terrorism.[9]

---

4. *See generally* President George W. Bush, President Discusses Creation of Military Tribunals to Try Suspected Terrorists (Sept. 6, 2006) (transcript *available at* http://www.whitehouse.gov/news/releases/2006/09/20060906–3.html) [hereinafter President's Sept. 6, 2006 Address]; President George W. Bush, Press Conference of the President (Sept. 15, 2006) (transcript *available at* http://www.whitehouse.gov/news/releases/2006/09/20060915–2.html). The authorization for the Program is discussed later in this Chapter.

5. President's Sept. 6, 2006 Address, *supra* note 4.

6. Because the Program under discussion in this Chapter is by its very nature secretive, I will use terms such as "reportedly" and "apparently" where specified facts have not been plainly established.

7. *See* Eur. Parl. Ass., Comm. on Legal Affairs and Human Rights, *Secret Detentions and Illegal Transfers of Detainees Involving Council of Europe Member States: Second Report*, ¶ 64, Doc. No. 11302 rev. (2007), *available at* http://assembly.coe.int/Documents/WorkingDocs/Doc07/edoc11302.pdf [hereinafter *Council of Europe June 2007 Report*].

8. D. Cameron Findlay, *Abducting Terrorists Overseas for Trial in the United States: Issues of International and Domestic Law*, 23 TEX. INT'L L.J. 1, 2–3 (1988); *see also* Dana Priest, *CIA's Assurances on Transferred Suspects Doubted*, WASH. POST, Mar. 17, 2005, at A01; Shaun Waterman, *Analysis: Rendition a Routine Practice*, UNITED PRESS INT'L, Mar. 9, 2005 (citing a former intelligence official knowledgeable about rendition who explained that rendition was approved in 1986 by President Reagan along with the establishment of the Counterterrorist Center). It should be noted that rendition to justice has also been used since the 1980s to bring individuals suspected of drug trafficking or arms dealing to the United States to face trial. *See* United States v. Noriega, 746 F.Supp. 1506, 1511 (S.D. Fla. 1990), *aff'd*, 117 F.3d 1206 (11th Cir.1997) (where U.S. military forces arrested former Panamanian leader Manuel Noriega in Panama City and transferred him to the United States for trial on drug charges).

9. *See* U.S. Gen. Accounting Office, GAO/NSIAD–99–135, Combating Terrorism: Issues to be Resolved to Improve Counterterrorism Operations 3 (1999). President Ronald Reagan's National Security Decision Directive 207 has only been partly declassified; the sections discussing rendition have not been made public. *See* National Security Decision

According to reports, when it was first approved, rendition to justice involved the apprehension of suspected terrorists by U.S. agents in (1) countries in which no government exercised effective control (i.e., "failed states" or states in chaos because of civil war or other massive unrest); (2) countries known to plan and support international terrorism; or (3) international waters or airspace.[10] These were locations where the U.S. government could not expect to obtain custody over an individual suspected of a crime using the traditional method of international extradition.

Extradition is a "formal process by which a person is surrendered by one state to another."[11] It is the usual method for transfer of suspects and fugitives, and it is designed to protect the sovereignty of the nation where the suspect has taken refuge while also allowing the requesting state to obtain jurisdiction over an individual who is suspected of committing a crime subject to its criminal jurisdiction.[12] Under U.S. law, extradition requires a valid treaty authorizing the representative of a foreign state to request the transfer of a named individual.[13] The request is followed by a judicial proceeding in which a federal judicial officer determines whether the crime is one covered by an extradition treaty, and whether there is probable cause to sustain the charge.[14] Once these prerequisites are satisfied, the judicial officer certifies the individual as extraditable to the Secretary of State.[15] The Secretary of State must then decide whether to surrender the alleged fugitive to the requesting foreign state.[16]

During the 1980s, the United States expanded the reach of its criminal law to cover a host of crimes against U.S. nationals or U.S. interests that occurred outside of U.S. territory.[17] At the same time, the United States experienced significant difficulties obtaining jurisdiction over suspected terrorists, in part because the United States did not have

---

Directive 207: The National Program for Combating Terrorism (Jan. 20, 1986), *available at* http://www.fas.org/irp/offdocs/nsdd/index.html.

10. Findlay, *supra* note 8, at 3 (citing a classified annex to a Presidential report on renditions to justice).

11. M. Cherif Bassiouni, International Extradition: United States Law & Practice 1 (5th ed. 2007).

12. Valerie Epps, *The Development of the Conceptual Framework Supporting International Extradition*, 25 Loy. L.A. Int'l & Comp. L. Rev. 369, 371–72 (2003).

13. *See* 18 U.S.C. § 3184 (2006).

14. Quinn v. Robinson, 783 F.2d 776, 787 (9th Cir. 1986).

15. 18 U.S.C. § 3184.

16. *Id.* §§ 3184, 3186; *see also* 22 C.F.R. § 95.2(b) (1999).

17. See Christopher L. Blakesley & Dan E. Stigall, *The Myopia of* U.S. v. Martinelli*: Extraterritorial Jurisdiction in the 21st Century*, 39 Geo. Wash. Int'l L. Rev. 1 (2007), for an overview of this issue.

valid extradition treaties with the countries most commonly harboring terrorists, and in part because those states sometimes asserted that the suspects were not eligible for extradition, since their crimes were "political" crimes, acts that have traditionally been excluded from extradition arrangements.[18] The rendition to justice policy was born of this frustration with what one former intelligence official has called "the enormously cumbersome and sometimes impossible process" of extradition.[19]

When carrying out renditions to justice, U.S. agents would apprehend the individual (sometimes luring suspects to the chosen location through elaborate ruses[20]) and would then forcibly transfer the person to the United States, where the individual would face indictment on criminal charges for specific acts of terrorism aimed at the United States or its citizens.[21] In sum, renditions to justice were a forcible means of obtaining personal jurisdiction over an individual who was sought on regular criminal charges.[22] While some cases of rendition involved allegations of mistreatment during abduction or interrogation, it has never been suggested that the purpose of this program was to subject the detainees to torture or cruel, inhuman or degrading treatment, or to hold them secretly. Once in the United States, the rendered individual would be treated like any other federal detainee awaiting trial.

Rendition to justice came to be seen as an imperative method for bringing suspected terrorists to the United States for trial during the 1990s. Although the document itself remains classified, President George H.W. Bush authorized specific procedures for renditions in 1993 through National Security Directive 77 ("NSD–77").[23] President Clinton followed the lead of Presidents Reagan and H.W. Bush by continuing the rendition program.[24] President Clinton signed Presidential Decision Directive 62 ("PDD–62") on May 22, 1998, setting up streamlined responsibilities

---

18. *See* Findlay, *supra* note 8, at 6–15.

19. *See* Waterman, *supra* note 8.

20. Consider, for example, the case of Fawaz Yunis, who was lured into international waters by undercover FBI agents posing as drug traffickers and then arrested and transferred to an American munitions ship. The D.C. Circuit rejected Yunis' legal objections to this method of gaining jurisdiction over him. *See* United States v. Yunis, 924 F.2d 1086 (D.C. Cir. 1991) (upholding jurisdiction to try Yunis); United States v. Yunis, 859 F.2d 953, 957 (D.C. Cir. 1988) (describing arrest).

21. Findlay, *supra* note 8, at 3–4.

22. *See generally* Findlay, *supra* note 8.

23. *See* Fed'n of Am. Scientists, National Security Directives (NSD) [Bush Administration 1989–1993], *available at* http://www.fas.org/irp/offdocs/nsd/index.html (listing NSD–77 as classified).

24. *See* Fed'n of Am. Scientists, Presidential Decision Directives [PDD] Clinton Administration 1993–2000, *available at* http://www.fas.org/irp/offdocs/pdd/index.html (containing the unclassified segments of PDD–39).

for ten major anti-terror programs, the first of which was called "Apprehension, Extradition, Rendition, and Prosecution."[25] Then–CIA Director George Tenet testified in 2000 that the CIA had rendered more than two dozen suspects between 1998 and 2000;[26] in 2004, he estimated the agency had conducted more than eighty renditions before September 11, 2001.[27]

Two important Clinton-era renditions must be included in this historical overview because they mark the beginning of an important shift in approach: the cases of Tal'at Fu'ad Qassim and the Tirana Cell. According to Human Rights Watch, Qassim was an Egyptian national who had been granted asylum in Denmark and traveled to Bosnia in the mid–1990s, reportedly to write about the war.[28] Concerned by the increasing globalization of terrorism and the radical Islamists who the United States saw as the central players, the United States demanded that the Bosnian government expel militants found inside its territory during the war. When the Bosnian government failed to do so, the U.S. government targeted Tal'at Fu'ad Qassim for rendition—to Egypt, not to the United States. According to news reports, Qassim was taken aboard a U.S. navy ship and interrogated before being transferred to Egyptian custody in the Adriatic Sea.[29] As Human Rights Watch reports, "Qassim's case is the first known rendition by the U.S. government to a third

---

25. PDD–62 has not been declassified. It is discussed in Nat'l Comm'n on Terrorist Attacks Upon the U.S., Staff Statement No. 5: Diplomacy (2004), *available at* http://govinfo.library.unt.edu/911/staff_statements/staff_statement_5.pdf. An unclassified summary of PDD–62 states: "To meet these challenges, President Clinton signed Presidential Decision Directive 62. This Directive creates a new and more systematic approach to fighting the terrorist threat of the next century. It reinforces the mission of the many U.S. agencies charged with roles in defeating terrorism; it also codifies and clarifies their activities in the wide range of U.S. counter-terrorism programs, from apprehension and prosecution of terrorists to increasing transportation security, enhancing response capabilities and protecting the computer-based systems that lie at the heart of America's economy." Press Release, The White House, Fact Sheet: Combating Terrorism: Presidential Decision Directive 62 (May 22, 1998), *available at* http://www.fas.org/irp/offdocs/pdd-62.htm.

26. *See* Waterman, *supra* note 8.

27. *Panel I Day Two of the Eighth Public Hearing of the National Commission on Terrorist Attacks Upon the United States* 30 (Mar. 24, 2004) (remarks of George Tenet, Director of Central Intelligence), *available at* http://govinfo.library.unt.edu/911/archive/hearing8/9–11Commission_Hearing_2004–03–24.pdf.

28. HUMAN RIGHTS WATCH, BLACK HOLE: THE FATE OF ISLAMISTS RENDERED TO EGYPT 19 (2005), *available at* http://hrw.org/reports/2005/egypt0505/egypt0505.pdf. Unless otherwise noted, the facts in this paragraph are taken from this publication.

29. *Id.* at 20 (citing Anthony Shadid, *Syria is Said to Hang Egypt Suspect Tied to Bin Laden*, BOSTON GLOBE, Nov. 20, 2001, at A1; Andrew Higgins & Christopher Cooper, *Cloak and Dagger: A CIA–Backed Team Used Brutal Means to Crack Terror Cell*, WALL ST. J., Nov. 20, 2001, at A1).

country with a record of torture."[30] Qassim was reportedly executed while in Egyptian custody. Three years later, the CIA worked with Albanian secret police to monitor the activities of a suspected terrorist cell made up of Egyptian nationals living in Tirana. After determining to their satisfaction that the men were engaged in terrorist activities, the Albanian police apprehended four men and handed them to the CIA, which in turn rendered the men to Egypt. Within a month, the CIA rendered another Egyptian national from Bulgaria to Egypt. The men were tried as part of a mass trial and alleged that they had been severely abused while in pre-trial detention. According to a former intelligence official discussing this new kind of rendition, in which suspected terrorists were transferred to third states instead of being taken to the United States: " '[t]he only requirement was that there be some kind of legal process (to which the rendered person would be subject)' in the receiving country."[31]

The model had been created. In the aftermath of 9/11, the complete transition would be made: intelligence-gathering, not trial, would become the purpose for transfer; the legal process requirement would be dropped; countries with a record of torture or secret CIA prisons hidden from the world would become the sites of detention; and rendition to justice would become extraordinary rendition.

El–Masri: Life in a CIA Prison in Afghanistan[32]

On the second night of his imprisonment in Afghanistan, Khaled El–Masri was interrogated by four masked men. One of the men asked him if he knew where he was. He replied, "Yes, I know, I'm in Kabul."[33] The man then replied, "It's a country without laws. And nobody knows that you are here. Do you know what that means?"

The men accused him of having been to a terrorist training camp in Afghanistan, and said that he was Egyptian; that his German passport had been forged. El–Masri suggested that the men speak with the German authorities, who would explain that he was in fact a German citizen. El–Masri was interrogated only three or four times while being held in Afghanistan; each time, he asked to see a representative of the German government. Two of the men who interrogated him identified themselves as Americans.

---

30. *Id.* It is impossible to confirm whether this was the first such transfer, since such actions were covert. One former intelligence official told UPI that this form of rendition was common, and even qualified "rendition to justice" in the United States as the exception to the norm of rendition to third states. *See* Waterman, *supra* note 8.

31. Quoted in Waterman, *supra* note 8.

32. Unless otherwise noted, the facts in this section are taken from: Declaration of Khaled El–Masri, *supra* note 1.

33. *See* Meek, *supra* note 2.

El–Masri discovered that he could communicate in a rudimentary way with other prisoners through the cell walls. It was through these communications that El–Masri learned he was in Afghanistan.[34] In March, he and others began a hunger strike, demanding that their basic human rights be respected. After refusing food for twenty-seven days, El–Masri was taken to meet with an American man who claimed to be the prison director, along with three other men. When asked why he was on hunger strike, El–Masri explained that he was protesting his abduction and detention without charge or contact with the outside world, and the inhumane conditions of his confinement. Claiming that he did not have the authority to release El–Masri, the prison director admitted that he knew El–Masri had not committed any crimes. On April 10, after thirty-seven days without food, El–Masri was force-fed; the next day he became very ill and was treated with antibiotics.

A few weeks later, El–Masri was taken to see an American man who said he was a psychologist; this man said he had come from Washington, D.C. to see El–Masri. After their conversation, the man told El–Masri that he could expect to be released soon. A few days later, the prison director came to see El–Masri with a man in uniform who spoke German and identified himself as "Sam." This man interrogated El–Masri, asking the same kinds of questions the Americans had asked. Although he would not answer when asked if he was a German official[35], from the way he looked and from his accent, El–Masri was certain that Sam was German.[36] Before Sam left, he told El–Masri that the authorities would now decide whether to release him, and that this assessment could take a week.

The next day, El–Masri resumed his protest hunger strike. That night, the German official, the American prison director, and a doctor came to his cell. They informed El–Masri that he would be released within eight days.

The Scope and Authorization of the Extraordinary Rendition Program

In many respects, the stories of men like Khaled El–Masri are among the main sources of information about the U.S. extraordinary rendition and secret detention Program. Although official acknowledgments about the Program continue to emerge, the U.S. government has

---

34. *See* Mirjam Gehrke, *German Seized by CIA Says He Feared for His Life*, DEUTSCHE WELLE, Jan. 21, 2006, *available at* http://www.dw-world.de/dw/article/0,2144,1862861,00.html.

35. See Meek, *supra* note 2.

36. *See* Christine Pöhlmann, *German Describes CIA Ordeal in Afghanistan*, AGENCE FRANCE-PRESSE, June 22, 2006.

not released comprehensive information about rendition and secret detention; still unconfirmed are the exact number and identities of people subject to "K–C–D" orders, the number and identities of people rendered to third countries for interrogation, and the number and identities of individuals held in secret CIA "black sites."

Concerning transfers to foreign governments, CIA Director Hayden has said that the number of individuals subject to rendition since 2001 is "mid-range, two figures," and investigative journalist Dana Priest has reported that her sources estimate that about seventy detainees have been subject to extraordinary rendition.[37] In an oft-cited 2005 *New Yorker* article, Jane Mayer estimated that there had been between 100 and 150 transferees.[38] Other estimates reach several thousand.[39] The Egyptian government alone has stated that approximately sixty to seventy detainees had been transferred to its custody between September 11, 2001, and May 2005.[40] Because of the confusion over definitions and the related practices involved in the U.S. government's "War on Terror" strategy, it is impossible to know with any certainty how many people have been subject to extraordinary rendition. One explanation for the range in estimates is that it appears likely that a larger number of individuals were secretly transferred to the custody of foreign governments, while comparatively few were held directly by the CIA in "black sites."

A presidential directive signed on September 17, 2001—less than one week after the attacks of September 11—purportedly provided the

---

37. *See* Council on Foreign Relations, *A Conversation with Michael Hayden*, Sept. 7, 2007, *available at* http://www.cfr.org/publication/14158/; Dana Priest, *CIA Holds Terror Suspects in Secret Prisons: Debate is Growing within Agency about the Legality and Morality of Overseas System Set up After 9/11*, Wash. Post., Nov. 2, 2005, at A1. For a comprehensive account of publicly available information about the Program, *see* Center for Human Rights and Global Justice, On the Record: U.S. Disclosures on Rendition, Secret Detention, and Coercive Interrogation (2008), *available at* http://www.chrgj.org/.

38. *See* Jane Mayer, *Outsourcing Torture: The Secret History of America's "Extraordinary Rendition" Program*, New Yorker, Feb. 14, 2005, at 106, 107 (citing Scott Horton); *see also CIA 'Outsourcing Torture,'* Agence France Presse, Feb. 7, 2005, *available at* http://www.commondreams.org/headlines05/0207–12.htm ("Scott Horton—an expert on international law who has examined CIA renditions—estimates that 150 people have been picked up in the CIA net since 2001.").

39. *See* Center for Human Rights and Global Justice (CHRGJ), NYU School of Law, Beyond Guantánamo: Transfers to Torture One Year After Rasul v. Bush 3 (2005), *available at* http://www.chrgj.org/docs/Beyond %20Guantanamo%20Report%20FINAL.pdf (quoting Jane Mayer: "One source knowledgeable about the rendition Program suggested that the number of *renditions* since September 11, 2001 may have reached as high as several thousand" (citation omitted)).

40. Shaun Waterman, *Terror Detainees Sent to Egypt; Official, U.S. Deny Torture is Condoned*, Wash. Times, May 16, 2005, at A4 (quoting the Prime Minister of Egypt).

CIA with legal authority for the Program.[41] Although the directive remains classified, the Council of Europe and the media have reported that it greatly expanded the CIA's authority to operate independently and to apprehend, transfer, detain, or even kill individuals designated for such treatment.[42] Attorneys from the Department of Justice, the CIA, and the Administration are reportedly involved in the designation of individuals who become eligible to be captured, detained, or even killed.[43]

On September 6, 2006, President Bush officially acknowledged that the U.S. government had created what he called a "separate program operated by the Central Intelligence Agency" to detain and interrogate individuals who were suspected of being "the key architects of the September the 11th attacks, and attacks on the USS Cole, an operative involved in the bombings of our embassies in Kenya and Tanzania, and individuals involved in other attacks that have taken the lives of innocent civilians across the world."[44] In a companion fact sheet, the Office of the Director of National Intelligence set out key facts concerning the Program.[45] It is important to note that these disclosures—and the information that has cumulated since—did not include anything about authorization to "kill" designated suspects, and what is known about this element of the Program, assuming there is such an element, remains obscure.

President Bush's September 6, 2006 statement came during a legislative battle in which he sought explicit authorization for military commissions to try suspected terrorists. The President sought such explicit authorization because the Supreme Court had—a few months earlier—struck down the existing military commissions system. In *Hamdan v. Rumsfeld*, the Court held that the commission created to try

---

41. The Presidential Directive has not been declassified, but the CIA admitted its existence during the course of a lawsuit by the ACLU. *See Leahy 'brushed off' on Secret Terror Docs*, UNITED PRESS INT'L, Jan. 3, 2007; Press Release, Am. Civil Liberties Union, CIA Finally Acknowledges Existence of Presidential Order on Detention Facilities Abroad (Nov. 14, 2006), *available at* http://www.aclu.org/safefree/torture/27382prs20061114.html.

42. *See Council of Europe June 2007 Report*, *supra* note 7, at 11–12; TYLER DRUMHELLER, ON THE BRINK: AN INSIDER'S ACCOUNT OF HOW THE WHITE HOUSE COMPROMISED AMERICAN INTELLIGENCE 35 (2006). With respect to killing, see Barton Gellman, *CIA Weighs 'Targeted Killing' Missions: Administration Believes Restraints Do Not Bar Singling Out Individual Terrorists*, WASH. POST, Oct. 28, 2001, at A01.

43. *See Council of Europe June 2007 Report*, *supra* note 7, at 12.

44. President's Sept. 6, 2006 Address, *supra* note 4.

45. *See* Office of the Director of National Intelligence, Summary of the High Value Terrorist Detainee Program (Sept. 6, 2006), *available at* http://www.dni.gov/announcements/content/TheHighValueDetaineeProgram.pdf; *see also* Office of the Director of National Intelligence, Biographies of High Value Terrorist Detainees Transferred to the U.S. Naval Base at Guantánamo Bay (Sept. 6, 2006), *available at* http://www.dni.gov/announcements/content/DetaineeBiographies.pdf.

individuals held at Guantánamo "lack[ed] power to proceed because its structure and procedures violate both the UCMJ and the Geneva Conventions."[46] In reaching this holding, the Court also signaled that Article 3 ("Common Article 3")—common to all four of the 1949 Geneva Conventions[47] and designed to provide minimum guarantees of humane treatment for all individuals detained in connection with any type of armed conflict—operates as a minimum floor for the treatment of individuals apprehended in the "War on Terror," at least those initially detained in Afghanistan. Soon after the *Hamdan* decision, the media reported that the White House believed the CIA to be bound by Common Article 3 under the *Hamdan* rule; the CIA did not comment on the issue.[48]

The CIA emptied out its "black sites"—at least temporarily—following the *Hamdan* decision. In his September 6 speech, President Bush announced the transfer of fourteen named "High-Value" detainees from CIA custody to the base at Guantánamo and stated that "[t]he current transfers mean that there are now no terrorists in the CIA program."[49] Human rights groups later reported on the cases of two individuals who had been held in "black sites" until soon after the *Hamdan* decision, when they were returned to their states of nationality.[50] Media reports of CIA agents purchasing insurance protection from potential lawsuits connected to the Program surfaced.[51] Government officials believed the extraordinary rendition and secret detention Program to be in jeopardy at this time. Explaining the need for the Program, the President said that "as more high-ranking terrorists are captured, the need to obtain

---

46. 548 U.S. 557 (2006).

47. *See* Geneva Convention Relative to the Treatment of Prisoners of War art. 3, Aug. 12, 1949, 6 U.S.T. 3316, 75 U.N.T.S. 135 [hereinafter Common Article 3].

48. *See* Mark Mazzetti & Kate Zernike, *White House Says Terror Detainees Hold Basic Rights*, N.Y. TIMES, July 12, 2006. For a discussion of the debate within the Administration concerning the applicability of Common Article 3 to terrorism suspects, *see* Tim Golden, *Detainee Memo Created Divide in White House*, N.Y. TIMES, Oct. 1, 2006, at A1.

49. President's Sept. 6, 2006 Address, *supra* note 4.

50. *See, e.g.* AMNESTY INT'L, UNITED STATES OF AMERICA: A CASE TO ANSWER: FROM ABU GHRAIB TO SECRET CIA CUSTODY: THE CASE OF KHALED AL-MAQTARI 26 (2008) [hereinafter THE CASE OF KHALED AL-MAQTARI]; HUMAN RIGHTS WATCH, GHOST PRISONER: TWO YEARS IN SECRET CIA DETENTION 24 (2007).

51. *See, e.g.,* Georg Mascolo & Matthias Gebauer, *Milan's Extraordinary Renditions Case: The CIA in the Dock*, SPIEGEL (HAMBURG), Jan. 10, 2007; Mayer, *supra* note 38; R. Jeffrey Smith, *Worried CIA Officers Buy Legal Insurance: Plans Fund Defense In Anti-Terror Cases*, WASH. POST, Sept. 11, 2006, at A01.

intelligence from them will remain critical—and having a CIA program for questioning terrorists will continue to be crucial to getting life-saving information."[52]

Congress would have to authorize the Program if it was to continue. Weeks after President Bush announced the existence of the Program, Congress passed the Military Commissions Act[53] (MCA), which sets out procedures for detaining, interrogating, and trying "unlawful enemy combatants" as defined in the Act.[54] President Bush considered the MCA sufficient approval of the Program,[55] although there is in fact no authorization for secret detention or extraordinary rendition in the law.[56] In July 2007, President Bush issued an executive order explicitly affirming that the CIA runs "a program of detention and interrogation."[57] In the last few years, a number of individuals have been held secretly by the CIA before being transferred to Guantánamo, and the CIA has acknowledged that the Program continues.[58]

In addition to the facts that were made public in September 2006, careful observers have been able to piece together a picture of the system based on a variety of sources, including: reports about released detainees;[59] investigations conducted by inter-governmental organizations such

52. President's Sept. 6, 2006 Address, *supra* note 4.

53. Military Commissions Act of 2006, Pub. L. No. 109–366, 120 Stat. 2600 (codified in scattered sections of 10, 18, 28 U.S.C.).

54. For a summary of the MCA's troubled relationship to international law, *see* John Cerone, *The Military Commissions Act of 2006: Examining the Relationship between the International Law of Armed Conflict and U.S. Law*, ASIL Insights, Nov. 13, 2006, *available at* http://www.asil.org/insights/2006/11/insights061114.html.

55. *See* President George W. Bush, President Bush Signs Military Commissions Act of 2006 (Oct. 17, 2006), *available at* http://www.whitehouse.gov/news/releases/2006/10/20061017-1.html (stating that "This bill will allow the Central Intelligence Agency to continue its program for questioning key terrorist leaders and operatives.").

56. In October 2006, John Bellinger, Legal Adviser to the Department of State, stated that that "[t]he act itself does not specifically address the CIA program." *See* John B. Bellinger III, State Department Legal Advisor, Foreign Press Center Briefing on the Military Commission Act of 2006 (Oct. 19, 2006), *available at* http://fpc.state.gov/fpc/74786.htm.

57. Exec. Order 13,440, 72 Fed. Reg. 40,707 (July 20, 2007).

58. *See* Press Release, Human Rights Watch, U.S.: Close CIA Prisons Still in Operation (Apr. 27, 2007), *available at* http://hrw.org/english/docs/2007/04/27/usdom15795.htm (discussing the CIA's secret detention and subsequent transfer of Abd Al-Hadi Al-Iraqi); *see also The Charlie Rose Show: Interview with Director Michael Hayden* (PBS television broadcast Oct. 22 & 23, 2007) (transcript *available at* https://www.cia.gov/news-information/press-releases-statements/press-release-archive-2007/interview-with-charlie-rose.html) (in which CIA Director Michael Hayden explains the continuation of the U.S. Program of rendition and CIA detention).

59. THE CASE OF KHALED AL-MAQTARI, *supra* note 50, at 26; AMNESTY INT'L, USA: BELOW THE RADAR: SECRET FLIGHTS TO TORTURE AND "DISAPPEARANCE," (2006); CHRGJ, SURVIVING THE DARKNESS: TESTIMONY FROM THE U.S. "BLACK SITES" (2007), *available at* http://www.chrgj.org/projects/docs/survivingthedarkness.pdf; Human Rights Watch, *supra* note 50, at 24.

as the Council of Europe and the European Union;[60] statements about specific aspects of the Program by various governmental agencies;[61] and documents released through litigation.[62]

What follows is a snapshot of the functioning and scope of the Program, based on these sources. The extraordinary rendition and secret detention Program is made up of three main components: apprehension and transfer operations, CIA "black sites," and sites in foreign countries where individuals are held at the behest of the United States. Apprehension and transfer involves a "rendition team" made up of individuals dressed entirely in black and wearing face masks. These individuals forcibly strip the detainee, subject him to a body cavity search, photograph him while naked, and dress him in a diaper before putting him in a new outfit. Detainees have reported being subjected to beatings during this process. The team next restrains the prisoner using handcuffs, ankle shackles, and chains, and deprives the detainee of sensory perception by covering his ears and eyes. Detainees are then placed aboard a plane (often a small, erstwhile civilian plane) and flown—sometimes for great distances.

Detainees are taken either to a secret CIA prison—a so-called "black site"—or delivered to a foreign government. Some detainees have experienced both fates. In the "black sites," guards dress in black and wear face masks, and detainees are often subjected to sensory manipulation including the use of excruciatingly loud music, horrifying sounds, pitch dark conditions, and sensory deprivation (e.g., through the use of constant white noise). Some detainees have been subjected to waterboarding—simulated drowning—and other "enhanced interrogation techniques" (or, as President Bush has called them, an "alternative set of procedures"[63]) reportedly approved for use on "high-value detainees."[64]

---

60. *See* Eur. Parl. Ass., Comm. on Legal Affairs and Human Rights, *Alleged Secret Detentions in Council of Europe Member States*, Doc. No. AS/Jur (2006) 03 rev. (2006), *available at* http://assembly.coe.int/CommitteeDocs/2006/20060124_Jdoc032006_E.pdf [hereinafter *Council of Europe January 2006 Report*].

61. For a detailed catalog of facts concerning the secret detention and extraordinary rendition Program that have been acknowledged by the U.S. government, see CHRGJ, *supra* note 37.

62. Press Release, Am. Civil Liberties Union, Newly Released Army Documents Point to Agreement Between Defense Department and CIA on "Ghost" Detainees, ACLU Says (Mar. 10, 2005), *available at* http://www.aclu.org/safefree/general/17597prs20050310.html. The declassified documents are available at American Civil Liberties Union: Torture FOIA, *available at* http://www.aclu.org/intlhumanrights/gen/13794res20050429.html. *See also* Press Release, Amnesty International, Center for Constitutional Rights & CHRGJ, Rights Groups Challenge CIA for Failure to Release More than 7000 Documents Relating to Secret Detention, Rendition, and Torture Program (June 26, 2008), *available at* http://www.chrgj.org/projects/detainees.html#Disappearances.

63. *See generally* President's Sept. 6, 2006 Address, *supra* note 4.

Detention in foreign facilities involves confinement in maddeningly small spaces (such as in the notorious *Far Falestin* prison in Syria[65]) and the use of torture such as *falaka* (beatings on the soles of the feet, reportedly used in Jordan[66]), sexual abuse (reportedly used in Jordan and Egypt[67]), and electric shocks (reportedly used in Egypt[68]). Whether in black sites or in foreign facilities, detainees are not given access to the outside world; they are not formally charged with any crime; and they are not allowed to seek the assistance of their governments.

El–Masri: Release[69]

On May 28, 2004, El–Masri was again handcuffed, shackled, and blindfolded. He was driven to an airstrip, and his blindfold was removed. His suitcase was returned to him, and he was allowed to change into his own clothes before his captors placed him in handcuffs, shoved earplugs into his ears, and covered his ears and eyes. He was led aboard a plane and strapped to a seat. During the flight, El–Masri became convinced that he was being taken to another country for execution. The German official who had visited him in prison accompanied him on this flight, and removed El–Masri's headphones during the flight. He told El–Masri that one of the reasons there had been such a long delay in releasing him was that the U.S. authorities wanted to ensure there was no evidence that he had been imprisoned by them in Afghanistan.[70] The official told El–Masri that he was being taken to a European country that was not Germany.

---

64. For admissions concerning waterboarding by former CIA Officer Daniel Kiriakou, see *CIA man defends "water-boarding,"* BBC News, Dec. 11, 2007, available at http://news.bbc.co.uk/2/hi/americas/7137750.stm; Darius Rejali, *5 Myths About Torture and Truth*, Wash. Post, Dec. 16, 2007, at B03; and Joby Warrick & Dan Eggen, *Waterboarding Recounted: Ex–CIA Officer Says It 'Probably Saved Lives' but Is Torture*, Wash. Post, Dec. 11, 2007, at A01. For a description of the six "enhanced interrogation techniques that were reportedly approved for use on 'high-value'" detainees, see Brian Ross & Richard Esposito, *CIA's Harsh Interrogation Techniques Described*, ABC News, Nov. 18, 2005, available at http://abcnews.go.com/WNT/Investigation/story?id=1322866.

65. Comm'n of Inquiry into the Actions of Canadian Officials in Relation to Maher Arar, *Report of Professor Stephen J. Toope, Fact Finder* 13–17 (2005), available at http://www.ararcommission.ca/eng/ToopeReport_final.pdf (describing Maher Arar's detention in *Far Falestin* prison).

66. *See, e.g.*, Amnesty Int'l., Amnesty International Report 2007: The State of the World's Human Rights 155 (2007), available at http://report2007.amnesty.org/document/15.

67. *Id.*

68. *See* Letter from Abu Omar while in an Egyptian prison, *translated in* Abu Omar, *This is How They Kidnapped Me*, Chi. Trib., Jan. 7, 2007, available at http://www.chicagotribune.com/news/nationworld/chi-cialetter-story,1,2033270.story.

69. Unless otherwise noted, the facts in this section are taken from Declaration of Khaled El–Masri, *supra* note 1.

70. Meek, *supra* note 2.

After the plane landed, the German official told El–Masri that some other people would help him get back to Germany. He was taken to a waiting vehicle, still blindfolded and handcuffed. This vehicle drove for more than three hours over winding, mountainous roads. During a brief stop, El–Masri was able to hear three men leaving the vehicle, and then three men getting into the vehicle. They drove for another three hours on what seemed to be both paved and unpaved roads. When the vehicle stopped for the last time, El–Masri was removed from the car and made to turn around; one of the men removed his blindfold, took off the handcuffs, and handed El–Masri his suitcase and passport. The man told El–Masri to walk down a path and not to look back.

Terrified that he was about to be shot in the back, El–Masri walked into the dark night; he heard the car leave. Soon, El–Masri encountered three armed men who asked for his passport. Seeing that he did not have a visa, the men accused El–Masri of being in Albania illegally; this was the first time El–Masri was told where he was. He was taken to a building where another official asked him why he was in Albania. El–Masri explained that he had been abducted in Macedonia and imprisoned in Afghanistan. The official laughed, saying that no one would believe such a story. The official told El–Masri that the officers would take him to the airport and put him on a flight to Germany.

Sure enough, officials accompanied El–Masri to the airport and took him through customs and immigration control. He boarded a plane that took him to Frankfurt International Airport. When he landed at 8:45 am on May 29, 2004, Khaled El–Masri was sixty pounds lighter than he had been when he left home almost six months before; he had grown a beard and now had long hair. Almost unrecognizable, El–Masri made his way home.

Is this Legal? Extraordinary Rendition and International Human Rights Law

Although there have been vigorous debates in the United States about the legality of the extraordinary rendition and secret detention Program, intergovernmental organizations such as the Council of Europe, the European Parliament, and numerous United Nations bodies have stated unequivocally that the Program contravenes international human rights law binding on the United States.[71]

---

71. *See* U.N. Comm. Against Torture, *Consideration of Reports Submitted by States Parties Under Article 19 of the Convention: Second Periodic Reports of States Parties Due in 1999: Addendum: United States of America*, ¶ 5, U.N. Doc. CAT/C/48/Add.3 (June 29, 2005) [hereinafter *U.S. Second Periodic Report to Committee Against Torture*] (considering U.S. report submitted May 6, 2005); U.N. Human Rights Comm., *Concluding Observations of the Human Rights Committee: United States of America*, U.N. Doc. CCPR/C/USA/CO/3/Rev.1 (Dec. 18, 2006); *Council of Europe June 2007 Report*, *supra* note 7;

The relevant human rights norms protecting against extraordinary rendition and secret detention include the following: the prohibition of *refoulement*, which proscribes transfers to a risk of torture; the prohibition of enforced disappearances, which prohibits the concealment of the fate and whereabouts of individuals deprived of their liberty; and the norm against torture and cruel, inhuman or degrading treatment.[72] This section will briefly summarize these norms in the context of the extraordinary rendition and secret detention Program.

The prohibition of *refoulement* is set out in a wide variety of human rights instruments.[73] Most relevant to the United States and its partners in the Program are the Convention Against Torture and Other Forms of Cruel, Inhuman or Degrading Treatment ("Torture Convention" or "CAT") and the International Covenant on Civil and Political Rights ("ICCPR"), which the U.S. government has ratified. CAT article 3 prohibits the transfer of individuals to states where they may be in danger of torture: "No State Party shall expel, return (*'refouler'*) or extradite a person to another State where there are substantial grounds for believing that he would be in danger of being subjected to torture." Article 7 of the ICCPR prohibits torture and cruel or degrading treatment; this article has been understood to implicitly include a *non-refoulement* rule. Both of these articles have been interpreted to apply to all forms of inter-state transfer of individuals, and therefore should be read to apply to informal transfers such as rendition. When extraordinary rendition involves transfer to a country where an individual is at real risk of torture or cruel, inhuman or degrading treatment, the transfer is prohibited by binding international human rights law.

Transfers to secret detention are likewise prohibited, in part because prolonged incommunicado detention of the type that detainees experience in CIA "black sites" has itself been found to constitute cruel and inhuman treatment or torture. In addition, secret detention is itself unlawful under international human rights law. The U.N. Committee Against Torture has found that secret detention is a *per se* violation of

---

Council of Europe June 2006 Report, supra note 60; Report on the Alleged Use of European Countries by the CIA for the Transportation and Illegal Detention of Prisoners, Eur. Parl. Doc. A6–0020/2007 (2007), *available at* http://www.europarl.europa.eu/comparl/tempcom/tdip/final_report_en.pdf; Draft Interim Report on the Alleged Use of European Countries by the CIA for the Transportation and Illegal Detention of Prisoners, Eur.Parl. Doc. A6–0213/2006 (2006), *available at* http://www.statewatch.org/cia/reports/ep-cia-interim-report-english.pdf.

72. Also relevant but not addressed here are, *inter alia*, rights against arbitrary detention, rights to consular access, and due process rights.

73. *See* Harold Hongju Koh & Michael J. Wishnie, *The Story of* Sale v. Haitian Centers Council: *Guantánamo and* Refoulement, Chapter 10 in this volume, for a discussion of the principle of *non-refoulement* as it applies to the United States in the refugee context.

the Torture Convention.[74] Further, when carried out in the manner used in the Program, secret detention amounts to enforced disappearance. The recently-concluded International Convention for the Protection of All Persons from Enforced Disappearance (adopted by the General Assembly in December 2006) defines enforced disappearance as:

> the arrest, detention, abduction or any other form of deprivation of liberty by agents of the State or by persons or groups of persons acting with the authorization, support or acquiescence of the State, followed by a refusal to acknowledge the deprivation of liberty or by concealment of the fate or whereabouts of the disappeared person, which place such a person outside the protection of the law. (Article 2)

While the United States has not ratified this convention, it is bound by the customary international law norm prohibiting enforced disappearance. In addition, a wide variety of other human rights norms are violated through rendition and secret detention, including: the prohibition on arbitrary detention; rights to due process and judicial guarantees; and the right to be free from cruel, inhuman and degrading treatment.

The U.S. government has focused a great deal of energy in the last several years on efforts to carve out legal space for its actions in the "War on Terror." Indeed, it has systematically produced legal arguments—pursuant to both international and domestic law—to support its actions. In relation to the extraordinary rendition and secret detention Program, the strategy has been to try to clear a space for actions free of international legal constraints.

The first argument is that human rights law only applies within the territory of a ratifying state—in other words, that human rights norms do not apply extraterritorially. In its reports to the United Nations treaty bodies monitoring the implementation of human rights treaties, the United States has consistently maintained that, unless explicitly specified otherwise, it is bound by human rights treaties only in activities it conducts within U.S. territory.[75] In other words, if you are outside

---

74. *See* Comm. Against Torture, *Consideration of Reports Submitted by States Parties Under Article 19 of the Convention: Conclusions and Recommendations of the Committee Against Torture; United States of America*, ¶ 17, U.N. Doc. CAT/C/USA/CO/2 (May 18, 2006) (finding that detaining individuals in secret sites constitutes a "per se" violation of the Convention), *available at* http://www.unhchr.ch/tbs/doc.nsf/898586b1dc7b4043c1256a 450044f331/e2d4f5b2dccc0a4cc12571ee00290ce0/$FILE/G0643225.pdf.

75. *See, e.g.,* U.N. Comm. Against Torture, *Consideration of Reports Submitted by States Parties Under Article 19 of the Convention: Initial Report of States Parties Due in 1995: Addendum: United States of America*, ¶¶ 183–88, U.N. Doc. CAT/C/28/Add.5 (Feb. 9, 2000) (considering U.S. report submitted Oct. 15, 1999), *available at* http://www.bayefsky. com/reports/usa_cat_c_28_add.5_1999.pdf. The U.S. government has made this argument

the United States but under the control of the U.S. government, you are unprotected by the human rights norms set out above.

While this argument may have traction under U.S. law, it ignores the relevant jurisprudence of international and regional human rights bodies.[76] Broadly speaking, human rights bodies have determined that treaties apply to two separate extraterritorial situations: cases where states have effective control over territory, and cases where states have power over an individual.[77] Under the effective control doctrine, human rights treaties would apply to places abroad that are under the control of the United States, as well as to the physical territory of the state itself. This means that human rights treaties would apply to U.S. conduct at Guantánamo and other locations where the United States has detention centers. If this were the only scenario in which human rights apply extraterritorially, human rights treaties would protect people in those spaces but not individuals transferred or detained by U.S. authorities in territories not under U.S. control (e.g., El-Masri's capture and rendition from Macedonia). The second scenario, however—governed by the personal control doctrine—extends to protect *all* individuals who are within the *personal control* of U.S. agents, no matter where they happen to be in the world.

The personal control doctrine is especially suitable to cases of transfer and detention, which involve physical custody of individuals by state agents. This reading ensures that human rights treaties fulfill their object and purpose—to protect those vulnerable to state abuses—instead of letting states avoid their duties by moving individuals farther and farther away from the protection of courts, oversight bodies, and humanitarian agencies. Under the personal control test, human rights law applies to all individuals who are apprehended and transferred by a

---

consistently in reports to the U.N. filed in recent years. *See* Margaret L. Satterthwaite, *Rendered Meaningless: Extraordinary Rendition and the Rule of Law*, 75 GEO. WASH. L. REV. 1333 (2007) at 1351–1354 [hereinafter Satterthwaite, *Rendered Meaningless*].

76. Although the U.S. Supreme Court has rejected the extraterritorial application of the *non-refoulement* rule set out in the United Nations Convention Relating to the Status of Refugees, *see* Harold Hongju Koh & Michael J. Wishnie, *The Story of* Sale v. Haitian Centers Council: *Guantánamo and* Refoulement, Chapter 10 in this volume, the extraterritorial application of the Convention Against Torture is a separate issue. Congress has passed legislation implementing the Convention's *non-refoulement* obligation, setting out U.S. policy as follows: "the United States [shall] not ... expel, extradite, or otherwise effect the involuntary return of any person to a country in which there are substantial grounds for believing the person would be in danger of being subjected to torture, *regardless of whether the person is physically present in the United States*." 8 U.S.C. § 1231 note (2000) (emphasis added). For an in-depth discussion of this issue, *see* Satterthwaite, *Rendered Meaningless*, *supra* note 75, at 1376–1379.

77. For citations and in-depth discussion of the doctrines discussed in this paragraph, *see* Satterthwaite, *Rendered Meaningless*, *supra* note 75, at 1351–1375.

state—here the United States. International human rights law therefore prevents transfers to countries where the individual is at risk of torture or secret detention.

In the instances in which the United States has directly defended aspects of the Program, it has emphasized the promises—so-called "diplomatic assurances"—that it obtains from cooperating countries concerning humane treatment of the detainees it transfers. Very little is known about the process for obtaining diplomatic assurances as part of the Program. Anonymous officials have told the media that CIA-initiated transfers have routinely been accompanied by assurances. One intelligence official specified that assurances are used whenever renditions were carried out with the purpose of delivering the detainee for interrogation, and not for trial. Recently retired CIA officers have said that verbal assurances are required by the CIA's Office of General Counsel whenever a rendition is carried out. Far from reducing the risk of torture, however, these assurances were known to be "a farce," according to a CIA officer who participated in the rendition Program.[78] The U.S. government has explained to the United Nations' human rights bodies that it relies on such assurances "as appropriate"; assurances are balanced against concerns that the individual may be at risk of torture in the custody of the country's officials.[79] This balancing approach is out of line with human rights standards concerning diplomatic assurances, which focus on safeguards that must accompany any use of assurances.[80] U.S. practice is in blatant violation of these safeguards.

Worse, if renditions are being conducted with the intent of subjecting an individual to coercive interrogations, the incentive structure is classically and horribly perverse: the sending country has an investment in the receiving country's abusive practices, and both states want those abuses to remain secret. As one official told *The Washington Post*, "They say they are not abusing them, and that satisfies the legal requirement, but we all know they do."[81]

At War with Al Qaeda? Extraordinary Rendition and International Humanitarian Law

As the case of Khaled El–Masri demonstrates, extraordinary rendition often takes place far from any traditional battlefield. Whether these operations qualify as part of an armed conflict that is governed by

---

78. Priest, *supra* note 8.

79. United States, List of Issues to be Considered During the Examination of the Second Periodic Report of the United States of America: Response of the United States of America, at 32–37, *available at* http://www.usmission.ch/Press2006/CAT–May5.pdf (submitted to the Comm. Against Torture).

80. Satterthwaite, *Rendered Meaningless*, *supra* note 75, at 1379–86.

81. Priest, *supra* note 8.

humanitarian law[82]—either its authorizing norms or its limiting rules—is hotly contested.[83] Briefly, the heart of the matter is this: humanitarian law authorizes—or at least accepts—the use of lethal force by privileged combatants (armies and militias that follow the rules of war), and limits the use of force and coercion in relation to protected persons (including prisoners of war, civilians, and those placed *hors de combat* because of injury or sickness). In relation to extraordinary rendition, the question is what law applies to the transfers and secret detention of individuals the United States asserts are unlawful combatants in a new kind of war.

Among the most controversial arguments the United States has made is that it is engaged in an armed conflict against Al Qaeda—or more broadly, against terrorism[84]—in which the entire world is literally a battlefield where unlawful combatants are subject to being killed, cap-

---

82. International humanitarian law—the law of armed conflict—is made up of both treaty law and customary international law. The most important treaties governing the treatment of individuals during times of armed conflict are the four Geneva Conventions of 1949. These treaties—which have been ratified by every state in the world—together set out basic rules of humane treatment. *See* Geneva Convention for the Amelioration of the Condition of the Wounded and Sick in Armed Forces in the Field, Aug. 12, 1949, 6 U.S.T. 3114, 75 U.N.T.S. 31 [hereinafter Geneva I]; Geneva Convention for the Amelioration of the Condition of Wounded, Sick, and Shipwrecked Members of Armed Forces at Sea, Aug. 12, 1949, 6 U.S.T. 3217, 75 U.N.T.S. 85 [hereinafter Geneva II]; Geneva Convention Relative to the Treatment of Prisoners of War, Aug. 12, 1949, 6 U.S.T. 3316, 75 U.N.T.S. 135 [hereinafter Geneva III]; and Geneva Convention Relative to the Protection of Civilian Persons in Time of War, Aug. 12, 1949, 6 U.S.T. 3516, 75 U.N.T.S. 287 [hereinafter Geneva IV].

83. In launching its attacks on Afghanistan, the Administration declared that it was engaged in an international armed conflict. At first, this approach was largely accepted by the international community, and the legality of the U.S. resort to force was, on the whole, accepted: the magnitude of the attacks on the World Trade Center and the Pentagon were deemed sufficient to trigger the inherent right of self-defense, and few countries argued that it was unlawful or inappropriate to target the Taliban as well as Al Qaeda in response. The controversy began when the United States declared that detainees picked up on the battlefield in Afghanistan were not entitled to protection under the Geneva Conventions—neither Geneva III (which protects prisoners of war) nor Geneva IV (which protects civilians). *See, e.g.,* Memorandum from Alberto Gonzales on Decision re Application of the Geneva Convention on Prisoners of War to the Conflict with al Qaeda and the Taliban to the President, (January 25, 2002), *reprinted in* THE TORTURE PAPERS 118–19 (Karen J. Greenberg & Joshua L. Dratel, eds., 2005) ("In my judgment, this new paradigm renders obsolete Geneva's strict limitations on questioning and renders quaint some of its provisions ...").

84. As Marco Sassòli explains:

Astonishingly ... the administration proceeded to declare that it was engaged in a single worldwide international armed conflict against a non-State actor (Al Qaeda) or perhaps also against a social or criminal phenomenon (terrorism) if not a moral category (evil). This worldwide conflict started—without the United States characterizing it as such at that time—at some point in the 1990s and will continue until victory.

tured or detained without notice (hence the potential to issue "K–C–D" orders).[85] This argument is aimed at legitimating the Administration's use of military or military-like techniques against a non-state enemy, while insulating its actions against that enemy from assessment under international humanitarian or human rights law. The argument proceeds generally as follows: the United States is engaged in an international armed conflict against a non-state enemy (Al Qaeda, a transnational terrorist network and its affiliates). As such, the conflict is not regulated by the protective norms of humanitarian law, which apply either to armed conflicts between nations ("international armed conflict," as described by Common Article 2 of the 1949 Geneva Conventions),[86] or to intrastate armed conflict ("non-international armed conflict," as described by Common Article 3 of the Geneva Conventions).[87] Because this new kind of armed conflict is not covered by the "quaint" provisions of international humanitarian law,[88] the United States is

---

Marco Sassòli, *Use and Abuse of the Laws of War in the "War on Terrorism,"* 22 LAW & INEQ. 195, 197–98 (2004).

85. The President determined on February 7, 2002, that the Geneva Conventions applied to the "present conflict with the Taliban," but found that "the Taliban detainees are unlawful combatants and, therefore, do not qualify as prisoners of war under article 4 of [the Third] Geneva [Convention]." Memorandum from President George W. Bush on Humane Treatment of al Qaeda and Taliban Detainees to the Vice President, *reprinted in* THE TORTURE PAPERS, *supra* note 83, at 134 (determining that "none of the provisions of Geneva apply to our conflict with al Qaeda in Afghanistan or elsewhere throughout the world . . ."). This decision was based on a series of memos prepared by Bush Administration officials, the State Department, and the military concerning the proper interpretation of several technical provisions of Geneva III. *See generally* memoranda *reprinted in* THE TORTURE PAPERS, *supra* note 83, at 138–43.

86. *See* Geneva III art. 2 (stating that the Convention shall apply to "all cases of declared war or of any other armed conflict").

87. Before the June 2006 *Hamdan* ruling, the United States denied that even Common Article 3 standards applied to detainees it determined were unlawful combatants, apparently concluding that such individuals are not protected by the Geneva Conventions at all, but instead, that as "enemy combatants" they essentially fall outside the laws of war. *See generally* memoranda *reprinted in* THE TORTURE PAPERS, *supra* note 83, at 138–43. This decision has been widely critiqued on the basis that—to use the words of the ICRC, writing in 1958:

> Every person in enemy hands must have some status under international law: he is either a prisoner of war and, as such, covered by the Third Convention, a civilian covered by the Fourth Convention, or again, a member of the medical personnel of the armed forces who is covered by the First Convention. *There is no* intermediate status; nobody in enemy hands can be outside the law.

INT'L COMM. OF THE RED CROSS, COMMENTARY: IV, GENEVA CONVENTION RELATIVE TO THE PROTECTION OF CIVILIAN PERSONS IN TIME OF WAR 51 (1958) (*principally authored by* Oscar M. Uhler & Henri Coursier; *edited by* Jean S. Pictet).

88. *See, e.g.,* Memorandum from Alberto R. Gonzales, *supra* note 83 ("In my judgment, this new paradigm renders obsolete Geneva's strict limitations on questioning and renders quaint some of its provisions . . .").

entitled to adapt its techniques to the circumstances without running afoul of the rules. One of these adaptations is the use of extraordinary rendition and secret detention.

In its interactions with United Nations human rights bodies, the United States has asserted that it is engaged in a "War on Terror" that is governed exclusively by the laws of armed conflict.[89] In making this assertion, the United States has argued that international humanitarian law is the applicable *lex specialis*,[90] i.e., that humanitarian law provides the relevant substantive rules regarding the treatment of individuals in the "War on Terror." In combination, the Administration's reference to the *lex specialis* rule[91] and its argument that it can "render" suspected terrorists as part of its "War on Terror," seem to indicate that the U.S. government believes that no law applies to protect individuals against such transfers. The legal vacuum is constructed as follows: since the transfers occur as part of an armed conflict, we must look to humanitarian law for any relevant rules concerning transfers. Al Qaeda members, however, are unprivileged combatants, and thus unprotected by rules found in the Geneva Conventions concerning the transfer of prisoners of war or other protected persons. Finally, the argument concludes, the rules of human rights law do not apply either, since humanitarian law operates as *lex specialis* to oust such rules from application. For this reason, suspected terrorists may be informally transferred from place to place without those transfers being unlawful, since no law applies.

A similar—though more textual—argument has been made in relation to secret detention. In the few instances in which the United States has defended the practice, it has alleged that certain individuals who pose a threat to security are not protected by the Geneva Conventions' provisions concerning access by the International Committee of the Red Cross ("ICRC") to detainees.[92] Simultaneously, the United States implies that the Geneva Conventions are the only relevant source of any obligations to allow access to detainees or to disclose the location of such detainees held in the context of armed conflict. In other words, the United States indicates that because such individuals are not covered by

---

89. *See* UNITED STATES, REPLY OF THE GOVERNMENT OF THE UNITED STATES OF AMERICA TO THE REPORT OF THE FIVE U.N. SPECIAL RAPPORTEURS ON DETAINEES IN GUANTÁNAMO BAY, CUBA 16 (2006), *available at* http://www.asil.org/pdfs/ilib0603212.pdf ("The United States is engaged in a continuing armed conflict against Al Qaeda, and customary law of war applies to the conduct of that war and related detention operations.").

90. *Id.* at 22.

91. The international law rule *lex specialis derogat legi generali* means that a special rule prevails over a general rule. *See* MALCOLM N. SHAW, INTERNATIONAL LAW 116 (5th ed., 2003).

92. *See, e.g.,* Steven R. Weisman, *U.S. Rebuffs Red Cross Request for Access to Detainees Held in Secret*, N.Y. TIMES, Dec. 10, 2005, at A10.

the Convention provisions concerning access to detainees, they are not protected against secret detention.[93] The ICRC has repeatedly sought access to detainees held in secret locations, and has expressed concern publicly about the practice.[94] Further, the ICRC has determined that enforced disappearance is unlawful under customary international humanitarian law, which binds all states as a general matter.[95]

With respect to international humanitarian law, there are three main responses to the Bush Administration's "War on Terror" approach to extraordinary rendition and secret detention. All begin with the common agreement that the current struggle against Al Qaeda and other transnational terrorist groups is not neatly governed by the laws of war. This is because international humanitarian law applies only to situations of armed conflict, and the definition of "armed conflict" is not easy to apply to the disparate circumstances of the "War on Terror" in a uniform manner.[96] Beyond cases in which two or more states' armies face off on a traditional battlefield, an armed conflict exists for the purposes of international humanitarian law only under the following circumstances:

---

93. *See, e.g.*, Sean McCormack, Spokesman, Dep't of State, Daily Press Briefing (May 12, 2006) (transcript *available at* http://www.state.gov/r/pa/prs/dpb/2006/66202.htm) ("Look, there are—under the Geneva Conventions there is a certain category of individual, and this is allowed for under the Geneva Conventions, individuals who forfeit their rights under Geneva Convention protections, and they do this through a variety of different actions. So there are a group of—there are allowances in the Geneva Convention for individuals who would not be covered by that convention and, therefore the party holding them would not be subject to the Geneva Conventions in providing access to those individuals.").

94. *See* ICRC, *U.S. Detention Related to the Events of 11 September 2001 and its Aftermath—The Role of the ICRC*, May 14, 2004, *available at* http://www.icrc.org/Web/Eng/siteeng0.nsf/iwpList74/73596F146DAB1A08C1256E9400469F48 (noting that the ICRC has "repeatedly appealed to the American authorities for access to people detained in undisclosed locations.... Beyond Bagram and Guantánamo Bay, the ICRC is increasingly concerned about the fate of an unknown number of people captured as part of the so-called global war on terror and held in undisclosed locations.").

95. *See* INTERNATIONAL RED CROSS, 1 CUSTOMARY INTERNATIONAL HUMANITARIAN LAW: RULES 340–343 (Jean–Marie Henckaerts & Louise Doswald–Beck eds., 2005).

96. Common Article 2 provides for the following rule of application: "the present Convention shall apply to all cases of declared war or of any other armed conflict which may arise between two or more of the High Contracting Parties, even if the state of war is not recognized by one of them." *See* art. 2 of Geneva I, Geneva II, Geneva III, and Geneva IV, *supra* note 82. The ICRC *Commentary* explains that the term "armed conflict" was chosen to avoid the potentially "endless" arguments that would arise if the word "war" was instead used; the emphasis was to be on the factual situation—the Conventions should apply to "[a]ny difference arising between two States and leading to the intervention of members of the armed forces"—not on the legal circumstances for such intervention. ICRC, COMMENTARY: III, GENEVA CONVENTION RELATIVE TO THE TREATMENT OF PRISONERS OF WAR 26 (1960) (*prepared by* Jean de Preux; *edited by* Jean S. Pictet).

a) if hostilities rise to a certain level and/or are protracted beyond what is known as mere internal disturbances or sporadic riots, b) if parties can be defined and identified, c) if the territorial bounds of the conflict can be identified and defined, and d) if the beginning and end of the conflict can be defined and identified.[97]

When these characteristics are absent, international humanitarian law treaties are not the controlling law, since their minimum threshold of applicability will not have been reached. These characteristics, which are drawn from treaty and customary law governing non-international armed conflicts, are not uniformly present in the "War on Terror."[98]

In the face of this mismatch, the Administration suggests that there is a legal vacuum. International legal scholars and advocates reject this approach, and tend to make three alternative arguments. The first asserts that the laws of war are not applicable to the "War on Terror," but human rights law continues to apply. A second argument posits that although the law is not perfectly suited to the current situation, the United States' conflict with Al Qaeda is best viewed as a non-international armed conflict, to which only the minimum rules applicable to such conflicts apply. The final argument accepts the administration's view that the United States is engaged in a new type of war. Rather than accepting that international humanitarian law is silent about this new form of conflict, however, this line of reasoning asserts that international humanitarian law should be read in conjunction with other rules of international law to protect the basic rights of all—including suspected terrorists. In the end, the problem with the Administration's arguments is that extraordinary rendition and secret detention are illegal under any of these paradigms—they violate both human rights law *and* international humanitarian law.

After *Hamdan*, the U.S. government appears to have accepted that its "War on Terror" activities are governed by Common Article 3.[99]

---

97. Gabor Rona, Legal Advisor, ICRC, Presentation at Workshop on the Protection of Human Rights While Countering Terrorism, Copenhagen: When is a War Not a War? The Proper Role of the Law of Armed Conflict in the "Global War on Terror" (Mar. 16, 2004) (*available at* http://www.icrc.org/web/eng/siteeng0.nsf/htmlall/5xcmnj?opendocument).

98. Of course, certain campaigns or operations in the "War on Terror" plainly entail armed conflict, including the wars in Afghanistan and Iraq. Those operations are limited in space and time, however, and are distinct from the concept of a "War on Terror" that is not limited by geography.

99. Soon after the Supreme Court delivered its judgment in *Hamdan*, Deputy Defense Secretary Gordon England issued a memo stating that "[t]he Supreme Court has determined that Common Article 3 to the Geneva Conventions of 1949 applies as a matter of law to the conflict with Al Qaeda." Memorandum from Gordon England, Deputy Def. Sec'y, to the Secretaries of the Military Departments (July 7, 2006), *available at* http://graphics8.nytimes.com/packages/pdf/politics/060711pentagon_memo.pdf. Although Secretary England stated that all Department of Defense operations other than the military

While there was some confusion concerning the application of Common Article 3 to the CIA's activities,[100] the issue was settled on July 20, 2007, when President Bush issued an executive order stating that Common Article 3 "shall apply to a program of detention and interrogation operated by the Central Intelligence Agency."[101] After "reaffirming" that terrorism suspects are "unlawful combatants" not eligible for protection as prisoners of war, President Bush "determine[d] that Common Article 3 shall apply to a program of detention and interrogation operated by the Central Intelligence Agency as set forth in this section."[102] While this would seem to bring the United States closer to compliance with international legal standards, the Order also purports to peg the humane treatment standards of Common Article 3 to standards set out in domestic law, and concludes that the CIA's detention and interrogation Program is compliant with relevant law, including Common Article 3 as defined in the Order. While the Order certainly has some domestic legal effect, it plainly did not clarify U.S. compliance as a matter of international law.[103]

Common Article 3 protects all individuals who have been detained from—among other things—"violence to life and person, in particular murder of all kinds, mutilation, cruel treatment and torture" and "outrages upon personal dignity, in particular humiliating and degrading treatment." This language should be interpreted to prohibit secret detention, since—as discussed above—undisclosed detention, in itself, has been found to violate norms against torture and cruel, inhuman or degrading treatment. The humane treatment provisions in Common Article 3 should also be read to include protection against transfer to a

---

commissions found to be impermissible by the Supreme Court were in line with Common Article 3, he ordered Department of Defense officials to review all policies and directives to ensure they were in compliance with this provision. *Id.*; *see also* Donna Miles, *England Memo Underscores Policy on Humane Treatment of Detainees*, AM. FORCES PRESS SERVICE, July 11, 2006, *available at* http://www.defenselink.mil/news/NewsArticle.aspx?ID=114. John Bellinger, Legal Adviser to the Department of State, has indicated that his Department understands the *Hamdan* decision to have extended Common Article 3 to the general "conflict with al Qaeda." John B. Bellinger, Legal Advisor, Dep't of State, Foreign Press Center Briefing: The Military Commission Act of 2006, at 1 (Oct. 19, 2006), *available at* http://fpc.state.gov/fpc/74786.htm.

100. *See* Mark Mazzetti & Kate Zernike, *White House Says Terror Detainees Have Basic Geneva Rights*, N.Y. TIMES, July 12, 2006, at A1. For a discussion of the debate within the Administration concerning the applicability of Common Article 3 to terrorism suspects, *see* Tim Golden, *Detainee Memo Created Divide in White House*, N.Y. TIMES, Oct. 1, 2006, at A1.

101. Exec. Order 13,440, 72 Fed. Reg. 40,707 (July 20, 2007).

102. *Id.*

103. For a comprehensive discussion of the ways in which this executive order condones activities that contravene international law, *see* AMNESTY INT'L, USA: LAW AND EXECUTIVE DISORDER: PRESIDENT GIVES GREEN LIGHT TO SECRET DETENTION PROGRAM (2007).

country or location where the individual is at risk of torture or cruel treatment. Applying the same logic used by international bodies interpreting human rights treaties, the protection against torture and cruel or degrading treatment in Common Article 3 should be interpreted to include a protection against *non-refoulement* to the same kind of treatment; this is necessary to ensure the prohibition on torture, and the humane principles on which it is built, has real meaning.[104] Further, the fact that Common Article 3 does not include an explicit *non-refoulement* rule is not dispositive: at the time it was drafted, this provision was largely designed for application in the context of civil wars and other intra-state conflicts.[105] Extraordinary rendition and secret detention are therefore both prohibited by Common Article 3.[106]

---

104. *See* Soering v. United Kingdom, 161 Eur. Ct. H.R. (ser. A) at ¶ 88 (1989) (holding that "[i]t would hardly be compatible with the underlying values of the Convention, that 'common heritage of political traditions, ideals, freedom and the rule of law' to which the Preamble refers, were a Contracting State knowingly to surrender a fugitive to another State where there were substantial grounds for believing that he would be in danger of being subjected to torture, however heinous the crime allegedly committed. Extradition in such circumstances, while not explicitly referred to in the brief and general wording of Article 3 (art. 3), would plainly be contrary to the spirit and intendment of the Article, and in the Court's view this inherent obligation not to extradite also extends to cases in which the fugitive would be faced in the receiving State by a real risk of exposure to inhuman or degrading treatment or punishment proscribed by that Article."); *see also* Satterthwaite, *Rendered Meaningless*, *supra* note 75, at 1357 n. 141 and accompanying text (discussing Human Rights Committee's construction of Article 7 of the ICCPR).

105. Unlike Geneva III and IV, which contain explicit rules concerning inter-state transfer of protected persons, therefore, Common Article 3 contains only the most basic guarantees required for situations of non-international armed conflict. Although it was not envisioned at the time that states would transfer among themselves fighters in non-international armed conflicts, this failure of imagination should not be taken as a limitation on the protection against *refoulement*.

106. A comparatively more difficult question is whether the United States is *obliged to apprehend instead of killing* suspected Al Qaeda operatives under Common Article 3. In other words, even if certain ways of carrying out the "capture" and "detain" parts of a "K–C–D" order are unlawful, is the U.S. government within its rights to instead kill designated individuals? This question must be addressed because non-state fighters are not protected against attack when they are taking an "active part in the hostilities" in a non-international armed conflict. Serious debate rages over what types of activities trigger this loss of immunity and whether individuals deemed to be "enemy combatants" by the U.S. government have, by definition, been found to have taken such an active part, making them legitimate targets for military marksmen or CIA drones. In other words, under humanitarian law, the application of Common Article 3 standards to the "War on Terror" may not bar the United States from killing members of Al Qaeda in situations of armed conflict, even if the United States had not attempted to arrest or detain them. However, reading international humanitarian law together with human rights law produces a rule that does require states to prefer the apprehension of terrorist suspects over killing them. For a discussion of these issues, *see, e.g.*, Philip B. Heymann & Juliette N. Kayyem, *Long–Term Strategy Project for Preserving Security and Democratic Freedoms in the War on Terrorism* (2004), *available at* http://www.mipt.org/pdf/Long–Term–Legal–Strategy.pdf;

Further, international authorities have found that international humanitarian law must be read in conjunction with international human rights law. The International Court of Justice explained the relationship between humanitarian law and human rights law in its 1996 *Advisory Opinion on the Legality of the Threat or Use of Nuclear Weapons*,[107] where it stated plainly that international human rights law continues to apply in times of armed conflict. The *lex specialis* rule, operating as a conflicts-of-law norm, requires that when rights have incongruous content in times of armed conflict, humanitarian law must necessarily inform the interpretation of such rights. When a conflict arises between norms, the *lex specialis* rule requires preference of international humanitarian law. In such cases, international humanitarian law allows for the justification of what would otherwise be a violation of human rights law. A soldier shooting an enemy on the battlefield looks like a human rights violation (the deprivation of life without due process) until the international humanitarian law rule is applied (privileged combatants may kill other combatants, or civilians taking a direct role in hostilities). In the context of extraordinary rendition, there is no conflict between norms: the rules of non-international armed conflict prohibit torture and cruel treatment. Human rights law prohibits the same kind of treatment, but also provides more specific—and harmonious—content, prohibiting not only torture and cruel treatment, but also adding precision by prohibiting *refoulement* to such treatment.

El–Masri: The Search for Justice[108]

"Those responsible have to take responsibility, and should be held to account."
—Khaled El–Masri[109]

At first, Khaled El–Masri did not tell anyone about the ordeal he had suffered. It would sound too outlandish, he thought, and he worried

---

Emmanuel Gross, *Thwarting Terrorist Acts by Attacking the Perpetrators or Their Commanders as an Act of Self–Defense: Human Rights Versus the State's Duty to Protect its Citizens*, 15 TEMP. INT'L & COMP. L.J. 195, 245–46 (2001); *see also* Jonathan Ulrich, Note, *The Gloves Were Never On: Defining the President's Authority to Order Targeted Killing in the War Against Terrorism*, 45 VA. J. INT'L L. 1029 (2005).

107. Legality of the Threat or Use of Nuclear Weapons, Advisory Opinion, 1996 I.C.J. 226 (July 8, 1996).

108. Unless otherwise noted, the facts in this section are taken from Declaration of Khaled El–Masri, *supra* note 1; Declaration of Manfred Gnjidic in Support of Plaintiff's Opposition to the United States' Motion to Dismiss, or in the Alternative, for Summary Judgment, El–Masri v. Tenet, 437 F. Supp. 2d 530 (E.D. Va. 2006) (No. 1:05cv1417), *aff'd sub nom*. El–Masri v. U.S., 479 F.3d 296 (4th Cir. 2007), *cert. denied,* 128 S.Ct. 373 (2007), *available at* http://www.aclu.org/pdfs/safefree/gnjidic_decl_exh.pdf; Declaration of Steven Macpherson Watt in Support of Plaintiff's Opposition to the United States' Motion to Dismiss, or in the Alternative, for Summary Judgment, El–Masri v. Tenet, 437 F. Supp. 2d 530 (No. 1:05cv1417), *available at* http://www.aclu.org/safefree/torture/25530lgl20060511.html; Cameron Abadi, *Disappeared but Not Silenced*, AMNESTY INT'L MAGAZINE, Spring 2007, *available at* http://www.amnestyusa.org/spring-2007/disappeared-but-not-silenced/page.do?id=1105397&n1=2&n2=19&n3=397 (interview with Khaled El–Masri); and interviews

109. See note 109 on page 563.

that no one would believe him. More importantly, those detaining him had threatened him. If he told his story, he worried that he would be kidnapped again. His house was empty when he returned; he learned that his wife had gone to Lebanon with their children to stay with her family when El–Masri had not returned from his vacation.[110] The family was soon reunited in Germany, and El–Masri told his wife what had happened to him.[111]

Despite his fears, El–Masri made an appointment with a lawyer named Manfred Gnjidic. On June 3, 2004—only a week after he was released—El–Masri told Gnjidic his story. Gnjidic asked El–Masri to write out his story, to make drawings of the hotel room in Macedonia and the facility in Afghanistan, and to gather all the physical evidence he had that might help prove that he was telling the truth. Gnjidic also wrote a letter to German Chancellor Gerhard Schroeder and the German Minister of Foreign Affairs. In response to these letters, the Office of the Public Prosecutor opened an investigation into the kidnapping, and contacted Gnjidic to set up an interview with El–Masri. Under German law, the Office of the Public Prosecutor is under an obligation to investigate suspected crimes; the prosecutor's office interviewed El–Masri numerous times and performed a radioactive isotope analysis of his hair. By confirming that El–Masri had been in a South Asian country and that he had been deprived of food, the analysis lent support to his story of a hunger strike while in detention in Afghanistan.

In June 2005, Steven Watt, an attorney with the American Civil Liberties Union ("ACLU") in New York, travelled to Germany to meet with El–Masri and Gnjidic. He had learned of El–Masri's ordeal several months earlier, and had spent time investigating the case and potential claims that El–Masri might have under U.S. and international law.[112] Watt was impressed with El–Masri's resolve and bravery in light of the legal obstacles Watt explained they would face if El–Masri decided to go

---

with Steven Watt, Senior Staff Attorney, ACLU Human Rights Program, and Ben Wizner, Staff Attorney, ACLU National Security Program, in New York City, N.Y. (Aug. 24, 2007). Quotes from Steven Watt and Ben Wizner, as well as information about legal strategy are drawn from interviews, *supra*.

109. Meek, *supra* note 2.

110. *Id.*

111. *Id.*

112. El–Masri's story was first told in a major U.S. news publication in Don Van Natta, Jr. & Souad Mekhennet, *German's Claim of Kidnapping Brings Investigation of U.S. Link,* N.Y. TIMES, Jan. 9, 2005, at 11.

forward with a U.S. case. Knowing that the case would be stymied by a number of significant legal and political challenges, Watt explained the situation several times to his potential new client, eager to ensure El–Masri understood what they were up against so that he could make an informed choice about the lawsuit. "In many ways, he understood better than I did," Watt said. "He knew the case was an opportunity to tell his story and he wanted to do it for that reason."[113] El–Masri made clear that his goals were not monetary; instead, he sought an acknowledgement from the U.S. government that it had wrongly detained him, and an apology from those responsible.[114]

After meeting with El–Masri, Watt felt sure that the case presented the opportunity Watt and his colleagues had sought for years—the ability to directly challenge the extraordinary rendition of an individual through kidnapping on foreign soil. Before moving to the ACLU in November 2004, Watt had worked at the Center for Constitutional Rights ("CCR"), and he had been on the legal team representing Canadian citizen Maher Arar, who was apprehended and rendered to Syria while changing planes at JFK International airport in New York in September 2002.[115] Working closely with Canadian lawyers who were pressuring the Canadian government to create a commission of inquiry into the Arar case, CCR attorneys filed suit on behalf of Arar in the U.S. District Court for the Eastern District of New York on January 22, 2004, while Watt was still at CCR.[116] The suit named then-Attorney General John Ashcroft, then-Deputy Attorney General Larry Thompson, then-FBI Director Robert Mueller, as well as other U.S. immigration officials as defendants. It alleged that these defendants had violated Arar's constitutional due process rights and had conspired in his torture in Syria in contravention of the Torture Victim Protection Act. Although the case was dismissed by the district court,[117] it brought a great deal of attention to the extraordinary rendition policy and sparked a national

---

113. Interview with Steven Watt, Senior Staff Attorney, ACLU Human Rights Program, in New York City, N.Y. (Mar. 25, 2008).

114. *Id.*

115. For a comprehensive accounting of the Arar case, *see* Comm'n of Inquiry into the Actions of Canadian Officials in Relation to Maher Arar, *Report of the Events Relating to Maher Arar: Analysis and Recommendations*, (2006), *available at* http://www.ararcommission.ca/eng/AR_English.pdf [hereinafter *Arar Commission of Inquiry Final Report*].

116. Attorneys central to the case have included David Cole, Maria LaHood, Jules Lobel, Barbara Olshansky, and Steven Watt.

117. At the time of writing, the case was still pending before the Second Circuit. *See* 414 F. Supp. 2d 250 (E.D.N.Y. 2006), *aff'd by* Arar v. Ashcroft, 532 F.3d 157 (2d Cir. 2008), *reh'g en banc granted by* Order of the Second Circuit Court of Appeals of Aug. 12, 2008 (on file with author).

debate that until then had not included the important focal point of a human story.

El–Masri's experience was similar to Arar's in many respects: both men were spirited away without charge on suspicions of having ties to Al Qaeda that later evaporated;[118] both were citizens of Western democracies that were allies of the United States; both had experienced ill-treatment and horrible conditions of confinement; and both men sought justice. Each man, however, represented a different side of the extraordinary rendition and secret detention Program: Arar had been transferred from the United States to Syria, where he was tortured by Syrians at the behest of the United States. El–Masri had been abducted abroad—in Macedonia—and was sent to a secret CIA prison in Afghanistan, where he was ill-treated by U.S. agents.

Moreover, like Arar, no evidence tied El–Masri to terrorism. In fact, as was apparent from the questions that interrogators asked El–Masri while he was in detention, it appeared that the reason behind El–Masri's abduction was a terrible mistake: the similarity of his name (Khaled El–Masri) with a suspected Al Qaeda leader (Khalid El Masri or Khalid al Masri).[119] Where the German El–Masri had been born in Kuwait to Lebanese parents in 1963, the Egyptian El Masri had been an associate of the Hamburg Cell in Germany in the lead-up to 9/11.[120]

For Watt and his colleagues at the ACLU, these facts underlined the importance of El–Masri's story. Here was someone who could speak for

---

118. Commissioner Justice Dennis O'Connor of the Inquiry into the Actions of Canadian Officials in Relation to Maher Arar stated:

> I am able to say categorically that there is no evidence to indicate that Mr. Arar has committed any offence or that his activities constitute a threat to the security of Canada. The public can be confident that Canadian investigators have thoroughly and exhaustively followed all information leads available to them in connection with Mr. Arar's activities and associations. This was not a case where investigators were unable to effectively pursue their investigative goals because of a lack of resources or time constraints. On the contrary, Canadian investigators made extensive efforts to find any information that could implicate Mr. Arar in terrorist activities. They did so over a lengthy period of time, even after Mr. Arar's case became a cause célèbre. The results speak for themselves: they found none.

Arar Commission of Inquiry Final Report, supra note 115, at 59. Media accounts indicate that both then-CIA Director George Tenet and then-National Security Council Director Condoleezza Rice ordered El–Masri's release once they realized he was innocent. *See* Lisa Myers, Aram Roston & NBC Investigative Unit, *CIA Accused of Detaining Innocent Man: If the Agency Knew He Was the Wrong Man, Why Was He Held?*, MSNBC, April 21, 2005, *available at* http://www.msnbc.msn.com/id/7591918.

119. *See* Dana Priest, *Wrongful Imprisonment: Anatomy of a CIA Mistake*, WASH. POST, Dec. 4, 2005, at A01.

120. NAT'L COMM'N ON TERRORIST ATTACKS UPON THE U.S., THE 9/11 COMMISSION REPORT 165–66 (2004), *available at* http://www.9-11commission.gov/report/911Report.pdf.

the reported several dozen CIA mistakes or "erroneous renditions"—here renditions to secret detention in a CIA prison.[121] As ACLU attorney Ben Wizner emphasized, here was someone who was utterly innocent, but who had nonetheless been disappeared by the U.S. government for months.[122] While both Watt and Wizner strongly believe that extraordinary rendition is wrong regardless of the individual's culpability, both also emphasize the important role of the "innocent victim" in test case litigation. Because they sought to make El–Masri the "face" of extraordinary rendition—the symbol of U.S. violations in the "War on Terror"—the lawyers felt it was important to ensure that he had not committed any crimes of terrorism. An innocent victim would disarm the legal team's opponents by focusing the public's attention on the lack of safeguards in the system, and by making impotent the argument that rendition and torture are "necessary" to stop a hardened enemy.

Between June 2005 and December 2005, the ACLU attorneys worked with Manfred Gnjidic and Khaled El–Masri to prepare a legal challenge to the rendition and secret detention Program. This preparatory work involved the development of a media strategy, investigative work, and legal drafting. By December 2005, the case was ready to be filed. Khaled El–Masri agreed to travel to the United States for the filing of the suit. When his airplane arrived in Atlanta from Germany on December 3, 2005, however, El–Masri was refused entry and sent back to Germany. The expulsion reportedly was carried out on the basis of information that customs officials received "from other American agencies"[123]—presumably the CIA. El–Masri later told reporters that the experience was very frightening: "My heart was beating very fast," he said, "I have remembered that time, what has happened to me, when they kidnapped me to Afghanistan. I have remembered and was afraid."[124]

El–Masri v. Tenet was filed on December 6, 2005 in the U.S. District Court for the Eastern District of Virginia.[125] The complaint named former CIA director George Tenet and other CIA officials as defendants,

---

121. See Priest, *supra* note 119.

122. Ben Wizner explained the importance of innocence this way: "Unless we had an innocent person, the debate would not have been about the rule of law. It would have been about whether torture works." Interview with Ben Wizner, *supra* note 108.

123. Scott Shane & Souad Mekhennet, *German Held in Afghan Jail Files Lawsuit*, N.Y. Times, Dec. 7, 2005, at A25 (citing U.S. Customs & Border Protection spokesperson Kristi Clemens).

124. *Id.*

125. The facts in this paragraph are drawn from the complaint in El–Masri v. Tenet, 437 F. Supp. 2d 530 (E.D. Va. 2006) (No. 1:05cv1417), *aff'd sub nom.* El–Masri v. U.S., 479 F.3d 296 (4th Cir. 2007), *cert. denied*, 128 S.Ct. 373 (2007), *available at* http://www.aclu.org/safefree/extraordinaryrendition/22211lgl20051206.html.

alleging that they violated both U.S. and international law when they abducted El–Masri. More specifically, the complaint alleged, pursuant to *Bivens v. Six Unknown Named Agents of Federal Bureau of Narcotics*,[126] that the CIA agents violated El–Masri's Fifth Amendment due process rights by subjecting him to treatment that "shocks the conscience" and by detaining him absent legal process. The complaint also alleged that the CIA agents arbitrarily detained him, tortured him, and subjected him to cruel, inhuman or degrading treatment cognizable under the Alien Tort Statute. With respect to Tenet, the complaint alleged that because he had actual and constructive knowledge of these actions, he—at a minimum—expressly and tacitly authorized the unlawful conduct of his subordinates, making him liable; it also alleged that he affirmatively ordered or condoned the abuse, and that he was responsible for the policy of extraordinary rendition, through which such abuse was authorized. The suit also named three corporations as defendants, claiming that—because they owned and operated the plane used to transfer El–Masri and because they knew or should have known what would befall him in Afghanistan—these corporations had colluded in the violation of his human and civil rights. Specifically, the complaint alleged that the airplane companies conspired and/or aided and abetted in the arbitrary detention, torture, cruel, inhuman, and degrading treatment that El–Masri suffered.

One of the greatest advocacy successes of the lawsuit was the media cascade that was created when the complaint was filed concurrently with a visit that Secretary of State Condoleezza Rice was making to Europe. This visit was scheduled in wake of revelations—most notably those published in an article by investigative journalist Dana Priest in *The Washington Post*[127]—of an archipelago of secret detention sites run by the CIA, some of them in Eastern Europe. Before she set off on December 5, 2005, Secretary Rice made a statement defending the policy of rendition:

> The United States and many other countries are waging a war against terrorism. For our country this war often takes the form of conventional military operations in places like Afghanistan and Iraq. Sometimes this is a political struggle, a war of ideas. It is a struggle waged also by our law enforcement agencies. Often we engage the enemy through the cooperation of our intelligence services with their foreign counterparts.... One of the difficult issues in this new kind of conflict is what to do with captured individuals who we know or believe to be terrorists.... The captured terrorists of the 21st century do not fit easily into traditional systems of criminal or

---

126. 403 U.S. 388 (1971).

127. Priest, *supra* note 37.

military justice, which were designed for different needs. We have to adapt.[128]

While aimed at quelling European protests against extraordinary rendition, this statement merely stoked the flames. After a meeting with Chancellor Angela Merkel in Germany, Rice was asked about the El-Masri case. She declined to comment. Chancellor Merkel was not so circumspect. "The American administration has admitted that this man was erroneously taken," she said through an interpreter.[129] Although the statement would later be retracted by her aides, in many ways the Chancellor was merely confirming something that had been reported a few days earlier in *The Washington Post*: that a U.S. official had informed the German interior minister "that the CIA had wrongfully imprisoned one of its citizens, Khaled Masri, for five months, and would soon release him.... There was also a request: that the German government not disclose what it had been told, even if Masri went public."[130] A few days later, the German Interior Ministry publicly confirmed that it had been informed by the U.S. government in May 2004 that the CIA may have mistakenly abducted El–Masri.[131] What followed was a flurry of media accounts covering the El–Masri case and probing the wisdom of the extraordinary rendition policy. In many ways, the filing of the suit itself was a huge victory: it allowed El–Masri to tell his story, it prompted media coverage and further investigation by journalists of both the particulars of El–Masri's experience and the Program more generally, and it "forced powerful people to answer uncomfortable questions," according to Wizner.[132]

Things did not go so well in court. On March 8, 2006, the United States filed a statement of interest and assertion of a formal claim of state secrets privilege along with a motion to stay court proceedings pending resolution of the privilege claim; Judge Ellis granted the motion. The next week, the United States filed a motion to intervene as defendant in the case and to dismiss the case as precluded by the state secrets privilege (or, in the alternative, for summary judgment). The government filed two declarations by Porter Goss as Director of the CIA: one public and one classified. In his public declaration, Goss argued that the claims alleged by El–Masri, and the potential defenses against those

---

128. Condoleezza Rice, U.S. Sec'y of State, Remarks Upon Her Departure for Europe (Dec. 5, 2005) (transcript *available at* http://www.state.gov/secretary/rm/2005/57602.htm).

129. Glenn Kessler, *Rice to Admit German's Abduction Was an Error*, Wash. Post, Dec. 6, 2005, at A18.

130. Priest, *supra* note 119.

131. Jeffrey Fleishman, *U.S. Envoy May Have Told Germany of CIA Error*, Ft. Worth Star-Telegram, Dec. 8, 2005, at A10.

132. Interview with Ben Wizner, *supra* note 108.

claims would force the CIA to admit or deny the existence of clandestine CIA activities, and that therefore dismissal of the suit was the only proper outcome.[133] The court quickly granted the motion to intervene and took under consideration the motion to dismiss.

The state secrets privilege is a common law privilege that is intended to protect against the disclosure of sensitive governmental information during civil litigation. The privilege protects evidence that, if disclosed, would harm national security. Procedurally, the government may intervene in any civil case (even when it is not a party to the suit) to invoke the state secrets privilege through a filing with the court. This filing must include an affidavit by the head of the relevant department or agency invoking the privilege after personal consideration of the matter.[134]

On April 11, the ACLU filed papers in opposition to the U.S. motion to dismiss, arguing that the facts central to the case were not state secrets, that the case should proceed and allow for discovery of non-privileged evidence, and that the court had options for how to proceed with the case in a way that would not require the United States to reveal any state secrets. Along with its motion and memorandum of law, the ACLU filed an extensive declaration by Khaled El–Masri, in which he explained his abduction, detention, and ill-treatment in his own words. The declaration was striking in its detail and clarity. Attorney Steven Watt also filed a declaration setting forth the extensive facts that had already been made public about the extraordinary rendition Program as a general matter, and about El–Masri's experience more specifically. The purpose of both declarations was to demonstrate that the state secrets privilege was inapposite: not only did El–Masri have the right and ability to talk about his own experience in the Program, but the U.S. government had itself admitted the existence of the rendition policy.

The ACLU's filings were unavailing: one month later, on May 12, 2006, Judge Ellis dismissed the case, holding that his hands were tied by existing law on the state secrets privilege:

> It is important to emphasize that the result reached here is required by settled, controlling law. It is in no way an adjudication of, or comment on, the merit or lack of merit of El–Masri's complaint. Nor does this ruling comment or rule in any way on the truth or falsity

---

133. Formal Claim of State Secrets Privilege by Porter J. Goss, Director, Central Intelligence Agency, El–Masri v. Tenet, 437 F. Supp. 2d 530 (E.D. Va. 2006) (No. 1:05cv1417), aff'd sub nom. El–Masri v. U.S., 479 F.3d 296 (4th Cir. 2007), cert. denied, 128 S.Ct. 373 (2007), available at http://www.aclu.org/safefree/torture/25531gl20060511.html.

134. For more on the state secrets privilege, see LOUIS FISHER, IN THE NAME OF NATIONAL SECURITY: UNCHECKED PRESIDENTIAL POWER AND THE REYNOLDS CASE (2006), and Robert M. Chesney, State Secrets and the Limits of National Security Litigation, 75 GEO. WASH. L. REV. 1249 (2007).

of his factual allegations; they may be true or false, in whole or in part. Further, it is also important that nothing in this ruling should be taken as a sign of judicial approval or disapproval of rendition programs; it is not intended to do either. In times of war, our country, chiefly through the Executive Branch, must often take exceptional steps to thwart the enemy. Of course, reasonable and patriotic Americans are still free to disagree about the propriety and efficacy of those exceptional steps. But what this decision holds is that these steps are not proper grist for the judicial mill where, as here, state secrets are at the center of the suit and the privilege is validly invoked.[135]

Judge Ellis' order concludes with one of the most striking passages in any case brought so far in the "War on Terror":

Finally, it is worth noting that putting aside all the legal issues, if El–Masri's allegations are true or essentially true, then all fair-minded people, including those who believe that state secrets must be protected, that this lawsuit cannot proceed, and that renditions are a necessary step to take in this war, must also agree that El–Masri has suffered injuries as a result of our country's mistake and deserves a remedy. Yet, it is also clear from the result reached here that the only sources of that remedy must be the Executive Branch or the Legislative Branch, not the Judicial Branch.[136]

Attorney Steven Watt vividly recalled the moment that he called Khaled El–Masri to tell him about the judge's ruling; it was undoubtedly one of the most difficult moments for him in the case. When Watt explained that the ACLU was prepared to appeal the case, El–Masri confided in him that—in Watt's recollection of El–Masri's words—"my biggest concern was that you were going to give up on me."[137] Reflecting on this reaction, Watt explained that El–Masri's words reminded him that the human rights lawyer always needs to ask himself if he is doing more harm than good and if the process of reliving events through interviews, being shut down by the courts, or being under a press microscope is not too much for a survivor-turned-plaintiff.

Watt assured El–Masri of the organization's commitment—and his legal team's personal commitment—to his case. El–Masri was emphatic in his desire to appeal. As the legal team prepared their filings for the Fourth Circuit, they also worked on a strategy that would reach beyond the court. This strategy was buoyed by several important developments in Europe. In April, a Committee of the European Parliament visited

---

135. Order Granting Motion to Dismiss at 16, El–Masri v. Tenet, 437 F. Supp. 2d 530 (E.D. Va. 2006), *available at* http://www.aclu.org/safefree/torture/27015lgl20060512.html.

136. *Id.*

137. Interview with Steven Watt, *supra* note 108.

Macedonia to investigate El–Masri's abduction.[138] On June 7, 2006, the Council of Europe released a report on extraordinary rendition and secret detention following an extensive investigation by Swiss Senator Dick Marty. The report found that El–Masri's account was accurate, and placed the case in the context of European collusion with what it characterized as systematic violations of human rights.[139] In Germany, the Parliament launched an investigation into the case.[140] In September 2006, German prosecutors said that they were seeking—and receiving—assistance from Spain in tracing the movements within Europe of individual CIA agents believed to be responsible for El–Masri's transfer from Macedonia to Afghanistan.[141]

By late autumn, the plans were set: El–Masri would again fly to the United States for the appeal. This time, he would be in the courtroom when attorney Ben Wizner argued his case. The ACLU was able to secure assurances that El–Masri would not be turned away at the U.S. border, and he bravely boarded a plane again. El–Masri arrived safely and attended the oral argument of his case before the Fourth Circuit Court of Appeals on November 28, 2006. The next day, he met with Congressional staffers and journalists to discuss the extraordinary rendition Program. This advocacy, aimed at ensuring that the American public understood that rendition was a policy with dire human impact, also had the effect of empowering El–Masri. "He may not have gotten an apology from the Administration," Wizner explained, "but he got a lot of apologies from Hill staffers, people who attended events where he spoke, and even a group of Germans who recognized him in New York City."

On January 31, 2007, while El–Masri awaited the outcome of his federal appeal, German prosecutors issued arrest warrants for thirteen individuals they identified as having been the crew and passengers on the flight from Macedonia to Afghanistan.[142] The individuals were suspected of involvement in the false imprisonment and torture of El–Masri.[143] The CIA declined to comment on the arrest warrants; the U.S.

---

138. European Parliament, Temporary Comm. on the Alleged Use of European Countries by the CIA for the Transport and Illegal Detention of Prisoners, Notice to Members No. 2: Report of the TDIP Committee Delegation to the Former Yugoslav Republic of Macedonia (June 6, 2006), *available at* http://www.europarl.europa.eu/comparl/tempcom/tdip/notices/pe374316_en.pdf.

139. *Council of Europe January 2006 Report*, *supra* note 60.

140. *See El–Masri Testifies Before German Parliament*, DER SPIEGEL, June 23, 2006.

141. *See Germany Tracing U.S. Agents Who Seized Masri*, AGENCE FRANCE PRESSE, Sept. 21, 2006.

142. *See German Arrest Warrants for 13 Suspected CIA Agents*, AGENCE FRANCE PRESSE, Jan. 31, 2007.

143. *See El–Masri Kidnapping Case: Germany Issues Arrest Warrants for 13 CIA Agents in El–Masri Case*, DER SPIEGEL, Jan. 31, 2007.

Department of Justice refused to assist German investigators in their criminal probe;[144] and the Department of State declined comment.[145] In February, the German government forwarded the arrest warrants to Interpol.[146]

There was no legal victory in the American courts, however. On March 2, 2007, the Fourth Circuit published its opinion in the case. In a unanimous opinion, the three-judge panel concluded that because of the classified nature of the extraordinary rendition Program, the facts that El–Masri would need to bring forward to make out his claims, and those the defendants would need to rely upon to defend themselves were reasonably likely to include privileged state secrets information. The Court held that it was not enough to show that El–Masri's experience in the rendition Program had been publicly reported around the world because "the public information does not include the facts that are central to litigating his action."[147] In conclusion, the Court held that the "central facts—the CIA means and methods that form the subject matter of El–Masri's claim—remain state secrets."[148] For this reason, the Fourth Circuit affirmed the district court's dismissal of the suit.

Although the legal team was terribly disappointed about the outcome, they were especially frustrated that neither court had even explored the numerous alternative approaches to proceeding with the case that they had forwarded in their filings. For example, the ACLU had argued that the district court should at least allow for discovery of non-privileged information before determining that the case could not proceed without disclosure of privileged information. They had also presented solutions that other courts had used to protect sensitive information, including *in camera* review of materials, the use of redaction where needed, and the provision of unclassified summaries of relevant information in substitution for direct evidence. Despite this disappointment, the legal team faced this setback in the same spirit as they had greeted the dismissal of the case by the district court. "Our goal has always been to end the extraordinary rendition program" in addition to obtaining redress for Khaled El–Masri, Ben Wizner explained. Preparing a petition for *certiorari* to the United States Supreme Court was "another opportunity for public education."

---

144. *See* Mark Landler, Stephen Grey & Mark Mazzetti, *German Court Confronts U.S. on Abduction*, N.Y. TIMES, Feb. 1, 2007, at A1.

145. *See Germany Issues Arrest Warrants for CIA Agent "Kidnappers,"* EVENING STANDARD (U.K.), Feb. 1, 2007.

146. *See U.S. Displeased Over German Hunt for CIA Agents*, DER SPIEGEL, Mar. 5, 2007.

147. El–Masri v. U.S., 479 F.3d 296, 311 (4th Cir. 2007), *cert. denied*, 128 S.Ct. 373 (2007).

148. *Id.*

As the ACLU worked on the petition, terrible news reached the legal team: Khaled El–Masri had been placed in a psychiatric institution following his arrest on suspicion of arson. Attorney Manfred Gnjidic traced these events directly to the abuse El–Masri had suffered in secret detention. The experience had made El–Masri a "psychological wreck."[149] The team pressed on, more motivated than ever in light of these developments.

On May 30, 2007, the ACLU filed its petition for *certiorari*. The petition argued that recent cases had "unmoored" the state secrets privilege from its "evidentiary origins" by using the privilege to dismiss cases at the pleading stage.[150] Further, this expansion of the privilege was being used to shield from judicial inquiry grave governmental misconduct.[151] Arguing that there was "conflict and confusion in the lower courts" concerning the scope and application of the privilege, the ACLU argued that the time was ripe for Supreme Court review of the doctrine.[152] In its opposition to the petition for certiorari, the government argued that the district court and the Fourth Circuit had been correct in their ruling, and that dismissing El–Masri's complaint was the only proper avenue since litigating the case would require the disclosure of properly privileged state secrets information.[153]

With the dual goals of obtaining Supreme Court review and educating the public, the legal team solicited *amicus curiae* briefs from influential players. *Amici* included the Constitution Project and the New York City Bar Association. One of the most important *amicus* briefs was that filed by Swiss Senator Dick Marty of the Council of Europe. Marty's brief, prepared by the law firm Lovells LLP, argued that the facts surrounding El–Masri's case could not be considered state secrets, since they had been revealed and reported through inter-governmental organizations such as the Council of Europe as well as the media and other sources.[154] The brief asserted that the United States' failure to abide by international law was destroying its standing in the community of nations and focused on the international opprobrium with which the

---

149. Robert Barnes, *Supreme Court Won't Review Alleged CIA Abduction*, WASH. POST, Oct. 10, 2007, at A04.

150. Petition for Writ of Certiorari at 12, El–Masri v. U.S., 128 S.Ct. 373 (2007) (No. 06:1613).

151. *Id.* at 10–14.

152. *Id.* at 15–24.

153. Brief for the United States in Opposition, El–Masri v. U.S., 128 S.Ct. 373 (No. 06:1613).

154. Brief for Amicus Curiae Senator Dick Marty, Chairman of the Legal Affairs & Human Rights Committee and Rapporteur of the Parliamentary Assembly of the Council of Europe in Support of Petitioner, El–Masri v. U.S., 479 F.3d 296 (4th Cir. 2007) (No. 06:1613), *cert. denied*, 128 S.Ct. 373 (2007).

extraordinary rendition Program had been greeted. Urging the Supreme Court to exercise its power of review, the brief asked the Supreme Court to ensure that El–Masri had an opportunity to obtain justice through law.[155]

While the petition for *certiorari* was pending, the German government decided not to request the extradition of the thirteen alleged CIA agents who were the subject of arrest warrants for El–Masri's abduction. Media reports attributed this decision to the German government's desire to avoid "an open conflict with the American authorities."[156] The U.S. Department of Justice declined to comment on the development, telling the Associated Press that the United States does "not discuss whether it has or has not received an extradition request from a given country or our communication with any country with respect to such requests."[157]

On October 9, 2007, the Supreme Court rejected the ACLU's petition for *certiorari*. Although this was another great disappointment, the legal team feels that the larger goals of the case were met, outside the courtroom. In the end, Ben Wizner insists, "we did not lose this case; the CIA lost the El–Masri case." Certainly, when Americans think of the extraordinary rendition Program, they think of Khaled El–Masri and the CIA's grave mistake. Almost from the moment the story broke, El–Masri's experience became a cautionary tale that demonstrated the errors built into the system. As Wizner explains, "[T]he only place in the world where Khaled El–Masri's allegations cannot be discussed is in a federal courtroom."

Steven Watt agrees. "This case was ultimately not about winning a lawsuit." It was about speaking the truth, exposing human rights violations, and empowering one individual who had been wronged. From the outset, Khaled El–Masri was hopeful that the very act of bringing the case would help others who were still caught up in the extraordinary rendition and secret detention Program: "I think that we can all benefit from what happens in my case, including others who are still in prison in other parts of the world without the rule of law."[158]

---

155. *Id.*

156. *Germany 'Drops CIA Extradition,'* BBC, Sept. 23, 2007. On June 9, 2008, lawyers from the European Center for Constitutional and Human Rights filed "a lawsuit against the German Government at the Berlin administration court for its failure to demand the extradition of 13 CIA agents suspected of having illegally 'rendered' Mr. El Masri from Macedonia to a US prison in Kabul, Afghanistan." Press Release, Rights groups demand investigation of CIA's Extraordinary Rendition Program, Lawsuits against Germany, US and Macedonia seek justice for Khaled El Masri (June 9, 2008), *available at* http://www.justiceinitiative.org/db/resource2?res_id=104096.

157. *Id.*

158. Desmond Butler, *Man Who Claims CIA Tortured Him in Secret Prison Recounts Story on Capitol Hill*, Assoc. Press, Nov. 29, 2006.

Conclusion: Internationalizing the Search for Justice

On April 9, 2008, El–Masri's ACLU attorneys filed a petition against the United States before the Inter–American Commission on Human Rights ("IACHR").[159] The petition charged the United States with violating El–Masri's rights to be free from torture, arbitrary detention, and enforced disappearance.[160] The petition also alleged that—due to the application of the state secrets doctrine—El–Masri was deprived of the right of effective access to a court and that his right to a remedy for the human rights violations he suffered had been violated.[161] These rights are all protected by the American Declaration of the Rights and Duties of Man ("American Declaration"), which applies to the United States through its membership in the Organization of American States ("OAS").[162] The IACHR may take jurisdiction over petitions that allege violations of the American Declaration by the United States, making it one of the only international human rights venues with jurisdiction over complaints by individuals whose rights are violated by the U.S. government.[163] Victims may be heard during hearings before the IACHR, and the body may issue written decisions and recommendations to states found to have violated the human rights of petitioners.[164]

---

159. Petition Alleging Violations of the Human Rights of Khaled El–Masri by the United States of America with a Request for an Investigation and Hearing on the Merits, April 9, 2008, *available at* http://www.aclu.org/safefree/torture/34837lgl20080409.html.

160. *Id.* at 39–63, 84–85.

161. *Id.* at 77–85.

162. *See* American Declaration of the Rights and Duties of Man, O.A.S. Res. XXX, Int'l Conference of Am. States, 9th Conference, OEA/Ser.L/V/I.4 Rev. XX (May 2, 1948) arts. I, XVII, XXV, XXVI, XXVII, XXVIII.

163. The Commission applies the American Declaration to States that have not ratified the American Convention. The Commission held, in *Roach v. United States*, that the Charter of the O.A.S. indicated the direct application of the Declaration to a Member State which was not a party to the Convention. *See* Roach v. United States, Case 9647, Inter–Amer. C.H.R., Rep. No. 3/87, ¶¶ 46–49 (Sept. 22, 1987), *available at* http://www.cidh.org/annualrep/86.87eng/EUU9647.htm ("As a consequence of articles 3j, 16, 51e, 112 and 150 of the Charter, the provisions of other instruments of the OAS on human rights [including the American Declaration of the Rights and Duties of Man] acquired binding force."). The Inter–American Court of Human Rights has approved of this practice, asserting that "given the provisions of Article 29(d) [of the Convention] ... States cannot escape the obligations they have as members of the OAS under the Declaration, notwithstanding the fact that the Convention is the governing instrument for the State Parties thereto." *Interpretation of the American Declaration of the Rights and Duties of Man Within the Framework of Article 64 of the American Convention on Human Rights*, Advisory Opinion, OC–10/89, Inter–Am. Ct. H.R. (ser. A) No. 10, ¶ 46 (July 14, 1989).

164. *See* Rules of Procedure of the Inter–Am. C.H.R., arts. 38, 43, 45, *available at* http://www.cidh.org/basicos/English/Basic18.Rules%20of%20Procedure%20of%20the%20Commission.htm.

Despite the ability of the Inter-American Commission to take jurisdiction over human rights cases against the United States, the U.S. government has a long history of largely ignoring the rulings of the IACHR.[165] For this reason, the ACLU's resort to the IACHR was as much an act of creative advocacy as it was a continuation of the search for legal redress. By seeking the assistance of the IACHR—one of two principal human rights bodies of the OAS—the ACLU was invoking the powerful case law that the IACHR and the Inter-American Court of Human Rights had developed to counter abductions and secret detentions carried out by state agencies. Since the 1980s, the Inter-American Court of Human Rights and the Inter-American Commission on Human Rights have together developed and applied a jurisprudence clearly proscribing enforced disappearances. This jurisprudence developed in response to the abductions carried out by Latin American dictatorships in the 1970s and 1980s, and it began with one of the most celebrated cases ever decided by the Inter-American Court, *Velásquez Rodríguez v. Honduras*.[166] In this case, the Inter-American Court found the state of Honduras responsible for the "disappearance" of Manfredo Velásquez, holding that the abduction and secret detention entailed grave violations of the right to life, personal liberty, and humane treatment.[167]

By calling on this jurisprudence in its petition on behalf of Khaled El-Masri, the ACLU was arguing that—regardless of the motive, the identity of the individual secretly detained, and the status of the state responsible—the act of enforced disappearance was a violation of basic human rights guaranteed to every individual. By internationalizing El-Masri's search for justice, the ACLU was working to ensure that the denial of *certiorari* by the U.S. Supreme Court was not the last chapter in his story.[168] Instead, the resort to international human rights advocacy opened a new chapter, one advocates hope will include vindication for El-Masri in his search for justice. They also hope that the IACHR will place the U.S. program of rendition and secret detention in the same category as earlier programs of enforced disappearance. Such a decision

---

165. *See generally* Richard J. Wilson, *The United States' Position on the Death Penalty in the Inter-American Human Rights System*, 42 SANTA CLARA L. REV. 1159–1190 (2002) (discussing U.S. attitude toward the IACHR).

166. Initially field with the IACHR in 1981, the case was referred to the Court in 1986 and decided by the Court in 1988. *See* JO M. PASQUALUCCI, THE PRACTICE AND PROCEDURE OF THE INTER-AMERICAN COURT OF HUMAN RIGHTS 13–18 (2003).

167. *See Velásquez Rodríguez Case*, (Merits), Inter-Am. Ct.H.R., Ser. C, No. 4 (1988) (holding the state of Honduras responsible for the "disappearance" of Manfredo Velásquez, which entailed violations of the right to life, personal liberty, and humane treatment).

168. El-Masri's attorneys have also teamed up with the Open Society Institute and attorneys in Albania and Macedonia to file requests for information about El-Masri's case in both countries, as well as a criminal complaint in Macedonia concerning El-Masri's detention there prior to his rendition to Afghanistan. *See* Press Release, *supra* note 156.

might—with time and political change—help achieve a transformation in how the United States engages in the fight against terrorism. With pressure from advocates and the moral condemnation of international human rights bodies, the U.S. government might be persuaded that terrorism—a form of lawlessness involving the negation of human dignity—is best fought within the bounds of the rule of law, and through the affirmation of the human rights and dignity of all.

Contributors to *Human Rights Advocacy Stories*

S. James Anaya is James J. Lenoir Professor of Human Rights Law and Policy at the University of Arizona James E. Rogers College of Law, where he teaches and conducts research in the areas of international law and organizations, human rights, constitutional law, and issues concerning indigenous peoples. On May 1, 2008 he assumed the position of United Nations Special Rapporteur on the situation of human rights and fundamental freedoms of indigenous people, having been appointed to that position by the U.N. Human Rights Council for an initial period of three years. Professor Anaya received his B.A. from the University of New Mexico (1980) and his J.D. from Harvard Law School (1983). From 1988 to 1999 Professor Anaya was on the law faculty at the University of Iowa, and he has been a visiting professor at Harvard Law School, Universidad de Deusto, the University of Toronto, and the University of Tulsa. Professor Anaya has lectured at universities, conferences, and training sessions throughout the world; and he has represented indigenous groups from many parts of North and Central American before courts and international organizations. He has successfully litigated major indigenous rights cases within the Inter–American human rights system, including the landmark case decided by the Inter–American Court of Human Rights, *Mayagna (Sumo) Community of Awas Tingni v. Nicaragua*. Among his numerous publications is his acclaimed book, *Indigenous Peoples in International Law* (2d ed., Oxford University Press, 2004). He is also a co-author of *International Human Rights: Problems of Law, Policy, and Practice* (4th ed., 2006) (with Richard B. Lillich, Hurst Hannum, & Dinah L. Shelton).

Ari S. Bassin is a Project Officer with the International Organization for Migration's Police Reform Project in Aceh, Indonesia, working on post-conflict security sector reform. The project works with the police and civil society to facilitate reform and build trust through training and capacity building in human rights and community policing. Mr. Bassin received a B.A. from Duke University, an M.P.P. from the University of Sydney, and a J.D. from New York University School of Law, where he was an Articles Editor with the *New York University Law Review*. He has worked as a Consultant for the International Center for Transitional Justice, the Harvard Center for Humanitarian Policy and Conflict Research, and Kontras (The Commission for "'the Disappeared' " and Victims of Violence), where he concentrated on projects promoting transitional justice in Iraq, Sudan, Uganda, Sierra Leone, Indonesia, Timor Leste, Cambodia, and Burma. He has published the following papers: *"Dead Men Tell No Tales": Rule 92* BIS—*How the Ad Hoc International Criminal Tribunals Unnecessarily Silence the Dead* (*New York University Law Review*) and *Was the Dujail Trial Fair?* (*Journal of International Criminal Justice*, co-authored with Miranda Sissons).

Karima Bennoune graduated from a joint program in law and Middle Eastern and North African studies at the University of Michigan, earning a J.D. *cum laude* from the law school and an M.A. from the Rackham Graduate School, as well as a Graduate Certificate in Women's Studies. From 1995 until 1999, she was based in London as a legal adviser at Amnesty International. Currently, she is a Professor of Law and the Arthur L. Dickson Scholar at the Rutgers School of Law–Newark. During academic year 2008–2009, Bennoune is a Visiting Professor at the University of Michigan Law School. Her publications have appeared in many academic journals, including the *American Journal of International Law*, the *Columbia Journal of Transnational Law*, the *European Journal of International Law*, and the *Michigan Journal of International Law*. Her most recent article, *Terror/Torture*, appeared as the lead article in the *Berkeley Journal of International Law* in 2008. Bennoune is the first Arab–American to win the Derrick Bell Award from the Association of American Law Schools Section on Minority Groups. She has been a member of the Executive Council of the American Society of International Law and has served on the Board of Directors of Amnesty International USA. Currently, she sits on the Board of Trustees of the Center for Constitutional Rights. Her human rights field missions have included Afghanistan, Bangladesh, Lebanon, Pakistan, South Korea, southern Thailand, and Tunisia.

Jonathan M. Berger is a senior researcher and head of policy and research at the AIDS Law Project in Johannesburg, South Africa. In addition to an undergraduate professional degree in architecture, he has an LL.B. from the University of the Witwatersrand, Johannesburg, and an LL.M from the University of Toronto. Prior to joining the AIDS Law Project, Jonathan served as a law clerk to Justice Catherine M. O'Regan of the Constitutional Court of South Africa. Before that, he served as the legal education and advice officer at the National Coalition for Gay and Lesbian Equality. Jonathan represents the law and human rights sector on the Programme Implementation Committee of the South African National AIDS Council. He is also an honorary research fellow at the

University of the Witwatersrand, Johannesburg, where—as part of a collective—he teaches an LL.B. course on HIV/AIDS and the law, and co-teaches an LL.M. course on medicines, rights and regulation. Until late 2007, Jonathan was a member of the board of the Lesbian and Gay Equality Project. He was integrally involved in the Constitutional Court challenge to the exclusion of same-sex couples from the marriage laws of South Africa. He also participated in lobbying and advocacy efforts leading up to the adoption of the Civil Union Act, 2006, which—amongst other things—recognizes a marriage between two persons of the same sex. In addition to a number of popular and academic articles and essays, his major publications include *Litigating for Social Justice in Post-Apartheid South Africa: a Focus on Health and Education* in *Courting Social Justice: Judicial Enforcement of Social and Economic Rights in the Developing World* (Varun Gauri & Daniel Brinks, eds., Cambridge University Press, 2008); *Health & Democracy: A Guide to Human Rights, Health Law and Policy in Post-Apartheid South Africa* (co-edited with Adila Hassim and Mark Heywood, Cape Town, SiberInk, 2007); *Patents and Public Health: Principle, Politics and Paradox*, in *Proceedings of the British Academy* (co-authored with Justice Edwin Cameron, 2005); and *Resexualising the Epidemic: Desire, Risk and HIV Prevention*, in *Development Update* (2005).

Mark Bromley helped launch the Council for Global Equality in 2008 to encourage a clearer and stronger U.S. voice on international lesbian, gay, bisexual and transgender human rights concerns. Mr. Bromley previously worked for more than eleven years at Global Rights, where he served in various program management positions. During his tenure at Global Rights, he coordinated donor relations and helped open field offices in Bosnia and Herzegovina, Burundi, Morocco, Nigeria and India. In 2005, he launched an organization-wide Lesbian, Gay, Bisexual, Transgender and Intersex Initiative. Mr. Bromley has also regularly monitored developments within the U.N. human rights system. He conducted research on sexual violence in support of the International Criminal Tribunals for Rwanda and for the former Yugoslavia, and he reviewed international law standards in legal briefs filed by Global Rights, as *amicus curiae*, in human rights cases before U.S. and international courts. From 2001–2002, Mr. Bromley served as a Foreign Policy Fellow in the office of U.S. Senator Russ Feingold. During that period, he staffed Senator Feingold's work on the Senate Foreign Relations Committee, including the Senator's Chairmanship of the Africa Subcommittee. Mr. Bromley holds a J.D. degree from the University of Virginia School of Law and a BSFS from the School of Foreign Service at Georgetown University. He has published on human rights and international law issues, and has served as an adjunct professor for the human rights clinic at the University of Virginia School of Law and at Nova Southeastern University, Shepard Broad Law Center.

Maia S. Campbell is a project attorney for the University of Arizona Indigenous Peoples Law and Policy Program advocating before international bodies for the Awas Tingni Mayangna community in Nicaragua and the Maya communities of Toledo District, Belize. Ms. Campbell also currently serves as a consultant for the Special Procedures Division of the United Nations Office of the High Commissioner for Human Rights.

Doug Ford is Lecturer in Human Rights at the University of Virginia School of Law and the Director of the Immigration Clinic, a community service partnership with the Legal Aid Justice Center. With his students, the Clinic represents people from around the world with immigration claims based on persecution, abuse and other grounds. His research has spanned issues from the intersection of human rights and international humanitarian law, to the rights of missing persons and their families, and detention standards for asylum seekers and other immigrant detainees. He graduated from Bowdoin College with an A.B. in 1983, and Northeastern University School of Law in 1996. He has worked as a journalist, including several years in Venezuela, and worked with non-governmental organizations, chiefly Physicians for Human Rights (PHR). He served as Deputy Director of PHR's Bosnia Projects from 1996 to 1999 and was a researcher and contributor to reports on issues ranging from massive violations in Chechnya and Kosovo, to substandard incarceration in the United States, and the right to health in Mexico. Most recently he was contributor and legal advisor to *Underground America, Narratives of Undocumented Lives* (Peter Orner, ed., McSweeney's Books 2008).

Jayne Huckerby has been Research Director at the New York University School of Law Center for Human Rights and Global Justice since 2006. She holds a BA.LLB (Hons 1) from the University of Sydney and a LL.M. from New York University, where she was a Vanderbilt Fellow, recipient of the David H. Moses Memorial Prize, Graduate Editor on the Journal of International Law and Politics and an International Law and Human Rights Fellow at the United Nations High Commissioner for Refugees. She has worked as a human rights adviser for inter-governmental and non-governmental organizations, including the Global Alliance Against Traffic in Women (GAATW), International Center for Transitional Justice, International Service for Human Rights, and United Nations Development Fund for Women (UNIFEM), specializing in the areas of gender, transitional justice, human rights of non-citizens, and human rights and counter-terrorism. Prior to joining the Center she also worked with the law firm Baker & McKenzie in Chicago, Sydney and London.

CONTRIBUTORS

Aziz Z. Huq will join the University of Chicago Law School faculty as an associate professor of law in September 2009. At the time of this writing, he directs the Liberty and National Security project at the Brennan Center for Justice at New York University School of Law and teaches as an adjunct at NYU School of Law. As a senior consulting analyst for the International Crisis Group, he has researched rule-of-law and constitutional issues in Afghanistan (2002–03), Pakistan (2004), and Nepal (2005, 2006). He graduated *summa cum laude* from both the University of North Carolina at Chapel Hill (1996) and Columbia Law School (2001). He clerked for Justice Ruth Bader Ginsburg of the Supreme Court of the United States, and for Judge Robert D. Sack of the U.S. Court of Appeals for the Second Circuit.

Deena R. Hurwitz is Associate Professor, General Faculty at the University of Virginia School of Law, and director of the Human Rights Program and the International Human Rights Law Clinic. Prior to that, she was the Robert M. Cover/Allard K. Lowenstein Fellow in International Human Rights at Yale Law School, where she co-taught the Lowenstein Human Rights Law Clinic. There she supervised Clinic students working with the plaintiffs' attorneys in the Sabra and Shatila case. She also taught International Human Rights at Yale College. Before entering academia, Professor Hurwitz served as a legal counselor with the Washington Office of the U.N. High Commissioner for Refugees. In 1997, she worked in Ramallah, Palestine with the Centre for International Human Rights Enforcement. From 1997 to 1999, she worked first with the Organization for Security and Cooperation in Europe (OSCE) Human Rights Office in Bosnia–Herzegovina and then directed Global Rights' (formerly the International Human Rights Law Group) Bosnia Program. Professor Hurwitz has been a consultant with the Open Society Justice Initiative in Afghanistan and Lebanon on clinical legal education. She received her J.D. from Northeastern University School of Law and B.A. in Community Studies from the University of California, Santa Cruz. Before attending law school, she was a staff member for more than ten years at the Santa Cruz Resource Center for Nonviolence, where among other things, she co-founded the Middle East Program. Between 1981 and 1993, she led U.S. citizens on study tours of the Middle East, and spent a sabbatical year (1989–1990) in Israel and Palestine. Professor Hurwitz authored *Lawyering for Justice and the Inevitability of International Human Rights Clinics* (*Yale Journal of International Law*, 2003) and edited a book, *Walking the Red Line: Israelis in Search of Justice for Palestine* (New Society Publishers, 1992). She is a member of the Bar of the Commonwealth of Massachusetts.

Amy Kapczynski is Assistant Professor at the University of California, Berkeley School of Law (Boalt Hall). She has written articles on constitutional law, intellectual property law and global health, and social movement theory in the field of intellectual property. Her current scholarship focuses on the intersections between international law, intellectual property, and global health. In 2002, she co-founded Universities Allied for Essential Medicines, a student-based group that seeks to change university practices to increase access to medicines and research on neglected diseases. After graduating from Yale Law School, she served as a law clerk for Judge Guido Calabresi on the U.S. Court of Appeals for the Second Circuit, as well as Justices Sandra Day O'Connor and Stephen G. Breyer of the U.S. Supreme Court. She also spent two years as a post-doctoral fellow in Law and Public Health at Yale Law School and the Yale School of Public Health.

Harold Hongju Koh is Dean and Gerard C. & Bernice Latrobe Smith Professor of International Law at Yale Law School, where he has taught since 1985. He served as law clerk to Justice Harry A. Blackmun from 1981–82; Attorney–Adviser at the Office of Legal Counsel, U.S. Department of Justice from 1983–85; and U.S. Assistant Secretary of State for Democracy, Human Rights and Labor from 1998–2001. He is co-founder of the Allard K. Lowenstein International Human Rights Clinic at Yale Law School, has been on the Board of Editors of the *American Journal of International Law* and Foundation Press Casebook Series, and has served on the Boards of Directors of Human Rights First, Interrights, and Human Rights Watch. He was Counsel of Record in *Haitian Centers Council v. Sale* (S. Ct. 1993) and *Cuban American Bar Association v. Christopher* (11th Cir. 1995), and Counsel to Amici Curiae Former U.S. Officials in *Rasul v. Bush* (S. Ct. 2004), Counsel to Amici Curiae Madeleine K. Albright and 21 Former Senior U.S. Diplomats in *Hamdan v. Rumsfeld* (S. Ct. 2006) and Co-counsel to Amici Curiae Professors of Constitutional Law and Federal Jurisdiction in *Boumediene v. Bush* (S. Ct. 2008). He is the author of many books and articles on international law and human rights including, most recently, *Transnational Litigation in United States Courts* (Foundation Press 2008).

Smita Narula is Associate Professor of Clinical Law and Faculty Director of the Center for Human Rights and Global Justice at New York University School of Law. Her research and clinical work focuses on key human rights issues including: caste-based discrimination; the rise of Hindu nationalism; racial profiling in the "War on Terror"; economic and social rights; and the accountability of corporations and international financial institutions for human rights abuses. She has authored numerous articles, reports, book chapters, and essays on the above subjects. Before joining NYU in 2003, she spent six years at Human Rights Watch, first as the organization's India researcher and later as Senior Researcher for South Asia. Narula has conducted a number of on-site investigations of human rights violations in South Asia and is co-founder of India's National Campaign on Dalit Human

Rights and the International Dalit Solidarity Network. She received her Masters in International Development from Brown University and her J.D. from Harvard Law School where she was editor-in-chief of the *Harvard Human Rights Journal*. Before law school, she worked on HIV and public health at UNICEF and the United Nations Development Fund. Narula has also taught human rights advocacy and documentation at Columbia University's Center for the Study of Human Rights. In 2008, she was appointed legal advisor to the U.N. Special Rapporteur on the Right to Food.

Alison J. Nathan is the 2008–2009 Alexander Fellow at New York University School of Law. She specializes in civil and criminal procedure, federal courts, habeas, and the constitutionality of the U.S. death penalty system. Her current research focuses on the death penalty, habeas corpus, and civil procedure. She has previously published on topics including the death penalty and constitutional law. From September 2006 to July 2008, Nathan was a Visiting Assistant Professor of Law at Fordham University School of Law, where she taught classes in civil procedure and death penalty jurisprudence. Nathan graduated *magna cum laude* from Cornell Law School in 2000 where she served as Editor-in-Chief of the *Cornell Law Review*. Following law school, she clerked for Judge Betty B. Fletcher on the U.S. Court of Appeals for the Ninth Circuit in Seattle. She then clerked for Associate Justice John Paul Stevens of the Supreme Court of the United States during 2001–2002. Nathan then entered private practice as a litigation associate at the law firm of Wilmer Cutler Pickering Hale and Dorr LLP, practicing first in Washington, D.C. and then New York. Her practice focused on complex civil litigation, with an emphasis on Supreme Court and appellate advocacy.

Katie Redford is the co-founder and U.S. Office director of EarthRights International. As an international human rights lawyer, she has recently been selected as an Ashoka Global Fellow for her innovative use of international law to hold transnational corporate and government actors accountable in U.S. courts for human rights abuses committed overseas. Redford is widely published in the field of human rights, international law and corporate accountability, and has been profiled in numerous books, most recently in *Your America: Democracy's Local Heroes*, and *Be Bold* and the award winning documentary film, *Total Denial*. Redford is a graduate of the University of Virginia School of Law, where she received the Robert F. Kennedy Award for Human Rights and Public Service. She is a member of the Bar of the Commonwealth of Massachusetts and served as counsel to plaintiffs in ERI's landmark case *Doe v. Unocal*. She received an Echoing Green Fellowship in 1995 to establish ERI, and since that time has split her time between ERI's Thailand and U.S. offices, while also serving as an adjunct professor of law at both UVA and the Washington College of Law at American University.

Sir Nigel Rodley is Professor of Law and Chair of the Human Rights Centre, University of Essex. He obtained an LL.B. from the University of Leeds (1963), an LL.M. from Columbia University, New York (1965), an LL.M. from New York University (1970) and a Ph.D. from the University of Essex (1993). His first academic post was as Assistant Professor of Law at Dalhousie University, Halifax, Nova Scotia, Canada (1965–68). In 1968–69 he served as an Associate Economic Affairs Officer at United Nations headquarters in New York, working on legal and institutional aspects of international economic co-operation. In 1969–70 he was Visiting Lecturer in Political Science at the Graduate Faculty of the New School of Social Research (New York) and in 1970–72 was also a Research Fellow at the New York University Centre for International Studies. Returning to the United Kingdom in 1973, he became the first Legal Adviser of the International Secretariat of Amnesty International, a position he held until 1990. During the same period he taught Public International Law at the London School of Economics and Political Science (part time). In 1990 he was appointed Reader in Law at the University of Essex, becoming Professor of Law in 1994. He was Dean of the School of Law 1992 to 1995 and has been Chair of the Human Rights Centre since 2004. In March 1993 he was designated Special Rapporteur on Torture by the U.N. Commission on Human Rights, serving in this capacity until 2001. Since 2001 he has been a member of the U.N. Human Rights Committee (Vice–Chair 2003–4), a position to which he has twice been elected by the States Parties to the International Covenant on Civil and Political Rights (as the UK's nominated candidate). He was elected a Commissioner of the International Commission of Jurists in 2003. He is a Trustee of the Medical Foundation for the Care of Victims of Torture. Nigel Rodley was awarded a KBE in the 1998/99 New Year's Honours List, "for services to human rights and international law." He received an honorary LL.D. from Dalhousie University in 2000 and in 2005 received (jointly with Professor Theodoor Van Boven and Judge Pieter Kooijmans) the American Society of International Law's Goler T. Butcher medal for "outstanding contributions to ... international human rights law." Publications include: *International Law in the Western Hemisphere* (co-editor with C.N. Ronning, Nijhoff 1974); *Enhancing Global Human Rights* (co-author with J.I. Dominguez, B. Wood and R.A. Falk; McGraw Hill 1979); *The Treatment of Prisoners under International Law* (Clarendon Press/UNESCO 1987, 2d ed. 1999); *To Loose the Bands of Wickedness: International Intervention in Defence of Human Rights* (ed., Brassey's 1992) and *International Responses to Traumatic Stress* (co-editor with Y. Danieli and L. Weisaeth; Baywood/UN 1995).

Margaret L. Satterthwaite is Associate Professor of Clinical Law and a Faculty Director of the Center for Human Rights and Global Justice at New York University School of Law. Professor Satterthwaite's recent scholarship includes *Rendered Meaningless: Extraordinary Rendition and the Rule of Law* (*George Washington Law Review*, 2007), *The Trust in Indicators: Measuring Human Rights* (with AnnJanette Rosga, *Berkeley Journal of International Law*, forthcoming, 2009) and *From Rendition to Justice to Rendition to Torture: Informal Transfer Under International Law and the Prospects for Enforcement in U.S. Courts* (in progress). Professor Satterthwaite serves on the Advisory Panel of Experts to the U.N. Special Rapporteur on Protecting Human Rights While Countering Terrorism (Professor Martin Scheinin), the National Security Task Force of the New York City Bar Association, and is Co–Chair of the Human Rights Interest Group of the American Society of International Law. Along with her students and colleagues, Professor Satterthwaite represents several individuals who were subject to extraordinary rendition and secret detention by the United States. She has worked for a variety of human rights organizations, including Amnesty International, Human Rights First, and the *Commission de Verité et de Justice* (Haitian Truth and Justice Commission). She graduated *magna cum laude* from NYU School of Law and served as a law clerk to Judge Betty B. Fletcher of the U.S. Court of Appeals for the Ninth Circuit in 1999–2000 and to the judges of the International Court of Justice in 2001–2002.

Beth Stephens is Professor of Law at the Rutgers–Camden School of Law, where she has taught since 1996. Professor Stephens has written extensively on the enforcement of international human rights norms in domestic courts, on topics that include the U.S. constitutional framework for human rights litigation; accountability mechanisms in other domestic legal systems; the legal obligations of corporations for human rights abuses; and international remedies for violence against women. She is the co-author of *International Human Rights Litigation in U.S. Courts* (2d ed. 2008). Professor Stephens litigated human rights cases as a staff attorney at the Center for Constitutional Rights (CCR), New York, from 1990 to 1996 and continues to assist on litigation as a cooperating attorney for CCR and a member of the Board of Directors of the Center for Justice and Accountability in San Francisco. A graduate of Harvard University and the University of California, Berkeley School of Law (Boalt Hall), she served as a law clerk to Chief Justice Rose Bird of the California Supreme Court. She lived in Nicaragua for six years in the 1980s, studying the changing legal system. Professor Stephens participated in the legal team that filed *Doe v. Unocal*.

Beth Van Schaack is Associate Professor of Law with Santa Clara University School of Law, where she teaches and writes in the areas of human rights, transitional justice, international criminal law, public international law, international humanitarian law and civil procedure. Professor Van Schaack joined the law faculty from private practice at Morrison & Foerster LLP. As a Senior Associate at "MoFo," Professor Van Schaack practiced in the areas of commercial law, intellectual property, international law, and human rights. In particular, she was trial counsel for *Romagoza v. Garcia*, a human rights case on behalf of three Salvadoran refugees that resulted in a plaintiffs' award of $54.6 million. She was also on the criminal defense team for John Walker Lindh, the "American Taliban." Prior to entering private practice, Professor Van Schaack was Acting Executive Director and Staff Attorney with the Center for Justice and Accountability, a non-profit law firm in San Francisco dedicated to the representation of victims of torture and other grave human rights abuses. She was also a law clerk with the Office of the Prosecutor of the International Criminal Tribunal for the Former Yugoslavia. Since 1995, she has served as a legal advisor to the Documentation Center of Cambodia, an organization dedicated to staging a legal accounting for the crimes committed during the Khmer Rouge era in Cambodia. In 2006, she served as Prosecutor for the International Citizen's Tribunal for Sudan, presided over by Nobel Laureate Wole Soyinka, which presented the case under international criminal law against President Omar Al–Bashir of Sudan. Professor Van Schaack is a graduate of Stanford University and Yale Law School.

Paul van Zyl is a co-founder and the Executive Vice–President of the International Center for Transitional Justice (ICTJ), an organization that assists countries pursuing accountability for past mass atrocity or human rights abuse. The ICTJ was founded in 2001 in response to a growing recognition that facing legacies of past abuse and injustice is crucial to promoting human rights around the world. By helping to address past crimes, transitional justice can help to break vicious cycles of violence and reduce the likelihood of future conflict. He has acted as an adviser and consultant to human rights organizations, governments, international organizations, and foundations on transitional justice issues in numerous countries. From 1995 to 1998, he served as Executive Secretary of the Truth and Reconciliation Commission in South Africa, helping to establish the Commission, develop its structure and modus operandi and manage its operations. He has also worked as a researcher for the Goldstone Commission, as a department head at the Centre for the Study of Violence and Reconciliation in Johannesburg, and as an associate at Davis Polk and Wardwell in New York. Throughout his career, Mr. van Zyl has received a number of academic and professional honors. He was selected as a Young Global Leader by the World Economic Forum in 2008 and a TED Fellow in 2007, and was named as one of New York's "Top 15 Lawyers Under 40" by New York Lawyer

Magazine. He is currently a member of the Monitor Talent Network and the World Economic Forum's Global Agenda Council on Fragile States, and has served as an advisor to the Sundance Documentary Film Program. In tandem with his work at the ICTJ, Mr. van Zyl serves as director of New York University School of Law's Transitional Justice Program, and teaches law both in New York and Singapore. He obtained a B.A. and an LL.B. from the University of the Witwatersrand in Johannesburg and an LL.M. in International Law from the University of Leiden in the Netherlands. Following these studies, he was accepted into the prestigious Hauser Global Scholars Program at New York University School of Law, where he completed a LL.M. in Corporate Law.

Kristen Walker, LL.B. (Hons), BSc, LL.M. (Melb), LL.M. (Columbia), is an Associate Professor of Law at the University of Melbourne and a barrister. Her areas of expertise include Australian constitutional law, refugee law and law and sexuality. Professor Walker's recent scholarship includes *Damned Whores and the Border Police: Sex Workers and Refugee Status in Australia*, in the *Melbourne University Law Review* (2007); *The Same–Sex Marriage Debate in Australia*, in the *International Journal of Human Rights* (2007); and *A Stronger Role for Customary International Law in Domestic Law* (with Andrew Mitchell), in *The Fluid State: International Law and National Legal Systems* (Charlesworth, Chiam, Hovell and Williams, eds., 2005). She has recently appeared in cases involving prisoners' right to vote under the Australian Constitution, discrimination by blood banks against men who have sex with men, and the imposition of "control orders" against persons suspected of terrorism. Professor Walker has also taught subjects on gender and international human rights law at Columbia Law School and at the James E. Rogers School of Law at the University of Arizona. She has degrees in law and science from the University of Melbourne and a Master of Laws from Columbia Law School, and she served as a law clerk to Sir Anthony Mason, then Chief Justice of Australia. She has also worked as a volunteer with the National Gay and Lesbian Task Force Policy Institute and Lambda Legal Defense and Education Fund.

Michael J. Wishnie is Clinical Professor of Law at Yale Law School. Professor Wishnie's teaching, scholarship, and law practice have focused on immigration, labor and employment, habeas corpus, civil rights, and administrative law. For years, he and his students have represented grassroots organizations and their members in a range of litigation, legislative, media, and community education matters. Professor Wishnie is also a Non–Resident Fellow of the Migration Policy Institute and frequently handles cases as a cooperating attorney for the American Civil Liberties Union Immigrants' Rights Project. He is a graduate of Yale College and Yale Law School and served as a law clerk to Judge H. Lee Sarokin of the U.S. District Court of New Jersey and

U.S. Court of Appeals for the Third Circuit and to Justices Harry A. Blackmun and Stephen G. Breyer of the Supreme Court.

†